AF180408

RESEARCH HANDBOOK ON REDD+ AND INTERNATIONAL LAW

RESEARCH HANDBOOKS IN CLIMATE LAW

Series Editor: Jonathan Verschuuren, *Tilburg University, the Netherlands*

This important and timely series brings together critical and thought-provoking contributions on the most pressing topics and issues within the field of climate law. The volumes in this significant series cover a wide array of the effects of climate change on such diverse fields as trade, human rights, energy, disasters, finance, and migration.

Each *Research Handbook* comprises specially-commissioned chapters from leading academics, and practitioners, as well as those with an emerging reputation and is written with a global readership in mind. Equally useful as reference tools or high-level introductions to specific topics, issues and debates, these *Handbooks* will be used by academic researchers, postgraduate students, practising lawyers and lawyers in policy circles.

Research Handbook on REDD+ and International Law

Edited by

Christina Voigt

Professor, Faculty of Law, University of Oslo, Norway

RESEARCH HANDBOOKS IN CLIMATE LAW

Edward Elgar
PUBLISHING

Cheltenham, UK • Northampton, MA, USA

© Christina Voigt 2016

All rights reserved. No part of this publication may be reproduced, stored in a retrieval system or transmitted in any form or by any means, electronic, mechanical or photocopying, recording, or otherwise without the prior permission of the publisher.

Published by
Edward Elgar Publishing Limited
The Lypiatts
15 Lansdown Road
Cheltenham
Glos GL50 2JA
UK

Edward Elgar Publishing, Inc.
William Pratt House
9 Dewey Court
Northampton
Massachusetts 01060
USA

A catalogue record for this book
is available from the British Library

Library of Congress Control Number: 2015952682

This book is available electronically in the Elgaronline
Law subject collection
DOI 10.4337/9781783478316

MIX
Paper from
responsible sources
FSC® C013604
FSC
www.fsc.org

ISBN 978 1 78347 830 9 (cased)
ISBN 978 1 78347 831 6 (eBook)

Typeset by Servis Filmsetting Ltd, Stockport, Cheshire
Printed and bound by CPI Group (UK) Ltd, Croydon, CR0 4YY

And then. . .the forest. Forest in singular, not forests, because it constitutes a unity. Forest and forest and an occasional river, for hours, while flying several hundred kilometres per hour. Further north, the rivers grow bigger, wider. Some are dark as strong tea, some are muddy. But overall, the forest. Flying at thousands of meters high, all one can see up to the horizon, to the right and left side of the plane, is forest. An ocean of green.

(F. L. C.)

Contents

Figures

Tables

Contributors

Harro van Asselt, Dr, Professor of Climate Law and Policy, University of Eastern Finland, School of Law, and Senior Research Fellow and NORD-STAR postdoctoral fellow, Stockholm Environmental Institute, Oxford Centre.

Reginald Rex Barrer, Senior Associate Researcher, Ateneo de Manila University School of Government, Philippines.

Marie-Claire Cordonier Segger, Dr, Senior Legal Expert, International Development Law Organization (IDLO), Rome, Italy, Senior Director, Centre for International Sustainable Development Law (CISDL) Montreal, Canada, Senior Research Associate, CIFOR, Affiliated Fellow of the Lauterpacht Centre and Visiting Professor, University of Chile, Faculty of Law.

John Costenbader, Senior Consultant, Carbon Markets and Forestry at Climate Focus, Washington, DC.

Patricia Elias, Independent consultant at Elias Consulting LLC.

Felipe Ferreira, MSc, Acting Head of the Division of Climate and Ozone, Ministry of Foreign Affairs, Brazil.

Markus Gehring, MA (Cantab), LLM (Yale), PhD (Hamburg), Deputy Director of the Centre for European Legal Studies (CELS), Fellow and Director of Studies in Law at Hughes, University of Cambridge and a Fellow of the Lauterpacht Centre for International Law.

Kirsty Gover, Associate Professor, Melbourne Law School, University of Melbourne, Australia.

Joyeeta Gupta, Professor of Environment and Development in the Global South, University of Amsterdam and Professor of Law and Policy in Water Resources and Environment at the UNESCO-IHE Institute for Water Management, Delft, the Netherlands.

Kristen Hite, Independent consultant and Adjunct Professor of Global Administrative Law and International Environmental Law, University of Maryland, Francis King Carey School of Law.

Peter Horne, Master of Laws (Australian National University), Bachelor of Laws (Monash University).

Sébastien Jodoin, Assistant Professor in the Faculty of Law of McGill University, Montreal, Canada and Faculty Associate of the Governance, Environment and Markets Initiative at Yale University, New Haven, Connecticut.

Paul Keenlyside, Climate, Forest and Land-use Consultant for Climate Focus, Washington, DC.

Antonio G.M. La Viña, Dean, Ateneo de Manila University School of Government, Philippines and civil society adviser to the Philippine delegation to the UNFCCC negotiations.

Alaya de Leon, Senior Associate Researcher, Ateneo de Manila University School of Government, Philippines and civil society adviser to the Philippine delegation to the UNFCCC negotiations.

Andrew Long, Independent researcher.

Constance L. McDermott, Dr, James Martin Senior Fellow in Forest Governance and Chair of the Environmental Change Institute's Forest Governance Programme, Oxford University.

Ernesto Roessing Neto, PhD Researcher at the Institute for European Studies, Vrije Universiteit Brussel, Belgium and Assistant Professor at the Universidade do Estado do Amazonas, Manaus, Brazil.

Charlie Parker, Executive Director at Climate Focus North America, Inc., Washington, DC.

Annalisa Savaresi, PhD, Research and Teaching Fellow in Global Environmental Law, University of Edinburgh Law School, UK.

Michaela Schwedeler, Trainee DG Environment at the European Commission.

Charlotte Streck, PhD and MSc, Director of Climate Focus, an international climate change law and policy consulting firm with offices in Amsterdam, Bangkok, Bogota, Lisbon and Washington, DC.

Christina Voigt, Dr, Professor of Law, University of Oslo, Department of Public and International Law/Center of Excellence – PluriCourts, Norway, and principal legal adviser to the Norwegian delegation to the UNFCCC.

Andrew Wardell, Dr, Senior Manager, CIFOR, Indonesia.

Margaret A. Young, Associate Professor, Melbourne Law School, University of Melbourne, Australia.

Oran R. Young, Professor Emeritus, Bren School of Environmental Science and Management, University of California, Santa Barbara.

Foreword

This volume, consisting of a collection of essays examining the emerging institutional and governance arrangement known as REDD+ (reducing emissions of greenhouse gases from deforestation and forest degradation) from a multiplicity of perspectives, provides an excellent opportunity to think about what students of governance know as "the problem of interplay."[1] This concern, which has become the focus of a considerable volume of research in recent years, directs attention to the fact that regimes or governance systems do not exist in a vacuum. They can and often do interact with one another in ways that have significant consequences, not only for the attainment of stated goals but also as sources of more or less prominent unintended consequences or side effects.

In the case of REDD+, this is partly a matter of thinking about interactions between this initiative and other elements of the regime complex dealing with climate.[2] There is some disagreement about the exact contribution of deforestation and forest degradation to global greenhouse gas (GHG) emissions.[3] Nonetheless, trees not only store carbon; they also remove carbon from the atmosphere by fixing carbon as they grow. A successful effort to protect forests would make a real difference with regard to addressing the problem of climate change. The question, then, is how does REDD+ dovetail with other elements of the climate regime? Does this initiative compete for a finite pot of funds available to deal with climate change, so that investing in REDD+ would reduce resources available to support other efforts to combat climate change? Or conversely, is REDD+ likely to increase the overall pool of resources available for

---

1 Oran R. Young et al., *Institutional Dimensions of Global Environmental Change (IDGEC) Science Plan*, Report No. 9. Bonn: IHDP, 1999; Oran R. Young, Leslie A. King and Heike Schroeder (eds), *Institutions and Environmental Change: Principal Findings, Applications, and Research Frontiers*. Cambridge: MIT Press, 2008.

2 Robert O. Keohane and David G. Victor, "The Regime Complex for Climate," *Perspectives on Politics*, 9 (2011): 7–23.

3 Authoritative sources generally include deforestation as a component of a larger category of emissions from "land use changes." The Global Carbon Project (www.globalcarbonproject.org/), perhaps the most authoritative source, indicates that land use changes accounted for 36 percent of annual emissions in 1960 but less than 10 percent of emissions in 2013.

efforts to address climate change, either because it taps funds that are not available to support other elements of the climate regime, or because success in dealing with deforestation and forest degradation is likely to produce demonstrable effects showing what can be done in combating climate change when we get the relevant governance arrangements right?

Even more important is the observation that forests produce a variety of values that have little or nothing to do with climate change. Wood products are important commodities. Harvested sustainably, forests can provide the raw materials needed to support a thriving industry for the indefinite future. Forests provide essential habitat for numerous species, especially in tropical regions where each hectare of forest typically hosts a unique assemblage of species and where there are many species that have yet to be identified by scientists. Forests are important to subsistence gatherers who depend on them for a variety of valuable products ranging from nuts and mushrooms to firewood. Forests provide ecosystem services, including the prevention of soil erosion and the maintenance of hydrological systems. Beyond this, forests have aesthetic value and have been an important source of inspiration for creative writers and poets. Think of Thoreau's classic work on *The Maine Woods* or the evocative opening lines of Longfellow's famous narrative poem, *Evangeline*: "This is the forest primeval, the murmuring pines and the hemlocks."[4]

This leads us to think about the regimes created to protect these other values associated with forests and to ask whether REDD+ is compatible with these arrangements or even interacts with them in a synergistic manner. Among the most prominent of these arrangements are the Convention on Biological Diversity (CBD) with its mandate to promote conservation at the genetic, species, and ecosystem levels, the International Tropical Timber Agreement (ITTA) aimed primarily at regulating plywood markets to prevent overharvesting in Southeast Asia, the non-governmental Forest Stewardship Council (FSC) established to encourage sustainable harvesting of wood products on a global basis, and the Convention on the Conservation of Migratory Species concerned with habitats of critical importance to migratory species. All these arrangements operate at the international level. In addition, there are municipal regimes that include provisions applicable to the management of forests. These address an array of issues, including the preservation of endangered

---

[4] These are iconic nineteenth-century American contributions to nature writing. Many Americans of my generation were expected to memorize sizable chunks of *Evangeline*. But nature writing in other cultures includes similar contributions.

species and the protection of wilderness areas as well as the production of wood products.

Is REDD+ likely to prove beneficial or harmful from the perspective of those responsible for operating these other regimes? Responding to this question poses issues relating to what the regimes literature characterizes as horizontal and vertical interplay. Are programmes sponsored under REDD+ likely to be well-received by those seeking to fulfill the goals of the CBD? And what about the interplay between REDD+ activities and the efforts of those seeking to maximize income from the sale of forest products? How will international arrangements like those envisioned under REDD+ interact with national measures designed to protect endangered species or set aside tracts of forest as components of wilderness systems?

One interesting issue that runs through many of these concerns relates to the harvest of wood products.[5] There is a debate about whether the protection of old growth forests is the best option from the point of view of climate change. Mature trees store large quantities of carbon, especially in their root systems. Yet younger, fast-growing trees may fix more carbon than mature trees that are not growing so fast. The promotion of dubious practices, such as the wholesale destruction of existing forests to make way for oil palm plantations, as contributions to combating climate change constitutes a distinct danger in this context. Intact forests provide a variety of ecosystem services, and the majesty of old growth forests is undoubtedly a source of inspiration for many of those who derive value from non-consumptive uses of forests. Viewed from this broader perspective, decisions about harvesting wood products are complex; they raise important questions that extend well beyond the usual calculations of sustainable yields that are the stock in trade of silviculturalists or the calculations relating to profit maximization that occupy the attention of forest economists.

In my view, it is always desirable to treat applied analyses, like the essays in this book on various aspects of REDD+, as opportunities to work back and forth between theoretical concerns and more applied or practical matters. Many analysts who began to think hard about the phenomenon of institutional interplay in the 2000s were motivated by a concern that unconnected institutional arrangements would interfere with one another and might well give rise to conflicts. Such interactions might make it difficult to attain the goals of individual arrangements or lead to

[5] Valentin Bellassen and Sebastiaan Luyssaert, "Carbon Sequestration: Managing Forests in Uncertain Times," *Nature*, 506 (13 February 2014): 153–5.

counterproductive battles for primacy among the proponents of interacting regimes. But reality has turned out to be considerably more complex than we anticipated.[6] Interactions can give rise to complementarity as well as conflict. Consider the ozone regime as a prominent example. Most ozone-depleting substances (ODSs) are also GHGs. So far, the success of the ozone regime in phasing out a wide range of ODSs has produced reductions in GHG emissions that exceed reductions achieved via the UN Framework Convention on Climate Change (UNFCCC) together with the Kyoto Protocol by a wide margin.[7] Hydrofluorocarbons (HFCs), on the other hand, are not ODSs, a fact that has made them attractive to those looking for substitutes for ODSs in various uses. But HFCs are powerful GHGs. In this case, what seems attractive from the perspective of protecting stratospheric ozone intensifies the problem of dealing with GHGs. As this example suggests, it is important to explore ways to alleviate conflicts of this sort, once the significance of the problem is fully documented. In the case of HFCs, efforts are underway to find alternatives to these chemicals for various uses. Negotiations aimed at reaching an agreement to phase out HFCs under the terms of the Montreal Protocol are advancing steadily; they may reach a successful outcome during the course of 2016.

More generally, however, we need to encourage sustained research both to identify the conditions under which institutional interplay will lead to complementarity or conflict and to identify best practices in dealing with such conflicts when they do arise. The detailed analysis of various aspects of REDD+ set forth in the contributions to this volume provide a welcome opportunity to contribute to this larger agenda in thinking about the phenomenon of institutional interplay.

Oran R. Young
Wolcott, VT
July 2015

---

6 Sebastian Oberthür and Thomas Gehring (eds), *Institutional Interaction in Global Environmental Governance: Synergy and Conflict among Global and EU Policies*. Cambridge: MIT Press, 2006; Sebastian Oberthür and Olav Shram Stokke (eds), *Managing Institutional Complexity: Regime Interplay and Global Environmental Change*. Cambridge: MIT Press, 2011.

7 "The deepest cuts," *The Economist*, 20 September 2014. URL: www.economist.com/news/briefing/2168680-our-guide-actions-have-done-most-slow-global-warming-deepest-cuts.

Acknowledgements

This book is the result of a collective effort by all authors, all of whom over the years have significantly contributed to the theoretical or practical development of REDD+ and/or are involved in the negotiations under the UNFCCC. For all of us REDD+ is important in many ways.

I would like to express my sincere gratitude to each and every one of the authors for making time and energy available for writing the respective chapters. Being able to draw upon the immensely rich knowledge and expertise of the authors was a truly humbling and rewarding experience. The book is an attempt to garner and share this richness.

I would also like to thank Stephanie Schmölzer and Eirik Torsvoll at Pluricourts (University of Oslo) for their excellent assistance. My special thanks go further to Laura Mann and Elizabeth Clack at Edward Elgar Publishing and to Jonathan Verschuuren as the series editor for entrusting me with this book project and for seeing it through.

Christina Voigt
Oslo, March 2016

Abbreviations

ACHR	American Convention on Human Rights
ADP	Ad Hoc Working Group on the Durban Platform for Enhanced Action
AfDB	African Development Bank
AFOLU	Agriculture, Forestry and Other Land Use
ASEAN	Association of Southeast Asian Nations
AWG-KP	Ad Hoc Working Group on Further Commitments for Annex I Parties under the Kyoto Protocol
AWG-LCA	Ad Hoc Working Group on Long-term Cooperative Action
BCCRF	Bangladesh Climate Change Resilience Fund
BeRT	Benefits and Risk Tool
BIT	Bilateral Investment Treaty
BNDES	Brazilian National Development Bank
BUR	Biennial Update Reports
CANZUS states	Canada, Australia, New Zealand and the United States
CAO	Compliance Advisor/Ombudsman
CARB	California's Air Resources Board
CBD	United Nations Convention on Biological Diversity
CBFF	Congo Basin Forest Fund
CCB	Climate, Community and Biodiversity
CCBA	Climate, Community and Biodiversity Alliance
CCPR	Human Rights Committee on Civil and Political Rights
CDM	Clean Development Mechanism
CERD	Convention on the Elimination of Racial Discrimination
CESCR	Committee on Economic, Social and Cultural Rights
CfRN	Coalition for Rainforest Nations
CFS	Carbon Fix Standard
CIEL	Centre for International Environmental Law
CIFOR	Centre for International Forestry Research
CISDL	Centre for International Sustainable Development Law
CITES	Convention on the International Trade in Endangered Species of Wild Flora and Fauna
COMIFAC	Central African Forest Commission

COP	Conference of the Parties
COP/MOP	Conference of the Parties serving as the meeting of the Parties to the Kyoto Protocol
CPF	Collaborative Partnership on Forest
CSD	Commission on Sustainable Development
CSO	Civil Society Organization
CTIF	Technology and Innovation Fund under the Convention on the International Trade in Endangered Species of Wild Flora and Fauna
DFID	Department for International Development of the United Kingdom
DLDD	Desertification/Land Degradation and the Effects of Drought
ECOSOC	UN Economic and Social Council
EE	Executing Entity
EPA	Economic Partnership Agreement
ERC	Emission reduction credit
ETS	Emissions Trading System
EU	European Union
FAO	United Nations Food and Agriculture Organization
FCPF	Forest Carbon Partnership Facility
FIP	Forest Investment Partnership
FLEGT	Forest Law Enforcement, Governance and Trade
FMRL	Forest Management Reference Levels
FPIC	Free, prior and informed consent
FREDDI	Trust Fund for REDD+ in Indonesia
FREL/FRL	Forest Reference Emission Level and/or Forest Reference Level
FSC	Forest Stewardship Council
FTA	Free Trade Agreement
GATT	General Agreement on Tariffs and Trade
GCF	Green Climate Fund
GCF	Governors' Forests and Climate Taskforce
GEF	Global Environment Facility
GHG	Greenhouse gas
GRIF	Guyana REDD+ Investment Fund
HFLE	High-forest–low-emissions
HRA	Human Rights Act
IAComHR	Inter-American Commission on Human Rights
IACtHR	Inter-American Court of Human Rights
IADB	Inter-American Development Bank
ICA	International Consultation and Analysis

ICCPR	International Covenant on Civil and Political Rights
ICCTF	Indonesia Climate Change Trust Fund
ICERD	International Convention on the Prohibition of All Forms of Racial Discrimination
ICESCR	International Covenant on Economic, Social and Cultural Rights
ICJ	International Court of Justice
ICSID	International Centre for Settlement of Investment Disputes
ICTSD	International Centre for Trade and Sustainable Development
IDB	Inter-American Development Bank
IDLO	International Development Law Organization
IE	Implementing entity
IEA	International Energy Agency
IFC	International Finance Corporation
IFF	Intergovernmental Forum on Forests
IIA	International Investment Agreement
ILC	International Law Commission
ILO	International Labour Organization
INDC	Intended Nationally Determined Contributions
IPCC	Intergovernmental Panel on Climate Change
IPF	Intergovernmental Panel on Forests
IPO	Indigenous Peoples' Organization
IPP	Indigenous Peoples' Plan
ITTA	International Tropical Timber Agreement
ITTC	International Tropical Timber Council
ITTO	International Tropical Timber Organization
IUFRO	International Union of Forest Research Organizations
JI	Joint implementation
JLG	Joint Liaison Group of the Rio Conventions
JNR	Jurisdictional and Nested REDD+ Framework
KP	Kyoto Protocol
LoI	Letter of Intent
LULUCF	Land Use, Land-Use Change and Forestry
MDB	Multilateral Development Bank
MEA	Multilateral Environmental Agreement
MFA	Ministry of Foreign Affairs
MIGA	Multilateral Investment Guarantee Agency
MRV	Measuring, reporting and verification
MYPOW	Multi-Year Programs of Work
NAFTA	North American Free Trade Agreement

NAMA	Nationally appropriate mitigation actions
NAP	National Action Programme
NAPA	National Adaptation Programmes of Action
NBSAP	National Biodiversity Strategies and Action Plan
NCP	National Contact Point
NDA	National Designated Authority
NE/NFP	National Entity or National Focal Point for REDD+
NGO	Non-Governmental Organization
NHRI	National Human Rights Institution
NIE	National Implementing Entity
NLBI	Non-Legally Binding Instrument on All Types of Forests
NPD	National Programme Document
NZBORA	New Zealand's Bill of Rights Act
ODA	Official Development Assistance
ODS	Ozone-depleting substance
OECD	Organisation for Economic Co-operation and Development
OP	Operational Policy
PEFC	Programme for the Endorsement of Forest Certification
PES	Payment for Ecosystem Services
PMF	Performance Measurement Framework
PNG	Papua New Guinea
PoW	CBD programme of work
QELRC	Quantified Emission Limitation and Reduction Commitments
RDA	Racial Discrimination Act
RED	Reducing Emissions from Deforestation
REDD+	Reducing Emissions from Deforestation and Forest Degradation and the role of conservation, sustainable management of forests and enhancement of forest carbon stocks in developing countries
REDD+ SES	REDD+ Social and Environmental Standards
REL/RL	Reference Emission Level/Reference Level
RL	Forest reference emission levels and/or forest reference levels
R-PP	Readiness Preparation Proposal
R-SWG	REDD+ Safeguards Working Group
SBI	Subsidiary Body for Implementation
SBSTA	Subsidiary Body on Scientific and Technical Advice
SEPC	Social and Environmental Principles and Criteria

SESA	Strategic Environmental and Social Assessment
SESG	Special Envoy of the Secretary General
SFM	Sustainable Forest Management
SIA	Sustainability Impact Assessment
SIS	Safeguard Information System
TBT	Agreement on Technical Barriers to Trade
TDCA	Trade, Development and Cooperation Agreement
TOR	Terms of reference
UN	United Nations
UNCCD	United Nations Convention to Combat Desertification
UNCED	United Nations Conference on Environment and Development
UNCITRAL	United Nations Commission on International Trade Law
UNDHR	United Nations Declaration on Human Rights
UNDP	United Nations Development Programme
UNDRIP	United Nations Declaration on the Rights of Indigenous Peoples
UNECE	United Nations Economic Commission for Europe
UNFCCC	United Nations Framework Convention on Climate Change
UNFF	United Nations Forum on Forests
UNPFII	United Nations Permanent Forum on Indigenous Issues
UN-REDD	United Nations Collaborative Programme on Reducing Emissions from Deforestation and Forest Degradation in Developing Countries
USAID	United States Agency for International Development
VAT	Value added tax
VCLT	Vienna Convention on the Law of Treaties
VCS	Verified Carbon Standard
VPA	Voluntary Partnership Agreement
WCST	Wildlife Conservation Society of Tanzania
WFR	Warsaw Framework for REDD+
WMO	World Meteorological Organization
WRI	World Resource Institute
WTO	World Trade Organization
WWF	World Wide Fund for Nature

Table of cases and legislation

DOMESTIC LEGISLATION

INTERNATIONAL TREATIES

EU LEGISLATION

CASES

ICJ

Regional Courts

Investment Arbitration

WTO Dispute Settlement

Domestic Courts

Introduction: the kaleidoscopic world of REDD+

Christina Voigt

REDD+ is a phenomenon. Arguably, no other aspect of the climate regime established under the UNFCCC is characterized by the intersection of as many and as varied international and national legal instruments.

Neither has any other climate aspect attracted the attention of the legal community working with questions of regime interaction and interplay, consistency and/or fragmentation of international law and polycentricity to the extent REDD+ has. The purpose of this book is to capitalize on this work and to inquire how and to what extent REDD+ is embedded in the international legal framework.

The research handbook takes a qualitative approach and looks at REDD+ from the perspective of international law. It attempts to analyze the challenges, innovations, shortcomings, and successes that are already part of the international legal framework for REDD+ or can be expected to arise.

Complexity is inherent in the very idea of REDD+. Conceived as an incentive instrument under the UNFCCC for developing countries to adopt and scale up climate mitigation actions in the forest sector, it mirrors in its design the pluralistic interests – and trade-offs – that characterize that sector. Perhaps more than any other sector, the forest sector amplifies multiple objectives, ranging from resource exploitation, land management, agriculture, food and fuel production, ecosystem services, biodiversity protection to providing people with livelihoods, amenities, and sanctuaries.

Already the acronym "REDD+," which aims at capturing under one and the same heading such widely differing activities as reducing emissions from deforestation and from forest degradation (the "REDD") as well as conservation and enhancement of forest carbon stocks and the sustainable management of forests (the "+"), gives an indication of the concept's multi-faceted character.[1] Underlying the (surprising) diversity of REDD+ activities is the understanding that slowing, halting, and eventually revers-

[1] See Chapter 1, "History and future of REDD+ in the UNFCCC: Issues and challenges" by Antonio G.M. La Viña, Alaya de Leon, and Reginald Rex Barrer.

ing forest cover and carbon loss will have to comprise of a range of policy approaches, national circumstances taken into account. Yet each activity comes with its own set of challenges and opportunities, some more readily explored than others.

REDD+ aims at incentivizing mitigation action in developing countries and at capturing and channeling developed countries' financial resources to do so. As a "bridging tool" between those countries that provide support and those that receive it, REDD+ is built upon clear methodologies and a robust framework for measuring, reporting, and verification as well as a high degree of transparency which is singular in the regulatory scheme under the UNFCCC. Importantly, the UNFCCC REDD+ framework has achieved a careful balance between environmental integrity and stringency of requirements to obtain financial support, while allowing for flexibility to accommodate the diversity of REDD+ countries and to allow for broad participation.[2]

However, the interface between the internationally agreed guidelines for REDD+ and national policy- and law-making is broad and diffuse. UNFCCC guidance on REDD+, if implemented, significantly delimits the sovereign space of those developing countries wishing to engage in REDD+, in particular if *ex post* payments for verifiably achieved emission reductions are being sought. Such "vertical interface" between the national and the international legal framework raises interesting questions pertaining to the role and force of international law vis-à-vis sovereignty claims over natural resources which both are of importance to the territorial state and also of collective importance to the global community. Which normative parameters for countries' exercise of sovereign discretion can legitimately be designed by international rules, and which levers for implementation, e.g. incentives or conditionalities, are politically feasible?

Another important aspect of REDD+ is the "horizontal interface" between REDD+ as a climate mitigation and finance instrument under the UNFCCC and *other* areas of international law. REDD+ is of indisputable relevance to various international legal regimes and vice versa. Multiple international legal instruments (already or potentially) interact with REDD+, both in terms of designing and implementing REDD+ policies at the national level, and carving out the legitimate normative space for REDD+ in the wider frame of international law.

---

[2] See Chapter 2, "The Warsaw Framework for REDD+: Implications for national implementation and results-based finance" by Christina Voigt and Felipe Ferreira.

As mentioned above, the genesis of REDD+ is a case example par excellence of regime interaction and interplay. REDD+ begs (and, to a certain extent, answers) questions as to the consequences of such interaction: is it synergetic or conflicting, does it develop ad hoc and chaotic or with a certain degree of consistency and foresight, does it lead to stronger integration or rather intensifies fragmentation?[3] Are we witnessing an emerging puzzle of international instruments where the pieces fall into their (normative) place, or is what we see a constant re-alignment of the law to the ever-changing political priorities, or, interestingly, both? Like a kaleidoscope, where external "shocks" do not lead to disruption but renewal, the continuous re-configuration of the colorful mosaic (of norms) in response to changing circumstances is proof of the REDD+ regime's strength, durability and resilience.

Regime interaction does and will occur for many reasons and in many ways. In the absence of a neutral ground to manage it, it should be viewed as a necessary and welcome way to adapt REDD+ to the realities of a pluricentric international legal system.[4]

With regard to REDD+, the interaction mirrors the diverse but overlapping axes of interests crossing the forest sector, most prominent among them (1) economic and developmental interests in the forest resource base with regard to timber, agricultural land, or extraction of sub-soil minerals and hydrocarbons, (2) interests that recognize forests as home and host for biological diversity and a multitude of ecological services, (3) interests in the human dimension of forests in terms of livelihoods, rights of forest-dependent people as well as participatory arrangements in decision-making, and (4) interests in good governance – especially in addressing corruption and other fiduciary risks,[5] legitimacy and multilevel governance,[6] adaptive management,[7] and the rule of law.[8]

---

[3] See Chapter 3, "The institutional complex for REDD+: A 'benevolent jigsaw'?" by Harro van Asselt and Constance L. McDermott, as well as Chapter 4, "REDD+ and interacting legal regimes" by Margaret A. Young.

[4] On the notion of "regime management," see Martti Koskenniemi, "Hegemonic Regimes" in: Margaret A. Young (ed.), *Regime Interaction in International Law: Facing Fragmentation* (Cambridge University Press, 2012), 305.

[5] See Chapter 12, "Managing fiduciary risk in REDD+" by Paul Keenlyside, John Costenbader, and Charlie Parker.

[6] See Chapter 10, "REDD+ and multilevel governance beyond the climate negotiations" by Ernesto Roessing Neto and Joyeeta Gupta.

[7] See Chapter 14, "Rediscovering ambition, implementation and operationalization" by Patricia Elias.

[8] See Chapter 15, "Adjudicating disputes across scales: global administrative law considerations for REDD+" by Kristen Hite and Chapter 9, "REDD+,

Accordingly, one such axis runs along addressing the drivers of deforestation and forest degradation through direct or indirect regulation. The necessary legal measures, however, may have implications for countries which have committed to trade liberalization and/or investment protection.

REDD+ may in itself be described as a form of sustainable investment in the forest sector. In this light, the role of international trade and investment rules is nuanced,[9] serving as either sword or shield for the policies, economic incentives, and other laws which address drivers and enhance forest protection, with potential to encourage climate-friendly investments in sustainable landscapes.[10]

A second axis deals with the impacts of deforestation and enhancement of forest carbon stocks and the sustainable management of forests for the protection of biological diversity and ecosystems as well as wildlife and species protection for which a whole range of international legal instruments exist, most prominent among them the Convention on Biological Diversity.[11]

A third axis addresses the social dimensions of REDD+, in particular its interplay with a number of human rights instruments. REDD+ policy approaches – or the absence thereof – can have significant implications for stakeholders' substantive and procedural human rights recognized in relevant international human rights agreements. Landowners, indigenous peoples, local communities, as well as affected individuals may hold rights that could be impacted by REDD+ policies. On the other hand, the explicit recognition of indigenous peoples' rights and rights of local communities in the context of REDD+ safeguards has, arguably, led to increased visibility and gains in the recognition of those rights.[12]

An important feature of the UNFCCC framework for REDD+ is thus the introduction of safeguards.[13] REDD+ safeguards direct

---

tenure and indigenous property: The promise and peril of a 'human rights-based approach'" by Kirsty Gover.

[9] See Chapter 8, "Addressing drivers of deforestation and forest degradation through international law" by Charlotte Streck and Michaela Schwedeler.

[10] See Chapter 13, "REDD+ instruments, international investment rules and sustainable landscapes" by Marie-Claire Cordonier Segger, Markus Gehring, and Andrew Wardell.

[11] See Chapter 7, "The Convention on Biological Diversity and REDD+" by Andrew Long and Chapter 11, "Seeing the forest for the trees: Getting post-Earth Summit forest protection back on track" by Peter Horne.

[12] See Chapter 6, "The human rights of indigenous peoples and forest-dependent communities in the complex legal framework for REDD+" by Sébastien Jodoin.

[13] Decision 1/CP.16, The Cancun Agreements: Outcome of the Work of the Ad Hoc Working Group on Long-term Cooperative Action under the

implementation and support of REDD+ activities beyond mitigation actions, aiming at avoiding negative social and environmental impacts and at promoting additional benefits as well as rights and interests of stakeholders.[14] In REDD+ parlance, safeguards need to be "addressed and respected" throughout the implementation of all REDD+ activities in an open and transparent manner. It is the concept of safeguards which explicitly recognizes the interplay of REDD+ with other areas of international law, most notably relevant international agreements with regard to the protection of human rights and conservation and sustainable use of biodiversity. Arguably, it was also the safeguard concept which triggered scholarly reflections on regime interaction in the context of REDD+ in the first place. In any case, safeguards and their implementation provide valid and valuable ground for such reflection. While developing countries currently are coming forward with information on how all safeguards have been addressed and respected throughout the implementation of REDD+ activities,[15] empirical data is becoming accessible and accumulating which can help to back up – or reject – claims of *de jure* and/or *de facto* regime interplay between REDD+ and other international legal agreements in the context of national implementation.

The method applied in this book is reminiscent of a hermeneutic exercise where scholars, consultants, and practitioners were invited to analyze the UNFCCC framework for REDD+ as well as documents, agreements, and practice outside the UNFCCC with the aim of achieving a (more or less) coherent understanding of the interplay and interaction between REDD+ and the wider spectrum of international legal instruments. Such an approach necessarily leads to some overlaps and repetition. However, the message that emerges from this exegesis is clear: REDD+ is a mosaic of overlapping instruments. Rather than calling for more coherence, the embeddedness of REDD+ in the international

---

Convention, UN Doc. FCCC/CP/2010/7/Add.1, 15 March 2011, Appendix I, paragraph 2, (a)–(g).

14 See Chapter 5, "The legal status and role of safeguards" by Annalisa Savaresi.

15 Decision 12/CP.17 states that developing country Parties should periodically provide a summary of information on how all the safeguards are being addressed and respected. The information should be provided in a way that ensures transparency, consistency, comprehensiveness, and effectiveness. The summary should contain information about which REDD+ activity or activities are covered and include information on national circumstances relevant to addressing and respecting the safeguards, a description of each safeguard in accordance with national circumstances, a description of existing systems and processes relevant to addressing and respecting safeguards, as well as information on how each safeguard has been addressed and respected.

legal framework and the diversity that lies in the interplay of different legal regimes should be recognized as adding strength, resilience, and legitimacy to REDD+.

REDD+ is an experiment of scale. Diverse levels and sites of governance allow for the experimentation, testing, and diffusion of best practices and, eventually, standards. REDD+ is polycentric, dynamic, adaptive, and flexible. This is the reality which needs to be acknowledged by policy-makers as well as scholars. The fluid, kaleidoscopic diversity of legal instruments, regime interplay, and the interaction of governance arrangements offer perhaps the best "fit" between the complex challenge of addressing deforestation and the need for an adequate and flexible legal and institutional framework governing REDD+.[16]

With the finalization of the formal REDD+ negotiations under the UNFCCC in 2015 and the integration of the existing framework in the Paris Agreement, REDD+ is elevated to a new phase where robust methodologies and assurances of adequate and predictable support should lead to upscaled implementation. The main goal of REDD+ is to enhance action and support to slow, halt, and reverse forest cover and carbon loss in developing countries, as part of the global effort against climate change. Interaction with various international legal instruments helps to ensure that this goal is achieved while respecting also other concerns and interests of the global community.

The new Paris climate agreement encourages Parties to take action to implement and support the existing framework for REDD+ under the UNFCCC.[17] Parties may therefore choose to build upon the international guidance and decisions already agreed for REDD+ for their nationally determined mitigation contributions with regard to terrestrial emissions and removals. However, the ambition to address all main emission sources and sinks will mean that REDD+ methodologies only cover a fragment of land-based emissions. The development of a common framework for all parties for all sectors, including the land sector, will take time and its outcome remains uncertain. One thing, however, is certain. The complexity of issues and interests to be taken into account will only increase when further objectives such as food and energy security, agriculture, land management, and sustainable finance and investment in land use are added to the picture. All of these diverse interests neither will, can, nor perhaps

---

[16] On the notion of "institutional fit", see Oran R. Young, *Institutional Dimensions of Environmental Change: Fit, Interplay, and Scale* (Cambridge: MIT Press, 2002).

[17] Decision 1/CP.21, *Adoption of the Paris Agreement*, Annex, Art. 5.1; FCCC/CP/2015/L.9.

should be addressed under the UNFCCC. Interaction and interplay with other legal instruments will therefore remain high on the legal and political agenda.

This book, it is hoped, gives impetus to further research on the possibilities and limitations, promises and consequences of such interplay.

PART I

REDD+ IN THE UN CLIMATE REGIME: HISTORY, DESIGN, GOVERNANCE AND INSTITUTIONAL ARCHITECTURE

1. History and future of REDD+ in the UNFCCC: issues and challenges

Antonio G.M. La Viña, Alaya de Leon and Reginald Rex Barrer[*1]

1. INTRODUCTION

One of the most complex issues that the Parties to the UNFCCC had to address since the UNFCCC entered into force is how to approach the land-use sector, including forestry and agriculture. The land-use sector adds a major contribution to global emissions, and climate change will have serious impacts on the sector. The Intergovernmental Panel on Climate Change (IPCC) has stated that emissions from land-use change, primarily deforestation, are estimated to contribute up to 17 percent of global greenhouse gas (GHG) emissions (IPCC, 2007).[2] While there is still debate and uncertainty about how big the contribution of land-use processes to GHG emissions is in general, the land-use sector – particularly forestry and agriculture activities in both developed and developing countries – "provides opportunities for quick and meaningful gains in both adaptation and mitigation."[3]

After initial resistance by some Parties, there is now broad agreement that the regulation of activities in the land-use sector, both as mitigation and adaptation, needs to be included in the global regime on climate change. But disagreement remains as to exactly what activities should be included, methodological issues, concerns regarding safeguards, and

* All websites cited in this chapter were accessed on 1 October 2015.

1 La Viña, de Leon and Barrer are civil society advisers to the Philippine delegation to the UNFCCC negotiations but this article does not necessarily reflect the position of the Philippines in those negotiations.

2 Rogner, H.-H., Zhou, D., Bradley, R., Crabbé, P., Edenhofer, O., Hare, B. (Australia), Kuijpers, L. and Yamaguchi, M. (2007), "Introduction", in Metz, B., Davidson, O.R., Bosch, P.R., Dave, R. and Meyer L.A. (eds), *Climate Change 2007: Mitigation. Contribution of Working Group III to the Fourth Assessment Report of the Intergovernmental Panel on Climate Change*, Cambridge, UK and New York: Cambridge University Press.

3 Morgan, J., Dagnet, Y. and Tirpak, D. (2014), *Elements and Ideas for the 2015 Paris Agreement*, Washington, DC: World Resources Institute.

the implications for climate finance in the case of developing countries. There is also a concern whether the rules on the forest and land-use sector in developed countries (Annex I Parties in the Kyoto Protocol), adopted by the Conference of the Parties (COP) through various decisions since 1997 should be harmonized with the rules formulated and adopted more recently by the COP for developing countries implementing REDD+ programs.

It should be noted that while Parties and stakeholders have recognized the importance of agriculture for both adaptation and mitigation, its inclusion in the latter has been more controversial, with many developing countries concerned about the impact of such inclusion on an economic sector that is critical to their food security and economies. Thus a phased approach has been suggested that would see the inclusion of agriculture at a later stage which might be more acceptable.[4]

2. LEGAL HISTORY OF REDD+ IN THE UNFCCC[5]

Both the UNFCCC and Kyoto Protocol (KP) acknowledge the importance of forests in GHG mitigation and adaptation.

Under the UNFCCC, all Parties are mandated to promote, along with sustainable management, conserving and enhancing GHG sinks and reservoirs, including biomass and forests, and to cooperate on this endeavor.[6] Forests in developing countries are highlighted in several provisions, with a mandate to protect and rehabilitate areas affected by drought and desertification, particularly in Africa, and the need for Parties to "give full consideration" to meeting the needs of developing countries related to climate change, especially those with "forested areas and areas liable to forest decay."

The KP, adopted in 1997, included provisions on land use, land-use change and forestry (LULUCF) activities in developed (Annex I) countries, allowing them to credit to their reduction or stabilization targets removals in the LULUCF sector.[7] Forests in developing countries were

---

4 Ibid.

5 For a more comprehensive history of REDD+, see La Viña, A.G.M. and de Leon, A. (2014), "Two Global Challenges, One Solution: International Cooperation to Combat Climate Change and Tropical Deforestation." CGD Working Paper 388. Washington, DC: Center for Global Development. http://www.cgdev.org/sites/default/files/CGD-Climate-Forest-Paper-Series-14-LaVina-DeLeon-International-Cooperation_0.pdf.

6 UNFCCC, Article 4, 1(d).

7 Articles 3.3 and 3.4 KP.

however excluded from the LULUCF sector because developing countries did not have economy-wide legally binding mitigation targets under the KP. Notwithstanding this exclusion, the Clean Development Mechanism (CDM), created as a flexibility mechanism under the Protocol, provided options for developed countries to meet their emission reduction targets by investing in "offset projects" in developing countries.[8] Among the eligible carbon sequestration projects were afforestation and reforestation; those related to forest conservation, i.e. avoiding or reducing deforestation and forest degradation, are currently not eligible under the mechanism.

2.1 COP 11 – Montreal

Avoided deforestation was formally introduced under the ambit of the UNFCCC in 2005. At COP 11 in Montreal, Papua New Guinea (PNG) and Costa Rica, leading the Coalition for Rainforest Nations (CfRN), made a joint submission entitled "Reducing Emissions from Deforestation in Developing Countries: Approaches to Stimulate Action," supported by several other Latin American and African countries.[9] This is considered the introduction of "RED" (Reducing Emissions from Deforestation) into the UNFCCC process and in line with this proposal, the COP invited Parties and observer organizations to make submissions on "issues relating to reducing emissions from deforestation in developing countries" for consideration by the Subsidiary Body on Scientific and Technical Advice (SBSTA).[10] SBSTA was also to report on its findings by December 2007 and organize a related workshop in the interim.[11] This decision began a two-year process for exploring methodological and policy issues around RED, but which would continue well beyond the Bali COP in 2007. This involved a series of workshops and a significant number of submissions of views from Parties and observer organizations.

2.2 COP 13 – Bali

In 2007, the COP formally launched a focused work plan, with timelines for decisions, on reducing emissions from deforestation and forest degradation in developing countries; and the role of conservation, sustainable management of forests and enhancement of forest carbon stocks

---

8 Article 12 KP.
9 UNFCCC, FCCC/CP/2005/MISC.1, 11 November 2005.
10 UNFCCC, FCCC/CP/2005/L.2, 6 December 2005.
11 UNFCCC, FCCC/CP/2005/L.2.

in developing countries with the aim of completing discussions by 2009 in Copenhagen. COP 13 produced the Bali Road Map to guide negotiations towards reaching a new climate agreement by 2009 in Copenhagen, with the goal of ensuring that a new agreement would be in place by the time the Kyoto Protocol ended in 2012. The road map was a set of decisions identifying negotiating "tracks" or key areas of work for the Parties. It included the Bali Action Plan, which provided "a comprehensive process to enable the full, effective and sustained implementation of the Convention through long-term cooperative action," prompting the establishment of the Ad Hoc Working Group on Long-term Cooperative Action (AWG-LCA) under the UNFCCC, working in parallel with the Ad Hoc Working Group on Further Commitments for Annex I Parties under the Kyoto Protocol (AWG-KP).

The Bali Action Plan provided five "building blocks" around which the Parties' future work would revolve (outside the Kyoto Protocol): shared vision, mitigation, adaptation, technology transfer and finance. The mitigation track includes "policy approaches and positive incentives on issues relating to reducing emissions from deforestation and forest degradation in developing countries; and the role of conservation, sustainable management of forests and enhancement of forest carbon stocks in developing countries" (REDD+).[12] It was a promising step that among the agreements reached in Bali was Decision 2/CP.13 on "Reducing emissions from deforestation in developing countries: approaches to stimulate action," which established a work program on REDD+ and showed "Parties' commitment to include REDD+ in a post-2012 climate agreement."

It was in fact at this point that, "acknowledging that forest degradation also leads to emissions, and needs to be addressed when reducing emissions from deforestation,"[13] "RED" was expanded to include forest degradation, the role of conservation, sustainable management of forests and enhancement of forest carbon stocks in the scope of methodological issues to be explored by SBSTA. However, because of the semicolon separating "policy approaches and positive incentives" for the first two activities ("REDD") and "the role" of the last three (the "plus"), it is argued that only emission reductions from REDD were considered eligible for compensation at this point.[14] Aside from encouraging support for activities, exploring actions and options, mobilization of resources and use of

---

12 UNFCCC, The Bali Action Plan, paragraph 1(b3).

13 UNFCCC Decision 2/CP.13.

14 Holloway, V. and Giandomenico, E. (2009), "Carbon Planet White Paper: The History of REDD Policy," *Carbon Planet Limited*, 4 December.

the most recent IPCC guidelines in undertaking REDD-related activities, Parties were asked to make submissions on methodological issues.[15]

2.3 COP 15 and 16 – Copenhagen and Cancún

In 2008, SBSTA identified the main methodological issues on REDD+ that needed to be elaborated: estimation and monitoring, reference emission levels, displacement of emissions, national and subnational approaches, capacity-building, effectiveness of actions and cross-cutting issues. It also decided to take note of "methodologically relevant" outcomes on the discussions on policy approaches and positive incentives under the AWG-LCA, which also held its first workshop on these issues that year.[16] It was at this time that the "plus" in REDD+ – the role of conservation, sustainable management of forests and enhancement of forest carbon stocks – was explicitly recognized as additional activities in tropical forests that could be compensated, when SBSTA dropped the semicolon that appeared between the sets of activities since Bali. This was reportedly a response to pressure from countries such as India, which wanted the same level of priority to be given to all five activities.[17]

The 2009 COP in Copenhagen was disappointing for failing to complete a legally-binding instrument to take effect in 2013, at the end of the first commitment period of the KP, and to cover other areas of agreement set out in the Bali Road Map. The Copenhagen Accord, which the COP merely "took note of," recognized the "crucial role" of REDD+ and of enhancing the function of forests in removing GHGs from the atmosphere, in the context of the provision of positive incentives through the establishment of a REDD+ mechanism, among others.[18] The provision of "scaled up, new and additional, predictable and adequate funding" for REDD+ from a "wide variety" of sources, along with improved access by developing countries, was also covered by the Accord.

But while the COP failed to adopt the Copenhagen Accord, it reached agreement on a core set of methodological guidance for REDD+. The COP decision now referred to the five activities related to REDD+, and requested developing country Parties to identify drivers of deforestation and forest degradation and means to address them, and in-country activities that contribute to REDD+ results; and to be guided by the

---

15 UNFCCC Decision 2/CP.13.
16 UNFCCC, FCCC/SBSTA/2008/6.
17 Holloway and Giandomenico, "Carbon Planet White Paper".
18 UNFCCC Decision 2/CP.15.

most recent IPCC guidance and guidelines as the basis for estimating the impacts of REDD+ activities. They were also asked to establish national forest monitoring systems, and subnational systems as a part of national systems as appropriate.[19]

It was in Cancún in 2010 that the requirements for REDD+ as an approach, i.e. the elements and standards that need to be in place, were laid out, and the first "requirements" associated with REDD+ were agreed. The Cancún Agreements enumerate the five REDD+ activities and the elements that developing country Parties who want to participate in REDD+ need to develop: a national strategy or action plan, national forest reference emission level and/or forest reference level (FREL/FRL), national forest monitoring system and safeguard information system (SIS). Related issues were identified – drivers of deforestation and forest degradation, land tenure, forest governance, gender considerations and safeguards – which need to be addressed in the strategies and action plans to be developed.[20]

Cancún was also an important turning point for the REDD+ discussions because it saw the establishment of the seven REDD+ safeguards,[21] which aim to manage the impacts of and address risks associated with REDD+.[22] Broad participation and respect for the knowledge and rights of indigenous peoples and local communities had been recognized in previous decisions and SBSTA conclusions, but it was in Cancún that addressing and respecting not only environmental integrity but also transparent governance, human rights and protection of social well-being were recognized as an integral part of any effort to achieve emissions reduction through REDD+.

The COP decided that setting up a REDD+ system in each country should be undertaken in phases, while also recognizing that countries are in different stages of development and have varying capacities and capabilities, and so may proceed through the phases in their own time and manner. Ultimately, countries would be able to produce emissions reduction results that are fully measured, reported and verified. In every phase, countries also need to ensure that the safeguards are promoted

19 UNFCCC Decision 4/CP.15.

20 UNFCCC Decision 1/CP.16.

21 UNFCCC Decision 1/CP.16, Appendix I, paragraph 2.

22 See Chapter 5 by Analisa Savaresi in this book. See also: Jagger, P., Lawlor, K., Brockhaus, M., Fernanda Gebara, M., Sonwa, D.J. and Resosudarmo, I.A.P (2012), "REDD+ safeguards in national policy discourse and pilot projects," in Angelsen, A. et al. (eds), *Analysing REDD+: Challenges and Choices*, Indonesia: Center for International Forestry Research, 301–16.

and supported, and developed countries in particular were urged to provide support to developing countries undertaking these activities. The COP also mandated the AWG-LCA in its subsequent session to explore financing options for the full implementation of the results-based actions.

2.4 COP 17 and 18 – Durban and Doha

From 2011 onward, Parties made concerted efforts to negotiate the specifics of methodological guidance, policy approaches and positive incentives for REDD+. In Durban in 2011, the COP agreed on methodological guidance on two elements defined in the Cancún work program: safeguards information systems and modalities relating to FREL/FRL.[23] However, guidance on these two elements was not completed and more work was carried out in subsequent sessions. On the other hand, considerable progress was made in the REDD+ finance discussion. Parties agreed that "results-based finance provided to developing country Parties that is new, additional and predictable may come from a wide variety of sources, public and private, bilateral and multilateral, including alternative sources," and that both market-based and non-market-based approaches could be developed to generate finance.[24]

The Doha COP in 2012, in the context of the endpoint of the Bali Action Plan, adopted a work program to focus on ways and means to transfer payments for results-based actions, ways to incentivize non-carbon benefits, and ways to improve the coordination of results-based finance. The COP also mandated SBSTA and the Subsidiary Body on Implementation (SBI) to jointly address the need to improve coordination of support and to consider existing institutional arrangements or "potential governance alternatives,"[25] and SBSTA to consider how non-market-based approaches such as joint mitigation and adaptation activities could be developed, and explore methodological issues related to non-carbon benefits associated with REDD+ activities.

2.5 COP 19 – Warsaw

In 2013, after eight years of negotiations, international guidance on all the fundamental elements of REDD+ was considered complete. COP 19 in Poland produced the "Warsaw Framework for REDD+," a total of seven

---

23 UNFCCC Decision 12/CP.17.
24 UNFCCC Decision 2/CP.17, paragraphs 65–7.
25 UNFCCC Decision 1/CP.18.

decisions completing the "package" of REDD+ rules and procedures needed to get results-based actions and payments off the ground.[26] The framework included decisions on:

- Methodological guidance on:
  - modalities for national forest monitoring systems;
  - timing and frequency of the provision of information on safeguards;
  - addressing drivers of deforestation and forest degradation;
  - measurement, reporting and verification (MRV) of emission reductions;
  - technical assessment of forest reference emission levels/forest reference levels;
- Coordination of support for REDD+ activities, including institutional arrangements; and
- Results-based finance for REDD+.

Together with previous agreements on methodological issues, policy approaches and positive incentives, these decisions provide a "complete" set of guidance for countries on the elements and standards that need to be developed for REDD+ for developing countries aiming to produce and report on emissions reduction results, on the one hand, and modes and mechanisms for how these efforts may be supported and their results financed or incentivized, on the other.

3. REDD+ AT COP 20 IN LIMA

Two agenda items were on the table for REDD+ at COP 20 in Lima in 2014: the need for further guidance on SIS and non-market-based approaches for REDD+. Among other reasons, progress on these items was hampered by the limited amount of time allocated for REDD+ discussions to give way to sessions of the Ad Hoc Working Group on the Durban Platform for Enhanced Action (ADP), under which the new climate change agreement, to be adopted in 2015 and to take effect in 2020, is being negotiated.

Developed countries and many developing countries began with widely differing views on the need for further guidance on SIS: developed

---

[26] For an in-depth analysis of the Warsaw Framework for REDD+, see Chapter 2 by Christina Voigt and Felipe Ferreira in this book.

countries viewed further guidance as helpful for countries to level off expectations and clarify understanding of what the reporting requirement on safeguards entailed, while many developing countries considered additional guidance unnecessary to begin implementation and a potential burden. Some potentially significant progress was made in discussing the provision of "indicative elements" of SIS summaries, but without enough time to complete agreed text, the agenda item was pushed to the next SBSTA session in June of 2015.

Draft language on non-market-based approaches for REDD+ was also proposed and Parties began discussion but ran out of time. No COP decision or SBSTA conclusion on REDD+ came out of Lima and the two agenda items were pushed forward to the next SBSTA session in Bonn in June 2015. These were taken up together with a third agenda item on incentivizing non-carbon benefits.[27]

With the ADP negotiations well underway, there was limited time allotted for REDD+-specific negotiations in Bonn. Yet in a manner reminiscent of the push to reach several decisions in Warsaw, the Parties were able to conclude negotiations on all three agenda items, which agreements the SBSTA has recommended to the COP for adoption. At the same time, Parties balanced attention to these topics with that of land use, and rights and land use, in the new agreement. There seems to be broad agreement that the land sector would/should play a central role in the new climate regime, and its explicit inclusion in the agreement text has been put forward by some Parties and supported by observer organizations/civil society. It is the question of what this inclusion would look like that is now being deliberated, including how REDD+ should be treated in relation to other land sector uses/issues under the Convention (i.e. LULUCF and Agriculture).

4. PROSPECTS FOR REDD+ IN THE PARIS AGREEMENT

As early as Warsaw, many governments and non-government actors expressed agreement that the land sector – including LULUCF, Agriculture, REDD+ and afforestation/reforestation under the CDM – should be included in the purview of the 2015 agreement to be adopted in Paris. In-depth discussions on potential arrangements and approaches

---

[27] For the result of those negotiations, see Chapter 2 by Christina Voigt and Felipe Ferreira in this book.

have been ongoing, not only in bilateral and multilateral forums and among non-governmental organizations (NGOs) and indigenous peoples' organizations, but also in the ADP itself. The future of REDD+ within this new regime is still unclear at this point, although the advantages of increased integration of land sector approaches in managing terrestrial carbon have been repeatedly pointed out in various forums, meetings, analyses, reports and discussions, both formal and informal. Among the benefits of increased integration are promoting synergies between mitigation and adaptation, and helping to "address complementary issues in the land-use sector, such as food security, energy and water supply."[28] On the other hand, the interaction among different land uses and climate is by nature complicated, such that approaching them in isolation, while trying to achieve cross-cutting or common objectives, is not only difficult[29] but likely to be counter-productive.

Aside from a high-level panel on the land sector and forests at the Warsaw COP, several reports and discussion papers have been devoted to this issue, including one on "Understanding Land Use in the UNFCCC"[30] with a separate summary for policymakers.[31] This report gives a comprehensive background and history of land use under the Convention and known issues surrounding the various modalities, including elaborating on "special features"[32] that make land use unique and that may merit special consideration of the sector in the new climate agreement: the legacy effect, non-permanence, non-anthropogenic and indirect effects, and complexities of estimation. The UNFCCC also produced a technical paper compiling "information on the mitigation benefits of actions, initiatives and options to enhance mitigation ambition,"[33] which includes findings

---

28 Korwin, S., Rey, D., Reeve, R. and Daviet, F. (2015), *Sustainable Land-Use in the Paris Agreement: Safeguarding Rights, Biodiversity and the Climate*, Norway: Rainforest Foundation Norway, Friends of the Earth.

29 Shames, S., Scherr, S.J., Wallace, C. and Hatcher, J. (2011), *Integrating Agendas for Forests, Agriculture and Climate Change Mitigation: Rationale and Recommendations for Landscape Strategies, National Policy and International Climate Action*, Ecoagriculture Discussion Paper No. 7, Washington, DC: Ecoagriculture Partners and Rights and Resources Initiative.

30 Iversen, P., Lee, D. and Rocha, M. (2014), *Understanding Land Use in the UNFCCC*.

31 Iversen, P., Lee, D. and Rocha, M. (2014), *Understanding Land Use in the UNFCCC, Summary for Policymakers*.

32 Iversen, P., Lee, D. and Rocha, M., *Understanding Land Use in the UNFCCC*, 11–20.

33 UNFCCC (2014), *Updated Compilation of Information on the Mitigation Benefits of Actions, Initiatives and Options to Enhance Mitigation Ambition*. FCCC/TP/2014/13, 26 November.

on land use and the land sector. A couple of reports have honed in on land use in a future climate agreement and propose specific approaches and options both for Parties' consideration in the ADP negotiations[34] and for application at national level, say in preparing their Intended Nationally Determined Contributions (INDCs).[35]

Some discussion papers, distributed at the Lima COP to facilitate Parties' thinking on the matter, go to the next step and focus on the need for a land sector approach that goes beyond "mitigation 'plus' co-benefits," and instead present a more holistic framework of establishing "enabling conditions" for sustainable land use. One paper talks about comprehensive land-use planning as a rights-based approach,[36] and another delves into sustainable land use and the role of good governance, rights and biodiversity conservation, asserting that the UNFCCC needs to evolve beyond a "risk-based approach" to one that incentivizes social and environmental protection, and good governance, as enabling conditions in a multi-objective framework that moves over time towards a more integrated approach.[37] This latter paper picks up highlights from a longer and more detailed report on sustainable land use released after the COP.[38]

4.1 A Landscape, Integrated Mitigation-Adaptation Approach

Korwin et al. have pointed out that the UNFCCC's traditional risk-based approach to protecting the social and environmental integrity of mitigation actions from the land-use sector is not adequate to achieve this objective. They call for a paradigm shift and cite the example of REDD+, which includes safeguards that require countries to be more proactive in enhancing governance, rights and biodiversity. Adopting safeguards could

---

[34] Estrada, M., Lee, D., Murray, B., O'Sulllivan, R., Penman, J. and Streck, C. (2014), "Land Use in a Future Climate Agreement," prepared with support from cooperative agreement # S-LMAQM-13-CA-1128 with U.S. Department of State.

[35] Elias, P., Funk, J. and Greenglass, N. (2014), *Positioning the Land-Use Sector to Contribute to post-2020 Climate Mitigation*, International Union for the Conservation of Nature and the Environmental Defense Fund. http://cmsdata.iucn.org/downloads/land_use_white_paper.pdf.

[36] Center for International Environmental Law (CIEL) et al. (2014), *Comprehensive Land-Use Planning: A Rights-Based Approach. Discussion Paper for Addressing the Land Sector under the ADP*, June.

[37] REDD+ Safeguards Working Group (R-SWG) (2014), *Discussion Paper on Sustainable Land-Use in the Post-2020 Agreement – The Role of Good Governance, Rights and Biodiversity Conservation*. Supplemented by R-SWG (2014), *Ensuring Sustainable Land-Use: Recommendations to the ADP on Safeguards.*

[38] Korwin et al. *Sustainable Land-Use in the Paris Agreement.*

potentially stimulate a shift towards a view of social, environmental and governance provisions as "enabling conditions" for effective and sustainable climate actions. In this regard, "the UNFCCC's treatment of the land-use sector under the 2015 agreement should go beyond an exclusive GHG focus to one that acknowledges good governance, a rights-based approach and biodiversity conservation as fundamental enabling conditions to ensure the effectiveness and permanence of climate actions."[39]

Ideally, the Paris agreement should ensure a more integrated approach to land-use management. That is, land use must be dealt with in a way that integrates environmental, social and governance considerations in the agreement to ensure the effectiveness, equity and permanence of the Parties' mitigation actions. Further, in its own right, the land-use sector must achieve genuine and permanent reduction in GHG emissions instead of substituting for substantive action in other sectors to reduce emission from fossil fuels.[40] If these are not done, there are significant risks that mitigation actions in the land-use sector will result in negative impacts on key ecosystem/landscape values/services, such as ecosystem resilience (and therefore adaptation), livelihoods and food security.

Landscapes have historically been segregated by sector resulting in fragmented and isolated management decisions. These in turn cause unsustainable land use, leading to higher GHG emissions, loss of ecosystem services and unnecessary risks for livelihoods and agricultural production. A landscape approach aims to recognize the relationship between different land uses and the various stakeholders by integrating them into a joint management process. This provides the opportunity to better handle trade-offs and realize synergies in the landscape. A landscape approach will ensure cross-sectoral integration where mitigation actions in the land-use sector do not undermine adaptation objectives and vice-versa.[41] "Landscape approaches" seek to provide tools and concepts for allocating and managing land to achieve social, economic and environmental objectives in areas where agriculture, mining, and other productive land uses compete with environmental and biodiversity goals.[42]

The Center for International Environmental Law (CIEL) argues in favor of "a comprehensive approach to land-use planning, which is not

---

39 Ibid.

40 Ibid.

41 Global Landscapes Forum Outcome Statement.

42 Sayer, J., Sunderland, T., Ghazoul, J., Pfund, J.L., Sheil, D., Meijaard, E., Venter, M., et al. (2013), "Ten Principles for a Landscape Approach to Reconciling Agriculture, Conservation, and Other Competing Land Uses," *Proceedings of the National Academy of Sciences* 110, no. 21: 8349–56.

focused solely on mitigation action, but on establishing a broad framework for the development and support of policies and measures to enhance and protect land-sector resources and the wealth of benefits derived from those resources."[43] It points out that "incentivizing emission reductions from land use will require a range of measures and approaches – many of which are non-quantifiable."[44] From a practical point of view, developing countries with significant land-use emissions could employ a range of approaches such as commitments based on policies and measures, and other qualitative approaches, which can be characterized as comprehensive land-use planning.

4.2 Inclusion of Safeguards in 2015 Agreement

The landscape approach should be accompanied by a rights-based approach to climate action. The Paris agreement should adopt an approach that builds on the precedent of the REDD+ safeguards and extends similar provisions for all countries to ensure the social and environmental sustainability of climate actions in the land-use sector.[45] For CIEL, good forest governance and addressing tenure rights are the first steps to tackling deforestation and forest degradation, such that comprehensive land-use planning should include indicators for improvements in forest governance and recognizing tenure rights. A comprehensive land-use planning approach under the ADP could enhance ambitious mitigation across all sectors, while protecting ecosystem health and rights to land, livelihoods and food-security.[46]

4.3 Harmonizing REDD+ and LULUCF in the Paris Agreement

One important decision that the UNFCCC COP might have to make soon, in the Paris Agreement or through a process launched at COP 21, is whether to harmonize the rules for an expanded REDD+ with the older rules for LULUCF of developed countries.

The UNFCCC sets specific requirements for all Parties concerning the promotion of actions on mitigation and reporting requirements of anthropogenic emissions by sources and removals by sinks, including from the agriculture and forestry sector. In 1997, with the adoption of the KP,

---

43 CIEL et al. *Comprehensive Land-Use Planning.*

44 Ibid.

45 R-SWG, *Discussion Paper on Sustainable Land-Use in the Post-2020 Agreement.*

46 CIEL et al. *Comprehensive Land-Use Planning.*

the commitments of Annex I Parties were to be measured and reported through the "net changes in greenhouse gas emissions by sources and removals by sinks" through LULUCF activities since 1990 as stated in Article 3.3 of the KP. The information to be reported under the KP during the commitment periods was supplementary information to that reported under Article 4.1(a) of the Convention. This meant that Parties were not supposed to submit two separate inventories but should provide any information required under the KP as supplementary, within the inventory report, to show each Party's compliance with its commitments.

As a further condition under the KP, Annex I Parties were to annually report emissions by sources and removals by sinks of CO_2 and other GHGs resulting namely from afforestation, reforestation and deforestation since 1990; and any human-induced or supplemental activities as stated under Article 3.3, such as forest management, revegetation, cropland management and grazing land management. Further, Annex I Parties must ensure that their GHG emissions "do not exceed their assigned amounts, referred to as the Party's quantified emission limitation and reduction commitments (QELRC)." Put another way, a Party's QELRC represents the ceiling of the amount of GHG emissions a Party commits to meet, compared to its previously reported emissions. To achieve their QELRC, each Party should promote sustainable development by implementing policies and measures; for example, the protection of and enhancement of sinks and reservoirs and the promotion of sustainable forms of agriculture.[47]

In COP 7 in 2001, the Marrakesh Accords included the adoption of the rules governing LULUCF activities. Specifically, in Decision 11 of said COP, these included three main elements, namely, a set of principles governing LULUCF activities; definitions for Article 3.3, and activities and agreed activities under Article 3, paragraph 4 of the KP; and a four-tier capping system limiting the use of LULUCF activities to meet emission targets.[48]

The principles in the Marrakesh Accords governing LULUCF were intended to address the concern that LULUCF activities should support the environmental integrity of the KP. The principles emphasize the importance of, among others, (1) sound science as basis, (2) methodological consistency, (3) consistency with the aim of the KP as stated in Article 3, (4) biodiversity conservation and sustainable use of natural resources, and that

---

[47] UNFCCC, Articles 3.3 and 3.4.

[48] UNFCCC (2001), Report of the Conference of the Parties on its Seventh Session, held at Marrakesh from 29 October to 10 November 2001, Addendum, Part Two: Action taken by the Conference of the Parties, Decision 11/CP. 7 Land Use, Land-Use Change and Forestry.

(4) LULUCF accounting is not an implication of transfer of commitments to ensuing periods. Also, the principles specified the exclusion of naturally occurring removals, including such removals from indirect anthropogenic effects, from the system and that the release of GHGs into the atmosphere, for example from forest fires, must be accounted for.[49]

Further, common definitions on LULUCF activities were established for consistency and comparability among Parties. These activities included definitions of *forest*, *afforestation*, *reforestation*, *deforestation* and also for four additional LULUCF activities previously identified under Article 3.3. Parties were given the choice to include any of these activities in meeting their emission targets, and the choice is then fixed for the first commitment period.[50]

The four-tier capping system limited the extent to which Parties can account for emissions and removals from specific LULUCF activities for the first commitment period. This capping system specifically limits Parties through the following:

> **Tier 1**: If a Party's afforestation, reforestation and deforestation activities result in more emissions than removals, a Party may offset these emissions through forest management activities, up to a total level of 9 megatons of carbon per year for the five-year commitment period.
> **Tier 2**: The extent to which forest management activities can be accounted to meet targets beyond 9 megatons of carbon per year is subject to an individual cap for each Party, specified in an appendix to the decision on LULUCF. This cap includes joint implementation projects involving forest management.
> **Tier 3**: Emissions and removals from cropland management, grazing land management and revegetation can be accounted for to help meet targets on a net basis, such as carbon stocks during 1990, times five, will be subtracted from the changes in carbon stocks during the first commitment period, in the lands where these activities will take place.
> **Tier 4**: Only afforestation and reforestation projects are eligible under the CDM. GHG removals from such projects may only be used to help meet emission targets up to 1 percent of a Party's base year emissions for each year of the commitment period.[51]

4.4 Reporting Requirements under the First Commitment Period

Parties are expected to begin reporting at the onset of the activity or the start of the commitment period, whichever of the two comes later. To ensure Party commitment compliance, Parties also have to annually report supplementary LULUCF-related information under the provisions

---

49 Ibid.
50 Ibid.
51 Ibid.

of the KP and the Marrakesh Accords. This was also as elaborated by good practice guidance in accordance with relevant decisions of the COP/MOP on LULUCF activities stated in Article 5.2.[52]

The good practice guidance for LULUCF activities under Article 3.3 and 3.4 of the KP specified that for the first commitment period ending in 2012, Annex I Parties that have ratified the KP shall apply the IPCC Good Practice Guidance for LULUCF in providing information on anthropogenic GHG emissions by sources and removals by sinks from LULUCF activities.[53] As further support to the submission of information on GHG emissions by sources and removals by sinks, Parties adopted tables of common reporting formats for LULUCF activities.[54]

4.5 Reporting Requirements under the Second Commitment Period

For the second commitment period, Annex I Parties are to apply the 2006 IPCC Guidelines for National Greenhouse Gas Inventories.[55] In support of this requirement for Annex I Parties, Appendix I to Decision 2/CMP.6 provided for forest management reference levels (FMRL), set transparently in accordance with the provision contained in that decision.[56] The

---

[52] UNFCCC (2005a), Report of the Conference of the Parties serving as the meeting of the Parties to the Kyoto Protocol on its first session, held at Montreal from 28 November to 10 December 2005, Addendum, Part Two: Action taken by the Conference of the Parties serving as the meeting of the Parties to the Kyoto Protocol at its first session, Decision 15/CMP.1 Guidelines for the Preparation of the Information required under Article 7 of the Kyoto Protocol.

[53] Ibid; IPCC (Penman, J., Gytarsky, M., Hiraishi, T., Krug, T., Kruger, D., Pipatti, R., Buendia, L., Miwa, K., Ngara, T., Tanabe, K. and Wagner, F. (eds)) (2003) *Good Practice Guidance for Land Use. Land-Use Change and Forestry*, Hayama, Japan: IPCC.

[54] Report of the Conference of the Parties on its eleventh session, held at Montreal from 28 November to 10 December 2005, Addendum, Part Two: Action taken by the Conference of the Parties at its eleventh session, Decision 14/CP.11 Tables of the Common Reporting Format for Land Use, Land-Use Change and Forestry.

[55] UNFCCC (2013), Report of the Conference of the Parties serving as the meeting of the Parties to the Kyoto Protocol on its ninth session, held in Warsaw from 11 to 23 November 2013, Addendum, Part Two: Action taken by the Conference of the Parties serving as the meeting of the Parties to the Kyoto Protocol at its ninth session, Decision 6/CMP.9 Guidance for reporting information on activities under Article 3, paragraphs 3 and 4, of the Kyoto Protocol.

[56] UNFCCC (2010), Report of the Conference of the Parties serving as the meeting of the Parties to the Kyoto Protocol on its sixth session, held in Cancún from 29 November to 10 December 2010, Addendum, Part Two: Action taken by the Conference of the Parties serving as the meeting of the Parties to the Kyoto

UNFCCC Secretariat reported the key conclusions of the FRML review process in a synthesis report.[57]

This decision also specified that Annex I Parties shall apply the revised supplementary methods and Good Practice Guidance Arising from the KP consistent with Decision 2/CMP.7 and Annex I of Decision 24/CP.19 for the purpose of providing information referred to above in the second commitment period, and the remaining regulations in Decision 6/CMP.9.

4.6 Accounting of LULUCF Activities under the Kyoto Protocol

The Convention and the KP differ in accounting for emissions and removals from LULUCF activities. The Convention includes all emissions and removals from LULUCF in a Party's total emissions. On the other hand, the KP only accounts for emissions and removals from specific LULUCF activities defined under Article 3.3 and 3.4 of the Protocol. It is mandatory that each Annex I Party account for emissions and removals in the commitment period on land where these activities have occurred. Further, under Article 3.4 of the Protocol, activities are restricted to forestland management, cropland management, grazing land management and/or revegetation.

In the second commitment period, activities under Article 3.4 have also included wetland drainage and rewetting. Accounting for these additional LULUCF activities differs between the first and second commitment periods.

Rules for accounting for LULUCF activities under the KP in the first commitment period were enumerated in the Annex to Decision 16/CMP.1 (UNFCCC 2005b).[58] For the second commitment period, accounting rules for LULUCF activities under the KP were provided in the Annex to Decision 2/CMP.7. The Annex to this decision confirmed definitions

---

Protocol at its sixth session, Decision 2/CMP.6 The Cancún Agreements: Land use, land-use change and forestry.

[57] UNFCCC (2011a), Ad Hoc Working Group on Further Commitments for Annex I Parties under the Kyoto Protocol sixteenth session, part four, Durban, 29 November 2011, Agenda item 3: Consideration of further commitments for Annex I Parties under the Kyoto Protocol, Synthesis Report of the Technical Assessments of the Forest Management Reference Level Submissions.

[58] UNFCCC (2005b), Report of the Conference of the Parties serving as the meeting of the Parties to the Kyoto Protocol on its first session, held at Montreal from 28 November to 10 December 2005, Addendum, Part Two: Action taken by the Conference of the Parties serving as the meeting of the Parties to the Kyoto Protocol at its first session, Decision 16/CMP.1 Land use, land-use change and forestry.

already previously stated in the Annex to Decision 16/CMP.1 and added definitions on natural disturbances and wetland drainage and rewetting, as well as the modalities, rules and guidelines for accounting of LULUCF activities under Articles 3.3 and 3.4 of the KP in the second commitment period, and the principles to govern LULUCF project activities under Article 12 of the KP.

There are clear differences in the treatment of REDD+ compared to LULUCF. LULUCF itself is treated distinctively under the UNFCCC and the KP. Reporting requirements and accounting for GHG emissions vary and give a reflection of the relative significance of LULUCF in the latter. Principles for example were provided under the Marrakesh Accords to support the integrity of the KP. Definitions were also established for LULUCF activities. Harmonizing rules that will be applicable to both REDD+ and LULUCF is an immediate key consideration.

5. RECOMMENDATIONS

Following the discussion in this chapter, the expansion of REDD+ into other land uses in developing countries must include the following:

- *Integration of climate mitigation and adaptation in land use through a landscape approach*. Land-use activities, policies and actions should be pursued with the alignment of both mitigation and adaptation objectives, with a view to achieving multiple social, environmental and governance objectives. This is best achieved through a landscape approach.
- *Transparency and effectiveness in governance*. The critical importance of transparency in the land sector, particularly through governance and accounting, should be paramount, with the inclusion of social, environmental and governance safeguards. Land use must be treated separately with the importance of ecological integrity, governance and rights as enabling conditions.
- *Recognition and respect for the rights and full participation of all relevant stakeholders*. Low-emission development, and in particular in the land-use sector, should happen through the full participation of civil society, indigenous peoples, local communities and women, ensuring the recognition and legal enforcement of rights, including participation, human, land tenure rights, and of the importance of traditional knowledge and indigenous knowledge; in accordance with good governance, as part of a rights-based approach to climate action.

- *Conservation and enhancement of natural forests and biodiversity.* Countries should implement land-use activities and policies with emphasis on the conservation and enhancement of natural forests and biodiversity that will not result in the conversion of natural forests into other land uses. Also, there should be a clear recognition that biodiversity is essential for increasing ecosystem resilience (adaptation) and to ensure the permanence and effectiveness of mitigation actions, as well as a recognition of other carbon-rich lands or ecosystems, e.g., peatlands, and the establishment of social and environmental safeguards for these ecosystems.
- *Consistency with international conventions and agreements.* Parties must harmonize the implementation of land-use activities/policies/actions in alignment with other international laws, specifically with the CBD and the Convention to Combat Desertification, consistently with and not prejudicing the implementation of the 2015 Sustainable Development Goals.
- *Harmonization of REDD+ and LULUCF rules.* What is needed is a new set of rules for measurement, reporting and verification (including accounting) that brings about a convergence and harmonization of the existing LULUCF and REDD+ rules, with ensuring transparency, comparability, and environmental integrity are the most important considerations.

2. The Warsaw Framework for REDD+: implications for national implementation and results-based finance•

*Christina Voigt and Felipe Ferreira**

1. INTRODUCTION

The adoption of the Warsaw Framework for REDD+ (WFR)[1] in 2013 has to a large extent concluded negotiations on REDD+ under the UNFCCC.[2] The WFR established a structure that is flexible enough to

• This chapter is a reprint of the same article published in 2 *Carbon and Climate Law Review* 2015, 113–129, with the generous permission by Lexxion. All websites cited in this chapter were accessed on 1 October 2015.

* Both authors have been involved in negotiations under the UNFCCC, as part of the Norwegian and Brazilian delegations, respectively. During the negotiations that led to the adoption of the WFR, Christina Voigt was co-chair of the COP work programme on results-based finance and Felipe Ferreira was lead REDD+ negotiator for the Brazilian delegation. The views expressed in this article are personal and the sole responsibility of the authors. They do not necessarily reflect the views of the Norwegian or Brazilian government.

[1] The WFR consists of the following UNFCCC COP decisions: Decision 9/CP.19, Work Programme on Results-based Finance to Progress the Full Implementation of the Activities Referred to in Decision 1/CP.16, Paragraph 70; Decision 10/CP.19, Coordination of Support for the Implementation of Activities in Relation to Mitigation Actions in the Forest Sector by Developing Countries, Including Institutional Arrangements; Decision 11/CP.19, Modalities for National Forest Monitoring Systems; Decision 12/CP.19, The Timing and the Frequency of Presentations of the Summary of Information on how all the Safeguards Referred to in Decision 1/CP.16, Appendix I, are being Addressed and Respected; Decision 13/CP.19, Guidelines and Procedures for the Technical Assessment of Submissions from Parties on Proposed Forest Reference Emission Levels and/or Forest Reference Levels; Decision 14/CP.19, Modalities for Measuring, Reporting and Verifying; Decision 15/CP.19, Addressing the Drivers of Deforestation and Forest Degradation, UN Doc. FCCC/CP/2013/10/Add.1, 31 January 2014.

[2] UNFCCC COP 21 in Paris, December 2015, adopted three further decisions on REDD+: Alternative policy approaches, such as joint mitigation and adaptation approaches for the integral and sustainable management of forests; further guidance on ensuring transparency, consistency, comprehensiveness and effectiveness when informing on how all the safeguards referred to in Decision 1/CP.16, Appendix I, are being addressed and respected, and methodological issues related

accommodate a large variety of circumstances and capabilities of developing countries, while at the same time establishing a robust and clear framework fulfilling the criteria for a results-based approach for financing mitigation actions in the forest sector, including independent verification.

The concept of results-based finance links payments directly to verified results. It focuses on rewarding positive outcomes of recipients' actions, as opposed to traditional support modalities which can include the provision of an upfront grant or concessional financing. In those cases, the key aspect is that there is very little or no attempt for transfers to be contingent on the results provided by the recipient.

In the case of REDD+, results are defined as mitigation outcomes, i.e. GHG emission reductions and/or enhancements in forest cover and carbon stocks (sinks) measured against a benchmark (forest reference emission level (REL) and/or forest reference level (RL)) expressed in tonnes of carbon dioxide equivalents per year.

Together with previous decisions, the WFR sets, *inter alia*, the general criteria for developing countries to access results-based finance for their mitigation actions in the forest sector. Moreover, the WFR attributes to the Green Climate Fund (GCF) a "key role" among the entities channeling results-based finance to REDD+ and requests it to consistently apply UNFCCC methodological guidance on REDD+, while encouraging financing entities not under the UNFCCC to do the same.

This chapter describes the WFR and indicates some of its implications, especially centralization and increased transparency, for the implementation of REDD+ in developing countries, in particular in the context of accessing results-based finance. Rather than a commentary of each decision, it outlines the WFR from the perspective of access to results-based payments and measuring, reporting and verification (MRV) processes for REDD+ actions. The WFR has increased transparency and coordination of these processes as well as centralized them at the national level in developing countries, by linking MRV processes to reporting obligations of Parties under the UNFCCC and by inviting Parties to establish a voluntary "national entity or focal point" for REDD+. Sub-national elements are only envisaged as interim solutions in close coordination with national authorities. This has significant implications for the implementation of REDD+.

---

to non-carbon benefits resulting from the implementation of the activities referred to in Decision 1/CP.16, paragraph 70. These decisions did not change the content of the Warsaw Framework to any extent and marked the formal conclusion of UNFCCC negotiations on REDD+ (Decisions 16, 17 and 18/CP.21, FCCC/CP/2015/10/Add., 29 January 2016).

The chapter is structured in the following way: after a discussion of the phased approach to REDD+ and the placement of the concept of results-based finance in this context, the chapter will in detail describe the criteria which, according to the WFR, need to be in place in order to access results-based finance for REDD+ activities, with a particular focus on the MRV system. Following this description, the role of the GCF is analyzed. Moreover, the analysis of the MRV system will show how the WFR has centralized processes and procedures for obtaining results-based finance on the national (as opposed to sub-national or project-based) level. The chapter concludes by indicating some of the implications of the WFR for national REDD+ implementation and access to results-based payments.

2. A PHASED APPROACH TO REDD+?

One of the most prominent features of REDD+ under the UNFCCC is that finance for REDD+, ultimately, will be based on achieved results in terms of GHG emission reductions measured against a benchmark (forest REL and/or forest RL) expressed in tonnes of carbon dioxide equivalents per year. It is, however, understood that REDD+ is complex and implementation depends on Parties' national circumstances, capacities and level of support, according to which Parties will move at their own pace.

The conceptualization of REDD+ therefore foresees a gradual increase in Parties' actions and support towards the "collective aim to slow, halt and reverse forest cover and carbon loss."[3] Right from the beginning of discussions around REDD+, it was expected that Parties would need to first go through a process of national policy analysis and design, consultation, consensus building, testing and evaluation, before moving to full-scale implementation – leading to results-based finance. Whereas the elements listed in Decision 1/CP.16, paragraph 71 established a common set of requirements for developing countries undertaking REDD+ activities, the so-called "phased approach" would seek to retain flexibility while establishing national government ownership of the process, as well as a commitment from key actors, as essential prerequisites for successful REDD+ planning and implementation.[4]

---

[3] Decision 1/CP.16, The Cancun Agreements: Outcome of the Work of the Ad Hoc Working Group on Long-term Cooperative Action under the Convention, UN Doc. FCCC/CP/2010/7/Add.1, 15 March 2011, Preamble of Section C.

[4] Arild Angelsen, Sandra Brown and Cyril Loisel, *Reducing Emissions from Deforestation and Forest Degradation (REDD): An Options Assessment Report* (Washington, DC: Meridian Institute 2009), at 3.

Accordingly, Decision 1/CP.16, paragraph 73 made explicit reference to this progression by stating that REDD+ activities "should be implemented in phases, beginning with the development of national strategies or action plans . . . followed by the implementation of national policies and measures . . . and results-based demonstration activities, and evolving into results-based actions that should be fully measured, reported and verified."

Such a flexible approach was considered necessary to accommodate the differing capabilities of developing countries. Accordingly, Parties agreed that the implementation of REDD+ activities, including the choice of a starting phase, "depends on national circumstances, capacities and capabilities of each developing country Party, and the level of support received."[5]

As a consequence, many developing countries have increased their capacity in forest-management related issues and strengthened their institutional capacity and coordination.[6] Fewer countries, however, have already implemented changes in their policy and legal frameworks that would eventually lead to a decrease in forest-related emissions. What could be perceived as lack of progress is not surprising, given the fact that the WFR was only adopted in 2013. Prior to its adoption, uncertainties remained as to the methodological and financial framework for REDD+ activities. For this reason, the WFR was hailed as a "signature" achievement[7] and an important assurance to the REDD+ community, in particular developing countries.

Despite the suggestion in Decision 1/CP.16 that REDD+ should over time gradually evolve towards results-based finance, there is no specific requirement for developing countries on when or how to follow these steps. The phased approach may suggest that national strategies or action plans should be the first item in the process towards results-based finance, but this may not necessarily be the case, for instance, for countries who already have established policy and legal frameworks for the forest sector.[8]

---

[5] Decision 1/CP.16, at para. 74.

[6] For an overview, see for example, Voluntary REDD+ Database, available at: www.fao.org/forestry/vrd/; an overview over countries with national REDD+ programmes relevant to the UN-REDD programme at: www.un-redd.org/Partner_Countries/tabid/102663/Default.aspx; and an overview over those countries that participate at the Forest Carbon Partnership Facility at www.forestcarbonpartnership.org/redd-countries.

[7] Matt McGrath, "'Signature' Achievement on Forests at UN Climate Talks," BBC News, 22 November 2013, available at: www.bbc.com/news/science-environment-25060843.

[8] The case of Brazil clearly illustrates this point. The policy and legal framework that led to a large portion of the decrease of emissions in the forest sector was

Ultimately, under the WFR, it is not gradual progression on the phased approach that grants access to results-based finance: according to Decision 9/CP.19, paragraph 3, *all* of the elements referred to in Decision 1/CP.16, paragraph 71, should be in place in order to access results-based payments.

Before exploring the elements required to obtain results-based finance in more detail, we would like to briefly turn to the concept of results-based finance.

3. RESULTS-BASED FINANCE

Results-based approaches have for over a decade been of increasing interest in official development assistance, especially in the health and education sectors,[9] but also increasingly in the environmental sector.[10]

In general, results-based finance is a financing approach where payments are made only after a quantified outcome has verifiably been achieved. Such an approach is usually characterized by the following criteria: (1) the disbursement of funds is contingent on the delivery of pre-determined results, (2) the recipient country has discretion over how results are achieved, under mutually agreed parameters, and (3) independent verification acts as the trigger for disbursement.[11]

---

already in place in 2005. Brazil's subnational forest REL for the Amazon biome was submitted and assessed in 2014, its results verified by September 2015 (document FCCC/SBI/ICA/2015/TATR.1/BRA), but the country published its national REDD+ strategy only on December 2, 2015 (available at http://redd.mma.gov.br/images/Publicacoes/Enredd_Final.pdf).

[9] See, for example, Amanda Melina Gritter, *Results-Based Financing. Evidence from Performance-Based Financing in the Health Sector* (Bonn: German Development Institute, Discussion paper 6/2013); Javier Pereira and Carlos Villota, *Hitting the Target?: Evaluating the Effectiveness of Results-Based Approaches to Aid* (Brussels: European Network on Debt and Development 2012); Mark Pearson, Martin Johnson and Robin Ellison, *Review of Major Results Based Aid (RBA) and Results Based Financing (RBF) Schemes: Final Report* (London: DFID Human Development Resource Centre 2010).

[10] See, for example, Craig Hanson, Suzanne Ozment and Cornis Van der Lugt, *Nature in Performance Integrating – Ecosystem Services into Business Performance Systems* (Washington, DC: World Resources Institute 2012); Jeffrey Milder, Sara Scherr and Carina Bracer, "Trends and Future Potential of Payment for Ecosystem Services to Alleviate Rural Poverty in Developing Countries," 15(2): 4 *Ecology and Society* (2010).

[11] See, for example, Nancy Birdsall and William D. Savedoff, *Cash on Delivery: A new Approach to Foreign Aid* (Washington, DC: Center for Global Development, 2010); Department for International Development, UK, "Strategy for Payment by Results: Sharpening Incentives to Perform," 26 June 2014,

The introduction and increasing use of results-based funding is an attempt in international efforts to make development assistance more effective.[12] In the past, assistance in general – and health funding in particular – has often failed to deliver the desired results. Proponents of results-based finance argue that, in comparison to traditional aid modalities, this mode might deliver results with more effectiveness and efficiency, transparency, less intrusiveness, lower transaction costs and increased "country-ownership" by recipient countries.

Nevertheless, the increasing theoretical and practical importance of results-based funding is also based on the expectation that these approaches allow donors (governments and financial entities) and implementing domestic governments to link funding more closely to measurable results than other financing modalities do. This has gained particular importance in a time of political pressure on budget allocations.[13]

Having said that, results-based approaches might also hold certain challenges. One such challenge is that progress may be slow or uneven. There are many reasons for this and they vary from country to country. The requirements for results-based finance are (and have to be) quite strict. This poses important challenges regarding the fact that effective results-based finance requires from the outset a certain level of capacity, from operational management and assessment to strategic planning to budgeting. Progress on implementation may therefore be slow and concentrated within those actors with the largest capabilities.[14]

---

available at www.gov.uk/government/publications/dfids-strategy-for-payment-by-results-sharpening-incentives-to-perform and the World Bank, "Program-for-Results Financing," March 2015, available at http://siteresources.worldbank.org/PROJECTS/Resources/40940-1244163232994/6180403-1340125811295/PforR_Overview_update2015.pdf.

[12] Rita Perakis and William Savedoff, *Does Results-Based Aid Change Anything? Pecuniary Interests, Attention, Accountability and Discretion in Four Case Studies* (Washington, DC: Center for Global Development, CGD Policy Paper 052, February 2015).

[13] Gritter, *Results-Based Financing. Evidence from Performance-Based Financing in the Health Sector*. For a discussion on results-based approaches, see Pereira and Villota, *Hitting the Target?: Evaluating the Effectiveness of Results-Based Approaches to Aid*, 9.

[14] See, for a discussion: John Mayne, "Challenges and Lessons in Implementing Results-Based Management," 13: 1 *Evaluation* (January 2007), 87–109. See also: Robert Behn, *Rethinking Democratic Accountability* (Washington, DC: Brookings Institute 2000); Annette Binnendijk, *Results-Based Management in the Development Cooperation Agencies: A Review of Experience*, Background Report (Paris: DAC OECD Working Party on Aid Evaluation 2000). Available at: http://www.oecd.org/development/evaluation/dcdndep/31950852.pdf.

Despite these challenges, the concept of results-based finance has gained traction within REDD+ as a means to make actions in the forest sector more effective and to increase recipient accountability as well as transparency. For these – and perhaps more – reasons, many countries view results-based payments as the principal mechanism that will provide "positive incentives" for effective REDD+ actions.

4. CRITERIA FOR OBTAINING RESULTS-BASED FINANCE FOR REDD+ ACTIONS

Results-based finance for REDD+ links payments to GHG emission reductions and enhancements in forest cover and forest carbon stocks. Results-based payments for mitigation actions in the forest sector in developing countries provide financial incentives and disburse resources against demonstrated and independently verified results that are largely within the control of the recipient developing country. In the context of REDD+, results-based finance could leverage private and public investment into activities that reduce GHG emissions and promote removals. The credibility and acceptance of results-based finance frameworks, however, depend on the rigor of the applied measurement methodologies, the conservativeness of the RL, and the transparency of the payment scheme.

For results-based finance for REDD+ actions, there have to be at least four components in place: (1) a clear agreement on the definition of results, (2) an understanding of what needs to be in place in order to trigger potential payments, (3) a set of commonly agreed parameters to frame the discretion left to implementing developing country Parties, and (4) a well-designed MRV system that can give reasonable confidence that results have been achieved.

With regards to the first point, UNFCCC Parties have agreed that – under the WFR and other related decisions – REDD+ results are defined as mitigation results: in the context of results-based payments for REDD+, the results are to be measured against an assessed forest REL and/or forest RL and to be expressed in tonnes of carbon dioxide equivalent per year.[15]

The second component – a clear understanding of what needs to be in place to trigger results-based payments – is something the WFR has

[15] Decision 12/CP.17, Guidance on Systems for Providing Information on how Safeguards are Addressed and Respected and Modalities relating to Forest Reference Emission Levels and Forest Reference Levels as referred to in Decision 1/CP.16, UN Doc. FCCC/CP/2011/9/Add.2, 15 March 2012, at paras. 7–15; Decision 14/CP.19, at para. 4; and Decision 13/CP.19.

clarified. Importantly, it requires that those REDD+ actions for which results-based payments are being sought need to be fully measured, reported and verified in accordance with Decisions 13/CP.19 and 14/CP.19.[16] UNFCCC Parties have recognized this as a prerequisite for obtaining and receiving results-based finance, necessary to give reasonable confidence that results have been achieved. The MRV process is a critical, complex and central element for obtaining and receiving results-based finance and is, therefore, dealt with comprehensively in section 5 below.

Furthermore, in order to obtain and receive results-based finance, developing countries should have "in place" a compound of criteria, most notably those contained in Decision 1/CP.16, paragraph 71.[17] The criteria are the following:

4.1 National Strategy or Action Plan

Effectively undertaking REDD+ activities presupposes a national architecture or governance structure that facilitates comprehensive actions and delivers mitigation outcomes that are effective, efficient and equitable. The overall responsibility for REDD+ and its implementation lies with the national government whose task it is to develop a national REDD+ strategy or action plan.[18] Such a process entails coordinating and strengthening existing institutional and legal arrangements with respect to mitigation actions in the forest sector as well as identifying and initiating necessary policy reforms at national and subnational levels.[19] A national REDD+ strategy may, thus, also comprise of various sub-national elements.

It is worth noting here that a *national* strategy ought to cover the entire relevant territory of a developing country Party. While subnational approaches as interim measures are recognized for national forest RELs and/or forest RLs as well as national forest monitoring systems, no such sub-national or sub-jurisdictional option is provided for REDD+ strategy development under the UNFCCC.[20]

---

16 Decision 9/CP.19, at para. 3.

17 Ibid.

18 Decision 1/CP.16, at para. 71(a).

19 Angelsen et al., *Reducing Emissions from Deforestation and Forest Degradation (REDD): An Options Assessment Report* (Washington, DC: Meridian Institute, 2009).

20 However, there seems to be a shared understanding that REDD+ activities may be *implemented* through subnational entities or shared competence between national and subnational governance entities. Countries may also prioritize certain geographical areas for action due to them being "hot spots" for deforestation activities or areas where actions will have a particular impact.

Further, developing country Parties are requested, when developing their national strategies or action plans, to address a catalogue of issues, *inter alia*, drivers of deforestation and forest degradation, land tenure issues, forest governance issues, gender considerations and the safeguards, ensuring full and effective participation of relevant stakeholders including indigenous peoples and local communities.[21]

Despite this list of elements, the concrete scope and approach to national REDD+ strategies or action plans is rather open and allows developing countries flexibility. National REDD+ strategies or action plans that are currently being developed in the context of national circumstances differ significantly from country to country.[22] They range from identifying REDD+ actions as a part in the overall climate change policy, embedding REDD+ into broader development strategies, to specific national strategies.[23] Also, countries may choose to include all REDD+ activities listed in Decision 1/CP.16, paragraph 70, or single out one or some of them according to prevailing national circumstances.[24] Finally, countries can choose to embark on and implement emission reduction policies prior to finalizing a national REDD+ strategy. However, the WFR clarified that a *national* REDD+ strategy or action plan ultimately needs to be in place by the time a developing country Party wants to proceed to obtaining and receiving results-based finance.

4.2 National Forest REL and/or Forest RL

Reference levels are a critical design element of REDD+, since there is a need for estimating benchmarks for assessing each developing country Party's performance in implementing REDD+ activities and measuring emission reductions due to REDD+ actions. Developing country Parties are therefore invited, on a voluntary basis and when deemed appropriate, to submit proposed forest RELs and/or forest RLs, in accordance with Decision 1/CP.16, paragraph 71(b).[25] RLs are to be expressed in

---

[21] Decision 1/CP.16, at para. 72.

[22] See, for example, Josefina Braña Varela, Donna Lee, Daniela Rey and Steven Swan, *REDD+ Safeguards: Practical Considerations for Developing a Summary of Information* (Washington, DC: Meridian Institute 2014).

[23] See, for example, *REDD+ National Strategy* (Jakarta: Indonesia REDD+ Taskforce 2012) available at: www.unorcid.org/upload/doc_lib/Indonesia%20REDD+%20National%20Strategy.pdf.

[24] See, for example, Republic of Tanzania, *National REDD+ Strategy*, 2nd draft (2012).

[25] Decision 12/CP.17, at para. 13.

tonnes of CO_{2eq} per annum. In establishing RLs Parties should take into account historic data, potentially adjusted for national circumstances.[26] Such adjustment is particularly important for countries with high forest carbon stocks but low historic deforestation rates relative to global average.[27]

The modalities for forest emission levels and/or forest reference levels further require consistency with each country's national greenhouse gas inventory, and allow for a step-wise approach that enables Parties to improve their RL over time due to better data, improved methodologies and, where appropriate, additional pools.[28] It is further acknowledged that RLs should periodically be updated taking into account new knowledge, new trends and modifications of scopes and methodologies.

The guidelines for submissions of information on reference levels are contained in the annex to Decision 12/CP.17 and include the principles of transparency, completeness, consistency, accuracy and comprehensiveness as well as being guided by the most recent IPCC guidelines and guidance. Consistent with the step-wise approach, Parties may commence with elaborating subnational RLs as an interim measure. However, it is important to note that, in the context of results-based finance, the transition to a *national* RL remains the final goal and that the assessment of proposed RLs is a mandatory *requirement*, and the basis of the MRV process.[29] The assessment of the RL against the requirements described above is a crucial part of the MRV process which is detailed in section 5.

---

[26] Decision 4/CP.15, Methodological Guidance for Activities relating to Reducing Emissions from Deforestation and Forest Degradation and the Role of Conservation, Sustainable Management of Forests and Enhancement of Forest Carbon Stocks in Developing Countries, UN Doc. FCCC/CP/2009/11/Add.1, 30 March 2010, at para. 7 and Decision 12/CP.17, at para. 9.

[27] So called High-forest–low-emissions (HFLE) countries would otherwise have little incentive to participate in a system based on RLs calculated from historical deforestation data alone because their emissions are small and thus have little room for reduction. If these countries do not participate, there is the risk of leakage from participating countries into these countries, which could threaten the environmental integrity of the whole system. National circumstances in this context could include the following: baseline above historic emissions, conservation activities, stage in forest transition, development plans. See Arild Angelsen, Doug Boucher, Sandra Brown et al., *Modalities for REDD+ Reference Levels: Technical and Procedural Issues* (Washington, DC: Meridian Institute 2011).

[28] Decision 12/CP.17, at paras. 7–15.

[29] Decision 1/CP.16, at para. 71(b), Decision 12/CP.17, at para. 11, and Decision 13/CP.19.

4.3 National Forest Monitoring System

Forest monitoring is a key issue in REDD+ policy and development. Because REDD+ is ultimately based on the premise of payments for mitigation results, it is critically important that measurements of emissions and removals are as accurate as possible, meaning they have low uncertainty.[30] Meeting these measurement and monitoring needs requires consistent and frequent images of forest landscapes, which can only be accomplished using a combination of remote sensing that has been calibrated and validated with measurements on the ground.[31]

Moreover, monitoring of natural forest cover and biodiversity can also, where appropriate, demonstrate how countries address and respect (some of) the safeguards of REDD+.[32]

Decision 4/CP.15 already requested developing country Parties to establish robust and transparent national forest monitoring systems and provided some guidance. The WFR reaffirms this guidance, including the use of a combination of remote sensing and ground-based forest carbon inventory approaches, and refers its technical aspects to the most recent applicable IPCC guidance and guidelines.[33]

The WFR sets further parameters for what constitutes a "robust"[34] monitoring system: data and information provided through such systems should be transparent, consistent over time, suitable for measurement, report and verification of REDD+ activities, as well as consistent with other methodological guidance developed under the UNFCCC for MRV of mitigation actions in general.[35]

---

30 Arild Angelsen, Maria Brockhaus, William D. Sunderlin and Louis V. Verchot, *Analysing REDD+ – Challenges and Choices* (Bogor: CIFOR 2012); Martin Herold, Rosa Román-Cuesta, Danilo Mollicone et al., "Options for Monitoring and Estimating Historical Carbon Emissions from Forest Degradation in the Context of REDD+," 6:13 *Carbon Balance and Management* (2011); Martin Herold and Margaret Skutsch, "Monitoring, Reporting and Verification for National REDD+ Programmes: Two Proposals," 6 *Environmental Research Letters* (2011).

31 Scott J. Goetz, Matthew Hansen, Richard A. Houghton et al., *Measurement and Monitoring for REDD+: The Needs, Current Technological Capabilities, and Future Potential*, Working Paper 392, CGD Climate and Forest Paper Series 17 (Washington, DC: Center for Global Development 2014).

32 Decision 11/CP.19, at para. 5.

33 Ibid, at para. 2.

34 Decision 4/CP.15 at para. 1(d) already identified the provision of estimates that are transparent, consistent, as far as possible accurate, and that reduce uncertainties already as qualifiers for "robust" national forest monitoring systems (Decision 4/CP.15).

35 Decision 11/CP.19, at para. 3.

The flexible, progressive nature of REDD+ under the UNFCCC is reinforced by the recognition that national forest monitoring systems should build upon existing systems (including, as an interim measure, subnational systems), be flexible, allow for improvement and reflect the phased approach, as appropriate.[36]

Although neither the WFR, nor previous decisions, explicitly determine any specific order for the development of the elements listed in Decision 1/CP.16, paragraph 71, there is a sequential logic intrinsic to the MRV process that requires forest monitoring systems to be in place *before* a country can develop a reference level and present results from their REDD+ actions. Results depend on estimating emissions and changes in forest area or forest carbon stocks over time. This estimation, in turn, can only occur with forest monitoring systems in place – thus making such systems the cornerstone of the MRV process.[37]

4.4 Safeguard Information System

An important feature of the UNFCCC framework for REDD+ is the introduction of safeguards. REDD+ safeguards direct implementation and support of REDD+ activities beyond mitigation actions, aiming at avoiding negative impacts and at promoting selected rights and interests of stakeholders.[38]

Accordingly, Decision 1/CP.16 provides that REDD+ activities should promote and support a set of social and environmental safeguards.[39] In order to ensure transparency of the implementation of these safeguards, the

---

36 Ibid at para. 4.

37 This point may be carried further. Forest monitoring systems are arguably the most important of the elements listed in Decision 1/CP.16, para. 71, because of their relationship with the development and effectiveness of all other elements (Decision 1/CP.16). Besides their role in the MRV process, forest monitoring systems are to a large extent the source of the information required for the development and follow-up of national strategies or action plans, as well as to feed safeguard information systems. See also Decision 11/CP.19, at para. 5 which acknowledges that forest monitoring systems may provide relevant information on how safeguards are being addressed and respected.

38 There is a large amount of literature on this aspect of REDD+. For an overview, see Chapter 5 by Annalisa Savaresi, "The Legal Status and Role of Safeguards," in this book; also: Constance L. McDermotte, Lauren Coada, Ariella Helfgotta and Heike Schroeder, "Operationalizing Social Safeguards in REDD+: Actors, Interests and Ideas," 21 *Environmental Science & Policy* (2012), 63 *et seq.*, at p. 72; Braña Varela, *REDD+ Safeguards: Practical Considerations for Developing a Summary of Information.*

39 Decision 1/CP.16, at Appendix I, para. 2 (a–g).

same decision requests developing countries to develop a system for providing information (SIS) on how all of the safeguards are being addressed and respected in the implementation of REDD+ activities throughout *all* phases.

Decision 12/CP.17 specifies that safeguard information systems must be implemented at the national level for all REDD+ activities regardless of the source or type of financing and through a country-driven approach. The decision further clarifies that the safeguard information system should provide consistent, comprehensive and transparent information that is accessible by all stakeholders and is updated regularly, that should be flexible to allow improvements over time and should provide information on how all of the safeguards are being addressed and respected.

4.5 Most Recent Summary of Safeguard Information

Decision 12/CP.17 further agrees that developing country Parties should periodically provide a summary of information on how all the safeguards are being addressed and respected.[40] The information can come from the SIS or other information systems or sources but should be provided in a way that ensures transparency, consistency, comprehensiveness and effectiveness. The summary should contain information about which REDD+ activity or activities are covered and include information on national circumstances relevant to addressing and respecting the safeguards, a description of each safeguard in accordance with national circumstances, a description of existing systems (including, for example, the SIS) and processes relevant to addressing and respecting safeguards as well as information on how each safeguard has been addressed and respected. Developing countries are encouraged to add additional information as they see fit and to step-wise improve the information.[41] The summary is to be provided by a national authority after the start of the implementation of REDD+ activities and included in the national communications from developing country Parties, as well as, on a voluntary basis, via the REDD+ Web Platform.[42]

---

[40] Braña Varela, *REDD+ Safeguards: Practical Considerations for Developing a Summary of Information*. It should be noted that although the summary of information and the SIS are intrinsically linked, the summary can inform the UNFCCC on the status of addressing and respecting safeguards prior to the establishment and full operationalization of the SIS.

[41] Decision 17/CP.21 Further Guidance on ensuring transparency, consistency, comprehensiveness and effectiveness when informing on how all the safeguards referred to in Decision 1/CP.16, Appendix I, are being addressed and respected.

[42] Decision 12/CP.17, paras. 3 and 4.

The WFR further states that developing countries seeking to obtain and receive results-based payments for REDD+ activities should provide the *most recent* summary of information on how *all* of the safeguards have been addressed and respected before they can receive results-based payments.[43]

The rationale for the requirement of providing the most *recent* summary is to give donors the transparency and assurance that for the relevant period for which results-based payments are being provided, all safeguards have been addressed and respected. Donors may have to offer evidence to their constituencies that finance spent on REDD+ is for achieved results that cause no environmental or social harm.

Following that line of thought, the argument can be made that "the most recent summary" should correspond to the period for which results-based payments are being sought – although the decision is not explicit on this matter. According to the guidelines for national communications from developing countries, the minimum frequency for providing a summary of information is every four years.[44] In practice, considering this long period might not be consistent with opportunities to access results-based finance, it is reasonable to expect a more frequent submission of summaries on safeguards – for instance every two years, along with results presented through the Biennial Update Reports.

5. MEASUREMENT, REPORTING AND VERIFICATION AT THE CORE OF RESULTS-BASED FINANCE FOR REDD+

As mentioned above, a well-designed MRV system that can give reasonable confidence that results have been achieved is critical to any results-based approach. In this sense, UNFCCC Parties decided that REDD+ actions should be fully measured, reported and verified "in accordance with Decisions 13/CP.19 and 14/CP.19."[45]

Decisions 13/CP.19 and 14/CP.19 refer, respectively, to the assessment of forest RELs and/or forest RLs and to the modalities for measuring,

---

[43] Decision 9/CP.19, para. 4.

[44] Arts. 4(1) and 12 of the United Nations Framework Convention on Climate Change, New York, 9 May 1992, in force 21 March 1994; Decision 17/CP.8, Guidelines for the Preparation of National Communications from Parties not included in Annex I to the Convention, UN Doc. FCCC/CP/2002/7/Add.2, 28 March 2003.

[45] Decision 9/CP.19, at para. 3.

reporting and verifying REDD+ actions and their results. Since REDD+ results are to be measured in relation to their RL, both decisions are closely interrelated; they establish, in practical terms, one periodical and continuous process, starting with the assessment of RLs.

The assessment of RLs and the following steps of the MRV process, including the insertion of information on results and respective payments in the Lima information hub (see 5.3 below), form interlinked elements that aim at securing certainty and transparency for results-based REDD+ actions.

5.1 Measurement: Assessment of RLs

While the process for the technical assessment of RLs was already established in Durban in 2011 by Decision 12/CP.17, paragraph 15, it was not until the WFR was adopted that Parties set out detailed guidance for this process. According to Decision 13/CP.19, the technical assessment will be conducted, on a yearly basis, by a team of land use, land-use change and forestry (LULUCF) experts selected from the roster of experts, under coordination of the UNFCCC Secretariat. Each reference level submission will be assessed by two experts, one from a developed country and one from a developing country – neither a national of the Party being assessed, nor funded by that Party. These characteristics offer assurances of the independence of this aspect of the MRV process and effectively mark the beginning of its international component. It is a lengthy process though: it can take up to 9–10 months from the submission of a proposed reference level to the publication of the final report.[46]

Once again reflecting the need for REDD+ to be technically robust, while flexible enough to allow for broad participation, Decision 13/CP.19 establishes a process where the team of experts will assess the degree to which the information provided is in accordance with the guidelines internationally agreed in Decision 12/CP.17, in a "facilitative, non-intrusive" technical manner, with a view to supporting the progressive improvement of the reference levels.[47] It is worth noting nevertheless that the scope of the assessment goes into considerably more detail than Decision 12/CP.17, by including, inter alia, its consistency with national greenhouse gas inventories; the use of historical data; pools, gases and activities included; the

---

[46] See Annex of Decision 13/CP.19 for the objective, scope and procedures of the assessment (Decision 13/CP.19).

[47] Ibid. See, for example, "Report of the Technical Assessment of the Proposed Forest Reference Emission Level of Brazil submitted in 2014," FCCC/TAR/2014/BRA (1 December 2014), http://unfccc.int/resource/docs/2014/tar/bra01.pdf.

definition of forest used; and whether assumptions on relevant policies and plans have been provided. For Parties seeking results-based payments, the technical assessment of the reference level has a particular weight, because the verification process is to a large extent based on the consistency between results and the assessed reference levels.

5.2 Reporting and Verification: Biennial Update Reports and International Consultation and Analysis

After the RL assessment procedure, REDD+ results are to be measured against the assessed RL, in tonnes of carbon dioxide equivalent per year,[48] reported through a technical annex to the Biennial Update Reports (BUR)[49] and verified through the International Consultation and Analysis (ICA) process agreed upon in Decision 2/CP.17.[50]

The BUR and the ICA process are part of enhanced MRV provisions for developing countries' mitigation actions under the UNFCCC, decided in the Cancun Agreements.[51] Under these, developing countries are to submit BURs, besides their regular national communications, "containing updates of national greenhouse gas inventories, including a national inventory report and information on mitigation actions, needs and support received."[52]

In response to concerns by some donor countries that the ICA process[53]

---

[48] Decision 14/CP.19, at para. 4.

[49] Decision 14/CP.19, at para. 6.

[50] Decision 14/CP.19, at paras. 10 and 11.

[51] Decision 1/CP.16, at paras. 48–67. Decisions 2/CP.17, Outcome of the Work of the Ad Hoc Working Group on Long-term Cooperative Action under the Convention, UN Doc. FCCC/CP/2011/9/Add.1, 15 March 2012, at paras. 32–62, Annexes III and IV; and Decision 20/CP.19, Composition, Modalities and Procedures of the Team of Technical Experts under International Consultation and Analysis, UN Doc. FCCC/CP/2013/10/Add.2, 31 January 2014, set up the guidelines for preparing the biennial update reports, as well as the modalities and procedures for the international consultation and analysis process.

[52] Decision 1/CP.16, at para. 60(c).

[53] ICA is the agreed international component of MRV of developing countries' mitigation actions more broadly, not just for REDD+. In general terms, it consists of two steps. The first is an "analysis [of the BUR] by technical experts in consultation with the Party concerned" in a manner that is "non-intrusive, non-punitive and respectful of national sovereignty." The analysis under the ICA is to be conducted by a team from the UNFCCC roster of experts, resulting in a summary report, and this will be subject to the second step: a "facilitative sharing of views" conducted by the SBI, in the form of open workshops, including the opportunity for questions and answers to the developing country concerned. The first round of

alone might not be stringent enough for the purpose of results-based payments (as opposed to traditional modalities of international support), the WFR effectively created additional layers for the MRV process of REDD+ results. Pursuant to Decision 14/CP.19, paragraphs 1, 3 and 6, REDD+ actions will be subject to the ICA process together with other mitigation actions by developing countries, regardless of the point along the "phased approach" when those actions are being carried out. Paragraphs 7–14 of the same decision, however, go further, requesting developing countries seeking to obtain and receive payments for results-based actions to supply in their BUR a technical annex on REDD+.

This technical annex will be subject to a specific analysis and a separate technical report by two LULUCF experts from the UNFCCC roster of experts (one from a developing and one from a developed country Party), to be included in the technical team responsible for the ICA upon request of the developing country concerned.[54] This additional layer of reporting and verification procedures offers further reassurances of the independence and technical quality of the MRV process with regard to REDD+ results, while at the same time keeping REDD+ consistent with the methodologies and guidance established for developing countries' mitigation actions under the UNFCCC.

For Parties seeking results-based payments, the elements to be included in the technical annex to the BUR are listed in the annex to Decision 14/CP.19. They can be broadly described as summary information linking REDD+ results to their corresponding assessed reference level, along with information that demonstrates that the methodologies used to produce the results are consistent with the assessed reference level and that allow for the reconstruction of the results. The focus of the technical annex is clearly on the relationship between the results and the assessed reference level.[55]

The verification procedure for REDD+ results conducted by the LULUCF experts under the ICA looks, *inter alia*, at the extent to which the data and information provided are transparent, consistent, complete[56] and accurate – and, most importantly, at the demonstration of the consistency of the results with the assessed reference level.[57] It may be

analysis will be conducted in 2015, for those countries that already submitted their BUR and will be repeated, accordingly, on a biannual basis (see Decision 1/CP.16, at para. 63 and Decision 2/CP.17, at Annex IV, para. 3).

[54] Decision 14/CP.19, at paras. 7–10.

[55] Decision 14/CP.19, at Annex.

[56] Complete means here the provision of information that allows for the reconstruction of the results.

[57] Decision 14/CP.19, at para. 11.

argued that, because of the close interrelation between the verification of results and the assessed reference level, Decisions 13 and 14/CP.19 jointly create, effectively, a two-step international verification process, conducted by independent experts, under the auspices of the UNFCCC. This verification process may be described as a *continuous cycle* that follows the timelines of the ICA.

The final outcome of the MRV process is a technical report by the LULUCF experts, to be published by the UNFCCC Secretariat, containing the respective country's technical annex on REDD+ results, the analysis conducted by the experts, as well as areas for technical improvement on data and methodologies and any comments or responses related to areas of further improvement or capacity-building needs.[58]

5.3 MRV and Transparency: Lima Information Hub

Once the MRV process is finalized, and all the documentation regarding REDD+ results and the requirements for obtaining results-based payments[59] are available, these will be published, along with related reports, in the "Lima Information Hub for REDD-plus" (Lima Info Hub).[60] The purpose of the Lima Info Hub is to increase transparency on results-based actions and on the corresponding payments, as well as on information related to the requirements to obtain and receive results-based finance. By linking mitigation results to their corresponding payments, it also serves as a tracking tool to avoid the possibility of double-counting results and/or payments – assuming that developed country Parties and entities providing results-based finance will want their payments recognized under the UNFCCC and inserted in the Lima Info Hub.[61]

Unlike other online tools developed outside the UNFCCC[62], the Lima Info Hub relates exclusively to results-based payments, not to readiness financing.[63]

---

58 Decision 14/CP.19, at para. 14.

59 See the list in Decision 9/CP.19, para. 11 (a–e) (Decision 9/CP.19).

60 http://redd.unfccc.int/info-hub.html. COP20 operationalized the information hub established by Decision 9/CP.19, at para. 9, and named it the "Lima Information Hub for REDD-plus" (Decision 9/CP.19). See "Report of the Conference of the Parties on its twentieth Session, held in Lima from 1 to 14 December 2014," UN Doc. FCCC/CP/2014/10, 2 February 2015, at para. 50.

61 Decision 9/CP.19, at paras. 9–15.

62 Such as the Voluntary REDD+ Database available at: http://www.fao.org/forestry/vrd/.

63 Further details on the design of the information hub are available at "Report on the Expert Meeting on an Information Hub for Information on the Results of

The actual effect of the Lima Info Hub might not be restricted to being a repository for REDD+ activities. In practical terms, by publicizing the information on the criteria established in Decision 1/CP.16, paragraph 71, and the outcomes of the MRV process, the Lima Info Hub serves implicitly as international recognition that a developing country is in a position to obtain and receive results-based payments. The insertion of information, however, "does not create any rights or obligations for any Party or other entity," i.e. it does not automatically entitle developing countries to receive payments, nor pre-determines conditions or any arrangements to that end.[64] It should be underlined that the insertion of information on results-based payments in the Lima Info Hub is to be done "in consultation with the developing country Party concerned, taking into full account Decision 10/CP.19, paragraph 2."

Being in a position to obtain and receive results-based payments, however, is not the same as being granted payments – there is still the matter of carrying out payment arrangements with a partner from the "wide variety of sources, public and private, bilateral and multilateral, including alternative sources"[65] channeling results-based finance to developing countries, most notably the Green Climate Fund.

6. RELATIONSHIP BETWEEN THE WFR AND MARKET MECHANISMS

The WFR, including the MRV process previously described, apply to REDD+ activities irrespective of the source or approach for financing REDD+, be it public or private, market or non-market. The matter of market approaches to REDD+, however, remains unresolved and highly polarized.[66]

While Parties have considered that "appropriate market-based

---

the Activities referred to in Decision 1/CP.16, paragraph 70, and Results-based Payments," UN Doc. FCCC/SBI/2014/INF.13, 14 October 2014.

[64] Decision 9/CP.19, at para. 16.

[65] Decision 9/CP.19, at para. 1; and Decision 2/CP.17, at para. 65.

[66] A number of countries are in favor of using market approaches, including offsetting, while, for example, Brazil, upon the adoption of the WFR, made an interpretative statement of Decision 9/CP.19, paras. 16–18, underlining that in order to ensure the environmental integrity of REDD+, results-based payments are not to be used to offset mitigation commitments by Annex I Parties (Decision 9/CP.19). See "Report of the Conference of the Parties on its nineteenth Session, held in Warsaw from 11 to 23 November 2013," UN Doc. FCCC/CP/2013/10/Corr.1, 20 June 2014.

approaches could be developed by the COP,"[67] they also later agreed that "nothing under this decision and its implementation prejudges any future decision with regard to the eligibility or non-eligibility"[68] of REDD+ activities to market-based mechanisms currently under discussion under the UNFCCC. The COP has further agreed that "results-based actions that may be eligible to appropriate market based approaches that could be developed by the Conference of the Parties (. . .) may be subject to any further specific modalities for verification consistent with any relevant decision of the Conference of the Parties."[69]

The possible development of market approaches for supporting REDD+ actions is, therefore, not only contingent upon the conditions established in Decision 2/CP.17 paragraph 66,[70] but also upon resolving the matter of "eligibility or non-eligibility" of REDD+ activities for market-based mechanisms. This maintains the existing uncertainties to market-based approaches for REDD+.[71]

It is worth noting further that "the information on results included on the information hub should be linked to the same results reflected on any other relevant future system that may be developed under the Convention."[72] This language could be understood as making reference to, for example, the possible development of systems to avoid double counting of mitigation units from market mechanisms developed and/or recognized under the UNFCCC. It could imply that the possibility of trading REDD+ mitigation results would be accompanied by the deduction of tonnes of CO_{2eq} from developing countries' national greenhouse gas accounting in the new agreement under the UNFCCC, currently being negotiated.

---

67 Decision 1/CP.16, at para. 66.

68 Decision 9/CP.19, at para. 18.

69 Decision 14/CP.19, at para. 15.

70 The conditions are: ensuring that environmental integrity is preserved, that the provisions of Decision 1/CP.16, Appendices I and II, are fully respected and should be consistent with the relevant provisions of existing and future decisions on these matters.

71 Market analysts have noted such uncertainty – see, for instance, Nicolas Kreibich, "Sending Mixed Signals to the Markets," 4 *Carbon Mechanisms Review* (2013), available at: www.jiko-bmub.de/files/basisinformationen/application/pdf/cmr-04-2013-english-web.pdf.

72 Decision 9/CP.19, at para. 17.

7. ACCESS TO RESULTS-BASED PAYMENTS

7.1 Financing Sources within the UNFCCC

(a) "Key" role of the GCF

In order to effectively implement and scale-up REDD+ actions the availability of finance is critical. For results-based finance, Parties have agreed that the sources may cover a wide variety, public and private, bilateral and multilateral, including alternative sources. Such a broad array of differing financing sources and corresponding entities is deemed a necessary condition for garnering adequate and predictable results-based finance – while it admittedly raises challenges in relation to coordination of support.

Among those financing entities, the WFR allocates to the Green Climate Fund a key role in channeling results-based finance to developing countries in a fair and balanced manner.[73] The explicit attribution of such a role to the GCF seeks to offer some degree of assurance to developing countries on the scale, adequacy and predictability of results-based finance for REDD+.

The COP has explicitly requested the GCF to apply the UNFCCC methodological guidance when providing results-based finance.[74] Accordingly, the Fund's Board has developed a specific logic model and performance measurement framework (PMF) for results-based payments for REDD+, following the WFR's methodological guidance.

The initial logic model for REDD+ results-based payments and the PMF were both adopted at the Board's eighth meeting in October 2014[75] and are integral to the GCF's mitigation logic model.[76] They show the way in which results-based payments for REDD+ contribute to the achievement of the GCF's overall mitigation objectives directly at the level of paradigm shift, i.e. shift to low-emission sustainable development pathways, and impacts in the Fund's overall mitigation logic model, providing the rationale for providing results-based payments.

When designing the initial logic model and the PMF, the Board has

---

[73] Ibid, at para. 5.

[74] Ibid, at para. 7.

[75] Green Climate Fund, Meeting of the Board, *Initial Logic Model and Performance Measurement Framework for REDD+ Results-based Payments*, GCF/B.08/08/Rev.01, 17 October 2014.

[76] Green Climate Fund, Meeting of the Board, *Initial Results Management Framework*, GCF/B.07/04, 7 May 2014. Results-based payments will partly contribute to the achievement of result 4.0 in the mitigation logic model, which includes also activities in the land use sector other than REDD+.

considered that "the body of REDD+ decisions define the requirements for recognizing developing countries' results-based actions and enabling them to receive results-based payments." The logic model defines its programme outcomes as the five REDD+ activities listed in Decision 1/CP.16, paragraph 70, expressed in tCO_{2eq}. Programmes outcomes can only be on the scale of national and, as an interim measure, sub-national levels. The Fund will disburse results-based payments in accordance with the guidance in Decision 9/CP.19 which – as explained above – requires, *inter alia*:

- results in tCO_{2eq} that have undergone technical analysis as referred to in 14/CP.19;
- an REL/RL that has undergone technical assessment as referred to in 13/CP.19;
- the most recent summary of information showing how all the safeguards referred to in Decision1/CP.16 have been addressed and respected, consistent with Decisions 1/CP.16, 12/CP.17, 9/CP.19 and 12/CP.19;
- a national strategy or action plan as referred to in 1/CP.16;
- information on the national forest monitoring system as referred to in 14/CP.19.

The source for the above information provided to the GCF will be the Lima Info Hub.

It is important to reiterate, however, that the expressed results do not establish payment rights. The operationalization and actual disbursement of results-based payments for REDD+ is to be considered in the context of the GCF's overall investment framework and in line with the Funds allocation policy. At least during this initial phase of the Fund's operationalization, until the Board develops specific modalities for disbursing results-based payments for REDD+ and/or calls for funding proposals, developing countries (or entities they nominate to obtain and receive results-based payments on their behalf) must submit their results through the proposal approval process outlined in the Board's Decision B.07/03.

(b) GCF national designated authority and the REDD+ national entity or national focal point

The GCF has recently opened accreditation procedures for implementing entities and intermediaries, as a first step for the GCF to start financing projects and programmes. All entities seeking accreditation are required, *inter alia*, to demonstrate that they meet Fiduciary Standards and Social and Environmental Safeguards, among other requirements. According to the Fund's agreed procedures, finance will flow from the Fund to implementing entities (IEs) and intermediaries – who will manage, oversee and intermediate resources to the executing entities (EEs). Funding proposals will be also be subject to a no-objection procedure by developing countries' national designated authorities (NDAs).[77]

It is important to point out the different, yet complementary, roles of the entities described above and the national entity or national focal point for REDD+ referred to in the WFR (henceforth "NE/NFP") – where they exist. The WFR invites interested Parties to designate an NE/NFP "to serve as liaison" on matters related to coordination of support.[78] The same Decision, in its paragraph 2, notes that the NE/NFP of developing countries, if designated, may nominate entities to obtain and receive results-based payments on behalf of the developing country concerned, "consistent with any specific operational modalities of the financing entities providing them with support."

As referred to in section 5.3 above, the insertion of information on results-based payments in the Lima Info Hub is to be done in consultation with the developing country Party concerned, especially the NE/NFP where a developing country Party has chosen to designate it – undoubtedly information on payments to the entities the NE/NFP has nominated, since the insertion of information is to be done "taking into full account Decision 10/CP.19, paragraph 2."[79] Entities submitting proposals to the GCF for results-based payments, therefore, should preferably be among those nominated by the NE/NFP, with a view to ensuring proper recognition in the Lima Info Hub.

At the same time, the nomination by the NE/NFP, *per se*, is not enough to access results-based payments under the GCF – entities submitting proposals to the GCF must also fulfill its operational modalities, including accreditation and the no-objection procedures. It follows that there is need for coordination between developing countries' NDA and NE/NFP where they exist, in order to ensure effective proposal procedures for REDD+ results-based payments.

---

[77] Green Climate Fund, Meeting of the Board, *Guiding Framework and Procedures for Accrediting National, Regional and International Implementing Entities and Intermediaries, including the Fund's fiduciary Principles and Standards and environmental and social Safeguards*, GCF/B.07/02, 7 May 2014.

[78] Decision 10/CP.19, at paras. 1, 4 and 5.

[79] Decision 9/CP.19, at para. 13.

7.2 Financing Entities outside the UNFCCC

As explained above, finance for REDD+ results can come from a variety of different sources and corresponding entities, including entities outside the UNFCCC, such as multilateral funds or public or private donors.

While the GCF and other financing entities under the UNFCCC are explicitly *requested* to apply UNFCCC methodological guidance on REDD+ when providing results-based finance for REDD+ actions, other entities outside the UNFCCC are only *encouraged* to do so, "in order to improve the effectiveness and coordination of results based finance."[80] The distinction between the request and encouragement is due to the fact that the COP has no normative powers with regard to entities that do not operate under its guidance and/or accountability.

The application by other entities financing REDD+ of the methodological guidance multilaterally agreed under the WFR and other relevant UNFCCC decisions is nevertheless key for the effectiveness and coordination of REDD+ results-based finance. For developing countries, having a common set of rules and requirements allows for clarity and predictability in relation to what is expected of them to access results-based finance. For financing entities providing or aiming to provide results-based finance, the application of the WFR provides independent assurances that results have been achieved, without the (expensive) need to maintain structures for MRV and oversight of the development and implementation of REDD+ activities – which could, therefore, reduce transaction costs.

Financing entities outside the UNFCCC may, of course, choose not to apply the methodological guidance on REDD+ developed under the UNFCCC. In this case, however, there is a considerable risk of redundancies and duplications with regard to the requirements to obtain results-based finance. A multitude of different requirements and procedures for each financing entity, in turn, raises transaction costs for developing countries. It may also increase the chances of double counting of results and payments. The widespread application of the UNFCCC methodologies is thus an important factor in the coordination of support to REDD+ activities.

Without prejudice to specific rules and regulations of financial entities, the WFR provides a common platform for harmonizing results-based finance to developing countries. The adoption of multilaterally agreed guidelines under the UNFCCC offers a clear understanding on what constitutes mitigation results, what is required to achieve them and how to

---

80 Ibid, at paras. 6 and 7.

measure, report and verify them. Confidence on this understanding also sets the basis to enable other entities to participate in the effort to scale-up results-based finance for forests. So far, sources of REDD+ financing have been concentrated in multilateral funds or large bilateral donors. WFR can be seen as a common platform with potential for harmonizing guidelines, while recognizing that different financial entities and donors may also have specific requirements in order to fulfill their rules and regulations.

By creating a common set of rules and reducing transaction costs, in particular for MRV, the WFR offers the possibility for a whole new set of smaller actors, including the private sector, to provide results-based finance on a broader scale, with immediate recognition on the international level. The potential for private sector participation will depend largely on arrangements between the private actors and national authorities responsible for REDD+, but it is worth noting that the WFR provides a uniform and independent standard that is analogous to *public* verification and registration. The key point here is the fact that REDD+ results under the WFR have the international recognition that a certain level of environmental integrity and the safeguards have been met. Governmental and international recognition further allow for innovative uses to leverage private finance to REDD+, as part of payment for ecosystem services or tax rebates, for instance.

8. SUMMARY AND CONCLUSIONS: IMPLICATIONS OF THE WFR FOR NATIONAL REDD+ IMPLEMENTATION AND ACCESS TO RESULTS-BASED PAYMENTS

After many years of negotiation, the WFR has finalized a robust framework for effective and sustained implementation of REDD+ activities, aiming at environmental integrity and tangible results, while allowing flexibility to accommodate the diversity of REDD+ countries. The finalization of the requirements of the MRV process is a critical element. REDD+ under the UNFCCC is the outcome of a delicate balance between stringency of requirements to obtain financial support, flexibility to allow broad participation, while at the same time keeping consistency with other obligations under the UNFCCC and with other relevant international agreements.

The WFR has achieved this balanced outcome by establishing the components for effective results-based finance identified above: (1) a clear agreement on the definition of results, (2) an understanding of what needs to be in place in order to trigger potential payments, (3) a significant degree of discretion left to implementing developing country Parties, based on commonly agreed parameters, and (4) a well-designed MRV system that can give reasonable confidence that results have been achieved. The WFR, therefore, offers a common set of rules for the implementation of REDD+ results-based actions and the requirements to obtain and receive results-based payments.

The WFR clearly recalls and builds on earlier decisions on REDD+. However, in the context of results-based finance it has added further layers of transparency and clarity. These have six distinct implications.

First, the WFR stresses the *accumulative* nature of the elements contained in paragraph 71 of Decision 1/CP.16 and of the provision of the most recent summary of information on how all of the safeguards have been addressed and respected by stating that all these elements need to be in place by the time results-based payments are being sought.

Second, the WFR infuses a *stronger degree of normative bindingness* to the pre-existing elements of REDD+. As a consequence of the WFR, results-based finance has been made *contingent upon the implementation* ("in place") of all elements as well as upon increased transparency, including on safeguards. It is difficult to perceive financing entities allocating results-based payments to country Parties that provide selective, inconclusive or inconsistent information on their REDD+ activities – or negative information on how they address and respect all of the safeguards. Ultimately, this provides a powerful incentive towards implementation.

Third, the WRF has had a consolidating and *streamlining effect* by providing a framework that not only builds upon, but allocates a more *systematically integrated* place and role to the pre-existing UNFCCC COP decisions on REDD+. Furthermore, by encouraging entities outside the UNFCCC which finance REDD+ activities to apply methodological guidance consistent with all pre-existing decisions on REDD+, the WRF aims at streamlining and harmonizing policy development and practice and to avoid possible tensions, fragmentation, inconsistencies and incompatibilities.

Fourth, in the context of results-based finance, the WFR embraced a *centralized, national level approach.* Although the approach based on the national scale of REDD+ activities (as opposed to the project level scale) is not something particularly new,[81] the WFR has taken this a step

[81] As previously mentioned, Decision 1/CP.16 at para. 70 refers to *national* strategies or action plans, *national* RLs (allowing subnational RLs only as an interim measure) and *national* forest monitoring systems (Decision 1/CP.16).

further – by centralizing at the national level the procedures to fulfill the requirements of results-based finance, as well as the receipt of support from financing entities under the UNFCCC.[82]

Such a centralized approach is critical to avoiding double counting of REDD-results as well as promoting better coordination of implementation and support. While developing countries have flexibility to implement REDD+ actions *per se* at the scale and levels that best suit their national circumstances, *access* to results-based finance is contingent upon procedures under the authority, or at least coordination, of national agencies. Such centralization has occurred mainly through two ways: (1) by linking the MRV process to national reporting obligations under the UNFCCC, and (2) by creating the possibility of setting up a national entity or national focal point for REDD+ with the prerogative to nominate other entities to obtain and receive the corresponding payments on their behalf.

Regarding (1), as we have seen in section 5, the entire MRV process for REDD+ is coupled with international procedures applicable to developing country Parties under the UNFCCC – namely, the assessment of RLs, the provision of the summary of information on safeguards through national communications, the reporting of results through the BUR and their verification through the ICA process. Hence, only national governments (i.e. the UNFCCC Parties) are accountable under the MRV process. Under the UNFCCC, even in cases where subnational agencies or institutions are effectively those implementing REDD+ activities, *it is the national government that ultimately assumes accountability for REDD+ results* to the international community.

Centralization, therefore, imposes important caveats to subnational jurisdictional approaches, which recently have been the object of increased interest in the literature on REDD+. Subnational actors simply cannot implement the internationally agreed MRV process independently from national governments. Thus, they may not achieve recognition under the UNFCCC of their results-based actions without close coordination with, and recognition by, national authorities.

Concerning (2), the WFR enhances developing countries' prerogative to determine who is authorized to obtain and receive results-based payments on their behalf, although, as we have seen in section 5.4, this does not necessarily mean that results-based finance has to flow through the national

---

Except for early demonstration activities, none of the provisions for REDD+, in any UNFCCC decision, apply to the project level scale.

[82] And other financing entities if they choose to apply UNFCCC REDD+ methodology.

government. However, a competent national authority – be it the national entity or national focal point or not – controls the recognition of the linkage between results-based actions and their corresponding payments if payments are to be inserted in the Lima Info Hub. In the case of the GCF, it is unlikely that results-based payments would be provided to entities not recognized by the competent national authority, particularly considering the accreditation requirements and the no-objection procedure required by the Fund.

Fifth, the level and robustness of *transparency and accountability* promoted by the WFR in general are without precedent and could be an example for other performance-based approaches. Centralization may, in fact, lead to further increased transparency and accountability beyond points (1) and (2) raised above, as it implies that there is a responsible national agency for REDD+ actions and results. Accountability is further strengthened by the need to align the implementation and results of REDD+ activities to other obligations under the UNFCCC, such as national communications, inventories, the BUR and ICA process.

At the international level, increased transparency and accountability under a common set of rules create a system that, for the purposes of results-based finance, provides incentives for aiming at higher standards. It is to be expected that results-based finance will be directed to those Parties who can demonstrate robust results and transparent information, including on safeguards, leading other actors to follow suit and improve over time.

Sixth, the WFR also has governance implications in terms of intersectoral and inter-agency *coordination*. At the domestic level, national authorities' accountability for REDD+ results requires increasing the level of national inter-agency coordination, including those responsible for other obligations under the UNFCCC and the multiple stakeholders involved in implementing REDD+ activities at all levels.

To illustrate this point, the MRV process, in itself, requires coordination among different institutions involved in forest monitoring systems, national greenhouse gases inventories and national communications to the UNFCCC, taking into account that the timing and frequency of the MRV process is dependent upon timelines and processes conducted by the UNFCCC Secretariat and the Subsidiary Body of Implementation. Therefore, while the implementation of most of the elements referred to in Decision 1/CP.16, paragraph 71 depends solely on national circumstances, capabilities and support received, undergoing the MRV process requires careful planning and coordination. Because the assessment of the reference level may take up to 9–10 months and the ICA process occurs on a biennial basis, missing a window of opportunity may lead to delaying access to results-based finance.

Likewise, with regard to obtaining and receiving results-based payments, the designation of entities to obtain and receive such finance will likely demand great coordination efforts between the national and, where necessary, sub-national agencies involved as well as financial entities, with a view to ensure that results-based finance benefits those actors that are responsible for implementing and strengthening REDD+ actions, in a fair and balanced manner.

With regard to coordinating developing countries' approaches to gradually move towards results-based finance, it is worth noting the need for a holistic readiness support, covering all elements that need to be *in place* in order for developing country Parties to access results-based finance. Financing each element in isolation, without consideration for their coherence, may fail to deliver results-based actions that are "fully measured, reported and verified, in accordance with Decisions 13/CP.19 and 14/CP.19" – and thus hinder access to results-based finance.

One final observation relates to the general concept of results-based finance described above as applied in the context of REDD+. While, conceptually, results-based finance is largely described as a financing approach where the recipient country has total discretion over how results are achieved, within REDD+ we see a *practical application* of the results-based approach to climate change finance on a multilateral level, where the recipient country still retains a large degree of discretion and flexibility, but it becomes apparent that the WFR sets up significant parameters to such exercise of discretion – and these are most pronounced in the requirements that need to be in place in order to access results-based finance, the different types of guidance to be applied, as well as the MRV process.

With all that having been said, it remains important to stress that the progression to results-based payments first and foremost requires the effective and sustained *implementation* of REDD+ activities. The Paris Agreement has given a strong signal to this extent by encouraging Parties to implement and support, including through results-based payments, the existing framework for REDD+.[83] The inclusion of REDD+ activities by many developing countries as part of their intended nationally determined contributions[84] is already proof of the importance and

[83] Decision 1/CP.21 Adoption of the Paris Agreement (FCCC/CP/2015/10, 29 January 2016), Annex, Art. 5.2

[84] For an overview of submitted Intended Nationally Determined Contributions (INDCs) see: http://unfccc.int/focus/indc_portal/items/8766.php.

widespread willingness of taking effective mitigation action in the forest sector from 2020 onwards. The main goal of REDD+ is to enhance action and support to slow, halt and reverse forest cover and carbon loss in developing countries, as part of the global effort against climate change. The full implementation of the WFR, through enhanced transparency, robust methodologies, clear requirements for linking verified REDD+ activities to results-based finance, coordination and centralization under national accountability is an important lever for bringing us closer to this goal.

PART II

REDD+ LINKAGES TO OTHER INTERNATIONAL AGREEMENTS

3. The institutional complex for REDD+: a 'benevolent jigsaw'?

*Harro van Asselt and Constance L. McDermott**+

1. INTRODUCTION

Officially situated under the umbrella of the UNFCCC, REDD+ is of undeniable relevance to a host of other international legal regimes, including those for human rights, biological diversity and trade. All of these regimes, like REDD+, interact with the diverse drivers and impacts of deforestation. The emergence of REDD+ further needs to be viewed in the context of several decades of developments in international forest law and governance. And while public international law continues to develop as a mosaic of overlapping legal instruments, a range of new transnational public, private and public–private governance arrangements have started to fill gaps by setting standards, financing and helping to put REDD+ in practice.

These various international legal instruments and transnational governance arrangements both influence, and are impacted by, rule development on REDD+ under the UNFCCC, giving rise to two overarching questions. The first question is whether the outcomes of such interactions can be viewed as synergetic, with the resulting legal system forming a 'benevolent jigsaw',[1] or whether they lead to a situation of 'conflictive fragmentation'.[2] Second, to the extent that the implications of institutional complexity can

---

* Harro van Asselt is grateful for support from the Swedish Research Council Formas (project Navigating Institutional Complexity in Global Climate Governance) and Sida (project Orchestrating International Climate Policy). Constance McDermott would like to acknowledge funding from the European Union Seventh Framework Programme (grant agreement no. FP7-282887; Future-oriented integrated management of European forest landscapes (INTEGRAL)).

+ All websites cited in this chapter were accessed on 1 October 2015.

1 Stephen Humphreys, 'Structural Ambiguity: Technology Transfer in Three Regimes' in Margaret A. Young (ed.), *Regime Interaction in International Law: Facing Fragmentation* (CUP 2012), 175, 181.

2 Frank Biermann et al., 'The Fragmentation of Global Governance Architectures: A Framework for Analysis' (2009) 9 *Global Envtl Pol* 14, 20–21. On the types of consequences of regime interactions, see Harro van Asselt, *The Fragmentation of Global Climate Governance: Consequences and Management of Regime Interactions* (Edward Elgar 2014), 52–8.

be seen as negative, the question arises to what extent states and non-state actors can do something about it.[3]

This chapter tackles these two questions by situating REDD+ in the context of debates on the benefits and drawbacks of the fragmentation of international law and polycentric governance. The chapter begins with a mapping of the 'institutional complex'[4] for REDD+, showing which aspects of REDD+ are covered by the various international regimes and other governance arrangements, and examining which actions, if any, have been undertaken vis-à-vis REDD+. It proceeds to identify some of the main implications of institutional complexity, highlighting the opportunities offered and risks posed by the diversity of institutions. The chapter then discusses how coordination efforts could help to manage institutional complexity. It concludes that a greater level of coordination may help to establish a more productive division of labour between the various legal regimes and governance arrangements; however, it cautions that the trade-offs inherent in the very idea of REDD+ limit the degree of coordination, making full coordination neither possible nor even desirable (given conflicting interests and unequal power relations), and suggests that the international legal system for REDD+ is likely to remain pluralistic in the future.

---

[3] On approaches to such 'interplay management', see Sebastian Oberthür, 'Interplay Management: Enhancing Environmental Policy Integration among International Institutions' (2009) 9 *Intl Envtl Agreements* 371; and Harro van Asselt, 'Legal and Political Approaches in Interplay Management: Dealing with the Fragmentation of Global Climate Governance', in Sebastian Oberthür and Olav S. Stokke (eds), *Managing Institutional Complexity: Regime Interplay and Global Environmental Change* (MIT Press 2011) 59.

[4] An institutional complex has been defined as 'a set of two or more international institutions that are interdependent and as such interact to co-govern a particular issue area in international relations'. Sebastian Oberthür and Justyna Pożarowska, 'Managing Institutional Complexity and Fragmentation: The Nagoya Protocol and the Global Governance of Genetic Resources' (2013) 13 *Global Envtl Pol* 100, 102. This definition is slightly more encompassing to another notion similarly used in the recent literature, namely that of 'regime complex'. See Kal Raustiala and David G. Victor, 'The Regime Complex for Plant Genetic Resources' (2004) 58 *Intl Org* 277; and Robert O. Keohane and David G. Victor, 'The Regime Complex for Climate Change' (2011) 9 *Perspectives on Politics* 7; Amandine Orsini, Jean-Frédéric Morin and Oran Young, 'Regime Complexes: A Buzz, a Boom, or a Bust for Global Governance?' (2013) 19 *Global Governance* 27. The notion of 'institutional complexity' acknowledges the relevance of international institutions that do not qualify as 'regimes'. Cf. Fariborz Zelli and Harro van Asselt, 'The Institutional Fragmentation of Global Environmental Governance: Causes, Consequences, and Responses' (2013) 13 *Global Envtl Pol* 1, 7.

2. MAPPING THE INSTITUTIONAL COMPLEX

This section discusses the various international legal instruments and transnational governance arrangements relevant for REDD+. It starts with an overview of developments in various international regimes of relevance to REDD+, and follows with a discussion of transnational governance arrangements and financial institutions. Though the overview is by no means exhaustive, it offers a sketch of the intricate legal and governance system applicable to REDD+.

2.1 International Forest Law and Governance

Although REDD+ analyses often start with the UNFCCC, it is important to remember that REDD+ is just one of the latest chapters in several decades of developments in international forest law and governance.[5] International forest governance began to gain momentum in the mid-twentieth century, catalysed by growing concern over the acceleration of tropical forest loss. This initial focus on the tropics was reflected in the establishment of the International Tropical Timber Organization (ITTO) under the UN, and the enactment of a series of International Tropical Timber Agreements in 1983, 1994 and 2006. From its inception, the ITTO has played the role of international facilitator rather than regulator, promoting sustainable forest management and trade in tropical timber through collaboration, finance and support to tropical producer countries.[6]

By the 1992 Earth Summit in Rio, pressure had risen for a more authoritative response to global forest loss. Yet while the Earth Summit witnessed the birth of several multilateral environmental agreements, it notably failed to reach agreement on a global forest convention. Nevertheless, a core outcome of the Earth Summit was to expand global debates around international forest governance from the tropics to forests worldwide.[7] In addition, countries adopted a set of non-legally

---

[5] See generally David Humphreys, *Logjam: Deforestation and the Crisis of Global Governance* (Earthscan 2006); and Anja Eikermann, *Forests in International Law* (Springer 2015).

[6] For an account of the role of the ITTO in sustainable forest management, see Duncan Poore, *Changing Landscapes: The Development of the International Tropical Timber Organization and Its Influence on Tropical Forest Management* (Earthscan 2003).

[7] David Humphreys, *Forest Politics: The Evolution of International Cooperation* (Earthscan 1996), 83–104.

binding 'Forest Principles'[8] and included a chapter on deforestation in Agenda 21.[9]

Since then, a plethora of initiatives have emerged in the area of global forest governance, contributing to an emerging body of 'soft law'.[10] This includes a series of intergovernmental panels and forums that emerged out of Rio as platforms for discussing international action on forests. These began with the Intergovernmental Panel on Forests (IPF), followed by the Intergovernmental Forum on Forests (IFF), which together produced 270 'proposals for action' to promote the management, conservation and sustainable development of forests.[11] In 2000, the United Nations Forum on Forests (UNFF) was established as a more permanent body.

Throughout these negotiating processes several key points of contention frustrated efforts to create legally binding decisions. Among these were the sovereign rights of states to govern their forests as they chose, including the right of developing countries to clear and develop their forest frontiers much as developed countries had done over preceding centuries. Unlike the problems of ozone depletion or climate change, it was argued, deforestation was not a transboundary environmental problem that justified foreign interference. Furthermore, there was a major lack of international finance to compensate developing countries should they agree to forgo development for forest conservation.[12]

At the same time, a significant and shifting group of countries argued strongly for a legally binding forest agreement. In many cases the 'pro' countries contained large, export-dependent forest industries concerned that increasing domestic environmental regulation and/or international environmental pressures might lessen their international competitiveness. From this perspective, an international legal agreement would serve to 'level the playing field' and enhance the reputation of the industry as a whole.[13]

---

8 'Non-legally Binding Authoritative Statement of Principles for a Global Consensus on the Management, Conservation and Sustainable Development of All Types of Forests, in Report of the United Nations Conference on Environment and Development (Rio de Janeiro, 3–14 June 1992)', UN Doc A/CONF.151/26 (Vol. III) (14 August 1992) Annex III.

9 Agenda 21, in 'Report of the United Nations Conference on Environment and Development (Rio de Janeiro, 3–14 June 1992)', UN Doc A/CONF.151/26 (Vol. I) (12 August 1992) Annex II, Chapter 11.

10 Humphreys, *Logjam*, 114–15.

11 UNFF, 'The IPF and IFF Proposals for Action: Main Actors and Degree of Action' (Secretariat of the UNFF 2002).

12 Humphreys, *Logjam*.

13 Ibid.

Fuelled by such motives for international cooperation, in 2008 the UNFF produced a 'non-legally binding instrument on forests'.[14] While the instrument lacked binding rules, it nevertheless included the first internationally agreed goal to reduce global forest loss. It also spurred the European Union (EU), a long-time supporter of a global forest convention, to pursue a region-wide 'legally binding agreement on forests in Europe'.[15]

Civil society actors, meanwhile, were growing increasingly frustrated with the slow pace of progress in the international forums. This led to the launch, in 1993, of the FSC as a non-state, market-based 'forest certification' scheme. The FSC established a multi-stakeholder decision-making structure to set international standards for environmentally and socially responsible forestry. The FSC also adopted a type of law 'enforcement', in the form of third-party auditing to verify that products carrying a green label indeed were produced in accordance with FSC standards. Forest producers that achieved certification under the FSC could attach the FSC label on their product, thus strengthening their access to green markets.[16]

However, the FSC lacked sovereign authority to write international rules. No sooner was the FSC launched, than industry and producer associations responded by forming competing national schemes, thus contributing to the fragmentation of forest governance. These competing schemes have since joined under the umbrella of the Programme for the Endorsement of Forest Certification (PEFC). To date certification has grown very rapidly across both programmes; as of November 2014 there were about 183 million hectares certified under the FSC and 265 million hectares certified under PEFC.[17] This represents about 11 per cent of the world's forests, and about 28.3 per cent of global roundwood production.[18]

---

[14] UN General Assembly, 'Resolution 62/98, Non-legally Binding Instrument on All Types of Forests', UN Doc A/RES/62/98 (31 January 2008). See also Katharina Kunzmann, 'The Non-legally Binding Instrument on All Types of Forests – Towards a Legal Regime for Sustainable Forest Management?' (2008) 9 *German L J* 981.

[15] See http://www.foresteurope.org/en/LBA.

[16] See also Philipp Pattberg, 'What Role for Private Rule-Making in Global Environmental Governance? Analysing the Forest Stewardship Council (FSC)' (2005) 5 *Intl Envtl Agreements* 175.

[17] FSC, 'Global FSC Certificates: Types and Distribution' (November 2014), https://ic.fsc.org/preview.facts-and-figures-november-2014.a-3810.pdf; PEFC, 'Global Statistics: SFM & CoC Certification' (November 2014), http://www.pefc.org/images/documents/PEFC_Global_Certificates_-_November_2014.pdf.

[18] UN Economic Commission for Europe (UNECE) and Food and Agriculture Organization (FAO), *Forest Products Annual Market Review 2012–2013* (UNECE and FAO 2013).

While such growth is globally significant, it is distributed very unevenly; the majority of the certified area is located in the global North and dominated by large-scale industry.[19]

The reasons for this uneven growth illustrate some of the core limitations of non-state, market-based forest governance. First, forest certification standards generally require compliance with forest laws; this is not surprising, given that the schemes themselves are legal entities with corresponding liabilities. But such legality requirements can only be met where there is effective state control, including the presence of secure forest tenure and effective law enforcement. The absence of these preconditions in many tropical forest areas, and particularly areas dominated by small and medium forest enterprises, excludes large swaths of the world's forests from certification. Another factor limiting certification's growth relates to the structure of global markets. Much of the timber harvested in the tropics is sold domestically where there is little market demand or incentive for certification.[20]

The limitations of both certification and global intergovernmental negotiations spurred a renewed focus in the early 2000s on legality. It was noted that much of the world's trade in tropical timber was not only uncertifiable, but also illegal. By refocusing attention on legality it was possible to find new common ground among a range of formerly conflicting interests: from international NGOs focused on environmental conservation and social welfare, to forest industry players concerned that illegal logging was undercutting timber prices, to governments unable to capture tax revenues or exert control over forest areas.[21] Unlike a global forest convention, agreement to tackle illegal logging did not threaten state sovereignty but rather strengthened it. Likewise, it did not require global-scale agreement, but could involve agreements at the plurilateral, bilateral and even unilateral levels. Unlike non-state, market-based certification, state-backed efforts to enforce legality were (presumably) independent of markets, not subject to competition among competing schemes, and could be imposed across entire national jurisdictions.

---

[19] Ibid.

[20] Constance L. McDermott, 'Certification and Equity: Applying an "Equity Framework" to Compare Certification Schemes across Product Sectors and Scales' (2013) 33 *Envtl Sci & Pol'y* 428.

[21] Benjamin Cashore and Michael W. Stone, 'Can Legality Verification Rescue Global Forest Governance?: Analyzing the Potential of Public and Private Policy Intersection to Ameliorate Forest Challenges in Southeast Asia' (2012) 18 *Forest Pol'y & Economics* 13; Feja Lesniewska and Constance L. McDermott, 'FLEGT VPAs: Laying a Pathway to Sustainability via Legality: Lessons from Ghana and Indonesia' (2014) 48 *Forest Pol'y & Economics* 16.

A wide range of illegal logging initiatives have since emerged.[22] This includes the World Bank-initiated regional forest law enforcement and governance initiatives in East Asia and the Pacific, Africa and Eurasia. It includes unilateral legal actions in the United States (a 2008 amendment to the Lacey Act),[23] the EU (the 2010 EU Timber Regulation)[24] and Australia (the 2012 Illegal Logging Prohibition Act)[25] involving new legislation that bans the import of wood products produced in violation of the laws of the country of origin. And it includes the EU Forest Law Enforcement, Governance and Trade (FLEGT) Action Plan and its associated bilateral Voluntary Partnership Agreements (VPAs). The EU FLEGT VPAs involve agreements with individual developing countries to develop a system of 'legality licensing'. Once operational, only licensed timber from VPA countries can be legally imported into the EU.[26]

The effectiveness of these legality initiatives remains to be seen. To date, there are few examples of prosecution under unilateral bans on trade in illegal timber, and there are as yet no fully operational FLEGT licensed timber systems. Meanwhile, the 2010s have seen a wave of new international forest commitments and pledges. This includes the UN's 2014 New York Declaration on Forests, with ambitious targets to end natural forest loss by 2030, restore at least 350 million hectares of forests and degraded landscapes, also by 2030, and more.[27] Likewise, forest conservation and sustainable use is included in the UN's Sustainable Development Goals, which were adopted in September 2015.[28]

---

[22] Constance L. McDermott, 'REDDuced: From Sustainability to Legality to Units of Carbon – The Search for Common Interests in International Forest Governance' (2014) 35 *Envtl Sci & Pol'y* 12.

[23] 16 USC §§ 3371–8 (Lacey Act).

[24] Regulation (EU) No. 995/2010 of the European Parliament and of the Council of 20 October 2010 laying down the obligations of operators who place timber and timber products on the market, [2010] OJ L295/23.

[25] Illegal Logging Prohibition Act 2012 (Cth), http://www.comlaw.gov.au/Details/C2012A00166.

[26] The EU's approach is described in: Communication from the Commission to the Council and the European Parliament, Forest Law Enforcement, Governance and Trade (FLEGT): Proposal for an EU Action Plan, COM(2003)251 final.

[27] New York Declaration on Forests and Action Agenda (23 September 2014), http://www.un.org/climatechange/summit/wp-content/uploads/sites/2/2014/07/New-York-Declaration-on-Forest-%E2%80%93-Action-Statement-and-Action-Plan.pdf.

[28] UN General Assembly, 'Resolution 70/1, Transforming our World: the 2030 Agenda for Sustainable Development', UN Doc A/RES/70/1 (21 October 2015) Goal 15.

2.2 International Climate Change Law

Against this backdrop of evolving international forest law and governance, deforestation moved high up the agenda of the climate negotiations in the mid-2000s, as discussed in greater detail elsewhere in this book.[29] Much of the emerging body of international law on REDD+ can be found in the decisions adopted by the COP to the UNFCCC. The 2010 Cancún Agreements provided initial guidance, suggesting that the objective for REDD+ is 'to slow, halt and reverse forest cover and carbon loss'.[30] The decision further suggested that REDD+ activities should take place in three phases, starting with national planning, followed by implementation of policies and measures and, eventually, results-based actions.[31] It also requested developing country Parties to put in place the necessary infrastructure for undertaking REDD+ activities, including the development of a national strategy, a national REL and a national monitoring system,[32] and specifies that certain social and environmental safeguards must be respected in the implementation of REDD+ activities (see Box 3.1).[33]

BOX 3.1 REDD+ SAFEGUARDS UNDER THE UNFCCC[34]

- Consistency with the objectives of national forest programmes and relevant international conventions and agreements;
- Transparent and effective national forest governance structures;
- Respect for the knowledge and rights of indigenous peoples and members of local communities, taking into account relevant international obligations, national circumstances and laws and acknowledging the UN Declaration on the Rights of Indigenous Peoples (UNDRIP);
- Full and effective participation of relevant stakeholders (particularly indigenous and local communities);
- Consistency with conservation of natural forests and biological diversity;
- Actions to address the risks of reversals;
- Actions to reduce displacement of emissions.

---

29 See Chapter 1 by La Vina et al. in this book.

30 UNFCCC, 'Decision 1/CP.16, Outcome of the Work of the Ad Hoc Working Group on Long-term Cooperative Action under the Convention', UN Doc FCCC/CP/2010/7/Add.1 (15 March 2011) Part C, preamble.

31 Ibid. para 73.

32 Ibid. para 71.

33 Ibid. para 72 and Appendix I.

34 Ibid. Appendix I, para 2.

Significant further progress was made in 2013 in Warsaw, where Parties adopted a set of decisions known as the 'Warsaw Framework for REDD+'.[35] The decisions concern the coordination of results-based finance,[36] institutional arrangements at the national level,[37] guidance on forest monitoring systems,[38] information on safeguards,[39] the assessment of reference levels,[40] modalities for MRV[41] and a general decision encouraging Parties to address the drivers of deforestation.[42] While the Warsaw Framework has been seen as one of the main positive outcomes of the 2013 meeting,[43] it leaves several questions unaddressed. Notably, Parties could not agree on an international body to oversee REDD+ finance, and there is still no guidance on where exactly such finance should come from (beyond the recognition that it 'may come from a variety of sources, public and private, bilateral and multilateral, including alternative sources');[44] in particular, the possible role of market mechanisms in REDD+ financing remains unclear.[45] As a result, REDD+ finance remains somewhat

---

[35] See Chapter 2 by Christina Voigt and Felipe Ferreira in this book, as well as: Maria Eugenia Recio, 'The Warsaw Framework and the Future of REDD+' (2014) 24 *YbIEL* 37; Annalisa Savaresi, 'Forests and Climate Change: An International Law-making Odyssey' (2015; on file with authors).

[36] UNFCCC, 'Decision 9/CP.19, Work Programme on Results-based Finance to Progress the Full Implementation of the Activities Referred to in Decision 1/CP.16, Paragraph 70', UN Doc FCCC/CP/2013/10/Add.1 (31 January 2014).

[37] UNFCCC, 'Decision 10/CP.19, Coordination of Support for the Implementation of Activities in Relation to Mitigation Actions in the Forest Sector by Developing Countries, Including Institutional Arrangements', UN Doc FCCC/CP/2013/10/Add.1 (31 January 2014).

[38] UNFCCC, 'Decision 11/CP.19, Modalities for National Forest Monitoring Systems', UN Doc FCCC/CP/2013/10/Add.1 (31 January 2014).

[39] UNFCCC, 'Decision 12/CP.19, The Timing and the Frequency of Presentations of the Summary of Information on How All the Safeguards Referred to in Decision 1/CP.16, Appendix I, Are Being Addressed and Respected', UN Doc FCCC/CP/2013/10/Add.1 (31 January 2014).

[40] UNFCCC, 'Decision 13/CP.19, Guidelines and Procedures for the Technical Assessment of Submissions from Parties on Proposed Forest Reference Emission Levels and/or Forest Reference Levels', UN Doc FCCC/CP/2013/10/Add.1 (31 January 2014).

[41] UNFCCC, 'Decision 14/CP.19, Modalities for Measuring, Reporting and Verifying', UN Doc FCCC/CP/2013/10/Add.1 (31 January 2014).

[42] UNFCCC, 'Decision 15/CP.19, Addressing the Drivers of Deforestation and Forest Degradation', UN Doc FCCC/CP/2013/10/Add.1 (31 January 2014).

[43] See, e.g., Fred Stolle and Ariana Alisjahbana, 'Warsaw Meeting Makes Progress on Forests, REDD+' (20 December 2013), http://www.wri.org/blog/2013/12/warsaw-climate-meeting-makes-progress-forests-redd.

[44] Decision 9/CP.19 para 1.

[45] Recio 48–9.

unpredictable, which may in turn have ramifications for countries' efforts to tackle deforestation.[46]

In the climate change negotiations, REDD+ is still being discussed in different contexts. REDD+ has been suggested as a possible 'nationally determined contribution' under the Paris Agreement; it has been discussed as an example for both market-based and non-market-based approaches under the same agreement; and it has been suggested that a separate window be created for REDD+ under the GCF.[47] Notwithstanding these various options, the Warsaw Framework has had a streamlining effect, with the set of decisions forming a common starting point for the future of REDD+ under the UNFCCC.[48]

2.3 International Biodiversity Law

In addition to the UNFCCC, another treaty agreed at the 1992 Earth Summit, the CBD,[49] has been deemed by some as the most important global legal instrument contributing to the international forests regime.[50] Forests, as part of and habitat for terrestrial biological diversity, have always been within the scope of the CBD. Parties to the treaty became more active in this area after 1996, when they launched a forest work programme.[51] One of the main policy documents of the CBD, the Strategic Plan for Biodiversity 2011–2020, containing the Aichi biodiversity targets, specifies several non-legally binding targets related to forest biodiversity. It states that by 2020 the rate of loss of natural habitats, including forests, needs to be at least halved (and where feasible brought to zero);[52] areas under forestry need to be managed sustainably;[53] and the contribution of biodiversity to carbon stocks needs to be enhanced, including at least 15 per cent of degraded ecosystems.[54]

---

46 Ibid. 68.

47 Ibid. 65–7.

48 For instance, the Warsaw Framework was referred to on several occasions in the negotiating text for a 2015 agreement, developed by Parties in Geneva in February 2015. See https://unfccc.int/files/bodies/awg/application/pdf/negotiating_text_12022015@2200.pdf.

49 United Nations Convention on Biological Diversity (adopted 5 June 1992; entered into force 29 December 1992), 1760 UNTS 79.

50 Humphreys 191.

51 van Asselt 128–9.

52 CBD, 'Decision X/2, The Strategic Plan for Biodiversity 2011–2020 and the Aichi Biodiversity Targets', UN Doc UNEP/CBD/COP/DEC/X/2 (29 October 2010) Annex, Target 5.

53 Ibid. Annex, Target 7.

54 Ibid. Annex, Target 15.

The emergence of REDD+ on the agenda of the UNFCCC formed an impetus for further activity by the CBD on the overlap between the climate and biodiversity regimes.[55] This included a set of decisions calling on Parties to the climate treaties to incorporate biodiversity considerations into their climate policies.[56] One such decision, adopted in 2008, requested Parties and other relevant stakeholders to ensure that REDD+ would not undermine the objectives of the CBD or its forest work programme; to involve biodiversity experts; and to respect the rights of indigenous and local communities.[57]

In Nagoya in 2010, Parties adopted a lengthy decision on biodiversity and climate change, which contained proposals to link the CBD more strongly to the REDD+ discussions under the UNFCCC. More specifically, it offered recommendations to minimize the biodiversity impacts of forestry activities.[58] The decision also requested the CBD secretariat to collaborate with other international bureaucracies and with CBD Parties to contribute to the discussion on, and possible development of, biodiversity safeguards for REDD+.[59] The CBD secretariat was also asked to identify possible indicators for monitoring how REDD+ could contribute to the objectives of the CBD.[60] This resulted in a document published by the secretariat in 2012, providing advice on REDD+ safeguards and indicators for biodiversity impacts of REDD+. The document highlights existing environmental and social safeguards developed in the context of transnational governance arrangements (see section 2.6), and recommends countries undertaking REDD+ activities to apply them.[61] It also provides

---

[55] For analyses, see Elisa Morgera, 'Far Away, So Close: A Legal Analysis of the Increasing Interactions between the Convention on Biological Diversity and Climate Change Law' (2009) 2 *Climate L* 85; Annalisa Savaresi, 'Reducing Emissions from Deforestation in Developing Countries under the UNFCCC: Caveats and Opportunities for Biodiversity' (2011) 21 *YbIEL* 81; Harro van Asselt, 'Managing the Fragmentation of International Environmental Law: Forests at the Intersection of the Climate and Biodiversity Regimes' (2012) 44 *NYUJILP* 1205.

[56] See, e.g., CBD, 'Decision VIII/30, Biodiversity and Climate Change: Guidance to Promote Synergy among Activities for Biodiversity Conservation, Mitigating or Adapting to Climate Change and Combating Land Degradation', UN Doc UNEP/CBD/COP/8/31 (15 June 2006) paras 1–2.

[57] CBD, 'Decision IX/5, Forest Biodiversity', UN Doc UNEP/CBD/COP/9/29 (9 October 2008) para 2(a).

[58] CBD, 'Decision X/33, Biodiversity and Climate Change', UN Doc UNEP/CBD/COP/10/27 (20 January 2011) para 8(p).

[59] Ibid. para 9(g).

[60] Ibid. para 9(h).

[61] CBD, 'Advice on the Application of Relevant REDD+ Safeguards for Biodiversity, and on Possible Indicators and Potential Mechanisms to Assess

an overview of how existing indicators for achieving the Aichi targets could be used as indicators for the monitoring of biodiversity impacts of REDD+. Nevertheless, to appease concerns from UNFCCC Parties, the CBD secretariat made clear that it did not intend to pre-empt the work on reference levels and safeguards for REDD+ under the UNFCCC, and suggested only considering modalities for monitoring the biodiversity impacts of REDD when the discussions in the climate regime had 'progressed further'.[62]

At the CBD COP in Hyderabad in 2012, Parties were only able to agree to 'take note with appreciation' of an Annex to a decision, which provides guidance on how to safeguard biodiversity in the implementation of REDD+ activities at the national level, drawing on the document prepared by the CBD secretariat.[63] At the request of Parties, the CBD secretariat continues to document experiences and lessons learned, and monitor progress on the implementation of biodiversity safeguards related to REDD+.[64] In addition, in 2014 the CBD endorsed its own 'Voluntary Guidelines on Safeguards in Biodiversity Financing Mechanisms', which refer to a set of six finance mechanisms including funding for climate change.[65]

2.4 International Human Rights Law

The emergence of REDD+ has drawn attention to the plight of forest-dwelling and forest-dependent communities. Specifically, concerns have been raised that REDD+ activities may affect the rights and livelihoods of indigenous and local communities, and calls have been made to facilitate stakeholder participation in the further development of REDD+.[66]

Impacts of REDD+ Measures on Biodiversity. Note by the Secretary', UN Doc UNEP/CBD/SBSTTA/16/9 (6 March 2012) 12–13.

[62] Ibid. 13.

[63] CBD, 'Decision XI/19, Biodiversity and Climate Change Related Issues: Advice on the Application of Relevant Safeguards for Biodiversity with Regard to Policy Approaches and Positive Incentives on Issues Relating to Reducing Emissions from Deforestation and Forest Degradation in Developing Countries; and the Role of Conservation, Sustainable Management of Forests and Enhancement of Forest Carbon Stocks in Developing Countries', UN Doc UNEP/CBD/COP/DEC/XI/19 (5 December 2012) para 9 and Annex.

[64] See, e.g., CBD, 'Biodiversity and Climate Change. Note by the Executive Secretary', UN Doc UNEP/CBD/COP/12/21 (30 September 2014).

[65] The guidelines can be found in: CBD, 'Draft Options for Voluntary Guidelines on Safeguards in Biodiversity Financing Mechanisms', UN Doc UNEP/CBD/COP/12/13/Add.4 (28 August 2014).

[66] See, e.g., Jacob Phelps, Edward L. Webb and Arun Agarwal, 'Does REDD Threaten to Recentralize Forest Governance?' (2010) 328 *Science* 312;

These concerns have led to new questions about the role of (international) human rights law in governing REDD+.[67] The relevance of this body of law needs to be seen against the backdrop of growing calls for a human rights-based approach to international climate policy.[68] In the REDD+ context, the focus has been on both substantive and procedural rights. Substantive human rights violations may, for instance, involve the granting of logging concessions with disregard for indigenous communities.[69] The discussion about procedural rights has centred on the effective participation of indigenous and local communities in decision-making about REDD+ (both at the international and the national levels).

Indigenous peoples enjoy special protection under the International Labour Organization (ILO)'s Convention 169.[70] While this Convention

---

Rosemary Lyster, 'REDD+, Transparency, Participation and Resource Rights: The Role of Law' (2011) 14 *Envtl Sci & Pol'y* 118; Robert Fisher and Rosemary Lyster, 'Land and Resource Tenure: The Rights of Indigenous Peoples and Forest Dwellers', in Rosemary Lyster, Catherine MacKenzie and Constance McDermott (eds), *Law, Tropical Forests and Carbon: The Case of REDD+* (CUP 2013) 187.

[67] Annalisa Savaresi, 'The Human Rights Dimension of REDD' (2012) 21 *RECIEL* 102; Annalisa Savaresi, 'REDD+ and Human Rights: Addressing Synergies between International Regimes' (2013) 18 *Ecology & Society* 5.

[68] See, e.g., Stephen Humphreys (ed.), *Human Rights and Climate Change* (CUP 2009); John H. Knox, 'Climate Change and Human Rights Law' (2009) 50 *Va J Intl L* 163; Lavanya Rajamani, 'The Increasing Currency and Relevance of Rights-Based Perspectives in the International Negotiations on Climate Change' (2010) 22 *J Envtl L* 391; International Bar Association, *Achieving Justice and Human Rights in an Era of Climate Disruption* (IBA 2014). See also UN Human Rights Council, 'Resolution 26/27, Human Rights and Climate Change', UN Doc A/HRC/26/L.33/Rev.1 (25 June 2014); and UN Office of the High Commissioner for Human Rights, 'A New Climate Change Agreement Must Include Human Rights Protections for All: An Open Letter from Special Procedures mandate-holders of the Human Rights Council to the State Parties to the UN Framework Convention on Climate Change on the occasion of the meeting of the Ad Hoc Working Group on the Durban Platform for Enhanced Action in Bonn (20–25 October 2014)', http://www.ohchr.org/Documents/HRBodies/SP/SP_To_UNFCCC.pdf.

[69] Savaresi, 'The Human Rights Dimension of REDD', 105–6.

[70] Convention (No. 169) Concerning Indigenous and Tribal Peoples in Independent Countries (adopted 27 June 1989; entered into force 5 September 1991) 28 ILM 1382. The convention is not the only relevant human rights instrument for the REDD+ context. See ClientEarth and World Resources Institute, *Lessons from International and Regional Instruments: A ClientEarth and World Resources Institute Submission to SBSTA* (ClientEarth and WRI 2011) (citing a range of other international and regional instruments with reference to the UNFCCC's safeguard provisions, such as the Universal Declaration on Human Rights and the International Covenant on Civil and Political Rights).

has not been widely ratified, further provisions are included in the UNDRIP,[71] which was adopted by the UN General Assembly. UNDRIP specifies that indigenous peoples cannot be subject to removal by force, and may not be relocated without their free, prior and informed consent (FPIC).[72] The principle of FPIC also applies more broadly to cases where governments intend to adopt legislative or other measures that may affect indigenous peoples.[73] Furthermore, the Declaration specifies that indigenous peoples have the rights 'to the lands, territories and resources which they have traditionally owned, occupied or otherwise used or acquired', and 'to own, use, develop and control the lands, territories and resources that they possess'.[74] States, in return, need to 'give legal recognition and protection to these lands, territories and resources . . . with due respect to the customs, traditions and land tenure systems of the indigenous peoples concerned'.[75] Although the Declaration is not legally binding, it 'includes several key provisions which correspond to existing State obligations under customary international law', and other provisions 'express the aspirations of the world's indigenous peoples, as well as of States, in their move to improve existing standards for the safeguarding of indigenous peoples' human rights'.[76] Moreover, through the Cancún Agreements (see Box 3.1, p. 70) a reference to UNDRIP is included in the REDD+ safeguards.[77]

2.5 International Trade Law

International trade law is relevant to trade-related measures that aim to tackle the drivers of deforestation.[78] As discussed in section 2.1, trade

---

71 UN General Assembly, 'Resolution 61/295, Declaration on the Rights of Indigenous Peoples', UN Doc A/RES/61/295 (2 October 2007).

72 Ibid. Article 10.

73 Ibid. Article 19.

74 Ibid. Article 26(1–2).

75 Ibid. Article 26(3).

76 International Law Association, 'Resolution No. 5/2012, Rights of Indigenous Peoples' (ILA 2012).

77 Decision 1/CP.16 (n 30) Appendix I, para 2(c). The decision, more generally, also emphasizes 'that Parties should, in all climate change related actions, fully respect human rights'. Ibid. para 8.

78 For instance, trade in and consumption of products such as beef and soybeans has been identified as a major driver of Brazilian deforestation. Jonas Karstensen, Glen P. Peters and Robbie M. Andrew, 'Attribution of CO_2 Emissions from Brazilian Deforestation to Consumers between 1990 and 2010' (2013) 8 *Envtl Research Letters* 024005.

measures targeting illegally logged timber are already in force in several jurisdictions, including the EU,[79] Australia[80] and the United States.[81] Such measures could be extended to other products such as agricultural commodities (e.g. palm oil, soy or beef). As Brack and Bailey point out, '[s]ince forest conversion for agricultural commodities is the main competitor to sustainable forestry, successful attempts to restrict trade in unsustainable or deforestation-related commodities should make REDD+ policies more viable'.[82] However, the adoption of such measures could lead to concerns about their compatibility with the agreements of the World Trade Organization (WTO).[83]

Under these agreements, countries have made commitments to liberalize trade (notably by lowering tariffs), and refrain from discrimination against other WTO Members. Measures that restrict trade in timber or agricultural commodities with a view to avoiding deforestation may thus contravene the existing disciplines under the relevant agreements, notably the General Agreement on Tariffs and Trade (GATT).[84] For instance, one relevant question is whether illegally logged and 'legal' timber can be considered 'like products' under Article III of the GATT. If this is the case, measures targeting illegal logging may violate the WTO's 'national treatment' principle.[85] The WTO-compatibility of measures targeting illegal logging – such as the EU's Timber Regulation[86] and Australia's Illegal Logging Prohibition Bill[87] – has been questioned by analysts, although ultimately it is important to remember that the outcomes of a

---

[79] E.g., Regulation (EU) No. 995/2010.

[80] Australian Illegal Logging Prohibition Act (Cth).

[81] Lacey Act (n 23).

[82] Duncan Brack with Rob Bailey, 'Ending Global Deforestation: Policy Options for Consumer Countries' (Chatham House and Forest Trends 2013) 2.

[83] The issue has indeed come up in the negotiations. See Kate Horner, Niranjali Amerasinghe and Sebastian Bock, 'REDD: Addressing the Drivers – A Case for the WTO?' (2013), http://www.ciel.org/Publications/REDD_WTO_4Jun2013.pdf.

[84] General Agreement on Tariffs and Trade (adopted 15 April 1994; entered into force 1 January 1995) 1867 UNTS 187.

[85] On the 'like products' debate in the context of the WTO see, e.g., Won-Mog Choi, *'Like Products' in International Trade Law* (OUP 2003).

[86] Akiva Fishman and Krystof Obidzinski, 'European Union Timber Regulation: Is It Legal?' (2014) 23 *RECIEL* 258.

[87] Andrew Mitchell and Glyn Ayres, 'Out of Crooked Timber: The Consistency of Australia's Illegal Logging Prohibition Bill with the WTO Agreement' (2012) 29 *Envtl & Planning L J* 462.

WTO dispute with respect to these and other measures would be hard to predict.[88]

Other trade-related measures that governments can adopt include sustainable public procurement,[89] lowering tariffs for sustainable timber or certain agricultural commodities[90] and standards and regulations (e.g. building standards related to timber or sustainability criteria for biofuels).[91] Each of these measures can also be examined in the light of international trade law, but their legal acceptability will depend first and foremost on their specific design.

2.6 Transnational Governance of REDD+

Transnational governance refers to transboundary cooperation involving 'the authoritative steering of network constituents to achieve public goals'.[92] This definition covers authoritative steering that cannot be neatly classified as (public or private) international law,[93] including non-governmental sources of authority. While the environmental, trade and human rights regimes discussed above draw on multiple sources of authority, the pluralism of transnational governance is perhaps most notable in the case of REDD+. This section therefore organizes the analysis of REDD+ law and governance around three key sources of transnational authority. These are fund-based authority (rooted in direct control of financial flows), market-based authority (rooted more diffusely in market demand) and 'hybrid' approaches

---

88 Duncan Brack, *Combating Illegal Logging: Interaction with WTO Rules* (Chatham House 2013) 14.

89 Public procurement measures targeting illegally logged timber have already been adopted by a wide range of countries (26 as of 2014), with more countries likely to follow. See Duncan Brack, *Promoting Legal and Sustainable Timber: Using Public Procurement Policy* (Chatham House 2014).

90 However, lowering tariffs for timber may have little effect given that such tariffs are already close to zero in many countries; lowering tariffs for agricultural commodities may be more effective, but would likely be highly contested. Brack and Bailey 23–5.

91 Ibid. 26–9.

92 Liliana B. Andonova, Michele M. Betsill and Harriet Bulkeley, 'Transnational Climate Governance' (2009) *Global Envtl Pol* 52, 53.

93 Ibid. This definition is broader than that of 'transnational law', a term used by Philip Jessup in 1956 to denote 'all law which regulates actions or events that transcend national frontiers . . . [including] public and private international law . . . [and] other rules which do not wholly fit into such standard categories'. Philip C. Jessup, *Transnational Law* (Yale UP 1956) 2.

governed by a combination of government, fund- and/or market-based authority.[94]

Fund-based authority has been instrumental in putting REDD+ into practice.[95] One important funding initiative is the UN-REDD programme, which was created in 2008 to help countries prepare for REDD+, and to provide technical and scientific support with respect to issues such as MRV and the achievement of multiple benefits.[96] The programme was established by three UN agencies – the Food and Agriculture Organization (FAO), the UN Environment Programme (UNEP) and the UN Development Programme (UNDP) – and is governed by a policy board that brings together partner countries, donors and international organizations, as well as members of civil society and indigenous peoples.[97] Another key initiative, the Forest Carbon Partnership Facility (FCPF), was launched by the World Bank in 2008, in an effort to bolster what it considers its pioneering role in the area of carbon finance and forest carbon conservation and sequestration. It serves the dual goal of building capacity for implementing REDD+ in developing countries (through its Readiness Fund), and testing the feasibility of performance-based payments for REDD+ through pilot activities in five countries (through its Carbon Fund). Another World Bank initiative, the Forest Investment Programme (FIP), also seeks to build capacity for REDD+, and aims to support national policies and measures to implement REDD+. Unlike UN-REDD, the FCPF and FIP are governed by donor and partner countries only.[98] Regional funding mechanisms administered by regional banks have also been created in recent years, including the Congo Basin Forest

---

[94] For a discussion of these categories, see Constance McDermott et al., 'Governance for REDD+, Forest Management and Biodiversity: Existing Approaches and Future Options' in John A. Parotta, Christoph Wildburger and Stephanie Mansourian (eds), *Understanding Relationships between Biodiversity, Carbon, Forests and People: The Key to Achieving REDD+ Objectives* (IUFRO 2013) 115, 123–5.

[95] For an evaluation of Norway's initiative, see Norad, *Real-Time Evaluation of Norway's International Climate and Forest Initiative Synthesising Report 2007–2013* (Norad 2014).

[96] UN Collaborative Programme on Reducing Emissions from Deforestation and Forest Degradation in Developing Countries (UN-REDD), 'Framework Document' (20 June 2008). UN-REDD has 58 partner countries: http://www.un-redd.org/partner_countries/tabid/102663/default.aspx.

[97] UN-REDD, 'UN-REDD Programme Rules of Procedure and Operational Guidance' (UN-REDD 2009) 3.

[98] International Bank for Reconstruction and Development, 'Charter Establishing the Forest Carbon Partnership Facility' (23 December 2014) Section 11.

Fund and the Amazon Fund. In addition to these multi-donor initiatives, individual governments have also become active in REDD+ finance. Perhaps the best example is Norway, which has concluded bilateral agreements with Brazil, Guyana, Indonesia and Tanzania under which performance-based payments for REDD+ activities are made.[99] Another notable transnational initiative that employs fund-based authority is the Governors' Climate and Forests Task Force, which brings together various states and provinces from Brazil, Indonesia, Mexico, Nigeria, Peru, Spain and the United States,[100] and which established a fund for REDD+ activities in 2013.[101]

Market-based and hybrid authority can be observed primarily in the wide range of standard-setting initiatives that have emerged in recent years. Several years of intergovernmental discussions on REDD+ did not lead to any clear or legally binding standards for implementing REDD+ activities. This niche was occupied by a growing number of private and public–private initiatives, most of which were associated with voluntary markets for forest carbon. These initiatives include standards for MRV of avoided emissions,[102] as well as standards to ensure that REDD+ activities are socially and environmentally responsible.[103] A notable example is the Climate Community and Biodiversity Alliance (CCBA), a partnership of non-governmental organizations, which has developed standards for terrestrial carbon mitigation projects, addressing the various safeguards of the UNFCCC.[104] Other examples of private standards relevant to

---

[99] See Norway, 'The Government of Norway's International Climate and Forest Initiative' (Norad 2012). For an evaluation of the initiative, see Norad, *Real-Time Evaluation of Norway's International Climate and Forest Initiative Synthesising Report 2007–2013* (Norad 2014).

[100] http://www.gcftaskforce.org/.

[101] http://www.gcffund.org/.

[102] Rachel Cracknell, 'From Project-based to Nested REDD+: Monitoring, Reporting and Verifying (MRV) Standards for Carbon Accounting' (WWF 2012).

[103] See, e.g., Constance L. McDermott et al., 'Operationalizing Social Safeguards in REDD+: Actors, Interests and Ideas' (2012) 21 *Envtl Sci & Pol'y* 63; Stephanie Roe et al., *Safeguards in REDD+ and Forest Carbon Standards: A Review of Social, Environmental and Procedural Concepts and Application* (Climate Focus 2013); Albert Abraham Arhin, 'Safeguards and Dangerguards: A Framework for Unpacking the Black Box of Safeguards for REDD+' (2014) 45 *Forest Pol'y & Economics* 24.

[104] The most recent edition of the CCBA standards can be found at: https://s3.amazonaws.com/CCBA/Third_Edition/CCB_Standards_Third_Edition_December_2013.pdf. For an analysis, see Isabel Melo, Esther Turnhout and Bas Arts, 'Integrating Multiple Benefits in Market-based Climate Mitigation Schemes:

REDD+ activities include the Verified Carbon Standard (VCS),[105] the Global Conservation Standard,[106] the Gold Standard[107] and the Plan Vivo standard.[108] Together with CARE International, the CCBA is also involved in the REDD+ Social and Environmental Standards (REDD+ SES) initiative, an example of hybrid governance. Unlike the CCBA's standards, the REDD+ SES are not intended for use in project-level certification. Rather, this initiative engages public actors at national and subnational levels as well as civil society representatives in developing detailed national-level REDD+ safeguards.[109]

3. IMPLICATIONS OF INSTITUTIONAL COMPLEXITY

The picture emerging from the preceding overview is one of an intricate mosaic of international legal instruments, international organizations, bilateral agreements, private, public–private and subnational initiatives.[110] Although the UNFCCC discussions on REDD+ have played an important role in this institutional complex, it becomes apparent that rule development under the climate regime needs to be viewed in its wider context. But what are the implications – in terms of opportunities and risks – of this growing institutional complexity?

One positive consequence may be the creation of a new division of labour between the UNFCCC and other legal instruments and governance arrangements.[111] Although there may have been initial hopes that REDD+

The Case of the Climate, Community and Biodiversity Certification Scheme' (2014) 35 *Envtl Sci & Pol'y* 49.

[105] http://www.v-c-s.org/.

[106] http://www.globalconservationstandard.org/.

[107] http://www.goldstandard.org/luf.

[108] http://www.planvivo.org/docs/Plan-Vivo-Standard-2013.pdf. For a discussion of voluntary standards, see Eduard Merger, Michael Dutschke and Louis Verchot, 'Options for REDD+ Voluntary Certification to Ensure Net GHG Benefits, Poverty Alleviation, Sustainable Management of Forests and Biodiversity Conservation' (2011) 2 *Forests* 550.

[109] http://www.redd-standards.org/.

[110] Even this picture of REDD+ governance is incomplete, as ultimately national laws and policies exert influence on REDD+ activities. However, this chapter retains a focus on international and transnational efforts.

[111] Cf. Thomas Gehring and Benjamin Faude, 'A Theory of Emerging Order within Institutional Complexes: How Competition among Regulatory International Institutions Leads to Institutional Adaptation and Division of Labor' (2014) 9 *Rev Intl Organizations* 471. See also Michele Betsill et al., 'Building

under the UNFCCC would evolve into a hard law instrument governing deforestation, such a scenario has become increasingly unlikely.[112] Not only are the rules developed thus far incomplete, but they also leave significant discretion for policymakers at the national and subnational level, for instance with respect to MRV and the implementation of safeguards. These regulatory lacunae allow other legal regimes and transnational governance arrangements to play a role – an opportunity they have indeed grasped.[113] Transnational governance arrangements have offered more detailed guidance in areas not (yet) covered by the UNFCCC. For instance, Abbott points out that the 'VCS recently adopted a standard for "jurisdictional REDD" because international rules were lagging behind a recognized need'.[114] Such divisions of labour need not be limited to the UNFCCC and transnational governance. Given their expertise in their respective issue areas, international legal instruments in the areas of human rights and biodiversity protection could better inform the formulation, implementation, and monitoring and reporting of safeguards at the national level, and add flesh to the UNFCCC's broadly formulated safeguard provisions.[115]

A further potential benefit of institutional complexity in REDD+ law and governance meshes well with the advantages highlighted by Ostrom's concept of polycentricity[116] as well as the literature on (global) experimentalist governance:[117] the diverse sites of governance allow for

---

Productive Links between the UNFCCC and the Broader Global Climate Governance Landscape' (2015) 15 *Global Envtl Pol* 1.

112 Annecoos Wiersema, 'Climate Change, Forests, and International Law: REDD's Descent into Irrelevance' (2014) 47 *Vand J Transnat'l L* 1.

113 The prospective role of transnational governance initiatives, such as certification, is discussed by Andrew Long, 'Global Climate Governance to Enhance Biodiversity and Well-Being: Integrating Non-State Networks and Public International Law in Tropical Forests' (2011) 41 *Envtl L* 951; and Kelly Levin, Benjamin Cashore and Jonathan Koppell, 'Can Non-State Certification Systems Bolster State-centered Efforts to Promote Sustainable Development through the Clean Development Mechanism?' (2009) 44 *Wake For L Rev* 777, 791.

114 Kenneth W. Abbott, 'Strengthening the Transnational Regime Complex for Climate Change' (2014) 3 *Transnat'l Envtl L* 57, 75.

115 For specific suggestions, see Daniela Rey et al., *A Guide to Understanding and Implementing the UNFCCC REDD+ Safeguards* (ClientEarth 2013).

116 See, e.g., Elinor Ostrom, 'Polycentric Systems for Coping with Collective Action and Global Environmental Change' (2010) 20 *Global Envtl Change* 550.

117 On experimentalist governance (mainly in the context of the EU), see Charles F. Sabel and Jonathan Zeitlin, 'Experimentalist Governance' in David Levi-Faur (ed.), *The Oxford Handbook of Governance* (OUP 2012) 169. On experimentalist governance in the global context, see Gráinne de Búrca, Robert O. Keohane

experimentation and the diffusion of best practices. Different transnational governance arrangements have offered an opportunity to test the usefulness of standards,[118] and to pave the way for 'REDD+ readiness' through a variety of funding mechanisms. Indeed, REDD+ itself can be viewed as an experiment in putting the concept of payments for ecosystem services in practice.[119] Moreover, the pluralist system allows for the coexistence of alternative governance frameworks that support a different balance of power, and different social and cultural models of governance. This could help offer a voice to those actors (e.g. indigenous and local communities) that often struggle to be heard.[120]

Notwithstanding the potential benefits of institutional complexity, the possible drawbacks also merit discussion. One such drawback is that rules and standards developed in different institutions may be at odds with each other. Even though the UNFCCC has now developed safeguards, there are still legitimate concerns that REDD+ as conceived in the climate change negotiations could have negative implications for social and environmental issues. In other words, there may still be tensions with international biodiversity and human rights law. For example, the rules do not necessarily prevent 'biodiversity leakage' (i.e. avoided deforestation in areas with low levels of biodiversity leads to an increase in deforestation in other areas with high levels of biodiversity) or 'land-grabbing' that leads to the displacement of local forest-dwelling communities.[121] It has therefore been suggested that further actions are needed to ensure that REDD+ delivers multiple benefits, as opposed to the 'do-no-harm' approach of safeguards.[122] Another tension in the institutional complex has already been highlighted above: new regulatory schemes targeting illegal logging

---

and Charles Sabel, 'New Modes of Pluralist Global Governance' (2013) 45 *NYUJILP* 723; and Gráinne de Búrca, Robert O. Keohane and Charles Sabel, 'Global Experimentalist Governance' (2014) 44 *Brit J Polit Sci* 477.

[118] For a review, see Merger, Dutschke and Verchot, who suggest that a combination of different standards should be used.

[119] Esteve Corbera, 'Problematizing REDD+ as an Experiment in Payments for Ecosystem Services' (2012) 4 *Current Opinion in Environmental Sustainability* 612.

[120] Naomi Johnstone, 'Indonesia in the "REDD": Climate Change, Indigenous Peoples and Global Legal Pluralism' (2010) 12 *Asian-Pacific L & Pol'y J* 93.

[121] Celia A. Harvey, Barney Dickson and Cyril Kormos, 'Opportunities for Achieving Biodiversity Conservation through REDD' (2010) 3 *Conservation Letters* 53, 55. Anne M. Larson et al., 'Land Tenure and REDD+: The Good, the Bad and the Ugly' (2013) 23 *Global Envtl Change* 678.

[122] For a discussion in the context of biodiversity, see ibid. 57–9; and Josil P. Murray and Julia P.G. Jones, *Safeguarding Biodiversity in REDD+* (CIFOR 2014), http://www.cifor.org/publications/pdf_files/SafeguardBrief/5193-brief.pdf.

may be in conflict with international trade law. However, the jury is still out on this issue, both with respect to the effectiveness of such schemes in addressing deforestation as well as their compatibility with WTO law.

Potential tensions and incompatibilities are not limited to international legal regimes. For instance, McDermott and colleagues note that the safeguards under the FCPF can be characterized as 'risk-based', emphasizing economic valuation of risks to minimize costs, whereas UN-REDD's safeguard policies are more 'rights-based', focused on the rights of indigenous and local communities.[123] Hence the implementation of these standards would have a different impact on the implementation of REDD+ activities on the ground.

Another negative implication of the sheer diversity of international and transnational institutions could be its impacts on marginalized communities. The proliferation of standards (both related to carbon and non-carbon benefits), channels of finance, capacity-building initiatives and discussion forums presents a challenge to any actor interested in REDD+ in practice. This challenge is disproportionately large for those actors, including indigenous and local communities, who have limited resources to navigate the various processes.[124]

4. MANAGING INSTITUTIONAL COMPLEXITY

While the polycentric image of REDD+ governance may thus sound appealing, some level of coordination may be warranted. Coordination may reduce tensions between different legal instruments and governance arrangements[125] or help harmonize existing standards.[126] This need is acknowledged also by those advocating a pluralist approach to governing REDD+. For instance, Boyd suggests that

> [p]lural, polycentric, nested forms of new governance hold considerable appeal in the abstract, but we need much more experience, more thick description,

---

[123] McDermott et al. See also Savaresi, 'REDD+ and Human Rights', 3–4.

[124] For instance, the complex governance system in Peru is suggested to lead to the social exclusion of certain communities. Fariborz Zelli et al., *Reducing Emissions from Deforestation and Forest Degradation (REDD) in Peru: A Challenge to Social Inclusion and Multi-level Governance* (German Development Institute 2014).

[125] For a similar discussion of the need for coordination in other cases in international climate change law and governance, see Harro van Asselt and Fariborz Zelli, 'Connect the Dots: Managing the Fragmentation of Global Climate Governance' (2014) 16 *Envtl Economics & Pol'y Studies* 137.

[126] As suggested by Merger, Dutschke and Verchot, 574.

> of how these forms of governance are taking shape in various environmental domains, and how enabling environments *that allow for coordination and translation across the diversity of normative orders* can be constructed in a manner that builds upon the informal processes and institutions that all formal order depends upon.[127]

The question then becomes: how can we best navigate the complex web of legal regimes and transnational governance arrangements?

Coordination between different REDD+-related institutions is already taking place to some extent, and has taken various forms. For example, concerns about diverging safeguards and sustainability requirements stemming from the FCPF, the FIP and UN-REDD were acknowledged by each of the institutions,[128] and spurred the development of the 'Common Approach' under the FCPF, which is meant to ensure that the various organizations implementing the FCPF use the same set of safeguards.[129] In addition, the FCPF and UN-REDD have developed joint guidelines for stakeholder engagement.[130] Coordination between different international legal regimes has been more challenging, but a dialogue between the administrative bodies of the UNFCCC and the CBD on issues of overlap, including REDD+, is taking place through the Joint Liaison Group of the Rio Conventions. However, while the CBD secretariat has actively sought to 'market' the linkages between climate change and biodiversity,[131] the mandates of the bureaucratic bodies of international legal regimes do not extend to decision-making (i.e. they cannot develop rules to implement the treaties they serve), meaning that their capacity to reduce tensions or enhance synergies remains limited.[132]

---

[127] William Boyd, 'Climate Change, Fragmentation, and the Challenges of Global Environmental Law: Elements of a Post-Copenhagen Assemblage' (2011) 32 *U Pa J Intl L* 458, 516 (emphasis added). A similar, more general argument is made by Krisch who, in his defence of legal pluralism in a 'postnational' world, argues that 'interface norms' are needed to coordinate different legal systems. Nico Krisch, *Beyond Constitutionalism: The Pluralist Structure of Postnational Law* (OUP 2010) 285ff.

[128] World Bank, 'Enhancing Cooperation and Coherence among Multilateral REDD+ Institutions to Support REDD+ Activities' (6 November 2010) 2.

[129] Forest Carbon Partnership Facility (FCPF) Readiness Fund, 'Common Approach to Environmental and Social Safeguards for Multiple Delivery Partners' (9 August 2012).

[130] 'Guidelines on Stakeholder Engagement in REDD+ Readiness With a Focus on the Participation of Indigenous Peoples and Other Forest-Dependent Communities' (20 April 2012).

[131] Sikina Jinnah, 'Marketing Linkages: Secretariat Governance of the Climate-Biodiversity Interface' (2011) 11 *Global Envtl Pol* 23.

[132] van Asselt 234–5.

Coordination can also take place unilaterally, through actions taken by only one institution.[133] A good example is the CBD COP, which has adopted a series of decisions with a view to avoiding (and responding to) conflicts and promoting synergies on various biodiversity-related issues. However, while the CBD has been argued to be instrumental in highlighting biodiversity concerns in UNFCCC decisions in the past,[134] the guidance on safeguards developed under the CBD was of limited influence on the development of safeguards under the UNFCCC.[135]

While some level of coordination has been possible, two further questions emerge. First, is enhanced coordination possible? Second, and more importantly, is it even desirable? Parties to the UNFCCC seemed to have answered both questions in the affirmative, at least with respect to coordination of support for the implementation of REDD+ activities. In Warsaw in 2013, they recognized 'the need for effective and transparent coordination of support for the implementation of the activities'.[136] Yet even this call for coordination through improved flows of information between the UNFCCC and other multilateral and bilateral initiatives financing REDD+ activities was contested, with some donors maintaining that decisions concerning REDD+ finance are within their sovereign rights.[137] In the absence of a coordination mechanism (e.g. a REDD+ Committee)[138] under the UNFCCC, some Parties have pointed to the possible role of the REDD+ Partnership in the coordination of the web of institutions until agreement is reached on coordination within the UNFCCC.[139] This partnership is an intergovernmental platform, which was established in 2010 with a view to taking concrete action, 'including improving the effectiveness,

---

133 Ibid. 71.

134 Farhana Yamin and Joanna Depledge, *The International Climate Change Regime: A Guide to Rules, Institutions, and Procedures* (CUP 2004) 523–4.

135 For a discussion, see Till Pistorius, Dinah Benick and Sabine Reinecke, 'REDD+ and Safeguards under the UNFCCC and the CBD' in Till Pistorius and Christine Schmitt (eds), *The Protection of Forests under Global Biodiversity and Climate Policies* (Federal Agency for Nature Conservation 2013) 7.

136 Decision 10/CP.19, preamble; see also para 3.

137 Recio 65–6.

138 Similar committees have been established under the UNFCCC, with respect to finance (the Standing Committee on Finance), adaptation (the Adaptation Committee), and technology (the Technology Executive Committee). Each of these is mandated to support the coordination of activities inside and outside the UNFCCC.

139 See Submission by Ireland and the European Commission on behalf of the European Union and its member States, in UNFCCC, 'Views on the matters referred to in decision 1/CP.18, paragraphs 34 and 35', UN Doc FCCC/SB/2013/MISC.3 (26 April 2013) 30.

efficiency, transparency and coordination of REDD+ initiatives and financial instruments, to facilitate among other things knowledge transfer, capacity enhancement, mitigation actions and technology development and transfer'.[140] However, it is unclear whether the partnership would be able to effectively manage the network of institutions or whether the existing fault lines in the climate negotiations will merely be replicated.[141] Moreover, it remains uncertain whether Parties to the UNFCCC really want to centralize coordination functions in the UNFCCC.[142]

This brief discussion illustrates how the feasibility of enhanced coordination may be constrained. Yet the more fundamental point may be that the web of institutions involved with REDD+ is not amenable to coordination. The diversity of institutions reflects the diverging interests of actors, and the different policy objectives attached to REDD+ by those actors. For some, REDD+ is about strengthening climate change mitigation policies, requiring institutions that help scaling up REDD+ activities as fast as possible, combined with strong MRV. Others see REDD+ as a possible vehicle to resolve the long-standing challenge of tackling deforestation, and point to the importance of ensuring sustainable forest management. Yet others view REDD+ as an opportunity to draw attention to the rights of indigenous and local communities living in or dependent on forests, necessitating a consideration of the relevance of human rights institutions. REDD+ can thus be viewed as a 'boundary object', meaning it is 'plastic, open to interpretation by different actors and valuable to each for different reasons', including its carbon and non-carbon benefits.[143] This insight provides an indication of why it is so difficult to enhance coordination. As Koskenniemi argues in his critique of regime interactions, '[i]n a world of hegemonic regimes, there is no "innocent" or impartial, neutral terrain from the perspective of which regime interaction could be managed'.[144] This means that the specific – and possibly conflicting – interests embedded in REDD+-related institutions may not easily be reconciled with

---

[140] http://www.fao.org/partnerships/redd-plus-partnership/en/. See also Sabine Reinecke, Till Pistorius and Michael Pregernig, 'UNFCCC and the REDD+ Partnership from a Networked Governance Perspective'(2014) 35 *Envtl Sci & Pol'y* 30.

[141] For an analysis, see Aarti Gupta, Till Pistorius and Marjanneke Vijge, 'Managing Pre-regime Complexity: The REDD+ Partnership as Bridge Institution' (2013; on file with authors).

[142] Recio, 66–7.

[143] McDermott et al. 64. See also William Boyd, 'Ways of Seeing in Environmental Law: How Deforestation Became an Object of Climate Governance' (2010) 37 *Ecology L Q* 843.

[144] Martti Koskenniemi, 'Hegemonic Regimes' in Young, 305, 320.

each other through enhanced coordination, and that instead the attention should shift to identifying the trade-offs that are required.[145]

5. CONCLUSIONS

It is a truism that REDD+ means different things to different people. While REDD+ under the UNFCCC has been established primarily to help achieve global climate change mitigation objectives, it addresses an issue – deforestation – that inevitably brings together a variety of actors and interests.[146] As a result, a range of policy goals are associated with REDD+. This is a reality that policymakers at the international and national levels need to grapple with, and that scholars and other analysts need to acknowledge.

The diverse set of international legal regimes and transnational governance arrangements discussed in this chapter are critical for tackling the multifaceted problem of deforestation.[147] Coordination can only go so far in addressing the risks and challenges associated with this resulting level of institutional complexity. Nevertheless, coordination can help with clarifying and balancing the trade-offs that need to be made in the development of coherent and effective REDD+ law and governance.

---

[145] Trade-offs in the context of 'greening' REDD+ are for example identified in Harro van Asselt, 'Integrating Biodiversity in the Climate Regime's Forest Rules: Options and Tradeoffs in Greening REDD Design' (2011) 20 *RECIEL* 139, 147–9.

[146] Boyd 523 (describing REDD+ as 'an emerging global assemblage of people, practices, organizations, laws, technologies, and territories that is taking shape at multiple sites around the world').

[147] On the notion of institutional fit, see Oran R. Young, *Institutional Dimensions of Environmental Change: Fit, Interplay, and Scale* (MIT Press 2002) 55–82.

4. REDD+ and interacting legal regimes

*Margaret A. Young**[1]

1. INTRODUCTION

International efforts to reduce emissions from deforestation and forest degradation are being developed under the auspices of the UNFCCC and other bodies. REDD+ schemes have emerged in response to the recognition that a large proportion of GHG emissions originate from forest-related activities.[2] REDD+ is based on the provision of incentives to encourage developing countries to avoid deforestation and forest degradation, sustainably manage forests, and conserve and enhance their forest carbon stocks.[3] Interventions occur in the context of existing and fragmented norms and institutions relating to forests. These include

* All websites cited in this chapter were accessed on 1 October 2015.

[1] An earlier version of this chapter was presented at the third UNITAR-Yale Conference on Environmental Governance and Democracy, and the author is grateful for comments from participants, especially Ben Cashore, Daniel Magraw and Annalisa Savaresi. The chapter has also benefited from comments from Christina Voigt, discussions with Tim Clairs and research assistance by Stephanie Niall and Cobi Smith. The author acknowledges the support of the Australian Research Council (ARC Discovery Project DP110100259 *Climate Change Law and Mitigation: Forest Carbon Sequestration and Indigenous and Local Community Rights*), and the comments of her co-investigators on this project: Lee Godden, Kirsty Gover and Maureen Tehan. Further insights from that project will be published as Maureen Tehan, Lee Godden, Margaret A. Young and Kirsty Gover, *Climate Change Responses and Indigenous and Forest Communities: International, National and Local Law Perspectives on REDD+* (Cambridge University Press, forthcoming).

[2] K.L. Denman et al., 'Couplings between Changes in the Climate System and Biogeochemistry' in S. Solomon et al. (eds), *Climate Change 2007: The Physical Science Basis. Contribution of Working Group I to the Fourth Assessment Report of the Intergovernmental Panel on Climate Change* (Cambridge University Press, 2007) 499; IPCC, *Climate Change 2013: The Physical Science Basis. Contribution of Working Group I to the Fifth Assessment Report of the Intergovernmental Panel on Climate Change* (Cambridge University Press, 2013).

[3] COP, UNFCCC, Decision 1/CP.16 ('The Cancún Agreements: Outcome of the Work of the Ad Hoc Working Group on Long-Term Cooperative Action under the Convention'), UN Doc FCCC/CP/2010/7/Add.1 (15 March 2011) para 70.

international legal regimes for the protection of biological diversity, forest management and timber trade regimes, food security initiatives and indigenous peoples' rights.

This chapter situates the development of REDD+ within the fragmentation of international law and discourses surrounding pluralism and the interaction of legal regimes.[4] It makes three points. First, REDD+ is itself emerging as an international regime, characterized by newly instituted and diffuse agencies (created from established bodies such as the FAO, the UNEP, the UNDP and the World Bank) and a broad range of state and non-state participants. Here, I draw on insights from public international law and international relations theory in identifying the development of special branches of laws and procedures responding to particular functional issues. Secondly, REDD+ is interacting with existing regimes both through state-controlled rules and procedures (such as the decisions of the UNFCCC COP) and non-state avenues. Regime interaction is not a neutral process of coordination or coherence. Indeed, REDD+ shows that climate change mitigation may conflict with the objectives of regimes for biodiversity protection, indigenous peoples' rights or food security. This is demonstrated with reference to the negotiation of REDD+ at the UNFCCC and associated mechanisms, as well as through the initial implementation of REDD+, when donor funds are provided to recipient states for capacity building and 'readiness' activities. Opportunities for states, international organizations and non-state actors to incorporate (or reject) norms, procedures and attitudes from other regimes are apparent. The third and final point is a normative one that builds from the observation that in interacting with existing regimes, the REDD+ regime is fluctuating between legally precise statements of rights-protections and a looser, experimentalist framework. I argue that a framework that allows for appropriate oversight of the activities of actors during regime interaction – which include but are not limited to states – should be maintained using rights or accountability mechanisms.

---

[4] Margaret A. Young, 'Introduction: The Productive Friction between Regimes' in Margaret A. Young (ed.), *Regime Interaction in International Law: Facing Fragmentation* (Cambridge University Press, 2012) 1.

2. REDD+'S EMERGENCE AS A REGIME

This section situates REDD+ in international law and law-making by arguing that it is emerging as a 'regime'.[5] Building on Krasner[6] and Fischer-Lescano and Teubner,[7] I have defined regimes as 'sets of norms, decision-making procedures and organizations coalescing around functional issue-areas and dominated by particular modes of behavior, assumptions and biases'.[8] The notion of 'regimes', while popular in international relations scholarship for many years, has become an important concept in understanding and analyzing the fragmentation of public international law. The concept is not restricted to the main sources of public international law (treaties or norms of customary international law) but also incorporates an institutional analysis and recognizes that participants of regimes can include a range of state and non-state actors. A related concept of 'regime complex'[9] also adds a richer understanding about loosely coupled arrangements between regimes. Moreover, drawing on insights from systems theory, it can be shown that the discourses *within* regimes have their own biases and preferences. These embedded biases and preferences, especially surrounding technical expertise, affect the interaction between regimes in unseen and important ways.[10]

The functional issue motivated by REDD+ is, broadly, the objective of the UNFCCC, namely the 'stabilization of greenhouse gas concentrations in the atmosphere at a level that would prevent dangerous anthropogenic interference with the climate system'.[11] (I note that this objective is similar but not identical to carbon sequestration schemes – which often adopt the

---

[5] For an extended discussion of REDD+'s emergence as a regime, see Maureen Tehan et al., *Climate Change Responses and Indigenous and Forest Communities* (forthcoming).

[6] Stephen Krasner, 'Structural Causes and Regime Consequences: Regimes as Intervening Variables' in Stephen Krasner (ed.), *International Regimes* (Cornell University Press, 1983) 1.

[7] Andreas Fischer-Lescano and Gunther Teubner, 'Regime-Collisions: The Vain Search for Legal Unity in the Fragmentation of Global Law' (2004) 25 *Michigan Journal of International Law* 999.

[8] Young, 'Introduction: The Productive Friction between Regimes', 11.

[9] Robert O. Keohane and David Victor, 'The Regime Complex for Climate Change' (2011) 9 *Perspectives on Politics* 7.

[10] Andrew Lang, 'Legal Regimes and Professional Knowledges: The Internal Politics of Regime Definition' in Young (ed.), *Regime Interaction in International Law: Facing Fragmentation*.

[11] UNFCCC, Article 2; see also Preamble to the Kyoto Protocol ('in pursuit of the ultimate objective of the [UNFCCC] as stated in its Article 2').

acronym REDD – that are developed as part of voluntary carbon markets. This chapter does not treat those schemes as part of the UNFCCC REDD+ regime; arguably they are more appropriately discussed in the context of REDD+ as an assemblage.)[12] UNFCCC parties have agreed to '[p]romote sustainable management, and promote and cooperate in the conservation and enhancement, as appropriate, of sinks and reservoirs of all greenhouse gases . . . including forests'.[13] Participation in such climate change mitigation is to be in accordance with parties' 'common but differentiated responsibilities and respective capabilities'.[14] They have also agreed to conclude a new climate agreement at the end of 2015, which would come into effect from 2020. This 'post-2020 agreement', as it is often termed, is expected to apply to all UNFCCC parties, including the United States, the EU and China. Forests and land use are expected to be included in the post-2020 agreement, and the broad aspiration of REDD+ is likely to continue in some form.

The issue motivating REDD+ within the UNFCCC has morphed over time. The early proposal to reduce emissions from deforestation (with the acronym RED)[15] was enlarged to include forest degradation (with the acronym REDD).[16] The role of conservation, the sustainable management of forests and the enhancement of forest carbon stocks (with the acronym REDD+) has been gradually acknowledged by parties,[17] and these objectives were later reworded to recognize REDD+ to encompass

---

[12] William Boyd, 'Climate Change, Fragmentation, and the Challenges of Global Environmental Law: Elements of a Post-Copenhagen Assemblage' (2010) 32 *University of Pennsylvania Journal of International Law* 457.

[13] UNFCCC, Article 4(1)(d).

[14] UNFCCC, Article 3(1); see also Article 4(1); Preamble.

[15] COP, UNFCCC, Item 6 of Provisional Agenda at Montreal ('Reducing Emissions from Deforestation in Developing Countries: Approaches to Stimulate Action') (Submission of Papua New Guinea and Costa Rica), UN Doc FCCC/CP/2005/Misc.1 (11 November 2005).

[16] See Chapter 1 by La Viña et al. in this book. COP, UNFCCC, Decision 2/CP.13 ('Reducing Emissions from Deforestation in Developing Countries: Approaches to Stimulate Action'), UN Doc FCCC/CP/2007/6/Add.1 (14 March 2008) 8.

[17] COP, UNFCCC, Decision 4/CP.15 ('Methodological Guidance for Activities Relating to Reducing Emissions from Deforestation and Forest Degradation and the Role of Conservation, Sustainable Management of Forests and Enhancement of Forest Carbon Stocks in Developing Countries'), UN Doc FCCC/CP/2009/11/Add.1 (30 March 2010) (acknowledging the importance of 'reducing emissions from deforestation and forest degradation, and the role of conservation, sustainable management of forests and enhancement of forest carbon stocks in developing countries').

'the conservation of forest carbon stocks; the sustainable management of forests and the enhancement of forest carbon stocks'.[18]

The norms and decision-making procedures have so far emerged from decisions of COP of the UNFCCC, reached by consensus as part of the UNFCCC processes.[19] These COP decisions – the most important of which are the Cancún Agreements and the WFR as discussed further below – are not treaties but are part of a growing body of 'autonomous institutional arrangements' that are subject to international institutional law.[20] Contrary to expectations, REDD+ is not currently developing as a hard-law regime.[21] In addition to the COP decisions, there have been a plethora of informal or soft-law processes which have developed outside of the UNFCCC negotiations but which influence and draw upon those negotiations. Adding to the complexity in ascertaining the source and subjects of international obligations is the fact that the funding for REDD+ schemes can come from 'a wide variety of sources, public and private, bilateral and multilateral',[22] with carbon credits and trade a possible future funding model.[23] Many soft-law processes are emerging through the work of international organizations that assist countries in building capacity to host REDD+ projects (known as 'readiness') and in channeling funds

---

[18] COP, UNFCCC, Decision 1/CP.16 ('The Cancún Agreements: Outcome of the Work of the Ad Hoc Working Group on Long-Term Cooperative Action under the Convention'), UN Doc FCCC/CP/2010/7/Add.1 (15 March 2011) para 70.

[19] Note that the requirement for consensus for COP decisions has emerged after failure to agree on draft Rules of Procedure (see draft Rule 42 (Voting)). See Draft Rules of Procedure of the Conference of the Parties and its Subsidiary Bodies in FCCC/CP/1996/2 (22 May 1996).

[20] On such arrangements, see Robin R. Churchill and Geir Ulfstein, 'Autonomous Institutional Arrangements in Multilateral Environmental Agreements: A Little-Noticed Phenomenon in International Law' (2000) 94 *American Journal of International Law* 623, 633.

[21] Annecoos Wiersema, 'Climate Change, Forests, and International Law: REDD's Descent into Irrelevance' (2014) 47 *Vanderbilt Journal of Transnational Law* 1.

[22] Decision 2/CP 17, 'Outcome of the Work of the Ad Hoc Working Group on Long-Term Cooperative Action under the Convention's Conference of the Parties, UNFCCC, Decision 12/CP.17 ('Guidance on Systems for Providing Information on How Safeguards Are Addressed and Respected and Modalities Relating to Forest Reference Emission Levels and Forest Reference Levels as Referred to in Decision 1/CP.16'), UN Doc FCCC/CP/2011/9/Add.2 (15 March 2012) para 65.

[23] It is outside the scope of the present chapter to elaborate on the likely development of funding arrangements for REDD+, but it is important to note that the form in which the arrangements will be made will have a major impact on REDD+'s relationship with other regimes, especially the WTO.

between those countries and donors. Examples that seek to evaluate (and modify) the behavior of recipient states are the 'Guidelines on Stakeholder Engagement for REDD+ Readiness with a Focus on the Participation of Indigenous Peoples and Other Forest-Dependent Communities'[24] and the 'Guidelines on Free, Prior and Informed Consent'.[25] Such guidelines to states seek consistency with UNFCCC COP decisions, but are also influenced by international institutional law and the constitutive documents of relevant international agencies. Partly in response to these processes, countries have generated their own guidelines and procedures as part of their national REDD+ strategies.[26]

The two most prominent international agencies guiding recipient states are linked to existing intergovernmental organizations. The first is the UN-REDD, established in 2008, which is a coalition of the FAO, UNEP and the UNDP. The second is the FCPF, launched in 2007, which is based within the World Bank but operates separately from the Bank's main funding programs. Within just these two sets of organizations, there are particular modes of behavior, assumptions and biases.[27] For example, a marked division in preferences as between these two sets of organizations relates to the differing attitude to the concept of FPIC, which I will discuss further below. Moreover, the FCPF has a clearer goal of establishing 'carbon-fund readiness' in its recipient countries than the UN-REDD, which is agnostic about whether REDD+ will develop into a carbon trading model. However, the organizations have often worked together: such as in developing the Guidelines on Stakeholder Engagement identified above.[28]

---

[24] UN-REDD and FCPF, 'Joint Guidelines on Stakeholder Engagement in REDD+ Readiness with a Focus on Indigenous Peoples and Other Forest-Dependent Communities' (2012), http://www.un-redd.org/Stakeholder_Engagement/Guidelines_On_Stakeholder_Engagement/tabid/55619/Default.aspx.

[25] UN-REDD, 'UN-REDD Programme Guidelines on Free, Prior and Informed Consent (FPIC)' (2012).

[26] See, e.g., Sophia Carodenuto and Kalame Fobissie, 'Operationalizing Free, Prior and Informed Consent (FPIC) for REDD+: Insights from the National FPIC Guidelines of Cameroon' (2015) 9 *Carbon & Climate Law Review* 156.

[27] This chapter is not based on ethnographic research into the practices of the organizations identified. In other contexts, however, empirical studies (not focused on REDD+) have suggested that cultural attitudes within the World Bank marginalize human rights concepts: see Galit A. Sarfaty, 'Why Culture Matters in International Institutions: The Marginality of Human Rights at the World Bank' (2009) 103 *American Journal of International Law* 647.

[28] See e.g. UN-REDD and FCPF Joint Guidelines on Stakeholder Engagement in REDD+ Readiness' (2012).

Aside from organizations that facilitate 'REDD+ readiness' and funding,[29] REDD+ has attracted the attention of a range of other actors, who will be affected by REDD+ schemes in various ways. Most notable are the indigenous peoples and forest-dwelling communities who depend on the forests for their culture and livelihood. There are also scientists and other experts (who are essential for any methodology that accounts for the value of carbon in forests); private investors seeking opportunities in carbon markets; and civil society groups. REDD+ is notable in that it has mobilized many voices. These actors are crucial in understanding REDD+ as it operates as a regime and also in understanding how it interacts with existing regimes, as will be discussed below.

3. REDD+ INTERACTS WITH EXISTING REGIMES

While the activities promoted by REDD+ schemes may be effective in sequestering carbon and achieving mitigation goals, there is a risk that valuing forests only for the carbon that they store may cause negative environmental and social impacts. These impacts could include the destruction of biological diversity (due to incentives to convert natural forests to monocultural forest plantations),[30] the displacement or loss of traditional knowledge and the elimination of subsistence and livelihood means.[31] Those other preferences are often represented in other existing regimes and this section considers how REDD+ interacts with those regimes.

---

[29] Although this chapter concentrates on the UN-REDD and the FCPF, there are a number of others, such as the interim REDD+ Partnership: see e.g. Till Pistorius and Sabine Reinecke, 'The interim REDD+ Partnership: Boost for Biodiversity Safeguards?' (2013) 36 *Forest Policy and Economics* 80.

[30] Risk to biodiversity, which is now addressed in the REDD+ Safeguards (discussed below) is identified, for example, by the Global Expert Workshop on Biodiversity Benefits from Reducing Emissions from Deforestation and Forest Degradation in Developing Countries, Nairobi, 20–23 September 2010 (UNEP/CBD/WS-REDD/1/3), para 6. But note that the Workshop identified the biggest risk to biodiversity is that 'a well-designed REDD-plus mechanism is not agreed upon and successfully implemented' (para 5).

[31] This risk is identified, for example, by IUFRO, by drawing on lessons from previous forestry-related interventions: see 'Understanding Relationships between Biodiversity, Carbon, Forests and People: The Key to Achieving REDD+ Objectives' (Global Assessment Report, International Union of Forest Research Organizations, 2012) 100 (Table 4.3).

3.1 Other Related Regimes

While not attempting an exhaustive list of forest-focused and forest-related regimes, this chapter points to a number of important examples. Some regimes seek to address agricultural and commodity expansion and logging – known drivers of deforestation – with varying degrees of success. The degree of their potential intersections with REDD+ is often determined by the local conditions surrounding the particular forests subject to REDD+ schemes – which may be threatened by the demand for charcoal fuel, palm oil, logging, agriculture or other development projects – and which may be subject to existing or future international oversight for a range of reasons quite separate from forest-related climate mitigation.

The most pertinent of these, perhaps, are legal arrangements surrounding forests and forestry, which have in the main devolved away from international laws and processes. As is well known, many states participating in the 1992 United Nations Conference on Environment and Development at Rio de Janiero unsuccessfully sought agreement to better protect the world's forests through an international convention, in tandem with the (successful) efforts to agree on the UNFCCC. Although the failure to agree upon a forest treaty has led to the description of a 'non-regime' for forests,[32] others argue that a broader set of processes represent part of a regime-complex or, more broadly, 'international forest governance'.[33]

If there is a dominant theme or ethos within the broad set of forest-focused international instruments, it is the recognition of national sovereignty over natural resources.[34] A deference to this view, rather than the often opposing view of forests as 'common heritage', is seen in non-legally binding declarations such as the 2007 General Assembly Resolution on a 'Non-legally Binding Instrument on All Types of Forests' (NLBI),[35] other decisions of the UNFF, proposals from the preceding IPF and the IFF and Rio's 'Non-Legally Binding Authoritative Statement of Principles for a Global Consensus on the Management, Conservation and Sustainable

---

[32] Radoslav S. Dimitrov et al., 'International Nonregimes: A Research Agenda' (2007) 9 *International Studies Review* 230, 231.

[33] Jeremy Rayner et al., 'Introduction' in Jeremy Rayner, Alexander Buck and Pia Katila (eds), *Embracing Complexity: Meeting the Challenges of International Forest Governance. A Global Assessment Report* (Global Forest Expert Panel on the International Forest Regime, IUFRO World Series vol. 28, 2010).

[34] See, e.g., recognition in the Forest Principles of the states' 'sovereign and inalienable right to utilize, manage and develop their forests': Forest Principles, Principle 2(a).

[35] United Nations General Assembly Resolution 62/97, 'Non-legally Binding Instrument on All Types of Forests', A/RED/62/98 (adopted 17 December 2007).

Development of All Types of Forests' (Forest Principles).[36] Tempering any appearance of toleration for rampant forest exploitation, however, is the endorsement of sustainable forest management, or 'SFM', a concept that recognizes the need to enhance the economic, social and environmental value of forests for the benefit of present and future generations.[37] While often observed to be a malleable concept, SFM has led to the development of criteria and indicators,[38] each generating particular path dependencies for forested countries. The intersection between REDD+ processes and SFM has become one of the many issues of regime interaction, as I will discuss further below.

In addition to these instruments, trade and logging regimes (with very diverse goals) include the Convention on the International Trade in Endangered Species of Wild Flora and Fauna (CITES) (which protects a number of tropical timber species from trade), the ITTA (which seeks to facilitate timber trade), and regional processes such as the FLEGT in the EU. These extend to private or transnational arrangements such as the timber certification schemes of the FSC.

The most relevant environmental regime is the CBD,[39] which promotes an 'ecosystem approach' and a holistic concern for forest protection.[40] The CBD seeks to establish systems of protected areas,[41] and sets in play a number of plans and targets for forest biodiversity. The CBD regime includes a number of additional protocols such as the Nagoya Protocol on Access to Genetic Resources and the Fair and Equitable Sharing of Benefits Arising from their Utilization, which came into force in 2014, and which deals with, among other things, the rights of indigenous peoples as holders

---

36 Forest Principles, United Nations General Assembly, Annex III ('Non-Legally Binding Authoritative Statement of Principles for a Global Consensus on the Management, Conservation and Sustainable Development of All Types of Forests'), UN Doc A/CONF.151/26 (Vol. III) (14 August 1992), 1992.

37 From the Ministerial Conference for the Protection of Forests in Europe in 1993; see also United Nations General Assembly Resolution 62/97, 'Non-legally Binding Instrument on All Types of Forests', A/RED/62/98 (adopted 17 December 2007), Preamble.

38 Constance McDermott et al., 'Mapping the Core Actors and Issues Defining International Forest Governance' in Jeremy Rayner et al. (eds), *Embracing Complexity: Meeting the Challenges of International Forest Governance*, 19, 30.

39 United Nations Convention on Biological Diversity (1992) 31 ILM 818 (in force 29 December 1993).

40 Harro van Asselt, 'Managing the Fragmentation of International Environmental Law: Forests at the Intersection of the Climate and Biodiversity Regimes' (2012) 44 *New York University Journal of International Law and Politics* 1205.

41 CBD, Article 8.

of traditional knowledge pertaining to genetic resources.[42] Financial support for developing countries to meet their biodiversity commitments and targets is pledged by other states through annual 'replenishments' of the Global Environment Facility (GEF).[43]

International financial institutions have played an increasingly important role in the governance of tropical forests in the past, and the World Bank in particular has been a key actor. Development cooperation between states has been conceptualized as a regime or set of regimes,[44] a distinctive aspect of which is broad-based goals or objectives (such as the Millennium Development Goals) rather than treaty provisions. World Bank funding for forest projects in developing countries – including the financing of commercial logging operations and efforts to promote SFM – has led to criticism and the evolution of internal strategies and policies.[45] Legal obligations within development regimes do not flow from treaty sources, but arise from the constitutive instruments of international financial institutions or at the transactional level of particular legal agreements underpinning specific projects.

Additional international regimes contain various protections for peoples

---

42 Entered into force 12 October 2014. See further Elisa Morgera, Elsa Tsioumani, Matthias Buck, *Unravelling the Nagoya Protocol: A Commentary on the Nagoya Protocol on Access and Benefit-sharing to the Convention on Biological Diversity* (Martinus Nijhoff, 2014).

43 See, e.g., Secretariat of the CBD, 'Donors replenish Global Environment Facility, but large funding gap for biodiversity remains' (Press Release, 22 April 2014). The GEF serves as the financial mechanism for the CBD. (It also serves as financial mechanism for other multilateral agreements including the UNFCCC, although since the Cancún Agreements there is a new 'Global Climate Fund': see further Richard B. Stewart, Bryce Rudyk and Kiri Mattes, 'Governing a Fragmented Climate Finance Regime' in Hassane Cissé, Daniel D. Bradlow and Benedict Kingsbury (eds), *The World Bank Legal Review: International Financial Institutions and Global Legal Governance* (World Bank; Martinus Nijhoff, 2012) vol. 3, 363, http://siteresources.worldbank.org/INTLAWJUSTICE/Resources/WBLegalReviewVol3.pdf).

44 Siobhán McInerney-Lankford, 'Human Rights and Development Regime Interaction and the Fragmentation of International Law' in Hassane Cissé et al. (eds), *The World Bank Legal Review: Legal Innovation and Empowerment for Development* (World Bank; Martinus Nijhoff, 2013) vol. 4, 123, 127, https://openknowledge.worldbank.org/bitstream/handle/10986/12229/NonAsciiFileName0.pdf.

45 See, e.g., the World Bank's Operational Policy (OP) 4.36–Forests, as described by Annie Petsonk, 'Legal Obligations and Institutions of Developing Countries: Rethinking Approaches to Forest Governance' in Hassane Cissé et al. (eds), *The World Bank Legal Review: International Financial Institutions and Global Legal Governance*, vol. 3, 293.

inhabiting or governing forested lands. The most significant treaty for indigenous peoples is the ILO Convention Concerning Indigenous and Tribal Peoples No. 169[46] (ILO Convention 169). A key instrument is the UNDRIP,[47] which is supported institutionally by UN bodies including the UN Permanent Forum on Indigenous Peoples,[48] an advisory body to the UN Economic and Social Council (ECOSOC) made up of both indigenous experts and state representatives. Human rights mechanisms flow from foundational instruments such as the Universal Declaration on Human Rights (UNDHR), the International Covenant on Civil and Political Rights (ICCPR)[49] and the International Covenant on Economic, Social and Cultural Rights (ICESCR),[50] among other treaties on the rights of children and the elimination of racial and gender discrimination.[51] Food security is supported by soft-law principles such as the FAO's Voluntary Guidelines on the Responsible Governance of Tenure of Land, Fisheries and Forests in the Context of National Food Security.[52]

It will already be clear that the state membership of these varied regimes is different: for example, the CBD has a large number of state ratifications

---

46 ILO, Convention Concerning Indigenous and Tribal Peoples in Independent Countries, opened for signature 27 June 1989, 1650 UNTS 383 (entered into force 5 September 1991).

47 United Nations General Assembly, Declaration on the Rights of Indigenous Peoples, A/RES/61/295 (13 September 2007).

48 Ibid., Article 42 (requiring bodies and states to 'follow up on the effectiveness of this Declaration'); see also Carsten Smith, Permanent Forum on Indigenous Issues, 'Draft General Comment No. 1 (2009), Article 42 of the Declaration on the Rights of Indigenous Peoples' (5 May 2009) UN Doc E/C.19/2009/CRP.12. The assumption of an institutional role is controversial, as states considered it to be a de facto attempt at changing the legal understanding of the Declaration and its mandates, and also considering other institutions such as the Expert Mechanism on the Rights of Indigenous Peoples and the Special Rapporteur on the Rights of Indigenous Peoples: see further Claire Charters, 'Multi-Sourced Equivalent Norms and the Legitimacy of Indigenous Peoples' Rights under International Law' in Tomer Broude and Yuval Shany (eds), *Multi-Sourced Equivalent Norms in International Law* (Hart Publishing, 2011) 289.

49 ICCPR, UN GA Res. 2200A (XXI), 21 UN GAOR Supp. No. 16, at 52, UN Doc A/6316 (1966), 999 UNTS 171 (entered into force 23 March 1976).

50 ICESCR, UN GA Res. 2200A (XXI), 21 UN GAOR Supp. No. 16, at 49, UN Doc A/6316 (1966), 993 UNTS 3 (entered into force 3 January 1976).

51 Convention on the Rights of the Child (CRC), UNTS 3, 28 ILM 1456 (entered into force 2 September 1990); Convention on the Elimination of All Forms of Discrimination against Women (CEDAW), UN Doc A/34/46, at 193 (1979), 1249 UNTS 14 (entered into force 3 September 1981); the International Convention on the Elimination of All Forms of Racial Discrimination (1966).

52 Endorsed by the Committee on World Food Security on 11 May 2012.

that largely mirror those of the UNFCCC (with a notable exception being that the United States is a party to the latter but not the former); in contrast, ILO Convention 169 has fewer than 30 parties (regionally concentrated) and the FSC is arguably non-state. This fragmentation is exemplified when one considers the different international obligations applying to countries participating in the FCPF or UN-REDD. Table 4.1 below provides a list of states that have participated in the funding mechanisms of FCPF or UN-REDD, together with selected forest-related international instruments to which they are also subject.[53]

One implication of considering the impact of fragmentation on REDD+ is that while it is possible to have a sense of interacting regimes, it is only possible to conclude on the degree of influence when one considers the obligations of specific states. Moreover, the obligations arise from different sources of law. Sources that are not treaties – such as UNDRIP – may be more determinative with a greater number of participating states, as they may be invoked as representing customary international law (discussed further below).

The resulting complexity is represented graphically by Figure 4.1 below. It is a static version of an online infographic of REDD+ and related international laws. The infographic enables a user to select a specific country (or sets of countries) participating in UN-REDD and/or the FCPF so as to identify the relevant applicable legal regimes (from a preselected and non-exhaustive list). Conversely, the user can select a specific legal instrument (or set of instruments) to identify the countries for whom these laws directly apply. The size of the balloon of each country and instrument provides further information. For example, the UNFCCC balloon is large because it is enjoys near universal application: *all* of the countries in the left hand column have ratified it. The ILO Convention 169, on the other hand, is accompanied by a small balloon, given its much smaller direct applicability – only 15 of the countries in the left hand column have ratified it.

---

[53] Data is drawn from the following websites last checked January 2016: http://www.unredd.net/index.php?option=com_unregions&view=overview&Itemid=495; https://forestcarbonpartnership.org/redd-countries-1; http://unfccc.int/parties_and_observers/parties/non_annex_i/items/2833.php; www.cbd.int/information/parties.shtml; www.cbd.int/abs/nagoya-protocol/signatories/; www.cites.org/eng/disc/parties/chronolo.php; www.ilo.org/dyn/normlex/en; www.un.org/press/en/2007/ga10612.doc.htm. See further https://dx.doi.org/10.4225/49/5567C4E16BB15. For a similar table developed by the Center for International Environmental Law (CIEL), which was published in November 2011 and updated 20 September 2013, see http://forestdefender.org/about/original-redd-rights-table.

Table 4.1 Selected international instruments applicable to countries participating in UN-REDD and/or the FCPF

Country	UNFCCC	CITES	CBD	Nagoya Protocol	ILO169	UNDRIP
Argentina[1, 2]	party	party	party		party	voted in favor
Bangladesh[2]	party	party	party			abstained
Belize[1]	party	party	party			voted in favor
Benin[3]	party	party	party	party		voted in favor
Bhutan[1, 3]	party	party	party	party		abstained
Bolivia, Plurinational State of[1, 3]	party	party	party		party	voted in favor
Burkina Faso[1, 3]	party	party	party	party		voted in favor
Cambodia[1, 3]	party	party	party	party		voted in favor
Cameroon[1, 3]	party	party	party			voted in favor
Central African Republic[1, 3]	party	party	party		party	voted in favor
Chad[3]	party	party	party			absent
Chile[1, 3]	party	party	party		party	voted in favor
Colombia[1, 3]	party	party	party		party	abstained
Congo, Democratic Republic of[1, 3]	party	party	party	party		voted in favor
Congo, Republic of[1, 2]	party	party	party	party		voted in favor
Costa Rica[1, 2]	party	party	party		party	voted in favor
Côte d'Ivoire[1, 2]	party	party	party	party		absent
Dominican Republic[1, 3]	party	party	party	party		voted in favor
Ecuador[3]	party	party	party		party	voted in favor
El Salvador[1, 3]	party	party	party			voted in favor
Equatorial Guinea[3]	party	party	party			absent
Ethiopia[1, 3]	party	party	party	party		absent
Fiji[1, 3]	party	party	party	party	party	absent
Gabon[1, 3]	party	party	party	party		voted in favor

Table 4.1 (continued)

Country	UNFCCC	CITES	CBD	Nagoya Protocol	ILO169	UNDRIP
Ghana[1,3]	party	party	party			voted in favor
Guatemala[1,3]	party	party	party	party	party	voted in favor
Guinea Bissau[3]	party	party	party	party		absent
Guyana[1,3]	party	party	party	party		voted in favor
Honduras[1,2]	party	party	party	party	party	voted in favor
Indonesia[1,3]	party	party	party	party		voted in favor
Kenya[1,3]	party	party	party	party		abstained
Lao People's Democratic Republic[1,3]	party	party	party	party		voted in favor
Liberia[1,3]	party	party	party	party		voted in favor
Madagascar[1,3]	party	party	party	party		voted in favor
Malawi[3]	party	party	party	party		voted in favor
Malaysia[3]	party	party	party			voted in favor
Mexico[1,3]	party	party	party	party	party	voted in favor
Mongolia[3]	party	party	party	party		voted in favor
Morocco[3]	party	party	party			absent
Mozambique[1]	party	party	party	party		voted in favor
Myanmar[3]	party	party	party	party		voted in favor
Nepal[1,2]	party	party	party		party	voted in favor
Nicaragua[1]	party	party	party		party	voted in favor
Nigeria[1,3]	party	party	party			abstained
Pakistan[1,3]	party	party	party	ratified but not yet party	party	voted in favor
Panama[1,3]	party	party	party			voted in favor

Papua New Guinea[1,3]	party	party	party			absent
Paraguay[1,3]	party	party	party		party	voted in favor
Peru[1,3]	party	party	party	party	party	voted in favor
Philippines[3]	party	party	party	party		voted in favor
Solomon Islands[3]	party	party	party			absent
South Sudan[3]	party		party			n/a
Sudan[1,3]	party	party	party	party		voted in favor
Sri Lanka[2]	party	party	party			voted in favor
Suriname[1,3]	party	party	party			voted in favor
Tanzania[1,3]	party	party	party			voted in favor
Thailand[1]	party	party	party			voted in favor
Togo[1,3]	party	party	party			absent
Tunisia[3]	party	party	party			voted in favor
Uganda[1,2]	party	party	party	party		absent
Uruguay[1]	party	party	party	party		voted in favor
Vanuatu[1]	party	party	party	party		absent
Vietnam[1,3]	party	party	party	party		voted in favor
Zambia[3]	party	party	party			voted in favor
Zimbabwe[3]	party	party	party			voted in favor

Notes:
1 Participant of the Forest Carbon Partnership Facility (FCPF)
2 UN-REDD programme partner member
3 UN-REDD programme partner observer

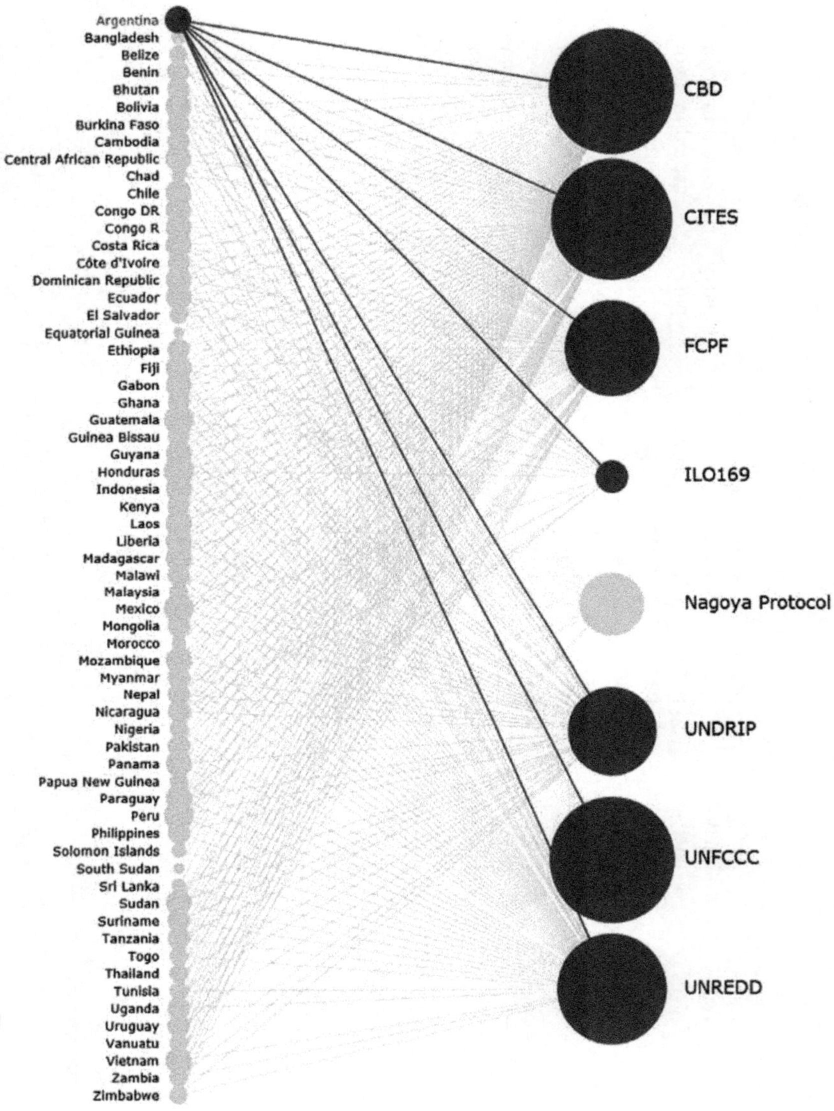

Figure 4.1 Infographic of international obligations of countries participating in UN-REDD and/or the FCPF[54]

[54] This infographic lists countries participating in UN-REDD and/or the FCPF and compares the applicability of selected international treaties and declarations. For the full infographic developed by Margaret Young and Cobi Smith,

The example in Figure 4.1 is a static representation of a user selecting one country (Argentina) and demonstrating the list of instruments which are applicable to that country (either because Argentina has ratified the relevant instrument (such as the CBD), has voted in favour of it (UNDRIP), or is participating in REDD+ funding arising from it (FCPF and UN-REDD)). Figure 4.1 thus emphasizes how Argentina's international legal obligations will impact on its REDD+ participation.

There is an important caveat about this infographic, and it is related to the fact that the list of legal instruments it contains is non-exhaustive. Because of size limitations, there are a range of other treaties, instruments and, importantly, norms of customary international law that are not included here. Indeed, it is important to emphasize that obligations arising from the listed international instruments coexist with norms of customary international law, which by definition bind all states and, due to a lack of specific supporting institutions, are often not considered to fall within international regimes. Of particular relevance in the current context, for example, is a purported obligation of states to consult with indigenous peoples on government policies or matters affecting them.[55] This obligation finds expression in the UNDRIP, but is also argued by some to have assumed the status of customary international law.[56] Customary international law protections such as these will impact on the intersecting regimes in the REDD+ context, as is explored further in the next part.

'Infographic of REDD+ and related international laws', see http://law.unimelb.edu.au/centres/creel/research/grants/climate-change-law-and-mitigation and http://cobismith.github.io/forestlaws/. The infographic was developed with the support of the Australian Research Council (ARC Discovery Project DP110100259). See further Tehan et al., *Climate Change Responses and Indigenous and Forest Communities*.

[55] Committee on the Rights of Indigenous Peoples, International Law Association (ILA) chaired by Siegfried Wiessner, 'Rights of Indigenous Peoples Final Report' (ILA, 2012) 4–7.

[56] A survey of relevant state and international practice conducted by a committee of experts assembled under the auspices of the ILA, and drawing on the work of the UN Special Rapporteur on Indigenous Peoples, found in 2010 the existence of such a norm of customary international law: this was cited by at least one international tribunal in 2011 (See *Grand River Enterprises Six Nations, Ltd., et al.* v. *United States of America*, 12 January 2011, available at http://www.state.gov/documents/organization/156820.pdf, para 210.) and reaffirmed in 2013: ILA, 'Sofia Conference (2012): Rights of Indigenous Peoples – Final Report' (2012) 29.

3.2 Regime Interaction and States

The presented list of forest-related regimes hints at the diversification and fragmentation of international laws relating to forest use and protection. Such diversification and fragmentation is a common feature of the international legal system,[57] and indeed in legal responses to the need for climate change mitigation.[58] What is clear from the public international law literature is that fragmentation creates real tensions for sovereignty.[59] States wish to ensure that they are bound *only* by the norms or decision-making procedures to which they have formally agreed (or to which they are otherwise obliged to follow as customary international law): for this reason, the International Law Commission (ILC) sought to find the common intention of states parties in resolving any conflicting norms in its 2006 seminal study.[60] Accordingly, the form in which REDD+ obligations may be entrenched in a post-2020 climate agreement, and even current legal agreements to create 'readiness' in recipient states, must be assessed according to existing international law obligations. For example, some REDD+ obligations may be subject to a customary international law obligation to consult with affected communities, as mentioned above. Similar arguments have been advanced with respect to the conceptually similar situation of a state seeking to inscribe indigenous properties on the World Heritage List according to the World Heritage Convention.[61] Moreover,

---

[57] UN International Law Commission, Fragmentation of International Law: Difficulties Arising from the Diversification and Expansion of International Law, Report of the Study Group of the International Law Commission (Finalised by Martti Koskenniemi), UN Doc. A/CN.4/L.682 and Add.1 and Corr.1 (2010).

[58] Margaret A. Young, 'Climate Change Law and Regime Interaction' (2011) 5 *Carbon & Climate Law Review* 147.

[59] Margaret A. Young, 'Fragmentation, Regime Interaction and Sovereignty' in Christine Chinkin and Freya Baetens (eds), *Sovereignty, Statehood and State Responsibility* (Cambridge University Press, 2015) 71.

[60] UN International Law Commission, *Fragmentation of International Law* (n 57).

[61] The three relevant scenarios identified by the ILA are when a state (1) proposes inscription of an indigenous property; or (2) refuses an indigenous community's request to propose the inscription of a property belonging to it; or (3) manages an indigenous property after its inscription: see International Law Association (2012), 18–20. The report concludes that there is a customary international law status of a right of indigenous peoples to recognition and preservation of their cultural identity, and this is a 'relevant rule of international law applicable in the relations between the parties to the World Heritage Convention', thus providing interpretative context to the World Heritage Convention pursuant to VCLT Article 31(3)(c).

given that almost all REDD+ recipient and donor countries are subject to general biodiversity obligations under the CBD (the only non-CBD parties being the US, Andorra and the Holy See), there is an argument that the ecosystem approach (which is increasingly dominant in the CBD regime) should underscore interpretations of REDD+.

At its most starkly positivist, however, the need to respect sovereignty has been interpreted by some decision-makers as leading to a requirement of parallel membership of regimes before the norms of those regimes have influence on one another. The related idea of 'self-contained regimes' isolates the applicable law and even sources of treaty interpretation within a regime in order to block exogenous norms: this idea has gained the support of some decision makers within the WTO.[62] Applied to the REDD+ context, this idea would clearly impact on the reception within the emerging REDD+ regime of norms and concepts from other regimes, where there is no parallel membership between UNFCCC parties and other relevant regimes. Indeed, during the REDD+ negotiations, a report prepared for Norway noted that a potential disadvantage of cross-referencing to human rights instruments in COP decisions was that some UNFCCC parties were not signatories of such agreements.[63]

Yet such stark closure is not generally apparent in the negotiation of REDD+. States *have* sought to control the sites of interaction with existing regimes, but not by making REDD+ self-contained. Instead, acting within the UNFCCC COPs, states have modified REDD+ to embrace or limit the influence of other regimes. This has been apparent in two main areas: the changing scope of REDD+ and the development of 'safeguards'.

The first of the two main ways in which states have mediated REDD+'s relationship with other regimes is through its scope. As identified above, the scope of REDD+ has developed over a series of COP decisions, which saw the focus change from RED to REDD to REDD+. These enlarged goals meant that the apparently simple aim of monitoring, reporting and verifying land use change (through remote sensing techniques) became

---

62 Anja Lindroos and Michael Mehling, 'Dispelling the Chimera of "Self-Contained Regimes" International Law and the WTO' (2005) 16 *European Journal of International Law* 857; Margaret A. Young, 'The WTO's Use of Relevant Rules of International Law: An Analysis of the Biotech Case' (2007) 56 *The International and Comparative Law Quarterly* 907.

63 Daniel Zarin et al., 'Reducing Emissions from Deforestation and Degradation (REDD): An Options Assessment' (Report Prepared for the Government of Norway, 2009) 26, http://www.redd-oar.org./links/REDD-OAR_en.pdf.

more complex,[64] involving questions of forest management that already preoccupied other regimes. There is evidence of highly contested and political choices in the COP decisions in response. For example, an early COP decision on demonstration activities used the language of 'sustainable forest management' and expressly noted 'inter alia, the relevant provisions of the United Nations Forum on Forests, the United Nations Convention to Combat Desertification and the Convention on Biological Diversity',[65] while later decisions used the different phraseology of 'sustainable management of forests'. The NLBI approach on SFM from the forest regime is therefore not as clearly endorsed as it could have been. Moreover, the general role of 'conservation' that featured in early 'plus' discussions was later constrained to a role of 'conservation of forest carbon stocks'. As such, delineating the scope of the REDD+ concept has had a marked effect on how REDD+ would be influenced by, and influence, other regimes.

The second of the two main ways in which states have mediated REDD+'s relationship with other regimes has been in agreeing on 'safeguards'. After deciding on REDD+'s scope, UNFCCC parties have incorporated norms and processes from other regimes through promoting particular objectives and activities to be achieved in the implementation of REDD+ projects. Finalized as the Cancún Agreements (named after the location of the relevant COP), parties have agreed that the following safeguards 'should be promoted and supported':

a. That actions complement or are consistent with the objectives of national forest programmes and *relevant international conventions and agreements*;

. . .

c. Respect for the knowledge and rights of indigenous peoples and members of local communities, by *taking into account relevant international obligations*, national circumstances and laws, and noting that the *United Nations General Assembly has adopted the United Nations Declaration on the Rights of Indigenous Peoples*;
d. The full and effective participation of relevant stakeholders, in particular indigenous peoples and local communities . . .

---

[64] Till Pistorius, 'From RED to REDD+: The Evolution of a Forest-Based Mitigation Approach for Developing Countries' (2012) 4 *Current Opinion in Environmental Sustainability* 638, 640.

[65] COP, UNFCCC, Decision 2/CP.13 ('Reducing Emissions from Deforestation in Developing Countries: Approaches to Stimulate Action'), UN Doc FCCC/CP/2007/6/Add.1 (14 March 2008) Annex on 'Indicative Guidance', para 8.

e. That actions are *consistent with the conservation of natural forests and biological diversity*, ensuring that the [REDD+ schemes] are not used for the conversion of natural forests, but are instead used to incentivize the protection and conservation of natural forests and their ecosystem services, and to enhance other social and environmental benefits . . . [Emphasis added]

In these safeguards, parties have recognized the imperative of ensuring that REDD+ actions do not conflict with the objectives of other international conventions and agreements. The issue of protecting the sovereignty of states that were not members of other regimes (i.e., ensuring that REDD+ parties did not become subject to other international conventions to which they had not consented) arose only obliquely. During the negotiations on this text, parties did not show a concern about explicitly quoting human rights treaties.[66] However, in the interests of not excluding specific treaties, parties used open-ended language and referred instead to 'relevant international obligations' (paragraph (c)). Where some restraint occurred was in the safeguard calling for consistency with biological diversity conservation (paragraph (e)). This does not refer to the CBD, which, it will be recalled, has not been ratified by the US.

It is prudent to note that the COP decisions on REDD+'s scope and safeguards are not subject to the law of treaties; they are not treaties (unless they serve to amend the UNFCCC or create or amend a Protocol). However, according to the law of treaties, the Cancún safeguards may well amount to 'subsequent practice'[67] relevant to interpreting the UNFCCC. In this way, the COP decision's references to existing international laws and conventions have distinct legal consequences. Of relevance, too, is the principle of 'systemic integration', which recognizes that 'whatever their subject matter, treaties are a creation of the international legal system and their operation is predicated upon that fact'.[68] In terms relevant to a post-2020 climate agreement: it is undeniably useful that states have recorded a general imperative for REDD+ obligations to be consistent with 'relevant

---

[66] Comment of UNFCCC country negotiator to author, 21 October 2014.

[67] Vienna Convention on the Law of Treaties (VCLT), Article 31(3(b) (treaty-interpreters may take into account 'any subsequent practice in the application of the treaty which establishes the agreement of the parties regarding its interpretation').

[68] UN International Law Commission, *Fragmentation of International Law: Difficulties Arising from the Diversification and Expansion of International Law, Conclusions of the Study Group of the International Law Commission* (A/CN.4/L.702) (18 July 2006) para 17.

international conventions and agreements' (paragraph (a)).[69] The future interpretation of REDD+ obligations by taking into account norms of the CBD does not necessarily require express reference to the CBD in the safeguards, nor does it require parallel membership as between a post-2020 agreement and the CBD. Moreover, state practice flowing from the safeguards could have systemic implications for the interaction of regimes at a domestic level, leading to policy coordination between government ministries such as agriculture, energy, forestry, trade, transportation and culture.[70] Indeed, in much of the evaluations of readiness preparations so far, states are reminded that REDD+ intersects with a whole range of other domestic policies and sectors, and that coordination between them is essential.[71]

Although they lack treaty status, the Cancún Agreement safeguards do seek to entrench certain legal obligations. The enforcement of the safeguards is linked to REDD+ funding and implementation. Rather than making adherence to the safeguards mandatory, the Cancún Agreements required developing countries to create a system for providing information on how the safeguards were being addressed and respected 'while respecting sovereignty'.[72] The requirement to provide information was

---

[69] COP, UNFCCC, Decision 1/CP.16 ('The Cancún Agreements: Outcome of the Work of the Ad Hoc Working Group on Long-Term Cooperative Action under the Convention'), UN Doc FCCC/CP/2010/7/Add.1 (15 March 2011) Annex. As noted by Savaresi, the choice to place this text in a COP decision can be contrasted to a choice to draft a conflict clause in the UNFCCC itself: see Annalisa Savaresi, 'The Role of REDD in the Harmonisation of Overlapping International Obligations' in Erkki J. Hollo, Kati Kulovesi and Michael Mehling (eds), *Climate Change and the Law* (Springer Netherlands, 2013) 391, 400. On conflict clauses in the CBD and UNCLOS, see Margaret A. Young, *Trading Fish, Saving Fish: The Interaction between Regimes in International Law* (Cambridge University Press, 2011) 50, 65.

[70] See, e.g., finding the need for policy coordination by The Forests Dialogue, 'Giving REDD+ Life: Integrating REDD+ with Broader Development Goals (The Forests Dialogue, 2012) (citing an example from Ghana, and observing that the Ministry of Energy had no contact with the REDD+ readiness process).

[71] The R-PP template, described below, indeed notes the need for 'some form of cross-sectoral REDD-plus working group . . . [to include] key agencies (e.g., agriculture, mining, transportation) and interest forest agency': see FCPF, 'Readiness Preparation Proposal (R-PP) Template Version 6, for Country Use' (2012) 8, https://www.forestcarbonpartnership.org/readiness-fund.

[72] COP, UNFCCC, Decision 1/CP.16 ('The Cancún Agreements: Outcome of the Work of the Ad Hoc Working Group on Long-Term Cooperative Action under the Convention'), UN Doc FCCC/CP/2010/7/Add.1 (15 March 2011) para 71(d).

considered to have been watered down after Cancún,[73] when the COP decision at Durban stated that 'national circumstances and respective capabilities' should be taken into account.[74] However, this was later strengthened at the Warsaw COP, when UNFCCC parties agreed that 'results-based payments' would not be paid to developing countries until they have provided 'the most recent summary of information on how all of the safeguards . . . have been addressed and respected'.[75] The implication of this requirement is that REDD+ funds are conditioned upon the provision by recipient countries of up-to-date information about adherence to safeguards. However, it is still relatively unclear whether this requirement is subject to transparency and oversight. A further COP decision on safeguards has reiterated that the summary of information 'should be provided periodically and be included in national communications, or communication channels agreed by the Conference of the Parties'.[76] Further, the summary could be provided '*on a voluntary basis*, via the web platform on the UNFCCC website' (emphasis added), and only after implementation of REDD+ activities has begun.[77] The Paris COP in 2015 is expected to provide guidance for developing countries 'to ensure transparency, consistency, comprehensiveness and effectiveness when informing on how all the safeguards are being addressed and respected'.[78]

By making funding contingent on a review of safeguards, the main drivers for the interaction between REDD+ and other regimes appear to

---

73 Rosemary Lyster, 'International Legal Frameworks for REDD+: Ensuring Legitimacy' in Rosemary Lyster, Catherine McKenzie and Constance McDermott (eds), *Law, Tropical Forests and Carbon: The Case of REDD+* (Cambridge University Press, 2013) 3, 13.

74 COP, UNFCCC, Decision 12/CP.17 ('Guidance on Systems for Providing Information on How Safeguards Are Addressed and Respected and Modalities Relating to Forest Reference Emission Levels and Forest Reference Levels as Referred to in Decision 1/CP.16'), UN Doc FCCC/CP/2011/9/Add.2 (15 March 2012) 16 para 1.

75 Decision 9/CP.19, 'Work Programme on results-based finance to progress the full implementation of the activities referred to in decision 1/CP.16, paragraph 70', COP, UNFCCC, Decisions 9-15/CP.19 ('Warsaw Framework for REDD-Plus'), UN Doc FCCC/CP/2013/10/Add.1 (31 January 2014) 24 para 4.

76 Decision 12/CP.19, 'The timing and the frequency of presentations of the summary of information on how all the safeguards referred to in decision 1/CP.16, appendix I, are being addressed and respected', ibid. 33 para 2.

77 'The timing and the frequency of presentations of the summary of information on how all the safeguards referred to in decision 1/CP.16, appendix I, are being addressed and respected', ibid. paras 3, 4.

78 SBSTA, Forty-second session, Bonn, Germany, 1–11 June 2015 (FCCC/SBSTA/2015/L.5/Add.1).

be the donors, which, as mentioned above, may be countries or private bodies, as mediated by the international institutions. Apart from this, there is no independent monitoring or review of a country's adherence to the safeguards. However, it is not inconceivable that the standards and guidelines of bodies such as the UN-REDD and the FCPF will provide the relevant benchmarks against which countries' conduct will be measured. As such, state conduct (either as fund recipient or donor) is not the only factor affecting the interactions of REDD+ with other regimes. Given this, studies of public international law's fragmentation should extend to an institutional analysis of 'regime interaction', not just in the resolution of conflicting norms at dispute settlement, but at the *ex ante* involvement of a range of actors in law-making, or the ongoing influence of institutional arrangements in the implementation of laws.[79] Such an analysis also calls for attention to issues such as 'path dependency, higher transaction costs, "tunnel vision" and even "solipsistic and imperial" tendencies within regimes'.[80] The remainder of this part considers this broader context.

3.3 Regime Interaction and International Organizations

In identifying forest-related regimes above, I noted their varying degrees of state membership. What is also apparent is that these regimes have different levels of institutional support and different procedures for non-state observership or participation. They also have their own cultures and biases. These are just some of the institutional factors that affect regimes' ability to coordinate with one another. In the REDD+ context, this has occurred both within the UNFCCC negotiations and in the preparation of the different phases of REDD+ implementation: first, when financial assistance is given to states for capacity-building to make them 'ready' to conduct REDD+ projects in forests (known as 'readiness') and second, in the implementation of the REDD+ projects themselves (including the proposed 'results-based payments', which have not yet occurred beyond pilot activities in a few selected countries).

Within the emerging REDD+ regime, the international organizations assisting in developing REDD+ 'readiness' and in testing pilot projects

---

[79] Margaret A. Young, 'Regime Interaction in Creating, Implementing and Enforcing International Law' in Young (ed.), *Regime Interaction in International Law: Facing Fragmentation*, 85; Jeffrey L. Dunoff, 'A New Approach to Regime Interaction' in Young (ed.), *Regime Interaction in International Law: Facing Fragmentation*, 136.

[80] Young, 'Introduction: The Productive Friction between Regimes', 11 (footnotes omitted).

are particularly influential in determining the modes of regime interaction. The UN-REDD (which, as a coalition of UNEP, UNDP and FAO, is itself based on regime interaction) and the World Bank's FCPF receive applications from countries for REDD+ readiness funding, which they accept or reject based on certain criteria. The criteria are set out in a template, known as the 'Readiness Preparation Proposal' or 'R-PP',[81] which seeks to follow the Cancún safeguards as well as be receptive to internal organizational policies or regulations.[82] These include social and environmental principles that have been influenced by existing international regimes. As such, the UN-REDD and the FCPF can act as gate-keepers for the entry into the emerging REDD+ regime of relevant norms and protections from existing international regimes.

One notable example of institutional influence in REDD+ activities relates to the issue of participation of indigenous peoples and the concept of FPIC. This can be termed, in informal parlance, a question of the 'C' in FPIC. The UN-REDD and the FCPF, although cooperating in developing guidelines on stakeholder engagement,[83] deviate in their approach to the concept of FPIC.[84] The World Bank's FCPF does not endorse the FPIC concept in its REDD+ projects; it adopts the consultative standard that is practiced in other Bank projects.[85] As such, FCPF REDD+ readiness projects will be arguably less responsive to norms from indigenous and human rights regimes than similar projects of the UN-REDD.

The ability of affected communities to seek redress for lack of adherence by states to the Cancún safeguards, once a REDD+ project has started to be implemented, is also linked to the identity and internal procedures of

---

[81] See UN-REDD and FCPF, *Readiness Preparation Proposal* (R-PP template, Version 6 Working Draft), April 4, 2012.

[82] For example, the UN-REDD cites its own 'Social and Environmental Principles and Criteria' (SEPC), developed with guidance from the UN-REDD Policy Board and through a public consultation process: R-PP, ibid. 3.

[83] UN-REDD and FCPF Joint Guidelines on Stakeholder Engagement in REDD+ Readiness' (2012), as discussed in Part 2 above.

[84] See further 'UN-REDD Programme Guidelines on Free, Prior and Informed Consent (FPIC)' (2012), discussed in Part 2 above.

[85] Note especially Operational Procedure 4.1; see further UN-REDD and FCPF, Joint Guidelines on Stakeholder Engagement in REDD+ Readiness (2012) para 7. Note that the FCPF will defer to high standards if these are used by the recipient state, such as has been attempted, for example, by Cameroon: see e.g. Carodenuto and Fobissie. It should also be noted that the World Bank's position is expected to move towards a consent-based FPIC model as part of its current operational review: see World Bank, *Environmental and Social Framework: Setting Environmental and Social Standards for Investment Project Financing* (second draft for consultation, 1 July 2015) 103–112.

the implementing international agency. For example, the FCPF Charter states that it 'must seek to ensure consistency with UNFCCC guidance on REDD'.[86] As such, the FCPF is bound to follow the Cancún safeguards, at least in the implementation of REDD+ projects (*after* the readiness stage).[87] Moreover, the FCPF is subject to the World Bank's existing operational policies and procedures, 'taking into account the need for effective participation of Forest-Dependent Indigenous Peoples and Forest Dwellers in decisions that may affect them, respecting their rights under national law and applicable international obligations'.[88] The implication is that affected communities could submit complaints to the World Bank's existing independent Inspection Panel for failures of the FCPF to adhere to the Cancún safeguards in REDD+ implementation. There are important precedents of such complaints outside of the REDD+ context. For example, members of the Cherangany-Sengwer communities living in the Cherangany Hills in Kenya claimed that they had been forcibly evicted from their lands within the forests as a result of a Bank-funded conservation project, and the Panel found that the Bank's relevant safeguard policies had not been correctly applied.[89] (The UN-REDD does not contain a similar procedure; at this stage its role has been limited to 'readiness' activities rather than implementation activities.)

Aside from the institutions charged with dispensing REDD+ readiness funds or otherwise implementing REDD+, there has been more direct influence of other regimes on the Cancún safeguards. For example, in 2012 parties to the CBD sought to influence the development of the REDD+ safeguards. In a dedicated COP decision, CBD parties asked the Executive Secretary to provide information on how REDD+ may

---

[86] International Bank for Reconstruction and Development, 'Charter Establishing the Forest Carbon Partnership Facility', 8 August 2013 section 3.1(c). 'UNFCCC guidance on REDD' is defined in the Charter as 'the body of rules, modalities, procedures and guidelines on REDD that is adopted under the auspices of the UNFCCC': Article 1.1.80.

[87] On a criticism of the lack of clarity over the application of World Bank policies at the REDD+ readiness phase or later implementation phase, see Kate Dooley et al., *Smoke and Mirrors: A Critical Assessment of the Forest Carbon Partnership Facility* (FERN and Forest Peoples Programme, 2011) 7.

[88] International Bank for Reconstruction and Development, Charter Establishing the Forest Carbon Partnership Facility, section 3.1(d).

[89] World Bank, 'Joint Statement from the World Bank Management and Inspection Panel', News Release, 2014/13/ECR (2 October 2014), http://ewebapps.worldbank.org/apps/ip/PanelCases/84%20-%20Press%20Release%20on%20Board%20Discussion%20%28English%29.pdf. See further, *Kenya – Natural Resource Management Project*, http://ewebapps.worldbank.org/apps/ip/Pages/ViewCase.aspx?CaseId=89.

affect the customary practices of indigenous and local communities.[90] This advice was intended to influence policy approaches for safeguards for biodiversity. The concept of adequate benefit-sharing developed within the CBD was also emphasized. As such, officials within the CBD secretariat (albeit with the formal request of states parties) sought to influence the development of the REDD+ regime.

A similar intervention was made by the UN Permanent Forum on Indigenous Issues in 2011. The Permanent Forum initiated a survey of the impact on indigenous peoples of REDD+ projects. Members of the Permanent Forum reported to the Forum in 2013 and noted that the impact of REDD+ could be positive or negative depending 'on the recognition of their rights, their level of participation and the nature and effectiveness of safeguards to be applied at the international and national levels'.[91] Of note, too, is the inclusion of the chairperson of the Permanent Forum on the Policy Board of the UN-REDD.[92]

The influence of international organizations on regime interaction in the REDD+ context is difficult to prove causally, but is apparent from discussions with officials and other participants. This gives rise to specific legal questions that are outside of the scope of the present chapter but should be considered in further studies. How the relevant organizations interact beyond the negotiation of REDD+ will be important. Of particular difficulty will be how a future carbon market (should one be implicated for REDD+ in a post-2020 climate agreement) distinguishes between institutional practices; such issues may well give rise to legal challenges within the trade regime. It is not far-fetched, for example, to devise a scenario where a state makes its import of carbon credits from REDD+ activities *conditional* on the recipient state's satisfactory support of indigenous rights and other protections. To counter any trade law claims of unjustifiable discrimination, the funding state could well invoke norms and standards from other regimes. These and other inter-regime scenarios are likely to develop in the context of the post-2020 climate agreement.

---

[90] CBD Decision XI/19, UNEP/CBDCOP/DEC/XI/19 (2012); see further Annalisa Savaresi, 'REDD+ and Human Rights: Addressing Synergies between International Regimes' (2013) 18 *Ecology & Society* 149.

[91] UN ECOSOC Permanent Forum on Indigenous Issues, Indigenous People's Rights and Safeguards in Projects Related to Reducing Emissions from Deforestation and Forest Degradation, UN Doc E/C 19/2013/7 (5 February 2013).

[92] UN-REDD and FCPF, Joint Guidelines on Stakeholder Engagement in REDD+ Readiness (2012), Annex 1.

3.4 Regime Interaction and Non-state Actors

A consideration of regime interaction in REDD+ would be incomplete without regard to the role and influence of non-state actors. Civil society groups including NGOs, academics and experts provide information, expertise, perspectives and experience. REDD+ has attracted the attention of civil society from its early stages, and many indigenous groups and other actors have been mobilized.

Perhaps the most significant group of interested parties is indigenous peoples, given that many of the projects will relate to forested lands governed or inhabited by them. Their engagement has been an ongoing challenge in the crafting of REDD+ and has received varied assessment. One study of the UNFCCC negotiations found that although alliances of indigenous peoples and forest communities have emerged, their ability to directly participate and affect outcomes in the REDD+ design process has been weak.[93] A later study was more positive: finding that indigenous peoples had substantially influenced the REDD+ agenda in a variety of ways.[94] Of particular relevance to regime interaction is the latter study's assessment of the inter-institutional knowledge and capacity-building brought by those groups.

Aside from the negotiation of REDD+ through the auspices of the UNFCCC, the scope for participation of non-state actors in the readiness activities and implementation of REDD+ continues to involve regime interaction. For example, there is a place for membership and observation on the UN-REDD Programme Policy Board.[95] Civil society groups have been active in observing and reporting on policy developments: the International Institute for Sustainable Development has provided reports about safeguard implementation after capacity-building workshops conducted in Africa in 2011; similarly, the World Resources Institute (WRI) has issued guidelines for instituting REDD+ safeguards at the national

---

[93] Heike Schroeder, 'Agency in International Climate Negotiations: The Case of Indigenous Peoples and Avoided Deforestation' (2010) 10 *International Environmental Agreements: Politics, Law & Economics* 317.

[94] Linda Wallbott, 'Indigenous Peoples in UN REDD+ Negotiations: "Importing Power" and Lobbying for Rights through Discursive Interplay Management' (2014) 19 *Ecology & Society* 166.

[95] UN-REDD and FCPF, Joint Guidelines on Stakeholder Engagement in REDD+ Readiness (2012), Annex 1. This Annex also refers to the potential for civil society engagement with the International Advisory Group on Forests, Rights and Climate Change, which is to advise the UN-REDD Policy Board.

level.[96] Groups such The Forests Dialogue provide innovative arrangements for dialogue and information-sharing, while the International Union of Forest Research Organizations (IUFRO) has sought to provide overarching expositions of the forest-focused and forest-related regimes.[97] Academics, activists and researchers also engage in advocacy, sometimes issuing 'declarations' writ large involving informal coalitions.[98] These are just some examples of the ongoing involvement of non-state actors in the field.

Important legal questions emerge from this non-state-led regime interaction. For states, sovereignty and legitimacy are clear concerns. More generally, democratic theory would seek to account for the involvement of non-state actors through representative or deliberative credentials. An important issue is the boundary question: if all 'affected people' are engaged in regime interaction, how are they identified? For example, is the Cancún Agreement's request that states address gender considerations in REDD+ national strategies and action plans[99] reconcilable with the participation of indigenous peoples who have under-inclusive power structures of their own? While a more extensive treatment of this issue is outside the scope of the present chapter, the following section provides some comments on the nature of regime interaction in the REDD+ context.

---

[96] Gaia Larsen and Florence Daviet, 'Safeguarding Forests and People: A Framework for Designing a National System to Implement REDD+ Safeguards' (World Resources Institute, November 2012), http://www.wri.org/publication/safeguarding-forests-and-people.

[97] IUFRO, 'Understanding Relationships between Biodiversity, Carbon, Forests and People: The Key to Achieving REDD+ Objectives'; Rayner et al.

[98] See, for two examples: 'Second Norwich Declaration on Environmental Justice: From Safeguarding to Mainstreaming Local Rights: Democratic Forest Governance as Pre-Requisite for a Just and Effective REDD+' (Declaration of Global Environmental Justice think tank held at the University of East Anglia, Norwich, UK, 14–16 May 2014), https://www.uea.ac.uk/documents/439774/6205791/Second+Norwich+Declaration+on+Global+Environmental+Justice.pdf/8c39f1a2-456f-4f68-9ee4-76f25b282251; Forest Peoples Programme, 'The Palangka Raya Declaration on Deforestation and the Rights of Forest Peoples' (Declaration of Looking Ahead: International workshop on Deforestation Drivers and the Rights of Forest Peoples, Palangka Raya, Central Kalimantan, Indonesia, 18 May 2014), http://www.forestpeoples.org/sites/fpp/files/news/2014/03/declaration_english.pdf.

[99] COP, UNFCCC, Decision 1/CP.16 ('The Cancún Agreements: Outcome of the Work of the Ad Hoc Working Group on Long-Term Cooperative Action under the Convention'), UN Doc FCCC/CP/2010/7/Add.1 (15 March 2011) para 72.

4. REGIME INTERACTION WITHIN A LEGAL FRAMEWORK

This chapter has argued that REDD+ can be conceptualized as an emerging regime, and that there is existing and potential interaction with other regimes within the international legal system. While this has occurred largely in the negotiation of REDD+ (and especially in the COP decisions such as the Cancún Agreement safeguards), many of the problems and opportunities surrounding REDD+'s further legal development and implementation will be concentrated in sites of interaction with existing international regimes. These 'sites of interaction' are themselves evolving and are apparent at different international, domestic and local law levels. As such, there is an ongoing need to account for REDD+'s influences on, and by, other forest-focused and forest-related regimes, and indeed other regimes in international law. In this final part, I argue for better understanding and legal accountability of the actors promoting or obstructing such interaction. This is not merely a question of 'learning lessons' or 'achieving coherence', but goes to more general issues of effectiveness, accountability and even legitimacy for REDD+.

An important research question is to ask whether the key actors in regime interaction – which include but are not limited to states – are subject to rights or accountability frameworks generated in part by a recognition of the phenomenon of fragmentation.[100] Research on global administrative law, with its attention to mechanisms of accountability, transparency and participation, is relevant to this inquiry.[101] Moreover, localized, contextualized implementation combined with avenues of peer-review is supported by emerging models of global experimentalist governance.[102] From a related research agenda, ideas of polycentric governance also support the pursuit of local, collective goals at different levels of government or private associations; indeed, this literature suggests that monitoring and rule enforcement are best devolved to a local level where trust and reciprocity can operate to achieve compliance.[103] While I support the

---

[100] Young, 'Fragmentation, Regime Interaction and Sovereignty'.

[101] Benedict Kingsbury, Nico Krisch and Richard B. Stewart, 'The Emergence of Global Administrative Law' (2005) 68 *Law and Contemporary Problems* 15. See further Hite's chapter in this volume.

[102] Gráinne de Búrca, Robert O. Keohane and Charles Sabel, 'New Modes of Pluralist Global Governance' (2013) 45 *New York University Journal of International Law and Politics* 723, 781.

[103] Harini Nagendra and Elinor Ostrom, 'Polycentric Governance of Multifunctional Forested Landscapes' (2012) 6 *International Journal of the Commons* 104.

call for clearer guarantees of rights in REDD+,[104] the approaches in these diverse literatures allow for deeper theoretical reflection on the different state and non-state entities who may hold correlative duties, and point to further research questions on the emerging REDD+ regime's interaction with other regimes. Three preliminary points are set out below.

First, for states, regime interaction flows from their existing international legal obligations as well as from the Cancún Agreement's safeguards and other practices. As noted above, the safeguards may yet be regarded as 'subsequent practice' in the interpretation of UNFCCC obligations. Separately, they may generate duties to cooperate in the same way that resolutions by international organizations, even if not binding, can found future obligations.[105] Furthermore, when UNFCCC developing countries are 'encouraged' to 'contribute to mitigation actions in the forest sector' as part of REDD+ COP decisions,[106] they act not only according to their obligations under treaties (including human rights treaties) and customary international law, but because adherence to the Cancún Agreement safeguards may be a precondition for the receipt of REDD+ funds. Their practice is made transparent through the WFR's 'safeguard information system'. Thus, the integration of the rights of indigenous peoples, biodiversity and social and environmental protections are a requirement for REDD+ recipient states through a combination of law and an experimentalist-orientated benchmarking and transparency provision.

These issues of regime interaction are not limited to REDD+ hosting states. Appropriate regime interaction also flows from obligations of donor countries. Indeed, calling for attention to the human rights obligations of states who are donors, partners or even just members of international financial institutions could improve those frameworks that 'are more usually the purview of broad policy commitments, programs, and process than of treaties'.[107] For example, if there is a principle of customary international law requiring government authorities to consult indigenous

---

[104] Savaresi (n 89).

[105] See, e.g., *Whaling in the Antarctic (Australia v Japan; New Zealand intervening)* ICJ Judgment (31 March 2014), available at http://www.icj-cij.org/docket/files/148/18136.pdf, para 137 (in that case, the Court found that Japan had failed to pay 'due regard' to resolutions of the International Whaling Commission, notwithstanding that such resolutions were not binding).

[106] The phrase is from the Cancún Agreements: COP, UNFCCC, Decision 1/CP.16 ('The Cancún Agreements: Outcome of the Work of the Ad Hoc Working Group on Long-Term Cooperative Action under the Convention'), UN Doc FCCC/CP/2010/7/Add.1 (15 March 2011) para 70.

[107] McInerney-Lankford, 'Human Rights and Development Regime Interaction and the Fragmentation of International Law' 153.

peoples on government policies or matters affecting them,[108] this will bind all states in REDD+ implementation. Even stronger protections – in substance if not in prospects for enforcement – flow from UNDRIP, which is supported by the recognition of FPIC in the UN-REDD Guidelines (but without any specific review procedures for affected communities). Protections such as FPIC and adequate benefit-sharing have been recognized as essential in situations where legal fragmentation implicates indigenous cultures.[109] To counter the suggestion that any obligations of states must be tied to the REDD+ projects occurring within their territory, regard could be had to other contexts of public international law, where states have assumed accountability – or at least some form of prescriptive jurisdiction – in faraway places.[110]

Secondly, rights and accountability mechanisms may be relevant for the activities of international organizations and other implementing agencies (including the FCPF and the UN-REDD). While international organizations do not have the same responsibilities as states, they are still subjects of public international law. The 'learning by doing' approach, articulated expressly by the World Bank's FCPF[111] and apparent also in practices of the UN-REDD may well be appropriate for an emerging regime such as REDD+ that is faced with existing pluralism and uncertainty, limited and yet-to-mature epistemic knowledge and the need for adaptive responses at multiple levels. Yet rights protections may be necessary in certain circumstances, particularly on issues affecting indigenous peoples: although rights predominantly are owed by states to individuals, UNDRIP acknowledges that the 'organs and specialized agencies of the United Nations systems and other intergovernmental organizations' shall

---

[108] Committee on the Rights of Indigenous Peoples, ILA chaired by Siegfried Wiessner, 4–7.

[109] Gunther Teubner and Peter Korth, 'Two Kinds of Legal Pluralism: Collision of Transnational Regimes in the Double Fragmentation of World Society' in Young (ed.), *Regime Interaction in International Law: Facing Fragmentation*, 23, 52.

[110] For example, UN peace-keeping usually involves the assumption of any liabilities by the host state (such as where a peace-keeping operation exercised the host government's authority in seizing private property), but in certain circumstances of peace-keeper misconduct, the relevant conduct may be attributed to the troop-contributing state or even the UN itself. A different example can be found in trade policy, where the trade laws of an importing state are sometimes said to represent an exercise of extraterritorial jurisdiction: see further Margaret A. Young, 'Trade Measures to Address Environmental Concerns in Faraway Places: Jurisdictional Issues' (2014) 23 *RECIEL* 302.

[111] International Bank for Reconstruction and Development, Charter Establishing the Forest Carbon Partnership Facility, Article 3.1(b).

contribute to the realization of its goals, and establish means to ensure participation of indigenous peoples.[112]

Organizations have obligations due to their own constitutive documents and procedures, external agreements and through implied powers. For example, the UN-REDD operates according to a 'human-rights approach'.[113] The FCPF is more restrained, as discussed above. Its position relates to a long controversy over whether enhanced recognition of human rights obligations by the World Bank flouts common understandings of its mandate.[114] Adopting or 'mainstreaming' a human-rights approach is seen by some as risking a return to didactic conditionality in the Bank's lending practices,[115] and by others as risking the co-option of human rights principles.[116] These perspectives underlie the difficulties faced by the REDD+ implementing agencies in incorporating norms and practices from other regimes.

Whether or not the relevant development regimes formally endorse a human-rights approach, the phenomenon of fragmentation could be argued to have created additional implied powers for international organizations.[117] Such implied powers build upon international institutional law and provide that in circumstances where regimes are dependent upon

---

[112] UNDRIP, Article 41.

[113] FAO, UNDP and UNEP, 'UN Collaborative Programme on Reducing Emissions from Deforestation and Forest Degradation in Developing Countries (UN-REDD). FAO, UNDP, UNEP Framework Document' (2008) 6, http://www.un-redd.org/Portals/15/documents/publications/UN-REDD_Framework Document.pdf.

[114] This relates to an asserted prohibition to enter into political decision-making: see Hassane Cissé, 'Should the Political Prohibition in Charters of International Financial Institutions Be Revisited?: The Case of the World Bank' in Hassane Cissé et al. (eds), *The World Bank Legal Review*, vol. 3, 59, http://siteresources.worldbank.org/INTLAWJUSTICE/Resources/WBLegalReviewVol3.pdf#page=77. See also Sarfaty, 'Why Culture Matters in International Institutions' 658–67.

[115] David Kinley, 'Human Rights and the World Bank: Practice, Politics, and Law' in Ana Palacio, Caroline Mary Sage and Michael J.V. Woolcock (eds), *The World Bank Legal Review: Law, Equity, and Development* (World Bank; Martinus Nijhoff, 2006) vol. 2, 353, 356, https://openknowledge.worldbank.org/bitstream/handle/10986/6899/568260PUB0REPL1INAL0PROOF0FULL0TEXT.pdf#page=367 and source cited therein.

[116] Martti Koskenniemi, 'Hegemonic Regimes' in Young (ed.), *Regime Interaction in International Law: Facing Fragmentation* 305, 319 (and sources cited therein).

[117] Margaret A. Young, *Trading Fish, Saving Fish: The Interaction between Regimes in International Law*, 273. This idea is elaborated in 271–8 and draws on jurisprudence of the International Court of Justice such as *Reparations for Injuries*

other regimes (such as in setting standards of conduct), international governmental organizations have the discretion to apply norms and facts from external sources 'because such collaboration is necessary for their functions'.[118] These implied powers are not boundless, of course. The often-observed risk of managerialism and technocratic decision-making, where unseen experts control global politics, could be exacerbated by an ability to act independently from express mandates.[119] One way to counter this risk is a requirement that such bodies be open and transparent in their practices. While the biases and cultural attitudes within these bodies are not erasable, enhanced transparency can lead to better understanding of the influence of their attitudes on regime interaction. It is encouraging, for example, that the FCPF has instituted regular meetings at which governments, forest-dependent indigenous peoples and forest dweller organizations, international and non-governmental organizations can participate;[120] these forums allow actors to commission and then comment on evaluations of the work of the FCPF, which are themselves made public.[121] A 2011 review commissioned by the 'participants committee' (of host and recipient states as well as potential financers) found that there had been high levels of transparency, 'in large part through the effective functioning of the FCPF website, but also through other processes such as

Suffered in the Service of the United Nations [1949] ICJ Reports 174 and *Legality of the Use by a State of Nuclear Weapons in Armed Conflict* [1966] ICJ Reports 66.

[118] Ibid.

[119] Ibid. 276–8 and sources cited therein.

[120] The participants committee is made up of donor and recipient states as well as private actors participating in the carbon fund: International Bank for Reconstruction and Development, Charter Establishing the Forest Carbon Partnership Facility, section 11. A larger 'participants assembly' can include representatives of international organizations, relevant NGOs, forest-dependent indigenous peoples and forest dwellers, and relevant private-sector entities as observers if invited: section 10.1(a).

[121] See Le Groupe-conseil baastel ltée and Nordic Agency for Development and Ecology, 'First Program Evaluation for the Forest Carbon Partnership Facility (FCPF): Evaluation Report' (2011) 30 (noting inter alia that much of the mutual learning taking place between the FCPF and the UNFCCC was due to the fact that many FCPF PC members are also UNFCCC negotiators). See also the Co-Chairs Summary of the FCPF Participants Committee (PC18) and Participants Assembly (PA7) at Arusha, Tanzania, 31 October–2 November 2014 (which noted inter alia that the upcoming review of the FCPF should include evaluation of the FCPF's relation to the frameworks of the UNFCCC: at 3). In addition to the FCPF Participants Committee-commissioned review, an earlier review is the Independent Evaluation Group, 'The Forest Carbon Partnership Facility' (Global Program Review vol. 6, issue 3, The World Bank Group, 2011) para 4.12 (noting inter alia that the FCPF 'has been a fair and inclusive program').

the conduct of PC meetings'.[122] Similarly, the UN-REDD has undergone an external evaluation at the request of the UN-REDD Policy Board.[123] The 2014 evaluation found that recognition of indigenous rights had been supported by its implementation of the Cancún safeguards, although the social and environmental safeguards were difficult to put in practice due in part to 'lack of clear guidance on how to implement, monitor and enforce these'.[124] There is an ongoing need for assessment on whether the practices of the relevant bodies meet the ideals of transparency and accountability.

Thirdly, non-state actors such as civil society groups, academics and research institutions and corporate interests play a major role in regime interaction. Non-state actors have an uncertain place in public international law, with individuals only emerging as rights holders in discrete areas such as human-rights regimes and investment treaties that guarantee particular protections; very little law imposes obligations outside of the territorial context of state regulation. Yet given their involvement and impact on regime interaction, greater attention to the accountability of non-state actors is needed. For businesses, guiding principles recommended by the UN require business enterprises to avoid causing or contributing to adverse human rights impacts;[125] these principles would seem to require that the entities providing private REDD+ funds respect the norms of human rights regimes. Of course, the limitation of such principles is that they do not necessarily lead to legal avenues for grievance and redress. It is encouraging that the 'Readiness Preparation Proposal' template for states, which as noted above seeks consistency with the Cancún safeguards, requires states seeking REDD+ readiness funds to propose some form of 'feedback and grievance mechanism'.[126] This mechanism aims to 'improve responsiveness to citizen concerns, help identify problems early, and foster

---

122 Le Groupe-conseil baastel ltée and Nordic Agency for Development and Ecology, 13.

123 Alain Frechette, Minoli de Bresser and Robert Hofstede, 'External Evaluation of the United Nations Collaborative Programme on Reducing Emissions from Deforestation and Forest Degradation in Developing Countries (the UN-REDD Programme)' (2014), http://www.un-redd.org/PolicyBoard/12thPolicyBoard/tabid/133354/Default.aspx>.

124 Ibid. vi.

125 John Ruggie, 'Report of the Special Representative of the Secretary-General on the Issue of Human Rights and Transnational Corporations and Other Business Enterprises: Guiding Principles on Business and Human Rights: Implementing the United Nations "Protect, Respect and Remedy" Framework', A/HRC/17/31 21 (March 2011).

126 UN-REDD and FCPF, *Readiness Preparation Proposal*, 16.

greater trust and accountability with program stakeholders'.[127] To impose accountability for businesses involved in REDD+, such a mechanism requires broad jurisdictional reach and effective domestic legal processes.

Civil society groups active in the sites of interaction between REDD+ and other regimes have much to offer in bridging understanding between regimes. Indeed, they may be essential in assisting lower-level actors with local and contextualized knowledge. Forms of accountability for these actors will recognize that their functions, constituencies and intended beneficiaries are different from states and international organizations.[128] They will also require conceptions of indigenous identity and membership.[129] Seeking to account for these participants in REDD+ interaction with other regimes requires that non-state actors are open about their credentials and interests. It also gives rise to ongoing strategic questions about particular forms of engagement – such as whether engaging in regime interaction risks assimilation or loss of identity and critical power.[130] Varied responses to such questions are visible so far, as is evident from the manifold positions taken by indigenous peoples on the REDD+ safeguards.[131] Perspectives such as these have an important deliberative place in the emerging REDD+ regime.

5. CONCLUSION

The development of the REDD+ regime at the UNFCCC has been influenced by existing international regimes. This influence has had major impacts, as reflected and recognized in the safeguards for social and environmental protection agreed by the COP at Cancún. Existing and potential normative and institutional interplay in the emerging REDD+ regime

---

[127] Ibid.

[128] Sasha Courville, 'Understanding NGO-Based Social and Environmental Regulatory Systems: Why We Need New Models of Accountability' in Michael W. Dowdle (ed.), *Public Accountability: Designs, Dilemmas and Experiences* (2006) 271; see further Young, *Trading Fish, Saving Fish: The Interaction between Regimes in International Law*, 282.

[129] On these questions, see Kirsty Gover, *Tribal Constitutionalism: States, Tribes, and the Governance of Membership* (Oxford University Press, 2010). See further Tehan et al., *Climate Change Responses and Indigenous and Forest Communities*.

[130] Koskenniemi, 'Hegemonic Regimes' 323.

[131] UN ECOSOC Permanent Forum on Indigenous Issues, Indigenous People's Rights and Safeguards in Projects Related to Reducing Emissions from Deforestation and Forest Degradation, UN Doc E/C 19/2013/7 (5 February 2013).

deserves closer analysis, and this chapter has sought to account for regime interaction by considering the activities of states, international organizations and non-state actors. In particular, it has sought to bring greater clarity to the issue of interacting regimes through infographics that can be used and modified online.

This chapter demonstrates that regime interaction does and will occur in many ways and for many purposes: not just for coordination but sometimes to prioritize one set of regime preferences over another, and sometimes to coopt a weaker regime. Calls for 'coherence' can miss these important aspects. The chapter has argued that a framework that allows for appropriate oversight and review of the activities of actors during regime interaction – which include but are not limited to states – should be maintained using rights or accountability mechanisms. Obligations to consult with affected indigenous peoples, which are held by states and relevant international organizations, are the minimum of such mechanisms. This research has institutional implications for the Cancún safeguards, which should be strengthened to ensure adequate scrutiny and review, for the structure of future funding of REDD+, for inter-agency monitoring and enforcement and for the post-2020 climate agreement. It also better accounts for the conditions of normative and institutional fragmentation that are an unavoidable aspect of the evolution and development of REDD+ within the system of international law.

5. The legal status and role of safeguards

Annalisa Savaresi[*+]

1. INTRODUCTION

The implementation of REDD+ activities and policies may have significant social and environmental impacts. On the one hand, restrictions upon forest uses associated with avoided deforestation and degradation may affect indigenous peoples and other forest-dependent communities' livelihood and means of subsistence. On the other, activities carried out to enhance forest carbon stocks, such as afforestation, may have negative impacts on biodiversity, by replacing biodiversity-rich non-forested landscapes with biodiversity-poor forest plantations. Furthermore, the implementation of REDD+ activities could be difficult in the context of faltering regulatory environments that tend to characterize forest governance in developing countries. Awareness of these potential trade-offs and risks prompted the IPCC to warn that forest-based mitigation activities need to avoid negative impacts associated with competition between land uses.[1]

Negotiations on REDD+ have witnessed a lively debate on how to avoid perverse outcomes and combine REDD+ activities and policies with the pursuit of co-benefits (or multiple benefits, as they have also been termed),[2] such as biodiversity conservation, improved forest governance and a wide array of societal advantages.

UNFCCC Parties' understanding on how to pursue this potential has evolved over time and is still in the process of forming. At the beginning of negotiations on REDD+, UNFCCC Parties merely recognized that

* The author gratefully acknowledges the support received from the LUC4C project (http://luc4c.eu) during the preparation of this piece.

\+ All websites cited in this chapter were accessed on 1 October 2015.

1 Gert J. Nabuurs and others, 'Forestry' in Bert Metz and others (eds.), *Climate Change 2007: Mitigation. Contribution of Working Group III to the Fourth Assessment Report of the Intergovernmental Panel on Climate Change* (Cambridge University Press 2007), at 543.

2 UN-REDD Programme, *Multiple Benefits-Issues and Options for REDD* (UN-REDD 2009), http://www.unredd.net/index.php?option=com_docman&task=doc_download&gid=472&Itemid=53.

REDD+ could promote co-benefits and complement the aims and objectives of other relevant international agreements and conventions.[3] They subsequently recognized the importance of promoting co-benefits,[4] and, eventually, of incentivizing so-called 'non-carbon benefits' for the long-term sustainability of REDD+ activities.[5] The term 'non-carbon benefits' has been generically used to refer to social, environmental and governance benefits produced by REDD+ activities that go beyond mere carbon storage, such as, for example, biodiversity conservation, poverty relief, or secure land and resource tenure. At the time of writing, the debate on non-carbon benefits of REDD+ is still ongoing, and UNFCCC Parties are in the process of debating what non-carbon benefits are; whether they should be reported and monitored, and if so how; and whether non-carbon benefits should attract specific payments.[6]

This range of 'collateral' considerations has enjoyed great prominence in the literature[7] and in policy discourses on REDD+.[8] Some commentators have emphasized how these considerations have taken center-stage, threatening to obfuscate the main purpose of REDD+.[9] Others, however,

---

[3] Decision 2/CP.13, Reducing emissions from deforestation in developing countries: approaches to stimulate action, UN Doc FCCC/CP/2007/6/Add.1, Preamble.

[4] Decision 4/CP.15, Methodological guidance for activities relating to reducing emissions from deforestation and forest degradation and the role of conservation, sustainable management of forests and enhancement of forest carbon stocks in developing countries, UN Doc FCCC/CP/2009/11/Add.1, Preamble.

[5] Decision 9/CP.19, Work programme on results-based finance to progress the full implementation of the activities referred to in decision 1/CP.16, paragraph 70, UN Doc FCCC/CP/2013/10/Add.1, para. 22.

[6] See Report of the Subsidiary Body for Scientific and Technological Advice on its thirty-eighth session, UN Doc FCCC/SBSTA/2013/3, paras. 45–7; and Methodological guidance for activities relating to reducing emissions from deforestation and forest degradation and the role of conservation, sustainable management of forests and enhancement of forest carbon stocks in developing countries, UN Doc FCCC/SBSTA/2014/L.8, para. 6.

[7] Compare the summary in Ingrid J. Visseren-Hamakers and others, 'Trade-Offs, Co-Benefits and Safeguards: Current Debates on the Breadth of REDD+' (2012) 4 *Current Opinion in Environmental Sustainability* 646.

[8] See e.g. UN-REDD Programme (n 2); Lera Miles, Emily Dunning and Nathalie Doswald, 'Safeguarding and Enhancing the Ecosystem Derived Benefits of REDD+' (UNEP World Conservation Monitoring Centre 2010), http://www.unep-wcmc.org/resources-and-data/safeguarding-and-enhancing-the-ecosystem-derived-benefits-of-redd.

[9] See for example, Arild Angelsen and Desmond McNeill, 'The Evolution of REDD+' in Arild Angelsen and others (eds), *Analyzing REDD+: Challenges and Choices* (CIFOR 2012), at 39 and 42.

BOX 5.1 REDD+ SAFEGUARDS IN THE DECISION 1/CP.16, CANCUN AGREEMENTS, APPENDIX I, PARA. 2

When undertaking the activities referred to in paragraph 70 of this decision, the following safeguards should be promoted and supported:

(a) That actions complement or are consistent with the objectives of national forest programmes and relevant international Conventions and agreements;
(b) Transparent and effective national forest governance structures, taking into account national legislation and sovereignty;
(c) Respect for the knowledge and rights of indigenous peoples and members of local communities, by taking into account relevant international obligations, national circumstances and laws, and noting that the United Nations General Assembly has adopted the United Nations Declaration on the Rights of Indigenous Peoples;
(d) The full and effective participation of relevant stakeholders, in particular indigenous peoples and local communities, in the actions referred to in paragraphs 70 and 72 of this decision;
(e) That actions are consistent with the conservation of natural forests and biological diversity, ensuring that the actions referred to in paragraph 70 of this decision are not used for the conversion of natural forests, but are instead used to incentivize the protection and conservation of natural forests and their ecosystem services, and to enhance other social and environmental benefits[1];
(f) Actions to address the risks of reversals;
(g) Actions to reduce displacement of emissions.

1. Taking into account the need for sustainable livelihoods of indigenous peoples and local communities and their interdependence on forests in most countries, reflected in the United Nations Declaration on the Rights of Indigenous Peoples, as well as the International Mother Earth Day.

have noted how failure to consider the wider environmental and societal impacts of REDD+ would undermine forest carbon sequestration.[10]

This latter perspective prevailed and in 2010 the UNFCCC COP adopted a list of broadly worded safeguards that Parties should promote and respect in the implementation of REDD+ activities (see box 5.1).[11]

[10] See e.g. Frances Seymour, 'Forests, Climate Change and Human Rights: Managing Risks and Trade-Offs,' *Human Rights and Climate Change* (Cambridge University Press 2009).

[11] Decision 1/CP.16, Cancún Agreements, UN Doc FCCC/CP/2010/7/Add.1, Appendix I, para. 2.

These safeguards acknowledge that REDD+ activities should avoid causing harm and enhance 'other social and environmental benefits.'[12] Therefore, REDD+ safeguards aim to ensure that REDD+ activities avoid negative impacts and provide benefits to host countries and affected communities, beyond mere carbon sequestration.

From the perspective of international law, these safeguards raise two fundamental questions. The first is that of the role of safeguards in the emerging legal framework on REDD+. The second is that of the relationship of safeguards with the well-established bodies of international law on forests, the protection of human rights and the conservation of biodiversity.

This chapter analyzes these two questions. First, it assesses the legal nature of REDD+ safeguards and their role in the climate regime. Then, it places REDD+ safeguards in the context of general international law, assessing their relationship with other areas of the law, most saliently, those on biodiversity, forests and human rights. Even though it remains to be seen how REDD+ safeguards will be concretely interpreted in practice and how much weight will be attached to their implementation in result-based payments, the conclusions provide some reflections on the role of safeguards in the emerging legal framework on REDD+.

2. THE STATUS OF REDD+ SAFEGUARDS IN GENERAL INTERNATIONAL LAW

There is no standard definition of safeguard in international law. The term is widely used in the practice of States and international organizations, such as the World Bank, to refer to measures making financial aid conditional on the prevention and mitigation of 'undue harm to people and their environment' that may result from funded activities.[13] These safeguards are typically part of conditions imposed upon countries receiving aid, and their fulfillment is a prerequisite for the provision of funding. Safeguards are often coupled with arrangements to monitor and verify their implementation. The consequences attached to lack of compliance with safeguards depend on whether conditionality is based on policy dialogue, agreement and support, or, rather, on recourse to sanctions or aid withdrawal.[14]

---

[12] Ibid., para. 2(e).

[13] Cf. for example the World Bank's environmental and social safeguard policies, http://go.worldbank.org/WTA1ODE7T0.

[14] Cesare Pinelli, 'Conditionality,' *Max Planck Encyclopaedia of Public International Law* (Oxford University Press 2013).

The UNFCCC COP is not in the habit of adopting safeguards or conditionalities for the provision of climate finance. The practice under the UNFCCC has instead been to leave such guidance to institutions entrusted to handle climate finance.[15] Controversially, the Parties to the KP have not adopted specific safeguards under the CDM, in spite of serious concerns regarding the environmental integrity and the contribution to sustainable development of registered project activities.[16]

Cognizant of lessons learnt through the CDM and of the specific potential trade-offs associated with forest-based mitigation, the UNFCCC COP has adopted an unprecedented list of safeguards for REDD+ activities.[17] These safeguards are not phrased like actual conditionalities for the provision of REDD+ funding. The wording introducing the safeguards merely says that they should be 'promoted and supported,' without providing any specific sanctions for lack of compliance. Nevertheless, the UNFCCC COP has subsequently clarified that, regardless of the source or type of financing, all REDD+ activities should be 'consistent with' safeguards.[18]

An embryonic system to monitor and verify the implementation of safeguards has also been laid out. Developing country Parties intending to undertake REDD+ activities are asked to adopt a system for providing information on how safeguards are being 'addressed and respected.'[19] Such information should be transparent, consistent, accessible by all relevant stakeholders, updated on a regular basis, country-driven, and build upon existing systems 'as appropriate.'[20] The provision of information on the implementation of safeguards is a requirement to receive REDD+

[15] Compare e.g. Global Environmental Facility Policy on Agency Minimum Standards on Environmental and Social Safeguards (2013); and Adaptation Fund Environmental and Social Policy (2013).

[16] Joelle de Sepibus, *The Environmental Integrity of the CDM Mechanism – A Legal Analysis of Its Institutional and Procedural Shortcomings* (Swiss National Centre of Competence in Research 2009), http://phase1.nccr-trade.org/images/stories/research/header_ip6/environmental%20integrity%20CDM.pdf; Lena Ruthner and others, *Study on the Integrity of the Clean Development Mechanism (CDM)* (2011), http://ec.europa.eu/clima/policies/ets/linking/docs/final_report_en.pdf.

[17] Decision 1/CP.16, Appendix I, para. 2.

[18] Decision 2/CP.17, Outcome of the work of the Ad Hoc Working Group on Long-term Cooperative Action under the Convention, UN Doc FCCC / CP/2011/9/Add.2, para. 63.

[19] Decision 1/CP.16, para. 71.

[20] Decision 12/CP.17, Guidance on systems for providing information on how safeguards are addressed and respected and modalities relating to forest reference emission levels and forest reference levels as referred to in decision 1/CP.16, UN Doc FCCC /CP/2011/9/Add.2, para. 2.

payments.[21] However, there is no indication on how compliance with this requirement will be assessed and what consequences may follow, should a party fail to comply with safeguards.

Information concerning compliance with safeguards is to be included in periodical national communications to the UNFCCC COP[22] and may also be published, on a voluntary basis, via a web platform on the UNFCCC website.[23] Developing country Parties should start providing such information after the start of the implementation of REDD+ activities. The frequency of subsequent submissions of information should be consistent with general arrangements for developing country Parties' national communications.[24]

The reporting requirements concerning the implementation of REDD+ safeguards, therefore, fall into the broader context of developing country Parties' obligations concerning MRV. Under the UNFCCC, developing country Parties are generally required to submit their first national communications within three years of entering the convention, and every four years thereafter.[25] The UNFCCC COP has subsequently established that developing country Parties should also submit biennial update reports, starting with December 2014.[26] These reports are to be subjected to an expert review process of international consultation and analysis.[27] Whether and how this process will specifically review the implementation of REDD+ safeguards, however, remains to be seen.

At the time of writing, only six developing country Parties have submitted biannual update reports.[28] It is therefore too early to say how implementation of REDD+ safeguards is being reported and how this is reviewed in the context of international consultation and analysis processes. More generally, UNFCCC COP guidance on REDD+ safeguards does not provide details on the types of evidence that countries might use to show compliance with safeguards or the ways in which such evidence should be collected, verified or reported. These matters are in the process of being further discussed in the context of the SBSTA, which since 2011

---

21 Decision 9/CP.19, para. 4.

22 Ibid., paras. 3–4.

23 Decision 12/CP.19, The timing and the frequency of presentations of the summary of information on how all the safeguards referred to in decision 1/CP.16, Appendix I, are being addressed and respected, para. 3.

24 Ibid., para. 4.

25 UNFCCC, Article 12.5.

26 Decision 2/CP.17, paras. 39–44.

27 Ibid., paras. 56–62.

28 The reports are available at: http://unfccc.int/national_reports/non-annex_i_natcom/reporting_on_climate_change/items/8722.php.

has been considering whether and how to give more guidance to Parties on the type of information to be provided on compliance with safeguards.[29]

In the meantime, the GCF, which is expected to function as the main source of REDD+ finance in the climate regime,[30] agreed on an initial framework for REDD+ results-based payments.[31] The framework reiterates that the provision of summaries of information on how safeguards are implemented is a prerequisite for REDD+ results-based payments.[32] Nevertheless, it is not clear how the content of these summaries will be assessed. Furthermore, there is a need to ascertain the compatibility of the GCF Environmental and Social Safeguards with REDD+ safeguards[33] and the consequences of lack of compliance. The GCF is therefore likely to assume a very prominent role in overseeing the implementation of REDD+ safeguards.

Taken together, all these elements provide important but inconclusive elements to ascertain the status of REDD+ safeguards in international law. UNFCCC COP decisions, such as that including REDD+ safeguards, have over the years filled the 'open-textured' provisions in the climate treaties with content, by adopting both 'hard' rules that Parties are expected to uphold,[34] as well as 'soft' guidance that Parties should take into account while interpreting their obligations.[35] Ultimately, whether

---

[29] The issue of types of information from systems for providing information on how the safeguards are being addressed and respected was addressed at the 41st session of the SBSTA in December 2014, but conclusions on the issue could not be adopted. The matter will be taken up again at the 42nd session of the SBSTA, in 2015.

[30] See Chapter 2 by Christina Voigt and Felipe Ferreira on results-based finance in this book. Decision 9/CP.19, Preamble and para. 5.

[31] GCF, Initial logic model and performance measurement framework for REDD+ results-based payments, GCF/B.08/08/Rev.01 (2014), Annex III.

[32] Ibid.

[33] GCF, Guiding framework and procedures for accrediting national, regional and international implementing entities and intermediaries, including the fund's fiduciary principles and standards and environmental and social safeguards, GCF/B.06/09 (2014).

[34] Building upon the mandate conferred upon them by the treaties, as for example, KP, Articles 3.4 and 12.7.

[35] Cf. Alan E. Boyle, 'Some Reflections on the Relationship of Treaties and Soft Law' (1999) 48 *International and Comparative Law Quarterly* 901, at 905. See also: Robin R. Churchill and Geir Ulfstein, 'Autonomous Institutional Arrangements in Multilateral Environmental Agreements: A Little-Noticed Phenomenon in International Law' (2000) 94 *American Journal of International Law* 623, at 642; and Jutta Brunnée, 'COPing with Consent: Law-Making Under Multilateral Environmental Agreements' (2002) 15 *Leiden Journal of International Law* 1, at 38.

decisions adopted by the UNFCCC COP acquire the guise of binding law is a matter of interpretation.[36]

In the case of REDD+ safeguards, the language in UNFCCC COP decisions is far from univocal. The Cancún Agreements do not say that safeguards are a prerequisite to carry out REDD+ activities. Subsequent COP decisions have however clarified that REDD+ activities should be consistent with safeguards, regardless of the source of funding;[37] and that Parties should provide information on how safeguards are addressed and respected to obtain results-based payments.[38] Together, these elements may be read in the sense to suggest that compliance with REDD+ safeguards is an actual legal obligation for UNFCCC Parties that decide to carry out REDD+ activities and that ask for international payments to do so. While some UNFCCC Parties have argued in favor of this interpretation,[39] only the practice of implementation will reveal whether compliance with safeguards is closely scrutinized and treated as a requirement for receiving REDD+ payments. In the meantime, much uncertainty surrounds what types of information should be provided concerning the implementation of safeguards. Parties' views on this issue greatly diverge,[40] and an evident tension exists between the need to ensure comparability and some degree of streamlining in the information Parties provide, on the one hand; and that to enable a country-driven approach that is not overly burdensome, on the other.

More generally, the overall uncertainty characterizing the status of

---

[36] See Harro van Asselt, Francesco Sindico and Michael Mehling, 'Global Climate Change and the Fragmentation of International Law' (2008) 30 *Law and Policy* 423, at 430. On the increasing informalization of the climate regime, see also Harro van Asselt, Michael Mehling and Clarisse Siebert, 'The Changing Architecture of International Climate Change Law' in Geert van Calster, Wim Vanderberghe and Leonie Reins (eds), *Research Handbook on Climate Change Mitigation Law* (Edward Elgar Publishing 2015), at 5; and Duncan French and Lavanya Rajamani, 'Climate Change and International Environmental Law: Musings on a Journey to Somewhere' (2013) 25 *Journal of Environmental Law* 437, at 446.

[37] Decision 2/CP.17, para. 63.

[38] Decision 9/CP.19, para. 4.

[39] The EU, for example, has argued: 'Safeguards are an inherent, integral part of REDD+ and therefore a requirement that must be fulfilled in order to obtain results-based payments.' See: Views on the issues referred to in decision 1/CP.18, paragraph 40. Submissions from Parties and admitted observer organizations, UN Doc FCCC/SBSTA/2014/MISC.4, at 33.

[40] Views on types of information from systems for providing information on how the safeguards are being addressed and respected and that may be provided by developing country Parties, FCCC/SBSTA/2014/MISC.7.

REDD+ under the climate regime reflects also on the legal status of REDD+ safeguards. As the next sections will show, the decision on whether to turn REDD+ into an offset mechanism à la CDM, or rather, into a means to provide financial assistance to developing countries in complying with their own emission reduction obligations is likely to have profound implications on the legal status of REDD+ safeguards.[41]

Another complicating factor is that the broad wording of REDD+ safeguards leaves much room for discretion to UNFCCC Parties. REDD-readiness practice has already provided ample evidence of the diverse ways in which REDD+ safeguards may be interpreted. Numerous developing countries have undertaken to create the conditions to perform REDD+ activities, either by adhering to inter-State initiatives,[42] or by entering into partnerships with international agencies. So while no actual results-based payments for REDD+ activities have been made, a vast REDD-readiness process has unfolded, resulting in a myriad of REDD-readiness arrangements established beyond the institutional scope of the UNFCCC, with no formal relation to it.

The REDD-readiness process has been mainly, although not exclusively, driven by two ad hoc international agencies:[43] the UN-REDD, constituted by the FAO of the UN, the UNDP and UNEP;[44] and the World Bank's FCPF.[45] These international agencies have entered into agreements with a large number of UNFCCC Parties willing to undertake REDD+ activities.[46]

In lack of more specific guidance from the UNFCCC Parties, the

---

[41] Annalisa Savaresi, 'Forests and Climate Change: An International Law-Making Odyssey,' presented at conference, Smart Mixes in Relation to Forest and Climate Change Governance, University of Amsterdam, Centre for International Law, March 2015.

[42] For an overview, see: http://www.fao.org/forestry/vrd/by/recipients.

[43] International agencies have been defined as international bodies constituted on the basis of a decision by an international organization, as opposed to a treaty or a form of bottom-up cooperation between national regulators. See Ayelet Berman and Ramses A. Wessel, 'The International Legal Form and Status of Informal International Lawmaking Bodies: Consequences for Accountability' in Joost Pauwelyn, Ramses Wessel and Jan Wouters (eds), *Informal International Lawmaking* (Oxford University Press 2012), 35, at 44.

[44] FAO, UNDP and UNEP, *UN Collaborative Programme on Reducing Emissions from Deforestation and Forest Degradation in Developing Countries (UN-REDD) Framework Document* (2008).

[45] The FCPF was launched by the World Bank in 2007: World Bank, *Charter Establishing the Forest Carbon Partnership Facility* (2013 edition).

[46] At the time of writing, the UN-REDD has partnered with 58 countries: http://www.un-redd.org/Partner_Countries/tabid/102663/Default.aspx. Forty-seven

UN-REDD and the FCPF have adopted standards to guide their partner countries in the REDD-readiness process, including on how to operationalize safeguards. In doing so, both the FCPF and the UN-REDD Programme have interpreted and filled with more precise content REDD+ safeguards, working as de facto alternative law-making forums, supplementing and complementing the decisions taken by the UNFCCC COP on the issue. While in fact the FCPF and the UN-REDD standards are mere internal rules, their incorporation into partnership and borrowing agreements makes them a determinant factor in the emerging body of law on REDD+.[47] Indeed, in the absence of more detailed guidance by the UNFCCC COP, standards by the UN-REDD and the FCPF have become the principal source to interpret REDD+ safeguards. The next section will investigate the chasm in the interpretation of REDD+ safeguards by these two institutions and the questions it raises on the relationship between REDD+ safeguards and other areas of international law.

For the present purposes, it is possible to conclude that REDD+ safeguards are unprecedented in the climate regime and break new ground on several counts. Five years after their adoption, however, there still is little clarity on their overall legal status. Formally, as part of a UNFCCC COP decision REDD+ safeguards are not legally binding on UNFCCC Parties. Substantially, the language in REDD+ safeguards is not univocal in conveying a sense of whether they ought to be regarded as conditionalities. The fact, however, that information on the implementation of safeguards is a requirement for receiving result-based payments seems to indicate that compliance with safeguards is mandatory and therefore a legal obligation for Parties seeking REDD+ results-based payments. Nevertheless, UNFCCC COP guidance says little on how compliance with safeguards will be assessed and what consequences may be associated with it. Therefore, unless the UNFCCC COP or the GCF provide further clarification on these issues, only when REDD+ results-based payments start to be disbursed will it be possible to gauge whether and how compliance with safeguards is treated as a legally binding obligation for developing country Parties asking for REDD+ results-based payments.

---

countries have adhered to the FCPF: https://www.forestcarbonpartnership.org/redd-country-participants.

[47] Laurence Boisson de Chazournes, 'Policy Guidance and Compliance: The World Bank Operational Standards' in Dinah Shelton (ed.), *Commitment and Compliance: The Role of Non-Binding Norms in the International Legal System* (Cambridge University Press 2000), at 282.

3. REDD+ SAFEGUARDS AND OTHER AREAS OF INTERNATIONAL LAW

The safeguards embedded in the Cancún Agreements focus on four core elements: the ecological and carbon integrity of REDD+ emission reductions; forest governance; the environmental and social impact of REDD+ activities; and their potential co-benefits.

The safeguards on the ecological and carbon integrity of REDD+ activities focus on avoiding reversal and reducing the displacement of emissions[48] and closely relate to UNFCCC Parties' reporting obligations.[49] The reporting of emissions and emission reductions in the land sector has long been a vexed question in the climate regime.[50] Presently, these matters are only sparsely covered in reporting obligations under the UNFCCC and the KP, leaving a wide margin of discretion to reporting Parties and a substantive gap in the frequency of reporting and level of detail required from developed and developing countries.[51] This matter could be looked at afresh in context of the new climate agreement to be adopted in 2015.[52] In this context, the succinct reference to addressing the risks of reversals in REDD+ safeguards could be translated into more specific reporting obligations to secure the ecological and carbon integrity of REDD+ emission reductions.

The nature of these obligations will greatly depend on whether REDD+

---

[48] Decision 1/CP.16, Appendix I, para. 2(f–g).

[49] Decision 4/CP.15; and Decision 11/CP.19, Modalities for national forest monitoring systems UN Doc FCCC/CP/2013/10/Add.1.

[50] For a summary, see Peter Iversen, Donna Lee and Marcelo Rocha, *Understanding Land Use in the UNFCCC* (Climate and Land Use Alliance 2014); Zoya E. Bailey, 'Sink That Sank the Hague: A Comment on the Kyoto Protocol' (2002) 16 *Temple International and Comparative Law Journal* 103; Eveline Trines, 'History and Context of LULUCF in the Climate Regime' in Charlotte Streck and others (eds), *Climate Change and Forests. Emerging Policy and Market Opportunities* (Chatham House 2008).

[51] The EU, for example, has maintained that continued implementation of existing rules would lower the actual stringency of the current emission reduction pledges and imply that reductions can be claimed without additional actions, which brings no real environmental benefit. European Commission, Communication from the Commission to the European Parliament, the Council, the European Economic and Social Committee and the Committee of the Regions, 'International climate policy post-Copenhagen: Acting now to reinvigorate global action on climate change,' COM/2010/0086, at 2.2.3.

[52] Charlie Parker and others, *The Land-Use Sector within the Post-2020 Climate Regime* (Nordic Council of Ministers 2014); Manuel Estrada and others, *Land Use in a Future Climate Agreement* (Meridian Institute 2014).

will eventually become a mere forest carbon offset program à la CDM, or rather, a means to assist developing countries in complying with their own emission reduction obligations under the 2015 agreement. While in the first scenario, the imposition of conditionalities concerning carbon integrity would be associated with the tradability of offsets on carbon markets, in the second, a certain level of equivalence between the reporting obligations of developed and developing countries would need to be ensured. It would, in other words, be necessary to ensure that developing country Parties' obligations are not disproportionately burdensome, when compared with those of developed ones.

The remainder of REDD+ safeguards have both a negative dimension – that connected to the prevention of harm – as well as a positive dimension – that related to the promotion of co-benefits and the pursuit of synergies with other forest-related instruments. From the perspective of international law, these safeguards raise interesting questions on the interplay between international law instruments.

In this regard, REDD+ safeguards specify that REDD+ actions should 'complement' or be 'consistent with' the objectives of 'relevant international conventions and agreements.'[53] This is a significant piece of interpretative guidance concerning the relationship between UNFCCC Parties' extant international obligations and those concerning REDD+. When faced with 'implementation conflicts' – i.e. conflicts engendered by implementation of perfectly compatible treaty obligations[54] – REDD+ activities and policies should be carried out in such a way as to support, rather than conflict with, the objectives of relevant international conventions and agreements. As the next sections will show, a wide range of treaties and practice may be regarded as relevant in this connection, as the plural formulation ('conventions and agreements') also suggests.

Before analyzing in detail the interplay between these bodies of law, it is necessary to highlight how REDD+ safeguards are also inextricably linked with the ongoing unresolved debate on the non-carbon benefits of REDD+. While in fact some Parties argue that non-carbon benefits are to be considered as an integral part of REDD+ safeguards,[55] others

---

[53] Decision 1/CP.16, Appendix I, para. 2(a).

[54] This term is used to refer to conflicts that are engendered by implementation of perfectly compatible treaty obligations. See Rudiger Wolfrum and Nele Matz, *Conflicts in International Environmental Law* (Springer 2003), at 24 and 96.

[55] The Philippines, for example, have argued: 'There is a clear linkage between NCBs and REDD-Plus safeguards. Reporting on NCBs could be partially covered by safeguards reporting mechanisms or safeguards information systems.' Views on the issues referred to in decision 1/CP.18 (2014), paragraph 40. Submissions from

argue that they are a collateral issue that should *not* be reported in the context of safeguard information systems, and, most crucially, should be addressed in other forums with relevant mandates, such as the CBD, the GCF or the FCPF.[56] Ultimately, if Parties to the UNFCCC decide to include non-carbon benefits in the information system that has been devised for REDD+ safeguards, this would be an important tool to scrutinize the flow of benefits to developing countries associated with REDD+. This would be particularly important if REDD+ should turn into an offset mechanism, like the CDM. The perceived lack of a system to ensure that countries hosting CDM projects receive concrete benefits, in fact, has been a major shortcoming in the functioning of that mechanism.[57]

While Parties to the UNFCCC are yet to make up their minds on this issue, standards adopted in the framework of the REDD-readiness processes provide important insights to foresee how this complex matter may be addressed. For example, the UN-REDD has not attempted to draw a distinction between carbon and non-carbon benefits of REDD+ activities. Instead, the FCPF has distinguished carbon and non-carbon benefits,[58] deciding that only the first be reported in benefit-sharing plans to be prepared to receive REDD+ results-based payments.[59] The FCPF has thus anticipated the UNFCCC Parties' decision on the delicate and controversial issue of non-carbon benefits by deciding what they are – at least in the

---

Parties and admitted observer organizations, at 33. Views on the issues referred to in decision 1/CP.18, para. 40. Submissions from Parties and admitted observer organizations, FCCC/SBSTA/2014/MISC.4, at 33.

[56] Compare the submission by the EU, ibid., at 28: 'the EU is of the opinion that there is no need for dedicated payments or price premiums for NCBs under the UNFCCC. Moreover, at international level this would add complexity (conceptually, technically and financially) to the REDD+ mechanism, thereby complicating and thus delaying implementation of REDD+'s primary objective and possibly even deviating from it. The EU does however see merit in (encouraging) discussions on NCBs in for[ums] with relevant mandates such as the CBD, the GCF and the FCPF and is interested to learn from pilot experiences how NCBs can be incentivized best.'

[57] High-Level Panel on the CDM Policy Dialogue, *Climate Change, Carbon Markets and the CDM: A Call to Action* (2012), at 18.

[58] The FCPF has defined non-carbon benefits as benefits 'produced by or in relation to the implementation and operation of' a REDD+ program, such as 'the improvement of local livelihoods, the building of transparent and effective forest governance structures, progress on securing land tenure, and enhancing or maintaining biodiversity and/or other ecosystem services.' FCPF Carbon Fund Methodological Framework (2013), at 32.

[59] Ibid., at 25.

context of FCPF payments – and that they should not be subjected to the same reporting requirements as carbon-related benefits.

The solution to these delicate questions makes it even more important to interpret REDD+ safeguards in a way that is consistent with the objectives of 'relevant international conventions and agreements.' Guidance provided in these instruments usefully complements REDD+ safeguards, supplementing them with an internationally agreed understanding on matters upon which States have already reached painstakingly negotiated consensus, such as forest biodiversity and the rights of forest-dependent communities. It is here argued that UNFCCC Parties should rely more systematically on this guidance, without attempting to 'reinvent the wheel.'[60] The next sections highlight points of synergies with existing bodies of law, as well as matters upon which further guidance may be needed, distinguishing between environmental and social impacts and co-benefits.

3.1 Environmental Safeguards

As negotiations progressed, much literature drew attention to biodiversity trade-offs associated with REDD+ activities, suggesting that they be applied selectively to different forest types.[61] This matter has only been partially addressed by the UNFCCC COP, which initially stated that REDD+ demonstration activities should be 'consistent with' sustainable forest management, noting, inter alia, the 'relevant provisions' of the United Nations Forum on Forests and the CBD.[62] This acknowledgement of the relevance

---

[60] This expression is also used by Elisa Morgera, 'No Need to Reinvent the Wheel for a Human Rights-Based Approach to Tackling Climate Change: The Contribution of International Biodiversity Law' in Erkki Hollo, Kati Kulovesi and Michael Mehling (eds), *Climate Change and the Law* (Springer 2013).

[61] See e.g. Till Pistorius et al., *Greening REDD+. Challenges and Opportunities for Forest Biodiversity Conservation* (University of Freiburg, Germany 2010), at 21; and Secretariat of the Convention on Biological Diversity, *REDD-plus and Biodiversity. CBD Technical Series No. 59* (Secretariat of the Convention on Biological Diversity 2011). For a detailed review, see Annalisa Savaresi, 'Reducing Emissions from Deforestation in Developing Countries under the UNFCCC: Caveats and Opportunities for Biodiversity' (2010) 21 *Yearbook of International Environmental Law* 81; and Annalisa Savaresi, 'Reducing Emissions from Deforestation in Developing Countries under the United Nations Framework Convention on Climate Change. A New Opportunity for Promoting Forest Conservation?' in Frank Maes and others (eds), *Biodiversity and Climate Change: Linkages at International, National and Local Levels* (Edward Elgar Publishing 2013).

[62] Decision 2/CP.13, Annex, para. 8.

of international biodiversity and forest instruments, however, does not appear in subsequent UNFCCC COP decisions dealing with REDD+. A few UNFCCC Parties have supported building on synergies between REDD+, the CBD and international forest instruments.[63] REDD+ safeguards, instead, do not mention the matter. Instead, they generically indicate that REDD+ activities should be 'consistent with the conservation of natural forests and biological diversity'; and should not be used for the conversion of natural forests,[64] but, rather, to incentivize their protection and conservation and to enhance other 'environmental benefits.'[65] Thus safeguards only timidly address the matter of overlaps between REDD+ and the vast body of law concerning forests and biodiversity. These two bodies of international law have inherently different characteristics.

On the one hand, no comprehensive international treaty on forests exists. Instead, States have cyclically rejected proposals to negotiate an all-encompassing forest treaty and, ultimately, to subject themselves to greater international scrutiny on how they manage their forests. Rather tellingly, there is no internationally agreed definition of what a forest is, and the understanding of this term is highly context-specific.[66] As a result, forest issues are addressed in an uncoordinated manner by a large number of international instruments and institutions.[67] The resulting legal landscape is greatly fragmented and consists of a heterogeneous set of instruments, which include treaties,[68] as well an array of informal instruments.[69] This fragmented body of law centers around two key notions:

---

[63] See UNFCCC, Views on methodological guidance for activities relating to reducing emissions from deforestation and forest degradation and the role of conservation, sustainable management of forests and enhancement of forest carbon stocks in developing countries. Submissions from Parties, UN Doc FCCC/SBSTA/2011/MISC.7, Submissions by Australia, at 6; European Union, at 59; El Salvador on behalf of Dominican Republic, El Salvador, Honduras and Panama, at 38–42; and Japan, at 82.

[64] Decision 1/CP.16, Appendix I, para. 2(e).

[65] Ibid.

[66] CBD SBSTTA, Background Report on Improving Forest Biodiversity Monitoring and Reporting, UN Doc UNEP/CBD/SBSTTA/16/INF/25, at 5.

[67] For a comprehensive overview, see Juergen Blaser and others, *Independent Assessment of the International Arrangement on Forests. Report of the Team of Independent Consultants*, New York: UNFF, September 2014, http://www.un.org/esa/forests/wp-content/uploads/2015/02/IAF-Assessement-Report-Final-12-Sep-2014.pdf.

[68] Such as the various editions of the ITTA of 1983, 1994, and 2006. ITTA 2006, into force 7 December 2011, UNTS vol. 2801, p. 1.

[69] These include: Non-Legally Binding Authoritative Statement of Principles for a Global Consensus on the Management, Conservation and Sustainable

that of States' sovereign right to exploit their forest resources; and that of sustainable forest management.[70] However, due to the considerable multiplication of standards on sustainable forest management, a common understanding of this crucial concept has remained surprisingly elusive and largely seems to lie in the eye of the beholder.[71] States' obligations in this regard are context-specific and depend on the interpretation of a layered set of international instruments of various legal natures.

On the other hand, the CBD is the main international treaty charged with protecting biodiversity. As seen with the UNFCCC, the body of law under the CBD has significantly grown by virtue of the work of its conference of the Parties (CBD COP). Much like the guidance of the UNFCCC COP, the legal significance of CBD COP decisions is a matter of interpretation. A distinguishing feature, however, is that CBD decisions are characterized by a markedly hortatory tone and rarely convey a sense of legally binding obligation.[72] Still, CBD COP decisions are a precious source of inter-governmentally agreed guidance on the interpretation of the CBD and on the means to achieve its objective. Most importantly, Parties to the UNFCCC and the CBD are virtually the same – with the salient exception of the US.

Both conventions deal with global environmental problems and establish regimes of almost universal application, which prohibit Parties from making specific reservations to their provisions.[73] The objectives of the conventions are not mutually exclusive, and instead feature several areas for mutually supportive action.[74] The existence of common interests is,

---

Development of All Types of Forests (Forest Principles), 31 ILM 881 (1992); and Non-legally Binding Instrument on Sustainable Forest Management of all Types of Forests, UNGA/Res/62/98; as well as decisions by treaty bodies, such as those established under the CBD and the ITTA.

[70] Forest Principles, at 1(a); and 2 (a).

[71] Diana Davenport, 'Forests and Sustainability' in Jeremy Rayner, Alexander Buck and Pia Katila (eds), *Embracing Complexity: Meeting the Challenges of International Forest Governance* (IUFRO 2011), at 87.

[72] On CBD COP decisions, see: Stuart R. Harrop and Diana J. Pritchard, 'A Hard Instrument Goes Soft: The Implications of the Convention on Biological Diversity's Current Trajectory' (2011) 21 *Global Environmental Change* 474.

[73] CBD, Article 34; and UNFCCC, Article 24.

[74] See Concetta M. Pontecorvo, 'Interdependence between Global Environmental Regimes: The Kyoto Protocol on Climate Change and Forest Protection' (1999) 59 *Heidelberg Journal of International Law* 705, at 742; and Frederic Jacquemont and Alejandro Caparrós, 'The Convention on Biological Diversity and the Climate Change Convention 10 Years After Rio: Towards a Synergy of the Two Regimes?' (2002) 11 *Review of European Community and International Environmental Law* 169, at 178; and Harro van Asselt, 'Managing the

inter alia, confirmed by the existence of the Joint Liaison Group, an informal forum for exchanging information, exploring opportunities for synergistic activities, and increasing coordination between the bureaucracies established under the so-called Rio Conventions.[75]

The CBD and the UNFCCC, however, view forests from different perspectives. While the CBD is concerned with forests as habitats and repositories of biodiversity, under the UNFCCC they are chiefly carbon sinks and sources. Despite these different approaches, both conventions address forest management to a certain degree and, when implementing REDD+ activities, Parties to both conventions are faced with implementation conflicts, as a focus on maximizing carbon sequestration may have negative impacts on biodiversity conservation. When faced with such implementation conflicts, Parties to both the CBD and the UNFCCC should consider the obligations and guidance adopted under both, interpreting them in a mutually supportive way, rather than in a conflicting fashion. This is explicitly conveyed in REDD+ safeguards and has been further elaborated upon in a series of CBD COP decisions, which, in a typically hortatory tone, draw attention to synergies and complementarities between the UNFCCC and the CBD on REDD+.[76]

Firstly, CBD Parties are encouraged to implement ecosystem-management activities, including the protection of natural forests, natural grasslands and peatlands, and the sustainable management of forests, with consideration of the use of native communities of forest species in reforestation activities.[77] Secondly, CBD Parties are invited to carry out REDD+ activities selectively; limiting the degradation and clearing of primary and secondary forests; converting only land of low biodiversity value or ecosystems largely composed of non-native species; avoiding invasive alien species; preventing the net reduction of carbon stocks in all organic carbon

---

Fragmentation of International Environmental Law: Forests at the Intersection of the Climate and Biodiversity Regimes' (2012) 44 *New York University Journal of International Law and Politics* 1205, at 1228–42.

[75] Decision 13/CP.8, Cooperation with Other Conventions, UN Doc FCCC/CP/2002/7/Add.1. This includes the Convention to Combat Desertification in Countries Experiencing Serious Drought and/or Desertification, Particularly in Africa, 33 ILM 1273 (1994), as well as the CBD and the UNFCCC.

[76] Decision IX/16, Biodiversity and Climate Change UN Doc UNEP/CBD/COP/9/29; CBD Decision X/33, Biodiversity and Climate Change UN Doc UNEP/CBD/COP/10/27; CBD Decision X/36, Forest Biodiversity UN Doc UNEP/CBD/COP/DEC/X/36; CBD Decision XI/19, Biodiversity and climate change related issues UN Doc UNEP/CBD/COP/11/35; and CBD Decision XI/21, Biodiversity and climate change UN Doc UNEP/CBD/COP/11/35.

[77] Decision X/33, at 8(n).

pools; and strategically locating afforestation activities within the landscape to enhance connectivity.[78] Most crucially, CBD Parties are invited to use strategic environmental assessments and environmental impact assessments to increase the positive impacts and to reduce the negative impacts of climate change mitigation and adaptation measures on biodiversity.[79]

In sum, CBD COP decisions have integrated guidance provided in REDD+ safeguards, taking a 'holistic' and proactive stance on the matter, which is fitted with the all-encompassing objective of the CBD and its efforts to promote concerted action under the Rio Conventions.[80] The CBD COP has, nevertheless, been cautious in underscoring that its guidance should not pre-empt any future decisions taken under the UNFCCC.[81] CBD guidance is phrased in a hortatory tone and hardly conveys legally binding obligations. Still, it provides very important elements on how CBD Parties should carry out REDD+ activities in light of their obligations under the CBD. And, as all UNFCCC Parties eligible to carry out REDD+ activities are also Parties to the CBD, these States should, by virtue of their obligations under the CBD, perform REDD+ activities in line with CBD guidance.

In addition to this interpretative work, the CBD treaty bodies have engaged in the debate on REDD+ safeguards under the UNFCCC by submitting views on methodological guidance for REDD+.[82] The submitted material includes a review of REDD+ safeguards and UN-REDD and the FCPF standards, suggesting that these do not cover all biodiversity-related risks raised by REDD+ activities equally or in sufficient detail.[83] Identified gaps include risks associated with afforestation in areas of high

---

[78] Ibid., at 8(o–p).

[79] Ibid., at 8(u).

[80] See Elisa Morgera, 'Faraway, So Close: A Legal Analysis of the Increasing Interactions between the Convention on Biological Diversity and Climate Change Law' (2011) 2 *Climate Law* 85, 91–2.

[81] Decision X/33, at 9(g–h).

[82] See e.g. CBD Secretariat, 'Submission by the Secretariat of the Convention on Biological Diversity to the Secretariat of the United Nations Framework Convention on Climate Change on methodological guidance for activities relating to reducing emissions from deforestation and forest degradation and the role of conservation, sustainable management of forests and enhancement of forest carbon stocks in developing countries (REDD-plus), specifically related to systems for providing information on how safeguards referred to in appendix I to UNFCCC decision 1/CP.16 are addressed and respected,' (2011).

[83] Ibid. This review is included in the summaries of a series of expert workshops on the links between biodiversity and REDD+ organized to support CBD Parties' efforts to address REDD+ in a way that contributes to the implementation of the CBD.

biodiversity value; the displacement of deforestation and forest degradation to areas of lower carbon value and high biodiversity value; and potential loss of traditional ecological knowledge.[84] The submission mentions that guidance provided in the framework of the CBD could partially fill these gaps, but emphasizes the need for further work on this issue.[85]

To conclude, the CBD Parties have engaged in the debate on REDD+ safeguards, making concrete efforts to build bridges between issues that are closely related both to the mandate of the CBD and the UNFCCC. This proactive approach, however, has been countered with apathy by UNFCCC Parties. A major obstacle affecting the integration of guidance supplied by the CBD within REDD+ is that the Parties have tended to interpret the conventions' mandate restrictively.[86]

3.2 Social Safeguards

The UNFCCC COP safeguards require that REDD+ activities promote and support transparent and effective national forest governance, public participation and respect the knowledge and rights of indigenous peoples and local communities; and, more generally, that they enhance other social benefits.[87] This *de minimis* guidance has not been further elaborated upon by the UNFCCC COP. Yet the notions of public participation, traditional knowledge and rights of indigenous peoples and local communities are conceptually linked to a diverse body of international law and

---

[84] Ibid., at 19.

[85] Ibid., at 29. For a detailed review, see Savaresi, 'Reducing Emissions from Deforestation in Developing Countries under the United Nations Framework Convention on Climate Change. A New Opportunity for Promoting Forest Conservation?' (n 61).

[86] See van Asselt, 'Managing the Fragmentation of International Environmental Law: Forests at the Intersection of the Climate and Biodiversity Regimes' (n 74) at 41, where the author quotes as an example the fact that Australia has expressed the view that the CBD and the UNCCD do not have a legitimate role in climate change mitigation. Compare UNFCCC SBSTA, 'Views on the Paper on Options for Enhanced Cooperation among the Three Rio Conventions, Submissions from Parties,' UN Doc FCCC/SBSTA/2006/MISC.4, submission by Australia, at 5. Along similar lines, see Brazil's submission on REDD+ non-carbon benefits: 'discussions regarding non-carbon benefits should be fully *consistent* with the respective mandates of each international regime, while preserving the *primacy* of UNFCCC over REDD+.' See Views on the issues referred to in decision 1/CP.18, paragraph 40. Submissions from Parties and admitted observer organizations, FCCC/SBSTA/2014/MISC.4, at 3–4 (emphasis added).

[87] Decision 1/CP.16, Appendix I, para. 2(c–e).

practice concerning, inter alia, non-discrimination;[88] self-determination;[89] a wide range of substantial and procedural human rights.[90]

The UNFCCC and REDD+ safeguards do not specifically mention human rights. Nevertheless, the implementation of climate change response measures, like REDD+, may have a host of implications on the enjoyment of several human rights. The Human Rights Council and its Special Rapporteurs and Independent Experts have increasingly drawn attention to the need to take into account the human rights implications of climate change response measures,[91] including REDD+.[92] In this regard, they suggested that international human rights law might strengthen international, regional and national climate change policy-making, promoting policy coherence, legitimacy and sustainable outcomes.[93]

So far there has been little uptake of these exhortations in international climate change law-making. In its sole reference to human rights to date, the UNFCCC COP has generically recognized that Parties should fully respect human rights 'in all climate change related actions.'[94] Since the UNFCCC does not contain any conflict clause, this assertion is a significant statement concerning the relationship between international climate and human rights law. When faced with implementation conflicts, obligations under the UNFCCC should be interpreted in such a way as to support, rather than conflict with, human rights. However, not all Parties to the UNFCCC have ratified human rights treaties, and adherence to the

---

88 International Convention on the Elimination of All Forms of Racial Discrimination (New York, 7 March 1966, in force 4 January 1969) 660 UNTS 195.

89 UNDRIP, UN General Assembly Resolution, Declaration on the Rights of Indigenous Peoples (2007) A/RES/61/295.

90 Such as those embedded in the ICCPR (New York, 16 December 1966, in force 23 March 1976), 999 UNTS 171; ICESCR (New York, 16 December 1966, 3 January 1976) 993 UNTS 3; and ILO Convention 169 Concerning Indigenous and Tribal Peoples in Independent Countries (Geneva, 27 June 1989, in force 5 September 1991) ILO/C169, as well as in regional human rights treaties. See Chapter 6 by Sebastien Jodoin in this book.

91 See the collection of references in Independent Expert on the issue of Human Rights Obligations relating to the enjoyment of a safe, clean, healthy and sustainable environment, Mapping Human Rights Obligations Relating to the Enjoyment of a Safe, Clean, Healthy and Sustainable Environment. Focus report on human rights and climate change (2014).

92 See e.g. Report of the Office of the United Nations High Commissioner for Human Rights on the Relationship between Climate Change and Human Rights, A/HRC/10/61 (2009), at 68.

93 Human Rights Council Resolution, Human Rights and Climate Change, 26/L.33 (2014), Preamble.

94 See Decision 1/CP.16, para. 8.

UNFCCC may not become an instrument to impose upon States obligations contained in instruments they have not adhered to. Therefore, the identification of relevant human rights law and practice depends on a host of circumstances, and most crucially, on the human rights treaties each UNFCCC Party has ratified.

In the case of REDD+, virtually all developing country Parties to the UNFCCC eligible to participate in REDD+ have ratified some human rights treaties.[95] In this vein, REDD+ social safeguards may be interpreted as implicit references to human rights obligations in international treaties UNFCCC Parties have ratified or may ratify in future.[96]

Only few UNFCCC Parties, however, have opined that the interpretation of REDD+ safeguards and their reporting be more closely linked with extant human rights law obligations.[97] This matter has been addressed in greater detail by the UN-REDD and the FCPF, which have nevertheless adopted almost opposite approaches to the issue.

The UN-REDD has adopted standards to support partner countries in implementing REDD+ safeguards.[98] The standards interpret the UNFCCC COP safeguards in light of human rights law and practice, drawing a human-rights-based approach to the work of the UN-REDD.[99]

---

[95] Virtually all developing country Parties to the UNFCCC eligible to participate in REDD+ have ratified the ICCPR, and the ICESCR. Several have also ratified regional human rights treaties.

[96] Annalisa Savaresi, 'The Role of REDD in Harmonizing Overlapping International Obligations' in Erkki Hollo, Kati Kulovesi and Michael Mehling (eds), *Climate Change and the Law. A Global Perspective* (Springer 2013), 412.

[97] For example, El Salvador (on behalf of the Dominican Republic, El Salvador, Honduras and Panama) and Switzerland. See: Views on Methodological Guidance for Activities Relating to Reducing Emissions from Deforestation and Forest degradation and the role of conservation, sustainable management of forests and enhancement of forest carbon stocks in developing countries. Submissions from Parties, UN Doc FCCC/SBSTA/2011/MISC.7. For example, Switzerland suggested that 'information systems for safeguards embody and reinforce the guidance and rules of existing environmental and human rights treaties, particularly UNDRIP and FLEGT, when relevant.' Ibid., at 100. Similarly, Chad, on behalf of Burundi, Cameroon, Central African Republic, Chad, Congo, Democratic Republic of the Congo, Equatorial Guinea, Gabon, Rwanda, and Sao Tome and Principe, suggested that safeguard information systems ensure consistence with international human rights law. Views on experiences and lessons learned from the development of systems for providing information on how all the safeguards are being addressed and respected and the challenges faced in developing such systems, UN Doc FCCC/SBSTA/2014/MISC.6, at 17.

[98] UN-REDD Social and Environmental Principles and Criteria (2012), at 3.

[99] Ibid., at 2: 'The SEPC reflect the UN-REDD Programme's responsibility to apply a human-rights based approach to its programming, uphold UN

First, UN-REDD-funded programs should respect and promote the recognition and exercise of the rights of indigenous peoples, local communities and other vulnerable and marginalized groups 'to land, territories and resources, including carbon.'[100] The standards also make specific reference to the need to respect and protect traditional knowledge[101] and cultural heritage and practices, and to ensure that the benefits from this knowledge are equitably shared.[102] Second, the design, planning and implementation of UN-REDD funded programs must 'promote sustainable livelihood and poverty reduction,'[103] and take into account potential synergies and trade-offs, respecting 'local and other stakeholders' values.'[104] There is an evident link between these standards and economic, social and cultural rights, but also with the rights of indigenous peoples and tribal communities to benefit from development,[105] and with notions, like that of benefit-sharing, which have been used in international human rights law and practice as a means to ensure that funded activities contribute to indigenous and other vulnerable communities' livelihoods.[106] Third, UN-REDD standards require that the design, planning and implementation of national REDD+ programs comply with 'democratic governance,'[107] going beyond the UNFCCC COP safeguards, to encompass a range of elements that are typically associated with procedural rights to access to information, justice and public participation.[108]

---

conventions, treaties and declarations, and apply the UN agencies' policies and procedures'.

[100] Ibid., Principle 2, Criterion 7.

[101] Ibid., at 13.

[102] Ibid., Criterion 11, footnote.

[103] Ibid., Principle 3.

[104] Ibid., Criterion 21.

[105] UNDRIP, Article 32.

[106] Report of the Special Rapporteur on the Rights of Indigenous Peoples, Extractive industries and indigenous peoples (2013) A/HRC/24/41, at 88; Human Rights Council, Expert Mechanism on the Rights of Indigenous Peoples, Advice No. 2, Indigenous peoples and the right to participate in decision-making, with a focus on extracting industries (2012) A/HRC/21/55, at 42; IACtHR, *Saramaka People* v. *Suriname* (Case No. 172), Judgment of 28 September 2008, 138–140; and ACHPR, *Centre for Minority Rights Development (Kenya) and Minority Rights Group International on behalf of Endorois Welfare Council* v. *Kenya* (Comm. No. 276/2003), Decision of 4 February 2010, at 297. See discussion in Annalisa Savaresi, *The Emergence of Benefit-Sharing under the Climate Regime. A Preliminary Exploration and Research Agenda.* (2014) http://papers.ssrn.com/sol3/papers.cfm?abstract_id=2524335, at 4.

[107] UN-REDD Social and Environmental Principles and Criteria, Principle 1.

[108] Ibid., Criteria 1–6, and at 8.

These standards are further elaborated upon in guidelines that partner countries should use to seek and obtain the FPIC of affected stakeholders for all activities supported by the UN-REDD. In line with established human rights law and practice,[109] the guidelines treat FPIC as a means to empower indigenous peoples, as well as other forest-dependent communities,[110] to determine the outcome of decision-making that affects them, rather than merely a right to be involved in such processes.[111] They also specify that no involuntary resettlement should take place as a result of REDD+ activities and/or policies.[112] The identification of indigenous peoples should take place by means of self-identification and not be dependent upon whether the national government has recognized a community as indigenous.[113]

As the UN-REDD standards have only recently been adopted, little evidence exists on how they have been implemented in practice. It already seems clear, however, that the UN-REDD has gone to great lengths to expand upon the UNFCCC COP safeguards, drawing on human rights law and practice. While the UN-REDD does not request partner countries to sign up to human rights treaties they have not ratified already, its standards openly draw upon human rights law and practice. And, although these standards are mere internal rules, their incorporation into partnership agreements makes them a source of legal obligations for partner countries.

There are no specific sanctions attached to breaches of UN-REDD standards. Still, agreements with partner countries include general clauses concerning suspension and resolution.[114] Coupled with the requirement that partner countries report information on implementation of the UN-REDD guidelines, in practice these standards may well work as conditionalities for the provision of assistance to partner countries. This in turn raises the question of the legitimacy of such conditionalities, since the

---

109 Compare: UNDRIP, Article 32.2; Human Rights Council, Expert Mechanism on the Rights of Indigenous Peoples, Advice No. 2, Indigenous peoples and the right to participate in decision-making (2011), para. 1; and *Saramaka People* v. *Suriname*, at 79–86. On the status of FPIC in international law, see International Law Association, 'Rights of Indigenous Peoples. Final Report' (2012), at 43–52.

110 UN-REDD Social and Environmental Principles and Criteria, at 12.

111 Ibid., at 20.

112 Ibid., at 10.

113 Ibid., at 29.

114 For example, Indonesia's National Joint Programme Document (2009), at 71, available at www.un-redd.org/AsiaPacific_NationalProgrammeDocument/tabid/106607/Default.aspx.

UN-REDD standards draw from obligations embedded in international treaties that not all Parties to the UNFCCC have ratified.[115] However, as States enter voluntarily into partnerships with the UN-REDD, they are expected to abide by its standards.

Similar considerations apply to the recently adopted GCF Environmental and Social Safeguards, which explicitly mention ensuring full respect of the human rights of indigenous peoples, and their FPIC, at least in certain circumstances.[116] While not all partner countries to the UN-REDD may have adhered to human rights treaties protecting the rights of indigenous peoples, the protection of these rights is expected to be a relevant criterion to obtain REDD+ results-based payments from the GCF.

Contrary to the UN-REDD, the FCPF has not elaborated specific standards for REDD-readiness activities. Instead, funded activities should comply with the World Bank's general Operational Policies and Procedures,[117] taking into account the need for 'effective participation' of forest-dependent indigenous peoples and forest dwellers in decisions that may affect them, respecting their rights 'under national law and applicable international obligations.'[118]

The World Bank Operational Policies have long raised criticism for subjecting the protection of the rights of indigenous peoples to a series of distinguo.[119] For example, indigenous peoples' FPIC is required only when the partner country has ratified ILO Convention 169[120] or adopted national legislation on the issue.[121] Partner countries are merely required to engage in a process of free, prior, and informed 'consultation,' rather than 'consent.'[122] When avoidance is not feasible, adverse effects should

---

115 See Chapter 9 of this volume by Kirsty Gover.

116 GCF, Guiding framework and procedures for accrediting national, regional and international implementing entities and intermediaries, including the fund's fiduciary principles and standards and environmental and social safeguards, at 1.7.

117 FCPF, Readiness Fund Common Environmental and Social Approach among Delivery Partners, at 14.

118 World Bank, Charter establishing the Forest Carbon Partnership Facility (2013 edition), Article 3, section 3.1(d).

119 Press Release, UN Special Rapporteur on the Rights of Indigenous Peoples (27 March 2013).

120 To date the Convention has been ratified by 22 States. See www.ilo.org/ilolex/cgi-lex/ratifce.pl?C169.

121 Guidelines on Stakeholder Engagement in REDD+ Readiness with a Focus on the Participation of Indigenous Peoples and Other Forest-Dependent Communities (2012), at 7.

122 World Bank OP 4.10 – Indigenous Peoples (2013 edn), at 1.

be 'minimized, mitigated, or compensated.'[123] Involuntary resettlement is openly contemplated.[124]

The FCPF approach has attracted some criticism. The UN Permanent Forum on Indigenous Issues has emphasized that 'displacement and exclusion of indigenous peoples from their forests, which may be triggered by projects funded by the Partnership Facility, should be avoided at all costs' and that the choice not to participate in REDD+ or in FCPF supported projects 'should be respected.'[125] An evaluation of the FCPF has specifically underscored the need to strengthen coordination with UN-REDD, and resolve differences with regard to advice given to participating countries on implementation of social safeguards. The reluctance of the World Bank to deal with human rights, however, is a major hindrance towards greater coordination with the UN-REDD.

The divergence in safeguards adopted under the FCPF and the UN-REDD has resulted in the fact that the same activities in the same countries may be subject to different standards, depending on which institution is handling the funding. To address this problem, the FCPF has decided that when the fulfillment of the partnership agreements is delegated to third institutions that deploy more stringent standards than its own, the more stringent standards prevail.[126] While this solution addresses questions associated with conflicts between standards, it also means that States that are partners solely to the FCPF can abide by the less stringent ones. So REDD+ activities in country partners to the UN-REDD are expected to follow a 'human-rights-based approach' and to secure FPIC. Instead, only when a partner country has ratified ILO Convention 169 or adopted national legislation on the issue does the FCPF require that FPIC be obtained.[127]

The interpretation of REDD+ safeguards by REDD-readiness processes has thus led to a fragmented landscape, where the UN-REDD

---

[123] Ibid.

[124] Ibid., at 20; and FCPF, Incorporating Environmental and Social Considerations into the Process of Getting Ready for REDDplus. Revised Draft (2010), at 2.

[125] See United Nations Permanent Forum on Indigenous Issues, Impact of Climate Change Mitigation Measures on Indigenous Peoples and on Their Territories and Lands (2008) E/C.19/2008/10, at 88.

[126] FCPF, Readiness Fund Common Environmental and Social Approach among Delivery Partners (2011), at 9.

[127] See Guidelines on Stakeholder Engagement in REDD+ Readiness with a Focus on the Participation of Indigenous Peoples and Other Forest-Dependent Communities (2012), at 6–7. For a commentary, see Annalisa Savaresi, 'The Human Rights Dimension of REDD' (2012) 21 *Review of European Community & International Environmental Law* 102, at 112.

and the FCPF have taken diverging stances on fundamental issues, such as involuntary resettlement and FPIC. The chasm in the approach to REDD+ safeguards adopted by the UN-REDD and the FCPF is ultimately down to the different institutional cultures and practices. Such discrepancy in standards is hardly conducive to the establishment of a level playing field enabling countries to carry out REDD+ activities on an equal footing. Therefore, further guidance from the UNFCCC COP on these crucial issues seems indispensable.

The UN-REDD experience has confirmed that there is ample scope to build upon human rights to interpret REDD+ safeguards. The added value of making reference to human rights lies in avoiding duplications and exploiting the consensus underpinning existing human rights law. Building explicit links with extant human rights instruments and practice, however, may be difficult, because not all State Parties eligible to carry out REDD+ activities are Parties to the same human rights treaties. The FCPF has reflected this fundamental challenge in its standards, which, very much like UNFCCC COP safeguards, merely make reference to 'relevant' international law, thus leaving it to partner countries to identify relevant law and its interplay with safeguards. This reluctance may, nevertheless, be superseded in the context of negotiations on a new climate agreement to be adopted in 2015, where the relationship between climate change and human rights is being looked at anew.[128]

4. CONCLUSIONS

This chapter has analyzed REDD+ safeguards, and the challenge of interpreting them in light of States' extant obligations concerning biodiversity, forests and human rights. Presently, ensuring that REDD+ safeguards are interpreted in line with States' international law obligations remains a matter left to the autonomous efforts of national decision-makers and single institutions, in what Sebastian Oberthür has aptly described as 'autonomous' or, at best, 'unilateral interplay management.' This approach is opposed to more systemic forms of interplay management, where coordination is carried out by a set of institutions together, or by an overarching international institution.[129] The risk that autonomous

---

128 For a review, see, Annalisa Savaresi and Jacques Hartmann, 'Human Rights in the 2015 Agreement' (Legal Response Initiative 2015).

129 Sebastian Oberthür, "Interplay Management Enhancing Environmental Policy Integration Among International Institutions," *International Environmental Agreements: Politics, Law and Economics* 9, No. 4 (2009): 371–91, at 376.

and unilateral interplay management endeavors end in incoherence is already palpable when one considers the divergence in REDD-readiness standards. This state of affairs poses considerable challenges for developed countries wishing to access funding, and faced each time with different standards. While this is not a matter arising only with regard to REDD+,[130] it is particularly concerning that such incoherence affects standards that are ultimately aimed at tackling the risk of perverse outcomes. It would therefore seem wise for UNFCCC Parties to adopt more specific guidance on this issue.

Experience accumulated with human rights, biodiversity and forest law and practice provides a precious aid on how to avoid perverse outcomes and pursue REDD+ co-benefits. So far guidance adopted by the UNFCCC COP has made little effort to draw upon these bodies of law. It has instead left a wide margin of discretion to UNFCCC Parties, by adopting a succinct list of very broadly worded safeguards.

Are these safeguards imposing actual conditionalities for UNFCCC Parties receiving REDD+ results-based payments? It would seem so. However, for the time being very little is known on the legal consequences to be attached to lack of compliance with safeguards, even though the suspension and withdrawal of funding would be an obvious option. The extent of Parties' obligations concerning the reporting of safeguards implementation is equally unclear and little is known on how Parties will report the implementation of REDD+ safeguards. In this state of uncertainty, there has been a proliferation of interpretations of REDD+ safeguards by REDD-readiness processes, which has engendered a great deal of confusion.

The complex debate on REDD+ safeguards boils down to concerns over striking the right balance between, on the one hand, avoiding perverse outcomes and pursuing co-benefits and, on the other, ensuring the feasibility of REDD+. There is furthermore an inherent tension between the need for international coordination and the respect for States' sovereignty. Ultimately, the solution to these questions greatly depends on whether REDD+ will be a mere facilitative mechanism to create the circumstances for developing countries to comply with their own emissions reduction obligations; or, rather, a mechanism for forest carbon offsets à la CDM. An exhaustive answer therefore will only be possible when the

---

[130] Compare the review of social and environmental safeguards adopted by bodies entrusted to handle climate finance under the UNFCCC in Annalisa Savaresi, *The Emergence of Benefit-Sharing under the Climate Regime. A Preliminary Exploration and Research Agenda* (n 107).

nature of REDD+ under the climate regime will be eventually clarified. Two main scenarios may be envisioned.

In the first scenario, the inclusion of REDD+ in the scope of the finance mechanism of the Convention would entail bringing REDD+ safeguards into line with those adopted by the GCF and/or the GEF, subjecting them to the same reporting and compliance regime.[131] Serious questions would, however, arise with regard to the legitimacy of REDD+ conditionalities concerning the pursuit of co-benefits: why should developing countries be asked to produce co-benefits when they reduce their emissions, when developed countries are not?

In the second scenario, REDD+ safeguards would become part of the legal framework established to render carbon credits generated with REDD+ activities fungible with the others traded on carbon markets, ensuring that they all comply with a minimum set of requirements, like those adopted in the context of the CDM.[132] In this context, safeguards would operate as actual conditionalities for REDD+ payments, and special premiums could be designed to reward the provision of co-benefits.[133]

UNFCCC Parties are still engaged in a soul-searching exercise on these issues. While they have unequivocally acknowledged the desirability of asking Parties implementing REDD+ activities to avoid perverse outcomes and pursue environmental and social co-benefits, they have been reluctant to provide guidance on how to go about it, and to draw upon existing international instruments designed to achieve these objectives. This is hardly surprising, and indeed is in line with the established law-making practice under the UNFCCC, which normally avoids providing detailed guidance to Parties on concrete action they should undertake in order to reduce their emissions. Implementation of climate response measures, however, has already provided ample evidence that there is a need to be especially vigilant over the risk of perverse outcomes. An obvious point of departure to tackle this risk would therefore be to vigorously explore

---

131 GEF Policy on Agency Minimum Standards on Environmental and Social Safeguards (2013); and Green Climate Fund, Guiding Framework and Procedures for Accrediting National, Regional and International Implementing Entities and Intermediaries, Including the Fund's Fiduciary Principles and Standards and Environmental and Social Safeguards (2014).

132 Decision 5/CMP.1, Modalities and procedures for afforestation and reforestation project activities under the clean development mechanism in the first commitment period of the Kyoto Protocol, UN Doc FCCC/KP/CMP/2005/8/Add.1.

133 Savaresi, 'Reducing Emissions from Deforestation in Developing Countries under the UNFCCC' (n 61), at 22–3.

ways to ensure that UNFCCC Parties' obligations concerning REDD+ are implemented in a mutually supportive fashion with those under related international instruments.

BIBLIOGRAPHY

Angelsen, A. and McNeill, D., 'The Evolution of REDD+' in Arild Angelsen and others (eds), *Analyzing REDD+: Challenges and Choices* (CIFOR 2012).

Bailey, Z.E., 'Sink that Sank The Hague: A Comment on the Kyoto Protocol' (2002) 16 *Temple International and Comparative Law Journal* 103.

Berman, A. and Wessel, R.A., 'The International Legal Form and Status of Informal International Lawmaking Bodies: Consequences for Accountability' in Joust Pauwelyn, Ramses Wessel and Jan Wouters (eds), *Informal International Lawmaking* (Oxford University Press 2012).

Blaser, J. and others, *Independent Assessment of the International Arrangement on Forests. Report of the Team of Independent Consultants*, New York: UNFF, September 2014, http://www.un.org/esa/forests/wp-content/uploads/2015/02/IAF-Assessement-Report-Final-12-Sep-2014.pdf.

Boisson de Chazournes, L., 'Policy Guidance and Compliance: The World Bank Operational Standards' in Dinah Shelton (ed.), *Commitment and Compliance: The Role of Non-Binding Norms in the International Legal System* (Cambridge University Press 2000).

Boyle, A.E., 'Some Reflections on the Relationship of Treaties and Soft Law' (1999) 48 *International and Comparative Law Quarterly* 901.

Brunnée, J., 'COPing with Consent: Law-Making under Multilateral Environmental Agreements' (2002) 15 *Leiden Journal of International Law* 1.

Churchill, R.R. and Ulfstein, G., 'Autonomous Institutional Arrangements in Multilateral Environmental Agreements: A Little-Noticed Phenomenon in International Law' (2000) 94 *American Journal of International Law* 623.

Davenport, D., 'Forests and Sustainability' in Jeremy Rayner, Alexander Buck and Pia Katila (eds), *Embracing Complexity: Meeting the Challenges of International Forest Governance* (IUFRO 2011).

De Sepibus, J., *The Environmental Integrity of the CDM Mechanism – A Legal Analysis of its Institutional and Procedural Shortcomings* (Swiss National Centre of Competence in Research 2009), http://phase1.nccr-trade.org/images/stories/research/header_ip6/environmental%20integrity%20CDM.pdf.

Estrada, M. and others, *Land Use in a Future Climate Agreement* (Meridian Institute 2014).

French, D. and Rajamani, L., 'Climate Change and International Environmental Law: Musings on a Journey to Somewhere' (2013) 25 *Journal of Environmental Law* 437.

Harrop, S.R. and Pritchard, D.J., 'A Hard Instrument Goes Soft: The Implications of the Convention on Biological Diversity's Current Trajectory' (2011) 21 *Global Environmental Change* 474.

High-Level Panel on the CDM Policy Dialogue, *Climate Change, Carbon Markets and the CDM: A Call to Action* (2012).

International Law Association, *Sofia Conference Report. Rights of Indigenous Peoples* (ILA 2012).

Iversen, P., Lee, D. and Rocha, M., *Understanding Land Use in the UNFCCC* (Climate and Land Use Alliance 2014).

Jacquemont, F. and Caparrós, A., 'The Convention on Biological Diversity and the Climate Change Convention 10 Years after Rio: Towards a Synergy of the Two Regimes?' (2002) 11 *Review of European Community and International Environmental Law* 169.

Miles, L., Dunning, E. and Doswald, N., 'Safeguarding and Enhancing the Ecosystem Derived Benefits of REDD+' (UNEP World Conservation Monitoring Centre 2010), http://www.

unep-wcmc.org/resources-and-data/safeguarding-and-enhancing-the-ecosystem-derived-benefits-of-redd.

Morgera, E., 'Faraway, So Close: A Legal Analysis of the Increasing Interactions between the Convention on Biological Diversity and Climate Change Law' (2011) 2 *Climate Law* 85.

Morgera, E., 'No Need to Reinvent the Wheel for a Human Rights-Based Approach to Tackling Climate Change: The Contribution of International Biodiversity Law' in Erkki Hollo, Kati Kulovesi and Michael Mehling (eds), *Climate Change and the Law* (Springer 2013).

Nabuurs, G.J. and others, 'Forestry' in Bert Metz and others (eds), *Climate Change 2007: Mitigation. Contribution of Working Group III to the Fourth Assessment Report of the Intergovernmental Panel on Climate Change* (Cambridge University Press 2007).

Oberthür, S., 'Interplay Management: Enhancing Environmental Policy Integration Among International Institutions' (2009) 9 *International Environmental Agreements: Politics, Law and Economics* 371.

Parker, C. and others, *The Land-Use Sector within the Post-2020 Climate Regime* (Nordic Council of Ministers 2014).

Pinelli, C., 'Conditionality,' *Max Planck Encyclopedia of Public International Law* (Oxford University Press 2013).

Pontecorvo, C.M., 'Interdependence between Global Environmental Regimes: The Kyoto Protocol on Climate Change and Forest Protection' (1999) 59 *Heidelberg Journal of International Law* 705.

Ruthner, L. and others, *Study on the Integrity of the Clean Development Mechanism (CDM)* (2011), http://ec.europa.eu/clima/policies/ets/linking/docs/final_report_en.pdf.

Savaresi, A., 'Reducing Emissions from Deforestation in Developing Countries under the UNFCCC: Caveats and Opportunities for Biodiversity' (2010) 21 *Yearbook of International Environmental Law* 81.

Savaresi, A., 'The Human Rights Dimension of REDD' (2012) 21 *Review of European Community and International Environmental Law* 102.

Savaresi, A., 'Reducing Emissions from Deforestation in Developing Countries under the United Nations Framework Convention on Climate Change. A New Opportunity for Promoting Forest Conservation?' in Frank Maes and others (eds), *Biodiversity and Climate Change: Linkages at International, National and Local Levels* (Edward Elgar Publishing 2013).

Savaresi, A., 'The Role of REDD in Harmonising Overlapping International Obligations' in Erkki Hollo, Kati Kulovesi and Michael Mehling (eds), *Climate Change and the Law. A Global Perspective* (Springer 2013).

Savaresi, A., *The Emergence of Benefit-Sharing under the Climate Regime. A Preliminary Exploration and Research Agenda* (2014), http://papers.ssrn.com/sol3/papers.cfm?abstract_id=2524335.

Savaresi, A., 'Forests and Climate Change: An International Law-Making Odyssey' (2015).

Savaresi, A. and Hartmann, J., *Human Rights in the 2015 Agreement* (Legal Response Initiative 2015).

Secretariat of the Convention on Biological Diversity, *REDD-plus and Biodiversity. CBD Technical Series No. 59* (Secretariat of the Convention on Biological Diversity 2011).

Seymour, F., 'Forests, Climate Change and Human Rights: Managing Risks and Trade-Offs,' *Human Rights and Climate Change* (Cambridge University Press 2009).

Trines, E., 'History and Context of LULUCF in the Climate Regime' in Charlotte Streck and others (eds), *Climate Change and Forests. Emerging Policy and Market Opportunities* (Chatham House 2008).

UN-REDD Programme, *Multiple Benefits-Issues and Options for REDD* (UN-REDD 2009), http://www.unredd.net/index.php?option=com_docman&task=doc_download&gid=472&Itemid=53.

Van Asselt, H., 'Managing the Fragmentation of International Environmental Law: Forests at the Intersection of the Climate and Biodiversity Regimes' (2012) 44 *New York University Journal of International Law and Politics* 1205.

Van Asselt, H., Sindico, F. and Mehling, M., 'Global Climate Change and the Fragmentation of International Law' (2008) 30 *Law and Policy* 423.
Van Asselt, H., Mehling, M. and Siebert, C., 'The Changing Architecture of International Climate Change Law' in Geert van Calster, Wim Vanderberghe and Leonie Reins (eds), *Research Handbook on Climate Change Mitigation Law* (Edward Elgar Publishing 2015).
Visseren-Hamakers, I.J. and others, 'Trade-Offs, Co-Benefits and Safeguards: Current Debates on the Breadth of REDD+' (2012) 4 *Current Opinion in Environmental Sustainability* 646.
Wolfrum, R. and Matz, N., *Conflicts in International Environmental Law* (Springer 2003).

6. The human rights of Indigenous Peoples and forest-dependent communities in the complex legal framework for REDD+

*Sébastien Jodoin**

1. INTRODUCTION

Few legal issues concerning REDD+ have arguably attracted more attention from scholars and practitioners than those relating to the recognition and protection of the human rights of Indigenous Peoples and forest-dependent communities in developing countries.[1] The salience of human rights to the development and implementation of REDD+ policies, programmes, and projects around the world results, in part, from increased awareness and concern over the adverse social implications of first-generation climate mitigation mechanisms, most notably the CDM and voluntary forest carbon offset projects carried out in developing countries.[2] REDD+ has also served as one of the first domains in transnational climate law and policy in which public and private actors have had to grapple with the need to abide by the emerging set of human rights principles, obligations, and standards that are redefining the field of natural resource management and conservation.[3]

* All websites cited in this chapter were accessed on 1 October 2015.

[1] See Chapter 5 by Annalisa Savaresi and Chapter 9 by Kirsty Glover in this volume. See also Annalisa Savaresi, "The Human Rights Dimension of REDD" (2012) 21:2 *Review of European Community & International Environmental Law* 102; Thomas Sikor and Johannes Stahl, "A Way Forward: Forest Rights in Times of REDD+" in Thomas Sikor and Johannes Stahl, eds, *Forests and People. Property, Governance, and Human Rights* (London, UK: Earthscan, 2011) 237; Robert Fischer and Rosemary Lyster, "Land and Resource Tenure: The Rights of Indigenous Peoples and Forest Dwellers" in Rosemary Lyster, Catherine Mckenzie and Constance K. McDermott, eds, *Law, Tropical Forests and Carbon: The Case of REDD+* (Cambridge, UK: Cambridge University Press, 2013) 187.

[2] Naomi Roht-Arriaza, "Human Rights in the Climate Change Regime" (2010) 1:2 *Journal of Human Rights and the Environment* 211 at 213–22.

[3] Frances Seymour, "Forests, Climate Change and Human Rights: Managing Risks and Trade-offs" in Stephen Humphreys, ed., *Human Rights and Climate Change* (Cambridge, UK: Cambridge University Press, 2009) 207–37.

This chapter discusses how the human rights both of Indigenous Peoples and forest-dependent communities have been addressed within the complex legal framework for REDD+. Adopting a legal pluralist perspective that sees law existing in and through multiple sites and forms that extend beyond those associated with the authority of sovereign states,[4] I conceive of REDD+ as being governed by a complex and heterogeneous array of sites of international and transnational law. Indeed, since its emergence in 2007, REDD+ has evolved into "a slew of unorchestrated, multi-level, multi-purpose and multi-actor projects and initiatives" that "permeates multiple spheres of decision-making and organisation, creates contested interests and claims, and translates into multiple implementation actions running ahead of policy processes and state-driven decisions."[5] One of the most obvious manifestations of the growing heterogeneity of REDD+ is provided by the distinction between jurisdictional REDD+ and project-based REDD+ activities. Jurisdictional REDD+ refers to multi-year programmes of policy reform, research, and capacity-building that over 60 governments have initiated across Africa, Asia, Latin America, and the Caribbean to prepare for the domestic implementation of REDD+. These programmes are supported by multilateral and bilateral assistance, and are designed in line with the guidance provided by the UNFCCC.[6] Conversely, project-based REDD+ refers to efforts to reduce carbon emissions from forest-based sources at the local level. These REDD+ projects generally aim to generate carbon credits that can be sold and traded on voluntary carbon markets and follow the standards set by private certification programmes for this purpose.[7]

In this chapter, I compare the manner in which two very different sites of law have addressed the human rights of Indigenous Peoples and forest-dependent communities in the legal norms that they have generated for REDD+: the UNFCCC and the CCBA. I selected these two sites of law because they each govern different types of REDD+ activities: while the

---

[4] See Roger Cotterrell, "Transnational Communities and the Concept of Law" (2008) 21(1) *Ratio Juris* 1; Ralf Michaels, "Global Legal Pluralism" (2009) 5:1 *Annual Review of Law & Social Science* 243; Gregory Shaffer, "Transnational Legal Process and State Change" (2012) 37:2 *Law & Social Inquiry* 229.

[5] Esteve Corbera and Heike Schroeder, "Governing and Implementing REDD+" (2011) 14:2 *Environmental Science & Policy* 89 at 93.

[6] See the chapters 1 and 3 in this volume, by La Viña et al., and Harro van Asselt and Constance L. McDermott respectively.

[7] Eduard Merger et al., "Options for REDD+ Voluntary Certification to Ensure Net GHG Benefits, Poverty Alleviation, Sustainable Management of Forests and Biodiversity Conservation" (2011) 2 *Forests* 550.

UNFCCC has provided authoritative guidance for the implementation of jurisdictional REDD+ by developing country governments, the CCBA has emerged as a leading certification programme, along with the carbon accounting standards set by the VCS, for the validation and verification of REDD+ projects. Moreover, because these two sites of law represent two very different forms of law-making, the UNFCCC being a multilateral environmental institution and the CCBA being a non-state certification programme, this comparison enables me to reflect on the role that differences between various forms and modes of law have played in the articulation of rights in the complex legal framework for REDD+.

The chapter begins by providing a brief overview of the international legal principles, standards, and issues that relate to the recognition and protection of the human rights of Indigenous Peoples and forest-dependent communities in the context of environmental governance (section 2). I then provide an analysis of whether and how these human rights have been recognized in the context of the UNFCCC (section 3) and the CCBA (section 4). Sections 2 and 3 open with a discussion of the role of each site of law in the complex legal framework for REDD+. I trace the development of the human rights of Indigenous Peoples and forest-dependent communities in these sites from 2005 to 2014. In my analysis, I draw on a range of primary and secondary sources as well as a set of semi-structured interviews that I completed from 2007 to 2014 with policy-makers, experts, and activists working on REDD+ around the world.[8] I conclude by identifying the key research questions that my analysis raises about the relationship between human rights and REDD+, and more broadly about the development and implementation of various forms of law with respect to REDD+.

---

[8] As part of a broader research project on the transnational legal process for REDD+, I completed 94 semi-structured élite interviews with individuals affiliated with international organizations, developing and developed country governments, corporations, and NGOs actively working on REDD+ around the world. The majority of the interviews were conducted, in person, in ten countries: Germany, Kenya, Indonesia, Italy, Norway, Panama, South Africa, Tanzania, United Kingdom, and the United States. Other interviews were conducted, through Skype, with interviewees based in some of these countries as well as in Australia, France, New Zealand, and Thailand. For a complete list of these interviews and further information on how they were conducted, see Sébastien Jodoin, "On-Line Appendix on REDD+ Fieldwork," (March 2015) available at: http://www.sjodoin.ca/data.

2. THE HUMAN RIGHTS OF INDIGENOUS PEOPLES AND FOREST-DEPENDENT COMMUNITIES IN THE CONTEXT OF ENVIRONMENTAL GOVERNANCE

Over the last three decades, human rights obligations, principles, and approaches have become increasingly relevant to the field of environmental governance,[9] most notably in contexts involving Indigenous Peoples[10] and forest-dependent communities.[11] In particular, a range of sources of international law and policy have increasingly recognized that the design and implementation of environmental laws, policies, and programmes must respect, protect, and fulfil a wide range of their procedural and substantive rights.

The procedural rights of Indigenous Peoples and forest-dependent communities in the context of environmental governance flow from the right to participation enshrined in international human rights law as well as the principle of public participation in international environmental law.[12] These procedural rights signify that communities should be given an opportunity to fully and effectively participate in decision-making processes that may affect their rights and should have access to administrative, judicial, and other accountability mechanisms in cases of human rights violations.[13] In addition, Indigenous Peoples benefit from an enhanced set

---

[9] Sébastien Jodoin, "Can Rights-Based Approaches Enhance Legitimacy and Cooperation in Conservation? A Relational Account" (2014) 15:3 *Human Rights Review* 283–303.

[10] Robert K. Hitchcock, "International Human Rights, the Environment, and Indigenous Peoples" (1994) 5 *Colorado Journal of Environmental Law and Policy* 1.

[11] Thomas Sikor and Johannes Stahl, "Introduction: The Rights-Based Agenda in International Forestry" in Sikor and Stahl, 1.

[12] See, e.g., *Declaration on Environment and Development*, Report of the United Nations Conference on Environment and Development, UN Doc. A/CONF.151/6/Rev.1 (1992), Principle 10 ("Environmental issues are best handled with the participation of all concerned citizens, at the relevant level. At the national level, each individual shall have appropriate access to information concerning the environment that is held by public authorities, including information on hazardous materials and activities in their communities, and the opportunity to participate in decision-making processes. States shall facilitate and encourage public awareness and participation by making information widely available. Effective access to judicial and administrative proceedings, including redress and remedy, shall be provided.") and Principle 22 ("Indigenous people and their communities and other local communities have a vital role in environmental management and development because of their knowledge and traditional practices.").

[13] See Office of the United Nations High Commissioner for Human Rights, "Report of the Office of the United Nations High Commissioner for Human

of procedural rights by virtue of their recognition as "peoples" and their right to self-determination under international law.[14] In particular, as is recognized in ILO Convention No. 169,[15] UNDRIP,[16] and the decisions of numerous international and regional human rights bodies,[17] Indigenous Peoples have the right to provide or withhold their FPIC to activities and measures that affect their rights, lands, and resources. As stated by the UN Working Group on Indigenous Populations, the principle of FPIC

> recognizes indigenous peoples' inherent and prior rights to their lands and resources and respects their legitimate authority to require that third parties enter into an equal and respectful relationship with them, based on the principle of informed consent . . . [and] requires processes that allow and support meaningful choices by indigenous peoples about their development path.[18]

The substantive rights of Indigenous Peoples and forest-dependent communities in the context of environmental governance include civil and political rights such as the rights to personal security, freedom of movement, and freedom from racial discrimination[19] as well as economic, social, and cultural rights such as the rights to housing, food, water,

---

Rights on the relationship between climate change and human rights," UN Doc. A/HRC/10/61, 15 January 2009, paras. 81–3.

[14] *United Nations Declaration on the Rights of Indigenous Peoples*, UN Human Rights Council Resolution 2006/2, 13 September 2007, UN Doc. A/RES/61/295, arts. 3, 4, and 5 [UNDRIP]. Article 19 of UNDRIP states that: "States shall consult and cooperate in good faith with the indigenous peoples concerned through their own representative institutions in order to obtain their free, prior and informed consent before adopting and implementing legislative or administrative measures that may affect them."

[15] *Convention concerning Indigenous and Tribal Peoples in Independent Countries*, ILO Convention 169, 72 ILO Official Bull. 59, 28 ILM 1382 (1989), arts. 4, 5 and 13–19.

[16] UNDRIP, arts. 10, 11(2), 19, 28, 29(2) and 32(2).

[17] See, e.g., IACtHR, *Maya Indigenous Communities and their Members against Belize* (Case No. 12.053), Report No. 40/04, 12 October 2004, at para. 142; IACtHR, *Saramaka People* v. *Suriname*, Preliminary Objections, Merits, Reparations, and Costs, Judgment of November 28, 2007, Series C No. 172, at para. 134; *African Commission on Human and Peoples Rights, Centre for Minority Rights Development (Kenya) and Minority Rights Group International on behalf of Endorois Welfare Council* (Case 276/2003), Judgment (2009) at para. 291.

[18] Commission on Human Rights, Sub-Commission on the Promotion and Protection of Human Rights, Working Group on Indigenous Populations, Twenty-second session, 9–13 July 2004, E/CN.4/Sub.2/AC.4/2004/4 p. 5.

[19] *International Covenant on Civil and Political Rights*, adopted 16 December 1966, UNGA Res. 2200A (XXI), 21 UN GAOR Supp. (No. 16) at 52, UN

health, an adequate standard of living, and culture.[20] All of these rights may be infringed or enhanced by the adoption and implementation of laws, measures, and programmes that seek to protect the environment and ensure the sustainable management of resources.[21] That said, the substantive right that is perhaps most relevant to environmental governance concerns the rights of communities to govern, access, and benefit from their traditional lands and resources. While there is no explicit right to land and resources in international human rights law,[22] such a right is intimately connected to several economic, social, and cultural rights, especially the entitlement to housing and the protection against forced evictions that form part of the right to an adequate standard of living.[23] Here again, Indigenous Peoples are generally understood as possessing a distinctive set of *sui generis* rights to land and resources in international law,[24] as recognized by UNDRIP,[25] ILO Convention No. 169,[26] and the decisions of regional human rights bodies.[27] These developments confirm that Indigenous Peoples possess rights to lands that they have

---

Doc. A/6316 (1966), 999 UNTS 171, entered into force 23 March 1976, arts. 9(1), 12(1), and 26(1).

[20] *International Covenant on Economic, Social and Cultural Rights*, adopted 16 December 1966, UNGA Res. 2200A (XXI), 21 UN GAOR Supp. (No. 16) at 49, UN Doc. A/6316 (1966), 993 UNTS 3, entered into force 3 January 1976, arts. 11, 12, and 15.

[21] Jessica Campese, "Rights-based Approaches to Conservation: An Overview of Concepts and Questions" in Jessica Campese, Terry Sunderland, Thomas Greiber, and Gonzalo Oviedo, eds, *Rights-based Approaches: Exploring Issues and Opportunities for Conservation* (Bogor, Indonesia: CIFOR and IUCN) 1.

[22] A right to property was included in the UNDHR, but was not included in either of the international covenants. See T.R.G. van Banning, *The Human Right to Property* (Intersentia: Oxford, 2002) at 36–47.

[23] UN Committee on Economic Social and Cultural Rights (CESCR), General Comment 4, The right to adequate housing (art. 11(1)), 13 December 1991, UN Doc. E/1992/23, at paras. 7–8.

[24] See generally Jérémie Gilbert and Cathal Doyle, "A New Dawn over the Land: Shedding Light on Collective Ownership and Consent" in Stephen Allen and Alexandra Xanthaki, eds, *Reflections on the UN Declaration on the Rights of Indigenous Peoples* (Portland, Oregon: Hart Publishing, 2011) 289.

[25] UNDRIP, arts. 25–27.

[26] ILO Convention No. 169, arts. 4, 5 and 13–19.

[27] See, e.g., *Mayagna (Sumo) Awas Tingni Community* v. *Nicaragua*, Series C, No. 79, at 153; *Case of the Indigenous Community Yakye Axa* v. *Paraguay*, Merits, Reparations and Costs, Judgment, IACtHR, Series C, No. 125 (June 17, 2005); IACtHR, *Saramaka People* v. *Suriname*, Preliminary Objections, Merits, Reparations, and Costs, Judgment of November 28, 2007, Series C No. 172.

traditionally owned, used, or occupied[28] or upon which their cultural practices, survival, and development depend.[29]

This brief review shows that Indigenous Peoples have made considerable gains in having their distinctive collective status and rights as "peoples" recognized in international law.[30] In this regard, while there is no universally accepted definition of the term "Indigenous Peoples,"[31] there is a working consensus in the United Nations over the criteria that may be used to identify Indigenous Peoples, namely:

> (i) priority in time, in terms of occupation and use of specific territory; (ii) voluntary perpetuation of cultural specificity, which can include aspects of their language, social organization, religion and spiritual values, modes of production, legal forms and institutions; (iii) self-identification, as well as recognition by other groups, or by State authorities, as differentiated collectives; and (iv) an experience of subjugation, marginalization, dispossession, exclusion or discrimination, whether these conditions persist or not.[32]

By contrast, forest-dependent communities do not possess a distinctive status or set of rights under international law, [33] nor do they hold explicit collective rights to FPIC or to their traditional lands and resources, or to FPIC under any existing international human rights instrument.[34] They must instead assert a broad set of claims based on generally applicable international human rights obligations or the rights held by Indigenous

---

28 See, e.g., UNDRIP, art. 26(1).

29 See, e.g., IACtHR, *Saramaka People* v. *Suriname*, Preliminary Objections, Merits, Reparations, and Costs, Judgment of November 28, 2007, Series C No. 172 at para. 122.

30 See generally Rhiannon Morgan, *Transforming Law and Institution. Indigenous Peoples, the United Nations and Human Rights* (Surrey, UK: Ashgate Press, 2011).

31 Alexandra Xanthaki, *Indigenous Rights and United Nations Standards: Self-Determination, Culture and Land* (Cambridge, UK: Cambridge University Press, 2007) at 9–10.

32 Erica-Irene Daes, Chairperson-Rapporteur, "Working Paper on the concept of 'indigenous people'" (United Nations Economic and Social Council, 10 June 1996), UN Doc. E/CN.4/Sub.2/AC.4/1996/2, at para. 70.

33 One possible definition of "forest-dependent communities" can be found in a protocol of the South African Development Community, in which they are defined as "A coherent, social group of persons with interests or rights related to forests or forest resources, in a particular area, which the persons hold or exercise communally in terms of an agreement, custom or law." (South African Development Community, *South African Development Community Protocol on Forestry* (Luanda, 3 October 2002) entered into force 17 July 2009, art. 2(1)).

34 David Takacs, "Environmental Democracy and Forest Carbon (REDD+)" (2014) 44 *Environmental Law* 71 at 92–4.

Peoples.[35] Indeed, existing decisions adopted by regional human rights bodies suggest that the protection of their collective rights depends upon a demonstration that they hold the status of Indigenous Peoples[36] or that they constitute "Tribal peoples" that share their key characteristics.[37] On the other hand, the importance of ensuring the participation of local communities, respecting their knowledge, and sharing benefits with them has most notably been recognized in the international regime for the protection of biodiversity.[38] In particular, the Nagoya Protocol adopted under the auspices of the CBD directs state parties to obtain the "prior informed consent or approval and involvement of indigenous and local communities" for access to their genetic resources and knowledge,[39] to implement mechanisms to share benefits with them,[40] and to take steps to strengthen their awareness and capacity in this field.[41] As Elisa Morgera has argued, these developments in international biodiversity law and policy reflect the influence of a rights-based approach to environmental governance and may offer useful lessons for the design and implementation of climate mechanisms such as REDD+.[42]

---

35 Sikor and Stahl, at 8.

36 See, e.g., *Centre for Minority Rights Development (Kenya) and Minority Rights Group International on behalf of Endorois Welfare Council* v. *Kenya* (February 2010) at paras. 161–2, 187, 212, and 226.

37 See, e.g., *Case of the Saramaka People* v. *Suriname*, IACtHR, Series C, No. 172 (28 November 2007) at paras. 79–86.

38 CBD, adopted 5 June 1992, 1760 UNTS 79, entered into force 29 December 1992, arts. 8(j), 10(c), and 17(2).

39 *Nagoya Protocol on Access to Genetic Resources and the Fair and Equitable Sharing of Benefits Arising from Their Utilization to the Convention on Biological Diversity*, UNEP/CBD/COP/DEC/X/1, 29 October 2010 Nagoya, Japan. Not yet in force, arts. 6 and 7.

40 Ibid., art. 5.

41 Ibid., arts. 21 and 22.

42 Elisa Morgera, "No Need to Reinvent the Wheel for a Human Rights-based Approach to Tackling Climate Change: The Contribution of International Biodiversity Law" in Erkki J. Hollo, Kati Kulovesi, and Michael Mehling, eds, *Climate Change and the Law: A Global Perspective* (New York, NY: Springer, 2013) 359.

3. THE DEVELOPMENT OF HUMAN RIGHTS IN UNFCCC DECISION-MAKING ON REDD+

3.1 The Nature and Role of the UNFCCC in the Complex Legal Framework for REDD+

Adopted in 1992 and in force since 1994, the UNFCCC is an international treaty that aims "to stabilize atmospheric concentrations of GHG at a level that would prevent human-induced actions from leading to 'dangerous interference' with the global climate system."[43] The UNFCCC follows the "convention/protocol" model that is typical of many other multilateral environmental agreements. It establishes a broad framework of objectives and a common platform for inter-governmental cooperation and dialogue and the adoption of follow-up agreements known as protocols that impose binding obligations upon states to undertake and support mitigation and adaptation efforts.[44] Comprised of all state parties to the UNFCCC and operating by consensus, the COP serves as the "supreme body" of the UNFCCC and is tasked with adopting decisions that promote its effective implementation.[45]

Over succeeding rounds in the negotiations to adopt a long-term agreement on climate change to succeed the KP, the UNFCCC COP has endorsed the concept of REDD+, affirming the "urgent need to take meaningful action" to reduce GHG emissions from forest-based sources in developing countries and recognizing that doing so could "promote co-benefits" and "complement the aims and objectives of other relevant international conventions and agreements."[46] The UNFCCC COP has thus encouraged states to "strengthen and support on-going efforts to reduce emissions from deforestation and forest degradation on a voluntary basis" as well as "to explore a range of actions, identify options and undertake efforts, including demonstration activities, to address the drivers of deforestation relevant to their national circumstances."[47] Since 2010,

---

[43] UNFCCC, 9 May 1992, 1771 UNTS 107, entered into force 21 March 1994, art. 2.

[44] Elisabeth DeSombre, *Global Environmental Institutions* (Abingdon, UK: Routledge, 2006) at 124.

[45] UNFCCC, art. 7.2.

[46] UNFCCC COP, Decision 2/CP.13, "Reducing emissions from deforestation in developing countries: approaches to stimulate action" in Report of the Conference of the Parties on its thirteenth session, Addendum, Part Two: Action taken by the Conference of the Parties at its thirteenth session, FCCC/CP/2007/6/Add.1 (14 March 2008), preamble.

[47] Ibid. at paras. 1 and 3.

the UNFCC COP has adopted a series of decisions that establish rules and provide methodological guidance for the domestic operationalization of REDD+ as part of the Cancún Agreements in 2010,[48] the Durban Platform in 2011,[49] and most recently the WFR in 2013.[50] Together, these decisions set the core modalities and requirements for the pursuit of jurisdictional REDD+ activities in developing countries.

3.2 The Rights of Indigenous Peoples and Forest-Dependent Communities in UNFCCC Decision-Making on REDD+

To begin with, the initial discussions on REDD+ within the UNFCCC largely neglected issues relating to the rights of Indigenous Peoples and forest-dependent communities. Indeed, the original proposal of RED submitted to the UNFCCC COP by the Coalition of Rainforest Nations in November 2005 did not refer to Indigenous Peoples, local communities, or their rights.[51] Likewise, in its December 2007 decision on approaches to stimulate early action on RED, the UNFCCC COP avoided rights-based language and merely acknowledged that "the *needs of local and indigenous communities* should be addressed when action is taken to reduce emissions from deforestation and forest degradation in developing countries."[52]

However, the formal launch of negotiations on REDD+ within the

---

48 UNFCCC, Decision 1/CP.16, "The Cancun Agreements: Outcome of the work of the Ad Hoc Working Group on long-term Cooperative Action under the Convention," in Report of the Conference of the Parties on its sixteenth session, Addendum, Part Two: Action taken by the Conference of the Parties, FCCC/CP/2010/7/Add.1 (15 March 2011) at paras. 68–79.

49 UNFCCC, Decision 2/CP.17, "Durban Platform for Enhanced Action: Outcome of the work of the Ad Hoc Working Group on Long-term Cooperative Action under the Convention," in Report of the Conference of the Parties on its sixteenth session, Addendum, Part Two: Action taken by the Conference of the Parties, FCCC/CP/2011/9/Add.1 (15 March 2012) at paras. 63–73.

50 UNFCCC COP, Decision 2/CP.17 at paras. 63–73; UNFCCC COP, Decisions 9/CP.19, 10/CP.19, 11/CP.19, 12/CP.19, 13/CP.19, 14/CP.19 and 15/CP.19, in Report of the Conference of the Parties on its nineteenth session, held in Warsaw from 11 to 23 November 2013, FCCC/CP/2013/10/Add.1 (31 January 2014).

51 Submission by the Governments of Papua New Guinea and Costa Rica, "Reducing Emissions from Deforestation in Developing Countries: Approaches to Stimulate Action" Eleventh Conference of the Parties to the UNFCCC: Agenda Item 6, available at: http://unfccc.int/resource/docs/2005/cop11/eng/misc01.pdf.

52 UNFCCC COP, Decision 2/CP.13, preamble [emphasis added].

UNFCCC in December 2007 and the subsequent proliferation of REDD+ programmes and activities around the world prompted a number of actors concerned with its potential adverse social impacts to initiate research and advocacy efforts in this new domain of transnational climate law.[53] Throughout 2008 and 2009, a growing array of Indigenous Peoples Organizations (IPOs) and NGOs thus began to press for greater recognition of the rights of Indigenous Peoples and local communities in the context of the international negotiations on REDD+.[54] It took some time for these advocacy efforts to bear fruit however.

At the 14th session of the UNFCCC held in December 2008 in Poznan, Poland, governments could not agree to include references to the rights of Indigenous Peoples and forest-dependent communities in developing SBSTA guidance on REDD+, referring instead to the need to "promote the full and effective participation of indigenous people and local communities, taking into account national circumstances and noting relevant international agreements."[55] Most strikingly, this SBSTA text referred to "Indigenous people" (singular) rather than "Indigenous Peoples" (plural), thus avoiding even an implicit reference to the international human rights obligations owed to Indigenous Peoples by virtue of their status as peoples under international law.[56] This clear aversion to the rights of Indigenous Peoples prompted the Indigenous Peoples' caucus to walk out of the UNFCCC negotiations under the rallying cry "No rights, no REDD"[57] and led the government of Denmark to take the unusual step of requesting

---

[53] See Jan Willem den Besten, Bas Arts, and Patrick Verkooijen, "The evolution of REDD+: An analysis of discursive-institutional dynamics" (2014) 35 *Environmental Science & Policy* 40 at 43–4.

[54] See Linda Wallbott, "Indigenous Peoples in UN REDD+ Negotiations: 'Importing Power' and Lobbying for Rights through Discursive Interplay Management" (2014) 19:1 *Ecology & Society*, art. 21 at 5–8.

[55] UNFCCC SBSTA, "Report of the Subsidiary Body for Scientific and Technological Advice on its twenty-ninth session, held in Poznan from 1 to 10 December 2008" FCCC/SBSTA/2008/13 (17 February 2009) Annex II, at para. 1(c).

[56] Wallbott, at 4–5; Heike Schroeder, "Agency in International Climate Negotiations: The Case of Indigenous Peoples and Avoided Deforestation" (2010) 10:4 *International Environmental Agreements* 317 at 327.

[57] Christopher Lang "'No rights, no REDD': Indigenous Peoples protest in Poznan" REDD-Monitor, 9 December 2008, available at: http://www.redd-monitor.org/2008/12/09/no-rights-no-redd-indigenous-peoples-protest-in-poznan/. See also Victoria Tauli-Corpuz, "International Human Rights Day 2008: A Sad Day for Indigenous Peoples" (10 December 2008), available at: http://www.forestpeoples.org/topics/un-framework-convention-climate-change-unfccc/news/2011/05/international-human-rights-day-200.

an official statement to the effect that its participation in these decisions "was without prejudice" to its support for indigenous rights.[58]

The tide would begin to turn in the Spring of 2009 as issues relating to human rights became an increasingly significant element of the negotiations on REDD+ within the UNFCCC.[59] Numerous governments employed rights language in their submissions to the SBSTA on issues relating to "Indigenous people and local communities for the development and application of methodologies" for REDD+.[60] In line with the terminology adopted in the CBD, the term "local communities" was now used by negotiators in the UNFCCC to encompass forest-dependent communities.[61] Furthermore, an influential report commissioned by the government of Norway on the design of a REDD+ mechanism within the UNFCCC and released in March 2009 included, among other elements, an overview of key principles and standards for understanding and assessing the effective participation of Indigenous Peoples and local communities, and presented options for respecting their rights and promoting their participation in REDD+ mechanisms created within the UNFCCC.[62] Finally, in their initial proposals for negotiating text on REDD+, the governments of Norway and Bolivia highlighted the importance of respecting the rights of Indigenous Peoples and local communities, and ensuring their full and effective participation in REDD+ activities. [63] Norway circulated draft legal

---

[58] UNFCCC COP, "Report of the Conference of the Parties on its fourteenth session, held in Poznan from 1 to 12 December 2008. Part One. Proceedings" FCCC/CP/2008/7 (19 March 2009), at fn. 15.

[59] REDD+ Fieldwork Interview 41 at 2.

[60] See the submissions by Bolivia, Ecuador, European Union, Guatemala, Mexico, Panama, Costa Rica, Switzerland (on behalf of the Environmental Integrity Group), and Tuvalu (UNFCCC SBSTA, "Issues Relating to Indigenous People and Local Communities for the Development and Application of Methodologies. Submissions from Parties." FCCC/SBSTA/2009/MISC.1 (10 March 2009).

[61] CBD, adopted 5 June 1992, 1760 UNTS 79, entered into force 29 December 1992, art. 8(j).

[62] Arild Angelsen et al., *Reducing Emissions from Deforestation and Forest Degradation (REDD): An Options Assessment Report* (Washington, DC: Meridian Institute, March 2009) at 25–8.

[63] See the submissions by Bolivia to the Ad Hoc Working Group on Long-Term Cooperative Action under the Convention, "Ideas and Proposals on the elements contained in paragraph 1 of the Bali Action Plan. Submissions from the Parties. Part 1" FCCC/AWGLCA/2009/MISC.4 (19 May 2009) 52 and by Norway to the Ad Hoc Working Group on Long-Term Cooperative Action under the Convention, "Ideas and Proposals on the elements contained in paragraph 1 of the Bali Action Plan. Submissions from the Parties. Part 2" FCCC/AWGLCA/2009/MISC.4 (19 May 2009) 51.

text on a REDD+ mechanism that proposed a number of principles for the protection of the rights of Indigenous Peoples and local communities, and introduced the notion of "safeguards" for REDD+.[64]

The first draft negotiating text developed for REDD+ by negotiators in May 2009 accordingly acknowledged the importance of respecting the rights of Indigenous Peoples and local communities, and explicitly referenced UNDRIP in doing so.[65] Moreover, a subsequent draft negotiating text discussed at different negotiation sessions from August to November 2009 included, for the time, a number of social and environmental safeguards, including a provision that included bracketed language referencing the rights enshrined in UNDRIP, including the right to FPIC.[66] This draft negotiating text formed the basis of vigorous exchanges between governments during the 15th session of the UNFCCC held in Copenhagen in December 2009.[67]

While the draft text on REDD+ was more or less finalized by the end of the Copenhagen conference,[68] the negotiations as a whole failed to deliver a new international agreement and the COP thus adopted a more limited decision on methodological guidance for REDD+ instead.[69] This decision merely reiterated "the need for full and effective engagement of indigenous peoples and local communities in, and the potential contribution of their knowledge to, monitoring and reporting of REDD+ activities"[70]

---

64 REDD+ Fieldwork Interview 41 at 1. See the submission by Norway to Ad Hoc Working Group on Long-Term Cooperative Action under the Convention, "Ideas and Proposals on the elements contained in paragraph 1 of the Bali Action Plan. Submissions from the Parties. Addendum" FCCC/AWGLCA/2009/MISC.4 (31 May 2009) 18.

65 Ad Hoc Working Group on Long-Term Cooperative Action under the Convention, "Negotiating Text" FCCC/AWGLCA/2009/8 (19 May 2009) at para. 109.

66 Report of the Ad Hoc Working Group on Long-term Cooperative Action under the Convention on its seventh session, held in Bangkok from 28 September to 9 October 2009, and Barcelona from 2 to 6 November 2009, 20 November 2009, FCCC/AWGLCA/2009/14, Item III.C, Policy approaches and positive incentives on issues relating to reducing emissions from deforestation and forest degradation in developing countries; and the role of conservation, sustainable management of forests and enhancement of forest carbon stocks in developing countries, at para. 4(e).

67 REDD+ Fieldwork Interview 41 at 1.

68 See UNFCCC COP, Report of the Ad Hoc Working Group on Long-term Cooperative Action under the Convention on its eighth session, held in Copenhagen from 7 to 15 December 2009, FCCC/AWGLCA/2009/17 (5 February 2010) at 34–7.

69 REDD+ Fieldwork Interview 41 at 1.

70 UNFCCC COP, Decision 4/CP.15, "Methodological guidance for activities relating to reducing emissions from deforestation and forest degradation and

and encouraged "the development of guidance for effective engagement of indigenous peoples and local communities in monitoring and reporting."[71] While this decision did not refer to indigenous or human rights, it did mark the formal emergence of the term "Indigenous Peoples" in the decision-making of the COP on REDD+.

The Cancún Agreements, adopted by the UNFCC COP one year later in December 2010, would thus serve as the vehicle for the first major decision on REDD+ within the UNFCCC. The Cancún Agreements specify that a national REDD+ strategy, one of the key elements of a country's REDD+ readiness efforts, must address the following issues: "drivers of deforestation and forest degradation, land tenure issues, forest governance issues, gender considerations and [environmental and social safeguards], ensuring the full and effective participation of relevant stakeholders, *inter alia*, indigenous peoples and local communities."[72] Moreover, the Cancún Agreements provide that the implementation of REDD+ should "promote" and "support" a set of social and environmental safeguards,[73] including the following two safeguards that are relevant to the rights of Indigenous Peoples and local communities:

> (c) Respect for the knowledge and rights of indigenous peoples and members of local communities, by taking into account relevant international obligations, national circumstances and laws, and noting that the United Nations General Assembly has adopted the United Nations Declaration on the Rights of Indigenous Peoples;
> (d) The full and effective participation of relevant stakeholders, in particular, indigenous peoples and local communities in [REDD+ activities];[74]

Finally, the Cancún Agreements establish that the fourth element of a developing country's national REDD+ readiness consists of the development of an information system for reporting on the way that environmental and social safeguards are "being addressed and respected" in REDD+ activities "while respecting sovereignty."[75]

The Cancún Agreements thus address both participatory and resource

---

the role of conservation, sustainable management of forests and enhancement of forest carbon stocks in developing countries" in Report of the Conference of the Parties on its fifteenth session, held in Copenhagen from 7 to 19 December 2009. Part Two: Action taken by the Conference of the Parties at its fifteenth session, FCCC/CP/2009/11/Add.1 (30 March 2010), preamble.

[71] Ibid. at para. 3.

[72] UNFCCC COP, Decision 1/CP.16, para. 72.

[73] UNFCCC COP, Decision 1/CP.16, para. 69.

[74] Decision 1/CP.16, Annex I, para. 2.

[75] UNFCCC COP, Decision 1/CP.16, para. 71(d).

rights in its paragraphs on REDD+. It conceives of land tenure issues and participatory rights as being central to the development of a national REDD+ strategy and also requires respect for the knowledge and rights of Indigenous Peoples and local communities in the context of REDD+. In doing so, the Cancún Agreements nonetheless adopt weaker language than the draft negotiating texts discussed during the summer and autumn of 2009. First, the expression "shall respect" safeguards used in previous drafts was replaced by the expression "promote and support." Second, the safeguards do not specifically refer to the right of Indigenous Peoples to FPIC. Third, the safeguards only "note" the adoption of UNDRIP, a drafting term of negligible legal import within the formal practices of the UNFCCC decision-making process.

After Cancún, issues relating to the rights of Indigenous Peoples and local communities receded somewhat from the UNFCCC negotiations on REDD+, which centred on the development of further guidance on readiness, finance, and MRV.[76] In this context, IPOs and NGOs lobbied governments to ensure that the final set of rules for REDD+ formulated by the UNFCCC COP would uphold and promote the rights of Indigenous Peoples and local communities, particularly with respect to the requirements of establishing safeguards information systems and the consideration of "non-carbon benefits" in the finance and governance of REDD+.[77] While many governments took the view that the carbon sequestration and climate mitigation potential of REDD+ should not be overburdened by social considerations and reporting mechanisms,[78] IPOs, NGOs, and their allies in government succeeded in building upon the gains made in Cancún. The Durban Platform, adopted by the COP at the 18th session of the UNFCCC in December 2011, specifies that safeguard information systems must be implemented at the national level for all REDD+ activities "regardless of the source or type of financing"[79] and through a "country-driven approach" that ultimately provides "transparent and consistent

---

[76] REDD+ Fieldwork Interview 7 at 12; REDD+ Fieldwork Interview 33 at 7; REDD+ Fieldwork Interview 42 at 1.

[77] REDD+ Fieldwork Interview 7 at 1–2. In fact, in early 2013, IPOs and NGOs formed the REDD+ Safeguards Working Group. Based at the Ateneo School of Government in the Philippines and bringing together more than 30 NGOs from the around the world, it seeks "to ensure effective implementation of safeguards and the achievement of benefits for communities, climate and biodiversity through the global REDD+ mechanism." (REDD+ Safeguards Working Group, "What We Do" available at: http://reddplussafeguards.com?page_id=103.

[78] REDD+ Fieldwork Interview 7 at 13; REDD+ Fieldwork Interview 33 at 8; REDD+ Fieldwork Interview 42 at 4–5; REDD– Fieldwork Interview 53 at 5.

[79] Decision 2/CP.17, para. 63.

information that is accessible by all relevant stakeholders and updated on a regular basis."[80] In addition, the WFR, adopted by the COP at the 19th session of the UNFCCC in November 2013, establishes that developing countries have to provide periodical summaries of this information to the COP whether through national communications or some other channel and on a web platform, on a voluntary basis.[81] Most importantly, the WFR also provides that developing countries seeking to obtain and receive results-based payments for REDD+ activities are obliged to "provide the most recent summary of information on how all of the safeguards [. . .] have been addressed and respected before they can receive results-based payments."[82]

Opinions on the value of the decisions adopted in Cancún, Durban, and Warsaw for respecting and protecting the rights of Indigenous Peoples and local communities continue to be divided among IPOs and NGOs. To be sure, these decisions fall short of fully incorporating the rights enshrined in UNDRIP or recognized by international and regional human rights bodies. Yet, compared with the initial reluctance of many governments to accord any importance to human rights issues in the initial stages of the development of REDD+, the final set of UNFCCC decisions reflects the clear advancement of international legal norms relating to the status and rights of Indigenous Peoples and the participation of local communities.[83]

4. THE DEVELOPMENT OF RIGHTS IN THE CLIMATE, COMMUNITY AND BIODIVERSITY STANDARDS

4.1 The Nature and Role of the CCBA in the Complex Legal Framework for REDD+

The CCBA is a non-governmental standard-setting programme that was established in 2003 by five international NGOs (Conservation

---

80 Decision 12/CP.17, para. 2.

81 UNFCCC, Decision 12/CP.19, "The timing and the frequency of presentations of the summary of information on how all the safeguards referred to in decision 1/CP.16, appendix I, are being addressed and respected" FCCC/CP/2013/10/Add.1 (31 January 2014).

82 UNFCCC, Decision 9/CP.19, "Work programme on results-based finance to progress the full implementation of the activities referred to in decision 1/CP.16, paragraph 70" FCCC/CP/2013/10/Add.1 (31 January 2014) at para. 4.

83 REDD+ Fieldwork Interview 7 at 12; REDD+ Fieldwork Interview 77 at 17; REDD+ Fieldwork Interview 82 at 1. See also Wallbott, at 5.

International, CARE International, the Rainforest Alliance, The Nature Conservancy, and the Wildlife Conservation Society) in order to foster "land management activities that credibly mitigate global climate change, improve the wellbeing and reduce the poverty of local communities, and conserve biodiversity."[84] The CCBA has most notably facilitated the drafting of the CCB Standards in order to promote "development of, and investment in, site-based projects that deliver credible and significant climate, community and biodiversity benefits in an integrated, sustainable manner."[85] The CCB Standards were first released in May 2005 and were subsequently revised in a second edition issued in December 2008 and a third edition launched in December 2013. Whereas the first edition was prepared on the basis of research, consultations, and pilot testing, the preparation of the second and third editions of CCB Standards followed a more transparent and inclusive process that was supervised by a multi-stakeholder steering committee (including representatives of Indigenous Peoples and other non-indigenous rural communities) in which a wide range of experts, affected stakeholders, and other interested parties were given the opportunity to provide feedback on the content of the standards and to receive written responses from the CCBA.[86]

The CCB Standards fulfil the typical functions of a certification programme: they set the rules for carrying out, monitoring, and evaluating projects, provide guidance and methodologies for the application of these rules, create a process for the accreditation of third-party auditors for the validation and verification of such projects, and establish procedures for addressing disputes and improprieties in the application of the standards.[87] The CCB Standards are not a fully fledged carbon accounting programme, however. They do not entail the quantitative certification of emissions reductions and do not lead to the issuance of

---

[84] CCBA, *Rules for the Use of the Climate Community & Biodiversity Standards*, 2013, available at: https://s3.amazonaws.com/CCBA/Third_Edition/Rules_for_the_Use_of_the_CCB_Standards_December_2013.pdf at 1.

[85] Ibid., at 1.

[86] CCBA, *Guidance for the Use of CCB Standards*, available at: https://s3.amazonaws.com/CCBA/Guidance_for_the_Use_of_the_CCB_Standards_May_2013.pdf at 1.

[87] Ibid. at 5–17. The validation of a project requires an assessment by an independent third party that the design of this project complies with the CCB Standards. This assessment is conducted through document review, a site visit, and stakeholder consultations. For a project to maintain its CCB validation, it must be verified every five years through a qualitative evaluation of its implementation. Verification includes document review and site visit of the project by a third-party auditor.

carbon credits that can be sold and traded through voluntary carbon markets and transactions.[88] The verification and validation that a REDD+ project has met the CCB Standards will enable that project to tag any carbon credits issued through another carbon accounting standard, such as the VCS,[89] to be tagged with a CCB label. As such, the CCB Standards offer project developers rules and guidance for the design and implementation of land-based climate mitigation projects "that simultaneously reduce or remove greenhouse gas emissions and generate positive impacts for local communities and the local environment,"[90] and moreover provide an independent demonstration to potential donors or investors that projects have delivered additional, net environmental, and social benefits.[91]

Although the CCBA predates the emergence of REDD+ within the UNFCCC and its standard-setting activities are addressed to a full range of land-based carbon projects, it has emerged, alongside the VCS Agriculture, Forestry and Other Land Use (AFOLU), as one of the most influential transnational sites of law for project-based REDD+ activities. In conjunction with the VCS AFOLU programme, the CCB Standards have become the leading standard for use in land-based climate mitigation activities around the world.[92] As of September 2014, ten REDD+ projects had been fully validated and verified under the CCB Standards, one REDD+ project is currently undergoing verification, and five REDD+ projects have been validated, but not yet verified. Of the ten REDD+ projects that have completed the verification stage, two are in Latin America, one is in Asia, and six are in Africa.[93] Given that most of the finance that currently exists for REDD+ projects originates in development aid or corporate social responsibility initiatives, the CCB label has increasingly been seen

---

[88] CCBA, *Rules for the Use of the CCB Standards*, at 3.

[89] The VCS provides the rules and requirements for the independent validation and verification of all carbon emission reduction projects and leads to the issuance of carbon credits that can be sold or traded on voluntary carbon markets.

[90] CCBA, *Rules for the Use of the CCB Standards*, at 3.

[91] CCBA, *CCB Standards Third Edition*, 2013, available at: https://s3.amazonaws.com/CCBA/Third_Edition/CCB_Standards_Third_Edition_December_2013.pdf at 7–8.

[92] 71 per cent of all forest carbon projects and transactions in 2013 were certified under both the VCS and the CCB Standards ((Molly Peters-Stanley, Gloria Gonzalez, and Daphne Yin, *Covering New Ground. State of the Forest Carbon Markets 2013* (Washington, DC: Ecosystem Marketplace, 2013) at xiv.

[93] CCBA, "Projects" available at: http://www.climate-standards.org/category/projects/.

by REDD+ practitioners and donors as a basic requirement for the design and implementation of REDD+ projects.[94]

4.2 The Rights of Indigenous Peoples and Forest-Dependent Communities in the CCB Standards

The first edition of the CCB Standards was designed as a checklist of criteria and indicators for project developers that covered four sections: general matters, climate impacts, community impacts, and biodiversity impacts.[95] In their first iteration, the CCB Standards included fifteen required criteria and eight optional criteria and provided for three levels of validation: an approved level in which a project met all required criteria, a silver level in which a project also fulfilled three optional criteria across three different sections, and a gold level in which a project satisfied an additional six optional criteria across each of the four sections.[96] In line with their objective of enabling land-based climate mitigation projects to achieve significant social benefits, the first edition of the CCB Standards also mandated the generation of net positive social and economic impacts for communities.[97] In order to meet this requirement, project developers had to use an "appropriate methodology [. . .] to estimate the net benefits to communities resulting from planned project activities," "document stakeholder dialogues and indicate if and how the project proposal was revised based on such input," and establish "a process for hearing, responding to and resolving community grievances within a reasonable time period."[98]

In addition to generating net benefits for communities within the boundaries of a project, project developers also had to "quantify and mitigate likely negative social and economic offsite impacts; namely, the decreased social and economic wellbeing of communities or people living outside the project boundary, resulting from project activities."[99] The first edition of the CCB Standards also required that "[t]here should be no

---

[94] REDD+ Fieldwork Interview 34 at 1–2; REDD+ Fieldwork Interview 47 at 7; REDD+ Fieldwork Interview 73 at 6; REDD+ Fieldwork Interview 77 at 3; REDD+ Fieldwork Interview 80 at 1. See also Rachel Godfrey Wood, *Carbon Finance and Pro-poor Co-benefits: The Gold Standard and Climate, Community and Biodiversity Standards* (London, UK: IIED, 2011) at 29.

[95] Ibid. at 6–7.

[96] Ibid. at 5.

[97] Ibid. at CM1.

[98] Ibid. at CM1.3.

[99] Ibid. at CM2.

significant land tenure disputes in the project area, or the project should fundamentally help to resolve these tenure issues"[100] and mandated that project proponents had to "guarantee" that the project "will not encroach uninvited on private property, community property, or government property" and does not lead to the involuntary "relocation of people."[101]

Despite these many positive elements, the first edition of the CCB Standards did not do much for the recognition and protection of the rights of Indigenous Peoples and local communities however. The first edition of the CCB Standards omitted any references to the status of Indigenous Peoples or their rights, such as their rights to resources, culture, or to FPIC to measures affecting their lands or rights. In fact, the only explicit use of rights language in the first edition of the CCB Standards related to labour rights (described as "worker rights"), which are included in the optional criteria on community involvement.[102] As a result some actors within the CCBA took the view that the first edition of the CCB Standards was largely titled towards its conservation objectives,[103] with less emphasis being placed on social considerations and almost no recognition of human rights standards and principles.

In February 2008, the CCBA launched a process to revise the CCB Standards in order to maintain their influence in a changing market affected by "opportunities related to REDD, potential use alongside new carbon verification standards and new methodological and technological approaches for evaluation of multiple benefits."[104] Released in December 2008, the second edition of the CCB Standards contained numerous and significant modifications in line with the discussions within the CCB Standards Committee and the feedback received from interested parties. In terms of structure, the second edition of the CCB Standards included fourteen (rather than fifteen) required criteria and three (rather than six) optional criteria and provided for only two levels of validation: an approved level in which a project met all required criteria and a gold level in which a project achieved exceptional social and environmental benefits by satisfying at least one optional criterion.[105] In terms of

---

100 Ibid. at G5.

101 Ibid. at G5.1 and G5.2.

102 Ibid.

103 REDD+ Fieldwork Interview 84 at 4.

104 CCBA, "Terms of reference, procedures and workplan for revision of the Climate, Community and Biodiversity Standards" (15 February 2008), available at: https://s3.amazonaws.com/CCBA/History_of_the_Standards/CCBS_Revision_TORS_15_Feb_updated_13_June_2008.pdf at 5.

105 Ibid. at 10–11.

substance, several requirements were added or strengthened across the general climate, community, and biodiversity sections, including a new indicator relating to REDD+ projects.[106] The most important changes implemented in the second iteration of the CCB Standards related to the recognition and protection of the rights of Indigenous Peoples and local communities.[107]

Whereas the first edition of the CCB Standards was devoid of rights-based language, references to the rights of Indigenous Peoples and local communities permeated its second edition.[108] The second edition of the CCB Standards most notably required the following from project developers: the description of "Indigenous Peoples" as well as "current land use and customary and legal property rights including community property" located in the project zone;[109] the effective participation of local communities and other stakeholders in the conception and implementation of the project, including through the establishment of a grievance mechanism;[110] assistance for the resolution of land tenure disputes in the project zone;[111] the approval of "appropriate authorities, including the established formal and/or traditional authorities customarily required by the communities";[112] respect for property rights (including community property such as "lands that communities have traditionally owned, occupied or otherwise used or acquired");[113] demonstration that a project "has obtained the free, prior, and informed consent of those whose rights will be affected by the project" ("in conformance with the *United Nations Declaration on the Rights of Indigenous Peoples*");[114] evidence that the project will not entail "the involuntary relocation of people or of the activities important for the livelihoods and culture of the communities," particularly activities that relate to "long-standing community land and resource usage in accordance with Indigenous Peoples' and local communities' customary laws,

[106] Ibid. at G2.3.
[107] REDD+ Fieldwork Interview 84 at 4.
[108] The second edition most notably included four references to Indigenous Peoples, three references to UNDRIP, and three references to the right to FPIC.
[109] CCBA, *Climate, Community and Biodiversity Project Design Standards Second Edition* (December 2008), available at: https://s3.amazonaws.com/CCBA/Upload/ccb_standards_second_edition_december_2008+(1).pdf at G1.5 and G1.6.
[110] Ibid. at G3.
[111] Ibid. at G5.
[112] Ibid. at G5.3.
[113] Ibid. at G5.3 and fn. 31.
[114] Ibid. at G5.4 and fn. 32.

values, customs, and traditions, including seasonal or cyclical use, rather than formal legal title to land and resources issued by the State";[115] the generation of "net positive impacts on the social and economic well-being of communities" (specifically defined in terms of their customary rights);[116] and the equitable sharing of costs and benefits with affected communities.[117] In addition to these requirements, the second edition of the CCB Standards included an optional criterion for the generation of exceptional community benefits that specifically aimed to reduce poverty within affected communities and entailed the use of "innovative approaches that enable poorer households to participate effectively in land-based carbon activities."[118]

The second edition of the CCB Standards thus constituted a clear progression in the recognition and protection of human rights within the CCBA. In particular, this edition of the CCB Standards incorporated several of the rights included in UNDRIP, such as the right to FPIC, rights to land, tenure, and resources, participatory rights, and protection against involuntary resettlement. Although the second edition of the CCB Standards was clearly designed on the basis of UNDRIP, it is striking that many of its criteria and indicators included requirements that applied both to Indigenous Peoples and local communities that did not hold this status. As such, the second edition of the CCB Standards reflected a willingness on the part of the CCBA to align itself with an emerging international consensus regarding indigenous rights as well as a desire to go beyond minimal standards and protections to ensure "high performance" for all communities, regardless of their formal status under international human rights law.[119]

By 2012, the CCB Standards had become the leading multiple-benefit standard for land-based climate mitigation projects, and its use has become standard practice for project-based REDD+ activities.[120] Since

---

115 Ibid. at G5.4 and fn. 33. The second edition of the CCB Standards also requires FPIC in the context of involuntary resettlement: "If any relocation of habitation or activities is undertaken within the terms of an agreement, the project proponents must demonstrate that the agreement was made with the free, prior, and informed consent of those concerned and includes provisions for just and fair compensation." (Ibid. at G5.4)

116 Ibid. at CM1 and fn. 41.

117 Ibid. at CM1.

118 Ibid. at GL2.

119 REDD+ Fieldwork Interview 77 at 6.

120 Molly Peters-Stanley, Katherine Hamilton, and Daphne Yin, *Leveraging the Landscape. State of the Forest Carbon Markets 2012* (Washington, DC: Ecosystem Marketplace, 2012) at 31.

the release of the second edition in 2008, the CCBA had received substantial feedback from project developers and other stakeholders regarding ways to improve and strengthen the CCB Standards.[121] In response, the CCBA launched a revision process in 2012 to develop a third edition with the specific objective of fostering "market interest and confidence in carbon credits from smallholder- and community-led projects."[122] In the end, the third (and current) edition of the CCB Standards included three notable changes that bolster the recognition and protection of the rights of Indigenous Peoples and local communities. First, the CCB Standards now contain a completely new criterion on stakeholder engagement that strengthens previous requirements relating to the full and effective participation and consent of affected communities and stakeholders.[123] This criterion most notably includes specific and comprehensive indicators relating to participatory rights, including access to information, consultation, participation in decision-making, and grievance procedures.[124] In addition, this criterion contains an indicator on issues of racial and sexual discrimination.[125]

Second, the third edition of the CCB Standards provides enhanced protections for the customary land and resource rights of Indigenous Peoples and local communities. It requires that project developers ensure that their project "respects and supports rights to lands, territories and resources, including the statutory and customary rights of Indigenous Peoples and others within Communities and Other Stakeholders."[126] In particular, the CCB Standards now require project developers to "[d]escribe and map statutory and customary tenure/use/access/management rights to lands, territories and resources in the Project Zone including individual and collective rights and including overlapping or conflicting rights," "describe measures needed and taken by the project to help to secure statutory rights," and "[d]emonstrate that all Property Rights are recognized, respected, and supported."[127] Finally, the CCB Standards mandate that the FPIC of "relevant Property Rights Holders has been obtained at every

---

121 CCBA, "Terms of reference, procedures and work plan for revision of CCB Standards including modifications that support smallholder- and community-led projects" (16 November 2012), available at: https://s3.amazonaws.com/CCBA/Upload/Revision+and+small/TOR+and+workplan+for+CCB+Standards+revision+11-19-12.pdfat 3.

122 Ibid. at 4.

123 CCBA, *CCB Standards Third Edition*, 2013 at G3.

124 Ibid. at G3.1–G3.6 and G3.7.

125 Ibid. at G3.6.

126 Ibid. at G5.

127 Ibid. at G5.1.

stage of the project"[128] (from design to implementation) in line with the comprehensive guidance that is now included among its indicators.[129]

Third, the optional criterion on exceptional community benefits has been completely revised. It now applies only to projects that are either led by communities or are explicitly aimed at reducing poverty.[130] And while this criterion previously focused on benefit-sharing *with* communities, it is now equally concerned with the equitable sharing of benefits *within* communities.[131] Lastly, the indicators related to this criterion include a special focus on the demonstration of net positive impacts, in terms of well-being as well as increased levels of participation in decision-making, for marginalized or vulnerable communities, marginalized or vulnerable members of communities, and women.[132]

As a result, just as the first edition of the CCB Standards may have been perceived as being inclined towards its environmental objectives, the third edition of the CCB Standards can be seen as reflecting an increased focus on human rights and social issues. In addition to providing clearer and more robust language relating to the participatory and resource rights of Indigenous Peoples and local communities, the CCB Standards also incorporate protections against discrimination based on gender, race, religion, or sexual orientation. While many of the criteria and indicators in the CCB Standards are clearly derived from international instruments on indigenous rights, the CCBA's inclination not to distinguish Indigenous Peoples from other local communities is manifest in this third edition. For instance, whereas the second edition of the CCB Standards referred to the specific need to identify "Indigenous Peoples" as part of the mapping of communities located in the project zone,[133] the third edition of the CCB Standards subsumes their identification within the broader definition of "communities,"[134] which are defined as "all groups of people—including Indigenous Peoples, mobile peoples and other local communities—who derive income, livelihood or cultural values and other contributions to well-being from the Project Area at the start of the project and/or under the with-project scenario."[135] As well, in its criterion and indicators that relate to legal status and property rights, the third edition of

---

128 Ibid. at G5.
129 Ibid. at G5.2.
130 Ibid. at GL2.
131 Ibid.
132 Ibid. at GL2.4 and GL2.5.
133 CCBA, *CCB Standards Second Edition* at G1.5
134 CCBA, *CCB Standards Third Edition*, at G1.5.
135 Ibid. at fn. 18.

the CCB Standards most notably extends the rights to lands, territories and resources, FPIC, and protection against involuntary settlement to all "Property Rights Holders,"[136] and not simply to Indigenous Peoples as is the case under UNDRIP.

5. CONCLUSION

This chapter has uncovered similarities and differences in how the human rights of Indigenous Peoples and forest-dependent communities have been addressed in two important sites of law within the complex legal framework for REDD+. On the whole, the adoption of human rights followed a similar trajectory in both the UNFCCC and CCBA. Whereas human rights issues, standards, and principles were initially accorded little recognition in the initial stages of law-making in either site, these eventually became an integral part of the legal infrastructure developed by the UNFCCC COP and the CCB Standards Committee for jurisdictional and project-based REDD+ activities. In both cases, the emergence of rights in the context of REDD+ are moreover related to the growing importance of human rights norms and perspectives to the fields of climate change[137] and conservation.[138] Finally, it is striking that both sites recognize, albeit in varying ways, the rights and interests of both Indigenous Peoples and other non-indigenous communities.

On the other hand, these two sites differ significantly in their conception and articulation of the rights of Indigenous Peoples and forest-dependent communities. To be sure, the CCBA goes much further than the UNFCCC in the extent and depth with which these rights are protected. Unlike the Cancún Agreements, the third edition of the CCB Standards most notably recognizes the importance of rights to lands and resources, FPIC, and protection against involuntary settlement. These levels of detail and ambition are not wholly surprising given the aim of the CCBA to

---

[136] Ibid. at G5.

[137] Lavanya Rajamani, "The Increasing Currency and Relevance of Rights-Based Perspectives in the International Negotiations on Climate Change" (2010) 22:3 *Journal of Environmental Law* 391.

[138] On the concept of rights-based approaches to conservation, see Jodoin. For instance, Conservation International, The Nature Conservancy, and the Wildlife Conservation Society are partners in both the CCBA and the Conservation Initiative on Human Rights: Conservation Initiative on Human Rights, "Conservation and Human Rights Framework" (2010) available at: https://iucn.org/about/work/programmes/social_policy/sp_themes_hrande/scpl_cihr/.

provide certification standards that could ensure that carbon sequestration projects would deliver multiple and significant social benefits beyond compliance with existing international law. As well, the multi-stakeholder structure and the iterative manner in which the CCB Standards were developed provided unique opportunities for adopting stronger rights and protections for Indigenous Peoples and forest-dependent communities than the UNFCCC's consensus-based, state-centred multilateral process and all of the political compromises that it might require on such a sensitive issue as indigenous rights. These factors also help explain why the UNFCCC and the CCBA differ in their treatment of the distinctive status and rights of Indigenous Peoples. While the Cancún Agreements maintain a clear distinction between the rights of Indigenous Peoples and forest-dependent communities that is more consistent with existing international instruments, the third edition of the CCB Standards essentially does away with this distinction and provides similar rights and protections to both categories of rights-holders.

This brief comparison of the development and articulation of human rights across these two sites of law for REDD+ raises numerous research questions that should be of interest to international legal scholars. One key research question relates to the complementarity and tensions between different rationales for integrating greater respect for the rights of Indigenous Peoples and forest-dependent communities in the design and implementation of REDD+ activities. For one thing, the recognition and protection of human rights in the context of REDD+ may result from a principled desire to uphold the rights and dignity of Indigenous Peoples and other communities as part of the broader struggle for environmental justice.[139] For another, respect for the rights, participation, and knowledge of indigenous and non-indigenous communities may also be justified for instrumental reasons due to the practical benefits that the engagement and empowerment of these communities may offer for efforts to reduce carbon emissions from forestry-based sources.[140] As I explore in my on-going research on the transnational legal process for REDD+, the differences between these two types of motivations may ultimately help explain variations in the manner and extent to which human rights are recognized and protected in the context of REDD+.

---

[139] David Schlosberg and David Carruthers, "Indigenous Struggles, Environmental Justice, and Community Capabilities" (2010) 10:4 *Global Environmental Politics* 12.

[140] Caleb Stevens et al., *Securing Rights, Combating Climate Change. How Strengthening Community Forest Rights Mitigates Climate Change* (Washington, DC: WRI and RRI, 2014).

Another key line of scholarly inquiry concerns the relationship between different sites of law in the complex legal framework for REDD+. The field of REDD+ is now governed by multiple sites of law that are characterized by different forms and modes of law-making.[141] As a comparison of the UNFCCC and the CCBA makes clear, sites of law for REDD+ vary in terms of the actors that are engaged in law-making, the deliberative character of the process of law-making, and the nature of authority as well as the degree of formalization that legal norms may ultimately embody as a result. In turn, these key differences in the nature of law-making may be expected to affect the effectiveness and future evolution of legal norms relating to the rights of Indigenous Peoples and forest-dependent communities within these two sites of law and beyond. As such, the complex legal framework for REDD+ offers a rich empirical environment for studying how different sites of law such as the UNFCCC and the CCBA operate and exert influence.[142] Other sites of law that are of particular interest with respect to the intersections between human rights and REDD+ that could form part of such an inquiry include the World Bank FCPF, the UN-REDD, and the REDD+ SES, each of which operates in very different ways.[143]

A related set of research questions could also address the increasing fragmentation between the rules that these different sites of law have provided for the design and implementation of REDD+.[144] As I have shown above, the heterogeneity of international law in the field of REDD+ is reflected not only in the different ways in which the UNFCCC and CCBA address the rights of Indigenous Peoples and forest-dependent communities, but also in the distinct types of REDD+ activities that they aim to govern, respectively jurisdictional REDD+ programmes and REDD+ projects. Additional research is needed to discuss the fragmentation of international

---

141 Corbera and Schroeder.

142 With respect to a multilateral environmental agreement like the UNFCCC, see Jutta Brunée, "COPing with Consent: Law-Making Under Multilateral Environmental Agreements" (2002) 15:1 *Leiden Journal of International Law* 1. With respect to a non-state certification programme like the CCBA, see Benjamin Cashore, Graeme Auld, and Deanna Newsom, *Governing Through Markets: Forest Certification and the Emergence of Non-State Authority* (New Haven: Yale University Press, 2004).

143 Nicholas Moss and Ruth Nussbaum, "A Review of Three REDD+ Safeguard Initiatives" FCPF and UN-REDD, June 2011, at 6–9.

144 See also Charlotte Streck and John Costenbader, *Standards for Results-Based REDD+ Finance Overview and Design Parameters Standards for Results-Based REDD+ Finance Overview and Design Parameters* (Washington, DC: Climate Focus, 2012).

law in the context of REDD+ and the opportunities that exist for greater divergence and convergence in the development and implementation of standards applicable to different types of REDD+ activities. Some scholars have already discussed how the experience of carrying out REDD+ projects could feed into the jurisdictional readiness efforts of developing countries in which they are implemented[145] as well as generate and disseminate lessons that may be of value for the pursuit of REDD+ in other countries.[146] In time, it will also be possible to explore the indirect and intersecting pathways through which the design and application of rights-related standards applicable to REDD+ projects may have exerted influence on a broader set of laws and governance arrangements in the forestry and natural resource sectors in developing countries.[147]

One final question that should be of interest to international legal scholars has to do with the normative implications of the diffusion and transformation of human rights as they have come into contact with multiple sites of law in the complex legal framework for REDD+. To be sure, the notion that a non-state market-driven system of governance such as a certification programme could serve to enhance the level of protection accorded to the rights of local populations in developing countries raises important questions about democratic legitimacy, participation, and accountability. Most importantly perhaps, the significant variation with which the distinctive character, status, and rights of Indigenous Peoples have been maintained or not raises fundamental questions about the normative basis upon which marginalized groups may claim special protections in international law.[148] In this regard, it will be important to compare the experience of developing and implementing human rights standards and protections in the context of other mechanisms (such as the CDM) or other regimes (such as biodiversity).

---

[145] Frances Seymour and Arild Angelsen, "Summary and Conclusions: REDD Wine in Old Wineskins?" in Arild Angelsen, ed., *Realising REDD+. National Strategy and Policy Options* (Bogor, Indonesia: CIFOR, 2009) 293 at 297.

[146] Pamela Jagger, Stibniati Atmadja, Subhrendu K. Pattanayak, Erin Sills, and William D. Sunderlin, "Learning While Doing. Evaluating Impacts of REDD+ Projects" in Angelsen, 281 at 281–2.

[147] Laura Bozzi et al., "The Role of Climate Private Voluntary Programs Affecting Forests: Assessing their Direct and Intersecting Effects" in *Business and Climate Policy: The Potentials and Pitfalls of Private Voluntary Programs* (Tokyo, Japan: United Nations University Press, 2012) 113–42.

[148] Compare Takacs with Patrick Macklem, "Indigenous Recognition in International Law: Theoretical Observations" (2008) 30 *Michigan Journal of International Law* 177 (discussing the unique status and rights held by Indigenous Peoples under international law).

While these lines of inquiry focus on the dynamic set of legal processes that underlie the recognition, articulation, and application of international human rights standards in the context of REDD+, this ambitious research agenda ultimately speaks to the broader set of research questions that one can pose about the nature and implications of the complex legal framework for REDD+. Given that issues relating to the rights of Indigenous Peoples and local communities speak to larger debates about the objectives, challenges, and opportunities of the development and implementation of REDD+,[149] additional research on human rights and REDD+ may assist us in understanding broader truths about international law in the field of REDD+.

---

149 Heike Schroeder and Constance McDermott, "Beyond Carbon: Enabling Justice and Equity in REDD+ Across Levels of Governance" (2014) 19:1 *Ecology & Society* 31.

7. The Convention on Biological Diversity and REDD+

*Andrew Long**

1. INTRODUCTION

The CBD interfaces with REDD+ because the development of REDD+ holds significant potential to impact biodiversity and ecosystem services in forested developing countries, and because securing long-term carbon emissions reductions in tropical forests will require improvements in forest management that may correspond with biodiversity preservation. Thus, the development of REDD+ is important to the CBD regime and, given its experience and expertise, that regime can play a significant role in making REDD+ effective and sustainable.

The CBD is particularly relevant to the emergence of REDD+ as a multiple benefit program, both in terms of making the case that REDD+ should be conceived of as a multiple benefit program and in operationalizing such a program. Accordingly, much of this chapter discusses REDD+ from a perspective that emphasizes non-carbon considerations, primarily biodiversity and social issues. Nonetheless, because carbon storage is the initial (and likely still the primary) motivation for REDD+, the chapter devotes some attention to explaining why REDD+ should be viewed in terms of multiple benefits and CBD's role in advancing this vision and operationalizing it. Concisely stated, a multiple benefits approach is increasingly recognized as necessary to the long-term viability and stability of REDD+, and CBD is well positioned to fulfill crucial functions in ensuring the legitimacy and accountability of REDD+ measures related to benefits other than carbon storage.

The CBD is also particularly motivated to support REDD+ because it is directly relevant to CBD's purpose and many of its goals, including the 2011–20 Strategic Plan for Biodiversity and the Aichi Biodiversity Targets created under it. As the CBD's institutional bodies recognize, REDD+ impacts on biodiversity may be positive or negative, depending on how and where it is implemented. A number of CBD decisions, technical

* All websites cited in this chapter were accessed on 1 October 2015.

reports, and publications address aspects of REDD+ directly, and the CBD has begun to engage substantively in REDD+ through formal recommendations for safeguards and indicators related to biodiversity protection. Beyond protection of biodiversity in REDD+ implementation, the CBD is particularly attuned to adaptation in forest ecosystems (including the relationship of forest adaptation to REDD+ mitigation goals) and issues concerning indigenous and local communities.

From the perspective of REDD+ participants, the CBD's involvement offers significant potential benefits at multiple scales. Most of these benefits flow from the ability of the CBD to bring significant institutional knowledge, resources, and relationships to the effort of creating a REDD+ program that will work on the ground to realize multiple benefits. At the global scale, the CBD's work in assessing and promoting best practices for REDD+ design and implementation may provide significant governance benefits because it has relatively high credibility on issues of biodiversity protection and securing related social benefits (including, for example, sustainable livelihoods). At the national level, the CBD's pre-existing role in the development of targets and planning mechanisms, as well as implementation strategies, offers perhaps the most direct pathways toward bringing global goals to fruition in specific forested developing countries. Finally, the CBD may assist local communities by promoting, investing (including through expertise), or otherwise facilitating the realization of social and environmental benefits that are most important to sustaining ecosystem services that local communities depend upon.

2. BACKGROUND: LINKAGES BETWEEN CBD AND REDD+

The underlying connection between the CBD and REDD+ grows from the overlap in the issues they address. Tropical forests are immensely important to biodiversity preservation, but preservation of tropical forests is not as easy as some early economic models advocating a forest-carbon mechanism may have assumed and, thus, the experience and expertise that CBD can bring to REDD+ efforts may prove important – even crucial – to developing the idea into a sustainable program that has a meaningful and lasting effect on climate change. But, there is more to the relationship than issue linkage. Institutional and governance considerations play an important role in determining whether issue linkage can produce beneficial synergies. Overall, CBD's approach to REDD+ suggests that the connections between the CBD and REDD+ are likely to prove significant, enduring, and mutually beneficial.

This section of the chapter provides a brief survey of the background necessary to understand these various linkages. It will briefly review relevant developments within the CBD regime to highlight the trends and developments that underlie its current strong interest and growing involvement in REDD+ development. It will then turn briefly to another angle on this relationship and provide context from a forestry perspective on REDD+ and CBD's increasing engagement with the mechanism.

3. THE CBD: REGIME EVOLUTION AND REDD+

The CBD was signed at the 1992 Rio Earth Summit, alongside the UNFCCC. It is a "framework" convention with three overarching objectives: "the conservation of biological diversity, the sustainable use of its components and the fair and equitable sharing of the benefits arising out of the utilization of genetic resources."[1] The CBD's benefit-sharing objective was recently further elaborated through a protocol, one of two protocols that have been negotiated under CBD and are now in force.[2] It is primarily the other two objectives – especially, the conservation of biological diversity, which is in many respects the central and essential objective of the Convention – that motivate the CBD's involvement in REDD+.[3]

[1] CBD, Art. 1.

[2] The Cartagena Protocol on Biosafety to the Convention on Biological Diversity was adopted on 29 January 2000 and entered into force on 11 September 2003. The Nagoya Protocol on Access to Genetic Resources and the Fair and Equitable Sharing of Benefits Arising from their Utilization (ABS) to the Convention on Biological Diversity was adopted on 29 October 2010 and entered into force on 12 October 2014, 90 days after the 50th instrument of ratification.

[3] Conservation of biodiversity has to be understood as CBD's central objective, although attention is often focused on the other, more economically motivated objectives, simply because the conservation of biodiversity is necessary to its sustainable use and to the production of the benefits that CBD seeks to ensure are equitably shared. Although it can be argued that, at times, the benefit-sharing objective of CBD may actually detract from its ability to meet its conservation goals, this chapter need not take a position on that issue and, due to its apparently limited relevance to REDD+, will not discuss the sharing of benefits from genetic resources in any significant depth. See e.g. Jim Chen, "Bioprospect Theory," 7 *Akron Intellectual Property Journal* 19 (2014) (suggesting that the efforts invested in debating biopiracy and related issues squander the world's "extremely small and fragile storehouse of political capital" that should be targeted squarely at biodiversity conservation or other massively important global environmental issues); but cf. Raphaël Billé et al., *COP 10 in Nagoya: A Success for Global Biodiversity Governance?* IDDRI Synthesis (2010), available at: http://www.iddri.org/Publications/Collections/Syntheses/Sy_1006_nagoya%20EN.pdf (suggesting

At least two features of the Convention's text, and evolution of practices therefrom, are relevant to understanding the CBD regime's involvement in REDD+. First, the text creates specific obligations and encouragements for member nations to generate information regarding biodiversity and plans for protecting it. Second, however, the Convention's language is particularly loose with respect to mandating any on-the-ground protection of biodiversity. While the first point is discussed in some detail in section 3.2 of this chapter, the second warrants a brief discussion here.

The Convention's embrace of broad aspirational goals, together with its design as a framework convention contemplating future development, have proven well-suited to institutional adaptation. Rather than focusing on specific and difficult to amend quantitative requirements for biodiversity protection in the way that, for example, the KP fostered UNFCCC attention to quantified emissions reduction requirements, the CBD regime has evolved into a particularly dynamic set of institutions that have explored and often expressly promoted a variety of novel governance approaches. Most notable in this regard are CBD's initiatives to build institutional linkages with other international regimes, including not only those with mandates expressly linked to biodiversity, but also those that relate to issues that affect biodiversity in a broad and long-term way, such as UNFCCC. In other words, the aspirational design of CBD's biodiversity provisions, while perhaps once viewed as grounds for criticizing the Convention, have proven capable of enabling the regime and its various bodies to orient toward the most significant developments and issues affecting biodiversity. CBD's interest and role in REDD+ development is a particularly significant example of this institutional flexibility.

The CBD has evolved in search of approaches to biodiversity conservation that will be effective. The history of efforts to reduce the closely related problems of biodiversity loss and tropical deforestation is marked by missed targets[4] and repeated failures to achieve significant

---

that the Nagoya Protocol is a formal success, but its importance will depend on decisions made by implementing nations). Sharing the benefits of REDD+ is an important issue with which CBD is increasingly concerned, as discussed below, but it has yet to be seen whether sharing benefits from genetic resources development is even relevant to REDD+ in any significant way.

[4] E.g. COP to the CBD, *Decision Adopted by the Conference of the Parties to the Convention on Biological Diversity at its Tenth Meeting*, UNEP/CBD/COP/DEC/X/2 at p. 7 (29 October 2010) ("The 2010 biodiversity target has not been achieved, at least not at the global level. The diversity of genes, species and ecosystems continues to decline, as the pressures on biodiversity remain constant or increase in intensity, mainly as a result of human actions.").

on-the-ground success.[5] CBD's attention to REDD+, in particular, grows from its work in two thematic areas: the forest biodiversity program area, with crossover into the climate change and biodiversity program area. In part, engagement with REDD+ can be understood as a response to frustration with pre-existing forestry efforts. The regime's interest in REDD+ is also informed by its work on the growing threats to biodiversity posed by climate change, and the need to account for them through measures aimed at mitigation, adaptation, or both. For example, in the pre-2010 period, two Ad-Hoc Technical Working Groups examined the interaction of climate change and biodiversity at the direction of the CBD COP.[6]

The present orientation of the CBD regime owes much to the 2010 COP meeting in Nagoya, Japan.[7] Along with adopting the Nagoya Protocol,[8] the COP adopted a strategic plan for the period 2011–2020 centered primarily on the Aichi Biodiversity Targets, that is of particular relevance for understanding the developing interest of the CBD regime in

---

[5] Regarding biodiversity, see e.g. Andrew Long, "Developing Linkages to Preserve Biodiversity," 21 *Yearbook of International Environmental Law* 1 (2012) ("In terms of actual species conservation across the globe, international biodiversity law is not working") and sources cited therein. Regarding tropical deforestation, see e.g. Andrew Long, "Re-orienting REDD Toward Sustainable Forestry: Adaptation and Polycentrism in Global Forest Governance," 6 *Tropical Conservation Science* 384, 386 (2013) ("Across the broad spectrum of international environmental law, there is no more striking example of negotiation failure than efforts to halt deforestation and promote sustainable forest management (SFM) in tropical forests") and sources cited therein.

[6] See generally Secretariat of the Convention on Biological Diversity, *Connecting Biodiversity and Climate Change: Mitigation and Adaptation: Report of the Second Ad Hoc Technical Expert Group on Biodiversity and Climate Change*, CBD Technical Series No. 41 (2009).

[7] The CBD adopted an approach based on setting targets for biodiversity in 2002 with the adoption of the *Strategic Plan for the Convention on Biological Diversity*, which established targets for 2010, further elaborated during the following COP. *Strategic Plan for the Convention on Biological Diversity*, COP 6 Decision VI/26 (2002); *Strategic Plan: Future Evaluation of Progress*, COP 7 Decision VII/30 (2004). The targets were framed as goals to be met by 2010. Although the 2010 goals were clearly found not to have been met, this target-based approach provides an important framework that offers broad value for global environmental governance efforts, and is the context within which the CBD's involvement with REDD+ developed. Further, CBD continued the goal-setting approach in 2010 by establishing a new set of targets for 2020. The process of establishing the 2020 targets (known as the Aichi Biodiversity Targets) at COP 10 in 2010 has helped to shape CDB's involvement with REDD+.

[8] The Nagoya Protocol was adopted on 29 October 2010 in Nagoya, Japan and entered into force on 12 October 2014, 90 days after the fiftieth instrument of ratification.

REDD+ at the time.[9] Ongoing implementation efforts toward meeting the Aichi Biodiversity Targets establish the overarching strategy within which CBD interfaces with REDD+. Further, part of the value of establishing the targets lies in connecting CBD with a broader global environmental governance network that includes other institutions, nongovernmental organizations, and others. Thus, the targets provide a lens for understanding CBD's connection with REDD+ both from within the regime and by placing the regime in a larger context.[10]

To see the relevance of REDD+ for current CBD efforts, it may be useful to consider the lead-up to COP 10. In its 2010 assessment, *Global Biodiversity Outlook 3*, CBD noted that dire predictions for terrestrial biodiversity are grounded to a significant degree in the predictions for tropical forests, including the effects of climate change on these important ecosystems.[11] For the period to 2100, the report identifies land-use change as "the main short-term threat, with climate change and the interactions between these two drivers, becoming increasingly important."[12] For example, the report recognizes a "high risk of dramatic loss of biodiversity and degradation of services from terrestrial ecosystems if certain thresholds are crossed," and cites the "plausible" scenario of a "self-perpetuating cycle" of dieback in the Amazon rainforest as one example.[13] The report's section that frames "alternative paths," which are essentially routes to more desirable outcomes, begins with the statement "[a]lleviating pressure from land use changes in the tropics is essential, if the negative impacts of loss of terrestrial biodiversity and associated ecosystem services are to be minimized" and lists "sustainable forest management" as one of the primary measures required to achieve this desirable outcome.[14] Further,

---

[9] COP to the CBD, *Decision Adopted by the Conference of the Parties to the Convention on Biological Diversity at its Tenth Meeting*, UNEP/CBD/COP/DEC/X/2 (29 October 2010) (stating, in paragraph 1 of the Annexed *Strategic Plan for Biodiversity 2011–2020 and the Aichi Biodiversity Targets*, "The purpose of the Strategic Plan for Biodiversity 2011–2020 is to promote effective implementation of the Convention through a strategic approach, comprising a shared vision, a mission, and strategic goals and targets ('the Aichi Biodiversity Targets'), that will inspire broad-based action by all Parties and stakeholders").

[10] Lisa M. Campbell et al., "Producing Targets for Conservation: Science and Politics at the Tenth Conference of the Parties to the Convention on Biological Diversity," 14 *Global Environmental Politics* 3, 41–63 (August 2014).

[11] Secretariat of the Convention on Biological Diversity, *Global Biodiversity Outlook 3*, at 74 (2010).

[12] Ibid.

[13] Ibid.

[14] Ibid. at 75.

the report highlights the importance of measures in the Brazilian Amazon to avoid dieback, noting that 20 per cent loss of original forest cover is predicted to be both a significant tipping point and the likely outcome of then-current trends by 2020. Although it endorses several types of measures in general, REDD+ is the only specific program under development named in the report for its potential to combat the alarming global terrestrial biodiversity trends.[15] This is indicative of the importance that REDD+ may hold for meeting CBD goals and illustrates why CBD views REDD+ as a particularly important development worthy of engagement. *Global Biodiversity Outlook 3* helped to frame the issues for the CBD's COP 10 meeting in Nagoya, Japan.[16]

The core rationale for the *Strategic Plan for Biodiversity 2011–2020* ("*Strategic Plan*") recognizes that biodiversity "underpins ecosystem functioning and the provision of ecosystem services essential for human well-being" and emphasizes the significance of biodiversity for furthering the objectives of the Millennium Development Goals, including poverty reduction.[17] Thus, CBD emphasizes the connection between biodiversity and human interests, particularly the needs of communities living in developing countries who depend upon ecosystem services directly. CBD seeks to advance sustainable use of biodiversity and to improve the framework for doing so through mainstreaming of biodiversity considerations into development planning and other governance areas. In many cases, this focus overlaps with the attention to tropical forests as among the most significant terrestrial habitats as well as perhaps the most threatened.

The *Strategic Plan* seeks (1) "to promote effective implementation" of the CBD by establishing global targets (the Aichi Biodiversity Targets) to "inspire broad-based action by all Parties and stakeholders," (2) "provide a flexible framework for the establishment of national and regional targets and for enhancing coherence in the implementation of the provisions of the Convention and the decisions of the Conference of the Parties," and (3) "serve as the basis for the development of communication tools capable of attracting the attention of and engaging stakeholders, thereby

---

15 Ibid. (cautioning that such mechanisms "must be carefully designed, as conserving areas of high carbon value will not necessarily conserve areas of high conservation importance" for biodiversity).

16 See e.g., COP to the CBD, *Decision Adopted by the Conference of the Parties to the Convention on Biological Diversity at its Tenth Meeting*, UNEP/CBD/COP/DEC/X/2 at p. 6 (29 October 2010) (referencing *Global Biodiversity Outlook 3* in explaining the rationale for CBD actions adopted by the decision).

17 Ibid.

facilitating the mainstreaming of biodiversity into broader national and global agendas."[18] The Strategic Plan states five broad "strategic goals" and several of the 20 Aichi Biodiversity Targets are grouped under each strategic goal. The goals are:

> Strategic goal A. Address the underlying causes of biodiversity loss by mainstreaming across government and society.
> Strategic goal B. Reduce the direct pressure on biodiversity and promote sustainable use.
> Strategic goal C. Improve the status of biodiversity by safeguarding ecosystems, species, and genetic diversity.
> Strategic goal D. Enhance the benefits to all from biodiversity and ecosystems services.
> Strategic goal E. Enhance implementation through participatory planning, knowledge management and capacity building.

Each of these strategic goals can be seen as relevant to REDD+, as can the biodiversity targets articulated under them. In 2011, the SBSTA of the CBD provided a study of the connections between CBD and REDD+.[19] The report highlights four of the Aichi Biodiversity Targets that are directly relevant to REDD+ development. As stated in *Biodiversity and REDD+*, these are:

(a) By 2020, the rate of loss of all natural habitats, including forests, is at least halved and where feasible brought close to zero, and degradation and fragmentation is significantly reduced (Target 5 of the Strategic Plan);
(b) By 2020 areas under forestry are managed sustainably, ensuring conservation of biodiversity (Target 7);
(c) By 2020, at least 17 per cent of terrestrial areas, especially areas of particular importance for biodiversity and ecosystem services, are conserved (Target 11);
(d) By 2020, ecosystem resilience and the contribution of biodiversity to carbon stocks has been enhanced, through conservation and restoration, including restoration of at least 15 per cent of degraded ecosystems, thereby contributing to climate change mitigation and adaptation and to combating desertification (Target 15).

These are complex and ambitious goals. As in other areas, the CBD has adopted a stance that builds on institutional and issue linkages to promote synergies that may operate at the system level to achieve them.[20] There is

---

18 Ibid. at p. 6.

19 Secretariat of the CBD, *Biodiversity and REDD+*, Technical Series No. 59 (2011).

20 See generally Andrew Long, "Developing Linkages to Preserve Biodiversity."

perhaps no geographic place or policy space where this is a more daunting task than the world's tropical forests.

4. THE FORESTRY CONTEXT OF REDD+: A SETTING FAVORABLE TO CBD ENGAGEMENT

International forest policy has long been among the most divisive and, frankly, unsuccessful corners of international environmental law. Tropical deforestation was among the top issues on the agenda prior to the 1992 Rio Earth Summit, along with climate change and biodiversity policy development. While the latter two issues led to the signing of framework conventions at Rio that have since played a primary role in shaping international policy (UNFCCC and CBD), negotiations related to tropical deforestation quickly descended into insurmountable divisions. The divisions and disagreements that underlaid the negotiation failures have been discussed in detail elsewhere, but a few points are relevant here.[21] Sands and Peel state the overarching global political dynamics well:

> International legal efforts to address forest issues have taken place in the context of the historical loss of the forests of developed countries, and of these states' efforts to ensure that the bulk of remaining forests in developing countries is preserved . . . Attempts by developed countries to "internationalize" forest issues have so far been largely unsuccessful . . . tropical forest resources of developed countries are carefully guarded as part of the national patrimony of these countries.[22]

For this reason, along with the persistent resistance of some developed countries to funding tropical forest-protection measures (due, in part, to significant domestic political actors' economic interest in exploiting them), forest governance has presented a particularly difficult challenge for international environmental law efforts. While the climate change

---

[21] UNCED produced the "Non-legally Binding Authoritative Statement of Principles for a Global Consensus on the Management, Conservation and Sustainable Development of All Types of Forests" (1992 Forest Principles). As Sands and Peel note, "[t]he weakness of this instrument reflects the lack of international consensus on the subject." Philippe Sands and Jacqueline Peel, *Principles of International Environmental Law* (3rd edn, Cambridge: Cambridge University Press, 2012) 497; see also Radaslov S. Dimitrov, "Hostage to Norms: States, Institutions and Global Forest Politics," 5 *Global Environmental Politics* 1, 7 (2005) ("The plan to include negotiations on a forest convention on the agenda for the 1992 UNCED was abandoned at the preparatory stage due to sharp disagreements among governments on the need for such a treaty").

[22] Sands and Peel.

and biodiversity agreements that emerged from the 1992 United Nations Conference on Environment and Development (UNCED) evolved into robust regimes, international governance of forests became a singularly bizarre and dysfunctional charade.[23] This result, seemingly very unfortunate at the time, is directly relevant to REDD+ development, and CBD's involvement with it, in at least two ways.

First, the lack of anything that could plausibly be described as an *effective* public international institution or regime to address the environmental significance of tropical forests fostered the development of intense interest in alternative approaches to governance. This has generated a wealth of governance experimentation, some significant and hard-won lessons about the complexity of forest governance, and a willingness to explore new governance ideas among many of the leading voices in tropical forest governance debates.

Second, the profoundly dysfunctional character of global forest governance – in which institutions apparently existed for the primary purpose of pre-empting effective governance[24] – created a wariness among NGOs, scholars, and others genuinely interested in tropical forest protection that has led to careful attention to on-the-ground results in a way that tends to expose potential problems rather than drown them in false hope. As a matter of governance *evolution*, therefore, it may be time to suggest that – without minimizing the massive losses of the past 25 years in terms of forest extent, biodiversity, and GHG emissions – the horrendous record of public international forest-protection initiatives prior to REDD+ played an important role in creating a socio-political climate that may be able to steer REDD+ development through the exceptionally complex minefield of climate–forest governance. As one of the most respected and competent major international regimes to have developed extensive expertise and experience in tropical forest issues, CBD is well positioned to play a mediating role between the battle-hardened perspective of forest-protection advocates and the sometimes overly optimistic arguments that carried REDD+ to prominence in the UNFCCC, and the broader epistemic community involved in global climate change governance.

---

[23] See generally David Humphrey, *Logjam: Deforestation and Crisis of Global Governance* (Routledge, 2006) (providing a thorough discussion of international politics regarding tropical forests during the 1990s and early 2000s).

[24] Dimitrov ("What is singular and what makes this case interesting is that the [UNFF] was deliberately designed not to deliver any policy output at all, and that *all* participating states wanted this . . . [Thus,] [t]he forest case demonstrates that sometimes states deliberately set up "decoy" international institutions to preempt governance").

Although the concept of "common but differentiated responsibilities" helped to smooth over the divide between developing and developed countries in negotiations related to climate change, at least from the 1992 UNCED through the 2001 US refusal to ratify the KP, there was never a similar conceptual umbrella for the quandary facing tropical forest negotiators. Accordingly, once the negotiations toward a global forests convention failed at UNCED, tropical forest policy entered a period that can be understood as a case study in failure, perverse incentives, and international dialogue that was often counterproductive, if it had any significant effect on forestry practices.[25] Unlike the climate change and biodiversity regimes, efforts to create meaningful international forest-protection law rarely produced anything more than explicitly non-binding agreements to broad and malleable principles.

The widespread support for REDD+, including the enthusiastic support of many international NGOs, grows in large part from the disappointment of prior efforts to promote forest protection through international law. By connecting forests with the more prominent and (in some respects, at least) more successful effort to mobilize the global community to take action on climate change, REDD+ has often seemed a promising means of re-invigorating efforts to combat deforestation.

The primary risk, from the perspective of forest-protection advocates, is that a climate–forest mechanism would be implemented in a way that prioritizes carbon at the expense of the broader environmental and social values of forest ecosystems. Forests face an extremely complex set of threats that suggest successful efforts to address deforestation will require complex multi-level governance that incorporates an understanding of the forests as heterogeneous socio-ecological systems and advances a goal of achieving long-term resilience.[26] For this reason, astute observers of forest policy noted that issues other than carbon storage were likely to play a key role in determining whether REDD+ would achieve its promised gains for forest protection (including, but not limited to, carbon storage), rather than merely joining a long list of formerly promising and ultimately failed efforts.[27]

To some degree, the "plus" in REDD+ is recognition that forests are

---

[25] Ibid.

[26] E.g. Timothy O. Randhir and Ayton Erol, "Emerging Threats to Forests: Resilience and Strategies at System Scale," 4 *American Journal of Plant Sciences* 739 (2013).

[27] E.g. Levin et al., "The Climate Regime as Global Forest Governance: Can Reduced Emissions from Deforestation and Forest Degradation (REDD) initiatives pass a 'dual effectiveness' test?" 10 *International Forestry Review* 538 (2008).

more than mere carbon stores and that such additional values must be taken into account if the mechanism is to succeed over the long term. CBD's expertise and institutional infrastructure related to biodiversity, with its complex web of interconnections to ecosystem services and social considerations, is one of the most valuable assets for ensuring that REDD+ fulfills its broader promise to the countries and local communities most directly connected to forest ecosystems while also advancing the carbon storage and economic goals that motivated the mechanism's acceptance by many developing countries seeking cost-effective ways to reduce carbon emissions globally. For that reason, CBD can give expression to many of the priorities of the forest-protection advocates in a manner that may have significant credibility at the international level.

Ecological and social issues beyond carbon storage are integral to REDD+ success because they are core determinates of whether the mechanism can be sustainable over the long term. From an economic perspective, therefore, these issues that once seemed secondary must be understood as primary factors in determining whether investment in particular REDD+ projects (such as those initiated by NGOs in cooperation with others) or measures (adopted by national governments, for example) are a wise investment over the long term. From a climate change perspective, the ecological and social questions of forest preservation are important not only because they relate to the long-term viability of carbon storage in the forests, but also because they can play a role in addressing adaptation concerns at a broader level. Thus, attention to maintaining forests as productive ecosystems and to the equity of the social systems affecting them has come to play an increasingly important role in establishing REDD+ as a workable long-term climate mechanism. In this way, it has also increasingly merged with the priorities of sustainable preservation of tropical forests that had long suffered from dysfunctional international forest law.

The issues other than carbon storage that affect the success of REDD+ can be loosely grouped into those related to "biodiversity" (often as a proxy for ecosystem services and other environmental considerations) and "social" (including governance and distribution of REDD+ benefits) considerations. These issues were initially viewed as secondary – potential "co-benefits" of carbon storage – particularly in the UNFCCC context, but have increasingly come to be understood as an essential component of a successful REDD+ mechanism.

The lynchpin in this nexus of interests is precisely the complex interconnection between human and ecological systems that CBD has increasingly targeted as the means of achieving its broad biodiversity preservation goals. Therefore, along with independent certification entities and NGOs that promote attention to ecological and social issues, CBD is well placed to play an important role in the development of REDD+ as a sustainable carbon storage and forest preservation mechanism over the long term.

Momentum for developing REDD+ into a mechanism or program that can realize multiple benefits coincides with the international community's increasing attention to adaptation concerns. Thus, REDD+'s multiple benefits can be understood as advancing both the mitigation and adaptation goals of the climate change regime.[28] While the connection may be somewhat less direct than in the case of UNFCCC, the CBD bodies also recognize that climate change mitigation and adaptation are priorities to meeting that Convention's overarching goals. Indeed, if REDD+ is understood broadly as a multiple benefit mechanism – rather than narrowly as a low-cost carbon storage opportunity – it corresponds rather closely with the CBD's fundamental objectives.[29] Not only does successful long-term sustainable management of tropical forests hold great promise for improving biodiversity preservation, it also tends to promote the development of sustainable economic use of biodiversity components and more equitable social arrangements in order to promote the long-term social sustainability of the measures incentivized through REDD+. In this broader sense, then, the goals of CBD are closely aligned with the priorities of REDD+ development.

5. MULTI-LEVEL GOVERNANCE AND CBD's ROLE(S) IN REDD+

REDD+ is a multi-level governance mechanism (or program) in that it necessarily operates at the international level and within national and subnational contexts. Accordingly, scalar and context-specific considerations play important roles in CBD's engagement with REDD+. This section will provide a brief theoretical framework for thinking about CBD's engagement with REDD+ as a global governance development, and also as it applies in more specific geographic contexts.

---

[28] See generally, Andrew Long, "REDD+, Adaptation, and Sustainable Forest Management: Toward Effective Polycentric Global Forest Governance," 6 *Tropical Conservation Science* 384 (2013).

[29] CBD, Art. 1.

6. GLOBAL ENGAGEMENT: CBD AND POLYCENTRIC GOVERNANCE OF REDD+

While many discussions of REDD+ and governance focus on the national or subnational governance considerations related to implementation, REDD+ may also hold important global governance lessons. This is especially true where it intersects with regimes such as the CBD. To understand the engagement of CBD, a major international regime in its own right, with the burgeoning development of REDD+, two theoretical contributions to the literature seem particularly helpful: (1) polycentric governance and (2) regime complexes in global environmental governance.

The initial insight behind polycentric governance is that hierarchical arrangements of authority may not always be the best available option. From this relatively simple insight emerges an increasingly complex literature on climate change governance, in particular, that recognizes the limitations of the Kyoto-style "top down" approach to a problem as complex (politically as well as socio-ecologically) as climate change.

REDD+, in many respects, epitomizes the types of governance arrangements that can be characterized as polycentric governance. Although the UNFCCC plays a particularly important role, it is not the "highest" authority in the sense that a federal government may have authority over states or provinces within it. The voluntary market, bilateral agreements, NGO-led efforts, and other contributors are giving rise to a plurality of experiences that constitute REDD+ and which interact with UNFCCC in a variety of ways. Even within any particular manifestation of REDD+, vertical authority need not be strictly hierarchical, but may be shared and divided in context-specific and sometimes novel ways. In many instances, especially those most closely aligned with public international law institutions, international actors may operate to incentivize, constrain, and monitor national actors who implement REDD+ on the ground. This is clearly not the only model of REDD+. In the voluntary market, for example, lines of authority do not fit within a traditional model and may not even resemble hierarchy. Instead, subnational states may collaborate independently of international or even national action, or may effectively bypass national governments and operate in direct collaboration with international organizations that cannot claim traditional legal authority "over" the activities on the ground.

While these innovative arrangements may, as the polycentric governance literature suggests, provide an important degree of flexibility for necessary experimentation to occur, they do also pose some challenges with regard to major governance considerations such as accountability and legitimacy. Much of the opposition and concern that has been voiced with regard to pricing forest carbon arises from these types of considerations. Concerns about so-called "carbon cowboys," who may exploit forest-carbon pricing for profit to the detriment of indigenous peoples or without securing any significant practical gains, illustrate the problem.

In the context of governance experimentation involving a wide array of international, national, and subnational actors who may or may not be formally connected to a well-defined legal regime, how does one distinguish legitimate from illegitimate efforts? And what lines of accountability protect the communities on the ground in and around forests, as well as the investors (public or private) who contribute? These, of course, are some of the issues that gave rise to the "safeguards" discussions under the UNFCCC and elsewhere, and they are real concerns. CBD's engagement is important for its ability to help sort out these governance challenges, as well as the social–environmental issues highlighted above.

7. NATIONAL AND SUBNATIONAL ENGAGEMENT: IMPLEMENTATION SUPPORT

Pre-existing experience with CBD's information-generation and monitoring provisions can provide a baseline and framework for designing, implementing, and monitoring REDD+ measures that achieve the safeguards and promote multiple benefits. National compliance with CBD provisions may establish the knowledge base necessary to address biodiversity-related concerns in REDD+ implementation.[30]

Among the most interesting aspects of this increasing engagement is the potential for CBD-driven activity to crossover into REDD+ development and implementation. For example, policy interest in biodiversity monitoring as a part of REDD+ – whether formally within the UNFCCC system or, more commonly, as an adjunct to other aspects of REDD+ – has grown significantly in recent years.

---

[30] See e.g. Till Pistorius et al., *Greening REDD+: Challenges and Opportunities for Forest Biodiversity Conservation* (Policy Paper, University of Freiburg, Germany (2010)) at 14 ("All developing countries that are currently preparing for REDD+ are Parties to the CBD. Most of them have elaborated national reports for the CBD that can help in developing national biodiversity objectives and indicators for REDD+").

8. FUNCTIONAL ROLE OF THE CBD IN REDD+: TOWARD MULTIPLE BENEFITS

8.1 Regime Complexes and Issue Linkage

Among the more useful concepts for understanding the global governance implications of CBD's role in REDD+ is the "regime complex" discussed, primarily, in international relations literature as a mode of governance that has emerged in the context of global environmental governance.[31] Perhaps the most careful and precise definition of a regime complex is "a network of three or more international regimes that relate to a common subject matter; exhibit overlapping membership; and generate substantive, normative, or operative interactions recognized as potentially problematic whether or not they are managed effectively."[32]

For the purposes of this chapter, a regime complex can be described as a system of institutions that arises from loose but meaningful couplings around a particular issue area.[33] This combines two key insights. First, that a regime complex is a system and, thus, has systemic properties, such as emergence from interacting components.[34] Second, it captures the essential feature of Keohane and Victor's description of a regime complex as a "loosely coupled set of specific regimes," thereby situating it between a fully integrated regime and a fully fragmented set of institutions.[35]

Regime complexes have been described for a range of international environmental concerns, beginning with Kal Raustiala and David Victor's article "The Regime Complex for Plant Genetic Resources," which coined the term (if not necessarily the concept). Although it seems arguable

---

[31] E.g. Amandine Orsini et al., "Regime Complexes: A Buzz, a Boom, or a Boost for Global Governance?" *Global Governance* 19, 27–39 (2013) (introducing a journal issue on regime complexes and providing background); see also Kal Raustiala and David Victor, "The Regime Complex for Plant Genetic Resources," *International Organizations* 58(2): 277–310 (2004) (coining the term).

[32] Orsini et al. For further discussion of the definition of a regime complex, see Andrew Long, "Complexity in Global Energy-Environment Governance," 15 *Minnesota Journal of Law, Science, & Technology* 1055 (2014) and sources cited therein.

[33] E.g. Thomas Gehring and Benjamin Faude, "Dynamics of Regime Complexes: Micro Foundations and Systemic Effects," *Global Governance* 19, 119–130 (2013) (discussing regime complexes as "systems of institutions").

[34] See generally Orsini (beginning its discussion of the concept by noting: "A group or a system has properties that differ from those of its constitutive parts").

[35] Robert O. Keohane and David G. Victor, "The Regime Complex for Climate Change," 9 *Perspectives on Politics* 7 (2011).

whether a regime complex exists for forest issues, despite the proliferation of instruments and institutions in the area,[36] there is little reason to doubt the existence of a regime complex for climate change. Indeed, Keohane and Victor offer a particularly helpful analysis of regime complexes using the climate change regime complex as their case study.[37]

The "regime complex" concept may help to understand the roles of various actors in the development of REDD+, which is part of the climate change regime (e.g., UNFCCC decisions provide a framework for at least some aspects of its development), but is also a part of something larger: the climate change regime complex. It is as an element of this larger system of loosely coupled institutions that CBD's role in REDD+ can best be understood. This point is implicit in Keohane and Victor's analysis of the climate change regime complex, which places the UNFCCC at the center but notes the growing significance of REDD+ in bringing together multiple actors in the loose couplings characteristic of regime complexes.

Keohane and Victor's analysis of the climate change regime complex

---

[36] There are two basic problems with attempting to define a regime complex for forestry. First, the variety of institutions and instruments that address forestry often work at cross purposes. See e.g. Peter Glück et al., "Core Components of the International Forest Regime Complex," in Jeremy Rayner, Alexander Buck, and Pia Katila (eds), *Embracing Complexity: Meeting the Challenges of International Forest Governance – A Global Assessment Report Prepared by the Global Forest Expert Panel on the International Forest Regime* (Vienna, IUFRO World Series vol. 28, 2010) (acknowledging this problem). More fundamentally, however, it is arguable, at best, whether all of the components of the regime complex actually share even the broadest, most general purpose that could give coherence to a regime complex. See ibid. (suggesting that interest in improved global forest governance, perhaps around the "sustainable forest management" concept may provide such coherence); but see Dimitrov (describing many of the would-be components as "decoys designed to pre-empt governance"). Forestry is particularly contested terrain in global politics and, thus, determining whether a regime complex exists in the area may be more a matter concerned with the definitional breadth of the regime complex concept than of studying the particular actors involved in forestry. No one disputes that many actors, for various reasons and in various contexts, want to preserve the right to destroy forests (including, for example, large-scale timber harvesting, as well as forest clearing to support plantation agriculture) in a way that virtually no actor could argue for a right to transform the climate or even eliminate biodiversity, both of which are purely byproducts of other activities and are not performed simply for the sake of doing so.

[37] Robert O. Keohane and David G. Victor, "The Regime Complex for Climate Change," 9 *Perspectives on Politics* 7 (2011). For background literature articulating Keohane's influential neoliberal institutionalist perspective on regimes, which influences his views on regime complexes, see e.g. Robert O. Keohane and Joseph S. Nye, Jr., *Power and Interdependence* (3rd edn, New York: Addison Wesley Longman, 2001 [1977]).

offers six normative criteria for assessing the value of particular couplings associated with a regime complex: coherence, accountability, determinacy, sustainability, epistemic quality, and fairness. These criteria offer one of the most helpful ways of understanding the value of CBD to REDD+, and thus frame the remaining normative discussion.

8.2 Normative Evaluation of CBD's Role in REDD+

CBD can play a valuable role in enhancing governance related to the safeguards in REDD+ and, ultimately, in developing multiple benefits, which can enhance the overall value of the program for climate change and other socio-ecological concerns (including, but not limited to, biodiversity conservation). Consideration of the factors suggested by Keohane and Victor for evaluating regime complex interaction – coherence, accountability, determinacy, sustainability, epistemic quality, and fairness – provides a way of probing the global governance impacts of CBD's involvement in REDD+, as elaborated below. It is not necessary to detail the contours of the climate change regime complex as a whole, nor even as it relates to REDD+ generally, in order to assess the potential role of CBD in this regard, as well as offering some tentative conclusions on the extent to which CBD is fulfilling this potential effectively. The evaluation is narrowly focused on CBD as it interacts with REDD+, and broader inquiries regarding the interaction of CBD's role with other systemic forces may be needed in future research for a more thorough understanding of overall REDD+ development, let alone the climate change regime as a whole.

Notably, the criteria applied not only describe the ways in which CBD may contribute to the climate change regime complex through REDD+, but also the extent to which REDD+ may contribute to the goals of CBD, which roughly align with an evolving biodiversity regime complex. Thus, although the analysis is relatively narrowly focused, it may serve multiple purposes.

(a) Epistemic quality and multiple benefits

CBD has played an important role in promoting a vision of REDD+ as a multiple benefit mechanism and in establishing the linkages between REDD+, biodiversity, and social/development concerns. Its engagement in this respect, and overall until recently, has primarily taken the form of information-generation, analysis, and dissemination. Thus, it has served to enhance the epistemic quality of REDD+ and, thereby, the climate change regime by providing a reliable source of information on the aspects of REDD+ that reach beyond carbon. In this respect, CBD may play a role that is similar in some ways to the role that IPCC plays in the broader discussions of climate change, albeit focused on the crossover between biodiversity and climate change in tropical forests.

Several CBD publications illustrate the point. For example, the 2009 publication *Connecting Biodiversity and Climate Change Mitigation and Adaptation* included among its "key messages" two relevant points. First, it urged the use of "Ecosystem-based adaptation, which integrates the use of biodiversity and ecosystem services into an overall adaptation strategy" in a way that would seem to promote a multiple benefit perspective on forest adaptation to climate change in collaboration with REDD+ development. Second, and more directly, the publication urges a multiple benefit approach to REDD+, stating:

> A portfolio of land use management activities, including the protection of natural forest and peatland carbon stocks, the sustainable management of forests, the use of native assemblages of forest species in reforestation activities, sustainable wetland management, restoration of degraded wetlands and sustainable agricultural practices can contribute to the objectives of both the UNFCCC and CBD. These activities, in addition to stringent reductions in fossil fuel emissions of greenhouse gases, play an important role in limiting increases in atmospheric greenhouse gas concentrations and human-induced climate change.[38]

Thus, just as REDD+ was beginning to gain solid support in the UNFCCC, CBD was urging the inclusion of biodiversity and social considerations in its implementation. Given the expertise and legitimacy with regard to ecosystem protection issues, and experience in tropical forests in particular, its endorsement of this view of REDD+ may have been significant in developing the credibility of REDD+ as a multiple benefit mechanism at a time when concerns regarding REDD+ non-climate implications were becoming prominent.

CBD has continued to develop the quality of information on this point. The 2011 publication *REDD+ and Biodiversity*, for example, provides a probing assessment of the risks and the potential benefits of REDD+ for biodiversity, both at the broad level and in examining particular experiences relevant to REDD+ development. Through this and other work, CBD has played a significant role in providing institutional support to the developing scientific and policy arguments for viewing REDD+ broadly as a mechanism with the potential to advance multiple policy objectives and, in particular, biodiversity conservation. Among other things, this work may be relevant to incorporating the concerns of REDD+ opponents into design and, thereby, transforming them into allies and supporters.

---

[38] https://www.cbd.int/doc/publications/cbd-ts-41-en.pdf at 10.

More recently, the CBD partnered with other organizations to produce the publication *Biodiversity and Livelihoods: REDD+ Benefits*, which examines the linkages between REDD+, biodiversity preservation and sustainable use, and social issues related to poverty and development. In it, CBD provides evidence and argument for an approach that emphasizes both biodiversity and development in REDD+ implementation. To the extent that the report is understood as credible, it provides a strong basis for developing REDD+ along lines that will address many of the social and ecological concerns that have been raised, thus building it into a multiple benefits program.

(b) Policy coherence and determinacy for ensuring multiple benefits

CBD's role in REDD+ development has gone beyond promoting multiple benefits through information, especially since COP 10 Decision X/33 in 2010. CBD has recently become active in articulating and promoting measures necessary to actualize the vision of REDD+ as a multiple benefits mechanism by taking steps to enhance the coherence of an approach to actualizing REDD+ safeguards and, perhaps, a multiple benefits approach.

Keohane and Victor discuss "coherence" of a regime complex in terms of compatibility and mutuality of reinforcement, citing the ability to channel resources from international emissions trading to compensation for developing country forest activities as an example.[39] The coherence promoted by CBD's recent work is similar, but relates to the ability of international incentives for forest-carbon activities to ensure or promote benefits beyond carbon.

Determinacy, as articulated by Keohane and Victor, relates to rules that have "a readily ascertainable normative content."[40] In other words, it relates to the ability of assessing compliance or evaluating quality in implementation. In the context of REDD+, CBD's contribution to determinacy relates to the ability to ensure that safeguards are being met or that multiple benefits are being achieved.

CBD has begun to play a significant role in the development of monitoring approaches to the "safeguards" required under UNFCCC decisions and in connection with broader efforts to promote biodiversity preservation through REDD+. While this work continues to improve epistemic quality, it also begins to enhance determinacy and coherence

---

[39] Keohane and Victor, at 16–17.

[40] Ibid. at 17 (quoting Thomas Franck, *The Power of Legitimacy among Nations* (New York, Oxford: Oxford University Press, 1990) at 52).

by providing a set of specific and measurable criteria for assessing the achievement of safeguards or multiple benefits that can be applied across contexts, thus strengthening the linkages within the regime complex and promoting the flow of resources to achieve goals related to biodiversity and social considerations as affected by REDD+.

Picking up on this and related themes in the broader dialogue, CBD has become actively involved in the development of REDD+ safeguards for biodiversity. For example, the SBSTA published draft advice on standards, indicators, and other monitoring tools related to the impact of REDD+ on biodiversity in 2012. It identified the following four areas of focus:

1. clarifying land tenure issues, and aiming for integrated land-use planning at the landscape level;
2. building on existing national biodiversity-related guidance and experience with the implementation of relevant decisions of the Convention on Biological Diversity;
3. developing and applying national level REDD+ safeguards, drawing upon the three main existing safeguard initiatives; and
4. using national safeguard processes to ensure that REDD+ achieves additional social and environmental benefits.

At COP 11, the CBD COP adopted Decision XI/19,[41] which formally embraced many of the SBSTA's recommendations on each of these areas. Although much of the language in the decision is couched as a warning of the risks against which the safeguards are designed to protect, the decision nonetheless also suggests the potential positive benefits, noting that along with reducing risks, the "Safeguards . . . may also enhance multiple benefits" of REDD+ development for biodiversity, "thereby supporting the credibility and long-term success of" the mechanism.[42]

(c) Accountability, fairness, and sustainability: CBD and the vitality of REDD+

REDD+ policy is developing quickly and the CBD's involvement appears to be growing deeper and more significant all the time. There is increasing

---

[41] The formal title of Decision XI/19 is *Biodiversity and climate change related issues: advice on the application of relevant safeguards for biodiversity with regard to policy approaches and positive incentives on issues relating to reducing emissions from deforestation and forest degradation in developing countries; and the role of conservation, sustainable management of forests and enhancement of forest carbon stocks in developing countries.*

[42] Decision XI/19 at paragraph 3.

reason to believe that the success of REDD+ in achieving multiple benefits on the ground, although it creates some trade-offs with regard to volume of carbon storage in the short term, may prove essential to the long-term success of REDD+.[43] CBD may play a crucial role in establishing REDD+ as a program with lasting value to the extent that it can help facilitate accountability through the development of coherent and determinate rules that will achieve results that are both ecologically sustainable and socially perceived as just (or fair) by participants. This is a tall order and the likelihood of success remains uncertain. Nonetheless, keeping these long-term goals in mind is important in assessing CBD's role, and in encouraging its continued development as an institution that can develop and promote the widespread adoption of policy rules based on accurate information.

It is important that efforts to develop a REDD+ program with long-term significance for climate change and tropical forest ecosystems do not suffer the illusion that this is a simple or quick fix. Forest politics has been a virtual case study in failure for multiple complex reasons, and REDD+ is no panacea. Achieving a REDD+ program that actually secures multiple benefits in a sustainable way "could be enormously challenging" and "is unlikely to be achieved as an isolated endeavor but rather as part of a larger effort to promote more holistic and synergistic multi-level governance for sustainable development."[44]

CBD's work in the development of standards contributes directly to accountability with regard to safeguards. Accountability is an especially important consideration for this developing aspect of REDD+ because increased accountability tends to promote legitimacy. In other words, by increasing confidence that safeguards provisions have concrete meaning and are being complied with (and, where relevant, multiple benefits are being realized), CBD's work tends to reduce concerns about the impact of REDD+ on biodiversity and social issues and may increase support. Further, CBD's technical expertise related to biodiversity is likely to increase the determinacy of standards through the development

---

43 See generally Ingrid J. Visseren-Hamakers et al., "Trade-offs, Co-benefits and Safeguards: Current Debates on the Breadth of REDD+," 4 *Current Opinion in Environmental Sustainability* 646–53 (2012) (reviewing the scientific literature and concluding that "many scholars have argued that both biodiversity and sustainable development are vital to REDD+ success, especially in the long term"). Similar points have been made in the legal literature. E.g. Andrew Long, "Global Climate Governance to Enhance Biodiversity and Well-Being: Integrating Non-State Networks and Public International Law in Tropical Forests," 41 *Environmental Law* 95, 126 (2011) ("REDD's success is fundamentally linked with its ability to generate cobenefits").

44 Visseren-Hamakers.

of scientifically valid and clearly defined content that can be applied to ensure compliance. Moreover, as CBD is one of several institutional actors involved in this work, it may increase the policy coherence at least in this limited topical area across multiple actors and geographical areas. As explained above, CBD's interaction with REDD+ has emphasized the importance of biodiversity and social issues for sustainability of REDD+ and the gains achieved, which includes CBD's involvement in promoting what Keohane and Victor describe as "fairness" as related to considerations such as benefit-sharing. Finally, CBD's recognized authority in the area of biodiversity policy (including the relationship to social issues) and its fairly extensive technical work related to REDD+ contribute significantly to the epistemic quality of REDD+ development as it relates to biodiversity.

REDD+ as a multiple benefit mechanism brings together many of the most challenging concerns of international and global environmental and social policy, some of which have heretofore appeared essentially intractable despite waves of policy initiatives over decades. If it succeeds in a meaningful way, it may be an indication of a level of maturation in global environmental governance that is necessary to enable real progress on the most difficult and pressing challenges of the twenty-first century.[45] In other words, it would represent the culmination of extensive practical and theoretical work in the past, social learning by doing, and more recent efforts to conceptualize, articulate, and implement.

9. CONCLUSION

REDD+ is directly relevant to the goals of the CBD, and CBD can serve as an influential voice in advocating and developing REDD+ in a manner that is sensitive to biodiversity and related social concerns. CBD's involvement may increase the ability of REDD+ to achieve multiple benefits as well as its ability to meet climate mitigation and adaptation priorities sustainably over the long term. CBD explicitly acknowledges the importance of REDD+ and has evolved to engage in its development. This relationship appears to be progressing in a way that can enhance forest governance for the benefit of both climate and biodiversity goals.

---

[45] See: Andrew Long, "Global Integrationist Multimodality: Global Environmental Governance and Fourth Generation Environmental Law," 21 *Journal of Environmental and Sustainability Law* 169 (2015) (discussing REDD+ in the larger context of global environmental governance evolution).

Several aspects of CBD's involvement in REDD+ reflect broader trends in the development of global environmental governance, primarily because REDD+ reflects the type of multi-institutional and multi-scalar cooperation that is likely necessary to address complex global environmental challenges. One aspect of this – CBD's significant role in developing REDD+ toward a more multi-issue focus – is central to CBD's involvement in REDD+ development. CBD's eager participation in the development of information and policy infrastructure for a multiple benefits form of REDD+, as well as safeguards mandated by UNFCCC decisions, helps to explain why it is becoming an increasingly important voice in REDD+ development and implementation. It may even prove among the more important actors in REDD+'s long-term success.

By enhancing the quality of knowledge and information related to socio-ecological aspects of REDD+, CBD may be enhancing the coherence of the climate change regime complex and promoting its determinacy. In turn, this work may also be contributing to the accountability and legitimacy of REDD+, at least insofar as REDD+ is understood as necessarily involving more than carbon storage, as appears not only necessary but also increasingly recognized. Ultimately, this work may lay a groundwork for meaningfully ensuring the fairness, legitimacy, and, if effective, sustainability of REDD+ benefits for forests and forest communities. To the extent that REDD+ furthers the goals of reducing climate change and promoting adaptation, and/or the conservation and sustainable use of biodiversity, the CBD's focus on the epistemic quality of REDD+ and growing involvement in realizing the benefits thereof directly contribute to the broader success of the climate change regime complex and to the realization of biodiversity-related goals.

PART III

GLOBAL GOVERNANCE FOR REDD+

8. Addressing drivers of deforestation and forest degradation through international law

*Charlotte Streck and Michaela Schwedeler**

1. INTRODUCTION: INTERNATIONAL LAW, DEFORESTATION AND REDD+

The reduction of deforestation depends on national commitment and effective policies in tropical countries that address drivers of deforestation. Forest conversion and exploitation are driven by global demand for commodities from forest regions, local and subsistence agriculture, fuel wood extraction and infrastructure development. In addition to these direct drivers, deforestation is also linked to indirect drivers. These indirect forces include international and national processes that influence human activities, such as changes in economic growth, population growth, commodity prices, diet shifts or technological change.

Accountability for reducing the impacts of economic production and trade of products generated on tropical forest lands is shared by all actors across the supply chains, from farmers to processors, traders, retailers and consumers. In addition, the legislators and policy makers are called upon to provide a policy environment that is conducive to forest conservation and sustainable land use. To address deforestation drivers, measures will need to be taken at the local, national or international level depending on where the driving factors operate. Different actors operate at each scale, though their decisions can be interrelated and influence each other. As international drivers of deforestation are difficult to control by national or subnational actors, such as national governments or local authorities, it is easier for these actors to concentrate on the sphere they can influence most. Consequently, the majority of the REDD+ strategies and interventions proposed by countries that have to deal with tropical deforestation issues focus on proximate and national drivers (Angelsen 2009, Kissinger et al. 2012, Sunderlin et al. 2014). That said, for REDD+ strategies to eventually be successful,

* All websites cited in this chapter were accessed on 1 October 2015.

actors at all three geographical scales will have to be reached, including international drivers.

International law has a role to play in addressing deforestation drivers. International legal instruments can formulate positive incentives for reducing deforestation, the most prominent example being the REDD+ framework under the UNFCCC. Treaties can on the other hand also create perverse incentives that – intentionally or not – drive deforestation. Liberalized trade, for example can lead to higher prices for agricultural commodities, increase deforestation and reduce welfare in resource abundant countries.

This chapter aims at analyzing international law instruments that can be used to assist tropical countries in reducing emissions from deforestation. We will set out by giving a brief overview over the main direct and indirect drivers of deforestation (section 2) which is followed by a discussion of the role of international law in reducing deforestation drivers (section 3). To illustrate the potential role of legal instruments in addressing drivers of deforestation, we describe in section 4 the role of the multilateral treaties, soft law instruments and regional agreements in more detail. Section 5 summarizes and concludes.

2. DRIVERS OF DEFORESTATION AND FOREST DEGRADATION

The deforestation and degradation of tropical forest areas are caused by a variety of direct and indirect factors. Direct drivers of deforestation are defined as all human activities that directly reduce forest cover, either completely resulting in deforestation or partially resulting in forest degradation (e.g. Geist and Lambin 2002, Schaeffer et al. 2005, Kissinger et al. 2012).

2.1 Underlying Causes and Global Trends

The drivers of deforestation and forest degradation are influenced and conditioned by a complex set of underlying circumstances which account for country- and region-specific differences. Any measures to deal with tropical deforestation and degradation have to take these indirect factors into account to be successful in the long run. The most important indirect drivers of deforestation include economic, technological, cultural, demographic, institutional and political factors (Figure 8.1) (Geist and Lambin 2002).

Geist and Lambin (2002) also showed that there are usually patterns of indirect driver interactions that underpin direct drivers. An example of this is the extension of roads into remote areas, which in turn enables logging

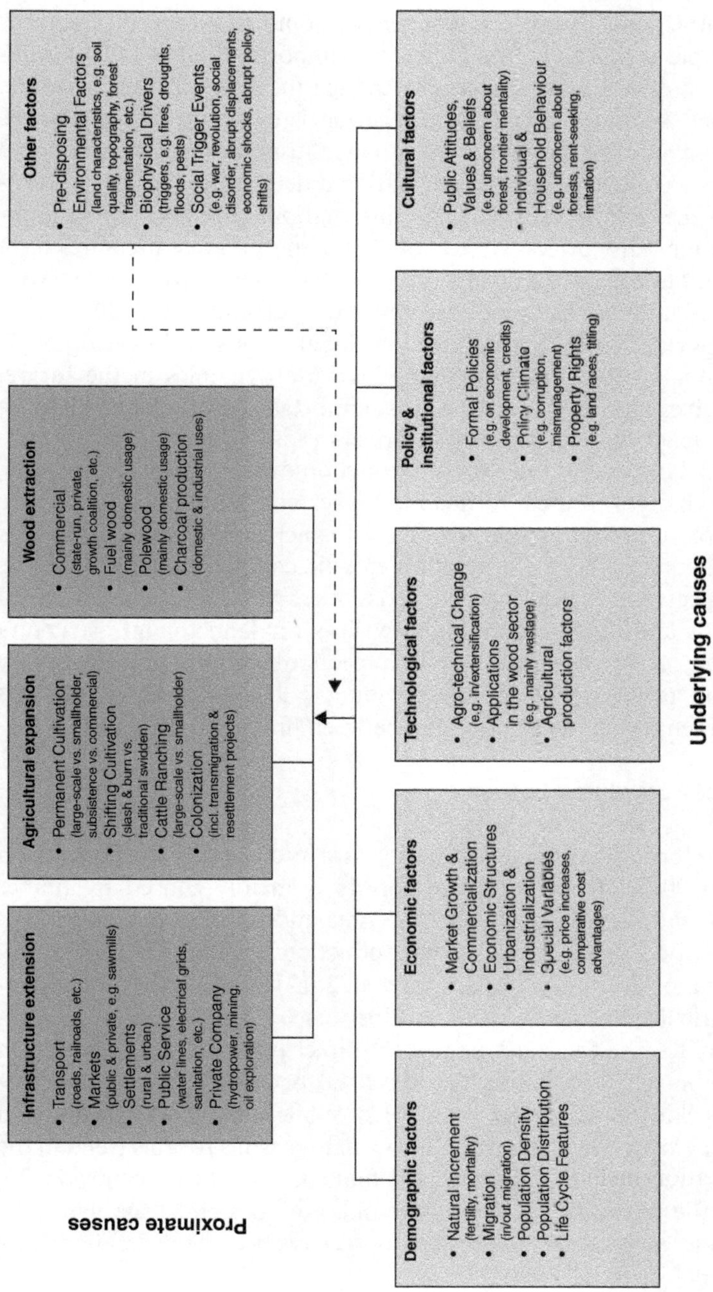

Source: Geist and Lambin 2002.

Figure 8.1 Direct and indirect drivers of deforestation and forest degradation

and wood extraction, but also the migration of settlers and the expansion of agricultural lands. Another characteristic of indirect drivers is that they act at multiple geographical scales, which is important to take into consideration when developing measures to change their strength or direction. Drivers that are more important at the local (e.g. poverty, subsistence farming) and national scales (e.g. governance structures, national policies) can be better controlled by local or national decision makers or governments, but they will have to adapt to international drivers such as international commodity prices. Up to now these international pressures have been difficult to control and many countries have only started to deal with the local and national factors of deforestation (Kissinger et al. 2012).

It is important to take a number of global trends and developments into account that are likely to shape land-use dynamics in the future. Table 8.1 gives an overview of the most important developments that are likely to impact indirect and direct drivers (Kissinger at al. 2012). The need to substantially increase food production over the next few decades, as well as changes in diets to include higher consumption of meat, are examples of some trends that are likely to increase pressure on forests (Rademaekers et al. 2010). Population growth, coupled with rapid income growth expected in many emerging economies, will also fuel the demand for minerals and timber products as well as for land for infrastructure development and urbanization. With economic development, energy demand will grow in many countries leading to likely increases in biofuels and thus intensifying the competition between different land uses.

2.2 Direct Agricultural Drivers

The major forces driving deforestation are food and fibre production (Houghton 2012). Degradation of forests is mainly caused by timber production and logging, particularly in Asia and Latin America, while in Africa fuel wood collection, charcoal production and livestock grazing are the more important causes (Kissinger et al. 2012) (Figure 8.2). The expansion of agricultural land, either for subsistence or commercial farming, is considered to be the most important direct cause of deforestation in tropical countries, accounting for about 80 per cent of tropical deforestation worldwide (Kissinger et al. 2012). While subsistence farming and population growth were identified as the main reasons for this trend in the 1980s, more recently it has been shown that commercial actors producing goods for the international commodity markets as well as supplying the growing cities in many developing countries have become the main drivers (DeFries et al. 2010, UCS 2011).

Deforestation is largely driven by the opportunity of farmers or

Table 8.1 Overview of major global trends important for governing drivers of deforestation and forest degradation in the future

Type	Major Future Trends
Global population	• Global increase, predominantly in urban areas, to 8.2 billion in 2030 • Largest increases in population in Africa (+235 million) and Asia and Pacific (+255 million) • Stabilized population level of 8 to 10 billion after 2050 due to rising living standards, urbanization, and declining birth rates
Economic growth	• Brazil, the Russian Federation, India and China are anticipated to continue growing over the next ten years at 8% per annum (OECD/FAO 2012) • Developing world will account for more than half of global economic growth throughout 2012/14 (World Bank 2012)
Agricultural commodities	• Overall, 70% increase in demand for food products by 2050 (FAO 2009)
Oil seeds	• 23% expansion of oil seed production between 2011–2020 (OECD/FAO 2011) • Two-thirds of global expansion is expected to occur in the developing world • Developing countries (particularly Asia), will likely continue to dominate the increase in vegetable oil (and oilseed meal) consumption (OECD/FAO 2011)
Oil palm	• 45% rise in palm oil output (mainly by Indonesia and Malaysia) (OECD/FAO 2011)
Meat	• 85% increase in the volume of meat produced by 2050 (FAO 2009) • Developing countries will account for about 78% of the additional output, mainly in Latin America (Brazil) • Growth in demand from large economies in Asia, Latin America and oil exporting countries (OECD/FAO 2011)
Biofuels	• Global production expected to increase rapidly over the next ten years • Ethanol increasing from 100 to 160 billion litres and biodiesel from 20 to 42 billion litres from 2010 to 2020 (OECD/FAO 2011)

Source: Kissinger et al. 2012.

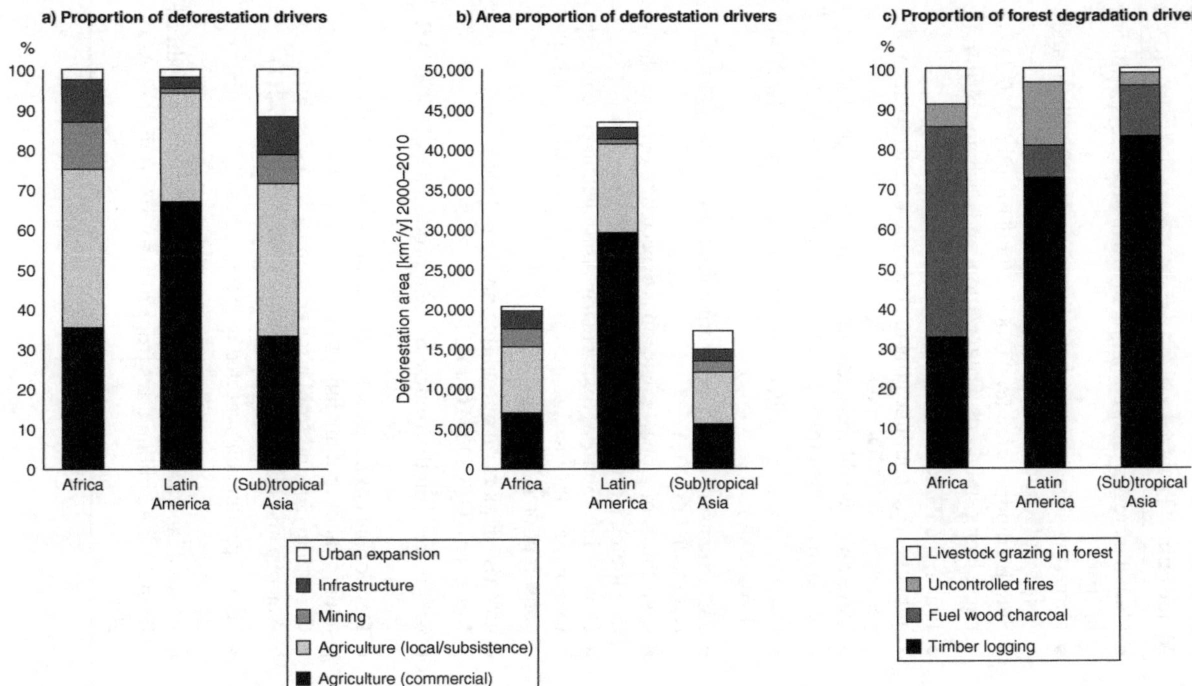

Source: Kissinger et al. 2012.

Figure 8.2 Direct drivers of deforestation and forest degradation

companies to capture forest rent by converting forests into pastures or croplands (Angelsen and Kaimowitz 2001). In Latin America, commercial agriculture, in particular the clearing of tropical forests for cattle ranching is a major driver of deforestation (Houghton 2012). Beef production differs from other kinds of livestock (pigs and chicken) because it relies on pasture and forage crops (rather than grain crops) to feed cattle. Stocking rates are generally very low, which results in the need for large amounts of land to produce small amounts of meat. This explains how cattle pasture has become one of the main drivers of deforestation in Latin America over the last few decades (Angelsen and Kaimowitz 1997, Boucher 2011).

The draining and burning of peatlands for agricultural production (mostly oil palm) in Southeast Asia is another major contributor to global GHG emissions. Much of the forest clearing in Southeast Asia is driven by industrial plantation industries. The Indonesian government encourages deforestation by designating vast tracts of forest land for conversion to plantations through issuing concessions to small groups of individuals on very favourable terms (Saxon and Roquemore 2011).

Another important deforestation driver is shifting cultivation, a type of small-scale farming that typically involves clearing the land, burning much of the plant material to fertilize the shallow tropical soils, planting and harvesting crops, and then abandoning the plot of land (letting the land go fallow) before moving to a new plot (Lininger 2011). During the fallow period, forests can regrow, and be burned again at a later date. Over the past decades, shortened fallow periods in many parts of the tropics resulted from population pressure, unclear land tenure rights or specific national policies fostering deforestation. Often, other farmers moved in behind shifting cultivators and established permanent pastures for cattle, other staples or cash crops.

While also contributing to deforestation, timber extraction and logging are the main drivers of forest degradation (Streck et al. 2013). Degradation patterns are regionally distinct: in Latin America and Asia, logging is the main driver while fuel wood and charcoal extraction drives forest degradation in Africa. Underlying these direct degradation drivers, there are two main types of value chains that can be considered demand-side drivers of deforestation and forest degradation in the tropics:

1. Local wood demand for energy and construction-related value chains, usually characterized by informality[1] and small-scale business.

---

[1] The word 'informal' is used to describe wood extraction and processing that falls outside of national legal frameworks surrounding forests. Although these

Table 8.2 Legal tools that can address drivers of deforestation

Tools	Instruments	Examples
Standards and Regulations	MEAs, investment and trade law	Permits (CITES), inclusion of forest species in CITES appendices
Goals and targets	MEAs (targets), soft law (declarations, announcements, voluntary submissions)	Aichi Biodiversity Targets, New York Declaration on Forests
Codes of conduct	Mostly soft law, voluntary initiatives	Forest certification
Transparency: MRV	MEAs	Reporting requirements under MEAs regarding treaty compliance
Positive incentives: financial	MEAs, bilateral cooperation, market mechanisms, UN and Bretton Woods Institutions, international finance institutions	MEAs: REDD+, CDM, GCF, bilateral, multilateral
Positive incentives: capacity building	MEAs, bilateral cooperation, UN and Bretton Woods Institutions, international finance institutions	UNFCCC REDD web platform: capacity building, workshops under the UNFCCC, the CDB, and other MEAs
Positive incentives: technology transfer	MEAs, bilateral cooperation, markets	Transfer of satellite, remote sensing technology under the UNFCCC, provisions under the Nagoya Protocol/CBD
Implementation partnerships	Soft law instruments, bilateral agreements, UN and Bretton Woods Institutions, international finance institutions	UN-REDD+, FCPF
Trade measures	MEAs, unilateral measures	Trade restrictions (CITES)

practices remain largely unregulated by law, they are socially accepted in many contexts and constitute a significant portion of livelihoods in tropically forested countries, which is why they are often distinguished from illegal forest activities.

2. International wood-based commodity value chains, characterized by industrially produced timber and related products, and large private investments.

3. ROLE OF INTERNATIONAL LAW

The classical approach of international public law relies on legally binding instruments negotiated between states that provide solutions to transnational and transboundary problems. Today however, much of international environmental law is preoccupied with regional or global concerns of various kinds (Brunné 2005), rather than with transboundary pollution problems. Climate change or the conservation of biodiversity provide examples for such global concerns that transcend the classical affairs to be regulated between neighbour states. Despite the many challenges that come with regulating global matters, international law remains decisively popular and the body of international law has steeply increased over the last decades. The subject matter of treaties has greatly diversified; today there is a treaty or declaration covering almost all aspects of life. Process, structure and content of legal agreements have also become more complex with hundreds of decisions taken under Multilateral Environmental Agreements (MEAs) and thousands of pages of guidance, party submissions and background papers produced. While in all this the state remains at the centre of international law, legal action has become more diverse, less hierarchical and more inclusive towards non-state actors. To the binding agreements come rules of customary international law, and a wealth of soft law instruments (Brown Weiss 2000).

The proliferation of legal instruments is particularly prominent in international environmental matters. But the increase in treaty numbers and international activity is not matched by success in halting environmental deterioration of our planet. Experts, policy makers and international lawyers also become increasingly doubtful about the extent to which international law can address the problems that it sets out to solve. As early as in 1989, the renowned international lawyer Philip Sands claimed that it is "doubtful whether traditional international law will succeed in establishing . . . effective procedures for protecting the environment" (Sands 1989). Today, nearly 30 years later, trust in the abilities of international law to regulate our environmental commons has cooled even further. The challenges are manifold: international law can hardly be enforced (Brunné 2005) and many agreements even lack a compliance regime; it applies only indirectly and depends on the transposition into national law; it is overburdened and often expectations as to what can be solved via legal means are too high; and finally it suffers from complexity and fragmentation. A 2006 Report of the *International Law Commission's Study Group on Fragmentation* shows how conflicts may arise between general and special international law and notes that "increasing attention will have to be given to the collision of norms and regimes and the rules, methods and techniques for dealing with such collisions" (ILC 2006).

Despite these shortcomings, MEAs formulate a number of "mechanisms for norm creation and adaptation, and to promote compliance in the context of polycentric problems where states are likely to be both perpetrator and victim" (Brunné 2005). Data collection, verification and reporting are at the core of many MEAs and help countries to identify causes and solutions for environmental problems. International reporting also makes performance transparent and comparable and it facilitates the exchange of views, international cooperation and support. The ongoing nature of MEA deliberations in the context of annual meeting of parties, subsidiary bodies, workshops and technical working groups enmeshes states in a variety of collective processes of deliberation, justification and judgment (Brunné 2005). MEAs also formulate a number of incentive systems designed to enable weaker parties to comply with treaty provisions. Financial mechanisms are established to channel funds towards project and programme proposals formulated by developing country parties. Capacity building and technology transfer should further enable treaty compliance. In addition to these tools that form part of almost all MEAs, coordination among MEAs and treaty bodies should promote synergies and harmonization between different instruments and mechanisms.

These different tools and instruments can also be found in MEAs and other legal texts that deal directly or indirectly with the conservation of tropical forests. While ultimately deforestation can only be stopped through policies and programmes on the ground, international law can certainly help create an enabling policy environment for forest conservation. Table 8.2 summarizes the instruments at the disposal of international law makers that can be used to address deforestation drivers.

There is currently no comprehensive forest convention or legally binding instrument focused primarily on forests. During the Rio Earth Summit in 1992 when the UNFCCC and the CDB were adopted, parties failed to reach agreement on a global forest convention. One of the reasons for that failure is that developing countries stood united in their claim that forests were a sovereign natural capital as opposed to a global commons (Humphreys 2005, van Asselt 2012). Instead of a treaty, the juridically weak "Non-Legally Binding Authoritative Statement of Principles for a Global Consensus on the Management, Conservation and Sustainable Development of all Types of Forests" (Forest Principles) was adopted (Ruis 2001). The added emphasis of "non-legally binding" regarding an instrument that would not be binding even without that emphasis indicates how sensitive the topic and how divergent the views in Rio were. In the institutional follow-up on the Forest Principles – the Intergovernmental Panel on Forests (IPF, 1995 to 1997), the IFF (1997 to 2000) and the UNFF (2000 to the present day) – the international will to arrive at a legally binding agreement has been increasingly on the wane (Ruis 2001). The various forums did however produce a substantial body of soft law including the 2008 Non-legally Binding Instrument on All Types of Forests.

The fact that there is no dedicated forest treaty does not mean that forests would not have been considered under international law. The UNFCCC, the CBD, the UN Convention to Combat Desertification (UNCCD) or the Ramsar Convention on Wetlands are environmental treaties with relevance for forests. Considering the many indigenous peoples that live in or close to forests, the Indigenous and Tribal Peoples Convention provides arguments for the protection of forests. The ITTA deals with the trade in tropical timber to ensure exports from sustainable sources. The WTO and its various legal instruments affect the policies of all sectors to a greater or lesser extent. Particularly relevant subsidiary tools related to forests are the GATT and the Agreement on Technical Barriers to Trade (TBT). There are also regional agreements such as the Central American Forest Convention, which is the only legally binding regional instrument focused exclusively on forests. Finally, demand-side instruments such as FLEGT aim to combat illegal logging by promoting trade in legally produced timber and through the strengthening of sustainable forest management.

4. INTERNATIONAL LAW INSTRUMENTS

International laws and agreements can provide regulatory architecture to guide global efforts to reduce the production or trade in illegal or unsustainably harvested forest commodities at both the demand and supply side of the market (Rautner et al. 2013). In the following sections we discuss a number of treaties and soft law agreements that provide context for forest protection by formulating goals, announcing initiatives and creating implementation partnerships.

4.1 UNFCCC

Despite recognizing the importance of forestry and agriculture in Articles 2 and 4[2] of the UNFCCC, the climate regime fails to formulate a coherent vision or set of incentives for encouraging mitigation in the land-use sector while maintaining the ecological and social functions of our landscapes. Quite the contrary, the UNFCCC and the KP formulate a fragmented set of rules, incentives and obligations. The KP considers forest emissions in developed countries, but fails to create incentives for reducing deforestation, the sector's highest source of emissions. Table 8.3 summarizes the objectives and instruments relevant to deforestation drivers under the UNFCCC/KP.

(a) REDD+ mechanism

This omission has been corrected in recent years, when the framework of "REDD+" defined rules that set incentives for reduced emissions from deforestation and forest degradation, the sustainable management of forests, conservation and the enhancement of forest carbon stocks. REDD+ establishes a framework of UNFCCC decisions that create incentives to reduce deforestation. Developed countries are called upon to provide significant financial support (Decision 1/CP.16, para. 76). Broad agreement on the arrangements for providing this support was reached at COP 19 in Warsaw in 2013. Countries reaffirmed previous decisions stating that "results-based finance" for REDD+ "may come from a variety of sources, public and private, bilateral and multilateral, including alternative sources" (Decision 9/CP.19, para. 1). The decision also confirms the key role to be played by the GCF in channelling results-based finance to developing countries, and provides guidance to the GCF on the application of finance. Financing entities outside the UNFCCC framework are "encouraged" to follow the same guidance, and it is likely that most will seek to do so in order to achieve coherence (Decision 9/CP.19, paras. 6–7).

Among the existing decisions, Decision 4/CP.15, Decision 1/CP.16 and Decision 15/CP.19 stress the need to address drivers of deforestation, whereby only the last decision from 2013 (1/CP/19 Warsaw) is dedicated to the drivers of deforestation. It is preceded by Decision 4/CP.15 from 2009 on "Methodological Guidance for Activities Relating to Reducing Emissions from Deforestation and Forest Degradation and the Role of Conservation, Sustainable Management of Forests and the

---

[2] UNFCCC art. 4.1(c): "all parties shall control, reduce or prevent anthropogenic emissions . . . in all relevant sectors, including the energy, transport, industry, agriculture, forestry and waste management sectors".

Enhancement of Forest Carbon Stocks in developing countries" which requests developing countries (1) to identify drivers of deforestation resulting in emissions including the means to address these drivers, and (2) identify activities that reduce emissions, increase removals and enhance forest carbon stocks. In Cancún, Decision 1/CP.16 (para. 72) requests countries that

> when developing and implementing their national strategies or action plans, to address, inter alia, the drivers of deforestation and forest degradation, land tenure issues, forest governance issues, gender considerations and the safeguards . . . ensuring the full and effective participation of relevant stakeholders, inter alia indigenous peoples and local communities.

This decision makes it clear that addressing drivers – rather than being a mere methodological issue – sits at the core of developing policies and measures that should address deforestation. However, both decisions – from 2009 and 2011 – still focus on developing countries when they call for action on deforestation drivers.

The decision that followed three years later recognized that when it comes to the implementation of REDD+ policies, the call to address deforestation drivers has to reach beyond developing countries. Local financial incentives can address local drivers with low opportunity costs, but the more structural and larger deforestation drivers need to be addressed by a mix of regulatory and demand-side measures by all countries. The decision from 2013 also acknowledges potential trade-offs when it states in its preamble that addressing deforestation drivers "may have an economic cost and implications for domestic resource". The decision stresses (again) that it is important for countries to address deforestation drivers as part of their national REDD+ plans (para. 1) and that drivers depend on the national context and circumstances (para. 2); however, it also recognized that the public and the private sector have to take action to reduce drivers (para. 3), that cooperation is essential and that information should be shared (paras. 4–5).

There are also several submissions by countries or groups of countries that develop proposals on how to address drivers of deforestation. A submission of Switzerland, Liechtenstein and Monaco from 2012 divides responsibilities of developing from those of developed countries in monitoring and addressing deforestation drivers. Developed countries should, among others, "foster responsible business conduct of their multinational companies operating abroad in activities related to deforestation and forest degradation (large-scale intensive agriculture, land-grabbing)", "address wasteful consumption", "increase public awareness of companies and consumers" and "promote responsible finance". Developing countries should, again, among others "address drivers across sectors and land-use activities i.e. agriculture, grazing land management, mining, and biofuels . . . including addressing drivers in multi-sectoral low carbon development planning", strengthen government and law enforcement, and clarify land titles.[3] This bifurcated obligation resonates with NGO submissions and an EU submission from the following year.[4]

(b) Cooperative sectoral approaches: agriculture

The UNFCCC decisions that mention drivers are not linked to the discussions on agricultural emissions under the UNFCCC. Consequently there is no link between the most important driver of land-use emissions (agriculture) and its source (forests).

Despite explicitly mentioning the need to address sector-specific emissions in Article 4(1)(c) of the Convention, the KP did not single out any sectoral action. The KP lists promotion of sustainable forest management practices, afforestation and reforestation, and sustainable forms of agriculture as ways for developed countries to achieve these emission reductions and limitation targets (KP, 1997: art. 2(1)(a)(ii)–(iii)). However, accounting for land-use emissions is limited to developed country parties, and the avoided deforestation is excluded from the offset mechanism, the CDM.

The Bali Action Plan introduced sector-specific approaches within the post-2012 negotiating framework (Decision 1/CP.13: para. 1(b)(iv)). As a result, from 2010 to 2012, agriculture was negotiated under the agenda item "cooperative sectoral approaches and sector-specific actions" in the context of the AWG-LCA. Thus, for the first time agriculture was discussed as a sector that required special attention. Building on a technical paper outlining opportunities in agriculture prepared by the UNFCCC Secretariat, the drafting group prepared a draft text in 2009 proposing the establishment of a work programme on agriculture. However, no agreement could be reached on this text before the AWG-LCA was dissolved in 2012.

(c) Methodological issues

The harmonization of the fragmented land-use accounting framework would further help to capture direct and indirect causes of deforestation.

---

[3] Submission of Switzerland, Liechtenstein and Monaco, Addressing Drivers of Deforestation and Forest Degradation and Robust and Transparent National Forest Monitoring Systems, 28 February 2012.

[4] CAN-submission on how to address drivers of deforestation, 20 February 2012. Submission from the EU and its member countries, Dublin 27 May 2013.

The 2006 Guidelines for National Greenhouse Gas Inventories, developed by the IPCC, reform the existing approach and integrate the LULUCF and agricultural sectors into a single agriculture, forestry, and other land uses (AFOLU) sector. This reflects the strong inter-linkages between emissions and removals from all types of land, and seeks to improve the consistency and completeness of the GHG estimation and reporting system (IPCC 2006). However, the COP has not yet adopted the 2006 IPCC Guidelines. In spite of the REDD+ acronym, which suggests a focus on particular mitigation activities (e.g., reduced deforestation and degradation, forest management, conservation, and forest carbon stock enhancement), many countries preparing for REDD+ work towards extending carbon monitoring to the whole forest sector. However, REDD+ itself remains limited to forest land and forest conversion, and does not take into account broader landscape impacts. Observers and parties alike have criticized the limitation on the forest sector and have argued that a more comprehensive landscape-based approach – also known as "Reducing Emissions from All Land Uses" – would provide a more comprehensive solution.[5]

4.2 The Convention on Biological Diversity

Contrary to the UNFCCC with its focus on forests as sinks and carbon pools, the CBD takes a holistic approach to conservation that is reflected in the "ecosystem approach"[6] adopted in 1995. The CBD is based on three core objectives, which relate to forest governance: the conservation of biological diversity, the sustainable use of its components, and the fair and equitable sharing of the benefits arising out of the utilization of genetic resources. While the treaty does not explicitly refer to forests, it has several provisions, work programmes and protocols, which could provide incentives for the protection of forests (see Table 8.4). Whereas the CDB conforms to the characteristics of other international hard laws, it fails to formulate standards or binding goals; the only strict unqualified obligation on parties being the submission of national reports (Harrop and Pritchard 2011). Relevant provisions include Article 6 of the CBD, which obliges parties to develop national biodiversity strategies and action plans

---

[5] See, e.g., World Agroforestry Centre, *Reference Emission Levels (REL) in the context of REDD and land-based NAMAs: forest transition stages can inform nested negotiations: Submission to SBBSTA UNFCCC February 28 2012*, available at http://www.asb.cgiar.org/PDFwebdocs/Reference%20Emission%20Levels%20-%20ICRAF%20submission%20to%20SBSTA.pdf.

[6] COP to the CBD Dec. II/8, Rep. of the 2nd Meeting, Nov. 6–17, 1995, UN Doc. UNEP/ CBD/COP/2/19 Annex II, 1, at 55 (Nov. 30, 1995).

Table 8.3 Deforestation, deforestation drivers and the UNFCCC

Relevant objectives	Instruments	Incentives	Limitations
Reducing emissions from deforestation, and increasing forest carbon stocks	REDD+ (Cancún Agreements, WFR). Transparency and exchange of views in the context of the UNFCCC (submission of reference levels, inclusion of REDD+ in country mitigation actions and contributions). Mandate to develop national plans, policies and measures for both developed and developing countries	Finance for REDD+ from public, private, multilateral, bilateral and possibly market sources (WFR). Capacity building from developed countries through bilateral and multilateral initiatives: FCPF, BioCarbon Fund, REDD+ readiness support. Demand-side and supply-chain measures by developed countries	No comprehensive accounting framework, data limitations. There is no link to the discussions on agriculture under the UNFCCC
Reducing emissions from LULUCF	Art. 3.3–3.4 KP	Reductions from the land-use sector (LULUCF) can be used to meet quantified emission limitations (targets)	Does not apply to developing countries. It is not clear whether LULUCF and REDD+ accounting will be integrated to a harmonized framework under a future climate treaty
Reducing emissions from agriculture, promoting forestation	Art. 12 KP	Afforestation/reforestation and agricultural projects focusing on methane (CH_4) and nitrous oxide (N_2O) are eligible under the CDM	Complicated processes and cumbersome rules have led to transaction costs that discourage parties from engaging. There is further very limited demand for CDM certificates on the market
Accounting and MRV	National communications, inventories, MRV for REDD+, CDM and mitigation actions	Mandates and obligations under the UNFCC and KP with capacity and financial support	Increasingly comprehensive, but not fully harmonized. Complex, lack of experts
Enhance adaptation of forest and land ecosystems	Nairobi Work Programme on Adaptation	Capacity building to identify adaptation needs, finance via the Adaptation Fund (KP) and, in future, the GCF	No link to the mitigation agenda, which in the land-use sector would be particularly important

(NBSAP) for the conservation and sustainable use of biological diversity.[7] These should be integrated into broader national plans for environment and development, particularly in the sectors of forestry, agriculture, fisheries, energy and transport. Parties are further required to identify and monitor essential components of biodiversity,[8] to establish protected areas to conserve biodiversity,[9] to identify incentive measures for the conservation and sustainable use of components of biological diversity,[10] to respect, preserve and maintain traditional knowledge and sustainable use of biological diversity with the involvement of indigenous peoples and local communities,[11] to undertake environmental impact assessments of proposed projects which are likely to have a significant adverse effect on biodiversity,[12] and to avoid or minimize adverse impacts from the use of biological resources.[13]

The CBD programmes of work (PoW)[14] are the primary instruments that parties employ to achieve the objectives formulated in the convention. The CBD's activities on forests started in 1996 with the request to develop a work programme for forest biodiversity. The PoW on forest biodiversity adopted in 1998 and expanded in 2002, consists now of three elements, 12 goals, 27 objectives and 130 activities. The PoW does not include quantified time-bound targets but it lists a broad range of possible activities which can be undertaken at the national level.[15] Further

---

[7] Article 6 of the CBD states: "Each Contracting Party shall, in accordance with its particular conditions and capabilities: (a) Develop national strategies, plans or programmes for the conservation and sustainable use of biological diversity or adapt for this purpose existing strategies, plans or programmes which shall reflect, inter alia, the measures set out in this Convention relevant to the Contracting Party concerned; and (b) integrate, as far as possible and as appropriate, the conservation and sustainable use of biological diversity into relevant sectoral or cross-sectoral plans, programmes and policies."

[8] CBD art. 7.

[9] CBD art. 8(a).

[10] CBD art. 11.

[11] CBD art. 8(j).

[12] CBD art. 14(1).

[13] CBD art. 10(b).

[14] The CBD COP has created seven thematic work programmes on agricultural biodiversity, dry and sub-humid lands biodiversity, forest biodiversity, inland waters biodiversity, island biodiversity, marine and coastal biodiversity, and mountain biodiversity; as well as five cross-cutting work programmes on incentive measures, the Global Taxonomy Initiative, protected areas, Article 8(j) (traditional knowledge), and technology transfer and cooperation. See http://www.cbd.int/programmes/.

[15] COP to the CBD Dec. VI/22, Rep. of the 6th Meeting, Apr. 7–19, 2002, UN Doc. UNEP/ CBD/COP/6/20 Annex I, 10 (May 27, 2002).

templates for promoting biodiversity governance, establishing protected areas, restoring degraded ecosystems and other measures are the Strategic Plan for Biodiversity 2011–2020 and the Aichi Biodiversity Targets.

While the CBD pursues a comprehensive approach to the protection of forests, the incentives for implementation are limited. The provisions of the treaty reflect the ways in which divergent positions were resolved during the complex negotiations. The result is a framework of general, flexible obligations which parties may apply through national laws and policies (McGraw 2002). The CBD has been intensely criticized for its vague and heavily qualified text fraught with loopholes and with no sanction mechanisms in cases of non-compliance (Morgera and Tsioumani 2011). In the absence of a mechanism to systematically and effectively monitor implementation and compliance at the national level, the CBD has been considered ineffective and with little impact on state practice. The design of NBSAPs and the PoW relies on a voluntary, cross-sectoral and national planning approach, presupposing the existence of sufficient capacity and incentives for the engagement of actors, including adequate infrastructure and institutional support, which cannot be taken for granted in many contexts (Rayner, Buck and Katila 2010).

The legal significance of the CBD may therefore be found in its soft law approach, reflected in its focus on global biodiversity targets. With almost universal membership, the biannual meetings of its COP are high-profile decision-making events where non-parties, international governmental and NGOs, indigenous peoples' representatives, prominent business associations and research institutes actively participate. Therefore, the CBD COP's normative activity is significant and demonstrates the intense, evolving and creative interpretation of the treaty by the international community (Morgera and Tsioumani 2011). While the conservation of forest carbon stocks and the conservation of biodiversity do not automatically coincide, there is a potential for co-benefits if appropriately designed. Given that the UNFCCC views forests first and foremost as sinks or sources of carbon dioxide emissions, the CBD's comprehensive and holistic approach can serve as an important flexible tool to ensure integrated forest conservation and management (van Asselt 2012). On the other hand, the CBD could also benefit from the climate regime's high political attention, financial support and capacity building. However, REDD+ may threaten biodiversity through the plantation of invasive species for fast carbon sequestration (Savaresi 2013). For example, reforestation projects with rapid-growing, often exotic monocultures that yield high carbon sequestration rates and economic returns often have little value for biodiversity conservation (Secretariat of the Convention on Biological Diversity 2008). Policies increasing the provision of carbon sequestration do not necessarily increase species conservation (Nelson et al.

Table 8.4 Deforestation, deforestation drivers and the CBD

Relevant objectives	Instruments	Incentives	Limitations
The conservation of biological diversity	Preparation of plans, strategies and programmes; mandate to establish protected areas; to adopt safeguards and policies that reduce negative impacts. Aichi Biodiversity Targets	Financial support via bilateral sources and the GEF. Capacity building. Incentive to share experience (soft approach). Technical and scientific cooperation. Formulation of indicators and biodiversity assessments	Largely voluntary. Insufficient financial support and lack of technical expertise to review plans, strategies and programmes
The sustainable use of biodiversity	Integration of biodiversity goals in cross-sectoral programmes; preparation of plans, strategies and programmes. Cross-cutting issue under the Convention. Programme on sustainable use of biodiversity	Identification of ecological services linked to biodiversity. Nagoya Protocol. Technology transfer. Finance, capacity building	Insufficient funds, incentives not always effective. Limited understanding on how to translate the objective into practice
More specifically: conservation of forests	Programme on forest biodiversity; specific recommendations on national forest and forest-related laws and policies	Finance and technology transfer to identified priorities for forest biodiversity; guidelines for national implementation of forest biodiversity targets	No link to agricultural programmes (programme on agricultural biodiversity). Insufficient funds. Soft law approach
Transparency, MRV	Parties prepare national reports on the status of implementation of the Convention. Biodiversity monitoring and assessments	Treaty compliance. The CBD helps to set the agenda and coordinate among the various biodiversity-concerned MEAs	No targets, no verification

2008). Hence, rules providing the wrong incentive could lead to tensions between the climate and biodiversity regimes.

4.3 Convention on International Trade in Endangered Species of Wild Fauna and Flora

CITES aims to protect identified plant and animal species from over-exploitation through international trade.[16] It contributes to the sustainability of forest resources, among others, by controlling trade in commercial timber (see Table 8.5). The main instrument of the treaty relevant for mitigating deforestation is its system of permits and certificates. While initially 18 tree species were listed in 1975, more than 400 tree species are listed in one of the Appendices today.[17] The majority of tree species are listed in Appendix II, which requires approval of an export permit by both importing and exporting nations and a confirmation that the export of the species "will not be detrimental for the survival of that species".[18] To protect tree species, CITES parties voted to list the species, and agreed to restrict international trade in the listed species and to control the trade through a system of import and export permits issued by national governments.[19] Each CITES party must pass its own implementing legislation and designate management authorities who are in charge of administering the licensing system.[20] To monitor the implementation of the convention, parties have to provide annual reports on import and export permits and biennial reports on national measures enacted to enforce the convention, which are reviewed by the Secretariat.[21]

Besides these general obligations, CITES creates several other incentives for countries to achieve the Convention's objectives. Through the ITTO-CITES programme[22] founded in 2007, the two Secretariats collaborate on a programme of activities, which seeks to ensure that international trade in CITES-listed timber species is consistent with their sustainable management and conservation. The programme provides capacity building projects and enhances the knowledge and skills of forest managers, enforcement and customs officers, forest owners and concessionaires. Programme assistance

---

16 The objectives are not explicitly stated in the convention; see http://cites.org/eng/disc/what.php.

17 See http://cites.org/eng/international_day_forests.

18 CITES art. IV(2)(a), (4).

19 CITES arts. II, III, IV, V.

20 CITES art. IX.

21 CITES art. 8.

22 http://cites.org/eng/prog/itto.php.

Table 8.5 Deforestation, deforestation drivers and the CITES

Relevant objectives	Instruments	Incentives	Limitations
Protecting wild animals and plants	Establishment of a system of permits and certificates	Obligation to report, trade sanctions and compliance regime. Cross-cutting capacity building, knowledge and outreach activities, trade sanctions. CITES Technology and Innovation Fund (CTIF)	Difficult listing procedure, lack of financial support and insufficient national enforcement

is available to countries which are, or have the potential to become, significant exporters of products from CITES-listed tree species.[23]

The incentive to comply with CITES is created by the imposition of penalties, such as trade sanctions and by facilitation, funding and capacity building. The combination of trade sanctions and capacity building has been effective, as they supplement each other (Reeve 2006). Under the threat of trade suspensions, parties increasingly seek technical assistance. On the other hand, improving national capacities facilitates the implementation of CITES, thereby avoiding non-compliance. While CITES is unique with its compliance regime, its effectiveness is tempered by the recognition that enforcement at the national level is extremely diverse and in some countries weak to non-existent (Reeve 2006). CITES legislation is often not adequately enforced due to a lack of political will, as well as a lack of financial and human resources. CITES is particularly dependent on the sanctions-based approach due to its lack of financial resources to support capacity building. The creation of the CTIF could significantly improve this.

4.4 International Tropical Timber Agreement

The ITTA adopted in 2006 is the only international legally binding instrument focusing specifically on forest resources (Rayner, Buck and

---

23 For an overview of the implementation of projects and recent news on the Programme see: http://cites.org/sites/default/files/common/prog/itto/CITES_Newsletter2014.pdf.

Katila, 2010). The first ITTA, ratified in 1985, established the ITTO, an intergovernmental organization with the mandate to promote the conservation and sustainable management, use and trade of tropical forest resources. Each ITTO member country is represented in the International Tropical Timber Council (ITTC), which is the decision-making and recommendatory body. The parties control over 90 per cent of all trade in tropical timbers and about 40 per cent of the remaining tropical forests. They are divided into producer and consumer countries, and the votes are split according to the main regions and allocated in proportion to trade and forests held.[24]

The overarching objective of the ITTA negotiated in 2006 is the promotion of trade in sustainable timber and of sustainable management of tropical timber producing forests (see Table 8.6).[25] Article 1 of the ITTA 2006 lists a wide variety of means to achieving its objectives, including improving forest law and governance, the use of forest certification, and the promotion of sustainable development and poverty alleviation. Positive incentives for the sustainable management of forests include non-invasive measures, such as increasing market transparency, providing trade and price data, reducing market-distorting illegal logging practices and providing a platform for producers and consumers of tropical wood rather than sanctions.

Despite its stated intentions, the ITTA has been criticized as being a "flawed commodities agreement that is deficient in required regulatory mechanisms or effective market intervention powers" (Nagtzaam 2014). Critical accounts have pointed to the effective veto coalition, which has hindered the entrenchment of higher order environmental values, such as conservation and allowed states to continue their exploitative behaviour of tropical gains. While the voting system allows all states with tropical forests to have a say in proceedings, states with large forest regions and export industries such as Malaysia, Indonesia and Brazil have a disproportionate say in the direction of the ITTO. As more votes are assigned to states with greater volumes of tropical timber exports, there is an incentive to continue to deforest. Both producer and consumer states block measures that aim to limit timber production due to a common interest to protect their economic interests and ensure that topical timber exports and imports are maintained (Nagtzaam 2014). Furthermore, financial resources, which depend on voluntary contributions, have not been adequate to comprehensively fund the programmes and activities that promote SFM and support capacity building and market access among ITTO producer member countries.

---

[24] See ITTA 2006 Annex A for the allocation of votes.

[25] ITTA 2006, art. 1.

Table 8.6 Deforestation, deforestation drivers and the ITTA

Relevant objectives	Instruments	Incentives	Limitations
To promote the sustainable management of tropical timber	ITTO. ITTO Action Plans. Guidelines on SFM. Council reports and policy documents	Market transparency, Financial assistance through ITTO, capacity building, transfer of technologies and technical cooperation	Equal focus on conservation and trade, few real incentives or penalties, no enforcement provisions

4.5 Convention Concerning Indigenous and Tribal Peoples in Independent Countries ILO Convention No. 169

The ILO Convention No. 169 on Indigenous and Tribal Peoples aims to protect the social, economic and cultural rights of indigenous peoples. Parties assume the responsibility for undertaking action to protect their rights with the participation of the peoples concerned, and to guarantee respect for their integrity. The Convention has only 20 parties, but its principles are respected beyond the small circle of parties. Once a party ratifies the Convention, a country has one year to align legislation, policies and programmes to the Convention before it becomes legally binding. Countries that have ratified the Convention are subject to supervision with regards to its implementation.

There is no specific focus within the framework of the ILO Convention related to forests, although its implementation programme includes activities such as ancestral domain management and environment and natural resource management (Ruis 2001). The Convention contains specific provisions on land that are framed by Article 13(1) which requires that governments recognize and respect the special spiritual, cultural and economic relationship that indigenous peoples have with their lands and territories (see Table 8.7). The following articles consider land rights, such as:

- Article 14, which states that "the rights of ownership and possession of the peoples concerned over the lands which they traditionally occupy shall be recognised";
- Article 15, which provides that the rights of people "to the natural resources pertaining to their lands shall be specially safeguarded",[26]

[26] Article 13(2) defines the term "lands" as used in arts. 15 and 16 as inclusive of "the concept of territories, which covers the total environment of the areas which the peoples concerned occupy or otherwise use".

Table 8.7 Deforestation, deforestation drivers and ILO 169

Relevant objectives	Instruments	Incentives	Limitations
Protection of indigenous lands	Consultations	Supervision of treaty application (art. 27)	Protection limited to a number of procedural steps that protect indigenous lands

including the right "to participate in the use, management and conservation of these resources" including sharing of benefits and receiving "fair compensation" for damage.

The protection extended by Article 15 is objectionable as it establishes mere obligation to consult (and no consent). It fails to account for the devastating effects that resource exploitation operations have on many aspects of indigenous peoples' lives and well-being (MacKay 2001). The procedures established are inadequate to secure the "recognition of and respect for the special spiritual and cultural relationship that indigenous peoples have with their lands and territories" (Article 13(1)).

4.6 World Trade Organization

Trade in timber and other forest products has significant effects on the rate and way of production of these products, which in turn has impacts on the rate of deforestation in exporting countries (Downes 1999). When trade affects agricultural output prices, it affects deforestation. Where prices go up, deforestation increases; where they go down, deforestation decreases (Robalino and Herrera 2009). Increases in agricultural and timber prices have lead to increases in deforestation in Mexico, Tanzania, Thailand, Brazil, Costa Rica, Australia and Brazil, to name but a few.

Trade agreements may have serious direct and indirect, positive and negative implications for forests (McDermott et al. 2007). In contrast to most MEAs, WTO agreements have strong teeth: they allow for the imposition of trade sanction if national law or practice is inconsistent with WTO rules. The objective of the WTO is to expand the production and trade in goods and services among others through the reduction of tariffs and other barriers to trade and the elimination of discriminatory treatment in international trade relations. Objectives also include allowing for the optimal use of the world's resources with the objective of sustainable development, seeking both to protect and preserve the environment.[27] However, despite these references to the environment, the predominant norm of the WTO is trade and investment liberalization without discrimination, which is built into all WTO agreements.

The status of forests under the principle of non-discrimination is thus still unclear and the application of WTO rules, as they have been interpreted to date, can interfere with national and possibly international laws and policies seeking to conserve the forests (Brack 2013). Eckersley (2004) argues that the awareness of vulnerability to a WTO challenge has a chilling effect on MEA negotiations. It prevents states from adopting and implementing trade restrictive obligations under MEAs in the light of the threat of a legal challenge. For example, environmental measures creating incentives to reduce deforestation, such as certification processes for sustainable timber, are seen as barriers to trade. As states cannot discriminate against "like products" (meaning products with similar characteristics or end uses) on grounds of their manufacture, it has been interpreted that states cannot discriminate between "sustainably managed" timber and timber from "unsustainable" sources (Rayner, Buck and Katila 2010). Further potential for conflict exists between the principle of non-discrimination and the ability of states to impose import restrictions to address biodiversity concerns (McDermott et al. 2007). Similarly, the provisions of CITES, the ITTA, the European Timber Regulation and other green-procurement initiatives could conflict with the trade regime. However, this has not yet been tested before a WTO dispute panel, as none of the treaty provisions have led to any WTO dispute (Brack 2013).

Despite these difficulties, states can adopt measures to address drivers of deforestation provided that a number of conditions to prevent the misuse of such measures for protectionist purposes are fulfilled (Howse and Eliason 2009). Such measures include the lowering of tariffs for sustainable as compared to unsustainable forest products, the adoption of bilateral or multilateral agreements between countries designed to restrict trade to an agreed definition of a "sustainable" product, the adoption of regulations differentiating between sustainable and unsustainable forest commodities, and public procurement policies for sustainable forest commodities (Legget 2013). Whether trade sanctions can be used to create an incentive for conservation is an ongoing discussion. Proponents claim that they could be an effective tool to reduce deforestation, whereas others argue that they cause perverse incentives by reducing the value of the stock of the resource, leading to depletion (Robalino and Herrera 2009).

---

27 Preamble of the Agreement establishing the World Trade Organization (Marrakesh Agreement).

Table 8.8 Deforestation, deforestation drivers and WTO law

Relevant objectives	Instruments	Incentives	Limitations
Increase international trade in goods and services	Non-discrimination rules. Trade agreements: GATT, GATS, etc.	Trade sanctions, reduction of barriers to trade, market access	Little scope for environmental protection
To allow for the optimal use of the world's resources with the objective of sustainable development, seeking both to protect and preserve the environment	Provisions allowing for trade restrictions imposed with the goal of conserving natural resources (e.g. art. XX GATT)	Protection of environmentally sustainable goods and services	Justification for environmentally motivated trade measures hard to find

While it can be concluded that WTO law does not create incentives to reduce deforestation, and that within the WTO there has been little effort invested to identify WTO-compatible measures that address drivers of deforestation, it seems that this is slowly starting to change (see Table 8.8). In January 2014, the EU together with 13 other WTO members pledged to launch negotiations to liberalize global trade in environmental goods, the so-called "green goods initiative". The initiative builds on a list of 54 environmental goods collected by the Asian-Pacific Economic Cooperation forum in 2012 to reduce import tariffs to 5 per cent or less by the end of 2015 (Vossenaar 2014). These negotiations for an "Environmental Goods Agreement" seek to eliminate tariffs on environmental goods on a plurilateral basis and to eventually include it in the WTO framework. Critical accounts have pointed to the difficulty of defining environmental goods and it has been argued that the initiative has little to offer unless the field of negotiations is widened to include a range of goods and services (de Melo and Wijil 2014). Others perceive it as the much-needed impetus for WTO negotiations, envisaging it as the stepping stone towards a multilateral treaty on the environment and predict a positive impact on the environment (McKenna 2014).

5. INCENTIVES AND DISINCENTIVES FOR DEFORESTATION IN SOFT LAW INSTRUMENTS

The "Rio Forest principles"[28] are the first international soft law agreement on forests, agreed at the UN Conference on Environment and Development in 1992. They are relevant because they lay the foundation for two principles, which have since dominated the negotiations on forests. These are firstly, the sovereign right of states to exploit their forest resources according to their own environmental policies, and secondly, SFM.[29] The concept of SFM has since been included in several international instruments and processes dealing with forests, including the ITTA, the CBD and the NLBI.

Following Rio, the IPF which was in operation between 1995–97 provided a setting for countries to debate and formally recognize the importance of a comprehensive forest policy framework for achieving SFM. Through the IPF, countries agreed on a common approach known as national forest programmes, and adopted a set of principles designed to guide their development and implementation. Today, national forest programmes processes are underway in more than 130 countries.

At present, the primary body responsible for the promotion of the management, conservation and sustainable development of forests is the UNFF (Rayner, Buck and Katila 2010). It facilitated the adoption of the NLBI in 2007, and defines a set of voluntary goals and principles. The NLBI seeks to achieve four global objectives on forests: (1) reverse forest loss, (2) enhance forest-based benefits, (3) significantly increase area of protected forests, and (4) mobilize financial resources. It creates objectives and policies at the international, regional and national level.[30] To achieve its objectives, the NLBI proposes to apply a mix of regulatory, financial and information policy tools, focusing on national forest programmes, which are based on criteria and indicators for SFM. Obligations are weak however: the NBLI merely "encourages" actors to "develop, promote and implement in a transparent manner voluntary instruments, such as voluntary certification systems or other appropriate mechanisms"

---

[28] United Nations Conference on Environment and Development, Statement of Principles for a Global Consensus on the Management, Conservation and Sustainable Development of All Types of Forests, June 13, 1992, 31 ILM 881.

[29] Non-Legally Binding Authoritative Statement of Principles for a Global Consensus on the Management, Conservation and Sustainable Development of all Types of Forests (Forest Principles) 1992.

[30] NLBI Annex para. 6(a–y).

(para. 2). NLBI stipulates that "Member States should submit, on a voluntary basis . . . national progress reports".

The most recently developed soft law instrument on forests is the New York Declaration on Forests, which was adopted in September 2014 and pledges to halve the rate of deforestation by 2020 and halt the loss of natural forests by 2030.[31] Not only government and NGOs but also major companies, including Unilever, Cargill and Asia Pulp and Paper, signed the declaration. The declaration has been criticized for its weak targets and origin.[32]

Together, these major soft law forest instruments establish a road map for the continued progress of forest policy at the international level. Their effectiveness is doubtful however, considering that the commitments that states have agreed on in international soft law on forests are so vague that their role in shifting state behaviour, if any, is limited (Humphreys 2009).

6. INCENTIVES AND DISINCENTIVES FOR DEFORESTATION IN REGIONAL INSTRUMENTS

Concurrent with the development of international collaborative efforts, the number and size of regional agreements and processes have grown. Albeit many regional instruments address deforestation, some only focus on tracking deforestation while others discourage forest conversion or prohibit forest conversion altogether (McDermott et al. 2007). Regional treaties and organizations have not always delivered better results than international agreements nor have they necessarily been more successful than individual states in creating incentives to implement the provisions of regional agreements. Their proliferation poses additional challenges for policy integration. For example, the Central African Forest Commission (COMIFAC) was created by the Yaoundé Declaration from 1999 with the mandate to coordinate and harmonize subregional policy and legislation affecting the conservation and sustainable management of the forests of Central Africa. It is charged inter alia with implementing the various SFM-based international initiatives, monitoring and coordinating REDD+

---

[31] See: http://www.un.org/climatechange/summit/wp-content/uploads/sites/2/2014/07/New-York-Declaration-on-Forest-–-Action-Statement-and-Action-Plan.pdf.

[32] See http://www.redd-monitor.org/2014/09/26/the-new-york-declaration-on-forests-an-agreement-to-continue-deforestation-until-2030/.

as well as FLEGT, and the CBD's access and benefit-sharing initiative. While this provides a great opportunity to improve forest management practices on several fronts simultaneously, in practice, COMIFAC finds itself overwhelmed in these efforts (Rayner, Buck and Katila 2010). The lack of coherent direction from the overlapping international regimes, the absence of an autonomous financing mechanism and the missing willingness of its signatory states to address their own shortcomings limit its effectiveness to create incentives that reduce deforestation.

Examples of more successful regional models include the Central American Forest Convention,[33] which is unique in its focus on forest management for subsistence purposes. As the only legally binding regional instrument focused exclusively on forests, it directs cooperation on regional-scale issues and encourages cooperation in national-level forest policy between member countries. The implementation of the convention has been satisfactory due to the wide participation and incorporation of civil society views and the mutual supportiveness of the various instruments it applies (Tarasofsky 1999).

Another regional instrument is the Association of Southeast Asian Nations (ASEAN), which has adopted the ASEAN Agreement on the Conservation of Nature and Natural Resources in 1985. The conservation treaty encompasses a broad range of natural resource issues, including forest resources, and it includes a range of generalized directory provisions to discourage deforestation.[34] However, with only three of the six required ratifications achieved so far, the treaty never entered into force.

7. UNILATERAL AND DEMAND-SIDE MEASURES

Over the past decade, a variety of demand-side measures to reduce incentives for deforestation have been developed by governments, the private sector and civil society. They include legislation, public procurement policies, voluntary bilateral agreements, multi-stakeholder roundtables, moratoria and independent certification. One of the most ambitious sets of measures aimed at illegal logging and forest governance adopted by a consumer country or bloc is the 2003 EU Action Plan for FLEGT (Brack 2013). FLEGT seeks to combat illegalities in the forest sector by using

---

[33] Regional Convention for the Management and Conservation of Natural Forest Ecosystems and the Development of Forest Plantations 1993.

[34] The Agreement requires parties to conserve habitats (art. 3(2)(a)), and to "take all necessary measures" to conserve forest cover (art. 6(1)), including natural forests (art. 6(2)(f) and (g)).

trade as the leverage to involve producers, traders and consumers in its implementation. The key instruments are the VPAs, which are legally binding bilateral trade agreements between the EU and timber exporting countries. They require that all timber exports are produced and traded in coherence with the legislation and the national licensing scheme of the originating country. They contain provisions on monitoring, licensing, transparency, participation of stakeholders, strengthening the capacity of government and civil society actors, policy and legal reforms and public procurement policies. Countries have several incentives to negotiate a VPA, including the strengthening of enforcement tools, increased tax revenues from the reduction in illegal logging and a priority position for development aid regarding FLEGT-related projects (Fishman and Obidzinski 2014). The FLEGT licensing system is supported by the EU Timber Regulation, which ensures due diligence and prevents illegal products from entering the EU through non-VPA countries.[35] Through these due diligence requirements for importers and the risk of penalties determined by the Member States, the EU Timber Regulation creates an additional incentive to negotiate and comply with the VPAs.

Other legislative action to avoid illegal logging includes the US Lacey Act, adopted in 2008, which prohibits the import, sale or trade of timber and timber products harvested in violation of an underlying law in the country of origin.[36] It requires importers to declare the country of origin, quantity and the plant species contained in their products and it has clear penalties for violations, such as deprivation of goods and vessels, fines and potentially imprisonment. In contrast to FLEGT, the Lacey Act does not engage in a dialogue for potential legal reforms in a country (Walker et al. 2013). Another country adopting unilateral measures to combat illegal logging is Australia, which adopted the Australian Illegal Logging Prohibition Bill in 2012. Modelled on the US Lacey Act, it prohibits the import of illegally logged timber.[37] Importers are required to conduct due diligence on raw logs to reduce the risk of processing illegally logged timber.

As these unilateral demand-side legislations are relatively new and are still being developed, it is too early to evaluate their impact. However, they have the potential to provide significant incentives for timber-exporting

---

[35] EU Timber Regulation No. 995/2010 came into effect in March 2013.

[36] See http://www.fws.gov/international/laws-treaties-agreements/us-conservation-laws/lacey-act.html.

[37] The Parliament of the Commonwealth of Australia. Illegal Logging Prohibition Bill 2012, available at http://www.aph.gov.au/Parliamentary_Business/Bills_Legislation/Bills_Search_Results/Result?bId=r4740.

countries to address the illegality in their forestry sectors. They can create a more predictable environment for finance, investment and aid, which facilitates the use of incentives to prevent deforestation. They can realign incentives in producer countries and modify the political economy of the forest and agricultural production sector in favour of certification by stimulating markets, creating new markets or challenging existing ones (Walker et al 2013). Besides creating a market incentive to reduce illegal logging, they can also help to create internationally agreed standards on what comprises sustainability and they can promote international cooperation on technology transfer and capacity building. However, to sustain the incentive to avoid deforestation through demand-side measures in the long term, it is important that the demand for legal or licensed timber is maintained (Walker et al 2013). Demand-side measures require considerable time and costs to achieve their objectives, which is reflected in the fact that there has been no trade in VPA licensed timber to date.[38] Furthermore, while there has been no formal claim so far, these legislations risk being in violation of WTO agreements (Fishman and Obidzinski 2014).

8. ANALYSIS AND CONCLUSIONS

In the absence of a comprehensive forest treaty that would provide for conservation and address deforestation drivers, a multitude of legal instruments has sought to fill the niche in global forest governance. The various instruments seek to promote forest conservation from their particular perspective, be it the protection of endangered species, the promotion of sustainably harvested timber, or the conservation of biodiversity. While all – and more, as our list remains incomplete – the instruments listed in this chapter seek to contribute to forest conservation, very few address deforestation directly. Not surprisingly, only the UNFCCC REDD+ framework includes decisions that call on countries to address deforestation drivers, something that seems obvious if REDD+ should succeed. Instruments that address illegality in the timber value chain address illegal logging as a deforestation driver. Most instruments however are concerned with the protection of a habitat or species and address the driving forces of destruction only indirectly through national plans or strategies.

It is not a given however that a global forest treaty would necessarily be more effective than the cumulative number of incentives, tools and mandates from different treaties, that is, if the cumulative

---

[38] See http://www.euflegt.efi.int/vpa.

effectiveness of the various instruments can unfold and display its effects, and is not restrained by conflicting mandates, lack of implementation, and overall treaty confusion. After all, each international instrument requires resources for implementation, and resources in human and financial capital that many countries do not have. If properly used, international law related to forests can be an important tool in the efforts to reduce deforestation. This is, however, premised on the existence of stable legal and political institutions. The strengthening of existing national and international institutions and the development of the rule of law are therefore essential for the achievement of treaty objectives.

Several tools can be used to strengthen governance and law enforcement and institutions. At the international level, synergies between different instruments can be reinforced to avoid duplication, overlap and confusion. Whereas several instruments aspired for the interaction with other forest-related programmes, such as the CBD and the ITTA, some still lack willingness to cooperate. In particular, the WTO should become more transparent and open in its negotiation processes and allow other MEA Secretariats to participate so that effective and trade-compliant measures can be deployed. Synergies should also be recognized with respect to the transfer of technology and financial resources.

Synergies between different instruments to improve their effectiveness can also be found at the national level. For example, in countries that implement both initiatives, REDD+ could support elements of FLEGT with its considerable financial support and political attention, whereas FLEGT could positively influence REDD+ by providing a potential model for legal reform, multi-stakeholder participatory processes, transparency and monitoring requirements. Considering that both REDD+ and FLEGT face similar challenges in their efforts to bring transformative change, building on synergies will help both to achieve their own and their overlapping goals (Broekhoven and Wit 2014).

Bilateral agreements can also be an interesting tool to address the drivers of deforestation. All bilateral trade agreements recently concluded by the EU (e.g. South Korea, Central America, Colombia and Peru, Singapore) include provisions on trade and sustainable development. These require adherence to existing key international labour and environmental standards and agreements, and the facilitation and promotion of trade in goods that contribute to sustainable development.[39] Some include a particular provision on trade in forest products, which commits parties to jointly improve forest law enforcement and governance and to promote

---

[39] See http://ec.europa.eu/trade/policy/policy-making/sustainable-development/.

trade in sustainable forest products.[40] While it is still too early to evaluate the impact of these provisions, they facilitate and promote discussions and action on the issue of trade in legal and sustainable forest and agricultural products (Brack 2013).

To effectively address drivers of deforestation, international law makers and national policy makers also have to carefully weigh the effects of adopted measures, not only directly but also indirectly. Here particular caution needs to be taken when evaluating trade liberalization and the associated impact on commodity prices. Regulation should steer agriculture away from expansion towards intensification. This requires safeguards that combine increases in agricultural production with the protection of natural resources.

Within this multitude of options and instruments, the UNFCCC may find its natural role in serving as a clearing-house to record different measures, provide transparency and help identifying synergies among different legal instruments. In this context, it is important that the focus on causes for deforestation does not get lost in a future climate treaty. While the tools to enforce any requests and mandates of the UNFCCC and its Protocol are weak, the various reporting requirements they formulate carry weight in their own right. They facilitate monitoring and evaluation processes within countries, inform stakeholders and support national policy making. In our view it is also essential that developed countries contribute their fair share in addressing deforestation drivers, and that they are held accountable in doing this. Ranging from deforestation-free public procurement, the WTO-compatible promotion of labelling, the monitoring of illegality, standards for responsible finance and the collaboration with the private sector, there are a multitude of activities that address powerful drivers of deforestation, often those that tropical forest countries are unable to address on their own.

BIBLIOGRAPHY

Angelsen, A., ed., 2009. *Realising REDD+, National Strategy and Policy Options*, Bogor, Indonesia: CIFOR, International Center for Forest Research.

Angelsen, A., 2010. "Policies for Reduced Deforestation and their impact on Agricultural Production", *Proceedings of the National Academy of Sciences* 107: 19639–44.

Angelsen A., Kaimowitz, D., 1997. "What Can We Learn from Economic Models of Deforestation?" Seminar paper, Bogor, Indonesia: CIFOR.

Angelsen, A., Kaimowitz D., 2001. "Agricultural Technology and Forests: A Recapitulation" (Chapter 21), and "Policy Recommendations" (Chapter 22), in Angelsen and Kaimowitz,

[40] EU–Central America Association Agreement, art. 289.

Agricultural Technologies and Tropical Deforestation, Wallingford, UK: CABI International.

Bodansky, D., 2000. "What's So Bad about Unilateral Action to Protect the Environment?" 11 *EJIL* 2, 339–47.

Boucher D., 2011. "Cattle and Pasture" (Chapter 5), in Boucher, D., Elias, P., Liniger, K., May-Tobin, C., Roquemore, S. and Saxon, E., 2011. *The Root of the Problem, What's Driving Tropical Deforestation Today*, Washington, DC: Union of Concerned Scientists.

Brack, D. 2013. *Controlling Illegal Logging: Consumer-Country Measures*, London, UK: Chatham House.

Brack, D., 2013. *Controlling Trade in Agricultural Commodities: Bilateral Agreements*, London, UK: Chatham House.

Broekhoven, G., Wit, M., eds., 2014. *Linking FLEGT and REDD+ to Improve Forest Governance*, Wageningen, the Netherlands: Tropenbos International, xx and 212.

Brown Weiss, E., 2000. "The Rise or the Fall of International Law?" 69 *Fordham L. Rev.* 345–72.

Brunné, J. in Beyerlin, U., Stoll, P., Wolfrum, R., eds., 2005. *Ensuring Compliance with Multilateral Environmental Agreements: A Dialogue between Practitioners and Academia*, Leiden/Boston: Brill, Nijhoff.

Cashore, B., Göhler, D., Hoogeveen, H., Rayner, J., Verkooijen, P., 2011. "Learning about Policy Learning: Designing a Global Forest Governance Learning Architecture", prepared for Workshop 3, Learning in Politics and Public Policy ECPR Joint Sessions of Workshops, St Gallen, 12–16 April 2011.

Chaytor, B., 2001. *The Development of Global Forest Policy: Overview of Legal and Institutional Frameworks.* Report commissioned by the Mining, Minerals and Sustainable Development Project of the International Institute for Environment and Development and the World Business Council for Sustainable Development.

De Melo, J., Vijil, M., 2014. *The Critical Mass Approach to Achieve a Deal on Green Goods and Services: What is on the Table? How Much to Expect?* Policy Research Working Paper, No. WPS 7061, Washington, DC: World Bank Group.

Defries, R.S., Rudel, T., Uriarte, M. and Hansen, M., 2010. "Deforestation driven by Urban Population Growth and Agricultural Trade in the Twenty-first Century", 3 *Nature Geoscience* 178–81.

Dixon, J., Gulliver, A., Gibbon, D., Hall, M., eds., 2001. *Farming Systems and Poverty: Improving Farmers' Livelihoods in a Changing World*, Washington, DC: FAO and the World Bank. (Available at: http://www.fao.org/3/a-ac349e.pdf).

Downes, D., 1999. *Assessing the Effects on Forests of Proposed Trade Liberalization in the Forest Product Sector: Comments Submitted to the Office of the United States Trade Representative and the Council on Environmental Equality*, Washington, DC: Center for International Environmental Law.

Eckersley, R., 2004. "The Big Chill: The WTO and Multilateral Environmental Agreements", 4 *Global Environmental Politics* 2, 24–50.

FAO, 2009. *How to Feed the World in 2050.* Discussion paper prepared for expert forum, 12–13 October, released 23 September.

Fishman, A., Obidzinski, K., 2014. "European Union Timber Regulation: Is It Legal?" 23 *Review of European, Comparative & International Environmental Law* 2, 258–74.

Geist, H.J., Lambin, E.R., 2002. "Proximate Causes and Underlying Driving Forces of Tropical Deforestation", 52 *BioScience* 2, 143–50.

Harrop, S., Pritchard, D., 2011. "A Hard Instrument Goes Soft: The Implications of the Convention on Biological Diversity's Current Trajectory", 21 *Global Environmental Change* 474–80.

Houghton, R.A., 2012. "Carbon Emissions and the Drivers of Deforestation and Forest Degradation in the Tropics", 4 *Current Opinion in Environmental Sustainability* 597–603.

Howse, R., Eliason A., 2009. "Domestic and International Strategies to Address Climate Change: An Overview of the WTO Legal Issues" in Cottier, T., Nartova, O., Bigdeli, S., eds., *International Trade Regulation and the Mitigation of Climate Change: World Trade Forum*, Cambridge, UK: Cambridge University Press.

Humphreys, D., 2005. "The Elusive Quest for a Global Forests Convention", 14 *Review of European, Comparative & International Environmental Law* 1, 1.

Humphreys, D., 2009. "Discourse as Ideology: Neoliberalism and the Limits of International Forest Policy", *Forest Policy and Economics* 11, 319–25.

ILC, 2006. Rep. of the Study Group of the International Law Commission, 58th Sess., May 1–June 9, July 3–Aug. 11, 2006, UN Doc. A/CN.4/L.682 (13 April 2006).

IPCC (Eggleston, H.S., Buendia, L., Miwa, K., Ngara, T. and Tanabe, K., eds.), 2006. 'Guidelines for National Greenhouse Gas Inventories', prepared by the National Greenhouse Gas Inventories Programme, Japan: IGES.

Kissinger, G., Herold, M., De Sy, V., 2012. *Drivers of Deforestation and Forest Degradation: A Synthesis Report for REDD+ Policymakers*, Vancouver, Canada: Lexeme Consulting.

Leggett, M., 2013. *Drivers of Deforestation and WTO rules: Conflicts and Solutions*, Oxford, UK: Global Canopy Programme.

Lininger, K., 2011. "Small-scale Farming and Shifting Cultivation" (Chapter 9), in Boucher, D., Elias, P., Liniger, K., May-Tobin, C., Roquemore, S. and Saxon, E., *The Root of the Problem, What's Driving Tropical Deforestation Today*, Washington, DC: Union of Concerned Scientists.

MacKay, F., 2001. *A Guide to Indigenous Peoples' Rights in the International Labour Organization*, Moreton-in-Marsh, UK: Forest Peoples Programme.

McDermott, C., O'Carroll, A., Wood, P. 2007. *International Forest Policy – the Instruments, Agreements and Processes that Shape it*, Department of Economic and Social Affairs, United Nations on Forests Secretariat.

McGraw, D., 2002. "The CBD – Key Characteristics and Implications for Implementation", 11 *Review of European, Comparative & International Environmental Law* 17–28.

McKenna, M., 2014. *The WTO Environmental Goods Agreements: Why Even a Small Step Forward Is a Good Step*, at http://blogs.worldbank.org/trade/wto-environmental-goods-agreement-why-even-small-step-forward-good-step.

Morgera, E., Tsioumani, E., 2011. "Yesterday, Today and Tomorrow: Looking Afresh at the Convention on Biological Diversity", 21 *Yearbook of International Environmental Law Study Group Report* (finalized by Martti Koskenniemi) (examining the impact of fragmentation of international law).

Mulliken, T., 2009. *The Role of CITES in Controlling the International Trade in Forest Products*, Rome: FAO.

Nagtzaam, G., 2014. "Into the Woods: Analyzing Normative Evolution and the International Tropical Timber Organization", 5 *Arts and Social Sciences Journal*, 2.

Nelson, E., Polasky, S., Lewis, D., Plantinga, A., Lonsdorf, E., White, B., Bael, D., Lawler, J., 2008. "Efficiency of Incentives to Jointly Increase Carbon Sequestration and Species Conservation on a Landscape", 105 *Proceedings of the National Academy of Sciences* 9471–6.

OECD/FAO, 2011. *Agricultural Outlook 2011–2020*, OECD Publishing and FAO.

OECD/FAO, 2012. *Agricultural Outlook 2012–2021*, OECD Publishing and FAO, http://dx.doi.org/10.1787/agr_outlook-2012-en.

Rademaekers, K., Eichler, L., Berg, J., Obersteiner, M., Havlik, P., 2010. "Study on the Evolution of Some Deforestation Drivers and their Potential Impacts on the Costs of an Avoiding Deforestation Scheme", prepared for the European Commission. Rotterdam, Netherlands: ECORYS and IIASA.

Rautner, M., Leggett, M., Davis, F., 2013. *The Little Book of the Big Deforestation Drivers*, Oxford, UK: Global Canopy Programme.

Rayner, J., Buck, A., Katila, P., 2010. "Embracing Complexity: Meeting the Challenges of International Forest Governance. A Global Assessment Report", IUFRO World Series vol. 28, Vienna.

Reeve, R., 2006. "Wildlife Trade, Sanctions and Compliance: Lessons from the CITES Regime", 82 *International Affairs* 881–97.

Robalino, J., Herrera L., 2009. *Trade and Deforestation: A Literature Review*, Geneva: World Trade Organization.

Ruis, Barbara M.G.S., 2001. "No Forest Convention but Ten Tree Treaties", *Unasylva*, No. 206, 52 *Global Conventions Related to Forests. An international journal of forestry and forest industries* 3, Rome: FAO. (Available at http://www.fao.org/docrep/003/y1237e/y1237e03.htm.)

Sands, P., 1989. "The Environment, Community and International Law", 30 *Harvard International Law Journal* 393.

Savaresi, A., 2013. "The Role of REDD+ in the Harmonisation of Overlapping International Obligations", in Hollo, E., Kulovesi K., Mehling, M., eds., *Climate Change and the Law*, New York: Springer, 391–418.

Saxon E., Roquemore, S., 2011. "Palm Oil" (Chapter 6), in Boucher, D., Elias, P., Liniger, K., May-Tobin, C., Roquemore, S. and Saxon, E., 2011. *The Root of the Problem, What's Driving Tropical Deforestation Today*, Washington, DC: Union of Concerned Scientists.

Scanlon, J., 2014. "Strengthening Front-line Action to Combat Wildlife and Forest Crimes", 2 *UN Chronicle* 16–19.

Schaeffer, R., Rodrigues, R.L.V., Laurance, W.F., Albernaz, A.K.M., Fearnside, P.M., Vasconcelos, H.L., Ferreira, L.V., 2005. "Underlying Causes of Deforestation", *Science* 18 February, 1046–7.

Schmidhuber, J., Bruinsma, J., Boedeker, G., 2009. *Capital Requirements for Agriculture in Developing Countries to 2050*, Rome: FAO, Economic and Social Development Department. (Available at ftp://ftp.fao.org/docrep/fao/012/ak974e/ak974e00.pdf.)

Secretariat of the Convention on Biological Diversity, 2008. *Biodiversity and Agriculture: Safeguarding Biodiversity and Securing Food for the World*, Montreal.

Secretariat of the Convention on Biological Diversity, 2009. *Connecting Biodiversity and Climate Change Mitigation and Adaptation: Report of the Second Ad Hoc Technical Expert Group on Biodiversity and Climate Change*, Technical Series No. 41, Montreal.

Streck, C., Burns, D., Guimares, L., 2012. *Towards Policies for Climate Change Mitigation: Incentives and Benefits for Smallholder Farmers*, Report No. 7, Copenhagen: CCAFS.

Streck, C., Schmidt, L., Tennigkeit, T., Bals, C., Gerber, K., 2013. *Financing REDD+ Catalyzing Private Finance through Public Support for REDD+*, Briefing Paper, Bonn: Germanwatch, March.

Sunderlin, W.D., Ekaputri, A.D., Sills, E.O., Duchelle, A.E., Kweka, D., Diprose, R., Doggart, N., Ball, S., Lima, R., Enright, A., Torres, J., Hartanto, H. and Toniolo, A., 2014. *The Challenge of Establishing REDD+ on the Ground: Insights from 23 Subnational Initiatives in Six Countries*, CIFOR Occasional Paper No. 104, Bogor, Indonesia: Center for International Forestry Research (CIFOR).

Tarasofsky, R., 1999. *Assessing the International Forest Regime*, Washington, DC: Island Press.

Union of Concerned Scientists (UCS), 2011. *The Root of the Problem – Drivers of Deforestation, What Is Driving Deforestation Today?*, June, Washington, DC.

van Asselt, H., 2012. "Managing the Fragmentation of International Environmental Law: Forests at the Intersection of the Climate and Biodiversity Regimes", 44 *Journal of International Law and Politics* 1205–78.

Vossenaar, R., 2014. *Identifying Products with Climate and Development Benefits for an Environmental Goods Agreement*, Issue Paper No. 19, Geneva: International Centre for Trade and Sustainable Development.

Walker, N., Patel, S., Davies, F., Milledge, S., Hulse, J., 2013. *Demand-side Interventions to Reduce Deforestation and Forest Degradation*. London: IIED.

World Bank, 2012. *Global Economic Prospects: Managing Growth in a Volatile World*, Volume 5, June, Washington, DC.

9. REDD+, tenure and indigenous property: the promise and peril of a 'human rights-based approach'

*Kirsty Gover**[1]

1. INTRODUCTION

In this chapter I argue that the emphasis in REDD+ policy and commentary on the need for 'secure and clear' tenure, coupled with a 'human rights-based' approach to programming suggests a bias in favour of property rights premised on current possession of land. Since states embarking on tenure reform in anticipation of REDD+ funding will need to address competing claims to forested land, the methodology so far endorsed by UN-REDD and the FAO could disadvantage communities claiming tenure rights based on prior possession. This is likely to affect indigenous communities claiming rights sourced in customary law, particularly where those rights are not enforceable in state law and are sought by communities that have been dispossessed of the land they claim. Human rights methodologies do not adequately address historic claims of this kind. I note that in contrast, the World Bank's operational policy OP 4.10 on indigenous peoples (which applies in principle to the FCPF in its administration of REDD+ funding), makes some provision, albeit limited, for the rights of indigenous peoples to land they no longer occupy, and provides for compensation where access to those lands cannot be secured.[2] However, the Bank's operational policies do not ordinarily apply to REDD readiness funding provided by the FCPF, and so will not

* All websites cited in this chapter were accessed on 1 October 2015.

[1] The research for this chapter was conducted as part of an Australian Research Council grant entitled *Climate Change Law and Mitigation: Forest Carbon Sequestration and Indigenous and Local Community Rights*. A version of the chapter will appear in Maureen Tehan, Lee Godden, Margaret Young and Kirsty Gover, *The Impact of Climate Change Mitigation on Indigenous and Forest Communities: International, National and Local Law Perspectives on REDD+* (Cambridge University Press forthcoming, 2016). Many thanks to the Melbourne Law Library Research Service and to Cate Reade for research assistance.

[2] World Bank, 'OP 4.10 – Indigenous Peoples' in *Operational Manual* (July 2005, rev April 2013) para 4, discussed below.

directly influence state tenure arrangements until REDD+ implementation is underway, leaving the field open in the REDD readiness phase to be shaped by the criteria and guidance developed by the UN-REDD and the FAO.

I argue in this chapter that REDD+ policy on tenure is at a nascent but crucial stage, and could benefit from consideration of the ways in which historic indigenous property claims have been conceptualised and addressed in North America and Australasia, and in the jurisprudence of international human rights bodies. In the absence of advice and standards that deal with claims based on prior possession in accordance with customary law, and in view of the incentives offered by REDD+ to powerful actors (including states) to reduce their liability by excluding indigenous claims and the time pressures inherent in the REDD+ agenda, as it stands REDD+ policy could encourage the consolidation of tenure arrangements that do not sufficiently account for the interests of indigenous and tribal peoples in forested lands.

In this chapter I examine the 'state of play' of tenure discourse in the REDD+ context. In section 1 I discuss, with a critical eye, the interventions on tenure that appear in the small body of policy and guidance offered to states by the UN-REDD and FCPF respectively, and the standards deployed by those bodies when evaluating R-PPs. These norms and standards relate in various (sometimes attenuated) ways to the decisions on REDD+ made by the UNFCCC, including the safeguard requirements identified in the 2010 Cancún Agreement. I identify within this body of policy a set of conceptual challenges that attends efforts to address indigenous property claims based on customary law where the dominant normative framework is premised on human rights: the difficulty of conceiving of property rights as human rights, the problem of circularity in property law, and the relation of these two conceptual hurdles to the official 'recognition' of indigenous customary property rights. I consider in particular the challenge of reconciling acts of recognition with the principles of equality and non-discrimination that underpin human rights law. In section 2 I consider the methods used to address these issues by courts in North America and Australasia, by international human rights bodies, and by the Inter-American Court of Human Rights (IACtHR). This body of jurisprudence, I argue, contains two conceptually distinct methodologies that govern the recognition of customary indigenous property rights, both of which could usefully inform the development of REDD+ policy on tenure.

2. WHAT ARE THE ENTRY POINTS FOR TENURE ISSUES IN REDD+ DISCOURSE?

2.1 The UN-REDD, the FCPF and the UNFCCC: Tenure Standards in REDD+

There is wide agreement among civil society actors, states and international bodies that adequate tenure arrangements will be a pivotal determinant of the success of REDD+ programmes at the state level, and of the REDD+ regime as a whole. In 2013, for example, a 'meeting of experts' convened by UN-REDD concluded that the need to address tenure issues in the REDD+ context was 'becoming increasingly urgent' and that there was a particular need for 'greater clarity over tenure and the recognition of customary rights to land by indigenous peoples and local communities'.[3] Notwithstanding the acknowledged importance of tenure arrangements, including the Cancún Agreement's direction to states to consider 'tenure issues' in the course of undertaking REDD+ activities, tenure policy is a late-starter in REDD+ debates. It was not until 2012, for example, that any policy advice on tenure reform was published by UN-REDD.[4] An external evaluation of UN-REDD conducted in 2014 found that while the Programme's emphasis on safeguards and on the principle of FPIC had attracted support for REDD+ from civil society and indigenous peoples, 'contentious issues such as tenure and benefit distribution remain unresolved challenges'[5] and 'relatively little has been done so far' in respect of 'land rights, carbon rights, tenure reform, and benefit sharing mechanisms under REDD+ scenarios',[6] adding that the UN-REDD Policy Board 'should make resource rights a priority area for Programmed interventions'.[7]

UN-REDD has been hesitant so far to offer substantive directions to

---

[3] UN-REDD, 'Background Paper for the Expert Meeting: Options for Addressing Tenure under REDD+' (25–27 February 2013) 3.

[4] Barney Dickson et al., 'REDD+ Beyond Carbon: Supporting Decisions on Safeguards and Multiple Benefits' (Policy Brief, UN-REDD 2012), http://theredddesk.org/resources/un-redd-policy-brief-redd-beyond-carbon-supporting-decisions-safeguards-and-multiple.

[5] Alain Frechette, Minoli de Bresser and Robert Hofstede, 'External Evaluation of the United Nations Collaborative Programme on Reducing Emissions from Deforestation and Forest Degradation in Developing Countries (the UN-REDD Programme)' (Evaluation Report, July 2014) iii, http://www.fao.org/evaluation/oed-home/oed-per/fr/?page=4&ipp=10.

[6] Ibid. 25.

[7] Ibid. ix.

states on optimal forest tenure arrangements. In its 2013 Policy Brief on tenure, UN-REDD acknowledged that tenure reform is 'an enormous, endogenous change process and requires a long-term perspective', and noted that 'resources available for REDD+ readiness are not sufficient to carry out national tenure reforms'.[8] Elsewhere UN-REDD and FAO officials noted the limitations imposed by the nature and scope of the REDD readiness phase, and suggested that '[t]he work on tenure under REDD+ must match the scope of the REDD+ instrument in terms of financial and human resources and the time frame for readiness'.[9] At its 2014 Policy Board meeting, for example, Board members were advised by officials that '[t]enure is too political an issue for a UN-REDD Programme blueprint to be put in place and the topic must instead be addressed at national level', and further, that UN-REDD's capacity to assist states in these endeavours were limited by the fact that '[t]enure is also often dealt with by ministries other than the one where REDD+ focal points work'.[10] At the same meeting however, more than half of the Policy Board Members in attendance 'rated addressing tenure issues as extremely important and an overwhelming majority believe[d] that tenure issues must be addressed at the very start of the REDD+ process'.[11] For now at least, however, tenure reform is an area within which the UN-REDD fears to tread too heavily.

The evidence to date suggests that states participating in REDD readiness preparations are themselves ill-equipped to address tenure issues in the context of REDD+, even while many recognise that it is a crucially important prerequisite for successful REDD+ implementation. A 2012 Country Needs Assessment conducted by the UN-REDD and FCPF concluded that 'legal frameworks to support the implementation of REDD+ and to resolve land tenure and carbon rights issues in the REDD+ context are needed in virtually all existing and nascent REDD+ country

---

[8] Dickson et al. (n 4) 6.

[9] UN-REDD, 'Background Paper' (n 3) 4. 'Currently, the tenure work has not yet been established in most REDD+ countries, and road maps for the tenure work still need to be developed. The legal framework for tenure is quite well developed in many countries, but compliance with the existing laws and regulations remains a major challenge for many governments and communities. REDD+ work on tenure therefore needs to be based on a solid analysis of the existing legal frameworks for tenure, in particular in view of the clarification of tenure systems and the formalization of customary tenure. In a nutshell: What is specifically needed in the improvement of tenure for effective REDD+ implementation?': ibid. 9.

[10] UN-REDD, 'Report of the Thirteenth Policy Board Meeting' (6–7 November 2014) 9–10.

[11] Ibid.

strategies'.[12] Likewise, civil society and policy bodies have expressed concern about the lack of reference to tenure in states' REDD+ readiness documents.[13] A recent report by the WRI surveyed 32 readiness proposals submitted to UN-REDD or the FCPF (26 R-PPs and 6 National Programme Documents (NPDs)), and observed that while most of the reviewed proposals identified the importance of clear and secure tenure for the success of REDD+ projects, only half went on to discuss 'existing tenure challenges' and fewer than one-third outlined 'specific next steps [for] address[ing] land tenure challenges'.[14] This the WRI thought was unsurprising, given that readiness proposals necessarily 'reflect preliminary thinking on REDD+ systems and strategies'.[15] They acknowledged also that tenure reforms 'can be costly and time consuming and that long-term sources of readiness financing have not yet been identified in most REDD+ countries'.[16] UN-REDD seems to agree, observing that even for those states that included tenure policies on forest conversion in their readiness documents, the complexity of competing claims to tenure in forested lands makes it likely that 'a range of challenges might prevent them from committing to policy reforms in relation to forest tenure.'[17]

Aside from the funding criteria deployed by the UN-REDD and FCPF, participating states are also obliged independently to meet obligations set out in the COP decisions of the UNFCCC. The formal entry point for tenure issues in REDD+ programming then, is the UNFCCC's 2010 COP decision (the 'Cancún Agreement'),[18] which sets out the basic parameters of the REDD+ regime, and outlines in an Appendix the 'safeguards'

---

[12] UN-REDD and FCPF, 'Country Needs Assessment: A Report on REDD+ Readiness Among UN-REDD Programme and Forest Carbon Partnership Facility Member Countries' (October 2012) 118.

[13] Sophie Chao, 'Forest Peoples: Numbers Across the World' (Forest Peoples Programme 2012), http://www.forestpeoples.org/sites/fpp/files/publication/2012/05/forest-peoples-numbers-across-world-final_0.pdf; Mary C. Thompson, Manali Baruah and Edward R Carr, 'Seeing REDD+ as a Project of Environmental Governance' (2011) 14 *Environmental Science & Policy* 100, 103.

[14] Lauren Goers Williams, 'Putting the Pieces Together for Good Governance of REDD+: An Analysis of 32 REDD+ Country Readiness Proposals' (Working Paper, World Resources Institute, March 2013) 14, http://www.wri.org/sites/default/files/pdf/putting_the_pieces_together_for_good_governance_of_redd.pdf; see also ibid. 8.

[15] Ibid. 5.

[16] Ibid. 7.

[17] Dickson et al. (n 4) 8.

[18] UNFCCC, 'Report of the Conference of the Parties on its Sixteenth Session' (Cancún, 29 November–10 December 2010) UN Doc FCCC/CP/2010/7/Add.1 (15 March 2011) para 72.

that recipient states should 'promote [] and support []' when undertaking REDD+ activities in their territories.[19] While the safeguards make no express reference to tenure, paragraph 72 of the decision itself requests states to consider 'land tenure issues' when developing and implementing their national REDD+ strategies.[20] The collection of principles, criteria, prompt questions and R-PP standards used by FCPF and UN-REDD to guide states through REDD readiness preparations is dense and complexly cross-referenced. Because these norms shape and drive state applications for REDD readiness funding however, they are currently the only 'enforceable' directions applicable to REDD+ recipient states, and so are for the time being the major interface between the policies favoured by international REDD+ agencies and the domestic law of participating states. For this reason they are considered in more detail below.

The link between the Cancún Agreement and the tenure standards adopted by the UN-REDD and the FCPF is somewhat opaque. Tenure appears in the UN-REDD's SEPC, which are 'consistent with' the UNFCCC's Cancún safeguards,[21] and in the FCPF's Strategic Environmental and Social Assessment (SESA) criteria which 'promote and support' the Cancún safeguards.[22] These criteria are reflected in the standards set out in the joint R-PP template that states must complete in order to receive REDD readiness funding (states must address either the UN-REDD SEPC criteria or the FCPF's SESA criteria in the R-PP, depending on which fund they are applying to).[23] To date, UN-REDD has not provided operational guidance on tenure, as it has done on

[19] Ibid. Appendix I(2).

[20] Ibid., para 72.

[21] UN-REDD, 'UN-REDD Programme Social and Environmental Principles and Criteria' (25–26 March 2012) UN Doc UN-REDD/PB8/2012/V/1 ('UN-REDD SEPC') 3. In the case of UN-REDD, the Programme has assigned 'principles' to the Cancún safeguards and the '[t]he criteria are the conditions that need to be met by UN-REDD Programme funded activities to contribute to the achievement of the principle': ibid.

[22] FCPF, 'World Bank Safeguard Policies and the UNFCCC REDD+ Safeguards' (28 August 2013) FMT Note CF-2013-3, 1, http://www.forestcarbonpartnership.org/, in response to FCPF, 'Recommendations of the Working Group on the Methodological and Pricing Approach for the Carbon Fund of the FCPF' (Participants Committee, 11 June 2012) FMT Note 2012-8, 8, https://www.forestcarbonpartnership.org/fcpf-templates-and-materials.

[23] See FCPF, 'Readiness Preparation Proposal (R-PP) Template' (Version 6, 20 April 2012) component 2d, 44, https://www.forestcarbonpartnership.org/fcpf-templates-and-materials. See also, UN-REDD, 'UN-REDD Programme Handbook for National Programmes and Other National-Level Activities' (2012) 13, http://www.unredd.net/index.php?option=com_docman&view=document&alias=8148-

stakeholder engagement, gender mainstreaming and FPIC.[24] UN-REDD has however identified 7 'social and environmental principles' and 24 corollary criteria to direct states in REDD readiness preparation, and has developed a draft 'Benefits and Risk Tool' (BeRT) to assist states to address the SEPC principles and criteria in their R-PP applications. In the REDD readiness phase of REDD+ programming, then, it is the point at which funding applications are submitted by states and evaluated by the UN-REDD Policy Board (or FCPF Facility Management Team) that the normative force of REDD+ tenure standards are brought to bear on states.

The UN-REDD's SEPC criteria on tenure illustrate the Programme's autonomy from the Treaty-based mechanisms of the UNFCCC, even in the course of developing evaluative standards that are 'consistent with' the UNFCCC's Cancún safeguards.[25] For example, because the Cancún safeguards make no express reference to tenure arrangements or property rights, the UN-REDD's advice on tenure is linked instead to the safeguards provision requesting states to promote and support respect for

> the knowledge and rights of indigenous peoples and members of local communities, by taking into account relevant international obligations, national circumstances and laws, and noting that the United Nations General Assembly has adopted the United Nations Declaration on the Rights of Indigenous Peoples.[26]

It is this provision, then, not the reference to 'tenure issues' in paragraph 72 of the decision, that underpins UN-REDD directions to states on the recognition of indigenous property rights. It appears in the UN-REDD SEPC as 'Principle 2', requiring states to '[r]espect and protect stakeholder rights in accordance with international obligations', notably, defining 'stakeholder rights' to include 'human rights, statutory and customary rights, and collective rights'.[27] The criteria that attend the principle accordingly require states to (inter alia), '[r]espect and promote the recognition

---

national-programmes-handbook-8148&category_slug=templates-forms-and-guidance-89&Itemid=134.

[24] UN-REDD, 'UN-REDD SEPC' (n 21) 16.

[25] Ibid. 3.

[26] UNFCCC, 'Tenth Session of the United Nations Permanent Forum on Indigenous Issues (UNPFII)' (February 2011) Appendix 1, 2(c), http://www.un.org/esa/socdev/unpfii/documents/session_10_UNFCCC.pdf; UN-REDD, 'Background Paper' (n 3) 11: '[T]he decision of the Convention on REDD+ clearly demands that the work on tenure under REDD+ goes well beyond forest boundaries.'

[27] UN-REDD, 'UN-REDD SEPC' (n 21) 5.

and exercise of the rights of indigenous peoples, local communities and other vulnerable and marginalized groups to land, territories and resources, including carbon'.[28] In the UN-REDD's BeRT tool, this criterion is expanded into three 'primary questions' (and many more 'guiding questions') asking states to consider whether there are 'existing policies and measures' in place, or 'specific actions' in the proposed REDD+ Programme, that 'respect and promote the recognition and exercise of equitable land tenure and carbon rights by indigenous peoples and local communities'.[29] To assist states to answer these questions, the tool also refers governments to guidelines and policy documents on forest tenure, including the FAO Voluntary Guidelines.[30]

As noted above, the UN-REDD's SEPC criteria are communicated to states in relatively more precise and concrete terms via the prompts and standards contained in the joint FCPF-UN-REDD R-PP templates. The template, however, defers substantive reporting on tenure reform to the final stages of the REDD readiness phase, so that it does not directly condition the supply of REDD+ funding. To complete the R-PP, states must submit an 'assessment of Land Use, Land Use Change Drivers, Forest Law, Policy and Governance', which includes information on 'pertinent laws, policies, and issues surrounding land tenure and resource rights, and traditional land use of indigenous people, extent of titled and untitled indigenous lands, indigenous claims for additional land "extensions" and process of land title demarcations'.[31] They are also directed to prepare a preliminary 'REDD+ Implementation Framework' which must address, inter alia, tenure issues such as

> [w]ho owns or uses the forest under statutory or customary law? Is there regulatory or legal clarity on who owns carbon benefits generated by REDD-plus activities? Is there a relationship between carbon ownership and land

---

[28] Ibid. Criterion 7, 5.

[29] UN-REDD, 'Draft Social and Environmental Principles and Criteria – Benefit and Risks Tool (SEPC-BeRT)' (2013) Principle 2, Criterion 7, http://www.unredd.net/index.php?option=com_docman&task=doc_download&gid=6352&Itemid=53. See also, UN-REDD, 'Benefit and Risks Tool (BeRT): Supporting Countries to Address and Respect the Cancun Safeguards', http://www.un-redd.org/multiple_benefits/sepc_bert/tabid/991/default.aspx.

[30] The BeRT tool text notes that 'The development of the BeRT has drawn on a rich body of relevant material, including in particular the REDD+ SES, the World Resources Institute's Governance of Forests Indicators Toolkit, One World Trust Accountability matrix and various multilateral institutions' safeguards policies, as well as Epple et al. (2011)': SEPC-BeRT (n 29) tab 1.

[31] R-PP Template (n 23) 33.

tenure? How would any land tenure, or carbon ownership, issues that arise be resolved or mediated?'[32]

Significantly, the R-PP template notes that in respect to the implementation framework, 'good practices are only just becoming evident for this component, as there is little experience to date', so in lieu of concrete standards, 'promising ideas' are offered instead.

The tenure standards deployed by the FCPF in the evaluation of REDD readiness funding applications have a different anatomy. The FCPF, like the UN-REDD, was formally established in 2008, but is a creature of the World Bank and operates entirely under its auspices. The FCPF's Charter confirms that its work is governed by the World Bank's ten Operational Policies and Procedures (also known as its 'safeguard policies') including OP 4.10 on Indigenous Peoples.[33] This Operational Policy has had a longstanding influence on the work of the Bank, and as with the other safeguard policies, non-compliance by Bank staff provides a basis for claims to be made to the World Bank Inspection Panel by affected groups.[34] At the time of writing consultations were underway on the revision of the policy, as part of the 'Review and Update of the World Bank Safeguard Policies' launched in 2012. A draft standard (draft Environmental and Social Standard 7) was circulated for comment on 30 July 2014[35] and

---

32 Ibid. 40.

33 Section 3.1(d) of the FCPF Charter provides that 'the operation of the Facility, including implementation of activities under Grant Agreements and Emission Reductions Programs, shall . . . comply with the World Bank's Operational Policies and Procedures, taking into account the need for effective participation of Forest-Dependent Indigenous Peoples and Forest Dwellers in decisions that may affect them, respecting their rights under national law and applicable international obligations': International Bank for Reconstruction and Development, 'Charter Establishing the Forest Carbon Partnership Facility' (24 October 2012), https://www.forestcarbonpartnership.org/sites/fcp/files/2013/FCPF%20Charter%20-%2010-24-12%20clean.pdf ('FCPF Charter').

34 Bank Information Center (BiC), 'SESA, Safeguards and the FCPF: A Guide for Civil Society' (January 2013), http://www.bicusa.org/wp-content/uploads/2013/01/SESA+informational+doc+for+PC6.pdf. Also Benedict Kingsbury, 'Operational Policies of International Institutions as Part of the Law-Making Process: The World Bank and Indigenous Peoples' in Ian Brownlie, Guy S. Goodwin-Gill and Stefan Talmon (eds), *The Reality of International Law: Essays in Honour of Ian Brownlie* (Oxford University Press 1999).

35 World Bank, 'Environmental and Social Framework: Setting Standards for Sustainable Development' – First Draft for Consultation (30 July 2014) 74–82, https://consultations.worldbank.org/consultation/review-and-update-world-bank-safeguard-policies.

revised on 1 July 2015,[36] but on its face does not substantively alter the tenure provisions of OP 4.10, which include most relevantly, paragraph 17. This paragraph sets out the tenure considerations that must be addressed by the Bank if an initial investigation shows that indigenous peoples will be affected by a proposed project:[37]

> If the project involves (a) activities that are contingent on establishing legally recognized rights to lands and territories that Indigenous Peoples have traditionally owned or customarily used or occupied (such as land titling projects), or (b) the acquisition of such lands, the IPP [Indigenous Peoples Plan] sets forth an action plan for the legal recognition of such ownership, occupation, or usage . . . Such legal recognition may take the following forms: (a) full legal recognition of existing customary land tenure systems of Indigenous Peoples; or (b) conversion of customary usage rights to communal and/or individual ownership rights. If neither option is possible under domestic law, the IPP includes measures for legal recognition of perpetual or long-term renewable custodial or use rights.[38]

Importantly, for the purposes of this chapter, while OP 4.10 identifies indigenous peoples as 'distinct, vulnerable, social and cultural group[s]'[39] with 'collective attachment to geographically distinct habitats or ancestral territories in the project area',[40] the policy also protects groups that have 'lost "collective attachment to geographically distinct habitats or ancestral territories in the project area" . . . because of forced severance'.[41] In order to qualify under this section of the policy, the loss must have occurred 'within the concerned group members' lifetime because of conflict, government resettlement programs, dispossession from their lands, natural calamities, or incorporation of such territories into an urban area'.[42] Thus while the policy is designed to protect people who occupy the land on which Bank-funded projects are to operate, and does not accommodate claims based on intergenerational historic loss, the policy does extend to groups who involuntarily lost possession of their land within living memory. In this respect the policy, when and if deployed

---

36 World Bank, 'Environmental and Social Framework: Setting Standards for Sustainable Development' – Second Draft for Consultation (1 July 2015) 102-111, https://consultations.worldbank.org/Data/hub/files/consultation-template/review-and-update-world-bank-safeguard-policies/en/materials/clean_second_draft_es_framework_final_draft_for_consultation_july_1_2015.pdf.

37 World Bank, 'OP 4.10' (n 2) para 17.

38 Ibid.

39 Ibid. para 4.

40 Ibid. para 4(b).

41 Ibid. para 4.

42 Ibid. para 4, fn 8.

by the FCPF in the REDD+ context, could extend to at least some non-occupant indigenous communities in a way that is not obviously contemplated by the FAO Guidelines.

In practice, however, the question of exactly how the World Bank operational polices are brought to bear on FCPF's evaluation of REDD readiness funding applications is controversial, and the Bank's advice on this point is somewhat ambivalent.[43] According to the Bank, while the FCPF constitutive documents specify that '[a]ny funding from the Bank would trigger the application of its safeguard policies',[44] in fact 'the FCPF Readiness Fund is not intended to fund projects or investments on the ground',[45] so that the formal process for ensuring compliance with the Bank's safeguard policies will ordinarily not apply to the provision of funding for REDD readiness preparations. For the purposes of applying its operational policies, then, the Bank draws a distinction between the financing of 'preparation' on the one hand, and financing 'the implementation of policies and projects' on the other.[46] It is only in respect of the latter that 'the safeguard instruments required by the safeguard policies would have to be prepared and applied as they are in standard Bank-financed projects'.[47] In short, while the safeguard policies apply in principle to all 'REDD readiness activities funded by the FCPF Readiness Fund', the Bank will not, except 'on an exceptional basis', enforce its operational policies at this stage. The tenure standards included in the World Bank's OP 4.10 on Indigenous Peoples, although offering a very high degree of protection where they are triggered, have been deferred beyond the REDD readiness phase, and are not likely to condition the allocation of funding by the FCPF until REDD+ *implementation* funding

---

43 Bank Information Center (n 34).

44 FCPF, 'Information Memorandum' (13 June 2008) 18, https://www.forestcarbonpartnership.org/readiness-fund. Including the selection of countries into the REDD Readiness Fund. FCPF, 'Incorporating Environmental and Social Considerations into the Process of Getting Ready for REDD' – Draft (Readiness Fund, 15 October 2009) FMT Note 2009-6, 1 (para 2(i)), http://www.forestcarbonpartnership.org/sites/fcp/files/Documents/tagged/FCPF_en_soc_guidelines_10-15-09.pdf. See also, FCPF, 'Incorporating Environmental and Social Considerations into the Process of Getting Ready for REDD' – 2010 update (Readiness Fund, 23 June 2010) FMT Note 2010-16, https://www.forestcarbonpartnership.org/sites/fcp/files/2014/June/FMT%20Note%202010-16%20SESA%20Mainstreaming.pdf.

45 FCPF, 'Incorporating Environmental and Social Considerations' (2009) (n 43) 3.

46 Ibid. 3.

47 Ibid.

is sought. For the foreseeable future, then, tenure issues in the REDD+ context will likely develop in line with the advice so far provided by the UN-REDD and FAO.

2.2 Tenure in REDD+: Debates and Controversies

There is no doubt that REDD+ has the potential to impact adversely on the well-being of indigenous and forest-dependent communities by incentivising others (including the state) to exclude them from forested lands.[48] REDD+ could also yield tenure-related 'co-benefits' for those communities, by encouraging the legal recognition and enforcement of their previously informal or de facto customary property rights, and by providing REDD+ payments to those communities in compensation for their emissions-reducing activities. As one might expect, then, existing UN-REDD advice on tenure references both risk-management and benefit-sharing goals. The report of UN-REDD's 2013 Expert Meeting on tenure, for example, identifies these as the two central instrumental values of tenure reform, observing that '[s]ecure tenure rights are the foundation for minimizing risks for investments into REDD+ and for sharing the benefits from carbon finance'.[49]

In risk-management reasoning, secure tenure is thought to directly discourage deforestation by allowing rights-holders to 'take into account future values in current decision-making', that is, to think prospectively about the long-term use of forested land rather than exploit or clear forests to prove ownership or in anticipation of losing access to the resource.[50] Secure and clear tenure is also sometimes presented as

---

[48] James Mayers et al., 'Forest-Based Climate Strategies: Making REDD and Other Initiatives Work' (IIED 2008), http://www.fern.org/publications/recommended-reading/forest-based-climate-strategies.

[49] UN-REDD, 'Background Paper' (n 3) 12.

[50] Ann-Kristin Rothe and Paul Munro-Faure, 'Tenure and REDD+: Developing Enabling Tenure Conditions for REDD+' (Policy Brief, UN-REDD 2013) 2, http://theredddesk.org/resources/tenure-and-redd-developing-enabling-tenure-conditions-redd. See Lisa Westholm, Robin Biddulph, Ida Hellmark and Anders Ekbom, 'REDD+ and Tenure: A Review of the Latest Developments in Research, Implementation and Public Policy Debates' in Randall A. Bluffstone and Elizabeth J.Z. Robinson (eds), *Forest Tenure Reform in Asia and Africa: Local Control for Improved Livelihoods, Forest Management, and Carbon Sequestration* (Routledge 2014) 224: 'if local community members are denied long-term benefits, they are more likely to look for short-term gains'. See also, Lorenzo Cotula and James Mayers, 'Tenure in REDD: Start-Point or Afterthought?' (IIED 2009) 6, http://pubs.iied.org/13554IIED.html?k=tenure%20in%20redd; United States Agency for International Development (USAID), 'Land Tenure and REDD+:

a prerequisite of effective participatory rights, because it is thought to provide a basis for identifying the holders of FPIC and to bolster their power to influence states and private sector actors in preparatory consultations.[51] Participatory rights, in this line of reasoning, also reduce community resistance to REDD+ projects and so ensure the stability and durability of those schemes. Conversely, insecure tenure is thought to increase the risk that a lack of community buy-in could undermine the success of REDD+ projects by increasing conflict over resources affected by (and benefits provided by) REDD+, and by creating uncertainty for donors and investors.[52]

On the other hand, secure and clear tenure has been presented in UN-REDD and FAO advice as a necessary basis for facilitating ex-post benefit-sharing. Tenure arrangements provide a way to identify the people and communities contributing to REDD+ climate change goals and so enable the equitable distribution of financial and co-benefits flowing from the operation of REDD projects.[53] In addition, secure and clear tenure is sometimes identified by the UN-REDD and FAO as a unqualified good or 'right', and so as an end in itself, either as a co-benefit of REDD+ or as a right vested in persons with 'legitimate' tenure claims. In this view REDD+ simply 'provides an opportunity to revise outdated tenure policy and legal frameworks [and] to strengthen formal and customary tenure rights'.[54] In a

---

Risks to Property Rights and Opportunities for Economic Growth' (Issue Brief 2013) 3, http://usaidlandtenure.net/issue-brief/land-tenure-and-redd: 'The lack of secure tenure for local populations is recognized as a principal driver of deforestation in many developing countries.'

[51] Cotula and Mayers (n 49) 3.

[52] Ibid. See also country concerns about REDD+ related tenure conflict in UN-REDD, 'Review of Tenure Issues and Needs Identified by UN-REDD Countries' (January 2013). Likewise the COP of the CBD has noted that a '[l]ack of benefits and/or lack of equitable distribution of benefits for relevant stakeholders, in particular for indigenous and local communities, are possible threats to the success of [REDD] activities': COP to the CBD, 'Decision Adopted by the Conference of the Parties to the Convention on Biological Diversity at its Eleventh Meeting' (5 December 2012) UN Doc UNEP/CBD/COP/DEC/XI/19, Annex, para 10, https://www.cbd.int/decision/cop/?id=13180. USAID, 'Land Tenure and REDD+' (n 49) 3–4.

[53] See Goers Williams (n 14) 14. See also, Crystal Davis, Ruth Nogueron and Anne-Gaelle Javelle, 'Analysis of Institutional Mechanisms for Sharing REDD+ Benefits' (Property Rights and Resource Governance Project, USAID March 2012), http://www.usaidlandtenure.net/content/analysis-institutional-mechanisms-sharing-redd-benefits.

[54] Dickson et al. (n 4) 1–2. See also, USAID, 'Land Tenure and REDD+' (n 49) 9.

2014 presentation to the UN-REDD Policy Board, for example, an FAO tenure specialist observed that:

> It's also important to remember that regardless of how REDD+ evolves, investment in securing tenure is widely recognized to be beneficial to communities and forests. Basically this is a win-win opportunity.[55]

How then, are states guided in the consideration of tenure issues in their REDD readiness activities? Since most of the advice and assistance UN-REDD provides is directed at states in the REDD readiness phase, and consistently with its human rights-based approach and extensive interventions on the participatory rights of indigenous peoples and forest-dwelling communities, to date the emphasis in UN-REDD advice has been on the ways in which security of tenure empowers communities to influence decision-making on REDD+ projects. In its 2013 policy brief, for example, after canvassing the various benefits attached to secure and clear tenure, the UN-REDD concluded that '[m]ost importantly, tenure security provides communities with some control over whether REDD+ will be implemented in their community and, if so, how it will affect their livelihoods'.[56] The FAO Voluntary Guidelines however, are not limited in scope to tenure issues impacted by REDD+, and take an expressly more development-focused approach, emphasising access to land as a means to ensure food security and reduce poverty. UN-REDD endorses the FAO Guidelines as a source of guidance for REDD+ participating states that 'can inform REDD+ countries that are developing their own strategies, policy and legal frameworks and activities' in relation to tenure reform.[57] Because of the heavy emphasis on these Guidelines in REDD+ programming on tenure, the lack of other sources within UN-REDD policy, and the non-application of World Bank safeguards in readiness preparations funded by the FCPF, the Voluntary Guidelines are likely to be a primary influence on the development of REDD+ policy and standards on tenure matters. For this reason, it is worth examining their content in some detail below, with a view to assessing their conceptual framing, and the impact of this framing on the interests of indigenous peoples.

---

[55] Amanda Bradley, FAO Tenure Specialist, in her presentation – 'Tenure and REDD+: Update and Key Messages' – at the Thirteenth UN-REDD Programme Policy Board meeting held in Arusha, Tanzania on 3–7 November 2014. For further information, see UN-REDD, 'Thirteenth Policy Board Meeting' (Arusha, Tanzania 3–7 November 2014), http://www.un-redd.org/PolicyBoard/13thPolicyBoard/tabid/794436/Default.aspx.

[56] Rothe and Munro-Faure (n 49) 2–3.

[57] Ibid. 6.

2.3 The FAO Guidelines

The FAO's policy on indigenous peoples expressly states that '[t]he rationale for engagement with indigenous peoples is grounded in FAO's mandate to achieve food security for all'.[58] Likewise, the Voluntary Guidelines are described in REDD+ literature as 'the first broad international consensus by governments, CSOs, the private sector, international organizations and academics on how to govern tenure in a way that increases national food security and promotes sustainable development'.[59] The emphasis on food security and development is significant. As will be discussed below, indigenous interests and land claims may or may not coincide with these goals, in the context of REDD+ or elsewhere.

As might be expected, the FAO Guidelines are pitched at the level of principle, and much of the advice they contain is of a procedural nature. The Guidelines urge inclusivity and participation in the design of tenure arrangements, and emphasise the need for rule of law principles to operate in the implementation of property law, including especially by ensuring that those laws are transparent and non-discriminatory, that documentary records of tenure arrangements are kept and made accessible, and that dispute-resolution mechanisms are available. Importantly, the Guidelines are not on their face confined to individualised private property, but aim instead to accommodate 'tenure rights in various forms, from limited use to full ownership',[60] and include 'all forms of tenure, including public, private, communal, collective, indigenous and customary'.[61] The key concept of 'tenure' used in the Guidelines is correspondingly broad, and is defined as

> the relationship, whether legally or customarily defined, among people, as individuals or groups, with respect to land . . . [as well as] rules invented by societies to regulate behaviour, . . . define how property rights to land are to be allocated within societies . . . [and] define how access is granted to rights to use, control, and transfer land, as well as associated responsibilities and restraints.[62]

---

[58] FAO, 'FAO Policy on Indigenous and Tribal Peoples' (2010) 7, http://www.fao.org/docrep/013/i1857e/i1857e00.htm.

[59] UN-REDD, 'Background Paper' (n 3) 5.

[60] FAO, 'Voluntary Guidelines on the Responsible Governance of Tenure of Land, Fisheries and Forests in the Context of National Food Security' (2012) 13 (para 8.8), http://www.fao.org/nr/tenure/voluntary-guidelines/en.

[61] Ibid. 2 (para 2.4).

[62] FAO, 'Land Tenure and Rural Development' (2002) 7, http://www.fao.org/docrep/005/y4307e/y4307e00.htm.

Accordingly, alongside exclusive possessory tenure rights, the Guidelines make reference to 'subsidiary tenure rights' (giving the example of 'gathering rights'), as well as to systems of regulation that extend beyond individual property, including 'systems of collective use and management' of publicly owned land and resources, and 'processes of allocation by the State'.[63] It is incumbent on states to 'determine which of the land, fisheries and forests they own or control will be retained and used by the public sector, and which of these will be allocated for use by others and under what conditions',[64] as well as to 'determine whether they retain any form of control over land, fisheries and forests that have been allocated'.[65]

Both UN-REDD and the FAO acknowledge that tenure is a composite concept comprised of a 'web of intersecting interests'.[66] The first point of note is that the FAO has deployed the concept of a 'bundle of rights' to give substance to the idea of tenure, an explanatory device that typically enumerates rights to use land, to control land, to recover 'rents and profits' from land users, and to transfer rights in land, and includes duties incumbent on property-holders.[67] The 'bundle of rights' idea is a pillar of western legal theories of property, used to complicate the classical common law conception of private property as a monolithic and absolute right vested in an individual to the exclusion of all others.[68] Accordingly, the Guidelines emphasise that 'no tenure right, including private ownership, is absolute'. Instead, all tenure rights are limited by the rights of third parties and by state intervention or regulation in the public interest, and all tenure rights are balanced against the duties of the rights-holder, including the duty to 'respect the long-term protection and sustainable use of land, fisheries and forests'.[69] Second, the FAO Guidelines draw on a distinction between 'formal' and 'informal' property rights. Formal rights are those that are 'explicitly acknowledged by the state and which may be protected using legal means'. In the Guidelines, formal rights are usually 'statutory rights', while informal property rights 'lack official recognition and protection' and may be illegal or 'extra-legal'. Customary property

---

63 'FAO Voluntary Guidelines' (n 59) 12 (para 8.3).

64 Ibid. 13 (para 8.5).

65 Ibid. 13 (para 8.8).

66 FAO, 'Land Tenure and Rural Development' (n 61) 7–8. See also, Rothe and Munro-Faure (n 49) 1.

67 FAO, 'Land Tenure and Rural Development' (n 61) 10.

68 See e.g., William Blackstone, *Commentaries on the Law of England*, vol. 2 (6th edn, Dublin 1775) (Eighteenth Century Collections Online) 8ff; and, on 'exclusion and exclusiveness', Felix S. Cohen, 'Dialogue on Private Property' (1954) 9(2) *Rutgers Law Review* 357, 370–1.

69 'FAO Voluntary Guidelines' (n 59) 6 (para 4.2).

rights, in the view of the FAO, are ordinarily informal and extra-legal in character, although the Organization concedes that the statutory recognition of customary rights in some countries (and in particular Africa), has 'blurred' this distinction in practice.[70]

Helpfully, then, the concept of tenure and tenure security used in UN-REDD and FAO advice is not dogmatically exclusive, but rather admits the possibility of multiple property rights coexisting in the same piece of land, an idea that is central to ways that property rights are conceived as a matter of law, at least in common law jurisdictions. The 'bundle of rights' approach, while attentive to the possibilities of addressing cross-claims by 'layering' property rights of different extents over a single parcel of land, does not on its own provide a way forward when that 'bundle' is contested, wholesale, by claimants who derive their rights from customary legal systems that predate that of the state. Where customary legal systems are implicated in property disputes, the legal questions become jurisdictional in form, involving conflicts of laws rather than conflicts of rights. In such circumstances the task is not simply to rank and allocate use and possessory rights over land, but to consider the ways in which customary legal systems and state legal systems can recognise and enforce rights sourced in normative systems external to the one in which enforcement will take place. In settler states the most difficult property-based conceptual impasses occur where rights-holders whose claims are legitimate in one legal system (usually customary law) find that their rights are not recognised in the other, and even more acutely, where third parties have acquired exclusive property rights to the claimed land that are recognised in the dominant legal system. The Guidelines advise that 'where informal tenure to land, fisheries and forests *exists*, States should acknowledge it in a manner that respects *existing* formal rights under national law' (emphasis added).[71] The real conundrum however, is how to decide that informal tenure 'exists' at all, as a matter of fact and law. This requires an 'act of recognition' in which political or judicial institutions of the state recognise the effectiveness of property rights based in customary law, determine the bases on which those rights can be enforced in state law, and select the rights that can be so recognised and enforced.

One of the most conceptually and politically fraught tasks for settler states and indigenous peoples, then, is to agree on the principles of justice that will govern such an exercise, and inform the redistribution of formal property rights where necessary. As will be discussed, courts are gener-

---

70 FAO, 'Land Tenure and Rural Development' (n 61) 11.
71 'FAO Voluntary Guidelines' (n 59) 16 (para 10.1).

ally reluctant to order the redistribution of property rights, because of the very complex questions of public policy involved. In the case of the common law doctrine of aboriginal title, for example, the rule of recognition deployed by judges typically provides that subsequent grants of property rights over indigenous territory will not be disturbed, so that where inconsistent grants have been made, pre-existing customary title will not find purchase in state law. In some settler states (but not all), where restitution is impossible because the grant of formal rights has 'extinguished' the possibility of asserting customary title in state forums, compensatory processes are provided instead, but these are ordinarily managed as negotiated political processes rather than litigated judicial ones. This draws attention to the fundamental assumptions at play in advice directed towards ensuring the 'security and clarity' of tenure. Security of tenure can be achieved in a variety of ways, and one of those ways is by denying the legal status of customary property rights. The legitimacy of security and clarity depends on the underpinning concepts of distributive and reparative justice by which those acts are to be judged. As Westholm et al. have pointed out, in the context of REDD+, 'clear and secure tenure does not per se imply equity'.[72]

Thus, while the Guidelines acknowledge that property rights are sometimes contested by claimants with equally 'legitimate' but differently justified claims, including competition between claims based on customary law and those based in state law, and that tenure is an aggregate 'bundled' concept that can accommodate multiple usage and possessory rights,[73] the concepts of security and clarity nonetheless drive policy advice towards the 'formalisation' of tenure arrangements. Setting aside the risks posed by state insistence on prioritising state grants over customary rights in formalisation processes, the formalisation of customary rights *qua* customary rights poses two types of risk to the holders of those rights. The first risk is endogenous, and points to the possibility that the content of customary law itself is not equitable, in which case recognition may enforce unjust allocations of property within a (formalised) customary system. This possibility receives almost no attention from UN-REDD

---

[72] Westholm et al. (n 49) 232.

[73] FAO, 'Land Tenure and Rural Development' (n 61) 9. Rothe and Munro-Faure (n 49) 3: 'Clarifying tenure in the REDD+ context is a complex endeavor, partly because several rights holders may have different rights over the same resources or share the same rights. These rights may also change over time depending on seasons and natural conditions. Primary and secondary rights may exist, and primary rights to trees may be allocated independently of primary rights to lands on which the trees grow.'

and the FAO. Indeed in the growing body of literature addressing tenure issues in REDD+ policy and programming, very few commentators have questioned the legitimacy of particular forms of property rights supported by customary laws. Yet custom is no guarantee of equity. Westholm et al. have put this problem in blunt terms; 'customary tenure arrangements are often not fair. Social institutions, just like statutory ones, may embody gender inequalities and unequal power relations.'[74]

The second risk is exogenous: the possibility that in formalising customary property rights, state law could compromise, undermine or extinguish some or all of those rights, or refuse recognition (and decline to protect) some rights that are legitimate in customary law. As to the first, UN-REDD's exploratory policies on tenure have noted the danger that customary rights could be compromised or extinguished by processes of statutory formalisation. UN-REDD has specified that '[g]iving customary and traditional rights statutory legal recognition should neither undermine local tenure systems nor simplify them', and that '[c]apturing their complexity and specificity is necessary for avoiding conflicts among local communities and ensuring that REDD+ is connected to the reality on the ground'.[75] Elsewhere the FAO has warned that '[i]ronically, attempts to increase the legal security of some may result in others losing their rights', especially use rights, but suggests that this would occur only in 'poorly designed' titling and registration projects, or where the state enforces 'existing rules that prevent access to resources', including forests.[76] Nowhere is it suggested that the loss of property rights is inevitable where formalisation is undertaken in respect of contested land, because some claimants will be successful at the expense of others. Attrition of this kind is especially likely where claims are equally legitimate and comparable in extent but premised on different legal systems, so that they are inconsistent and irreconcilable as matters of law and fact. This is significant, because it is the nature of property rights to be permanent and resistant to adjustment or reformulation, and to be constitutionally protected from state acquisition or diminishment, so that property disputes are more likely than other legal conflicts to be resolved on a 'winner takes all' basis. This makes property rights uniquely impervious to methods familiar to human rights law, such as provisions allowing states to impose 'justifiable limitations' on rights,[77]

---

[74] Westholm and others (n 49) 232.

[75] UN-REDD, 'Background Paper' (n 3) 13.

[76] FAO, 'Land Tenure and Rural Development' (n 61) 20–21.

[77] See Section 1 of the Canadian Charter of Human Rights and Freedoms, which 'guarantees the rights and freedoms set out in [the Charter] subject only to such reasonable limits prescribed by law as can be demonstrably justified in a free

or judicial methods of 'balancing' or 'proportionality' that are used to rank or reconcile otherwise conflicting rights.

These are serious questions for evolving REDD+ tenure policy. Some commentators have warned, for example, that in the REDD+ context, an emphasis on certainty could result in states asserting greater centralised control over forested land.[78] Others have suggested that the increased value of forested land, along with the prospect of REDD+ payments to governments 'may create a *dis*incentive for forest and conservation and other government authorities to resolve long-standing land disputes in forest areas'.[79] In fact, a 2014 independent evaluation of UN-REDD included the observation that 'REDD+ and the recent push to secure related carbon rights now threaten to recentralize forest rights and benefits altogether'.[80] This would reduce community control over forested lands, and so increase the likelihood that forest-dependent communities will be denied access to forest resources, and will not receive co-benefits allocated to reward local contributions to emission reductions.

These problems require not just the identification of legitimate property rights, but the identification of the right that is to take priority in the event of a conflict between two or more legitimate property rights. The concept of 'legitimacy' is thus the normative fulcrum on which the FAO Guidelines turn, but on its content they are notably silent. States are urged to 'take reasonable measures to identify, record and respect legitimate tenure right holders and their rights, whether formally recorded or not',[81] but the Guidelines do not offer a view on the features of land use, or of prior possessory title, that would comprise 'legitimate tenure rights' deserving of recognition, nor what to do when these conflict with the legitimate tenure rights of third parties. In short, the Guidelines offer advice on the *protection* of legitimate tenure rights, but not on how communities *demonstrate* that they have such rights. The position of non-occupants in cross-claims, in particular, is barely addressed. One tantalising reference mentions that policies governing the allocation of tenure rights 'should specify the means of allocation of rights, such as allocation based on historical use or other

---

and democratic society': Canadian Charter of Rights and Freedoms, Part I of the Constitution Act, 1982, being Schedule B to the Canada Act 1982 (UK), 1982, c 11. Identical wording is used in the New Zealand Bill of Rights Act 1990.

[78] USAID, 'Land Tenure and REDD+' (n 49) 7; Thompson, Baruah and Carr (n 13) 36.

[79] Ibid. 23.

[80] Frechette, de Bresser and Hofstede (n 5) 25.

[81] 'FAO Voluntary Guidelines' (n 59) 3.

means'.[82] In its statements specifically addressing indigenous peoples, however, the Guidelines revert to a current-use based approach, including where claims are made to ancestral lands. The Guidelines state that 'recognition should take into account the land, fisheries and forests that are *used* exclusively by a community and those that are shared' (emphasis added)[83] and further, that 'where indigenous peoples and other communities with customary tenure systems have legitimate tenure rights to the ancestral lands *on which they live*, States should recognize and protect these rights' (emphasis added)[84] – references that again imply that 'legitimate tenure rights' are those based on current occupancy or use.

What will be required by states then, if they are to take proper account of indigenous claims, is not a set of Guidelines directed to optimal 'outcomes' (security and clarity) but advice on how to assess the legitimacy of the rights that are to be secured and clarified. Methods and doctrines of this kind have been developed by courts in the settler states, but not, as will be described below, with much assistance from human rights principles. The vastly complicating aspect of REDD+-related advice on tenure then, is that in practice, the recognition of customary law as a source of legally enforceable property rights logically precedes the protection and enforcement of those customary rights in state law. The FAO's references to legitimate 'informal' or 'de facto'[85] rights that 'exist [] in reality' in contradistinction to formal rights that 'exist because of the formal law'[86] does little more than beg the question of recognition. By bracketing recognition, the approach taken by the FAO and UN-REDD to customary property raises issues of acute importance for indigenous peoples, because it leans towards the protection of current use, in recognition of the needs-based claims of communities dependent on forest resources for food security, without a corresponding justificatory basis that could support the (possibly competing) claims of prior occupants. It is possible, then, that the methods recommended in the Guidelines could encourage the formalisation of tenure rights that preclude or extinguish indigenous property rights, in furtherance of 'clear and secure' tenure rights for current users.

While the UN-REDD has usefully acknowledged that 'tenure rights are currently not recognised as human rights',[87] its guidance shows that the

---

82 Ibid. 13 (para 8.8).
83 Ibid. 15 (para 9.4).
84 Ibid. 15 (para 9.5).
85 See Edella Schlager and Elinor Ostrom, 'Property-Rights Regimes and Natural Resources: A Conceptual Analysis' (1992) 68(3) *Land Economics* 249, 254.
86 FAO, 'Land Tenure and Rural Development' (n 61) 12.
87 Rothe and Munro-Faure (n 49) 5.

'human rights based approach'[88] it adopts in its work is the primary lens brought to bear on questions involving indigenous tenure. This approach adds little to the concept of 'legitimacy' that animates the FAO Guidelines, because it does not contemplate conflict between rights, nor does it address the different logics underpinning property and human rights respectively, as is demonstrated by the positioning within the Guidelines of human and property rights as mutually supportive entitlements:

> Given that all human rights are universal, indivisible, interdependent and interrelated, the governance of tenure of land, fisheries and forests should not only take into account rights that are directly linked to access and use of land, fisheries and forests, but also all civil, political, economic, social and cultural rights.[89]

This ambivalence is also apparent in the Guidelines' treatment of indigenous-specific human rights instruments. States are advised that when addressing the tenure rights or claims of indigenous peoples, they must meet their commitments 'as appropriate' under the ILO Convention 169, the CBD and the UNDRIP,[90] and 'should remove and prohibit all forms of discrimination related to tenure rights'.[91] The question I pose in the remainder of this chapter is as follows: to what extent can human rights principles, including principles of equality and non-discrimination, assist indigenous peoples to secure title to their ancestral and traditional territories? In other words, are the types of human rights-based tenure reform anticipated by the UN-REDD and the FAO capable of 'doing justice' to tenure claims based on customary law in circumstances where a state has not recognised customary law as a source of legally enforceable property rights? The following section suggests that in the domestic law of states, the anti-discrimination principles that underpin human

---

[88] A 'human rights-based approach' being one of the five principles underpinning the United Nations Development Assistance Framework (UNDAF), as outlined in Frechette, de Bresser and Hofstede (n 5) para 53, and the 'UN Collaborative Programme on Reducing Emissions from Deforestation and Forest Degradation in Developing Countries (UN-REDD)', FAO, UNDP, UNEP Framework Document (2008) 7, http://www.un-redd.org/Portals/15/documents/publications/UN-REDD_FrameworkDocument.pdf. See also, FCPF, 'Readiness Preparation Proposal (R-PP) Template' (Version 5, 30 October 2010) 7, http://www.forestcarbonpartnership.org/sites/forestcarbonpartnership.org/files/Documents/PDF/Nov2010/PC7%202g%20R-PP%20Template%20v5%20Oct%2030%202010%20Annexes_0.pdf.

[89] 'FAO Voluntary Guidelines' (n 59) 7 (para 4.8).

[90] Ibid. 14–15 (para 9.3); see also 22 (para 12.7).

[91] Ibid. 4–5.

rights law can support judicial recognition of customary title, but do not *require* it, and in the absence of such recognition, the legislative allocation of property rights to indigenous groups can be categorised as a form of racially discriminatory preferential treatment. The IACtHR, however, has developed a jurisprudence in which it effectively performs the act of recognition itself in lieu of recognition by the state, and by doing so brings customary property rights within the protection of the American Convention's equality and property provisions. In sum, in order for human rights principles to protect, rather than imperil, indigenous customary property rights, those rights must first be recognised as legally enforceable. The advice offered by UN-REDD and the FAO does not (so far) guide states in determining when such recognition is required as a matter of justice.

3. INTERNATIONAL HUMAN RIGHTS AND PROPERTY LAW: CONCEPTUAL PROBLEMS

It is worth noting at the outset of this section that none of the major global international human rights instruments recognise a 'right to property' per se. Of the seven major international human rights instruments, only the UNDHR purports to protect property. Article 17 of the UNDHR provides that '[e]veryone has the right to own property alone as well as in association with others' and specifies that that '[n]o one shall be arbitrarily deprived of his property'. As will be discussed below, a similar provision appears as Article 21 of the regional American Convention on Human Rights (ACHR), and as Article 1 of Protocol 1 of the European Convention on Human Rights. These provisions, notably, do not on their face guarantee that a person will own any property at all, or that a person is entitled to be granted property by the state, but rather speak to the equal protection of any property rights a person has already acquired (in other words, property rights recognised in law). As discussed above, the question of whether property rights can properly be said to 'exist' in the absence of legal recognition is a fraught one. On this conundrum, international human rights law has little to add.

Throughout the FAO Guidelines, states and other actors are urged to respect and protect 'human rights and legitimate tenure rights',[92] and the Guidelines further note that '[g]eneral principles in international law provide protection that relate[s] to access to land; e.g. equality and

92 Ibid. 4.

non-discrimination in ownership and inheritance'.[93] Non-discrimination, however, can be a problematic concept for indigenous people and their claims. Put simply, because indigeneity is identified in international and domestic law as a cognate of race, recognition of distinctive property entitlements for indigenous peoples can appear in state law as a form of prohibited racial discrimination. States recognising indigenous property rights are from time to time challenged to show that these acts of recognition do not constitute racial discrimination against non-indigenous peoples or indigenous non-beneficiaries. The following section examines the ways that indigenous property claims, including prior possessory claims, have been considered in international law, before turning to a discussion of some of the strategies used in domestic law to overcome or avoid the implication of racial discrimination. Finally, I consider the approach taken by the IACtHR, which has developed a body of jurisprudence aimed at reconciling principles of equality and non-discrimination with distinctive indigenous rights to their ancestral lands, including rights that are not based on current occupancy or use. I take as my starting point the UNDRIP (2007), to which states are referred in the Cancún Agreement safeguards, the FAO Guidelines, in UN-REDD's policy brief on tenure and in the instructions to states applying to the UNREDD or FCPF for REDD readiness funding.

3.1 Indigenous Property in the UNDRIP

The UNDRIP is a Declaration, and therefore a General Assembly resolution not formally binding on states as a matter of international law on its own terms, although many of its provisions replicate and augment principles well established in international treaties and in international customary law. The extent to which the UNDRIP extends beyond the previously accepted categories and scope of human rights in international law, and the binding qualities of aspects of the UNDRIP that may be considered 'novel', is a matter of intense scholarly and political debate. The negotiation of the UNDRIP was a long and difficult process, spanning a total of 22 years. Some of the most difficult aspects of negotiations centred on the parts of the draft text that addressed indigenous rights to land and natural resources. These debates, and in particular, the concerns expressed by states that have recognised historic indigenous property rights, illustrate some of the complexities of reconciling customary and state-based sources of property rights. The central provision in question is Article 26 of the

---

93 Rothe and Munro-Faure (n 49) 5.

UNDRIP. This provides that '[i]ndigenous peoples have the right to the lands, territories and resources which they have traditionally owned, occupied or otherwise used or acquired', along with the 'right to own, use, [and] develop' those lands and resources. To comply with Article 26, states are obliged to 'give legal recognition and protection to these lands, territories and resources . . . with due respect to the customs, traditions and land tenure systems of the indigenous peoples concerned'.[94] Some states, including the CANZUS states (Canada, Australia, New Zealand and the United States) were concerned that the provision could entitle indigenous peoples 'as of right' to lands now owned or occupied by third parties. Canada, for example, argued that the phrase failed to make a necessary distinction between land 'over which indigenous people have or can establish legal rights' and land that they claim but do not (yet) have legal rights to.[95] The United States was similarly of the view that:

> [t]he use of the past tense suggests that lands 'traditionally occupied' at an earlier time – but not now – might be subject to the article. We cannot agree with a blanket statement that all existing legal rights of others to lands 'traditionally occupied' by indigenous persons at some much earlier time should in all cases be set aside regardless of the circumstances.[96]

Similar distributive problems were addressed by CANZUS states in their interventions on draft Article 27 (now Article 28), securing the rights of indigenous peoples to 'the restitution of the lands, territories and resources which they have traditionally owned or otherwise occupied or used' and providing that where this is not possible, indigenous peoples shall be provided 'compensation' in the form of 'lands, territories and resources equal in quality, size and legal status'.[97] The United States, for example, expressed its support for 'adequate legal procedures to ensure that claims of non-consensual confiscation or use of the lands or property are fairly resolved' but doubted that restitution was a viable means for resolving all historical land claims, suggesting instead that 'the declaration should call on states to consider the possibility of negotiated settlements, as

---

[94] Declaration on the Rights of Indigenous Peoples, UNGA Res 61/295 (13 September 2007) UN Doc A/RES/61/295.

[95] Canada, 'Preliminary Comments Part VI'. See also, Canada, 'Statement on Lands and Resources' (21 October 1999), doCip Doc 014a (on file with author).

[96] United States, 'Preliminary Comments Part VI (Land and Resources)' (28 November 1995), doCip Doc 030a (on file with author).

[97] UN Economic and Social Council, 'Report of the Sub-Commission on Prevention of Discrimination and Protection of Minorities on its Forty-Sixth Session' (28 October 1994) UN Doc E/CN.4/1995/2, 112 (art 27).

appropriate, when not otherwise required by law'.[98] Canada likewise suggested that the Article should include reference to the need for land claims settlement processes and noted that alternatives to restitution should be included in the Article, alongside market-based compensation.[99] When the four CANZUS states voted against the UNDRIP in 2007, all stated that Article 26 was one of the reasons that they could not endorse the Declaration.[100]

3.2 Indigenous Property and the UN Human Rights Treaty Bodies

As noted above, the FAO Guidelines do not address the claims of indigenous peoples that might be premised on historic or prior customary possession. They also make only a brief and oblique reference to the kinds of restitution that might be sought by dispossessed indigenous communities: '[w]here appropriate, the concerns of indigenous peoples regarding restitution should be addressed in the national context and in accordance with national law and legislation.'[101] This statement is notably less strongly framed than the provisions of the UNDRIP discussed above. It is also less strongly worded than the General Recommendation of the Committee administering the Convention on the Elimination of Racial Discrimination (the CERD Committee), which in 1997 called on state parties

> to recognize and protect the rights of indigenous peoples to own, develop, control and use their communal lands, territories and resources and, where they have been deprived of their lands and territories traditionally owned or otherwise inhabited or used without their free and informed consent, to take steps to return those lands and territories. Only when this is for factual reasons not possible, the right to restitution should be substituted by the right to just, fair and prompt compensation. Such compensation should as far as possible take the form of lands and territories.[102]

It seems clear that equality-based justifications for human rights are in some ways in tension with justifications based on the historic entitlements

---

[98] United States, 'Preliminary Comments Part VI (Land and Resources)' (28 November 1995), doCip Doc 030a (on file with author).

[99] Canada, 'Preliminary Comments, Part VI' (1995) doCip Doc 023a (on file with author).

[100] DoCip Comparison Table (on file with the author).

[101] 'FAO Voluntary Guidelines' (n 59) 25 (para 14.3).

[102] UN Committee on the Elimination of Racial Discrimination, 'General Recommendation No. 23: Indigenous Peoples' (18 August 1997) UN Doc A/52/18, Annex V at 122 ('CERD Committee General Recommendation 23') para 5.

of indigenous groups. The CERD Committee has promulgated a series of general recommendations that deal with the claims of indigenous peoples. These provide some avenues for the assertion of indigenous property rights, but are limited in ways that in most cases make them inadequate vehicles for the assertion of claims based on customary title and prior possession. First, the Convention includes provisions that require states to take special measures in order to 'secur[e] adequate advancement of certain racial or ethnic groups or individuals requiring such protection as may be necessary in order to ensure such groups or individuals equal enjoyment or exercise of human rights and fundamental freedoms'.[103] These measures, which the Committee accepts can be equated in most cases with 'affirmative action',[104] are subject to an important qualification. They may not 'lead to the maintenance of separate rights for different racial groups and . . . they shall not be continued after the objectives for which they were taken have been achieved'.[105] Special measures accordingly provide an equality-based justification for indigenous property rights where these are necessary to alleviate indigenous disadvantage relative to non-indigenous groups. Disadvantage, however, is not always an aspect of indigenous claims-making, nor is the scope of indigenous land claims necessarily tied to the material needs of the claimant community. The requirement of temporality, in addition, is a challenging one for indigenous peoples claiming property rights lost as a result of historic injustice. The justificatory basis of such rights does not evaporate when indigenous peoples enjoy equality (however measured) with non-indigenous members of a settler society. Instead, the rights find their basis in measures of continuity that connect contemporary communities with historic indigenous antecedents possessing the rights that are now claimed by indigenous groups, in perpetuity, as their successors. Since these may be difficult to defend as temporary special measures, they raise again the possibility that protections for indigenous

---

103 International Convention on the Elimination of All Forms of Racial Discrimination (adopted 21 December 1965, entered into force 4 January 1969) 660 UNTS 195 ('CERD') art 1(4); see also, art 2(2).

104 UN Committee on the Elimination of Racial Discrimination, 'General Recommendation No. 32: The Meaning and Scope of Special Measures in the International Convention on the Elimination of All Forms [of] Racial Discrimination' (24 September 2009) UN Doc CERD/C/GC/32 ('CERD Committee General Recommendation 32') 4 (para 12): 'The term "special measures" includes also measures that in some countries may be described as "affirmative measures", "affirmative action" or "positive action" in cases where they correspond to the provisions of articles 1(4) and 2(2) of the Convention.'

105 CERD art 1(4).

property may be perceived to conflict with norms of non-discrimination in international and domestic law.

This problem has been addressed in part by the CERD Committee in its 2009 General Recommendation 32 on special measures, passed two years after the adoption of the UNDRIP. In this recommendation, the CERD draws a distinction between 'special measures', and what it calls 'specific rights' vested in particular groups including indigenous peoples. Specific rights are not mentioned in the text of the CERD. According to the Committee, however, they include:

> the rights of persons belonging to minorities to enjoy their own culture, profess and practice their own religion and use their own language, the rights of indigenous peoples, including rights to lands traditionally occupied by them, and rights of women to non-identical treatment with men, such as the provision of maternity leave, on account of biological differences from men.[106]

These rights, the Committee observes, 'are permanent rights, recognized as such in human rights instruments, including those adopted in the context of the United Nations and its specialized agencies'.[107] The purpose of such rights is not to ensure substantive equality by addressing disadvantage, and the CERD Committee's recommendation offers no justification for specific rights other than its reference to rights extant in international legal instruments. Despite their promise then, these features of the CERD Committee's advice make 'specific rights' a rather precarious basis on which to justify the recognition of indigenous property rights in domestic law. To my knowledge, no state has so far attempted to do so. Special measures, on the other hand, *have* provided a justification for the recognition of indigenous land rights in Australia, while also placing limits on the scope of that recognition. The Australian example shows, then, the trade-offs that must be contended with when addressing indigenous property claims through the lens of anti-discrimination law. It is discussed here to highlight the awkward interface of human rights and indigenous property claims in the liberal democracies, and to show that indigenous and public actors have been able to navigate a path between these two theoretical frames to secure the recognition of some historic indigenous property rights, albeit in an imperfect and limited way. The methodology developed in Australia can be contrasted with that developed by the IACtHR. Together the approaches demonstrate the ways in which the tension between equality and property norms can be managed

---

106 CERD Committee General Recommendation 32 (n 101) para 15.
107 Ibid.

to allow and encourage the recognition of historic indigenous property rights.

3.3 Indigenous Property and Anti-discrimination Law in Australia: The Equal Protection of Property Rights (Once Recognised)

In contrast to the other CANZUS states, in Australia no historic treaties were signed with indigenous peoples and to date no constitutional recognition of indigenous property rights exists. As a consequence, federal anti-discrimination law has provided a major vehicle for the protection of indigenous common law property rights, bringing the competing logics of human rights and property into very sharp relief. The federal Racial Discrimination Act 1975 (RDA), which incorporates the International Convention on the Prohibition of All Forms of Racial Discrimination (ICERD) into Australian law, has been of pivotal importance in this enterprise. A central example is the landmark 1992 decision of the Australian High Court, *Mabo (No. 2)* v. *Queensland* ('*Mabo* (*No. 2*)'),[108] which provided the first recognition in Australian common law of property rights sourced in indigenous 'traditional laws and customs'. The High Court recognised that the customary property rights of indigenous Australians had legal effect in common law as 'native title' rights, which survived the acquisition of sovereignty by the British Crown and remained intact unless and until they were validly extinguished by a legislative or executive act or inconsistent grant, abandoned by traditional owners or voluntarily relinquished to the Crown. To be valid, an extinguishment would have to comply with the RDA's prohibition on racial discrimination, and where extinguishment had not occurred, rights premised in traditional laws and customs were entitled to be protected to the same degree as other property rights. In the lead judgment, Brennan J held that:

> Whatever the justification advanced in earlier days for refusing to recognize the rights and interests in land of the indigenous inhabitants of settled colonies, an unjust and discriminatory doctrine of that kind can no longer be accepted. The expectations of the international community accord in this respect with the contemporary values of the Australian people . . . A common law doctrine founded on unjust discrimination in the enjoyment of civil and political rights demands reconsideration. It is contrary both to international standards and to the fundamental values of our common law to entrench a discriminatory rule which, because of the supposed position on the scale of social organization of

108 *Mabo* v. *Queensland* (*No. 2*) (1992) 175 CLR 1 (High Court of Australia).

> the indigenous inhabitants of a settled colony, denies them a right to occupy their traditional lands.[109]

The important feature of this application of non-discrimination law to indigenous property claims is that while equal protection is owed to native title rights *once recognised*, anti-discrimination law, including the RDA, did not compel the *recognition* of those rights. In the logic of native title law, the fact that before 1992 the common law did not recognise 'native title' rights did not amount to discrimination. Similarly, the fact that non-proprietary aspects of traditional laws and customs continue to be denied legal force in the common law today is not regarded as racially discriminatory. In effect, the lack of recognition means there is no 'right' for anti-discrimination law to protect. The act of recognition effected by the High Court in *Mabo* (*No. 2*) was an augmentation of Australian common law that was influenced by the development of human rights and anti-discrimination law domestically and internationally, but it was not required by that body of law. In fact, as is illustrated below, in the absence of common law recognition of property rights emanating from customary law, grants of land to indigenous communities can appear as forms of racial discrimination.

In Australia, the interplay of anti-discrimination law and indigenous property rights in the pre-*Mabo* (*No. 2*) era had a very different character than it does today. A legislative grant of freehold title made by the South Australian government to the Anangu Pitjantjatjara Yankunytjatjara people in 1981, of land falling within their traditional territory, was considered by the High Court in the landmark case of *Gerhardy* v. *Brown* (1985). The Court found that the South Australian Act was a discriminatory measure in the terms of the RDA, and was saved from invalidation only because it was a temporary 'special measure' designed to overcome indigenous disadvantage, and so fell within the RDA's exemption for such measures.[110] At the time the grant was made, the doctrine of native title did not form part of Australian common law, so that in effect there were no existing property rights that could attract the protection of the RDA. In other words, because of the prohibition against racial discrimination in the RDA, in the eyes of the High Court, the legislation effected a *grant* of freehold property rights to the group, rather operating to *protect* customary property rights that already existed. In the *Mabo* (*No. 2*) judgment then, the High Court accomplished two tasks: it

---

[109] Ibid. 42 (Brennan J).
[110] *Gerhardy* v. *Brown* (1985) 159 CLR 70.

recognised that traditional laws and custom could generate common law property rights in the form of native title, and it confirmed (in reliance on its majority findings in *Mabo* v. *Queensland* (1988) ('*Mabo* (*No. 1*)') that by virtue of the RDA, all legal protections provided to persons in respect of their right to 'own and inherit property' now extended to holders of native title.[111]

Recalling the FAO's emphasis then, on the need to recognise 'legitimate' tenure rights, the use made in the Voluntary Guidelines of human rights and non-discrimination principles addresses the equal protection of property rights (as in the second branch of the findings in *Mabo* (*No. 2*), above), but not *recognition* as the prerequisite of protection. In effect the FAO Guidelines emphasise the equal treatment of property rights once recognised as 'legitimate', but leave open the question of the criteria on which 'legitimacy' is to be assessed. The application of human rights principles does not assist in this endeavour and in the absence of recognition, can undermine it.

It is for this reason, I argue, that human rights and non-discrimination principles have not been used to advance the recognition of indigenous property rights in those countries where other justificatory bases are available. In the other western settler states of Canada, the United States and New Zealand, historic indigenous property claims, including those based on common law doctrines of aboriginal title, find purchase in commitments made in historic treaties, and in indigenous-specific 'special trust relationships', doctrines of the 'honour of the Crown', and fiduciary responsibilities that attach primarily to the executive branches of settler governments and guide courts in statutory interpretation.[112] Matters arising from the negotiation of land claims settlements by settler executives are regarded as largely non-justiciable political questions. Accordingly, indigenous–state relationships in those countries are increasingly structured by political bargains and characterised by inter-governmental forms of relations, rather than human rights. Canada, for example, has provided constitutional protection

---

[111] *Mabo* v. *Queensland* (1988) 166 CLR 186, 219 per Brennan, Gaudron and Toohey JJ. Cited, in part, in *Mabo* (*No. 2*) 53 per Brennan J.

[112] See, for example, *Nor Nyawai & Ors* v. *Borneo Pulp Plantation Sdn Bhd & Ors* [2001] 2 CLJ 769 HC (refd) (Malaysia); *Kerajaan Negeri Selangor & Ors* v. *Sagong Tasi & Ors* [2005] 4 CLJ 169 (Malaysia); *Guerin* v. *The Queen* [1984] 2 SCR 335 (Canada); *Manitoba Metis Federation* v. *Canada (Attorney General)* [2013] 1 SCR 623 (Canada); *New Zealand Maori Council* v. *Attorney-General* [1987] 1 NZLR 641 (HC & CA) 664; *Te Runanga o Wharekauri Rekohu Inc.* v. *Attorney-General* [1993] 2 NZLR 301, 304.

to indigenous property and treaty rights in s 35 of the Constitution Act,[113] notably positioned outside of the human rights' protections of the Charter of Human Rights and Freedoms, and 'shielded' from the application of the Charter by s 25.[114] The Supreme Court has urged the settlement of s 35 claims by negotiation.[115] The non-discrimination provisions of New Zealand's Bill of Rights Act (NZBORA) and Human Rights Act (HRA) have never been used to advance Maori claims in New Zealand's courts,[116] even while Maori have successfully sought urgent action decisions by the CERD Committee on the discriminatory impacts of the New Zealand Foreshore and Seabed Act 2004 (now repealed); a statute that denied to Maori the right to litigate customary title claims to the foreshore.[117] The emphasis on inter-governmental avenues for claims-making in these countries is a reflection of the politically strategic choices of indigenous peoples, as well as of traditions of judicial deference to the executive in matters involving indigenous interests, and of the acknowledged limitation of non-discrimination norms in the resolution of disputes requiring the redistribution of property and expenditure of public resources.

3.4 The Inter-American Court Methodology: Equal Recognition of Property Rights

To this body of domestic law and practice the IACtHR and the Inter-American Commission on Human Rights (IAComHR) have contributed an extensive and growing body of jurisprudence on indigenous and tribal property rights, predominantly in respect of groups in Latin America. The Court has developed a judicial methodology by which to reconcile and combine the equality and property protections of the ACHR in order to direct states to formalise indigenous and tribal rights to traditional lands. In a series of cases decided in the last 15 years, the Court

---

113 Constitution Act 1982, being Schedule B to the Canada Act 1982 (UK), 1982, c 11.

114 Ibid. s 25.

115 See, for example, *Delgamuukw* v. *British Columbia* [1997] 3 SCR 1010 [186]: 'Ultimately, it is through negotiated settlements, with good faith and give and take on all sides, reinforced by the judgments of this Court, that we will achieve what . . . [is] a basic purpose of s 35(1) – "the reconciliation of the pre-existence of aboriginal societies with the sovereignty of the Crown".'

116 New Zealand Bill of Rights Act 1990 (NZBORA) s 20, Human Rights Act 1993 (HRA) s 21(1)(f). See Fleur Adcock, 'Maori and the Bill of Rights Act: A Case of Missed Opportunities?' (2013) 11 *NZJPL* 183, 199.

117 Committee on the Elimination of Racial Discrimination, 'Decision 1 (66): New Zealand Foreshore and Seabed Act 2004' (27 April 2005) UN Doc CERD/C/DEC/NZL/1, para 6.

and Commission have found that the failure of state parties to recognise that indigenous customary property rights have the same legal status and effect as the private property rights of other citizens has breached the non-discrimination and equality provisions of the ACHR (Articles 1(1) and 2), read in conjunction with its Article 21 property guarantee. Article 21 provides in relevant part that 'everyone has the right to the use and enjoyment of his property'.[118] The link between the two parts of the ACHR is summarised by the IACtHR as follows:

> [P]rotection of property under Article 21 of the Convention, read in conjunction with Articles 1(1) and 2 of said instrument, places upon States a positive obligation to adopt special measures that guarantee members of indigenous and tribal peoples the full and equal exercise of their right to the territories they have traditionally used and occupied.[119]

According to the IACtHR, then, the combination of the equality and property protections in the Inter-American Convention means that states may not deny the legal force of indigenous property rights to traditionally owned and occupied land where those rights are held in accordance with customary law.[120] In effect, once the Court has deemed the claimed rights to be 'property' in the terms of Article 21, the state cannot deny their legal status, even if they are not otherwise given legal effect in domestic law, and even if they have been regarded in state law as 'de facto' or 'informal' property rights only.[121] The novelty of this approach is that it entails the assertion by an international human rights body of the jurisdiction to determine the existence and legal effect of property rights not recognised in state law, as part of assessing a state's performance of its international human rights obligations. In this way, by deciding that customary law generates property rights in state law, the IACtHR has performed an

---

118 *Case of the Saramaka People* v. *Suriname*, IACHR Series C No. 18 (17 September 2003) ('*Saramaka* v. *Suriname*') [110]. See also, *Kuna Indigenous Peoples of Madungandi and Embera Indigenous People of Bayano and their Members* v. *Panama* (Advisory Opinion, Report No. 125/12) IAComHR (13 November 2012) 196; *Maya Indigenous Community of the Toledo District* v. *Belize* IACHR Report No. 40/04, OEA/Ser.L/V/II.122 Doc 5 rev 1 at 727 (12 October 2004) [193].

119 *Saramaka* v. *Suriname* (n 117) [91].

120 Ibid. [110]: 'This limitation on the recognition of the legal right of the members of the Saramaka people to fully enjoy the territory they have traditionally owned and occupied is incompatible with the State's obligations under Article 2 of the Convention to give legal effect to the rights recognized under Article 21 of such instrument.'

121 Ibid.

act of recognition equivalent in substance to that undertaken by the Australian High Court in *Mabo* (*No. 2*).

What might this add to the 'human rights based' approach currently deployed by UN-REDD? Importantly for the purposes of this chapter, until recently the jurisprudence of the IACtHR was focused on the current use and possessory rights of indigenous and tribal peoples, albeit use and possession in accordance with customary law. It has evolved more recently however, to accommodate the rights of indigenous and peoples who are no longer in possession of the lands they claim. This body of law could assist to give content to the concept of 'legitimacy' that is to trigger recognition in the terms used by the FAO and UN-REDD, where indigenous property rights are not recognised by the state, including in circumstances where claimants have been dispossessed.

The landmark 2001 case of *Mayagna* v. *Nicaragua*[122] addressed the rights of an indigenous community that was in possession of the lands it claimed. Later cases have addressed the claims of indigenous or tribal groups to lands they no longer occupy in two situations: first, where title to those lands has not been granted to third parties, so the land is effectively state-owned (*Moiwana Community* v. *Suriname*)[123] and second, where some of the claimed lands are now held by third parties as private property (*Yakye Axa* v. *Paraguay*, and *Sawhoyamaxa* v. *Paraguay*).[124] In situations where formal rights are held over indigenous lands by third parties, the Court has confined itself to acknowledging the need for restitution *of some kind*, including the possibility of lands in kind or monetary compensation, and has urged procedural fairness in the dispute-resolution processes associated with those claims.[125] In other words, the Court has left decisions on the allocation of competing rights to the state, but has articulated procedural considerations that the state must take into account in the course of such allocation, if it is to comply with its human rights obligations in the terms of the Convention.

In *Mayagna* v. *Nicaragua*,[126] the IACtHR found that the failure of the Nicaraguan state to 'delimit and demarcate' the lands *possessed* by the

---

[122] *The Mayagna (Sumo) Awas Tingni Community* v. *Nicaragua*, IACHR Series C No. 79 (31 August 2001) ('*Mayagna* v. *Nicaragua*').

[123] IACHR Series C No. 124 (15 June 2005).

[124] IACHR Series C No. 125 (17 June 2005) ('*Yakye Axa* v. *Paraguay*'); IACHR Series C No. 146 (29 March 2006).

[125] 'However, merely abstract or juridical recognition of indigenous lands, territories, or resources, is practically meaningless if the property is not physically delimited and established': *Yayke Axa* v. *Paraguay* (n 123) [143].

[126] *Mayagna* v. *Nicaragua* (n 121).

Mayagna (Sumo) Awas Tingni people 'violated the right to property protected by article 21 of the American Convention on Human Rights, to the detriment of the members of the Mayagna (Sumo) Awas Tingni Community, in connection with articles 1(1) and 2 of the Convention'.[127] According to the Commission, the case stands for the proposition that:

> States violate the right to equality before the law, equal protection of the law, and non-discrimination when . . . they do not grant indigenous peoples 'the protections necessary to exercise their right to property fully and equally with other members of the . . . population'.[128]

The crucial element in this reasoning (to borrow again from the FAO's direction to states to recognise 'legitimate tenure rights') is that the asserted rights were 'legitimate' because the indigenous community in question possessed the land, and possessed it in accordance with customary law. In these circumstances, and 'as a result of customary practices, possession of the land should suffice for indigenous communities lacking real title to property of the land to obtain official recognition of that property, and for consequent registration'.[129] Accordingly then:

> traditional possession of their lands by indigenous people has equivalent effects to those of a state-granted full property title; [and] traditional possession entitles indigenous people to demand official recognition and registration of property title.[130]

In a series of cases decided after 2004, however, the IACtHR has been asked to investigate the question of 'whether possession of the lands by the indigenous people is a requisite for official recognition of property title thereto'.[131] That is, it was asked to identify the attributes of 'legitimate

---

127 Ibid. [173(2)]. See also, *Saramaka* v. *Suriname* (n 117) para 91. *Saramaka People* v. *Suriname* (Preliminary Objections, Merits, Reparations, and Costs) IACHR Series C No. 172 (28 November 2007) [91].

128 *Kuna Indigenous People of Madungandi and Embera Indigenous People of Bayano and their Members* v. *Panama*, IACHR Report No. 58/09, Petition 12.354 (21 April 2009) [303]. See also [305]; and *Maya Indigenous Community of the Toledo District* v. *Belize*, IACHR Report No. 40/04, OEA/Ser.L/V/II.122 Doc 5 rev 1 at 727 (12 October 2004) [61] and [171].

129 *Mayagna* v. *Nicaragua* (n 121) [151].

130 *Sawhoyamaxa* v. *Paraguay* (n 123) [128]. See also, *Yayke Axa* v. *Paraguay* (n 123) [215], and see [143]: 'a strictly juridical or abstract recognition of indigenous lands, territories or resources lacks true meaning where the property has not been physically established and delimited'.

131 *Sawhoyamaxa* v. *Paraguay* (n 123) [126]. *Moiwana Community* v. *Suriname*, IACHR Series C No. 124 (15 June 2005) ('*Moiwana* v. *Suriname*') [134]; *Yayke*

tenure' when an indigenous or tribal community is no longer in possession of the land in question. In the 2005 case of *Moiwana* v. *Suriname* the Court found that the members of a dispossessed tribal community were 'legitimate owners of their traditional lands' and that their 'traditional occupancy' of the claimed land 'should suffice to obtain State recognition of their ownership'.[132] In that case, the community had been forcibly dispossessed and the claimed land had not been allocated by the state to third parties. In the 2006 case of *Sawhoyamaxa* v. *Paraguay*, the Court further extended its methodology on recognition, holding that the Sawhoyamaxa people had the right to claim the restitution of traditional lands which they no longer possessed, even though some of the land had been granted to third parties,[133] noting that the fact that these lands were in private ownership 'is not in itself an "objective and sufficient ground" barring restitution thereof'.[134] Significantly, the Court articulated a 'connection' test that could allow title to survive even when possession had been lost. Since the unique relationship between indigenous peoples and the land is the 'spiritual and material basis for indigenous identity', then according to the IACtHR, the right to claim traditional lands is enforceable 'as long as said relationship exists'.[135] The unique relationship may be expressed by, inter alia: 'spiritual or ceremonial ties; settlements or sporadic cultivation; seasonal or nomadic gathering, hunting and fishing; the use of natural resources associated with their customs and any other element characterizing their culture.'[136] When considering the circumstances in which third party title could be redistributed to the indigenous claimants, however, the IACtHR drew a distinction between the mandate of the Court to make determinations on state compliance with human rights, and the exclusive jurisdiction of the state to make decisions concerning the allocation of property rights, especially in cases involving competing claims:

> [T]he Court cannot decide that Sawhoyamaxa Community's property rights to traditional lands prevail over the right to property of private owners or vice versa, since the Court is not a domestic judicial authority with jurisdiction to decide disputes among private parties. This power is vested exclusively in the Paraguayan State. Nevertheless, the Court has competence to analyse whether

Axa v. *Paraguay* (n 123) [124]–[131].

132 *Moiwana* v. *Suriname* (n 130) [133] and [134].
133 *Sawhoyamaxa* v. *Paraguay* (n 123) [130].
134 Ibid. [214].
135 Ibid. [130].
136 Ibid. [131].

> the State ensured the human rights of the members of the Sawhoyamaxa Community.[137]

Accordingly, in this case, in order to comply with the Convention's equality and property protections, the state was required to grant rights to the claimed lands or *suitable alternative lands* to the Sawhoyamaxa within three years of the judgment 'irrespective of whether [those rights] be acquired by purchase or by condemnation'.[138] To comply with the order, the state was obliged to 'consider the possibility of purchasing these lands or the lawfulness, need and proportionality of condemning these lands in order to achieve a lawful purpose in a democratic society', and the Court noted that if

> restitution of ancestral lands to the members of the Sawhoyamaxa Community is not possible on objective and sufficient grounds, the State shall make over alternative lands, selected upon agreement with the aforementioned Indigenous Community, in accordance with the community's own decision-making and consultation procedures, values, practices and customs.[139]

Thus the allocation of customary lands to third parties did not 'extinguish' the customary title of indigenous peoples, providing that those people have maintained their unique 'spiritual and material' relationship to the land in question.

Finally, in the 2005 case of *Yake Axa* v. *Paraguay*, also involving the claims of a group no longer in possession of their traditional land, the Court outlined the criteria to be addressed 'when indigenous communal property and individual private property are in real or apparent contradiction'[140] so that the property rights of one or the other must be adjusted, finding that:

> [T]he American Convention itself and the jurisprudence of the Court provide guidelines to establish admissible restrictions to the enjoyment and exercise of rights, that is: a) they must be established by law; b) they must be necessary; c) they must be proportional, and d) their purpose must be to attain a legitimate goal in a democratic society.[141]

In addition, whatever balance is struck in the case of indigenous claims to traditional land must recognise the special significance of land as a

---

137 Ibid. [136].
138 Ibid. [215].
139 Ibid. [212]. See also [214].
140 *Yayke Axa* v. *Paraguay* (n 123) [144].
141 Ibid.

basis of indigenous cultural identity, and control of traditional territory 'as a necessary condition for reproduction of their culture, for their own development and to carry out their life aspirations'.[142] Accordingly while indigenous property rights need not always take priority over private third party rights, where there are 'concrete and justified reasons' preventing the state from returning traditional lands to the indigenous community, third party rights may legitimately be preserved, in which case compensation must be provided to indigenous peoples, in a manner and of a type 'primarily guided by the meaning of the land for them'.[143]

The IACtHR's approach to indigenous prior possessory claims can be summarised as follows. First, in the absence of evidence of current occupation and use, prior occupancy of the claimed land can suffice to engage the state's obligation to give legal effect to the claimed property rights. Where the land in question has not been allocated to third parties, traditional occupancy in accordance with customary law renders those rights 'legitimate' and deserving of legal protection. Where formal property rights to traditional lands have been vested in third parties, and indigenous claimants have maintained their unique spiritual and material relationship to those lands, their rights are prima facie legitimate and must be given legal effect. In those circumstances, where both third party and indigenous rights are 'legitimate', the Court will not itself decide on how disputes between those rights are to be resolved. It will, however, find a state to be in breach of the equality and property protections of the ACHR if that state limits the 'legitimate' rights of either party to the dispute, unless it does so in ways that are established by law, necessary, proportional, designed to attain a legitimate goal in a democratic society and which recognise the special significance of land as a basis of indigenous cultural identity. A refusal to give priority to indigenous rights to traditional lands where there are competing third party rights over the same land will be in compliance with the Convention only if there are 'concrete and justified' reasons for that refusal, in which case compensation must be provided in lieu of land in kind or property rights. In summary, the IACtHR has provided an expanded, much more subtle and balanced example of the way that UN-REDD's 'human right-based approach' could be brought to bear on the recognition of indigenous rights to forested land, one that deals not just with protection, but also recognition, and which encompasses claims based on prior possession as well as current use.

---

[142] Ibid. [146].
[143] Ibid. [149].

4. CONCLUSION

This chapter has addressed the consideration given to date to indigenous tenure issues in the evolving international discourse on REDD+. It has pointed out that tenure issues have to date only tentatively been addressed by the two major REDD+ funding bodies: the UN-REDD and the FCPF, and then primarily in criteria used to assess applications for REDD+ readiness funding, rather than in substantive operational guidance. The World Bank's operational policies do not apply directly during FCPF's funding of REDD readiness preparations, so that the FAO Voluntary Guidelines, as endorsed by UN-REDD, provide the most substantive advice to states to date on how to progress tenure reform in preparation for REDD+ implementation. I have suggested that these may disadvantage indigenous peoples relative to other property claimants, because of the Guidelines' emphasis on current use and food security needs of persons and communities occupying or using forested land. Since indigenous claims are more likely than others to be premised on prior possession in accordance with customary law, and because the historic non-recognition of customary law means that those communities are more likely than others to have been dispossessed, an emphasis on current occupation does not capture the circumstances in which many indigenous communities find themselves. Accordingly, the emphasis in REDD+ policy and guidance on the need for 'secure and clear' tenure, and a 'human rights-based' approach to programming, combine to raise the possibility that REDD+ could incentivise states to design tenure arrangements that deny the legal effect of some legitimate indigenous customary rights to forested land.

I have suggested that the 'human rights-based' approach to tenure reform so far endorsed by the UN-REDD and FAO is unlikely to provide a way forward on its own in contexts where title and possession are contested, because it imports concepts of racial discrimination that can frustrate the allocation of property rights to indigenous peoples or diminish their extent and duration. The Australian example serves to show the shortcomings of methods that address indigenous property claims through the lens of human rights law, because this body of law does not contain a justification for the recognition of customary title (although it can encourage such an act of recognition), and is directed instead to the equal protection of property rights *once recognised.* The jurisprudence of the IACtHR however, shows a promising way forward, in which the Court has directed states to recognise and protect indigenous title based on customary law in fulfilment of the Convention's property and equality protections, and to resolve disputes with due account of the significance of indigenous ties to traditional land. While this jurisprudence depends for its implementation on state acceptance of the Court's findings on the 'existence' of indigenous property rights as de jure, rather than de facto rights, it provides a methodology which mitigates the possibility that recognition could constitute racial discrimination. This set of judicial experiences and findings could usefully inform the development of advice on tenure reform in the REDD+ context, and perhaps help to address the bias in existing commentary towards protecting the current users of land, by providing a justification for the claims of indigenous asserting title based on prior or historic possession in accordance with customary law.

10. REDD+ and multilevel governance beyond the climate negotiations

*Ernesto Roessing Neto and Joyeeta Gupta**

1. INTRODUCTION

Forests have been on the global agenda for at least 50 years. However, forest governance at the global level has been scattered through different organizations and forums, and comprehensive efforts to govern it globally have failed.[1] The climate change discussions have re-energized forest governance efforts since the early days of the climate negotiations and particularly with the emergence of REDD on the agenda.[2] Having said that, discussions on forest management have nevertheless moved rather slowly within the climate negotiations, thus leading to the emergence of discussions and decisions in parallel forums. This chapter aims to present and discuss a few of these parallel legal developments, without attempting to be comprehensive.

One can distinguish four phases in forest governance and climate change.[3] The first pre-1990 phase recognized the role of forests in the climate change problem and included a provisional target on net forest growth in the Noordwijk Declaration on Climate Change.[4] The next phase (1990–97) focused on elaborating a forest policy commitment. Forest targets were delegated to a possible forest convention, while the 1992 UNFCCC stated that forests were both sources and sinks of greenhouse

---

* All websites cited in this chapter were accessed on 1 October 2015.

[1] David Humphreys, *Logjam: Deforestation and the Crisis of Global Governance* (Earthscan 2006) 214.

[2] Joyeeta Gupta et al., "Climate Change and Forests: From the Noordwijk Declaration to REDD" in Joyeeta Gupta, Nicolien van der Grijp and Onno Kuik (eds), *Climate Change, Forests and REDD: Lessons for Institutional Design* (Routledge 2013) 1–2.

[3] Constanze Haug and Joyeeta Gupta, "Global Forest Governance" in Joyeeta Gupta, Nicolien Van der Grijp and Onno Kuik (eds), *Climate Change, Forests and REDD: Lessons for Institutional Design* (Routledge 2013) 52–4.

[4] UNEP, IPCC and World Meteorological Organization (WMO), "Report of the Third Session of the WMO/UNEP Intergovernmental Panel on Climate Change (IPCC)", http://digital.library.unt.edu/ark:/67531/metadc11889/m1/46/, Appendix D, para. 21.

gases and that Parties should take appropriate measures.[5] In the third phase (1997–2005), the KP of 1997 was adopted and allowed developed countries to partially meet their mitigation targets through the use of sinks.[6] The KP's CDM acknowledged the importance of afforestation and reforestation measures by including these as possible measures to increase GHG absorption within its scope, although deforestation and forest degradation were ultimately not included in the mechanism.[7]

Over time, the focus moved towards finding ways to reward the efforts of developing countries in maintaining their forests. This led to the fourth phase, the birth of REDD+ within the UNFCCC in 2005, first as RED; eventually it grew to encompass deforestation (REDD) and ultimately also the "role of conservation, sustainable management of forests and enhancement of carbon stocks" (REDD+).[8] The overall idea for REDD+ is simple – to provide performance-based positive incentives to those who reduce deforestation and forest degradation – although in practice many issues must be addressed.[9]

One of the main issues related to REDD+ involves the need to ensure that emissions reductions are actually attained and properly measured, thus entailing the need to establish MRV procedures, as well as reference levels and measures to ensure permanence (i.e., to ensure that forests protected through REDD+ are not deforested in the future).[10]

Moreover, social and environmental safeguards are essential, in order to avoid practices which ultimately lead to emissions reductions from forests, but at the expense of the livelihoods of forest-dependent peoples and of other components of the forest ecosystem (such as biodiversity).[11]

REDD+ is expected to be implemented through a three-phased

---

[5] UNFCCC, United Nations Framework Convention on Climate Change 1992, Art. 4.d.

[6] UNFCCC, Kyoto Protocol to the United Nations Framework Convention on Climate Change 1997, Art. 3.3.

[7] Markus Lederer, "From CDM to REDD+ – What Do We Know for Setting up Effective and Legitimate Carbon Governance?" (2011) 70 *Ecological Economics* 1900, http://www.sciencedirect.com/science/article/pii/S0921800911000577.

[8] Till Pistorius, "From RED to REDD+: The Evolution of a Forest-Based Mitigation Approach for Developing Countries" (2012) 4 4/6 *Climate Systems* 638, 640, http://www.sciencedirect.com/science/article/pii/S1877343512000899.

[9] Ernesto Roessing Neto, "Forests and Climate Change: REDD+ as a Tool of Global Forest Governance" [2015] *The International Spectator* 64; 66.

[10] Contanze Haug and Joyeeta Gupta, "The Emergence of REDD on the Global Policy Agenda" in Joyeeta Gupta, Nicolien Van der Grijp and Onno Kuik (eds), *Climate Change, Forests and REDD: Lessons for Institutional Design* (Routledge 2013) 86.

[11] Ibid., 87–8.

approach: phase 1, known as readiness, which includes all the necessary preparatory work for REDD+, such as the establishment of institutional frameworks, capacity-building, and the implementation of a monitoring system; phase 2, which consists of the implementation of policies and demonstration activities, including pilot-projects; phase 3, which is the actual provision of results-based incentives based on accurate measurement of emissions reductions achieved under REDD+.[12]

As a result of this phased approach, there have been various efforts, at various levels, to address phases 1 and 2, in order to prepare the ground for phase 3 whenever it becomes operational. Also, the slow progress of negotiations within the UNFCCC may be a factor behind the design and implementation of these initiatives.[13]

Without attempting to be comprehensive, but rather aiming to provide an overview of cases which illustrate the multilevel governance process through which REDD+ is being implemented, this chapter presents a range of initiatives taking shape at various levels. Therefore, it starts by discussing multilateral developments on REDD+ (see section 2), bilateral agreements and processes on REDD+ (see section 3), national developments on REDD+ (see section 4), subnational activities (see section 5) and the activities of the private sector (see section 6) before drawing some conclusions on how the governance of REDD+ is proceeding.

2. MULTILATERAL DEVELOPMENTS

Forest governance has in one way or another been dealt with by a range of organizations (FAO, UNEP, GEF, UNDP, World Bank, ILO) and treaties (Ramsar, CBD, CCD, CITES, ITTA, United Nations Permanent Forum on Indigenous Issues (UNPFII)). But although there were many actors engaged, their interests in forest protection varied and resources were limited. The emergence of REDD, however, had a unifying effect in that it has brought many of these actors together to discuss ways of collaboration and ways of bringing together different interests in one coherent strategy. This was also possible because of the expectation of financial resources.

In 2007, the UNFCCC process yielded the "Bali Action Plan" at its

---

12 UNFCCC, The Cancún Agreements: Outcome of the work of the Ad Hoc Working Group on Long-term Cooperative Action under the Convention 2010 [Decision 1/CP.16] para. 73.

13 Haug and Gupta (n 10), 80.

13th Conference of the Parties (COP-13), which contained the basis for a new climate agreement to be adopted by 2009, and formally incorporated REDD into the convention's negotiating process.[14] In parallel, during COP-13, UNEP, UNDP and FAO supported the ongoing process on REDD within the UNFCCC through a parallel initiative called UN-REDD, aimed at helping developing countries prepare to implement REDD.[15]

In 2008, the FCPF was set up by the World Bank as a way to finance such projects: its Readiness Fund helps countries to develop capacity to implement, thus essentially helping countries to overcome phase 1 of REDD+; its Carbon Fund pays for emission reductions and develops methods for doing so, thus essentially addressing phase 2.[16] This initiative came as a follow-up to a long line of initiatives on forest financing ranging from the Prototype Carbon Fund in 2000 and some dozen funds to finance forest-related activities since then, including the BioCarbon Fund.[17]

At the UNFCCC's COP-15 in Copenhagen, expectations were high that a follow-up agreement on climate change with quantitative targets would be adopted. However, when this hope disappeared, 50 Parties to the convention jointly established the now defunct REDD+ Partnership. This Partnership hoped to push the process further by ensuring that countries were ready to implement and thereby encourage the donors to invest in this. The Partnership focused on knowledge-sharing. The Partnership did not intend to have a permanent character – but perhaps a pre-emptive character in that it wished that once adequate progress was made within the UNFCCC regime, it could become part of it.[18]

The UNFCCC process eventually proceeded after the relatively unsuccessful COP in Copenhagen, and REDD+ moved forward, albeit slowly, through a series of decisions adopted afterwards at COP-16, COP-17, COP-18, and most notably an ensemble of seven decisions on REDD+ adopted at COP-19, known as the WFR.[19] Overall, these decisions

---

14 UNFCCC, Bali Action Plan 2007 [Decision 1/CP.13] para. 1.b.iii.

15 Haug and Gupta (n 10) 81–2; Saša Danon and Daniele Bettiati, "Reducing Emissions from Deforestaton and Forest Degradation (REDD+) – What is behind the Idea and What is the Role of UN-REDD and Forest Carbon Partnership Facility (FCPF)?" (2012) 2 *South-East European Forestry* 95, 96, http://hrcak.srce.hr/index.php?show=clanak&id_clanak_jezik=120739.

16 Haug and Gupta (n 10), 82–3.

17 Ibid.

18 Ibid.

19 The decisions are Decision 1/CP.13 (Bali Action Plan); Decision 2/CP.13; Decision 4/CP.15; Decision 1/CP.16; Decision 2/CP.17; Decision 12/

provide elements for the development of REDD+ in areas such as financing, monitoring systems, transparency, safeguards, reference levels and verification. However, progress is still necessary if REDD+ is ever to move towards phase 3 within the UNFCCC, particularly in what relates to ensuring secure sources of funding for REDD+.[20]

As it is reflected in the Lima Call for Climate Action, REDD+ is expected to be part of the multilateral post-Kyoto climate change regime, although its institutional framework and operationalization are still not completely clear.[21] However, based on the development so far, REDD+ is expected to be regulated broadly at the multilateral level, through the UNFCCC, and to be implemented at the national level[22], thus meaning that Parties to the UNFCCC will ultimately be internationally responsible for developing (or ensuring that lower levels of government within them develop) the framework for implementing REDD+ on the ground.

It is expected that clearer contours for REDD+ will emerge during COP-21 in 2015, when a new legally binding instrument to succeed the KP is expected to be adopted. Nevertheless, this means that it will have taken at least eight years since the formal inclusion of REDD+ in the UNFCCC negotiations (in 2007 through the Bali Action Plan) before its actual establishment at the multilateral level, not to mention the subsequent period of time it may take for its full implementation on the ground.

Perhaps as a result of the combination of the slow progress at the multilateral stage with the need to prepare for the implementation of REDD+, bilateral processes related to REDD+ have sprung up, particularly aimed at spurring the development of phases 1 and 2 of REDD+, thus helping to lay the conditions for the implementation of phase 3 of REDD+ whenever it becomes operational. A brief account of some of such processes is provided in the following section.

CP.17; Decision 1/CP.18; Decision 9/CP.19; Decision 10/CP.19; Decision 11/CP.19; Decision 12/CP.19; Decision 13/CP.19; Decision 14/CP.19; Decision 15/CP.19.

20 William D. Sunderlin et al., *The Challenge of Establishing REDD+ on the Ground: Insights from 23 Subnational Initiatives in Six Countries* (CIFOR 2014), 104, 18, http://www.cifor.org/publications/pdf_files/occpapers/op-104.pdf.

21 UNFCCC, Lima Call for Climate Action 2014 [Decision 1/CP.20] para. 38; 92.

22 UNFCCC The Cancún Agreements: Outcome of the work of the Ad Hoc Working Group on Long-term Cooperative Action under the Convention (n 12) para. 71.

3. BILATERAL DEVELOPMENTS

The success of REDD+ depends on funding. In this sense, individual developed countries such as Australia, France, Germany, Japan, Norway, the United Kingdom and the United States have shown themselves able and willing to push the agenda forward through bilateral initiatives.[23]

Among initiatives espoused by such countries, the German and Norwegian initiatives are of particular interest, given the fact that they already rely, to a certain extent, on results-based financing, thus being an example of phase 2 of REDD+, but already serving as a prototype of how phase 3 of REDD+ could be operationalized.

Through its REDD Early Movers program, Germany has been providing financing to "pioneers in forest conservation, setting a precedent for others to follow", as it was the case in the funding provided to the Brazilian state of Acre in 2013 for emissions reductions achieved through forest conservation in 2012.[24] In essence, the program consists of providing financial incentives for countries and subnational entities which have, in the past, achieved deforestation reduction and are currently engaged in the preparation for REDD+.

In the case of Norway, the country, through its International Climate and Forest Initiative, has been engaging directly with countries such as Brazil, Indonesia and Guyana, to provide assistance in the design and implementation of REDD+. In the case of the bilateral cooperation between Norway and Brazil on REDD+, it is interesting to notice that, through a Memorandum of Understanding concluded by representatives of both States, further complemented by a series of agreements between the Brazilian National Development Bank (BNDES) and the Norwegian Foreign Ministry,[25] Brazil has received over 4.5 billion Norwegian Crowns on results-based transfers between 2009 and 2013.

---

[23] Charlotte Streck, "Financing REDD+: Matching Needs and Ends" (2012) 4 *Current Opinion in Environmental Sustainability* 628, 629, http://linkinghub.elsevier.com/retrieve/pii/S1877343512001376.

[24] KfW, "KfW Rewards Successful Forest Conservation" (5 February 2013), https://www.kfw-entwicklungsbank.de/International-financing/KfW-Entwicklungsbank/About-us/News/Newsm-Details_20353.html.

[25] Norwegian Ministry of Foreign Affairs and Banco Nacional de Desenvolvimento Econômico e Social – BNDES, Donation Agreement 2009, http://www.regjeringen.no/upload/MD/Vedlegg/Klima/klima_skogprosjektet/donation_agreement_bndes.25.03.09.pdf. The agreement was later amended in 2009, 2010, 2011 and 2012, and eventually superseded by a new one in 2013 (which was subsequently amended later in the same year). For more information, see http://www.amazonfund.gov.br/FundoAmazonia/fam/site_en/Esquerdo/doacoes/.

The bilateral cooperation between Brazil and Norway on REDD+ is particularly interesting, given that, by rewarding Brazil for past deforestation reduction efforts, it is a results-based system,[26] thus providing a testbed for the implementation of phase 3 of REDD+. The funding provided by Norway is channeled, through the Amazon Fund (managed by the BNDES), towards activities related to phases 1 and 2 of REDD+.[27]

These are just a few examples of how bilateral initiatives are helping to shape REDD+ at the global level. Many more bilateral initiatives aimed at the establishment of REDD+ exist. Overall, it is expected that bilateral, State-to-State initiatives on REDD+ will mobilize between circa USD 1.7 and 4.5 billion between 2006 and 2019.[28] Another study has estimated that around USD 936 million have flowed towards REDD+ through bilateral arrangements between 2009 and 2012.[29]

Although some actions may be results-based (thus resembling to a certain extent phase 3 of REDD+), such as is the case of Germany's Early Movers initiative and of the cooperation between Norway and Brazil, most of the bilateral initiatives for REDD+ are aimed at the development of activities which may be characterized as pertaining to phases 1 and 2 of REDD+, such as the establishment of national REDD+ strategies and the early implementation of pilot-projects.[30]

Given the need to develop national strategies and a national framework for REDD+, in order to prepare the ground for a future phase 3 of REDD+, many have focused on the national efforts towards the adoption of laws and policies on REDD+. In the next section, some of these are presented.

---

[26] Arild Angelsen, "REDD+ as Performance-Based Aid: General Lessons and Bilateral Agreements of Norway" (WIDER 2013) WIDER Working Paper 2013/135 15, http://hdl.handle.net/10419/93710.

[27] Ibid. 15–16; Fabiano Toni, "Decentralization and REDD+ in Brazil" (2011) 2 *Forests* 66, 74, http://www.mdpi.com/1999-4907/2/1/66.

[28] REDD+ Partnership, "Voluntary REDD+ Database" (2013), http://www.fao.org/forestry/vrd/by/recipients. The large difference stems from the fact that figures are voluntarily informed by recipient and funding countries.

[29] Kerstin Canby et al., "Tracking REDD+ Finance 2009–2012 – Finance Flows in Seven REDD+ Countries" (2014) *Forest Trends* 22, http://www.forest-trends.org/publication_details.php?publicationID=4802.

[30] Ibid. 28.

4. NATIONAL DEVELOPMENTS

The emergence of national policies and laws on climate change has been observed for many years. For instance, a study on 66 countries has shown that, in 2013, the group had adopted 487 "climate change-related laws or policies of equivalent status".[31]

Given that in many countries most or at least a significant portion of their respective emissions of GHGs result from deforestation and other forest-related activities, it is only natural to expect that several of these countries would move towards the incorporation of REDD+ into their climate change policies. In this sense, several countries have moved towards the adoption of national laws and policies on REDD+, as is the case in, among others, Brazil, Cameroon, Guyana, Indonesia, Papua New Guinea and Peru.[32]

In the case of Brazil, for instance, the country is relying on reducing deforestation to achieve most of the emissions reductions targets contained in its National Policy for Climate Change, which was made into law in 2009.[33] The Amazon Fund, which was established based on an initial bilateral understanding between Brazil and Norway (see section 3), is an important part of the policy, given that it channels donated funding to voluntary deforestation reduction projects.[34] Furthermore, proposed legislation on REDD+ remains under discussion in the country's Senate and in the country's Chamber of Deputies, in a process which started with a large and quick mobilization of various actors, despite moving at a slow pace.[35]

Indonesia, for its part, enacted the world's first national legal framework for REDD+, a ministerial regulation which would later be known

---

[31] M. Nachmany et al., *The GLOBE Climate Legislation Study: A Review of Climate Change Legislation in 66 Countries. Fourth Edition* (GLOBE International and the Grantham Research Institute, London School of Economics 2014) 24, http://globelegislators.org/publications/legislation/climate.

[32] Gupta et al. (n 3); John Costenbader (ed.), *Legal Frameworks for REDD: Design and Implementation at the National Level* (IUCN 2009).

[33] Peter H. May, Brent Millikan and Maria Fernanda Gebara, *The Context of REDD+ in Brazil* (2nd edn, CIFOR 2011) 37, http://www.cifor.org/publications/pdf_files/OccPapers/OP-55.pdf.

[34] Ibid.

[35] Alex Shankland and Leonardo Hasenclever, "Indigenous Peoples and the Regulation of REDD+ in Brazil: Beyond the War of the Worlds?" (2011) 42 *IDS Bulletin* 80, 83–5, http://dx.doi.org/10.1111/j.1759-5436.2011.00225.x. Updates on the discussion of the proposals may be consulted at http://www.senado.leg.br/atividade/materia/detalhes.asp?p_cod_mate=100082 (Senate) and http://www.camara.gov.br/proposicoesWeb/fichadetramitacao?idProposicao=491311 (Chamber of Deputies).

as the "Redd Regulation", which contained rules regarding the implementation of REDD projects in the country.[36] In tandem with international negotiations, Indonesia has since moved from a project-based approach towards a national approach for REDD+, thus leading to the enactment of its national REDD+ Strategy in 2012.[37]

Interestingly, the United States has also made a national move towards the enacting of laws and regulations related to REDD+ in the past, although this move has ultimately come to a halt. This refers to the now filed proposed bills discussed in the US Congress, namely the American Clean Energy and Security Act of 2009 and the American Power Act of 2010, both of which contained rules on the use of international REDD+ as part of the country's national policy on climate change.[38]

In the case of the United States, the rationale was working to achieve emissions reductions from forestry outside of the United States in order to help the country achieve its proposed targets, thus using REDD+ overseas to move part of the emissions reductions efforts out of the country, be it in the form of offset credits or direct State-to-State international cooperation. If any of the bills had passed through the US Congress, a unilaterally established framework for REDD+ would have emerged and presented an opportunity for developing countries to move more quickly towards receiving payments under REDD+, which could either have had positive impacts on the UNFCCC process (such as a quicker move towards REDD+ based on the blueprint already provided by the USA) or negative ones (such as undermining the multilateral process and subjecting REDD+ recipients to rules in whose drafting they had no participation).

Overall, there are many challenges for national policymakers, particularly in developing countries, when designing and implementing REDD+, most notably the fair and effective treatment of land ownership and of land use rights, benefit sharing, access to information, public participation and MRV.[39] Nevertheless, given that REDD+ is moving towards the multilateral establishment of broad guidelines and national implementation according to the specific needs and deforestation drivers

---

[36] Ministry of Forestry of the Republic of Indonesia, Ministerial Regulation p. 30/Menhut-II/2009 on Procedures for Reducing Emissions from Deforestation and Forest Degradation (Unofficial English Translation) [p. 30/Menhut-II/2009].

[37] Badan Pengelola REDD+, *Dokumen Satgas REDD+* (2014), http://www.reddplus.go.id/pustaka/dokumen/dokumen-satgas-redd.

[38] C2ES, *Comparison of the American Clean Energy Act of 2009 (Waxman-Markey) and the American Power Act (Kerry-Lieberman)* (June 2010) 10, http://www.c2es.org/federal/congress/111/comparison-waxman-markey-kerry-lieberman.

[39] Costenbader (n 32), 5.

in each country, they are ultimately important for the success of REDD+ at the global level.

Therefore, in developing countries, the development of national policies and laws on REDD+ ultimately relates to the multilateral level, given that they may be understood as part of the preparatory work encompassed by phases 1 and 2 of REDD+.

In the particular case of the United States, it made sense to pursue unilateral efforts with respect to REDD regardless of the multilateral REDD+ negotiations, in the context of a failed attempt to achieve a new multilateral agreement at COP-15 in 2009 and of non-ratification of the KP by the United States; also, it was unclear, at the time, what would be the future of the UNFCCC process.[40] Ultimately, both proposed laws failed to be enacted and we can only speculate about what their impacts on REDD+ could have been.

These national processes are also complemented by subnational ones, particularly in countries with a federal structure (either *de jure* or *de facto*), as is the case for Brazil, Indonesia, Mexico and the United States, given that subnational entities in such countries have, to a greater or lesser extent, legislative and executive powers in terms of environmental protection, the use of natural resources and forest management. Therefore, in the next section, some subnational developments are presented.

5. SUBNATIONAL DEVELOPMENTS

REDD+ is also being developed by subnational jurisdictions, i.e. provinces, states and the like. This is reflected, for instance, in the existence of the Governors' Forests and Climate Taskforce (GCF), a coalition of subnational jurisdictions from Brazil, Indonesia, Mexico, Nigeria, Peru, Spain and the United States which was established in 2008 with the initial objective of working collaboratively on the design of rules that could lead to the inclusion of REDD activities in cap-and-trade mechanisms, such as those emerging, at the time, in the East Coast of the United States and in California.[41]

The GCF has since moved towards being a broader coalition through which its members exchange experiences and lessons, employ joint efforts

---

[40] Feja Lesniewska, "REDD: The Copenhagen Effect" (2010) 6 *Law, Environment and Development Journal* 102, 105, http://www.lead-journal.org/2010-1.htm.

[41] GCF, *Joint Action Plan – Appendices* 1, http://www.gcftaskforce.org/documents/GCTF-1000-2009-031-AP.pdf.

to develop policies and programs towards sustainable rural development, engage with various stakeholders and seek financing for REDD+ from a variety of sources, including, besides carbon markets, public financing and efforts to reduce deforestation linked to global food supply chains.[42]

Within the GCF, 24 jurisdictions in five developing countries (Brazil, Indonesia, Mexico, Nigeria and Peru) are developing policies and enacting laws on REDD+.[43] These include, for instance, state laws in the Brazilian states of Amazonas, Acre and Mato Grosso, as well as various policies and regulations enacted in the Indonesian province of Aceh. Overall, the GCF includes 26 members, 23 from developing countries and three from developed countries (California and Illinois, in the US; Catalonia, in Spain), including over 20 percent of the globe's rainforests and most of the Brazilian and Peruvian portions of the Amazon.

The development of subnational policies may be seen as part of the broader effort to establish national REDD+ policy in federal countries.[44] However, subnational actions also have the potential to acquire an international dimension, as may be seen in the coordination of actions of various subnational jurisdictions through the GCF. In certain cases, however, this international dimension of subnational REDD+ actions may go beyond mere coordination, and result in direct engagement between subnational jurisdictions located in different countries, bypassing the national level of government, such as is the case of the international REDD+ efforts pursued by California.

California has statutory provisions on REDD+, treating it as one of the possible pathways to be pursued in its comprehensive climate change policy, similar to the inclusion of REDD+ in the defunct bills at the national level in the United States. California was one of the main driving forces behind the creation of the GCF in 2008, given the potential to work towards special partnerships with tropical jurisdictions for the Californian efforts towards the use of REDD+.[45]

---

42 GCF, *GCF Overview*, http://www.gcftaskforce.org/about/gcf_overview/.

43 GCF, *GCF Knowledge Database* (2013), http://www.gcftaskforce-database.org/Home.

44 Andrea A. Azevedo et al., *Mato Grosso No Caminho Para Desenvolvimento de Baixas Emissões: Custos E Benefícios Da Implementação Do Sistema Estadual de REDD+* (IPAM 2013) 7–8, http://www.ipam.org.br/biblioteca/livro/Mato-Grosso-no-Caminho-do-Desenvolvimento-de-Baixas-Emissoes-Custos-e-Beneficios-da-Implementacao-do-Sistema-Estadual-de-REDD-/682.

45 Jesse Lueders et al., *The California REDD+ Experience: The Ongoing Political History of California's Initiative to Include Jurisdictional REDD+ Offsets within its Cap-and-Trade System* (Center for Global Development 2014) Working Paper 386 8–9, http://cgdev.org.488elwb02.blackmesh.com/sites/default/

As a result, the collaboration involving Acre (Brazil), California (USA) and Chiapas (Mexico) has sprung up. This process emerged from within the GCF, in which all of the three states are members, but also went beyond it. The GCF remains a platform for interaction, for the exchange of experiences and for the financing of certain activities related to phase 1 of REDD+. The process involving Acre, California and Chiapas has evolved into the creation of a dedicated workgroup aiming to provide recommendations on pathways for the potential linkage of REDD+ programs pursued in Acre and Chiapas to the Californian climate change policy. The workgroup also conducted three workshops in California on the issue and published a draft report for public consultation prior to publishing its final recommendations. Currently, the linkage is subject to a definition by California's Air Resources Board (CARB), which is considering whether to enact rules regulating the linkage.

The key to the linkage involving these three states would be the generation of emissions offsets from the REDD+ programs implemented in Acre and Chiapas, which could ultimately be used by entities in California to fulfill part of their emissions reductions targets, albeit with a certain limit.[46] This would essentially entail that emissions reductions would be achieved in Acre and Chiapas, i.e., outside of California, reducing the local impact of the Californian climate change policy, but still contributing to climate change mitigation at the global level.

However, it is not clear if the linkage will actually move forward, given the many obstacles it faces. First, the financing of REDD+ through offsetting is a contentious issue: for instance, within the UNFCCC, the use of offsets to address deforestation was left out of the KP's CDM,[47] and Brazil (where the state of Acre is situated) opposes the financing of REDD+ via offsets.[48] Also, there has been vocal opposition from some groups specifically against this linkage.[49] Furthermore, the fact that the process is driven by subnational entities leaves it vulnerable to future federal measures (in any of the respective countries) against it, such as

---

files/CGD-Climate-Forest-Paper-Series-13-Lueders-Horowitz-et-al-California-REDD.pdf.

[46] California, Code of Regulations 2015 s 95854.

[47] Lederer (n 7), 1900.

[48] BASIC, *Joint Statement Issued at the Conclusion of the 16th BASIC Ministerial Meeting on Climate Change*, http://www.itamaraty.gov.br/index.php?option=com_tags&view=tag&id=516-grupo-de-paises-basic-brasil-africa-do-sul-india-e-china&lang=pt-BR.

[49] Gloria Gonzalez, "International REDD Faces Uphill Battle in California in 2014" *Ecosystem Marketplace* (8 October 2013), http://www.ecosystemmarketplace.com/pages/dynamic/article.page.php?page_id=9988.

federal legislation adding restrictions or forbidding the linkage, or the imposition of federal red tape.

Another issue related not only to the Californian process, but to subnational REDD+ processes in general, is their relation to the UNFCCC. Under the climate change regime, subnational REDD+ is only acceptable as an interim measure, and the ultimate goal is to have REDD+ implemented nationally.[50] Therefore, it is not clear how a system established, for instance, between California and Acre would fit into the architecture provided by the UNFCCC. Perhaps a way forward would be the accommodation of the process within the Brazilian and American national REDD+ actions, although the use of offsets as a source of financing could prevent this from happening (as a result of the previously discussed Brazilian opposition to REDD+ financing via offsets).

Nevertheless, whether the initiative involving Acre, California and Chiapas is to move forward or not, subnational laws and policies are to remain, albeit indirectly, part of the process of designing and implementing REDD+. Even if, within the UNFCCC, REDD+ is under the responsibility of sovereign States, REDD+ will ultimately be implemented on the ground through the works of various levels of government within national boundaries, thus entailing the participation of subnational jurisdictions and the consequent establishment of subnational institutions, laws and policies for REDD+.

Besides the multilateral, bilateral, national and subnational levels of governance, all ultimately linked to State actors, REDD+ is also being developed through the initiative of private entities, through the design and implementation of private standards, which may at times also influence the works of State actors. The next section sheds some light on the issue, focusing on two private standards related to REDD+.

6. REDD+ DEVELOPING THROUGH PRIVATE STANDARDS

REDD+ has also been developing through private rulemaking, by means of voluntary standards and their respective certification processes, as is the case of the Jurisdictional and Nested REDD+ Framework (JNR) of the VCS and of the certifications provided by the CCBA.

---

[50] UNFCCC The Cancún Agreements: Outcome of the work of the Ad Hoc Working Group on Long-term Cooperative Action under the Convention (n 12) para. 71.

The JNR is aimed at providing a pathway for REDD+ programs implemented at the jurisdictional level (such as national, state or provincial programs) to funding from the voluntary market.[51] It is focused on the accounting aspects of REDD+, that is, on the measurement of emissions and of emissions reductions, thus providing a certification which states that emissions offsets from such REDD+ programs amount to actual emission reductions obtained on the ground.

The CCBA does not address the precise measurement of carbon emissions, but is instead aimed at certifying that REDD+ activities are also delivering social and environmental benefits.[52] Given that voluntary markets operate out of the multilateral framework for REDD+, in which the adoption of safeguards is envisaged, it helps to provide participants in the voluntary market with assurances that emissions reductions represented by the credits transacted in the market have not been obtained through the performance of activities which are socially and environmentally detrimental.

Although such processes are voluntary in nature, thus not leading directly to the creation of mandatory rules for REDD+, they entail the creation of voluntary sets of rules which are adopted by actors willing to take part in voluntary markets for REDD+. Such markets allow for individuals and businesses to purchase credits resulting from emissions reductions, instead of pursuing these reductions themselves, and are based on the free will of the purchasers.[53] Various reasons exist for the recourse to voluntary markets, such as the offset of personal emissions and the branding of a company as environmentally conscious.

The VCS is currently one of the most influential private standards in the field, and it is developed through a process involving multiple stakeholders, with a governing body involving members such as industry associations and investors.[54] It is currently recognized by the Australian National

---

[51] VCS, *Jurisdictional & Nested REDD+: Scaling Up REDD+ Activities*, http://www.v-c-s.org/sites/v-c-s.org/files/FactSheet%20JNRI%202013%20-%20MidRes_2.pdf.

[52] Eduard Merger, Michael Dutschke and Louis Verchot, "Options for REDD+ Voluntary Certification to Ensure Net GHG Benefits, Poverty Alleviation, Sustainable Management of Forests and Biodiversity Conservation" (2011) 2 *Forests* 550, 554; 556, http://www.mdpi.com/1999-4907/2/2/550/.

[53] Michael Gillenwater et al., 'Policing the Voluntary Carbon Market' [2007] *Nature Reports Climate Change* 85, 128, http://www.nature.com/doifinder/10.1038/climate.2007.58.

[54] Adam G. Bumpus and Diana M. Liverman, "Accumulation by Decarbonization and the Governance of Carbon Offsets" (2008) 84 *Economic Geography* 127, 145–6, http://doi.wiley.com/10.1111/j.1944-8287.2008.tb00401.x.

Carbon Offset Standard[55] and, in terms of REDD+, has also been quite influential in the design of jurisdictional programs, such as in the case of the state of Acre (Brazil), which is developing its state-wide REDD+ program to conform to the standards established under the JNR initiative.[56] In the same way, the CCBA has been influential, having also been adopted by some States and subnational jurisdictions in the design of their programs.[57]

Besides the VCS and the CCBA, other private standards related to REDD+ exist, such as the FSC, the PEFC, the CarbonFix Standard (CFS), the Plan Vivo Standards, and SocialCarbon, although all of these are either only incidentally related to REDD+ (such as PEFC and FSC) or are not used as often as the VCS and the CCBA.[58]

Therefore, this private REDD+ rulemaking activity is also an important part of the overall multilevel governance structure for REDD+, adding to the activities performed at the other levels of governance. Furthermore, it also influences the development of REDD+ by State actors, as in the case of the use of CCBA and VCS standards as guidance for the design of programs in certain jurisdictions.

7. FINAL REMARKS

The examples discussed in the previous sections point to the development of REDD+ through a multilevel governance process, performed through different State and non-State actors. Although this may have been inevitable, due to the slow pace of negotiations within the UNFCCC, it adds complexity and may also be problematic in certain points.

On the one hand, we see the advantages of multiple actors becoming engaged in the REDD+ process, given that it speeds the process up and ensures that, although at different levels, all actors move in more or less the same direction. This becomes evident in the preparatory character (i.e. phases 1 and 2 of REDD+) of most of the initiatives

---

55 Australian Government – Department of the Environment, *NCOS Eligible Offsets*, http://www.environment.gov.au/node/35887.

56 Anthony Anderson et al., *O Sistema de Incentivos Por Serviços Ambientais Do Estado Do Acre, Brasil: Lições Para Políticas, Programas E Estratégias de REDD Jurisdicional* (WWF-Brazil 2013) 56, http://d3nehc6yl9qzo4.cloudfront.net/downloads/wwf_sisa.pdf.

57 Ibid.

58 Merger, Dutschke and Verchot (n 52) 554–6.

being performed at the bilateral, national and subnational levels, thus pointing to a process through which actors move to create the conditions for a quicker implementation of REDD+ at the multilateral level, particularly phase 3, once the UNFCCC negotiations yield more concrete results.

However, such multiple processes may also be pre-emptive of multilateral discussions within the UNFCCC; they may adopt rules and methods that are not established collectively. This becomes evident from the defunct initiative of the United States to build its own system for REDD+, which would have had to engage with tropical nations if a more democratic and comprehensive system were to be developed.

Although forests will not necessarily be more protected globally through a multilateral approach in lieu of a complex web of unilateral actions, moving ahead with the establishment of REDD+ systems which ignore the UNFCCC process may lead to conflicting rules on the issue, thus adding new difficulties to actors who are trying to mitigate climate change while reducing forest emissions. However, if the multilateral process ultimately fails in providing a firm blueprint for climate change mitigation and for reductions of emissions from forests, actions such as those of California may turn out to be one of the few ways through which incentives for reducing such emissions are developed.

Therefore, it remains to be seen what the UNFCCC process holds for the future of REDD+. Will it stop at the current provisions, particularly the WFR, thus providing only general guidelines on REDD+, without any additional institutional backing and, more importantly, without secure sources of funding for it? Or will it provide further institutional backing to the existing framework and a clear pathway for mobilizing resources for REDD+? There may be, in the end, two pathways through which REDD+ may be developed: (1) through a loose coordination across various levels ultimately aimed at laying the ground for the insertion of various activities within the framework provided by the UNFCCC process; (2) through various processes which ignore the UNFCCC to a greater or lesser extent, such as the Californian efforts towards REDD+ and the financing of REDD+ through voluntary markets based on private standards.

Ultimately, REDD+, regardless of the pathway to be pursued, seems to be evolving into a multilevel instrument involving actors globally, all the way down to the very local people living off the forests of the world. However, given the uncertainty surrounding the future of the multilateral climate change regime, particularly in relation to the mitigation actions to be performed by Parties to the UNFCCC and the long-term financing of REDD+, it is unclear whether REDD+ will ultimately lead to globally enhanced forest conservation and management, or whether it will be just another global forest initiative with limited impact. The number of initiatives in place, and of actors involved in them, seems to point to the fact that there exists hope that REDD+ will indeed lead to a positive outcome for forests.

11. Seeing the forest for the trees: getting post-Earth Summit forest protection back on track

*Peter Horne**

1. INTRODUCTION

According to the FAO, the world's forests cover over 4 billion hectares, which is approximately 31 per cent of the world's total land mass.[1] Of this total coverage, 36 per cent is 'primary forest' with no clear indications of human interference.[2]

Despite the significance of forests, only 13 per cent of total forest is within legally protected areas.[3] Multiple treaties, soft law instruments, guiding principles and international processes have been established at multilateral, regional and bilateral levels to promote sustainable forest management and address forest loss, but these have proven incapable of meeting their lofty goals.

This chapter considers the efforts at forest preservation that emerged from the 1992 UNCED and makes five recommendations for improving their synergies at a practical level.

These outcomes include the three 'Rio Conventions', which comprise the CBD,[4] the UNFCCC,[5] and the UNCCD.[6] The UNFF, the evolution of the Non-Legally Binding Authoritative Statement of Principles for a Global Consensus on the Management, Conservation and Sustainable Development of All Types of Forests ('Forest Principles')[7] and Chapter 11 of Agenda 21 are all considered.

* All websites cited in this chapter were accessed on 1 October 2015.
1 FAO (2010) 3.
2 Ibid. 5.
3 Ibid. 6.
4 1760 UNTS 79.
5 1771 UNTS 107.
6 UNTS 1954.
7 UNGA A/CONF.151/26 (Vol. III).

2. THE RIO CONVENTIONS: SUBSTANCE AND SYNERGY

UNCED was a defining moment in international environmental law, catalysing a boom in multilateral environmental efforts. While the Rio Conventions differ in scope, they epitomise the wide-ranging significance of forests through acknowledging their importance in the achievement of their respective goals and objectives.[8]

2.1 The Convention on Biological Diversity

The CBD's objective is a consistent international approach to the conservation of biological diversity, the sustainable use of its components, and the fair and equitable sharing of the benefits arising out of the utilisation of genetic resources.[9] Parties progress these objectives at the national level through NBSAPs.[10] At 3 November 2015, 184 CBD Parties (94 per cent) have submitted an NBSAP,[11] which are complemented by other common requirements such as country reporting.[12]

In 2010, the tenth COP to the CBD (CBD COP10) in Nagoya, Japan adopted the Strategic Plan for Biodiversity 2011–2020, which aims to establish an overarching framework for biodiversity and included the 20 Aichi Targets.[13] Through this decision, Parties undertook to revise their NBSAPs to incorporate the Strategic Plan and 26 have followed through on that commitment.[14]

While the word 'forest' is not used in the CBD text, given the fact that forests are among the world's most biologically rich terrestrial systems, their preservation is significant in CBD implementation.

Article 8 establishes requirements for in situ conservation that address protection areas,[15] regulation and management[16] and rehabilitation of degraded areas.[17] Additionally, several of the Aichi Targets relate specifically to forests:

---

8 Action on Forests (2012).
9 Article 1.
10 Ibid. Article 6.
11 http://www.cbd.int/doc/nbsap/nbsap-status.doc.
12 Article 26.
13 CBD decision X/2.
14 http://www.cbd.int/doc/nbsap/nbsap-status.doc.
15 Article 8(a).
16 Ibid. Article 8(c).
17 Ibid. Article 8(f).

(5) . . . the rate of loss of all natural habitats, including forests, is at least halved and where feasible brought close to zero, and degradation and fragmentation is significantly reduced.

(7) . . . areas under agriculture, aquaculture and forestry are managed sustainably, ensuring conservation of biodiversity.

(11) . . . at least 17 per cent of terrestrial and inland water . . . are conserved through effectively and equitably managed, ecologically representative and well connected systems of protected areas and other effective area-based conservation measures, and integrated into the wider landscapes and seascapes.

(14) . . . ecosystems that provide essential services, including services related to water, and contribute to health, livelihoods and well-being, are restored and safeguarded.

(15) . . . ecosystem resilience and the contribution of biodiversity to carbon stocks has been enhanced, through conservation and restoration, including restoration of at least 15 per cent of degraded ecosystems, thereby contributing to climate change mitigation and adaptation and to combating desertification.

Forest biodiversity has been one of the CBD's seven thematic work programmes since 2002,[18] and consists of 12 goals, 27 activities and 130 programmes under the three broad elements of conservation, sustainable use and benefit-sharing, institutional and socio-economic enabling environment, and knowledge, assessment and monitoring.

2.2 The United Nations Framework Convention on Climate Change

The UNFCCC is the primary multilateral mechanism for addressing climate change. Its ultimate objective is the stabilisation of atmospheric GHG concentrations at a level that would prevent dangerous anthropogenic climate change, in sufficient time to allow ecosystems to adapt naturally.[19] Article 4 describes a range of common obligations for its Parties, which include reporting, mitigation and adaptation planning and action, and general manifestations of cooperation.

Forests store 289 gigatonnes (Gt) of carbon in their biomass alone,[20] and the AFOLU sector accounts for about one quarter of net anthropogenic GHG emissions.[21] Ensuring the sustainable management of global forest stock is therefore a critical aspect of the international response to climate change.

---

[18] CBD decision VI/22.

[19] Article 2.

[20] Article 4.

[21] IPCC (2014) 25.

The UNFCCC references forestry as a sector requiring focus for both developing and implementing new measures to address GHG emissions (a 'source')[22] and to be sustainably managed for storage of GHGs (a 'sink').[23] Countries prone to forest decay are also referenced in the context of the need to address the impact of climate change response measures on developing countries.[24] In practice, forest issues are addressed through different methods dependent upon whether a country is developed (Annex I) or developing (non-Annex I). However, the fundamental consideration stems from forests functioning as both a source and a sink.

Developed countries operate under stringent sets of rules and commitments that originated from the KP, where the sectoral approach is referred to as LULUCF. Under LULUCF, developed country Parties report and account for the GHG emissions from sources and removals from sinks through the submission of their annual GHG national inventory reports.

Following the conclusion of the Kyoto Protocol, developing countries commenced a process for addressing their own forest emissions. This process culminated in the development of 'reducing emissions from deforestation and forest degradation and the role of conservation, sustainable management of forests and enhancement of forest carbon stocks in developing countries' (REDD+) in 2010,[25] culminating in the WFR in 2013.[26]

Forests are also a potential source of emission reduction units under the KP's CDM. Reforestation and afforestation activities hosted by developing country Parties can generate offset units that a developed country Party could use in meeting mitigation commitments under the KP. However, there has been negligible interest as these units are impermanent (applying only for the life of a commitment period or project), and their complexity increases transaction costs, making them financially unviable given the current state of the international carbon market.

2.3 The United Nations Convention to Combat Desertification

The UNCCD was designed to address the challenge of desertification and drought, with a particular focus on the arid drylands of Africa. The UNCCD defines desertification as 'land degradation in arid, semi-

22 Article 4(1)(c).
23 Ibid. Article 4(1)(d).
24 Ibid. Article 4(8)(c).
25 UNFCCC decision 1/CP.16.
26 UNFCCC decisions 9-15/CP.19.

arid and dry sub-humid areas resulting from various factors'.[27] 'Land degradation' is defined as:

> reduction or loss . . . of the biological or economic productivity and complexity of rainfed cropland, irrigated cropland, or range, pasture, forest and woodlands resulting from land uses or from a process or combination of processes.[28]

The UNCCD is therefore closely related to the other conventions, but unique in its more specific focus on interventions that would serve to aid the alleviation of poverty through restoring land and soil productivity and mitigating the effects of drought. At present approximately 40 per cent of the world's population live in areas with scarce water.

Parties to the UNCCD share a range of general obligations such as cooperation, information and technical exchange, and the promotion of integrated national approaches to implementation.[29] Parties also share a common reporting obligation through which they describe their efforts to implement the UNCCD.[30]

In addition to general obligations, Parties have obligations related to national circumstances. Affected country Parties (defined as those with land at least partially in arid, semi-arid and/or dry sub-humid areas)[31] are obliged to undertake a variety of measures such as prioritising the issue, establishing national strategies and priorities, addressing underlying causes and strengthening enabling environments.[32] Developed country Parties are obliged to provide support, including financial and technical.[33]

These obligations were further elaborated at UNCCD COP8 in Madrid, Spain in 2007 with the adoption of the ten-year strategic plan and framework (2008–18) ('the Strategy').[34] The Strategy has four strategic and five operational objectives intended to enhance implementation. Parties are urged to align their National Action Programmes (NAPs), the key implementation instrument for the UNCCD, with this Strategy.

The UNCCD adopted the slogan 'forests keep drylands working' for 2011, which indicates the importance of forests in addressing its core issues. Forests are highly effective at preventing desertification through

---

27 Article 1(a).
28 Ibid. Article 1(f).
29 Ibid. Article 4.
30 Ibid. Article 26.
31 Ibid. Article 1(h)–(i).
32 Ibid. Article 5,
33 Ibid. Articles 6, 20.
34 UNCCD decision 3/COP.8.

reducing water and wind erosion of soils, retaining nutrient cycling and stabilising water tables. Accordingly, forests are one of the six UNCCD thematic priorities and all affected country Parties are obliged to report on their forest cover. This informs policy makers, which has translated into the inclusion of afforestation, reforestation, and sustainable forest management and agroforestry efforts as sectoral components within their NAPs.

2.4 Synergies and Collaboration

At the highest level, the common thread across the Rio Conventions is an undertaking to pursue sustainable management of forests, which sees the Rio Conventions complement each other in implementation.

In 2001, the Joint Liaison Group of the Rio Conventions (JLG) was jointly established by COP to facilitate coordination. The JLG has a focus on collaboration at the secretariat level rather than implementation at end-user level, which has seen a variety of initiatives including the Rio Conventions Pavilion[35] (a platform to share technical expertise and report on progress) and a number of joint publications. The JLG identified synergies in three areas (gender, adaptation and forests), releasing the Action on Forests report in the lead-up to Rio+20 in 2012.

Action on Forests summarises the mandates and action programmes on forests under each convention and provides a high-level breakdown of synergies between the three. Specifically, the Aichi Biodiversity Targets for the CBD,[36] REDD+ under the UNFCCC[37] and combating desertification/land degradation and the effects of drought (DLDD) and SFM.[38] The report uses the five forest-related Aichi Targets as a base for cross-referencing decision elements to highlight synergies. These include reducing forest cover loss, effectively managing land use, increasing conservation areas, and the restoration of degraded lands.[39]

3. BEYOND THE RIO CONVENTIONS

While the primary focus of this paper is the Rio Conventions, it is also important to recognise that these are not the only relevant instruments in

---

35 www.riopavilion.org.
36 CBD decision X/2.
37 UNFCCC decision 1/CP.16.
38 UNCCD decision 4/COP.8.
39 Article 14.

play. For example, the Ramsar Convention on Wetlands,[40] the CITES,[41] and the World Heritage Convention[42] all address forests to some extent in their respective goals. There was also a process out of the UNCED outcome that has developed in parallel to the Rio Conventions that is worth considering.

3.1 The Forest Principles and Agenda 21

An international protection framework for forests was one of the most contentious aspects of UNCED, with significant effort invested by participants at a thematic level in the two weeks of the summit and the years leading up. Negotiations splintered largely along developed and developing country lines, with stalemates on key issues including the sovereign use of forests and the provision of finance for sustainable forest management in developing countries.

In place of a forest convention, countries left UNCED with a political declaration called the Forest Principles, which became Annex III of the UNCED report. The contentious nature of its substance is illustrated through countries taking the additional, legally unnecessary step of inserting 'non-legally binding' in the title.

The guiding objective of the Forest Principles as articulated in the preamble 'is to contribute to the management, conservation and sustainable development of forests and to provide for their multiple and complementary functions and uses'.[43] The Forest Principles address topics such as the need for holistic and coordinated approaches to forest issues, as well as the broader principles of the sovereign right to development, intergenerational equity, the need for support to address incremental costs to developing countries, and an encouragement to incorporate the cost of environmental practices into the trade of forest goods and services.

The other significant UNCED forest outcome was Chapter 11 of Agenda 21, which addressed efforts to combat deforestation. The impetus for Chapter 11 included the lack of institutional and policy frameworks to 'support and develop the multiple ecological, economic, social and cultural roles of trees, forests and forest lands'.[44] Chapter 11 focused on the need to promote holistic and coordinated efforts at national, jurisdictional

---

[40] 1971, 996 UNTS 245.
[41] 1973, 993 UNTS 243.
[42] 1971, 1037 UNTS 151.
[43] Ibid. (b).
[44] Agenda 21, Ch 11, para 1.

and local levels, community engagement and an appreciation for the multiple uses of forests. In many ways, the Forest Principles were successful in capturing the key principles of Chapter 11.

3.2 Post-UNCED Responses

After UNCED, the Commission on Sustainable Development (CSD) established the IPF with a two-year mandate to consider forest policy. IPF had five focus areas: cooperation and financial assistance, research, trade in forest goods and services, and organisations, institutions and instruments, drawn from the core aspects of both the Forest Principles and Chapter 11.

When the IPF concluded in 1997, the ECOSOC immediately established the IFF to carry on from where it left off, particularly in areas where the IPF could not achieve consensus. This again included the central issues of finance and other support as well as institutions and mechanisms. The IPF/IFF process concluded in 2000 with a combined 270 proposals to move towards sustainable forest management.

3.3 The Forum on Forests and the Non-Legally Binding Instrument

After the IPF/IFF process, ECOSOC established the UNFF in 2000 as one of its subsidiary bodies. The UNFF was mandated to promote 'the management, conservation and sustainable development of all types of forests and to strengthen long-term political commitment to this end'.[45] Every UN member is a member of UNFF.

The UNFF's most significant outcome to date is the NLBI, which was subsequently adopted by the UN General Assembly in December 2007.[46]

The NLBI states the three purposes of strengthening political commitment to sustainable forest management action, enhancing the contribution of forests to the Millennium Development Goals, and providing a framework for national action and international cooperation. It sets four Global Objectives on Forests, which aim to reverse the loss of forest cover worldwide, enhance forest-based benefits and improve the livelihoods of forest-dependent people, increase the area of sustainably managed forests and the proportion of their outputs, and mobilise financial resources from all sources, including from declining foreign aid, for sustainable forest management.

---

[45] ECOSOC 2000/35.

[46] UNGA A/C.2/62/L.5.

The UNFF operates in accordance with these four objectives, which it has expanded through its own Multi-Year Programs of Work (MYPOW). The UNFF decided to further strengthen the international arrangement on forests and develop a strategic framework for 2017–2030 at its eleventh session, which concluded in May 2015.

3.4 The Collaborative Partnership on Forests

Another useful piece of the international puzzle is the Collaborative Partnership on Forests (CPF), established in 2001 following an ECOSOC recommendation. The CPF is a voluntary and informal collaboration effort by 14 UN, international and regional bodies including the CBD, UNCCD and UNFCCC.

The CPF's mission is to promote the sustainable management of all types of forests and strengthen long-term political commitment to this end, principally by supporting the UNFF and enhancing cooperation and coordination on forest issues.

Among the CPF's key areas of work are efforts to streamline forest-related reporting by developing countries, harmonising forest-related definitions, promoting awareness (such as through the International Day of Forests), and through producing collaborative research and fact sheets on various forest issues.

4. COLLABORATION CASE STUDIES

The JLG, UNFF and CPF all represent efforts to collaborate at the macro-level, but it is also important to consider implementation efforts on the ground. Two useful examples of practical implementation in view of synergies are REDD+ under the UNFCCC, and the GEF funding envelope established for its most recent replenishment.

4.1 REDD+

Arguably, the primary driver of focus on the forest sector in recent years has been its role in a climate change context, and the recent emergence of REDD+. More than US$7.3 billion has been pledged to support REDD+,[47] although it is unclear how much of this has been delivered to date.

---

[47] Kerstin Canby, Gustavo Silva-Chávez, Jessica Breitfeller, Christine Lanser, Marigold Norman, Brian Schaap, 'Tracking REDD+ Finance:

REDD+ intends to incentivise the preservation of forest carbon through the source and sink aspects of the forest sector. UNFCCC decision 1/CP.16 described the five REDD+ actions as reducing emissions from deforestation and forest degradation, conservation of forest carbon stocks, sustainable management of forests and the enhancement of forest carbon stocks.[48]

REDD+ recognises the link to broader forest management efforts through overarching expectations and a range of 'safeguards' that 'should be promoted and supported'. While these include measures to avoid the risk of reversals (i.e. the subsequent release of stored forest carbon), the role of indigenous peoples and consistency with other actions under the UNFCCC, they also address areas that emphasise the necessary focus on synergies, including for actions to:

> Be consistent with the objective of environmental integrity and take into account the multiple functions of forests and other ecosystems;[49]
> Be consistent with Parties' national sustainable development needs and goals;[50]
> Be consistent with the adaptation needs of the country;[51]
> Promote sustainable management of forests;[52]
> [C]omplement or [be] consistent with the objectives of national forest programmes and relevant international conventions and agreements;[53]
> [Be] consistent with the conservation of natural forests and biological diversity, ensuring that the actions referred to in paragraph 70 of this decision are not used for the conversion of natural forests, but are instead used to incentivize the protection and conservation of natural forests and their ecosystem services, and to enhance other social and environmental benefits . . .[54]

Both the CBD and UNCCD have responded to the self-recognition of synergies with REDD+ and their respective objectives. Parties to the CBD established a process to develop indicators that may support the implementation of REDD+ in the context of managing the established safeguards.[55] The UNCCD invited all Parties to scale up their sustainable forest management policies and practices in support of biodiversity conservation.[56]

2009–2012 – Finance Flows in Seven REDD+ Countries', *Forest Trends* (November 2014).

48 UNFCCC decision 1/CP.16, 70.
49 Ibid. appendix I, 1(d).
50 Ibid. 1(f).
51 Ibid. 1(h).
52 Ibid. 1(k).
53 Ibid. 2(a).
54 Ibid. 2(e).
55 CBD decision X/33.
56 UNCCD decision 4/COP.8.

UNCCD COP10 adopted the Advocacy Policy Framework on climate change, which invites Parties to include DLDD considerations in national REDD+ programmes and include REDD+ considerations in NAPs.

4.2 The Global Environment Facility

As the GEF is an operating entity of the financial mechanism for each of the Rio Conventions, it is a useful case study from an implementation perspective.

The GEF released a revised strategy for sustainable forest management in the context of its sixth replenishment (GEF-6),[57] which targets the broader concept of sustainable forest management in response to lessons learned through previous implementation efforts. The strategy advocates actions at the landscape level, recognising the synergies between climate change, biodiversity and land degradation, as well as the link between the Rio Conventions and the alleviation of poverty.

Underpinning this effort will be a US$250 million funding envelope, where financial contributors will be encouraged to invest a portion of their allocation. The SFM envelope aims to demonstrate the linkage between climate change, biodiversity and land degradation objectives at the practical implementation level. Two integrated approach pilot projects have been identified and will focus on sustainable cities and removing deforestation from supply chains. The latter is also the subject of the new sustainable forest landscapes tranche of the World Bank's BioCarbon Fund.[58]

The recent establishment of the GCF notwithstanding, the GEF is the only functioning operating entity for the Rio Conventions and has over 20 years of experience in progressing implementation objectives. It has a track record of trialling new efforts (GEF-5 featured a similarly innovative envelope for REDD+) and works closely with its delivery partners on the ground. In many ways, the GEF is a prime example of Rio Convention collaboration and coordination in implementation.

5. RECOMMENDATIONS

It is clear from the above analysis of the Rio Convention approach to forests and consideration of the process that culminated in the UNFF and NLBI that there are clear synergies and overlaps that could be approached

---

57 GEF (2014).

58 http://biocarbonfund-isfl.org/.

in a more effective fashion. This paper has identified five areas where this could occur.

5.1 National Focal Points

A key challenge for all countries is in breaking down domestic siloing at government level. For example, the Australian Government national focal point for the UNFCCC is from the Department of Foreign Affairs and Trade, the CBD and UNCCD from the Department of the Environment, and the UNFF from the Department of Agriculture.

The separation of bureaucratic and ministerial interests is not uncommon across developed and developing countries, but leads to a practical disconnection in knowledge and expertise exchange. This adversely impacts the capacity of the representatives of state actors in each forum to effectively take a broader and more strategic and holistic approach to subject matter.

This could be addressed through appointing a single national forest focal point. Consistent with national forum focal points, this should be a senior public servant or junior minister, but the forest focal point would serve as the primary channel for all international communication on forests.

The Australian Government recently replaced its Ambassador for Climate Change at the expiration of his term with an Ambassador for the Environment. The expanded scope could serve as a means to facilitate greater internal government collaboration.

5.2 Country Reporting

A second area of improvement is in the way countries report on their forest sectors. Each of the Rio Conventions developed specific reporting tools that reflect a negotiated process and outcome that is fit for its specific objectives, touching on technical issues within a country's forest sector. While reporting is a necessary component of effective implementation, accountability and transparency mechanisms, there is scope to implement a common forest sector reporting mechanism.

The common mechanism would replace existing onerous and duplicative administrative burdens that currently occur at different times, with a single comprehensive tool to address the full spectrum of national forest indicators.

For example, reporting under the UNFCCC is different for developed and developing countries, but entails some combination of National Communications, Biennial Reports, and/or annual inventories. The CBD requires regular National Reports to demonstrate how the CBD objectives are being implemented, and the UNCCD requires Country Reports to track progress in a similar way. Additionally, the UNFF has established a voluntary reporting system to track progress towards the NLBI objectives. Countries are also required to provide reports to access financial and other forms of support from respective financial mechanisms, multilateral development banks and other providers of financial assistance (such as other governments).

As the text of the Rio Conventions only imposes the requirement of reporting, COPs have determined the scope and format through decisions. Current requirements could be amended to adopt a common reporting mechanism without amendments to the respective treaties. The CBD made an initial foray into this area through decision X/36, requesting the secretariat to work with the UNFF and the CPF to investigate ways of streamlining reporting. While this is a good start, it does not go far enough.

Common forest sector reporting would be of particular benefit to developing countries seeking support for implementation of forest actions, but hamstrung by the lack of both resources and technical expertise. In practice, this work is often contracted to private sector consultants who can effectively perform the function but do so in an uncoordinated fashion that does not serve to build lasting domestic capacity.

5.3 Implementation

The third area that would benefit from enhanced coordination is the method of proposing implementation action. As with reporting, countries are required to submit information on forest-related implementation efforts in different formats under each convention. Under the UNFCCC, the WFR established parameters for developing countries to report on their efforts. The CBD requires similar information from countries in their NBSAPS and from UNCCD countries through their respective NAPs. Again, there also exists a variety of separate implementation proposal formats for accessing support.

The practical reality of implementation is that countries will adopt measures that achieve a variety of ends. Accordingly, countries should look to adopt a common framework for the development and implementation of forest actions.

The move to a common implementation action framework would be easier than a move to a common reporting framework. While reporting requirements are driven by the need for global understanding, implementation arrangements are inherently determined by national circumstances. For example, engaging indigenous communities to perform traditional land management practices is an appropriate means to further the objectives of all three Rio Conventions. Under a common framework, this could be captured in all three forums through a single proposal.

As with the reporting obligation, the implementation obligations are broad and have been clarified through COP decisions. This also provides the legal capacity for the amendment of requirements through further COP decisions rather than treaty amendment.

5.4 Active Interdependence

In many ways, the fourth area – active interdependence – is a creature of the first three. The JLG is clear in its role as a facilitator of coordination between the respective Rio Convention secretariats, rather than an implementation body. The secretariats are independent entities designed to assist and facilitate party-driven convention processes, and accord this obligation appropriate respect. However, Parties in each forum have consistently demonstrated their desire to remain bound by narrow interpretation of each forum's mandate.

A potential way around this would be for COPs to empower the secretariats to actively pursue streamlining and rationalisation efforts in contrast to the current and more passive approach of identifying existing and emerging synergy.

This approach would likely prove to be contentious given the change in the current relationship between the COP and secretariat under each convention, as well as its departure from the traditional secretariat role. However, the impediments to this approach are political rather than legal. While Parties would be reluctant to relinquish any part of their ownership over the process, the COP possesses the legal capacity to provide this mandate to the secretariat.[59]

5.5 The Landscape Approach

While the final recommendation would serve to enhance synergies on forest action across the Rio Conventions, it goes somewhat further. Since UNCED it has been clear that arriving at a legally binding international framework on forests is highly unlikely for a range of reasons. Despite the progress that has been made, the key challenges of sovereign rights to development, developed and developing country divides and expectations of financial support have not been sufficiently addressed.

---

[59] CBD Article 24; UNFCCC Article 8; UNCCD Article 23.

Forests are critical to the objectives of the Rio Conventions, but they are also critical to other conventions that extend beyond international environmental law. For example, forests are a significant consideration for the international human rights framework as they can provide the means to achieve a number of universal rights such as rights to work, movement, and other housing, land and property rights.

Consequently we should start to move beyond the existing paradigm and recognise forests as part of a broader, multifunctional landscape. This landscape approach would recognise that forests are part of an interconnected web of biodiversity, climate change and land management concerns, equally networked to broader issues of agriculture, food security and human rights considerations.

6. CONCLUSION

Former FAO forestry director, Jack Westoby, once commented that 'forestry is not about trees, it is about people. And it is about trees only insofar as trees can serve the needs of people.' Westoby's comment is often repeated, but much like the development of approaches to forests under the Rio Conventions and the broader UNCED outcomes, it fails to tell the full picture.

The world recognised the importance of forests in 1992, but the legacy of the inability to arrive at a uniform approach is a series of disconnected, top-down mechanisms. This has led to duplication, competition and confusion in implementation, particularly in developing countries where the need for coordinated and effective approaches is often the greatest.

A common theme through the five recommendations in this paper is the need for all forest stakeholders to focus on forests from the bottom up, which is a key lesson from implementation experiences through REDD+ and the GEF. On the ground, synergies across objectives are clear but international frameworks are immaterial. This appreciation would logically lead to seeing the benefits of forests as a whole, and the relationship of forests within the broader landscape.

In the same way as Westoby saw the importance of forests to people but not of people to forests, the international community must see both the importance of forests to frameworks and of these frameworks to forests.

BIBLIOGRAPHY

Ambalam, Kannan, 'Challenges of Compliance with Multilateral Environmental Agreements: the case of the United Nations Convention to Combat Desertification in Africa' *Journal of Sustainable Development Studies*, Volume 5, Number 2, 2014.

Birnie, Patricia, Alan Boyle and Catherine Redgwell, *International Law and the Environment* (Oxford University Press: 2009).

Bodansky, Daniel, *The Art and Craft of International Environmental Law* (Harvard University Press: 2010).

CBD, UNCCD, UNFCCC, 'The Rio Conventions – Action on Forests', 2012.

Cowie, Annette, Uwe A. Schneider, Luca Montanarella, 'Potential Synergies between Existing Multilateral Environmental Agreements in the Implementation of Land Use, Land Use Change and Forestry Activities' *Environmental Science & Policy*, Volume 10, Issue 4, June 2007, 335–52.

Evans, Malcom (ed.), *International Law* (Oxford University Press: 2010).

Food and Agriculture Organization (FAO), 'Global Forest Resources: Key Findings', 2010.

Food and Agriculture Organization (FAO), 'State of the World's Forests', 2012.

Food and Agriculture Organization (FAO), 'State of the World's Forests', 2014.

Global Environment Facility (GEF), 'GEF-6 Sustainable Forest Management Strategy: Strengthened Support for Forests', 2014.

IPCC, 'Summary for Policymakers', in Ottmar et al. (eds) *Climate Change 2014, Mitigation of Climate Change. Contribution of Working Group III to the Fifth Assessment Report of the Intergovernmental Panel on Climate Change* (Cambridge University Press: 2014).

Mackey, Brendan et al., 'Policy Options for the World's Primary Forests in Multilateral Environmental Agreements' *Conservation Letters* 2014.

Pistorius, Till, Christine Schmitt, Dinah Benick and Steffen Entenmann, *Greening REDD+: Challenges and Opportunities for Forest Biodiversity Conservation* (University of Freiburg: 2010).

Rothwell, Donald, Stuart Kaye, Afshin Akhtarkhavari and Ruth Davis, *International Law: Cases and Materials with Australian Perspectives* (Cambridge University Press: 2011).

Scott, Karen, 'International Environmental Governance: Managing Fragmentation Through Institutional Connection' 12 *Melbourne J. of Int'l Law* 177.

Shaw, Malcom, *International Law* (Cambridge University Press: 2003).

UNCCD, 'REDD+ and Desertification', 2012.

Yamin, Farhana and Joanna Depledge, *The International Climate Change Regime: A Guide to Rules, Institutions and Procedures* (Cambridge University Press: 2004).

Convention on Biological Diversity, opened for signature 5 June 1992, 1760 UNTS 79 (entered into force 29 December 1993).

Declaration of the United Nations Conference on the Human Environment (Stockholm Decl-Binding Instrument on All Types of Forests (NLBI) UNGA A/C.2/62/L.5.

United Nations Convention to Combat Desertification in those Countries Experiencing Serious Drought and/or Desertification, Particularly in Africa, opened for signature 17 June 1994, 3 UNTS 1954 (entered into force 26 December 1996).

United Nations Framework Convention on Climate Change, opened for signature 9 May 1992, 1771 UNTS 107 (entered into force 21 March 1993).

Agenda 21 (United Nations: 1992).

Universal Declaration of Human Rights (adopted 10 December 1948) UNGA Res 217 A (III).

PART IV

REDD+ FINANCE, MARKETS AND INVESTMENT

12. Managing fiduciary risk in REDD+

*Paul Keenlyside, John Costenbader and Charlie Parker**

1. INTRODUCTION

The delivery of REDD+ finance to governments with weak institutions carries fiduciary risk. As noted by a report by the OECD on risk management in the delivery of aid in post-conflict and transitional states, "[e]xposure to corruption and fiduciary risk is an inevitable part of engagement in fragile states – but that does not mean that it has to be tolerated or that it cannot be managed."[1] The purpose of this chapter is to discuss why fiduciary risk is a major factor in the delivery of public REDD+ finance, explore how fiduciary risk has been managed to date with reference to a number of bilateral and multilateral REDD+ funds, and analyse the implications of fiduciary risk management choices for aid effectiveness in the REDD+ context.

The Paris Declaration on Aid Effectiveness acknowledges that using a recipient country's own systems of financial management, accounting, auditing and procurement will strengthen country capacity and increase aid effectiveness.[2] As part of the Accra Agenda for Action, donors have aimed to channel more than half of government-to-government assistance through domestic fiduciary systems.[3] However, as this note illustrates, few REDD+ funds are currently designed according to this approach.

This chapter begins in section 2 with an overview of fiduciary standards generally, and a description of how fiduciary standards have been framed in the context of public climate finance. Section 3 then describes why fiduciary risk might arise specifically in the flow of REDD+ finance. Section 4 sets out how fiduciary risk has been managed to date in existing REDD+ funds, with reference to other climate funds where illustrative.

---

* All websites cited in this chapter were accessed on 1 October 2015.

[1] OECD, *Managing Risks in Fragile and Transitional Contexts, The Price of Success* 146 (2011), available at http://www.oecd.org/dac/governance-peace/conflictandfragility/docs/managing%20risks.pdf.

[2] The Paris Declaration on Aid Effectiveness, para. 17, adopted in Paris, 2 March 2005, available at http://www.oecd.org/dac/effectiveness/34428351.pdf.

[3] Accra Agenda For Action, para. 15.e, adopted in Accra, 4 September 2008.

Four approaches are analysed in this section: the management of risk by domestic institutions of recipient country governments; the management of risk by international institutions tasked with fund management; the management of risk by donor country government institutions; and the management of risk by a combination of these. Finally, the chapter concludes with recommendations, based on the above analysis, for managing fiduciary risk in REDD+.

2. WHAT ARE FIDUCIARY STANDARDS?

Fiduciary standards refer to the standard of care that a person under a duty to act solely in the interest of another (commonly a trustee acting on behalf of a beneficiary) must exercise within the scope of that relationship.[4] In the context of international aid, fiduciary standards are designed to ensure that resources are used for their intended purpose and that resources are spent efficiently, enhancing "aid effectiveness."[5] The risk that resources will not be used efficiently or to their intended purpose is referred to as "fiduciary risk." Fiduciary risk can be mitigated by requiring the fund administrator to meet relevant fiduciary standards, typically in financial management (e.g., accounting and auditing), project oversight (e.g., monitoring and evaluation systems and procurement processes) and decision making (e.g., demonstrating transparent and accountable decision making through investigative functions and disclosures of conflicts of interest).

There is no commonly agreed set of "international fiduciary standards" in the aid context.[6] However, a number of funds including climate funds have established minimum fiduciary standards for organisations seeking to become implementing entities of those funds. In 2007, the GEF developed a set of minimum fiduciary standards in response to the recommendation of GEF donors to strengthen the accountability of GEF

---

[4] See Restatement (Third) of Trusts § 2, Comment *b* (2003).

[5] See, e.g., The Global Fund, *Fiduciary Arrangements for Grant Recipients*, para. 2 (2003), available at http://www.theglobalfund.org/documents/core/grants/Core_Fiduciary_Arrangements_en/.

[6] Laura Druce et al., *Direct Access to International Climate Finance and Associated Fiduciary Standards* 10 (April 2014), available at http://fs-unep-centre.org/sites/default/files/publications/directaccessengneu.pdf. See also GCF, *Business Model Framework: Access Modalities*, para. 11, GCF/B.05/08, 24 September 2013, available at http://gcfund.net/fileadmin/00_customer/documents/pdf/GCF_B05_08_BMF_Accreditation_fin_20130924.pdf, page 5.

agencies eligible for implementing and executing GEF funded projects.[7] The Adaptation Fund, which was designed to disburse through recipient country institutions (called National Implementing Entities (NIEs)) as well as multilateral institutions, has developed a set of fiduciary standards to guide the accreditation process of implementing entities.[8] More recently, the GCF has analysed the experience of these funds, among others, in order to arrive at its own fiduciary standards as part of its criteria for the accreditation of intermediaries and implementing entities.[9] The fiduciary standards of the three funds, which are summarised in Table 12.1 below, correspond relatively closely, and though they differ in how each component part is broken down, the same core institutional capacities for managing fiduciary risk are covered.

Fiduciary standards apply at two fundamental stages in the disbursement of aid. First are the fiduciary standards that development agencies are invariably required to follow in accordance with domestic laws within donor countries. For example, the UK's Department for International Development (DFID) or the USAID must have appropriate standards in place to ensure that they remain accountable to their national legislatures for their use of public resources.[10] Second are the fiduciary standards that aid recipients are required to follow in the handling and disbursement

---

[7] GEF, *Minimum Fiduciary Standards for GEF Partner Agencies, Policy: GA/PL/02*, available at https://www.thegef.org/gef/sites/thegef.org/files/documents/document/GA.PL_.02%20Minimum_Fiduciary_Standards.pdf.

[8] Adaptation Fund, *Report on Fiduciary Standards for Implementing Entities*, AFB/B.6/4, available at http://www.adaptation-fund.org/wp-content/uploads/2015/01/AFB.B.6.4_Fiduciary_Standards.pdf.

[9] GCF, *Guiding Framework and Procedures for Accrediting National, Regional and International Implementing Entities and Intermediaries, Including the Fund's Fiduciary Principles and Standards and Environmental and Social Safeguards (Progress Report)*, GCF/B.06/09, available at http://gcfund.net/fileadmin/00_customer/documents/pdf/GCF_B06_09_Guiding_Framework_for_Accreditation_fin_20140211.pdf.

[10] DFID's Accounting Officer (the Permanent Secretary) is accountable to Parliament for DFID's spending. The National Audit Office, on behalf of Parliament, scrutinises DFID's systems for ensuring effective management and proper use of the development budget. See DFID, *Managing Fiduciary Risk when Providing Financial Aid*, para. 141, 2011, available at https://www.gov.uk/government/uploads/system/uploads/attachment_data/file/67488/how-to-fiduciary-fin-aid.pdf. Pursuant to 31 USC § 3515, USAID is required to prepare consolidated financial statements for each fiscal year. Office of Management and Budget (OMB) Circular A-136, "Financial Reporting Requirements," requires USAID to submit a performance and accountability report, including audited financial statements, to OMB, the Department of the Treasury and the Government Accountability Office (GAO).

Table 12.1 Standards for finance

Green Climate Fund	Global Environment Facility	Adaptation Fund required competencies
BASIC FIDUCIARY STANDARDS Key administrative and financial capacities General management and administrative capacities (overall governance and oversight structure) Financial management and accounting Internal and external audit Control framework (internal oversight provisions) Procurement (relating to the general operations of the entity, as well as procurement in the context of the implementation and execution of funding proposals approved by the Fund) TRANSPARENCY AND ACCOUNTABILITY Code of ethics Disclosure of conflict of interest Capacity to prevent or deal with financial mismanagement and other forms of malpractices Investigation function SPECIALISED FIDUCIARY STANDARDS Project/programme preparation and appraisal (track record) Project/programme implementation, oversight and control Monitoring and evaluation Project-at-risk systems and related project risk management capabilities	AUDIT, FINANCIAL MANAGEMENTS AND CONTROL FRAMEWORK External financial audit Financial management and control frameworks Financial disclosure Code of ethics Internal audit PROJECT AND ACTIVITY PROCESS AND OVERSIGHT Project appraisal standards Procurement processes and guidelines Monitoring and project-at-risk systems Evaluation function INVESTIGATIONS Investigation function Hotline and whistleblower protection	FINANCIAL INTEGRITY The ability to accurately and regularly record transactions and balances to an appropriate standard as attested to by a competent entity The ability to safeguard, manage and disburse funds efficiently to recipients on a timely basis Legal status to contract with Adaptation Fund and third parties REQUISITE INSTITUTIONAL CAPACITY Procurement procedures which provide for transparent competition including effective means of redress Capacity to undertake monitoring and evaluation Ability to identify, develop and appraise project – ex ante and ex post – technically, legally, financially, economically, socially and environmentally (as appropriate) Competency to manage or oversee the execution of the project including ability to manage subrecipients, fit for purpose infrastructure and resource to support project delivery and implementation TRANSPARENCY AND SELF-INVESTIGATIVE POWERS Freedom to whistle-blow on issues of fraud and gross mismanagement Objective policy for self-regulation

of finance. For example, international organisations, multi-donor trust funds, recipient country governments and other implementing or executing entities will all have fiduciary standards in place governing how resources are disbursed or spent on procurement at the project delivery stage. This chapter focuses on the second stage, though to some extent fiduciary standards at stage two are shaped by the fiduciary standards required of donor agencies at the first stage.

3. FIDUCIARY RISK IN REDD+

Although fiduciary risk is a concern in the provision of all aid, ensuring transparency and accountability can be particularly problematic in the context of REDD+. This is due to two primary reasons: corruption levels in forestry sectors generally, and the design and delivery of REDD+ funds in particular. These are explained in more detail below.

3.1 Corruption and Forestry

The forestry sector regularly ranks as a problem sector for corruption in many developing countries.[11] Central and local government officials typically wield large discretionary powers, for example in the issuing of logging concessions, and decision making, though amenable to bribery, may not be open to public or judicial scrutiny.[12] Monitoring of wood production against permitted harvesting levels may also be left to local discretion,[13] as

---

[11] Forestry was ranked the most corrupt sector in Indonesia according to the 2012 Corruption Eradication Commission report. See Berni Moestafa, *Forest Misuse Costs Indonesia $7 Billion in Revenue, Report Says*, Bloomberg News, 10 November 2013, available at http://www.bloomberg.com/news/2013-11-10/forest-misuse-costs-indonesia-7-billion-in-revenue-report-says.html. See also Transparency International, *Forest Governance Integrity in Asia Pacific, Corruption and Forestry*, available at http://archive.transparency.org/regional_pages/asia_pacific/forest_governance_integrity/corruption_and_forestry and Janette Bulkan and John Palmer, "Breaking the Rings of Forest Corruption: Steps Towards Better Forest Governance," 18 *Forests, Trees and Livelihoods* 103 (2008) available at http://www.researchgate.net/publication/228983091_Breaking_the_rings_of_forest_corruption_steps_towards_better_forest_governance.

[12] This is identified as a problem in Indonesia's forestry sector. See Maira Martini, *Causes of Corruption in Indonesia* 7–8 (2012) available at http://www.u4.no/publications/causes-of-corruption-in-indonesia/downloadasset/2890.

[13] Transparency International, *Global Corruption Report: Climate Change* 300 (2011) available to download at http://www.transparency.org/whatwedo/publications/doc/gcr/.

centralised data collection on forest extent and wood production is often unreliable. Despite technological progress, difficulties tracking harvested wood mean legally and illegally harvested stock is often indistinguishable once it enters supply chains.[14] In addition, by their very nature, forestry activities tend to be conducted in remote regions where government institutions and the rule of law may be weaker. Further, rural and forest dwelling communities typically lack the influence, resources and – where they do have recognised title to the land – access to a reliable judicial system through which to enforce rights. Lastly, the financial rewards of forest clearance can be highly concentrated,[15] creating powerful networks of shared interests, and the social and environmental costs are widely shared, commonly falling hardest on marginalised groups. Penalties for illicit activities are often insufficient to create an effective deterrent.[16] As summarised by a World Bank note on illegal logging and corruption, "[w]ith limited oversight, abundant rents, and poor incentives, the opportunities for corruption [in the forest sector] abound."[17]

Exacerbating the corruption risk in the forestry sector is the fact that many REDD+ host countries are perceived as experiencing high levels of corruption generally. Of the top ten recipients of REDD+ finance,

---

[14] See Christian Nellemann, *Green Carbon, Black Trade: Illegal Logging, Tax Fraud and Laundering in the World's Tropical Forests. A Rapid Response Assessment* (2012), available at http://www.unep.org/pdf/RRAlogging_english_scr.pdf (noting than between 10 and 30 per cent of global timber supply is from illegal logging).

[15] In Southeast Asia for example, deforestation is driven for the most part by large-scale plantations. These are typically controlled by large agri-business companies that control a significant share of primary production of palm oil, rubber and other commodities. See Doug Boucher et al., *The Root of the Problem. What's Driving Tropical Deforestation Today?* 27 (2011) available at http://www.ucsusa.org/sites/default/files/legacy/assets/documents/global_warming/UCS_RootoftheProblem_DriversofDeforestation_FullReport.pdf.

[16] In Papua New Guinea, the maximum penalty for smuggling logs is a fine of $20,000, but the average log shipment is worth more than ten times that sum. See Sam Lawson, *Illegal Logging in Papua New Guinea* 13 (2014), available at http://www.chathamhouse.org/sites/files/chathamhouse/home/chatham/public_html/sites/default/files/20140400LoggingPapuaNewGuineaLawson.pdf. Penalties are tougher in Indonesia, including prison sentencing, but, a handful of high profile cases aside, investigation, prosecution and conviction rates are low. See Marilyne P. Goncalves et al., *Justice for Forests Improving Criminal Justice Efforts to Combat Illegal Logging* 1 (2012), available at http://siteresources.worldbank.org/EXTFINANCIALSECTOR/Resources/Illegal_Logging.pdf.

[17] World Bank, *Combating Illegal Logging and Corruption in the Forestry Sector* 13 (2006), available at http://siteresources.worldbank.org/INTENVMAT/64199955-1162240805462/21127309/6Combating.pdf.

Table 12.2 REDD+ countries, ordered according to amount of REDD+ funds received

REDD+ country (ordered according to amount of REDD+ funds received)	CPI 2013 country ranking (out of 177 countries)	CPI 2013 score (out of 100)
Brazil	72	42
Indonesia	114	32
D.R.C.	154	22
Mexico	106	34
Guyana	136	27
Peru	83	38
Tanzania	111	33
Burkina Faso	83	38
Lao PDR	140	26
Papua New Guinea	144	25

nine score less than 40/100 according to Transparency International's Corruption Perceptions Index, with an average score of 32/100 (see Table 12.2). This is unsurprising, as REDD+ countries with large forest cover face the institutional and economic challenges associated with many resource-rich developing countries, where "abundance" can invite corruption, inefficient bureaucracies and rent-seeking.[18]

3.2 Corruption in the Delivery of REDD+ Finance

The way in which REDD+ finance is currently delivered presents significant opportunities for the misallocation of funds. The financial landscape of REDD+ is highly complex, with numerous multilateral, bilateral and private funders providing resource streams that overlap and blend at the national level. Given that there is no consolidated REDD+ database tracking financial flows, and many REDD+ agreements are not publicly available, tracking where money is spent and what for is not straightforward. At the recipient country level, long distribution chains including centralised institutions, local government, private sector developers and NGOs increase the risk of corrupt intermediaries capturing funds before they reach intended beneficiaries. Where expected results from REDD+ investments are intangible and difficult to capture with "SMART"

[18] See Shannon M. Pendergast et al., *Corruption and the Curse of Natural Resources* (2008) available at http://economics.ca/2008/papers/0633.pdf.

indicators (e.g., "capacity building" at the REDD readiness stage), the effectiveness of expenditure can be difficult to quantify. Where outcomes are tangible (e.g., under a payment for performance system) there is the risk of misuse of indicators (e.g., baseline inflation during the development of forest reference levels).

4. MANAGING FIDUCIARY RISK IN REDD+

Robust fiduciary standards that introduce high levels of transparency and accountability are important to guard against the risks outlined above. The fiduciary risk attached to REDD+ finance, as with any other type of aid, can be managed at a number of levels in the disbursement chain. However, depending on the design of the REDD+ fund or agreement, one institution in the disbursement chain is typically responsible for the majority of fiduciary risk management. This can either be (1) a domestic institution of the recipient country government, (2) a multilateral institution tasked with fund management, (3) a donor country government institution, or (4) a combination of these. This section provides examples of each approach in the REDD+ context, with some examples from other types of climate finance where illustrative, and seeks to draw out strengths and/or weaknesses of each approach.

4.1 Fiduciary Risk Managed Domestically

The Norway–Brazil partnership on REDD+ is the pre-eminent example of a REDD+ agreement that devolves fiduciary responsibility to domestic institutions within the host country. Norwegian contributions are channelled through the Amazon Fund, a national level institution that has the ability to issue grants without further donor approval.[19] The Brazilian development bank, BNDES, manages Amazon Fund resources in compliance with Brazilian law and international financial reporting standards, and internal and external audits are conducted to ensure fiduciary standards are being met. External audits are conducted according to Brazilian technical accounting standards.[20] As part of the agreement, Norway has

---

[19] Donation Agreement entered into by and between the Norwegian Ministry of Foreign Affairs and Banco Nacional de Desenvolvimento Economico E Social (BNDES), Nor.– BNDES, 25 March 2009. Articles V (Contributions and Obligations of the BNDES) and IX (Selection of Projects and Procurement), available at http://www.regjeringen.no/upload/MD/Vedlegg/Klima/klima_skogprosjektet/donation_ agreement_bndes.25.03.09.pdf.

[20] Ibid. art. X.

reserved the right to withhold disbursements where financial management of the Amazon Fund is not "satisfactory."[21]

Reliance by a donor on domestic institutions and standards to manage fiduciary risk is relatively unusual for REDD+, and represents both the spirit of "mutual trust and cooperation" in which the Amazon Fund was conceived,[22] and the solid reputation of BNDES for fiduciary risk management. One view is that the Amazon Fund's strict adherence to agreed procedures, and the absence of claims of corruption or illegality, demonstrates the capacity of some developing country institutions to meet high fiduciary standards.[23] Observers have noted that the strictness of procedures within the Amazon Fund has led to the improvement of management standards downstream, with funds better managed by grantees implementing projects,[24] though this in turn has been partially responsible for slowing disbursement rates and has made it difficult for smaller organisations to access the fund.[25]

The success of the Amazon Fund has provided a model for devolving fiduciary responsibility that other REDD+ agreements may follow. It is likely that financial support for REDD+ in Peru, agreed in a Joint Declaration of Intent signed in September 2014 by Peru, Norway and Germany, will be provided through a national institution with fiduciary responsibilities for fund management.[26] The Declaration of Intent sets out three phases of the REDD+ partnership: preparation, transformation and contributions for verified emissions reductions. One of the deliverables of the first phase will be the design and implementation of a financial instrument that should "be managed according to established international

---

21 Ibid. art. XII.

22 Ibid. art. II.

23 See Maya Forstater et al., *The Effectiveness of Climate Finance: A Review of the Amazon Fund* 31 (2013) available at http://www.odi.org/sites/odi.org.uk/files/odi-assets/publications-opinion-files/8340.pdf. See also Norad, annexes, *Real-time Evaluation of Norway's International Climate and Forest Initiative. Synthesising Report 2007–2013* 229 (2014), available to download at http://www.norad.no/en/toolspublications/publications/2014/real-time-evaluation-of-norways-international-climate-and-forest-initiative.-synthesising-report-2007-2013/.

24 Norad, at 213.

25 Forstater et al., at 3.

26 See Joint Declaration of Intent between the Government of the Republic of Peru, the Government of the Kingdom of Norway and the Government of the Federal Republic of Germany on "Cooperation on Reducing Greenhouse Gas Emissions from Deforestation and Forest Degradation (REDD+1) and Promote Sustainable Development in Peru" 23 September 2014, available at https://www.regjeringen.no/contentassets/b324ccc0cf88419fab88f2f4c7101f20/declarationofintentperu.pdf.

standards – including fiduciary [and] governance [standards]."[27] Though it is not explicitly stated that this financial instrument will be a national fund, the declaration notes that the IDB "has committed to explore the provision of technical assistance to the Government of Peru to develop the proper fiduciary and financial mechanism."[28] As part of phase three of the partnership, donors commit to channelling financial contributions for verified emissions reductions through the agreed financial instrument.

There are also examples of climate finance being delivered with fiduciary responsibility devolved to the recipient country outside REDD+. The most notable case is under the Adaptation Fund, established in 2001 at the Marrakesh COP to the UNFCCC, with the central aim of financing "concrete adaptation projects and programmes in developing country Parties that are Parties to the [Kyoto] Protocol."[29]

In addition to traditional access through multilateral channels, the Adaptation Fund can also be accessed "directly" through national accredited institutions known as NIEs.[30] To be successful in the accreditation process, NIEs must satisfy certain fiduciary standards determined by the Adaptation Fund Board. Fiduciary standards cover three areas: financial integrity and management; institutional capacity; and transparency and self-investigative powers.[31] Key requirements are the periodic and independent auditing of transactions and balances, the presence of transparent procurement procedures and the capacity to undertake monitoring and evaluation.

The "direct access" modality is an innovation of the Adaptation Fund and is designed to improve the capacity of developing countries to manage funds and projects, strengthen country ownership over projects and elevate the profile of climate change and adaptation issues at the national level. Under direct access, NIEs are responsible for project implementation through executing entities and bear all financial, monitoring and reporting responsibilities.[32]

Despite the difficulties many national bodies have faced in meeting accreditation standards (less than a quarter of Adaptation Fund resources

---

27 Ibid. art. V.b.

28 Ibid. Technical support from the IADB.

29 Report of the Conference of the Parties on its Seventh Session, held at Marrakesh from 29 October to 10 November 2001, Decision 10/CP.7 para. 1. UN Doc. FCCC/CP/2001/13/Add.1.

30 Adaptation Fund Board, *Operational Policies and Guidelines for Parties to Access Resources from the Adaptation Fund*, paras. 26–7, available at http://unfccc.int/files/adaptation/implementing_adaptation/adaptation_funding_interface/application/pdf/afbguide.pdf.

31 Ibid. at para. 32.

32 Ibid. at para. 28.

have been channelled through NIEs, with only five out of 34 funded projects submitted through NIEs), there is nevertheless broad consensus on the need to scale-up direct access, and the Adaptation Fund has introduced a number of measures to that end, including a cap on the multilateral access modality and a Readiness Program to build capacity of NIE applicants.[33] While not all recipient countries will have the capability (or inclination) to accredit national entities at present, the lesson of the Adaptation Fund is that it is possible for even least developed countries to identify institutions that meet required fiduciary standards.

The experience of the Adaptation Fund has influenced the design of the GCF. The GCF Governing Instrument determined that in addition to access through multilateral implementing entities, GCF resources should be made available through NIEs accredited by the GCF Board.[34] Accreditation will be in accordance with the GCF's fiduciary standards, "with a view to enhancing country ownership." To that end, the GCF Board has been developing a guiding framework and procedures for accrediting national, regional and international implementing entities and intermediaries, and have drafted fiduciary principles and standards that such entities would have to meet. The GCF Board has agreed that such a framework should "accommodate different capacities and capabilities of countries."[35]

The benefits of using in-country systems to manage fiduciary risk are clear, and mirror the arguments frequently put forward for expanding direct access. These are increased country ownership, oversight and accountability, the harmonisation of international funds with national funds and systems, the reduction of transaction costs and the better targeting of funds at the project level.[36]

---

[33] See Charlie Parker et al., *Early Experiences in Adaptation Finance: Lessons from the Four Multilateral Climate Change Adaptation Funds* (2014), available at http://www.climatefocus.com/documents/files/early_experiences_in_adaptation_finance.pdf.

[34] See Governing Instrument of the Green Climate Fund, para. 47, establishing GCF direct access facility. For the latest progress on operationalising this facility, see Guiding Framework and Procedures for Accrediting National, Regional and International Implementing Entities and Intermediaries, Including the Fund's Fiduciary Principles and Standards and Environmental and Social Safeguards, GCF/B.07/02, available at http://gcfund.net/fileadmin/00_customer/documents/MOB201406-7th/GCF_B07_02_Guiding_Framework_for_Accreditation_fin_20140512_16.30_hrs.pdf.

[35] See GCF/B.05/08, Annex.

[36] See Alexander Froede and Claudia Assman, *Capacity Development for Direct Access to Climate Finance*, available at https://www.giz.de/expertise/downloads/giz2012-en-climate-finance-capacity-development.pdf.

Nevertheless, while donors should aim to increase direct access modalities for REDD+ finance, there is a limit within developing countries to absorb such finance. Many recipient countries will not have the institutional capacities to manage fiduciary risk in a manner that is consistent with accountability requirements placed on aid budgets in donor countries. Given that fiduciary risks are particularly pronounced within REDD+, it would be inadvisable to relax these standards.

4.2 Fiduciary Risk Managed Multilaterally

As a general rule, multilateral REDD+ funds require that beneficiaries comply with fiduciary standards of the relevant implementing entity, which will either be a multilateral development bank (MDB) or UN agency. Thus under the FCPF's Readiness Fund, each "delivery partner" applies their own fiduciary rules in supervising funds transferred by the World Bank.[37] Under the FIP, each operation must follow the fiduciary standards of the implementing MDB,[38] with each MDB discharging its responsibilities "with the same degree of care as it exercises with respect to its own resources."[39] UN-REDD's proposed Social and Environmental Principles and Criteria require that funded activities "ensure the transparency and accountability of fiduciary and fund management systems linked to REDD+ activities."[40] However, no further guidance is provided as to the standards according to which fiduciary systems are assessed, and in practice, activities will follow the rules and regulations of the participating UN-REDD organisations (UNDP, UNEP and FAO), which must in turn report to the Administrative Agent (the UN-REDD Multi-Donor Trust Fund).[41] Finally, the Congo Basin Forest Fund (CBFF) operates accord-

---

[37] FCPF Seventh Participants Committee Meeting, Resolution PC/7/2010/4 para. 6. available at https://www.forestcarbonpartnership.org/sites/forestcarbonpartnership.org/files/Documents/PDF/Nov2010/PC7%20Resolutions.pdf.

[38] FIP Investment Criteria and Financing Modalities, para. 88, available at https://www.climateinvestmentfunds.org/cif/sites/climateinvestmentfunds.org/files/FIP_Investment_Criteria_and_Financing_Modalities_final.pdf.

[39] Ibid. para. 89a.

[40] UN-REDD Programme Social and Environmental Principles and Criteria, Criterion 1, available at http://www.unredd.net/index.php?option=com_docman&task=doc_download&gid=6754&Itemid=53.

[41] See Standard Memorandum of Understanding (MOU) for Multi-Donor Trust Funds using Pass-Through Fund Management, United Nations Collaborative Programme on Reduced Emissions from Deforestation and Degradation in Developing Countries (UN-REDD), s.IV.1. available at http://mptf.undp.org/document/download/7248.

ing to the fiduciary management procedures of the African Development Bank (AfDB),[42] and projects funded by the CBFF must comply with all applicable AfDB policies.

In addition to the multilateral funds, a number of bilateral REDD+ agreements channel finance through multilateral entities, which apply their own fiduciary and operational policies to financed activities. Most prominent among these is the Norway–Guyana agreement, which established the Guyana REDD+ Investment Fund (GRIF), an international, multi-donor trust fund with the World Bank as trustee, that disburses through multilateral entities (termed partner entities) including the World Bank, Inter-American Development Bank (IADB) and UNDP.[43] Partner Entities of the GRIF release funds in "grant agreements" to Implementing Entities (the Government of Guyana is the main implementing entity) that deliver projects. For all investments of GRIF resources for which they provide operational services, partner entities are responsible for ensuring that the use of funds is consistent with their own fiduciary standards, and are responsible for supervising each project's adherence to these standards.[44] Where funds are used inconsistently with partner entity fiduciary standards (i.e. in a manner inconsistent with the grant agreement), the implementing entity must promptly return funds to the partner entity, and the partner entity must return funds to the GRIF. Thus projects managed by the Government of Guyana, as implementing entity, must meet fiduciary standards of the partner entity in order for funds to be disbursed, and once disbursed, there is considerable oversight of how funds are managed. The Letter of Intent (LoI) signed between Norway and Liberia in September 2014 appears to follow the same model as the GRIF, according to which Norway commits, on evidence of achieved emissions reductions in Liberia, to channel financial contributions through the World Bank.[45]

---

[42] CBFF Operational Procedures Manual, available at http://www.afdb.org/fileadmin/uploads/afdb/Documents/Policy-Documents/Congo%20Basin%20Forest%20Fund%20-%20Operational%20Procedures%20EN.pdf.

[43] See Administration Agreement (Guyana REDD-Plus Investment Fund) between Royal Norwegian Ministry of Foreign Affairs and International Development Association, 9 October 2010, available at https://www.regjeringen.no/globalassets/upload/md/vedlegg/klima/klima_skogprosjektet/guyana/aa.pdf.

[44] Ibid.

[45] Letter of Intent between the Government of the Republic of Liberia and the Government of the Kingdom of Norway on "Cooperation on Reducing Greenhouse Gas Emissions from Deforestation and Forest Degradation (REDD+1) and Developing Liberia's Agriculture Sector", art. VII.b., 23 September 2014, available at https://www.regjeringen.no/contentassets/b8b93fa03bda4ac893d-065d26d64075b/letterofintentliberia.pdf.

Fiduciary standards of MDBs and UN agencies do not align entirely, as evidenced by the mixed success of GEF agencies (that is, the MDBs, UN agencies and NGOs in complying with the GEF's minimum fiduciary standards).[46] Where fiduciary standards and the requirements relating to fiduciary risk do not align exactly, there is the risk that REDD+ host countries will expend unnecessary resources meeting different standards required by different implementing entities, in order to access resources for essentially the same activities. Thus a review of UN-REDD country evaluations noted the burden created by differing requirements of the three UN-REDD agencies (UNDP, UNEP and FAO), observing that while some processes have been streamlined, "there are still operational procedures such as fiduciary risk assessments . . . which are applied according to the requirements of the different implementing agencies."[47] Requiring beneficiary countries to demonstrate compliance with divergent standards increases transaction costs, slows disbursement and in general exacerbates problems associated with aid fragmentation. During ongoing discussions around the design of REDD+ within the UNFCCC, developing country Parties have noted that the different requirements, processes and standards of different financing channels can lead to uncoordinated implementation and inequitable allocation of funds.[48]

The capacity of multilateral entities to manage fiduciary risk makes them an attractive vehicle through which to channel REDD+ finance. This is particularly the case in lower capacity countries without institutions that can demonstrate long track records of reliable financial management. However, this arrangement can create parallel decision

---

[46] See GEF, *Status of the GEF Agencies with Respect to Minimum Fiduciary Standards*, GEF/C.35/5, 27 May 2009, available at http://www.thegef.org/gef/sites/thegef.org/files/documents/C.35.5_Fiduciary_Standards.pdf. GEF agencies are the Asian Development Bank, AfDB, Conservation International, the Development Bank of Southern Africa, the European Bank for Reconstruction and Development, the FAO, the IADB, the International Fund for Agricultural Development, International Union for Conservation of Nature, UNDP, UNEP, United Nations Industrial Development Organization (UNIDO), the World Bank and WWF. See http://www.thegef.org/gef/gef_agencies.

[47] Norad, *Real-Time Evaluation of Norway's International Climate and Forest Initiative Synthesising Report 2007–2013* Report 3/2014 32 (2014) available to download at http://www.norad.no/en/toolspublications/publications/2014/real-time-evaluation-of-norways-international-climate-and-forest-initiative.-synthesising-report-2007-2013/.

[48] See Report on the Workshops of the Work Programme on Results-Based Finance to Progress the Full Implementation of the Activities Referred to in Decision 1/CP.16, para. 70, available at http://unfccc.int/resource/docs/2013/cop19/eng/05.pdf.

making structures, where host country institutions design and approve projects, only to find that projects do not satisfy the implementing entities' fiduciary requirements.

Notwithstanding this, multilateral entities' fiduciary standards are generally comparable,[49] and most often conform to internationally accepted standards. This is unsurprising, given their experience managing multibillion-dollar trust funds.[50] Thus the main issue with relying on international entities for fiduciary responsibility is not variant standards of these entities and the duplicative efforts required by host countries to meet them. Rather, the main issue is that bypassing country-based institutions undermines country ownership, which can lead to delays and bottlenecks in the disbursement of finance and project implementation.

As noted above, under the GRIF arrangement, partner entities are responsible for the use of funds transferred to them by the trustee, and are required to show consistency with their own fiduciary policies and procedures for all investments for which they provide operational services. Essentially, this means that investments must be in line with international fiduciary and environmental standards. The Government of Guyana meanwhile is responsible for proposing, designing and approving projects that GRIF resources are used to finance. Thus partner entities can withhold finance for projects that have been approved by the Government of Guyana due to concerns around fiduciary risk.

A recent study highlighted that partner entities' focus on compliance with fiduciary standards has overshadowed the real aim of the GRIF, which is to channel finance quickly into low-carbon development so as to avert mining and logging projects.[51] Others have seen delays as the responsibility of the Government of Guyana for failing to develop fund-

---

[49] See *Meetings of the Transitional Committee for the Design of the Green Climate Fund, Report on the Survey of Relevant Funds and Institutions and Lessons Learned: A Note on the Results of Surveys and Interviews*, 10, TC-3/INF.2, 31 August 2011, available at http://unfccc.int/files/cancun_agreements/green_climate_fund/application/pdf/tc3_inf2_survey_final_corrected.pdf.

[50] The World Bank group held approximately USD 29 billion in trust in 2013, UNDP approximately USD 8 billion. See the World Bank Group, *2013 Trust Fund Annual Report* (2013) available at http://siteresources.worldbank.org/CFPEXT/Resources/299947-1274110249410/CFP_TFAR_AR13_High.pdf. See also UNDP multi-partner trust fund office gateway website, available at http://mptf.undp.org/.

[51] Nancy Birdsall and Jonah Busch, *Assessing Performance-Based Payments for Forest Conservation: Six Successes, Four Worries, and Six Possibilities to Explore of the Guyana Norway Agreement* 3 (2014) available at http://international.cgdev.org/sites/default/files/Birdsall_Busch_performance-based-aid-forest-conservation_2.pdf.

able project concept notes, and observe that partner entity standards are vital to prevent misuse of resources.[52] Yet to some extent, the tension between the desire to disburse quickly, and the desire to meet proper fiduciary standards, is inevitable where fiduciary risk is managed outside of the host country. The same issue has arisen in the CBFF, whereby donors place their funding with the AfDB precisely because of its fiduciary policies, yet also complain that AfDB procedures for financial management and procurement are too cumbersome to allow for timely disbursement.[53]

Furthermore, domestic capacity to manage fiduciary risk is unlikely to develop for as long as international funds do not rely on or transition towards domestic institutions, as with the multilateral REDD+ funds. It is commonly stated that the aim of REDD+ finance is to build readiness capacity and pilot REDD+ schemes in developing countries in order that these countries are able to access, in the future, scaled-up performance based payments for generating verified emissions reductions (this is the basis of the phased approach to REDD+ set out in the Cancún Agreements).[54] However, it is questionable whether this objective is being fully met where domestic institutions are bypassed due to capacity concerns.

4.3 Fiduciary Risk Managed by Donor Country

In 2008 Norway and Tanzania signed a LoI according to which Norway agreed to provide up to NOK 500 million (approximately USD 40 million) to fund REDD+ activities over five years.[55] Funds have been disbursed by the Royal Norwegian Embassy in Dar-es-Salaam to implementing partners in Tanzania: a mixture of domestic and international NGOs delivering pilot projects, and research institutions working on policy and research projects. Agreements have been formalised through contracts and grant

---

[52] Response of John Palmer to Birdsall and Busch (2014), published on REDD Monitor, 21 May 2014, available at http://www.redd-monitor.org/2014/05/21/a-debate-on-redd-in-guyana/.

[53] Operations evaluation department, African Development Bank group, trust fund management at the African Development Bank, an independent evaluation 14 (2013), available at http://www.afdb.org/fileadmin/uploads/opev/Documents/Trust%20Fund%20Management%20at%20the%20African%20Development%20Bank%20-%20EN.pdf.

[54] The Cancún Agreements: Outcome of the work of the Ad Hoc Working Group on Long-term Cooperative Action under the Convention, Decision 1/CP.16 para. 73, UN Doc FCCC/CP/2010/7/Add.1.

[55] Norad, at 311.

agreements entered into between the Norwegian Ministry of Foreign Affairs (MFA) and the implementing partners.

The choice to bypass the Tanzanian national government was informed by Norwegian concerns about government capacity to manage fiduciary risk, and in particular reported corruption within the Ministry of Natural Resources and Tourism, which had mismanaged previous Norwegian Official Development Assistance (ODA) contributions.[56] By disbursing through their Embassy, Norway retained greater control over fund management. For example, agreements permit close monitoring of project delivery, through scheduled and unscheduled visits to implementing partners.[57] It has been noted that these procedures helped to identify and rectify two instances of mismanagement within projects run by World Wide Fund for Nature (WWF) Tanzania (misuse of finance) and the Wildlife Conservation Society of Tanzania (failure to meet contractual obligations).[58]

However, lack of country ownership due to the decision to bypass government institutions has been highlighted as one of the major reasons for Tanzania's slow progress towards REDD+ readiness.[59] Tanzania has not established a national financing mechanism, has not developed a functional MRV system, and has not agreed upon a set of social and environmental safeguards or decided how safeguards will be monitored. Although it is widely acknowledged that Norwegian support has led to some ministerial capacity development, institutional capacity building has been limited and REDD+ infrastructure remains poorly financed absent Norway's contribution.

Further, while it has been possible to identify the financial irregularities noted above, their very existence indicates that operating through NGOs with embassy oversight is no guarantee of eliminating fiduciary risk.

---

[56] See U4, *Monitoring Aid: Lessons from a Natural Resources Programme in Tanzania* (2009) available at http://www.u4.no/publications/monitoring-aid-lessons-from-a-natural-resources-programme-in-tanzania/downloadasset/132. See also Eirik G. Jansen, "Don't Rock the Boat: Norway's Difficulties in Dealing with Corruption in Development Aid" in *Corruption, Grabbing and Development: Real World Challenges* 186 (Tina Søreide and Aled Williams eds., Edward Elgar Publishing Ltd.) (2014).

[57] See e.g., Contract between the Norwegian Ministry of Foreign Affairs (MFA) and the World Wide Fund for Nature Tanzania Country Office (WWF TCO) regarding Enhancing Tanzanian Capacity to Deliver Short and Long Term Data on Forest Carbon Stocks Across the Country, available at http://www.norway.go.tz/PageFiles/253880/WWF_contract.pdf.

[58] Norad, at 314–15.

[59] Ibid. at 312–13 and 326.

Following allegations of fraud in WWF Tanzania, Ernst and Young were asked to conduct a full forensic audit of the projects, which placed the level of fraud at approximately USD 400,000.[60] Norway's contract with the Wildlife Conservation Society of Tanzania (WCST) meanwhile was terminated after the organisation failed to meet contractual obligations,[61] including failure to provide satisfactory financial and audit reports or deliver desired results on the ground.[62]

Thus, the retention by donors of the responsibility for handling fiduciary risk may enable donors to retain control over projects and deliver quick results (it has been noted that the requirement to demonstrate results in a short time frame was another significant factor in the decision to disburse to NGOs). However, such retention of responsibility also diminishes country ownership, and may even discourage domestic investment required to develop domestic financial institutions and improve procedures to the point that a country is able to generate long term REDD+ results.

4.4 Fiduciary Risk Management Transitioned from International to Domestic Entity

The LoI agreed between Norway and Indonesia in 2010, which set out the Norway–Indonesia partnership on REDD+, determined that Indonesia would design and establish a funding instrument "managed by an internationally reputable financial institution."[63] A Joint Concept Note, agreed subsequent to the LoI, determined that a temporary funding instrument would be put in place to fund activities in the first phase of the agreement.[64]

---

[60] WWF International, *WWF International Board Report on Incidences of Fraud in Tanzania*, available at http://d2ouvy59p0dg6k.cloudfront.net/downloads/wwf_international_boardreport_on_the_incidence_of_fraud_in_wwf_tanzania.pdf.

[61] Norad, at 315.

[62] Finnigan Wa Simbeye, *Tanzania: Norway Stops Funding Conservation Projects*, AllAfrica, 4 August 2013, available at http://allafrica.com/stories/201308040036.html.

[63] See Letter of Intent between the Government of the Kingdom of Norway and the Government of the Republic of Indonesia on "Cooperating on Reducing Greenhouse Gas Emissions from Deforestation and Forest Degradation", 26 May 2010, available at http://www.regjeringen.no/upload/SMK/Vedlegg/2010/Indonesia_avtale.pdf.

[64] Indonesia–Norway Partnership Joint Concept Note, 12 March 2010, available at http://www.regjeringen.no/upload/MD/2011/vedlegg/klima/klima_skogprosjektet/Indonesia/jcn_indonesia_norway_redd_partnership_2010.pdf.

In 2010, Norway had concerns about the capacity of Indonesian financial institutions to provide sufficient administrative quality assurance and found that the risk of mismanagement was such that appointing an international entity as the initial fiduciary agent was essential to attract the confidence of other donors.[65] For this reason, the first funding phase was channelled through the UNDP Trust Fund under the project titled "Support to the Establishment of Indonesia REDD+ Infrastructure and Capacity," with funds subject to UNDP fiduciary standards.[66]

This interim financial arrangement will ultimately be replaced by a permanent funding instrument, the Trust Fund for REDD+ in Indonesia (FREDDI), once it is operational. Though no decisions have been taken on which financial institution will be responsible for the financial management of FREDDI, it is expected that an Indonesian institution will perform this function. Thus the Norway–Indonesia partnership is an example of a fund designed to transfer fiduciary responsibility from an international to a domestic institution.

This phased approach to managing fiduciary risk, entrusting financial management with multilateral entities for initial expenditure while simultaneously building domestic capacity, is also evident in the design of the Indonesia Climate Change Trust Fund (ICCTF). The ICCTF is a national, multi-donor trust fund established by the government of Indonesia as a vehicle through which to raise, coordinate and channel international climate finance in alignment with national spending priorities.[67] The ICCTF is designed to become operational in three phases, progressing from an "innovation fund" (phases 1 and 2) which channels grants from development partners, to a "transformation fund" (phase 3) which leverages finance from a wider range of sources (e.g., private investment, domestic budgets and potentially the carbon market).[68] UNDP has been appointed as trustee with fiduciary responsibility for the first phase. For the second phase, an Indonesian institution will share fund management with UNDP, before taking full control in the third phase.

---

[65] Norad, at 292–3.

[66] See UNDP Project Document, *Support to the Establishment of Indonesia REDD+ Infrastructure and Capacity*, available at http://www.undp.org/content/dam/undp/documents/projects/IDN/00060694_PRODOC%20REDD%2B.pdf.

[67] See *Indonesia Climate Change Trust Fund, Annual Report 2013*, available at http://icctf.or.id/App_ClientFile/a1780ed9-591c-4352-aff5-4763a3283033/Assets/ICCTF%20Annual%20Report%202013.pdf.

[68] See Christine Grüning et al., *Case Study: The Indonesia Climate Change Trust Fund (ICCTF)* 11 (2012), available at http://fs-unep-centre.org/sites/default/files/publications/icctf2012-08-16finalversion_1.pdf.

Management of phase 1 was entrusted to UNDP in order to secure donor confidence on the meeting of minimum fiduciary standards.[69] During this phase, resources have been invested in developing the capacity and procedures of the ICCTF to comply with international fiduciary standards, so that standards should remain high once fund management transitions to a national institution. Bank Mandiri, the largest commercial bank in Indonesia, has been appointed as national trustee and will serve as joint fund manager for phase 2.[70]

To date, capitalisation of the ICCTF has been disappointing, and developing capacity of the ICCTF has been challenging, with a number of questions remaining over the transparency of its financial management and procedures for combating fraud.[71] Yet the ICCTF does indicate how climate finance can be delivered in a way that mitigates up-front fiduciary risk in countries with weaker institutional track records, while developing and utilising national financial systems in a way that promotes country ownership.

A further example of this transitional approach to devolving fiduciary responsibility is the Bangladesh Climate Change Resilience Fund (BCCRF). The BCCRF was set up in 2010, growing out of a multi-donor trust fund initially established with contributions from the UK, in order to assist Bangladesh in responding to the impacts of climate change.[72] The World Bank has been selected to serve as trustee on an interim basis from 2010 to 2015, and is responsible for fiduciary management, transparency and accountability in the use of funds. After 2015, the Secretariat of the BCCRF will assume fiduciary responsibility for the fund. The Secretariat is based in Bangladesh's Ministry of Environment and Forests. During the interim period, the World Bank has committed to working closely with the Ministry to help build the capacity of the Secretariat,[73] though the effective development of the Secretariat has been hindered by the small amount of

---

[69] Aidy Halimanjaya et al., *The Effectiveness of Climate Finance: A Review of the Indonesia Climate Change Trust Fund* 14 (2014) available at http://mhpss.net/?get=150/The-Effectiveness-of-Climate-Finance_A-Review-of-the-Indonesia-Climate-Change-Trust-Fund.pdf.

[70] ICCTF Annual Report, at 14.

[71] Aidy Halimanjaya et al., at 22.

[72] See S. M. Munjurul Hannan Khan et al., *The Bangladesh National Climate Funds: A Brief History and Description of the Bangladesh Climate Change Trust Fund and the Bangladesh Climate Change Resilience Fund* (2012), available at https://ldcclimate.files.wordpress.com/2012/05/bangladeshnationalfund.pdf.

[73] World Bank news, *Bangladesh Climate Change Resilience Fund*, May 22, 2012, available at http://www.worldbank.org/en/news/feature/2012/05/22/bangladesh-climate-change-resilience-fund-bccrf.

funds (USD 0.2 million) that have been made available for that purpose.[74] Nevertheless, the BCCRF is expected to become the main funding channel for climate finance into Bangladesh in the future,[75] and has the potential to serve as national implementing entity for new funds such as the GCF.

5. CONCLUSION

Fiduciary risk is a major factor in the delivery of public REDD+ finance due to corruption in the forestry sector generally and opportunities for misallocation in the way REDD+ finance is delivered and tracked. This chapter has explored four options for managing fiduciary risk: (1) the management of risk by domestic institutions of recipient country governments, (2) the management of risk by international institutions tasked with fund management, (3) the management of risk by donor country government institutions, and (4) the transition of risk management from international to domestic institutions.

In general we find that managing fiduciary risk domestically increases host country ownership, oversight and accountability, it encourages the harmonisation of international funds with national funds and systems, and should reduce transaction costs while leading to the better targeting of funds at the project level. The example of the Amazon Fund demonstrates that higher capacity host countries have the ability to manage fiduciary risk effectively. Other upper-middle and high-income REDD+ countries such as Mexico, Costa Rica, Chile or Argentina would have similar capacity in place. However, the majority of REDD+ countries are lower-middle income countries and will not have the institutional capacities to manage fiduciary risk. Where this is the case, there are obvious attractions for using the fiduciary systems of multilateral entities, or retaining oversight by disbursing through their embassies. However, the case studies described in this chapter suggest that while this approach does not eliminate fiduciary risk, it does seriously undermine country ownership, can lead to duplicative compliance costs and can create bottlenecks in the

---

[74] International Center for Climate Change and Development, *Policy Brief, National Funding Entities for Local Adaptation: Lessons Learned from Bangladesh* (2014) available at http://www.icccad.net/wp-content/uploads/2014/07/CCG_Policy-Brief_May-2014.pdf.

[75] Bangladesh Climate Change Resilience Fund, newsletter, *Interview with Dr. Hasan Mahmud, Minister of Environment and Forests, Bangladesh*, November 2012, available at http://bccrf-bd.org//Documents/pdf/Newsletter%208Nov12%20-%20final.pdf.

disbursement process. Host country ownership will be particularly undermined where funds bypass host country institutions altogether and are channelled through NGOs with donor country oversight. One approach that can be used to minimise this outcome is to build a transition pathway from donor-provided fiduciary systems to in-country fiduciary systems, such as those assumed in Indonesia and Bangladesh in other climate mitigation activities.

To conclude, fiduciary risk should ideally be managed by host country institutions. Where domestic capacity is not in place, the fiduciary systems of international entities should be utilised. However, in this case, there should be parallel efforts to build the capacity of host country institutions, a process in place for transitioning fiduciary responsibility to host country institutions, and a clear timetable for working towards this transition.

13. REDD+ instruments, international investment rules and sustainable landscapes

*Marie-Claire Cordonier Segger, Markus Gehring and Andrew Wardell**+

1. INTRODUCTION

International rules to guide climate change responses, and to govern international investments, were not crafted as opposing poles. In the context of poverty eradication and sustainable development of a global green economy, these objectives are actually intended to be integrated and mutually supportive. In the 1997 UN General Assembly Special Session on Sustainable Development, at paragraph 23, countries noted that 'Economic development, social development and environmental protection are interdependent and mutually reinforcing components of sustainable development.' Calling for sustained economic growth, they further declared: 'Growth can foster development only if its benefits are fully shared. It must therefore also be guided by equity, justice and social and environmental considerations. Development, in turn, must involve measures that improve the human condition and the quality of life itself.' States further agreed, at paragraph 81, that:

> To stimulate higher levels of private investment, Governments should aim at ensuring macroeconomic stability, open trade and investment policies, and

* This chapter shares thoughts with authors' contributions to R. Rayfuse and S. Scott (eds), *International Law in the Era of Climate Change* (Cheltenham, UK: Edward Elgar 2012), p. 84 with A. Kent; O.C. Ruppel, C. Roschmann and K. Ruppel-Schlichting, *Climate Change: International Law and Global Governance* (Nomos 2013); with J. Hepburn, to D. Freestone and C. Streck (eds), *Legal Aspects of Carbon Trading Kyoto, Copenhagen, and Beyond* (Oxford: Oxford University Press 2009); and to C. Haywood, A. Wardell, M.C. Cordonier Segger and P. Holmgren, 'Legal Frameworks for Implementing REDD+ in Zambia, Mozambique and Tanzania: Opportunities for a Sustainable Landscapes Approach', 2 Carbon & Climate Law Review (2015), pp. 130–42. Authors thank Freedom-Kai Phillips in particular, alongside other CISDL jurists and researchers, for their invaluable insights and assistance in preparing this chapter.

+ All websites cited in this chapter were accessed on 1 October 2015.

> well-functioning legal and financial systems ... To ensure that such investments are supportive of sustainable development objectives, it is essential that the national Governments of both investor and recipient countries provide appropriate regulatory frameworks and incentives for private investment. Therefore further work should be undertaken on the design of appropriate policies and measures aimed at promoting long-term investment flows to developing countries ... Official development assistance donors and multilateral development banks are encouraged to strengthen their commitment to supporting investment in developing countries in a manner that jointly promotes economic growth, social development and environmental protection.[1]

Later, in the 2012 UN Conference on Sustainable Development Declaration on The Future We Want, countries further declared:

> we consider green economy ... as one of the important tools available for achieving sustainable development ... We emphasize that it should contribute to eradicating poverty as well as sustained economic growth, enhancing social inclusion, improving human welfare and creating opportunities for employment and decent work for all, while maintaining the healthy functioning of the Earth's ecosystems.[2]

This chapter focuses on the interactions between REDD+ as an international investment measure with climate and sustainable development objectives, and other currently evolving rules of international investment law. It considers current experience with REDD+ as an instrument to incentivise investment in forest sector GHG emissions mitigation towards more sustainable landscapes, recent concerns and opportunities raised through the interpretation of international investment agreements by the arbitral panels convened to hear disputes under the rules of the International Centre for Settlement of Investment Disputes (ICSID) or the United Nations Commission on International Trade Law (UNCITRAL), and recent trends and options for crafting the extensive and growing network of bilateral and regional investment treaties to support sustainable development. The chapter considers how investment law might best fail to frustrate, and perhaps even foster, more effective implementation of REDD+ in developing countries. With special attention to countries that have experienced growth in land-based investments over the past decade and depend on their natural resources, the chapter considers REDD+

---

[1] UN, A/Res/S/19-2. 'Programme for the Further Implementation of Agenda 21', New York, USA (19 September 1997) 23 and 81.

[2] UN, 'The Future We Want', United Nations Conference on Sustainable Development, Rio de Janiero, Brazil (22 June 2012) Outcome Document, United Nations Sustainable Development Knowledge Platform, http://sustainabledevelopment.un.org/futurewewant.html [The Future We Want].

legal issues to date and their key linkages with international investment legal frameworks. Among other studies, it draws on key findings from leading work by the Centre for International Forestry Research (CIFOR) and the International Development Law Organization (IDLO).[3]

The chapter is structured in five parts. Section 2 briefly reviews the global context, evolution and progress of REDD+ to date, approaching the instrument as a measure to encourage more sustainable investments in landscapes. From a survey of recent arbitral decisions, Section 3 then discusses how key principles of investment law are being interpreted by tribunals, demonstrating how investment rules can serve as sword or shield for REDD+. Section 4 briefly surveys how international legal frameworks for investment can better reflect global sustainable development goals, in a way which resembles similar previous refinements of trade law. Section 5 concludes with reflections on the importance of carefully crafting investment treaties, including through the correct use of process innovations such as sustainability impact assessments, to ensure that new international economic rules can foster the contributions of REDD+ to sustainable development of a global green economy.

Although, as this chapter discusses, climate change may not have made its presence known directly in many international investment disputes so far, global efforts to find solutions have already had effects on the regimes themselves in other ways. This chapter considers whether our existing international economic law regimes are adequate, in their current forms, to address the pressures and tensions that REDD+ and other climate measures engender. The ultimate outcomes of this debate are still being determined, as negotiators, policymakers, academics and tribunals continue to work towards equitable and sustainable responses to climate change. However, this chapter presents a few ways forward, setting out possibilities for future enhancements of the two regimes to ensure that climate change is and remains a defeasible issue. Ultimately, we suggest, climate change cooperation presents many challenges but, on balance, also opportunities for trade and investment law to provide a meaningful framework for global sustainable development.

---

[3] C. Dalupan et al., *Enabling Legal Frameworks for Sustainable Land Use Investments* (Bogor: CIFOR and IDLO 2015); P. Towela Sambo et al., *Enabling Legal Frameworks for Sustainable Land Use Investments in Zambia: Legal Assessment Report* (Bogor: CIFOR 2015); E. Chiziane et al., *Enabling Legal Frameworks for Sustainable Land Use Investments in Mozambique: Legal Assessment Report* (Bogor: CIFOR and IDLO 2015); R. Kibugi et al., *Enabling Legal Frameworks for Sustainable Land Use Investments in Tanzania: Legal Assessment Report* (Bogor: CIFOR and IDLO 2015).

2. REDD+ INVESTMENTS IN GLOBAL CONTEXT

Global trade and investment trends, leading to increasing food consumption, population growth, rising demand for resources-based imports, and growing purchase of agricultural and forest lands, are placing ever-greater pressure on communities and their landscapes.[4] Countries endowed with significant natural resources are experiencing economic growth, tied to exploitation of their lands and forests.[5] Across Africa, Latin America and Asia, especially, many countries' economic systems rely significantly on natural capital, and are attracting increasing numbers of land-based investments.[6] However, conversion of forested land, due in part to agricultural, mining, energy, forestry and other productive sector-specific investments, has resulted in widespread land degradation and ever-worsening pressure on the world's climatic systems. Currently, as International Energy Agency (IEA) data suggests, GHG emissions in 2012 were 58 per cent higher than in 1990. In relation to Article 2 of the UNFCCC, this suggests that despite billions of dollars of investments (and faith) in actions structured by the Parties, such as nationally appropriate mitigation actions (NAMAs), national adaptation programmes of

---

[4] This section draws upon authors' collaborative analysis with colleagues in C. Haywood et al., 'Legal Frameworks for Implementing REDD+ in Zambia, Mozambique and Tanzania: Opportunities for a Sustainable Landscapes Approach' (2 Carbon & Climate Law Review (2015), pp. 130–142), and they are indebted to these colleagues for excellent ideas, substantive insights and significant intellectual contributions in a series of world-leading CIFOR and IDLO research studies and beyond.

[5] K. Deininger and D. Byerlee, *Rising Global Interest in Farmland: Can it Yield Sustainable and Equitable Benefits?* (Washington, D.C.: World Bank Publications 2010) at p. 10.

[6] A. Almeida-Santos, L. Monge Roffarello and M. Filipe, *African Economic Outlook: Mozambique* (Tunis: AfDB, Paris: OECD and New York: UNDP 2013), http://www.africaneconomicoutlook.org/en/country-notes/southern-africa/mozambique/; P. Engbo Rasmussen, K. Munkoni and G. Lwanda, *African Economic Outlook: Zambia* (Tunis: AfDB, Paris: OECD and New York: UNDP 2013), http://www.africaneconomicoutlook.org/en/countries/southern-africa/zambia/; P. Charle, R. Dhliwayo and J. Loening, *African Economic Outlook: Tanzania* (Tunis: AfDB, Paris: OECD and New York: UNDP 2013), http://www.africaneconomicoutlook.org/en/countries/east-africa/tanzania/; Republic of Zambia, *Vision 2030* (Lusaka: 2006): Zambia's Vision 2030 identifies agriculture, energy, mining and forestry as key economic sectors; Government of Mozambique, *Agenda 2025: the Nation's Vision and Strategies* (Maputo: 2003): Agenda 2025 highlights the need to prioritise agriculture, industry, mining, tourism and infrastructure; Government of Tanzania, *National Development Vision 2025* (Dar-es-Salaam: 1999): Vision 2025 identifies agriculture and energy as key areas of growth.

action (NAPAs) and the CDM, overall global performance is still far from sufficient to achieve 'stabilization of greenhouse gas concentrations' and prevent dangerous anthropogenic climate change. Further, conversion of tropical forests is leading to increases in carbon dioxide (CO_2) emissions (nearly 12–15 per cent of global anthropogenic GHG gases), and driving the destruction of essential biodiversity which also provides the timber and non-timber forest products which sustain local livelihoods.[7] To halt forest loss and achieve sustainable and equitable outcomes for forest communities, a number of measures have been attempted in the past, including traditional conservation efforts, command-and-control measures, and new market-based instruments such as Payments for Ecosystem Services (PES), achieving only limited success at scale.

Consequently, the UNFCCC is crafting and adopting special measures to reduce emissions from deforestation and land degradation, seeking to simultaneously support enhancement of carbon stocks, conservation, and sustainable management of forests in developing countries (REDD+) as a climate mitigation instrument.[8] REDD+ was originally conceived as a PES system, linking sellers and buyers via voluntary, conditional agreements over a well-defined forest-based environmental service – or a change in land use presumed to produce that service.[9] The majority of funding, it was anticipated, would come from carbon markets, in line with an early conviction that avoiding deforestation would be 'quick, cheap and easy.'[10] It was initially assumed that 'avoided deforestation' would be integrated into international (compliance market) emissions trading, thereby reducing the international carbon permit price due to the anticipated low-cost credit supply from tropical forest regions. This was meant to result in a potential reduction of total compliance costs for industrialised countries.[11]

It has been hoped that REDD+ projects could prove to be among the

---

[7] See, for example, R.E. Gullison, P.C. Frumhoff, J.G. Canadell et al., 'Tropical Forests and Climate Policy', 316 *Science* (2007), at 985 et seq.

[8] For a detailed overview of the history of the REDD+ negotiations see: REDD+ Cambodia Programme, 'The Road from Bali to Warsaw: Collection of COP Decisions on REDD+' (Cambodia: 2014), http://www.cambodia-redd.org/wp-content/uploads/2014/05/F8-COP-Decisions-for-Web.pdf.

[9] S. Wunder, 'The Efficiency of Payments for Environmental Services in Tropical Conservation', 21(1) *Conservation Biology* (2007), p. 48 et seq.

[10] J. Stoltenberg, 'Comments made by the former Prime Minister of Norway during the Avoided Deforestation Partners Side Event at the Copenhagen COP 19' (Copenhagen: 16 December 2009).

[11] See generally, N. Anger and J. Sathaye, *Reducing Deforestation and Trading Emissions: Economic Implications for the post-Kyoto Carbon Market* (Mannheim: German Centre for European Economic Research (ZEW) 2008).

most feasible and financially affordable opportunities to reduce drivers of deforestation and mitigate climate change while providing other sustainable development benefits, and reserving future options for land-use and resources. Developed countries pledged 'fast start financing' after 2012 to advance REDD+ architecture, readiness and demonstration activities. International (global, regional and bilateral) legal instruments, guidelines and safeguards are being crafted and continuously updated as new REDD+ knowledge and experience become available. At least 50 developing countries are now in the process of developing national REDD+ strategies and plans through a number of multilateral and bilateral international initiatives. Over 400 REDD+ projects are being piloted to lay foundations for implementation of a REDD+ instrument.[12] Public and private sector investments in forests are relevant to three distinct types of REDD+ interventions: REDD+ policy and institutional capacity development, jurisdictional REDD+ programmes to mitigate GHG emissions through forests across subnational areas,[13] and individual REDD+ projects. Responding to early initial enthusiasm surrounding REDD+ as a global policy measure,[14] scholars and practitioners have also begun work to unravel complex political, technical and economic issues to be addressed in the design and implementation of national, jurisdictional and project-level REDD+ activities.[15] It is becoming clear that international investment law, like trade law, is an important strand of the complex and interwoven legal and governance tapestry in which the REDD+ financial instrument is situated, globally.

---

[12] For example, the Centre for International Forestry Research, 'Global database of REDD+ and other forest carbon projects. Interactive map' (2014), http://www.cifor.org/gcs/redd-map/.

[13] G. Fishbein and D. Lee, *Early Lessons from Jurisdictional REDD+ and Low Emissions Development Programs* (Arlington: The Nature Conservancy, FCPF and World Bank Group 2015).

[14] A. Angelsen (ed.), *Moving Ahead with REDD: Issues, Options and Implications* (Bogor: CIFOR 2008); J. Ebeling and M. Yasue, 'Generating Carbon Finance Through Avoided Deforestation and its Potential to Create Climate, Conservation and Human Development Benefits', *Philosophical Transactions of the Royal Society B*: 363 (2008) p. 1917 et seq; A. Angelsen, M. Brockhaus, M. Kanninen et al. (eds), *Realising REDD+: National Strategy and Policy Options* (Bogor: CIFOR 2009).

[15] See generally, W. Sunderlin et al., *The Challenge of Establishing REDD+ on the Ground* (Bogor: CIFOR 2013); G. Fishbein and D. Lee, *Early Lessons from Jurisdictional REDD+ and Low Emissions Development Programs* (Arlington: The Nature Conservancy, FCPF and World Bank Group 2015); P. Franks and A. Quesada-Aguilar, *Equitable REDD+ Exploring Concepts and Strategies* (London: International Institute for Environment and Development 2014).

REDD+ efforts represent only a partial contribution in the global response to climate change, of course. In the past decade, a small part of emission reduction activity has been directly linked to forests and land use. A total of 67 approved CDM afforestation and reforestation projects under the KP as of October 2013 represented only 0.75 per cent of all approved CDM projects.[16] Total REDD+ Voluntary Carbon Market 'over-the-counter sales' in 2014 only amounted to US$94 million, mitigating approximately 22.6 million metric tons of CO_2 equivalent, approximately 0.6 per cent of total GHG emissions in the same year.[17] Further, a large proportion of all REDD+ financing is still being provided by bilateral and multilateral ODA funds,[18] rather than through investments attracted on markets, at present.

This trend might require review. REDD+, initially conceived as an instrument to incentivise climate mitigation action in the forest sector, holds potential to encourage low-carbon landscape-level investments which meet private and public sustainability objectives.[19] In essence, REDD+ has already moved beyond carbon.[20] Alongside economic returns, REDD+ seeks to provide social and environmental benefits and depends on engaging stakeholders collaboratively towards more sustainable landscapes.[21] In this light, sustainable landscapes are 'a framework

---

[16] S. Danon and D. Bettiati, 'Reducing Emissions from Deforestation and Forest Degradation (REDD+) – What is Behind the Idea and What is the Role of UN-REDD and Forest Carbon Partnership Facility (FCPF)?', 2(2) *South-East European Forestry* (2011), pp. 95–9, at p. 95.

[17] M. Peters-Stanley and G. Gonzalez, *Sharing the Stage. State of the Voluntary Carbon Markets 2014* (Washington D.C.: Forest Trends' Ecosystem Marketplace 2014), at p. 6.

[18] Multiple estimates have been made of the long-term financing needed to reverse tropical deforestation and degradation. See inter alia N. Stern, *The Economics of Climate Change: The Stern Review* (Cambridge: Cambridge University Press 2006); and J. Eliasch, *Climate Change: Financing Global Forests. The Eliash Review* (London: UK Office of Climate Change 2008).

[19] J.A. Parrotta et al., 'Chapter 1 – Introduction' in J.A. Parrotta, C. Wildburger and S. Mansourian (eds), *Understanding Relationships between Biodiversity, Carbon, Forests and People: The Key to Achieving REDD+ Objectives. A Global Assessment Report*. IUFRO World Series Volume 31 (Vienna: International Union of Forest Research Organizations 2012) at p. 14.

[20] H. Schroeder and C. McDermott, 'Beyond Carbon: Enabling Justice and Equity in REDD+ Across Levels of Governance', 19(1) *Ecology and Society* (2014), pp. 31–2.

[21] O. Dubois, *Capacity to Manage Role Changes in Forestry. Introducing the '4Rs' Framework* (London: International Institute for Environment and Development 1998). The 4Rs framework defines stakeholders' roles by their Rights, Responsibilities, Returns/Revenues and Relationships, and seeks to

to integrate policy, practice and financing for multiple land uses, within a given area, to ensure equitable and sustainable use of land and resources while strengthening governance and measures to mitigate and adapt to climate change.'[22]

REDD+ could make important contributions in this regard. However, multiple governance and investment-related uncertainties have plagued REDD+ financing, including concerns as to whether national performance-based payments or the GCF will be effective, whether benefits will be distributed equitably, whether safeguards will be respected, and whether disputes will be resolved justly.[23] The absence of a fully fungible compliance market for forest carbon credits, other than those generated through CDM afforestation and reforestation activities, and the challenges faced by voluntary carbon markets, have resulted in REDD+ dependence on ODA.

Systems for administration of payments, should REDD+ financing be achieved at scale, also present particular concern. Opportunities remain for rent-seeking and benefit-capture by local elites, external project developers and different levels of government authorities, with the interests of remote forest-dependent communities especially at stake. Failure to establish effective, efficient and equitable REDD+ benefit-sharing systems may lead to perverse results. If poorly designed, REDD+ policies, measures and projects may bring new risks to forest communities through the loss of or reduced access to forest resources, conflicts within and among communities, and the potential destabilising effects of forest carbon financing in local economies.

Critically, the design of REDD+ benefit-sharing arrangements will influence their ability to achieve efficient, effective and equitable attribution (how and who generates emissions reductions), governance (how and who manages REDD+ funds), sourcing (who contributes and how REDD+ funds are raised) and disbursement (how and to whom REDD+ funds are delivered and distributed). Simply put, if REDD+ payments do not reach those who are directly responsible for protecting and managing forests, the additionality and permanence upon which forest carbon

---

improve collaboration between stakeholders in forestry management by assessing the different pressures and stakes at play.

22 Adapted from J. Sayer et al., 'Ten Principles for a Landscape Approach to Reconciling Agriculture, Conservation, and other Competing Land Uses', 110(21) *PNAS* (2013), pp. 8349–50 and C. Harvey et al., 'Climate-Smart Landscapes: Opportunities and Challenges for Integrating Adaptation and Mitigation in Tropical Agriculture', 7 *Conservation Letters* (2014), pp. 77–90.

23 GCF, 'Analysis of the Expected Role and Impact of the Green Climate Fund' GCF/B.09/06 (Seoul: 2015).

credits depend are difficult to assure for those investing public and/or private funds. The risk is that REDD+ would be unable to realise its potential as an investment incentive for GHG emission mitigation, or eventually for sustainable landscapes more broadly.

Situating implementation of REDD+ within the context of sustainable landscapes management has implications for legal analysis. It becomes clearer that REDD+ initiatives – as a type of investment – can face similar national governance challenges to other land-based investments, including complex multi-level governance systems,[24] inchoate decentralisation,[25] globalised trading patterns,[26] and insecure small-scale land users' and local communities' land tenure.[27] Such national barriers to REDD+ implementation are linked to multi-level land and forest governance; overlapping policy, legal and institutional frameworks; and decentralisation of government decision-making and implementation responsibilities, resulting in insecure land tenure rights compounded by an inadequate set of fiscal incentives for effective participatory forest governance.

Sustainable landscape approaches may also assist in addressing these challenges by ensuring greater harmonisation and alignment of policy and regulatory frameworks. Unlike earlier technocentric sectoral land-use planning methods, viewing REDD+ as a measure to encourage low-carbon investment in sustainable landscapes involves overcoming 'governance in silos.'[28] By moving beyond a narrow sector-specific (forestry) approach to

---

[24] See generally, E. Mwangi and D. Andrew Wardell, 'Multi-level Governance of Forest Resources', Part 1: 6(2) *International Journal of the Commons* (Special Issue) (2012), pp. 79 et seq and Part 2: 7(2) *International Journal of the Commons* (Special Issue) (2013), pp. 339 et seq.

[25] See generally, S.P.J. Batterbury and J.L. Fernando, 'Rescaling Governance and the Impacts of Political and Environmental Decentralization', 34(11) *World Development* (2006), pp. 1851 et seq.

[26] See generally, M.-C. Cordonier Segger, M. Gehring and A. Newcombe (eds), *Sustainable Development in World Investment Law* (Netherlands: Wolters Kluwer 2011) [Cordonier Segger, Gehring and Newcombe 2011] and M.-C. Cordonier Segger and Markus Gehring (eds), *Sustainable Development in World Trade Law* (Netherlands: Kluwer Law International 2005) [Cordonier Segger and Gehring 2005].

[27] See generally, W.D. Sunderlin, A. Duchelle, I Aju Pradnja Resosudarmo et al., 'How Are REDD+ Proponents Addressing Tenure Problems? Evidence from Brazil, Cameroon, Tanzania, Indonesia and Vietnam', 55 *World Development* (2014), pp. 37 et seq.

[28] D. Andrew Wardell, 'Moving Beyond Governance in Silos: Challenges and Opportunities in the Democratic Republic of Congo', policy presentation at the Xylaredd conference, Musee Royale de l'Afrique Centrale, Tervuren, Belgium, 26 May 2015.

climate change mitigation and by recognising REDD+ as an investment instrument, it may be possible to improve performance across a broader array of land uses to achieve emissions reductions and more sustainable development. Improvements in one sector become more likely to succeed over the long term if changes also occur in other sectors where investment is taking place.

To encourage this, outside the national REDD+ architecture, international incentives for REDD+ can be adopted to promote these investments over other, less sustainable land uses. Many developing countries have liberalised their investment frameworks, providing a strong set of incentives and simplifying their investment procedures, all with the aim of attracting large-scale private sector investments. The focus of these reforms has been economic growth. Investment laws do not typically mention sustainable development and rarely include tangible socioeconomic and environmental objectives.[29] Highly capitalised large-scale land and natural resources investments, irrespective of any sustainability considerations, enjoy incentives such as tax holidays, corporate income tax discounts or credits, deductions for capital costs, accelerated depreciation of capital equipment, deductions for foreign exchange losses, carry forward of losses, and a range of Value Added Tax (VAT)-related exemptions and other relief measures.[30] As documented by CIFOR and IDLO, even greater incentives are available for projects over US$500,000, in countries such as Zambia and Tanzania.[31]

Unfortunately, very little priority and many fewer incentives are provided for sustainable investments, including REDD+, within existing investment codes of both developed and developing countries, especially the most impoverished and vulnerable countries such as the DR Congo.[32] This state of affairs runs at cross purposes with commitments

---

[29] For example, the objective of the Zambia Development Agency Act is to 'foster economic growth and development by promoting trade and investment in Zambia through an efficient, effective and coordinated private sector-led economic development strategy.' Zambia Development Agency Act 2006 (Republic of Zambia), at Preamble.

[30] Investment Act 1997 (United Republic of Tanzania); Code of Fiscal Benefits 4/2009 (Republic of Mozambique); Zambia Development Agency Act 2006 (Republic of Zambia).

[31] Investment Act 1997 (United Republic of Tanzania), at s 20; Zambia Development Agency Act 2006 (Republic of Zambia), at ss 3 and 56.

[32] E. Kassongo, G.-J. Kounga, D. Andrew Wardell, M. Gehring, M.-C. Cordonier Segger and F. Perron-Welch, *Natural Resources Law and Governance for Sustainable Landscapes in the Democratic Republic of Congo Information Briefs* (Kisangani: CIFOR, CISDL and UNIKIS 2015).

to sustainable development, identified as a crucial policy objective in the post-2015 development agenda, and makes it difficult for sustainable investments to compete with other, purely profit-driven extractive investments.

In this context, the broader investment framework, including legal registration processes and fiscal and policy incentives, has important implications for all land and natural resources investments, including future REDD+ initiatives, at any scale of implementation. From this view, REDD+ gains a much better chance of achieving stable and long-lasting forest sector mitigation efforts, and even to contribute to broader aims of sustainability and poverty eradication, if international legal frameworks, including international investment treaties, can be crafted to help rather than hinder more sustainable investments.

3. REDD+ IN INTERNATIONAL INVESTMENT RULES

3.1 Investment Law as Sword or Shield for REDD+

Private sector investment can and does help to finance the adoption of low-carbon technologies and processes.[33] As the World Bank has argued in referring directly to climate change, 'private finance [is] now the biggest show in town.'[34] To provide a stable framework for this private sector investment, and of relevance to new laws related to REDD+ schemes and other incentives for more sustainable, low-carbon economic development, in recent decades more than 3,000 International Investment Agreements (IIAs) have been negotiated.[35]

These IIAs seek to create favourable conditions and stable frameworks for the treatment of foreign investors and investments, encouraging private sector investment in developing countries. They are supplemented

---

[33] D. Murphy, 'Technology in a Post 2012 Climate Regime', paper presented to 'A Way Forward: Canadian and International Perspectives on Post 2012 Climate Policy', 4 March 2008, Ottawa, Canada.

[34] M. Klein and T. Harford, *The Market for Aid* (Washington, D.C.: World Bank Publications 2005), p. 51.

[35] A. Newcombe and L. Paradell, *Law and Practice of Investment Treaties: Standards of Treatment* (Leiden: Kluwer Law International 2009), pp. 57–64 [Newcombe and Paradell]; UNCTAD Secretariat, 'International Investment Rulemaking', 22 May 2007, TD/B/COM.2/EM.21/2; UNCTAD, 'Latest Developments in Investor–State Dispute Settlement', IIA Monitor No. 1 (2008) UNCTAD/WEB/ITE.IIA/2008/3.

internationally by rules and dispute settlement procedures developed through the UNCITRAL and the ICSID. The IIA obligations normally guarantee a minimum standard of treatment, or 'fair and equitable treatment,' towards the foreign investor. They also guarantee non-discrimination to investors in 'like circumstances.' Some IIAs commit to 'stabilisation clauses' which can exclude IIA-covered investments from changes in the law of host States. IIAs may often, according to the OECD, provide for stability at the price of regulatory flexibility for countries.[36] Such principles and their application are important for current and future attempts to develop domestic rules to respond to the emerging climate change challenges. The 'legitimate expectations' of the investor regarding regulatory frameworks may become grounds for a challenge by a foreign investor towards an (unfavourable) change in circumstances due to new climate change regulations, including REDD+ schemes if these impose significant new costs on private firms.[37]

By December 2007, there were 280 known IIA arbitrations, in which foreign investors challenged governments in often confidential 'investor–State' dispute settlement proceedings by invoking investment agreement clauses.[38] Potentially, the disciplines imposed by these IIAs, measures and rule-making bodies could actually work to constrain carbon trading and related regulatory measures. However, it may be possible to design emissions trading systems carefully, to avoid becoming embroiled in disputes of this kind. It is also possible to design IIAs and trade agreements to ensure that legitimate new energy, transportation, forestry, waste management and other measures are, at a minimum, not frustrated but rather perhaps even promoted.

Indeed, IIAs could potentially promote sustainable development and climate change action by ensuring more stable investment environments and thus encouraging investors to provide private funds for CDM projects and for Joint Implementation (JI). However, in these accords, States have also agreed on disciplines that have been used recently to challenge regulatory measures related to sustainable development.[39] Although climate

---

[36] K. Gordon and J. Pohl, 'Investment Treaties over Time – Treaty Practice and Interpretation in a Changing World', *OECD Working Papers on International Investment* (Paris: OECD Publishing 2015/02), http://dx.doi.org/10.1787/5js7rhd8sq7h-en.

[37] K. Miles, 'International Investment Law and Climate Change: Issues in the Transition to a Low Carbon World', Society of International Economic Law, Inaugural Conference 2008 at p. 19 [Miles].

[38] *Supra*, Newcombe and Paradell, p. 59.

[39] *Supra*, Miles, p. 26. *Supra*, Cordonier Segger, Gehring and Newcombe 2011.

change disputes have not yet featured heavily in the investment regime, the principles arising from the disputes challenging other measures related to sustainable development could be applied to future, specifically climate-related disputes. As noted above, in IIAs, Parties often grant foreign investors the right to challenge host States in investor–State arbitral tribunals under UNCITRAL or ICSID rules, particularly on claims related to performance requirements, fair and equitable treatment, expropriation and transparency. These privileges may be used to challenge carbon-trading measures, depending on how new domestic schemes are designed, and how the IIAs are interpreted.[40] As with trade law, such challenges have both direct effects, where a State or its local authority that has 'lost' a dispute is required to compensate an investor or group of investors for the economic impact of new carbon regulations, or indirect regulatory effects, where environment and development regulators are stifled or 'chilled' from adopting or implementing carbon reduction measures due to threats of investor–State litigation.[41]

Indeed, a sustainable development-orientated survey of investment disputes and the principles used to resolve them reveals a handful of arbitrations related to climate change measures, if not to REDD+ as such.[42] While such disputes may not yet pose fundamental challenges to international climate instruments, both concerns and triumphs have been noted. By reasoning from existing case experience and positing analogous circumstances, it is possible to identify certain instances where investment law may act as a sword against sustainable investment incentives such as REDD+, and others where investment law may actually shield such measures.

In certain instances, investment rules can become a sword – wielded as a legal threat to shift burdens or require compensation from governments even in cases where regulatory changes have become necessary for the public interest in light of new scientific climate risk information, or used to prevent and weaken climate measures that could affect investor interests through regulatory chill. It is no surprise that climate change, as new risk data becomes available, has sparked a wide range of regulatory responses at international and national levels of government. A diverse

---

40 J. Werksman, K.A. Baumert and D.K. Navroz, 'Will International Investment Rules Obstruct Climate Protection Policies?' *Climate Notes* (Washington, D.C.: World Resources Institute 2001) [Werksman et al.].

41 F. Baetens, 'The Kyoto Protocol in Investor–State Arbitration: Reconciling Climate Change and Investment Protection Objectives', in *supra* Cordonier Segger, Gehring and Newcombe 2011, at 681.

42 Ibid.

arrangement of climate regulations including subsidies, taxes, traditional command-and-control measures such as standards, bans or prohibitions, and also market-based mechanisms, may then be assessed by international adjudicators in the trade and investment regimes, many of whom have little to no climate change or sustainable development expertise or even knowledge. Such measures, even taken in the public interest to mitigate climate change, can impact on existing investors in different ways. As a response, entrenched interests may seek to defend old technologies and ways of doing business by trying to challenge the new regulatory measures if they affect investments. Depending on the precise characterisation of the measure and its actual impact, the outcomes of legal challenges will likely differ. One possible effect of this is that the definitional boundaries of the regimes will be stretched, as adjudicators are pushed, for instance, to consider whether a particular impact is tantamount to expropriation under investment rules, without understanding its public aims or implications.

Such concerns have been raised due to cases such as the recently settled proceedings in *Vattenfall* v. *Germany I*.[43] There, the Swedish State-owned energy company Vattenfall challenged new regulations imposed on its coal-fired power plant project near Hamburg. Following local elections in 2008, the Green Party had entered power in a coalition in the Hamburg municipal government, and had imposed more onerous measures on the plant than had been expected by the investor – partly on grounds of the contribution made by the coal-fired plant to climate change. In response, the Vattenfall investor claimed violations of the Energy Charter Treaty,[44] and sought €1.4 billion in damages. Proceedings were suspended in March 2010 while the Parties sought a settlement, and the case sent seismic ripples of concern through other local governments seeking to back away from harmful fossil fuels. Depending on the damages involved in any settlement, *Vattenfall* could be an example of the 'sword' effect of such disputes.

In the *Bilcon* arbitration, which involved a decision not to open a quarry in Quebec due to likely environmental impacts, the majority of an arbitral panel found that Canada had treated the US investor unfairly and breached the minimum standard because the impact assessment had not investigated possible mitigation for the climate and other environmen-

---

[43] *Vattenfall AB, Vattenfall Europe AG, Vattenfall Europe Generation AG* v. *Federal Republic of Germany*, ICSID Case No. ARB/09/6 (11 March 2011), http://www.italaw.com/documents/VattenfallAward.pdf. In a more recent case, *Vattenfall II*, the company is challenging the decision by the German federal government to exit nuclear power.

[44] Energy Charter Treaty (1995) 34 ILM 360.

tal impacts of the proposed mining and port operation. In the opinion of the majority, outright governmental mistakes could trigger a breach while normal exercise of discretion would not have done so. This case is important for REDD+ because of the nature of government action for climate and other considerations, which often invokes an exercise of discretion. The *Bilcon* decision seems to indicate that arbitrators will apply a very strict standard to the exercise of such discretion in environmental or climate matters. While the reasons for this decision were mainly of a procedural nature, they triggered a strong dissent by Professor and Arbitrator Donald McRae, who criticised the choice of threshold of the other two arbitrators and argued that their decision was detrimental to the implementation of the environmental impact regime.[45] He warned against the 'chilling effect' and the 'remarkable step backwards in environmental protection.'[46] Indeed, if a developed country government such as Quebec was unable to meet the burden of demonstrating their correct exercise of discretion on public climate change and environmental concerns, it could be difficult for a developing country to do so.

Perhaps more closely related to REDD+, a very recent case concerns a decision by the Quebec government on a policy choice related to climate change effects and other likely ecological risks. In the *Lone Pine* arbitration,[47] the investor challenges a decision by the provincial government to prohibit fracking.[48] The (not yet resolved) arbitration highlights two issues. On one hand, subnational laws can be adopted for climate change purposes, impeding local investment as a public policy choice once new information about risks becomes available, and REDD+ is no exception if it limits existing uses of the land property. On the other hand, investment law may well be interpreted in a way that is respectful

---

45 *William Ralph Clayton, William Richard Clayton, Douglas Clayton, Daniel Clayton and Bilcon of Delaware Inc.* v. *Government of Canada*, UNCITRAL, PCA Case No. 2009-04, Award on Jurisdiction and Liability (2015), http://www.italaw.com/sites/default/files/case-documents/italaw4212.pdf [Bilcon].

46 Ibid., Bilcon, Donald McRae, 'Dissenting Opinion', at paras 48–51, http://www.italaw.com/sites/default/files/case-documents/italaw4213.pdf; L. Eric Peterson, 'In NAFTA Dissent, Donald McRae sees Chilling Effect – and "Remarkable Step Backwards in Environmental Protection" – Due to Majority Ruling', *IA Reporter*, 21 May 2015, http://tinyurl.com/pq63wjz.

47 *Lone Pine Resources Inc.* v. *The Government of Canada*, ICSID Case No. UNCT/15/2, First procedural order by the panel (2015), http://www.italaw.com/sites/default/files/case-documents/italaw4252.pdf.

48 See J. Hepburn 'On Heels of Bruising NAFTA Loss in Bilcon Case, Canada Offers First Sketch of its Defence to "Lone Pine" Fracking Arbitration', 30 March 2015, *IA Reporter*, http://tinyurl.com/qa4j86o.

of environmental and societal concerns.[49] In the context of REDD+, an analogous dispute might take place where the central government has made a commitment under REDD+ to forest an area sustainably, but the owner is a foreign investor who had purchased the land with the intention to clear cut. If the government does not adopt a broad REDD+ scheme but instead targets a particular area (due to its carbon capture potential or other unique social and ecological co-benefits for instance), the investor could attempt a claim under the fair and equitable treatment standard. While a modern interpretation would respect the legal framework and perhaps even the climate change public policy imperative, less open interpretations might see a discrimination against the foreign investor in such an instance. Investment law arbitrators are not always very knowledgeable about sustainable development concerns or legal frameworks, and this is a serious detriment to public confidence in such instances.

However, as noted above, investment treaties can also provide 'shields' for climate change measures, including REDD+. In such cases, respondent governments that had agreed to encourage renewable energy or other new technologies through subsidies or incentives, or to protect an area for carbon and ecological values, or to place increased scrutiny on climate-unfriendly projects, failed to comply with climate commitments or simply changed their approaches. If a political climate changes, the State may seek to roll back agreed incentives for climate mitigation investments, particularly if their popularity appears to become a fiscal burden or a possible source of valuable extra rents. Such disputes provide opportunities for investment tribunals to demonstrate the utility of investment protection for 'sustainable investments.' Arbitral processes have the potential to show how stable and clear international economic rules can encourage private sector investments which mitigate climate change and support more sustainable landscapes.

Certain investment tribunal cases on the horizon reflect this alternative 'shield' pattern of climate change disputes. Challenges are underway against Spain and the Czech Republic, brought by foreign investors in the renewable energy industries.[50] In the first dispute, Spain allegedly changed its renewable energy support regime in an abrupt and non-transparent manner. This gave rise to no fewer than 14 arbitrations against the Government of

---

[49] Ibid.

[50] A. Moralas, 'Impax, Hudson Seek Damages Over Spain Solar Subsidies', *Bloomburg Business* 8 March 2011, http://www.bloomberg.com/news/2011-03-08/impax-hudson-clean-energy-join-investors-suing-spain-on-solar-subsidy-cut.html.

Spain by renewable energy investors.[51] The investors claimed that the Government had reneged on their promise of a long-term, guaranteed favourable price for green energy produced by the investors' solar facilities, and that this constitutes a violation of applicable investment treaties. They argued that the policy change was not foreseeable and the main argument by Spain that the subsidies are very expensive was not accepted. Similarly, the Czech Republic has recently revealed that there are seven arbitrations proceedings concerning measures in the solar energy sector. Renewable energy investors from different countries have complained that the Czech Republic essentially repealed most of the existing incentives to invest in this area.[52] While only one of these arbitrations has resulted in a final award, they appear to highlight that investment law does not just act as a sword against the government but also as a shield for regression and lowering of environmental standards on which the investor relied.

Another dispute is under arbitration to address claims from an investor in the wilderness conservation and recreation industry that the relevant government authorities have not complied with their own protection regulations, reducing the value of the investment. A related arbitration is currently ongoing in the case of *Allard* against Barbados, where claims have been raised by a Canadian investor that the country's authorities permitted harm to a nature sanctuary.[53] In the context of REDD+, a similar dispute might take place where a government invites investment into REDD+ projects but at a later stage and in a manner unforeseeable for the investor, decides suddenly to change its policy and withdraw support for REDD+, agrees to permit other harmful uses for the forest that destroy the value of the REDD+ investment, or grants carbon rights over the agreed areas to other actors. In such a case, investment law might protect the REDD+ sustainable investors from seeing the commitments upon which they relied being rescinded without any compensation. The IIA would shield the REDD+ investor from the risk that a political decision abruptly degrades the value of the REDD+ investment, destroying the project.

Rather than automatically placing constraints or weakening climate mitigation and adaptation incentives of government authorities, directly

---

[51] C. Trevino, 'An Update on Renewable Energy Claims against Spain', *IA Reporter* 9 June 2015, http://tinyurl.com/oe6eo5a.

[52] L. Eric Peterson,. 'Solar Investors File Arbitration against Czech Republic; Intra-EU BITs and Energy Charter Treaty at Center of Dispute', *IA Reporter* 15 May 2013, http://tinyurl.com/ouxxub2.

[53] C. Trevino, 'Arbitrators Hearing UNCITRAL Claim by Canadian Investor that accuses Barbados of Presiding over Harm to Nature Sanctuary', *IA Reporter* 13 February 2015, http://tinyurl.com/qf3t3sp.

causing governance challenges for REDD+ and other instruments which seek to mobilise and encourage climate action and finance, the contribution of international economic law to REDD+ and sustainable development is more nuanced. While they cannot universally grant stability and a risk-free environment for sustainable investors either, the rules of IIAs have the potential to be used as either 'swords' or 'shields' for REDD+ measures to encourage investment in climate mitigation and sustainable landscapes. A great deal depends on the specific rules themselves, how they are crafted, and how they are implemented to encourage REDD+ investments.

3.2 REDD+ and Carbon-Trading Schemes in the Context of IIAs

Behind the recent disputes, several key aspects of law on sustainable development relating both to investment and to climate change are entwined and interacting. This is not surprising. As has been noted by the Centre for International Sustainable Development Law (CISDL), the International Centre for Trade and Sustainable Development (ICTSD) and others, the intersection between these regimes poses genuine challenges and opportunities.[54] International trade and investment treaty rules may affect the viability and effectiveness of new regulations to address climate change.[55] For Parties to the UNFCCC, its KP and any successors, economic incentives such as eco-labelling, carbon taxes, export bans and restrictions, emissions trading schemes, border carbon adjustments and subsidies on low-carbon technology, and also REDD+, can and should be adopted as mitigation measures likely to be undertaken in an effort to fulfil GHG-reduction commitments.[56] These measures have a direct

---

[54] M.-C. Cordonier Segger, M. Gehring, F. de Andrade Correa, P. Reynaud, A. Harrington and R. Mella, 'Climate Change and Sustainable Energy Measures in Regional Trade Agreements' (Geneva/Montreal: *CISDL/ICTSD Issue Paper 3* 2013), http://www.ictsd.org/downloads/2013/08/climate-change-and-sustainable-energy-measures-in-regional-trade-agreements-rtas.pdf [Cordonier Segger, Gehring et al. 2013]; C. Voigt, *Sustainable Development as a Principle of International Law – Resolving Conflicts between Climate Measures and WTO Law* (Leiden: Martinus Nijhoff 2009); D. Freestone and C. Streck (eds), *Making Kyoto Work* (Oxford: Oxford University Press 2002); M.A. Teehankee, I. Jegou and R. Jacques Rodrigues, 'Multilateral Negotiations at the Intersection of Trade and Climate Change: An Overview of Developing Countries' Priorities in UNCSD, UNFCCC and WTO Processes', *ICTSD Issue Paper No. 2* (2012).

[55] Ibid.; UNFCCC, Report of the Conference of the Parties on its seventeenth session, held in Durban from 28 November to 11 December 2011, FCCC/CP/2011/9/Add.1.

[56] Ibid.

correlation to the investment of a State and its private sector in the reduction of carbon and other GHGs on a practical level, by offering industry incentives to reduce GHG use and also by creating an educated public that is able to make environmentally informed choices. Such measures can also confer economic advantages or disadvantages for those subject to new domestic regulations or those that can access new international regimes.[57] In the context of investment law, several key issues arise in this regard.

First, on a nearly theoretical level, REDD+ carbon finance schemes may not always be classified as pure market-based instruments, in the absence of command-and-control origins. The very existence of a government-imposed cap on the amount of carbon that can be emitted by a given sector is evidently 'control' in nature, and the very granting of carbon rights for avoided emissions implies certain government activities. A cap establishes a performance requirement, but allows for the market to set the price of carbon emissions and for firms to choose abatement technologies or forest conservation and restoration techniques to meet the standard. However, even the introduction of new performance standards or a national REDD+ strategy and related land-use planning processes could pose questions under certain investment treaties. In US and Canadian investment treaties, Parties have sought to prevent or constrain the use of performance requirements or standards. These requirements have provided countries with a way to enhance the value of an investment for the national 'host' economy by mandating a certain way of producing a product such as sourcing local services, labour or content (local content requirement). Related measures help countries earn foreign exchange through export requirements. If examined out of context, even carbon caps may appear to be violations of prohibitions on performance requirements. In the context of REDD+, a related dispute might arise where an investor in REDD+ carbon might find that they are being compelled to sequester the carbon in a certain way, with requirements for certain sub-contracts, and can argue that the government authority violates commitments not to impose performance requirements on foreign investors. An arbitrator might even find that specific REDD+ obligations, such as additional safeguards or sustainability criteria, would be considered as the government requiring a certain performance by the investor.

Second, the actual legal nature of a carbon right or avoided emissions certificate may raise issues in investment law, just as the legal nature of

---

[57] Ibid.; D. Freestone and C. Streck (eds), *Legal Aspects of Carbon Trading: Kyoto, Copenhagen, and Beyond* (Oxford: Oxford University Press 2010) [Freestone and Streck].

an allowance has been flagged as an issue in the design of various US emissions trading systems. For instance, the SO_2 trading system under the Acid Rain programme of the 1990 Clean Air Act raised the issue of property rights. The possibility that an allowance would constitute a property right raised arguments in the US based on 'taking of property' under the Fifth Amendment of the US Constitution. In that instance, the issue was resolved by classifying the allowances as tradable goods which were, nevertheless, not property rights as such. [58] However, legal concerns remain that contractual or property rights might be subject to claims by those holding the credits, in the situation where regulations are introduced which alter the value of the allowance or avoided emissions carbon credit in question.[59] The decision to imbue carbon rights, credits and allowances with property-like status could potentially open governments to allegations of expropriation under investment treaties, should the value or quantity of the credits be reduced in the future. The potential for such an approach to engage international investment law disciplines is evident, and could lead to investor–State disputes. In the context of REDD+, there is still some distance to traverse before discussions focus on particular use of credits. However, it is not inconceivable that a REDD+ carbon investor might feel that their carbon rights had been invalidated through certain government action, or simply through the lack of consistent and reliable enforcement of existing economic, environmental or human rights laws, or agreed rules governing the issuance of emission certificates. This recognised, the 'quasi-property rights' character of emission certificates is now widely recognised and seen as a necessary condition of many emission trading schemes.

Third, just as for allowances in emissions trading, it is important to consider how carbon rights and emission reduction credits (ERCs) are allocated among the participants in a REDD+ climate finance scheme. The recognition of carbon rights and related ERCs by the government and investors vis-à-vis the actors, whether these are particular industry-specific actors, or 'carbon-intensive parties' or any other pre-determined set of actors, can be problematic in trade and investment terms. Carbon rights

---

[58] M. Gehring and C. Streck, 'Emissions Trading: Lessons from SOx and NOx Emissions Allowance and Credit Systems Legal Nature, Title, Transfer, and Taxation of Emission Allowances and Credits', 35 *Environmental Law Reporter* (2005), pp. 10219–35; J. Robinson, J. Barton, C. Dodwell, M. Heydon and L. Milton, *Climate Change Law: Emissions Trading in the EU and the UK* (London: Cameron May 2007) [Robinson et al.].

[59] N. Fichthorn and A. Wood, 'Preserving the SO_2 Market', *Environmental Finance* (September 2002).

and allocations indicate the degree to which carbon can be emitted within a system, and thereby 'pre-determine the overall environmental benefits that can be expected from the system.'[60] As with allocation of allowances, recognition of carbon rights is an intensely political process, and compromises are often necessary. Both trade and investment concerns can be triggered by allocations of credits which are discriminatory, or not 'fair and equitable.' For emissions trading allowances, allocations can affect the competitiveness of firms and operators within the domestic and international markets, and also raise concerns as to discrimination towards non-national actors which compete in the targeted market. Among various options open to designers of emission trading schemes, free allocation, allocation based on 'grandfathered rights,' allocation based on more modern 'baselines,' and partial auctioning all pose similar problems. If any non-national actors within the territory do not receive precisely the same allowances as comparable national actors, these firms can argue that they have been prejudiced in the market, as they incur higher costs to reduce their carbon output or find the resources to pay for their continued output. This could be held to violate trade obligations of non-discrimination and national treatment, but more importantly, it could also be characterised as going beyond the 'fair and equitable treatment' standard promised to foreign investors in most IIAs. The EU's Emissions Trading System (ETS) provides one possible example; there, in light of the EU's design choices, windfalls may have been received by certain parties through the free allocation process,[61] and this could have triggered investment disputes. The option of 100 per cent auctioning resolves many such concerns, though this can still entail competitive consequences depending on the frequency, size and accessibility of auctions, should it be shown that *in effect*, regulations made participation more challenging for foreign firms. In the ETS, this problem is difficult but not impossible to address. For instance, many ETS regulations have incorporated provisions specifically ensuring no distinction between national or foreign-owned companies. In the context of REDD+, a similar dispute might take place if a foreign investor has invested in a REDD+ project and expects to be able to sell carbon rights which are not secure, or to receive accredited avoided emissions credits,

---

60 M. Wemaere and C. Streck, 'Legal Ownership and Nature of Kyoto Units and EU Allowances', in D. Freestone and C. Streck (eds), *Legal Aspects of Implementing the Kyoto Protocol Mechanisms: Making Kyoto Work* (Oxford: Oxford University Press 2005), p. 41.

61 A.D. Ellerman and P. Joskow, *The European Union's Emission Trading System in Perspective* (Arlington: Pew Center 2008), http://www.c2es.org/docUploads/EU-ETS-In-Perspective-Report.pdf [Ellerman and Joskow].

but a government authority decides to change the regulations recognising the carbon rights, constrain or otherwise prevent the recognition or sale of the related credits, or to arbitrarily restrict the credits in some other form. In such a case, a foreign REDD+ investor might question whether the government authority had breached its obligations to provide fair and equitable treatment, and again, take the matter to an investor–State arbitral tribunal in order to request compensation.

A fourth basic issue that triggers both trade and investment rules involves the commitment to regulatory transparency, which may well support the designers of REDD+ climate finance or emissions trading schemes. It can be argued that REDD+ carbon markets may be more transparent and accessible than traditional command-and-control schemes, since just as for emissions trading, 'anyone wishing to challenge the environmental effectiveness of the trading regime can question directly the level of the overall cap rather than having to unravel the, often complex, relationship between specific controls applied to an individual plant and an ambient environmental quality standard.'[62] The transparency of domestic law and policymaking process is important to any potential investor.[63] However, as mentioned above, investors can benefit from investment treaty guarantees against changes in government policy (not just fiscal or tax policy, but also environment and development policy),[64] hoping to stabilise regulations for the lifetime of an investment.[65] A regulator may need to make it clear to potential investors that post-establishment decisions, such as governmental decisions influencing the investment after it has been made, will take State commitments under the UNFCCC and the KP into account. In the context of REDD+, many intricate rules may be required at national,

---

[62] *Supra* J. Robinson et al., note 58 at 45; J. Pauwelyn 'U.S. Federal Climate Policy and Competitiveness Concerns: The Limits and Options of International Trade Law', *Working Paper* 07-02 (New York: Duke University Press 2007), see also R.A. Stewart, 'Economic Incentives for Environmental Protection: Opportunities and Obstacles', in R.L. Revesz, P. Sands and R.A. Stewart (eds), *Environmental Law, the Economy and Sustainable Development* (Cambridge: Cambridge University Press 2000).

[63] The Preamble to the Aarhus Convention expressly calls for 'transparency in all branches of government' when implementing provisions related to the Aarhus Convention's aims: Convention on Access to Information, Public Participation in Decision-Making and Access to Justice in Environmental Matters (adopted 25 June 1998, entered into force 30 October 2001) 38 ILM 17.

[64] A. Ross-Robertson, 'Is the Environment Getting Squeezed out of Sustainable Development?', *Public Law* (2003), p. 249.

[65] S. Baughen, *International Trade and the Protection of the Environment* (New York: Cavendish 2007), Chapter 7.

regional and local levels, and one significant challenge involves the ability of governments to ensure that these multi-level and multi-sectoral sets of regulations can function coherently together. For example, the new DR Congo REDD+ law gives considerable discretion to different levels of government.[66] An investment claim might, as discussed, arise if these different levels of government contradict each other or take decisions in an arbitrary and clandestine way. A REDD+ investor would then benefit from a higher form of transparency guaranteed by the international investment agreement. Moreover, transparency works in many directions. As discussed elsewhere, impact assessments and other such requirements can contribute to stability rather than detract from it, by generating valuable investment intelligence and creating a more level playing field for investors.[67] To that end, by securing transparent policy decisions, States might insulate their new climate policies from formal investor–State challenges, while also contributing to their clarity and legitimacy.[68]

3.3 Climate Regulations and the Investors in the 'Like Circumstances' Debate

As seen in the *Methanex* v. *US* dispute,[69] not all investor–State tribunals are willing to interpret their jurisdiction over regulators very broadly. While some IIAs can be used to question environmental protection and sustainable development regulations, others clearly cannot be extended so far.[70] Still, where States enact measures, including emissions trading schemes, to favour low-carbon development over carbon-intensive projects, especially in developing countries where the forestry and extractive sectors are dominated by a few foreign investors (while not forgetting that domestic investors retain important stakes), these interests could well frame investor–State challenges in terms of discrimination. Where such allegations are raised, it will be important to secure an appropriate interpretation of the concept of

---

66 E. Kassongo, G.-J. Kounga, D. Andrew Wardell, M. Gehring, M.-C. Cordonier Segger and F. Perron-Welch, *Natural Resources Law and Governance for Sustainable Landscapes in the Democratic Republic of Congo Information Briefs* (Kisangani: CIFOR, CISDL and UNIKIS, 2015).

67 *Supra* Cordonier Segger, Gehring and Newcombe 2011.

68 R. Tarasofsky, 'Heating Up International Trade Law: Challenges and Opportunities Posed by Efforts to Combat Climate Change' (2008) 1 *CCLR* 7 [Tarasofsky].

69 *Methanex* v. *USA*, UNCITRAL, Award on Jurisdiction (28 August 2002), http://www.italaw.com/sites/default/files/case-documents/ita0518.pdf.

70 J.C. Lawrence, 'Chicken Little Revisited: NAFTA Regulatory Expropriations After *Methanex*', *Georgia Law Review* 41 (2006), p. 261.

'like circumstances.' Under the wording of a typical IIA, it is only where two parties are in 'like circumstances' and receive different treatment that tribunals would find discrimination. For future climate change measures, the inclusion of public interests and carbon emissions in one proposed project as compared to another which does not take such issues into account might serve to distinguish hitherto 'like' parties from one another.

The *Parkerings* v. *Lithuania* ICSID arbitration demonstrates this principle.[71] The case concerned two competing firms from Norway and the Netherlands in their tenders to construct and operate traffic facilities in the Lithuanian capital Vilnius. The Norwegian company, Parkerings, proposed a project that impacted on a UNESCO World Heritage site at the centre of Vilnius' old town. In response to this, the authorities imposed more onerous requirements on Parkerings' project than on its Dutch competitor's project, which posed no similar archaeological and cultural heritage issues. Parkerings then claimed discriminatory treatment in favour of its Dutch competitor. The tribunal's discussion of this claim turned on the concept of 'likeness.' The arbitrators ultimately found that the State could take a proposed project's impacts on the environment into account, when deciding how to treat different projects. In their view, '[t]he historical and archaeological preservation and environmental protection could be and in this case were a justification for the refusal of the project . . . the City of Vilnius did have legitimate grounds to distinguish between the two projects.'[72] The tribunal's approach has been welcomed in leading legal scholarship on these issues:

> This decision points to the ecological impact of an investor's project as a determinative factor in the like circumstances test. If this approach is followed in future investor–state disputes, then the potential for non-discrimination requirements in international investment agreements to frustrate climate change mitigation regulation will be significantly reduced.[73]

Learning from this experience, negotiators may need to recognise the importance of maintaining flexibility for climate change measures in investment treaties, while regulators must take care to design the rules for carbon trading, and clean technology investments, to avoid discrimination between industries in 'like circumstances.' This approach can extend to implementation of measures to encourage sustainable investments, such as REDD+.

---

[71] *Parkerings-Compagniet AS* v. *Republic of Lithuania*, ICSID Arbitration Case No. ARB/05/8, Award (11 September 2007), paras 375 and 392, http://www.italaw.com/cases/812 [*Parkerings* v. *Lithuania*].

[72] Ibid., *Parkerings* v. *Lithuania*, paras 392, 396.

[73] *Supra* Miles, p. 32.

For REDD+, it is assumed that there is a national legal or regulatory framework which is the same for domestic and foreign investors. This reduces the danger of being seen to treat two investors/projects differently. A government might decide to treat two REDD+ projects differently, due for instance to differing social or ecological conditions, and then a careful analysis of 'like circumstances' may be warranted. An arbitrator might well find a violation of 'like circumstances.' The recent *Bilcon* arbitration gave rise to concern in this respect. In that case, the majority of arbitrators decided that the investor did not have to show that a government authority had actually treated another investor more favourably under the rules; it was sufficient to show that rules had been violated. If this relatively low standard for 'like circumstances' is adopted by more arbitrators, that could mean an increase in REDD+ investment liability, but also a correspondingly greater level of security for REDD+ investors who have gained an additional 'shield' against an arbitrary government action which results in cancellation of their investment.

3.4 Indirect Expropriation and REDD+ Investments

Certain climate finance and GHG mitigation schemes may lead to investment law claims of 'indirect expropriation.'[74] States choose whether their measures will be limited to a particular sector or economy-wide in application, and which jurisdictions will be subjected to (or allowed entry into) the scheme. Emitters targeted by ETS can include both direct emitters of carbon, such as power plants or even car owners, and also those 'further upstream' in the chain of carbon use, such as oil companies or petroleum refiners. For instance, the EU's ETS covers power and industry sectors only,[75] and focuses simply on addressing CO_2 emissions.[76] Depending on the data collected and economic impact assessments, States decide whether their schemes will be comprehensive or simply sectoral, and whether partial coverage can achieve their objectives.

Such choices may affect the competitiveness of national companies against each other and against foreign companies. If investments in foreign investor-dominated sectors were seen as being unjustly targeted by stringent and costly requirements 'tantamount to expropriation' while other domestic investor-dominated heavy emitting sectors were excluded

---

[74] S. Huq and H. Reid, 'Benefit Sharing under the Clean Development Mechanism', in *supra* Freestone and Streck (eds), p. 229.

[75] Extensions to the scheme are, however, continually under review. Most recently, the aviation industry is intended to be subjected to the system.

[76] *Supra* Ellerman and Joskow.

from the scheme, challenges might be issued under IIAs. If investors found themselves unable to ensure that forests are not exploited, or a regulator decided to arbitrarily remove guarantees for REDD+, such measures could be characterised as indirect expropriation of the investment. Similarly, if the cost of carbon certificates becomes high enough to threaten the economic viability of certain investments (for instance fossil fuel exploration and development, or a coal-fired power plant), the carbon inclusion measure could also be deemed 'tantamount to expropriation.' The core debate focuses on who bears the risks of private investments in 'high carbon' sectors – host governments or investors? Essentially:

> if a government measure is undertaken for a clear public welfare purpose (such as health and safety, environment, public morals or order, etc.), and is non-discriminatory, but has the effect of harming a . . . foreign investor, under what circumstances can that measure be held to be an indirect expropriation, for which the government must pay compensation?[77]

As demonstrated in the *Ethyl* v. *Canada Case*,[78] claims of indirect expropriation can be made when new government measures affect the value of a foreign investment in a specific or unique industry. Such issues could arise for governments implementing climate change measures, particularly because, in some countries, carbon-intensive industries are dominated by multinational extractive enterprises with the necessary know-how and capital for exploration and development, but also the necessary foreign nationality to bring claims under investment treaties. Moreover, the repeal by Canada of its ban on a gasoline additive known as MMT following the *Ethyl* v. *Canada* case clearly demonstrated the indirect effect of a foreign investor challenge on government policy directions.[79]

In the context of REDD+, a similar dispute might take place in a situation where a government authority decides to overly restrict which parts of landscapes can be part of a REDD+ project in order to exclude other investors, or where the host government at national, regional or local levels suddenly decides to adopt new measures which directly or indirectly

---

[77] A. Cosbey, *NAFTA's Chapter 11 and the Environment*, Discussion Paper for CEC Public Workshop, Mexico City (24 March 2003), p. 3, http://www.iisd.org/pdf/2003/investment_jpac.pdf.

[78] *Ethyl Corporation* v. *Canada*, Award on Jurisdiction, 24 June 1998 (1999) 38 ILM 708.

[79] A. Newcombe, 'Regulatory Expropriation, Investment Protection and International Law: When Is Government Regulation Expropriatory and When Should Compensation Be Paid?' (LLM Thesis, University of Toronto 1999) (unpublished), http://ita.law.uvic.ca/documents/RegulatoryExpropriation.pdf.

take away the value of the REDD+ investment. In one possible scenario, a government might establish a national REDD+ framework and regulatory regime to support these investments, but then once international investors agree to participate, a change in policy or approach results in the repeal of all REDD+ commitments and resumption of policies which promote forest degradation and destruction. In such an instance, the international investor's acquisitions would become worthless for the purposes of REDD+, having been directly or indirectly expropriated, and the investors might seek compensation through an arbitral tribunal.

Indeed, if a developed State such as Canada or Australia could be perceived to have chilled its policy and regulatory decisions due to international investment law obligations, a smaller developing country might face even higher pressure. Whether or not the developing country could in fact afford to compensate for the expropriation is a particularly pressing challenge in the case of climate change measures, including emission trading schemes and REDD+ climate finance.

3.5 Stabilisation Clauses

A further aspect of international investment law can also be briefly noted. Certain IIAs contain so-called 'stabilisation clauses,' under which States agree to freeze the laws of a country to the time the investment was made, or not to apply new laws to the investment, or to bear the costs of all regulatory changes affecting an investment. These commitments could be problematic from the standpoint of ETS regulations, and a similar concern arises for REDD+. If the country has an IIA with a stabilisation clause, it may become risk adverse, and less adaptive, during a crucial and fragile period of development for the fledgling REDD+ investments. Nationally and internationally, REDD+ might be subject to significant changes, such as the adoption of more stringent safeguards. Such changes, once reflected in domestic regulatory regimes, could run counter to an IIA stabilisation clause. Most of those clauses would take the international dimension into account and recognise those changes as legitimate, but sudden or apparently arbitrary national policy shifts could be more difficult to justify.

In essence, if States are bound to continue treating the investment in a certain way, this may assist in the achievement of UNFCCC objectives, contributing to the stability and reliable functioning of the REDD+ investment. However, it may also serve to chill necessary regulatory changes that respond to new or emerging scientific discoveries that often drive the evolution and effectiveness of climate change regulations and governance systems.

4. CLIMATE CHANGE AS A CATALYST FOR MORE CAREFUL CRAFTING OF CONTEMPORARY TRADE AND INVESTMENT AGREEMENTS

To date, the experience of international economic law provides a mixed picture for REDD+ instruments, with some aspects of investment regimes offering sufficient flexibility to accommodate and even assist investors in REDD+, and other aspects potentially posing difficulties for REDD+ regulators or investors. Despite real risks within certain areas of trade and investment law that the regimes and their dispute settlement mechanisms are currently inadequate to deal with the challenges of climate change and sustainable development more broadly, there is also cause for cautious optimism.

Important countries responsible for the design of international trade and investment agreements are increasingly recognising the need for new rules which support climate change response and other sustainable development goals.[80] Indeed, more than 190 Parties to the UNFCCC, in their national communications, have pledged to adopt new national strategies and laws, backed by new or tailored institutions, to address climate change.[81] Countries such as Mexico, the Philippines and the UK have recently passed domestic legislation creating regulatory frameworks for the implementation of key UNFCCC commitments, encouraging the creation of carbon-trading markets including REDD+ in a concerted effort to mitigate their respective contributions to GHG emissions and to establish effective adaptation strategies.[82] Many other countries are currently undertaking similar legislative and policy reform measures to more efficiently manage climate change in an economic framework.[83] Evolving international economic regimes can significantly impact the effectiveness of these efforts, either fostering or frustrating the sustainable development

---

[80] This section shares thoughts with the authors' work in *supra* Cordonier Segger, Gehring et al., and with one author's foundational research in *Athena's Treaties* (forthcoming 2017).

[81] See UNFCC, National Reports, http://unfccc.int/national_reports/items/1408.php.

[82] IDLO, 'The New General Law of Climate Change in Mexico: Leading National Action to Transition to a Green Economy' (Mexico City/Rome: *IDLO Legal Working Paper*, 2012), http://www.idlo.org/Publications/MexicoClimateChangeLWB.pdf. See also United Kingdom Climate Change Act 2008, Chapter 27, http://www.legislation.gov.uk/ukpga/2008/27/contents.

[83] IDLO-CISDL, 'Compendium of Legal Best Practices on Climate Change Policy' (2007), http://www.mtnforum.org/sites/default/files/publication/files/climatechangecislmay2011.pdf.

of a low-carbon economy in the future. Along with increased awareness of other pressing and legitimate environmental and social objectives, climate change has sharpened the desire for more refined international trade and investment agreements. In legal, academic and other communities, there is a growing body of literature examining climate change response threats and potentials within trade and investment law.[84] Pressures, over time, have led to incremental changes in thinking within the trade and investment community, such that debates over issues in each regime have opened up, and linkages have been identified and studied.[85] Negotiators and adjudicators are more willing to engage with other regimes and other goals than in the past, and States have recognised the need to respect policy and regulatory space in order to achieve their own sustainable development goals.

The obligations of States under international trade and investment law might intersect with their efforts in certain aspects of climate change regulations, requiring careful work to design compatible measures to

---

[84] M.-C. Cordonier Segger, 'Integrating Social and Economic Development and Environmental Protection in World Trade Law', in Cordonier Segger and Gehring 2005, *supra*; A. Green, 'Climate Change, Regulatory Policy and the WTO: How Constraining Are Trade Rules?' *Journal of International Economic Law* 8 (2005), p. 143; B. Condon, 'Climate Change and Unresolved Issues in WTO Law', *Journal of International Economic Law* 12 (2009), p. 895; M. McKenzie, 'Climate Change and the Generalized System of Preferences', *Journal of International Economic Law* 11 (2008), p. 679; P. Veel, 'Carbon Tariffs and the WTO: An Evaluation of Feasible Policies', *Journal of International Economic Law* 12 (2009), p. 749; A. Green, 'Trade Rules and Climate Change Subsidies', *World Trade Review* 5 (2006), p. 377; M. Doelle, 'Climate Change and the WTO: Opportunities to Motivate State Action on Climate Change Through the World Trade Organization', *RECIEL* 13 (2004), p. 85; G. Goh, 'The World Trade Organization, Kyoto, and Energy Tax Adjustments at the Border', *Journal of World Trade* 38 (2004), p. 395; *supra* Miles; Werksman et al., Tarasofsky.

[85] For linkages between trade law and the environment, see, e.g.: J. Trachtman, 'Trade and . . . Problems, Cost-Benefit Analysis and Subsidiarity', *European Journal of International Law* 9 (1998), p. 32; D. Bethlehem et al., *The Oxford Handbook of International Trade Law* (Oxford: Oxford University Press 2009), Part IV; Cordonier Segger and Gehring 2005; S. Charnovitz, 'The WTO's Environmental Progress', *Journal of International Economic Law* 10 (2007), p. 685; H. Grosse Ruse-Khan, 'A Real Partnership for Development? Sustainable Development as a Treaty Objective in European Economic Partnership Agreements and Beyond', *Journal of International Economic Law* 13 (2010), p. 139; A. Green and T. Epps, 'The WTO, Science, and the Environment: Moving Towards Consistency', *Journal of International Economic Law* 10 (2007), p. 285. For discussion of investment linkages, see, e.g., Cordonier Segger, Gehring and Newcombe 2011, *supra*; S. Spears, 'The Quest for Policy Space in a New Generation of International Investment Agreements', *Journal of International Economic Law* 13 (2010), p. 1037.

establish REDD+ climate finance schemes, and may potentially lead to constraints on policy and law-making flexibility.[86] However, as noted in the 1987 Report of the World Commission on Environment and Development,[87] the 1992 Rio Declaration and Agenda 21,[88] the 2002 Johannesburg Declaration and Plan of Implementation[89] and the 2012 Rio Declaration on The Future We Want,[90] trade and investment could also provide important contributions to sustainable development. As in the international climate regime, in many trade agreements and IIAs, Parties explicitly highlight their shared commitment to sustainable development as part of the object or purpose of the treaty. Sustainable development is a key objective of the world community, not only in the abstract, but in the very arena that has most sought to encourage economic growth – investment and trade policy and law.[91] Measures to address climate change are an integral part of sustainable development, and if such statements of purpose are included, they are relevant to understand and interpret the agreements.

In regional trade and investment agreements, States have gone further in certain instances, seeking to promote sustainable development through the inclusion of innovative yet practical international instruments.[92] Several preventive provisions, cooperative mechanisms and new trade liberalisation enhancement initiatives can be identified. There are also important

---

[86] *Supra* Miles. See also S. Charnovitz, 'Trade and Climate: Potential Conflicts and Synergies' in *Beyond Kyoto: Advancing the International Effort against Climate Change* (Arlington: Pew Center 2003) at 141. And see D. Blanford and T. Josling, 'Greenhouse Gas Reduction Policies and Agriculture: Implication for Production Incentives and International Trade Disciplines', *ICTSD Issue No. 1* (2009); 'Trade, Climate Change and Global Competitiveness: Opportunities and Challenges for Sustainable Development in China and Beyond', *ICTSD, Selected Issue Briefs No. 3* (2008); 'A Comparative Assessment of How Trade Liberalization and the Economic Crisis Have Impacted India and South Africa', *ICTSD Information Note No. 13* (2010).

[87] World Commission on Environment and Development, *Our Common Future* (Oxford: Oxford University Press 1987).

[88] UN, 'Rio Declaration on Environment and Development' (1992) 31 ILM 874; United Nations Conference on Environment and Development, Rio de Janerio, Brazil (14 June 1992) Agenda 21, https://sustainabledevelopment.un.org/content/documents/Agenda21.pdf.

[89] UN, World Summit on Sustainable Development, 'Plan of Implementation of the World Summit on Sustainable Development', Johannesburg, South Africa (4 September 2002), http://www.un.org/esa/sustdev/documents/WSSD_POI_PD/English/WSSD_PlanImpl.pdf.

[90] *Supra* The Future We Want.

[91] *Supra* Gehring and Cordonier Segger 2005, Introduction.

[92] *Supra* Cordonier Segger, Gehring et al. 2013.

procedural innovations which can support sustainable development. Many legal options are available to States seeking to deliver on a commitment to sustainable development in a regional trade and investment regime, either as a principle or an objective.

First, States can include introductory and hortatory provisions which signal the Parties' commitment to sustainable development and climate change, such as preambular commitments to 'promote sustainable development' as a 'joint resolution' of the Parties to the accord, or other initial provisions which commit to engage in the accord in accordance with a 'principle of sustainable development.' For instance, the North American Free Trade Agreement (NAFTA) includes a reference to the need to 'promote sustainable development' within its Preamble.[93] Both the Canada–Chile Free Trade Agreement (FTA) and Chile–US FTA recognise the importance of strengthening capacity to protect the environment and promote sustainable development.[94] The EU–Chile Association Agreement goes further, committing to implement their accord in accordance with the 'principle of sustainable development,'[95] and even in original negotiating directives, the EU economic accord with Central America sought explicitly to 'harness globalisation in support of sustainable development' and 'ensure an appropriate balance between economic, social and environmental components in a sustainable development context.'[96] Indeed, in their Preamble, the Parties to the Japan–Switzerland Free Trade and Economic Partnership Agreement (EPA) also specifically highlight their determination 'to adequately address the challenges of climate change.'[97] In the EU–Columbia–Peru Agreement, Parties agree to 'promote international trade in such a way as to contribute to the objective of sustainable development' and recognise the benefit of considering environmental issues 'as part of a global

---

[93] North American FTA (1993) 32 ILM 289.

[94] Canada–Chile FTA (XXX) 36 ILM 1079; US–Chile FTA (XXX) 42 ILM 1026.

[95] EU–Chile Association Agreement (30 December 2002) http://ec.europa.eu/trade/issues/bilateral/countries/chile/eu/euchlagr_en.htm.

[96] Draft EU–Central America Negotiating Directive (2007), paras 3.4 and 3.7 engaging the EU with Costa Rica, El Salvador, Guatemala, Honduras, Nicaragua, Panama, http://www.bilaterals.org/?draft-eu-central-america.

[97] Agreement on Free Trade and Economic Partnership between Japan and the Swiss Confederation (2009) http://www.mofa.go.jp/region/europe/switzerland/epa0902/agreement.pdf, which notes 'DETERMINED, in implementing this Agreement, to seek to preserve and protect the environment, to promote the optimal use of natural resources in accordance with the objective of sustainable development and to adequately address the challenges of climate change.'

approach to trade and sustainable development.'[98] The incorporation of sustainable development concerns in preambles clarifies the object and purpose of the treaties themselves, providing guidance to the Parties. As has occurred in the WTO, preambular commitments on sustainable development were found to be useful to interpret the scope of general exceptions in a dispute on requirements that shrimp trawlers use turtle excluder devices to avoid harming endangered species.[99] Dispute settlement bodies thus refer to preambular commitments to interpret the operational provisions of economic accords.

Second, States can include provisions which create 'windows' or exemptions from trade rules, where trade obligations might otherwise constrain regulators and policymakers, mitigating their effects.[100] Over the past decades, many observers have raised the concerns that economic treaties might prevent or weaken the adoption and enforcement of legitimate measures for health, the environment and the conservation of natural resources.[101] To accommodate such policies, however, many treaties contain provisions that establish exceptions that work as windows in the economic disciplines, allowing regulatory measures that might otherwise not be permitted. Such exceptions may be particularly relevant for adaptation, mitigation and financing measures to respond to climate change in developing countries. Climate change is a new challenge for many regulators, and new measures are required to respond, including measures to stimulate development of clean-energy technologies that provide alternative ways to meet growing energy demand without increasing emissions. Without such windows in trade and investment treaties, both real and perceived conflicts might arise, chilling the new regulatory measures that are required. For instance, in trade and investment agreements, many States adopt general exceptions for measures related to the conservation of exhaustible living and non-living natural resources, and the use of measures, including environmental measures, necessary to protect

---

[98] Trade Agreement between the EU and its Member States, on the one Part, and Colombia and Peru, on the other Part, Article 267.1.

[99] United States – Import Prohibition of Certain Shrimp and Shrimp Products, DS 58 (2001); United States – Measures Relating to Shrimp from Thailand, DS 343 (2008), see *supra* Cordonier Segger and Gehring 2005.

[100] *Supra* Cordonier Segger, Gehring et al. 2013, at p. 12.

[101] G.P. Samson and W. Bradnee Chambers (eds), *Trade, Environment and the Millennium (Second Edition)* (United Nations University Press, 2002) 2; see N. Bernasconi-Osterwalder et al., *Environment and Trade: A Guide to WTO Jurisprudence* (Routledge, 2005); 'WTO Dispute Panel Rules against Canada in Renewables Case', ICTSD (January 18, 2013), http://ictsd.org/i/news/biores/152926/.

human, animal or plant life or health. These GATT Article XX-style exemptions are increasingly common in regional trade agreements, including those with investment chapters.[102] One example of such provisions is found in Korea–EU FTA, which provides in Article 2.15 a general exception by directly noting the Parties reliance on GATT Article XX, with Article 6.1(g) and Article 7.50 further noting that facilitation of trade is not to prejudice national security, health and the environment with Parties permitted to take protective non-discriminatory measures.[103]

States may further adopt specific exceptions in sections of the trade and investment treaty where it is clear that trade rules on inter alia sanitary and phytosanitary standards, TBTs, intellectual property rights, public procurement, services or investment might constrain the use of environmental and social measures. [104] As a further example, in the Central America–Dominican Republic FTA which also agrees investment law commitments, Parties adopted 1994 GATT-style general exceptions, but alongside, at Article 10.07 on Services, further environmental exceptions are provided. Along the same lines, in Article 13.13 on TBTs, there are specific exceptions for hazardous waste and the environment.[105]

Similar exceptions are also found in the 1998 CARICOM–Dominican Republic FTA at Article IV which requires Parties to use international standards, but is open to exceptions where these would be an ineffective or inappropriate means to fulfil its legitimate objectives, which explicitly include health, environment and sustainable development objectives.[106] If

---

[102] See CARIFORUM–EU EPA of 15 October 2008 at Part V in Article 224 on General Exceptions; in the Central America–Chile FTA of 18 October 1999 at Article 2002 on General Exceptions; in the Central America–Dominican Republic FTA of 16 April 1998 at Article 17.01 General Exceptions; in the Chile–Australia FTA of 30 July 2008 at Article 22.1; in the Chile–Colombia FTA of 27 November 2006 at Article 21.1 General Exceptions; in the Chile–MERCOSUR FTA of 25 June 1996 at Article 49; in the Chile–New Zealand, Singapore and Brunei Darussalam (P4) FTA of 18 July 2005 at ch. 19 General Exceptions; in the Costa Rica–Mexico FTA of 05 April 1994 at Article 18.01 General Exceptions; in the Costa Rica–China FTA at Article 159 General Exceptions which adopts the GATT Article XX *mutatis mutandis*; in the El Salvador–Taiwan FTA of 7 May 2007 at Article 16.02 on General Exceptions; and in the EU–South Africa TDCA of 1 January 2000 at Article 27 Exceptions.

[103] Korea–EU FTA (6 October 2010).

[104] *Supra* Cordonier Segger, Gehring and Newcombe 2011.

[105] *Supra* Central America–Dominican Republic FTA.

[106] Legitimate objectives, in the TBT Appendix, are defined as: 'Objectives such as safety, protection of human, animal or plant life or health, the environment or consumers (including matters relating to quality and identifiability of goods or services); or, sustainable development, considering, among other things, where

international standards advocated clearing of certain lands and obsolete agricultural practices, and a REDD+ measure sought to achieve climate and sustainable development objectives by going beyond the standard, this exception could be helpful. As another example, Article 150 of the EU–CARIFORUM EPA contains a specific exception for genetic resources, traditional knowledge and folklore in the subsection on standards concerning intellectual property rights. Article 150 notably indicates the Parties' commitment to: 'respect, preserve and maintain knowledge, innovations and practices of indigenous and local communities embodying traditional lifestyles relevant for the conservation and sustainable use of biological diversity.'[107] Such exceptions could assist in States' efforts to indicate that government measures to secure or enhance REDD+ biodiversity co-benefits are not meant to be prevented by the trade or investment disciplines. States may also insert 'reserved exceptions' to explicitly prevent an economic treaty from applying to socially or environmentally sensitive sectors. Of relevance to REDD+, such reserved exceptions may prevent investment disciplines from being applied to parks conservation, land-use planning, water or energy policy, among other natural resources; they can also reserve health and education sectors from services disciplines, as has been seen in the US–Chile FTA and the Canada–Chile FTA.[108] These 'reserved' exceptions can be linked to the findings of sustainability impact assessments or environmental assessments of the trade agreements. [109] States can also include general interpretive statements to guide potential areas where trade rules could otherwise constrain the use of measures agreed in other international (or regional) agreements.[110]

An example of such provisions is found in the Korea–EU FTA, which reaffirms the Parties' commitment to implement laws putting into practice obligations under MEAs to which they are a party including the Montreal Protocol and the KP.[111] Similar provisions are found in the Canada–Chile FTA,[112] the

---

appropriate, fundamental climatic, geographical, technological or infrastructural factors or scientific justification.' *Supra*, CARIFORUM–EU EPA.

[107] Ibid., EU–CARIFORUM EPA, at Article 150.

[108] *Supra* US–Chile FTA and Canada–Chile FTA.

[109] Ibid.

[110] Ibid.

[111] Ibid. at p. 17.

[112] Canada–Chile FTA Article A-04 (referencing the requirements of the Convention on International Trade in Endangered Species of Wild Fauna and Flora, the Montreal Protocol on Substances that Deplete the Ozone Layer, and the Basel Convention on the Control of Transboundary Movements of Hazardous Wastes and their Disposal).

Canada–Costa Rica FTA,[113] the Canada–Colombia FTA[114] and the US–Central America–Dominican Republic FTA,[115] among others.

In the investment chapters of certain economic accords, States are also adopting commitments not to lower health, safety, environmental and related standards to attract foreign investment, in order to prevent a 'race to the bottom.'[116] These provisions may favour REDD+ measures, preventing investment disciplines from inadvertently stifling the adoption of higher standards in response to climate adaptation or mitigation opportunities. Echoing Chapter 11 of the NAFTA, Section G-14 of the Canada–Chile FTA, signed on 5 December 1996, provides for these exceptions with the caveat that they cannot be waived in the event they cause issues for potential investors.[117] Insofar as climate change measures can be construed as health, safety or environmental measures, this RTA would prevent Parties from relaxing forest protection and other land-use planning requirements in order to encourage investment. As another example, the 2006 US–Peru FTA features a chapter on the environment, which agrees not to weaken or reduce the protections of environmental laws to encourage trade and investment, and also not to fail to effectively enforce environmental regulations in a manner affecting trade or investment.[118] Such provisions provide greater clarity to regulators as to whether other provisions of trade treaties might be intended to strike down or weaken new environmental laws or to prevent their enforcement. Following this trend, other IIAs have started to include similar provisions to prevent lower investment standards. The new version of the US Bilateral Investment Treaty (BIT) Model[119] expands obligations in the area of environment committing Parties not to waive or derogate from their domestic

---

[113] Canada–Costa Rica FTA, Article I.4.

[114] Canada–Colombia FTA, Annex 103.

[115] Dominican Republic–Central America–United States FTA, ch. 17.

[116] See NAFTA; Canada–Colombia FTA; Canada–Chile FTA; Canada–Peru FTA.

[117] '2. The Parties recognize that it is inappropriate to encourage investment by relaxing domestic health, safety or environmental measures. Accordingly, a Party should not waive or otherwise derogate from, or offer to waive or otherwise derogate from, such measures as an encouragement for the establishment, acquisition, expansion or retention in its territory of an investment of an investor. If a Party considers that the other Party has offered such an encouragement, it may request consultations with the other Party and the two Parties shall consult with a view to avoiding any such encouragement.'

[118] US–Peru FTA, Article 18.3 on Enforcement of Environmental Laws, 1(a).

[119] See 2012 US Model Bilateral Investment Treaty, http://www.state.gov/documents/organization/188371.pdf.

environmental laws as an encouragement for investment, and not to fail to effectively enforce their domestic labour and environmental laws as an encouragement for investment.[120]

Third, States can negotiate arrangements for 'value-added' but parallel (non-integrated) trade- and investment-related social and environmental cooperation, within the text of their trade or investment treaties, or alongside such agreements.[121] These may include the adoption of parallel agreements (or chapters, or both) for cooperation on environmental and social matters, and the development of institutions for social and environmental cooperation including carbon trading. They may also agree to adopt and implement common work programmes on specific environmental or social projects such as emissions monitoring and registration, particularly when accompanied by reliable capacity-building, technology transfer and financing commitments. They may also provide factual report or complaints mechanisms to provide recourse when it appears that environmental or social rules are being violated in order to gain trade- or investment-related advantages. One example of such provisions of direct relevance to REDD+ is found in the EU–Colombia–Peru Trade Agreement, signed on 26 June 2012, which indicates the Parties resolve to enhance efforts regarding climate change and commitment to sustainable use of natural resources.[122] For instance, the Canada–Peru Side Agreement on the Environment agrees on new collaboration to promote sustainable use of natural resources, forests management and use. It also highlights a commitment to the joint development of clean technologies, as a priority.[123] The 2010 EU–Central American EPA covers political dialogue, trade and cooperation measures. In Cooperation at Article 50, the Parties established a channel for cooperation on the environment.[124] Similarly, in the CARIFORUM–EU EPA,[125] the Parties agreed to cooperate, including by facilitating support for projects related to environmentally friendly products and technologies, including energy and forests.[126] Indeed, the

---

[120] Ibid., Article 12.1.

[121] *Supra*, Cordonier Segger, Gehring et al. 2013, at pp. 7–9.

[122] Ibid., at pp. 12–13.

[123] Agreement on the Environment between Canada and the Republic of Peru preamble.

[124] EU–Central America Association Agreement Article 50 (Cooperation on Environment), 65.

[125] CARIFORUM–EU EPA, Article 83.26.

[126] Ibid., at Article 138, '2. Subject to the provisions of Article 7 and 134, the Parties agree to cooperate, including by facilitating support, in the following areas: . . . (a) projects related to environmentally-friendly products, technologies, production processes, services, management and business methods, including those

EU has been very diligent in pursuing environmental and sustainable development collaboration. Commitments to encourage and support such cooperation have been adopted in the EU–South Africa Trade, Development and Cooperation Agreement (TDCA),[127] the EU–ESA EPA,[128] the EU–South Korea FTA[129] and the Mexico–EU Association Agreement.[130] Such provisions are not just found in the agreements that developed countries negotiate with developing countries. For instance, at Article 18.3 of the Chile–Colombia FTA, the Parties agree to support green markets.[131]

Fourth, States may include constructive 'sustainable development'-orientated trade and investment rule enhancement initiatives, where a positive 'triple-win' might be achieved within the trade agreement. These may include, for instance, sanitary and phytosanitary provisions which promote scientific cooperation and risk assessment to improve levels of health or environment protection; government procurement provisions which make public purchasing of low-carbon goods or services more affordable; TBT provisions to implement non-discriminatory certification processes and promote mutual recognition; intellectual property rights provisions which support low-carbon technology transfer or respect for traditional knowledge; investment provisions which privilege socially responsible corporations and low-carbon investments; measures to promote reductions in illegal trade in forestry products; measures to secure additional liberalisation of environmental goods and services such as low-carbon transportation; or measures to secure reductions in unsustainable fossil fuel development subsidies. One example of such provisions of direct relevance to REDD+ is found in the EU–Colombia–Peru FTA, which aims to promote trade and investment which facilitate access, use and dissemination of climate change mitigation, provides in Article 273 for the development of a timber verification system and in Article 275 measures to promote investment in climate change mitigation technologies.[132] The Canada–Peru FTA makes explicit reference, in the chapter entitled 'Investment', to corporate social responsibility and the need for Parties to encourage enterprises to incorporate such

---

related to appropriate water-saving and Clean Development Mechanism applications; (b) projects related to energy efficiency and renewable energy.'

127 EU–South Africa TDCA, Article 57.

128 EU–ESA EPA, Article 47.

129 EU–South Korea FTA, Article 13.6.

130 Mexico–EU FTA, Article 23.

131 Chile–Columbia FTA, Article 18.3(4).

132 *Supra*, Cordonier Segger, Gehring et al. 2013, at pp. 13–15.

standards into their internal policies.[133] As another example, Article 9 of the Japan–Switzerland Agreement includes a slightly more substantive obligation to 'encourage trade and dissemination of environmental products and environment-related services' in pursuit of 'climate-change-related goals.'[134] Similarly, the Korea–EU FTA includes an obligation in Article 13.6(2) to 'strive to facilitate and promote trade and foreign direct investment in environmental goods and services, including environmental technologies, sustainable renewable energy, energy efficient products and services and eco-labelled goods.'[135] Indeed, certain trade and investment accords have piloted provisions to encourage the development of a specific form of investment to address climate change: PES, supporting climate finance for reducing emissions from deforestation, and land degradation and more (REDD+).[136] For instance, in the EU–Central America Agreement, Article 289 on Trade in Forest Products provides that:

> In order to promote the sustainable management of forest resources, the Parties commit to work together to improve forest law enforcement and governance and to promote trade in legal and sustainable forest products through instruments that may include, inter alia: effective use of CITES with regard to endangered timber species; certification schemes for sustainably harvested forest products; regional or bilateral Forest Law Enforcement Governance and Trade ('FLEGT') Voluntary Partnership Agreements.[137]

Finally, certain procedural innovations can be undertaken by the parties during trade or investment negotiations to promote sustainable development, and secure the integration of environmental and social concerns into a trade and investment treaty. Such process changes may also assist parties and others in identifying useful innovations that might be included in a trade or investment agreement. For instance, States may undertake *ex ante* (or ongoing) environment, development, human rights or sustainability impact assessments and reviews of trade liberalisation policies and draft treaties. As examples, the EU Sustainability Impact Assessments (SIAs) carried out during the preparations for negotiations of the EU–Central America Association, the EU–South Korea FTA and

---

[133] Canada–Peru FTA, signed 29 May 2008, Chapter 8 'Investment', Article 810. See also A. Delfino et al., 'Corporate Social Responsibility and Climate Change', in *Climate Change: A Guide to Carbon Law and Practice* (London: Globe Business Publishing 2008), p. 157.

[134] *Supra* FTA Japan–Switzerland, at Article 9.

[135] *Supra* Cordonier Segger, Gehring et al. 2013, at p. 22.

[136] S. Mason-Case et al., *Lessons Learned in Legal Preparedness for REDD+* (IDLO, 2012).

[137] EU–Central America Agreement, Article 289.

the EU–Colombia–Peru FTA all uncovered serious vulnerabilities of the regions in question to climate change.[138] The outcomes of these assessments may be used to identify the areas where preventive, cooperative or enhancement initiatives could be useful in a trade or investment treaty. [139] States may also host consultations between economic, environment and development authorities. They may agree upon, or strengthen, diverse mechanisms to ensure transparency and public participation in trade negotiations, and they may also establish new mechanisms to inform tribunals about sustainable development issues, including amicus curiae, public participation and expert consultation measures.

It is not yet clear which strategies or instruments will have the most success in helping to integrate social and economic development and environmental protection. It is likely that no single measure can accommodate or even support all REDD+ and other climate finance instruments, or address all governance challenges. Rather, many different provisions may be needed throughout a new trade or investment agreement. Certain instruments, such as the normative or regulatory evaluation elements of *ex ante* SIAs, are still underdeveloped. Others, such as the new system of certification to ensure that forestry products traded from Peru to the United States are not obtained through illegal logging, are simply new.[140] Such provisions alone will not necessarily ensure that sustainable development priorities including climate change are given more weight by the Parties in complying with their obligations, or by dispute settlement bodies in interpreting agreements, as compared to the other relevant objectives of agreements. However, they appear likely to contribute to the achievement of a greater degree of integration in the trade agreements. This is an important first step towards preparing the trade and investment regimes for future climate change measures.

5. CONCLUSION

The economic activity associated with global trade and investment has been a significant cause of GHG emissions. At the same time, though, global trade and investment – re-orientated towards, for instance,

---

[138] *Supra*, Cordonier Segger and Gehring et al. 2013, at p. 26.

[139] Ibid.

[140] United States–Peru Trade Promotion Agreement, signed on 12 April 2006, https://ustr.gov/trade-agreements/free-trade-agreements/peru-tpa/final-text; ICTSD, 'US–Peru Bilateral to Address Illegal Logging, Boost MEA Implementation', *Bridges Trade BioRes* (22 June 2007), http://ictsd.net/i/news/biores/9122.

sustainable investments in forests and broader landscape management, new low-carbon technologies and environmental services – can be a crucial component of the world's response to climate change. This means that the connections between climate change and the international law governing trade and investment, and the effects of each upon the other, will continue to be highly important. Certainly, climate change may not yet be identifiable by itself as a specific factor driving the evolution of trade and investment rules. Indeed, climate-related disputes have not overrun the dockets of trade and investment tribunals, and those that have arisen so far in each regime have not yet represented jurisprudential watersheds. Certain recent trade and investment agreements do refer to climate change specifically, but these are still few, and often as part of an overarching commitment to environmental protection. Country commitments to address climate change have also had, and will have, more nuanced effects on trade and investment law in a range of ways.

First, REDD+, initially conceived as an instrument intended to incentivise mitigation action in the forest sector of developing and other countries, holds potential to expand into a mechanism to encourage low-carbon investments (from various inter-related sectors) towards more sustainable landscapes. Examining REDD+ from an investment and sustainable landscapes perspective, however, uncovers underlying law and governance challenges in many countries, which could greatly diminish the GHG emission mitigation potential of the instrument, and weaken its contribution to sustainability.

Second, climate change considerations have arguably broadened the scope of trade and investment law. As governments develop innovative and more detailed economic and other incentives aimed at mitigating and adapting to climate change, entrenched interests will naturally seek to challenge these, presenting new scenarios to adjudicators and pushing the definitional boundaries of the subjects. However, it is possible that investment law is not only a set of rules to protect established interests and limit governmental powers to influence foreign investment. Rather, investment law might also *promote* international investment in priority sectors for sustainable development and provide conditions more conducive to success in these sectors. In this light, domestic and international instruments for climate change and the low-carbon economy can be viewed as part of investment law, to be backed by investment protection policies, rules, governance and dispute settlement mechanisms. Instruments such as REDD+ and mechanisms such as the CDM can be recognised as investment incentives, formulated to promote beneficial economic activity to which there has long been commitment in international treaties, national development strategies, and local land-use plans, channelling global investment towards forest carbon mitigation, renewable energy sources, and even more sustainable landscapes.

Third, climate change has prompted serious analysis of whether existing trade and investment law regimes are adequate to deal with the tensions that it imposes. Much research has been done to identify features of the existing trade and investment law regimes that purport to threaten States' efforts to combat climate change, and decisions of un-transparent international investor–State arbitral tribunals still present mixed results. This work has demonstrated that there is indeed a risk that the existing regimes will have the effect of frustrating climate change measures and weakening desirable policies, measures and strategies to mitigate GHG emissions. Nevertheless, there is also cause for optimism. Key players in the trade and investment regimes have already begun to recognise the need for better rules in this respect. Along with increased awareness of other pressing and legitimate environmental and social objectives, the arrival of the climate change problem has sharpened the desire for more refined international trade and investment agreements.

Climate change is a major part of a debate on the wider effects of trade and investment that is now more enlightened than it was a decade or two ago. Particularly in academic and policy discourse on trade and investment, climate change routinely features as a key priority. Action on climate change calls for consideration of important factors previously downplayed in trade and investment law, such as integration between economic, environmental and social priorities, inter-generational equity, and commitments to low-carbon investment and technology transfer. Global efforts to achieve promises of sustainable development are leading to incremental changes in thinking among jurists and others working in the two regimes. Many recent FTAs and BITs demonstrate a greater concern for non-economic interests and greater flexibility to balance trade and investment commitments with other policy goals such as environmental protection, human rights or corporate social responsibility. Similarly, recent jurisprudence from investment tribunals has grappled far more openly with such issues than in the past. Such decisions suggest that, combined with the recent reorientations of trade and investment rules, there is likely to be sufficient flexibility in the regimes to accommodate the pressures of climate change, and even to encourage new investment instruments such as REDD+. Provided that these techniques and innovations continue to be supported by key actors in the regimes, the potential exists that trade and investment rules can foster, rather than frustrate, the efforts of REDD+ and other climate instruments to encourage low-carbon investment in sustainable landscapes.

PART V

FUTURE DEVELOPMENTS AND LEGAL CHALLENGES

14. Rediscovering ambition, implementation and operationalization

*Patricia Elias**

1. INTRODUCTION

In this chapter I will explore the rationale behind breaking the barriers to increasing REDD+ ambition and the need for, but challenges of, flexible operationalization and implementation of this emissions reductions and forests conservation mechanism.

Historically, destruction of tropical forests through deforestation and forest degradation causes the emissions of 5.3 Gt of CO_{2eq} annually.[1] The most common activities associated with deforestation and forest degradation in the tropics are those that are driven by the global commodity trade, most notably for palm oil, soy, beef and wood products.[2] However, REDD+ provides a durable and widely applicable vision for shifting towards a green economy in which these commodities are still produced, but their production is decoupled from deforestation and degradation. In many ways, the global nature of the drivers of deforestation and degradation present a financial challenge to REDD+ ambition.[3]

Another challenge to increasing ambition is the dependence of REDD+

* All websites cited in this chapter were accessed on 1 October 2015.

[1] http://www.forestemissions.org/~/media/Files/Projects/Carbon%20Emissions/CarbonEmissions_Policy%20Brief.pdf. This value was reached by consensus between two of the leading expert teams on forest emissions, after agreeing to look at the same time scale (2000–2005) and the same sources of emissions. Their original papers are: Baccini, A., Goetz, S.J., Walker, W.S., Lapore, N.T., Sun, M., et al. 2012. "Estimated Carbon Dioxide Emissions from Tropical Deforestation improved by Carbon-Density Maps." *Nature Climate Change*, 2, 182–5; and Harris, N.L., Brown, S., Hagen, S.C., Saatchi, S.S., Petrova, S., et al. 2012. "Baseline Map of Carbon Emissions from Deforestation in Tropical Regions." *Science*, 336, 1573–5.

[2] Hosonuma, N., Herold, M., De Sy, V., De Fries, R.S., Brockhaus, M., Verchot, L., Romijn, E. (2012). 'An Assessment of Deforestation and Forest Degradation Drivers in Developing Countries.' *Environmental Research Letters*, 7(4), 044009.

[3] Fisher, B., Edwards, D.P., Giam, X. and Wilcove, D.S. (2011). "The High Costs of Conserving Southeast Asia's Lowland Rainforests." *Frontiers in Ecology and the Environment*, 9(6), 329–34.

on action by developing countries as well as financing from developed countries. This means that ambition by all actors is necessary to fully achieve the emissions reductions potential of REDD+, and in essence ties the success of REDD+ to a global commitment to address climate change. Although it is still a relatively new concept, and there are numerous challenges to generating ambition, recent successes in REDD+ provide the promise that ambition can be rekindled.

Such successes in REDD+ can also be used as case studies for the challenges and opportunities of operationalizing the mechanism. On the one hand, REDD+ requires flexibility to be implemented in a large range of circumstances, but it also needs to meet some specific guidelines to ensure the validity of the results. Therefore, an adaptive management loop approach could be used to guide operationalization. Adaptive management is a system designed to achieve progress towards an explicit goal, which is iteratively assessed, and feedback mechanisms are used to adjust approaches in order to consistently work at meeting the goal. However, such a flexible approach is difficult to implement legally.[4]

Successful operationalization, including meeting established guidance and standards, is expected to generate increased interest in REDD+ and provide additional funding for the mechanism. This can be seen as a "positive feedback" loop for REDD+. Both this positive feedback loop and the adaptive management loop capture the challenges and opportunities for REDD+ operationalization.

Implementing REDD+ will require addressing legal issues, garnering finance and avoiding fragmentation. Existing evidence from implementation has indicated that REDD+ funding has proceeded along a different pathway than was originally envisioned, in which a variety of financing sources would be used to scale-up to the level of funding needed to significantly reduce emissions.[5] Finally, implementation will need to avoid fragmentation as REDD+ is implemented through a wide range of approaches, means and actors.

---

[4] Ruhl, J.B. and Fischman, R., 2010, "Adaptive Management in the Courts", 95 *Minnesota Law Review*, 2.

[5] Canby, K., Silva, G., Breitfeller, J., Lanswer, C., Normal, M. and Schapp, B. 2014. "Tracking REDD+ Finance: 2009–2012 – Finance Flows in Seven REDD+ Countries." *Forest Trends*.

2. INCREASING REDD+ AMBITION

2.1 The Important Challenge of REDD+ Ambition

Under the UNFCCC the global community has committed to "stabilization of greenhouse gas concentrations in the atmosphere at a level that would prevent dangerous anthropogenic interference with the climate system."[6] Through the UNFCCC Copenhagen Accord, it was agreed that this means keeping global warming to below 2°C.[7] Already, it is clear that global atmospheric temperatures will increase beyond 2°C, and that efforts to address climate change will likely mean a peak at many degrees higher, with the goal that the temperature could level-off closer to two degrees above pre-industrial levels.[8] Even so, there is increasing evidence that meeting the objective of the UNFCCC, as it has been interpreted through a 2°C target, may not be possible. Therefore, meeting such a goal would require a global effort to make steep and significant reductions in all of the emissions causing climate change, and no sector can be ignored for its mitigation potential.

Tropical deforestation causes about 10 percent of global GHG emissions,[9] and degradation contributes additional emissions. Therefore, ambition on REDD+ is necessary for any efforts that aim to meet the objective of the UNFCCC.

In addition to the benefits it confers as a solution to climate change, REDD+ is linked to many other social and environmental outcomes. For example, efforts to reduce deforestation can in theory (though may not necessarily if not appropriately designed) help reduce habitat loss and protect biodiversity,[10] improve local governance opportunities,[11] reduce illegal logging activities[12] and support the provision of other

---

6 UNFCCC. 1992, http://unfccc.int/resource/docs/convkp/conveng.pdf.

7 2/CP.15.

8 Sanford, T., Frumhoff, P.C., Luers, A. and Gulledge, J. 2014. "The Climate Policy Narrative for a Dangerously Warming World." *Nature Climate Change*, 4, 164–6.

9 http://www.forestemissions.org/~/media/Files/Projects/Carbon%20 Emissions/CarbonEmissions_Policy%20Brief.pdf.

10 Gardner, T.A. et al. 2012. "A Framework for Integrating Biodiversity Concerns into National REDD+ Programmes." *Biological Conservation*, 154, 61–71.

11 Blom, B., Sunderland, T. and Murdiyarso, D. 2010. "Getting REDD to Work Locally: Lessons Learned from Integrated Conservation and Development Projects." *Environmental Science & Policy*, 13(2), 164–72.

12 http://www.ccmss.org.mx/descargas/Lessons_for_REDD_from_measures_to_control_illegal_logging_in_Indonesia.pdf.

ecosystem services.[13] Therefore, regardless of the sources of finance, REDD+ provides a tool to place an economic value on the many ecosystem benefits it confers. This is something conservationists have been trying to do for decades with mixed success using various policy mechanisms.[14]

However, a major challenge to REDD+ ambition is that it is competing with high-value global commodity markets. The major causes of deforestation and degradation in the tropics are expansion of soy, cattle, and oil palm agriculture and logging.[15] Since production of such commodities provides economic growth within the producing country, it can be useful to envision REDD+ as a multi-faceted tool that drives sustainable development while also addressing climate change. The forest transition curve is a conceptual model that can be applied in understanding the role REDD+ can play in moving towards green economies.

2.2 The Forest Transition Curve

The fundamental theory behind REDD+ is to provide economic development while reducing the threat of the causes of deforestation. One approach, then, to understanding how REDD+ can succeed is to consider how it can alter the shape of the forest transition curve in developing countries (Figure 14.1). The forest transition curve is the shift from declining forest cover towards forest recovery.[16] Although the reasons why most developed countries have followed a similar curve in their economic development are varied, this has been well documented.[17]

The REDD+ mechanism, in essence, helps developing countries reach the right-hand end of the forest transition curve and achieve economic development, while avoiding the intermediate forest loss – it makes the transition shallower. Following this model, REDD+ is not a payment for avoided deforestation in perpetuity. Instead, it is a tool to move economically from one end of the forest transition curve to the other. This

---

[13] Kinzig, A.P., Perrings, C., Chapin III, F.S., Polasky, S., Smith, V.K., Tilman, D. and Turner II, B.L. 2011. "Paying for Ecosystem Services — Promise and Peril." *Science*, 334 (November), 603–4.

[14] Pfaff, A., Sills, E.O., Amacher, G.S., Coren, M.J., Lawlor, K. and Streck, C. 2010. "*Policy Impacts on Deforestation: Lessons Learned from Past Experiences to Inform New Initiatives*." Nicholas Institute.

[15] Hosonuma et al. (n 2).

[16] Rudel, T.K., Schneider, L. and Uriarte, M. 2010. "Forest Transitions: An Introduction." *Land Use Policy*, 27, 95–7.

[17] Uriarte, M., Schneider, L. and Rudel, T.K. 2010. "Synthesis: Land Transitions in the Tropics." *Biotropica*, 42(1), 59–62.

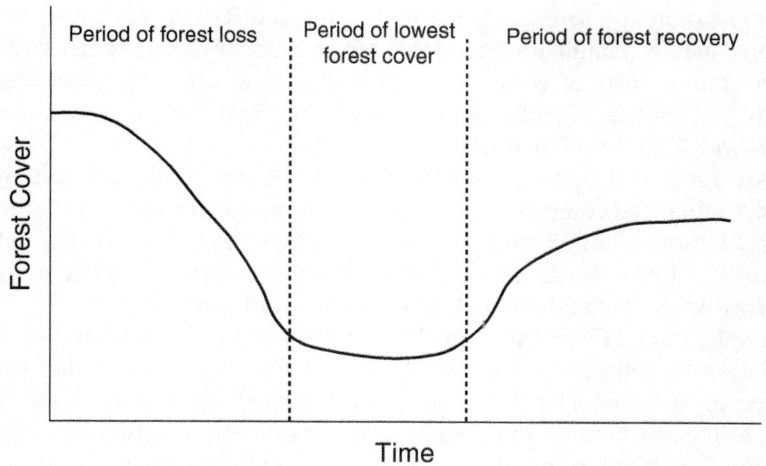

Figure 14.1 *The forest transition curve in which a country loses relative forest cover, reaches a low-point of forest cover, and then recovers forested area*

understanding of REDD+ provides a framework for analyzing how it may vary among countries and over time within the same country.

The forest transition curve can also provide a framework for understanding the UNFCCC REDD+ goal: "Parties should collectively aim to slow, halt and reverse forest cover and carbon loss, in accordance with national circumstances, consistent with the ultimate objective of the Convention, as stated in Article 2."[18] This goal, negotiated by countries, and included in the package of the 2010 Cancún Accords, suggests the global cooperation necessary to make REDD+ work. Indeed, to reach the full potential of flattening the forest transition curve of forested developing countries, a global effort will be necessary. This goal could be considered as a way to address the global aggregate forest transition curve, with all countries working towards moving economies to the right-hand side of the curve, while avoiding a low-point in global forest cover as an intermediate step.

2.3 Drivers of Deforestation

One of the purposes of REDD+ is to provide financial compensation for the lost opportunity costs of deforestation. The nature of the drivers of

---

[18] FCCC/CP/2010/7/Add.1.

deforestation and forest degradation means that REDD+ is largely competing against a number of goods traded on global markets. Therefore the opportunity costs of commodity development are homogeneously spatially distributed,[19] increasing the challenge of matching financial incentives with REDD+ outcomes.

An additional approach to addressing the drivers of deforestation, besides financial compensation, is to use international treaties or national laws. Although not all created with REDD+ in mind, there are a number of international treaties and national laws that attempt, in some way, to address some of the drivers of deforestation and forest degradation. For example, the CITES[20] can contribute to reducing deforestation and degradation by reducing the global demand for trade in species that cause forest destruction. The 2008 amendments to the United States Lacey Act can also contribute to addressing the drivers of deforestation and degradation.[21] This law prohibits the import of illegally produced forest products, thus reducing the demand for products that cause forest destruction. Finally, although the WTO is often seen as a barrier to addressing the drivers of deforestation, the organization recognizes that "members have the right to adopt trade-related measures to protect the environment."[22] Therefore, there are a number of law-based tools for addressing the drivers of deforestation which can contribute to increased ambition without requiring traditional financial payments.

2.4 The Role of Multiple Actors

Chapter 4 describes some of the opportunities and challenges associated with funding REDD+, that is considered the ambition of developed countries in creating a functional REDD+ mechanism. In many ways the ambition to fund REDD+ is likely to be tied to global ambition to address climate change. Therefore, the success of the negotiations in 2015 to develop a global agreement may be critical for REDD+ ambition from developed countries.

Incorporating REDD+, or a similar approach, into global agreements to address climate change is also important because land-use emissions are a major part of the emissions profiles of many countries.[23] Therefore,

---

19 Fisher et al. (n 3). Ahmed, S.E. and Ewers, R.M. 2012. "Spatial Pattern of Standing Timber Value across the Brazilian Amazon." *PloS One*, 7(5), e36099.

20 CITES 1973, Washington, DC.

21 Food, Conservation, and Energy Act of 2008, HR 2419.

22 http://www.wto.org/english/tratop_e/envir_e/envt_rules_intro_e.htm.

23 Land use emissions per country can be compared at faostat3.fao.org.

global mechanisms to address climate change should provide for the effective participation of those countries through effective incentives. Furthermore, specific considerations should be given for the legal and technical architecture to incorporate forest-related emissions reductions, depending on whether or not a country is receiving financial compensation for such actions.

Finally, the role of the private sector in addressing all global warming emissions needs to be considered. In sectors such as energy the connection between the private sector and emissions is direct. Although this relationship may be more difficult to make in degradation and deforestation, it is clear that, globally, most forest destruction is caused by global commodity markets for palm oil, beef, soy and wood products.[24] Therefore, ambitious REDD+ efforts must include the private sector. However, this has, to date, been a perpetual challenge for REDD+ action.[25]

There are indications that this may improve. In September 2014, 34 companies signed a statement to "cut natural forest loss in half by 2020, and strive to end it by 2030," along with efforts to restore forests, ultimately leading to a reduction of 4.5 to 8.8 billion tons of CO_2 per year.[26] This statement was also endorsed by a number of governments, civil society organizations and indigenous peoples' groups. However, this agreement was non-legally binding, and although the high-level political statement also included an action agenda, it remains to be seen if such cooperative efforts will result in changes of practice by companies. To increase the political momentum behind this announcement, the participating REDD+ countries signed the Lima Challenge in December 2014. This signaled their commitment to implementing large-scale mitigation action, and specifically indicated the emissions reductions potential they can achieve with international support.[27]

---

24 Rudel, T.K., DeFries, R., Asner, G.P. and Laurance, W.F. 2009. "Changing Drivers of Deforestation and New Opportunities in Conservation." *Conservation Biology*, 23(6), 1396–405.

25 See Chapters 10 and 12 (by Neto and Gupta, and Keenlyside et al., respectively) in this book.

26 http://www.un.org/climatechange/summit/wp-content/uploads/sites/2/2014/07/New-York-Declaration-on-Forest-—-Action-Statement-and-Action-Plan.pdf.

27 The Lima Challenge, signed by forested country signatories of the NY Declaration on Forests. Lima, Peru, December 2014.

2.5 Success as an Indicator of the Potential of Ambition

REDD+ success to date indicates that the mechanism can have an impact in reducing emissions,[28] but the fact that such activity has been concentrated in just a few countries also points to the potential for such efforts to expand and scale-up.[29]

In the Brazilian Amazon, deforestation is now 75 percent lower than the baseline.[30] The approaches to achieve emissions reductions in Brazil appear to be varied and diverse, but include legal reform, stricter enforcement of existing and new laws, interagency cooperation, differentiated licensing requirements for higher deforestation municipalities, voluntary action by the private sector, alterations in access to agricultural credit, and changes in agricultural commodity prices.[31]

2.6 Summary

As a source of global emissions, ambitiously reducing deforestation and forest degradation is critical to addressing climate change. REDD+ provides a tool to shift developing country economies away from ones that depend on forest destruction to ones in which a growing economy and financial expansion are decoupled from forest loss. This can be done by engaging the multiple actors that are part of the drivers of deforestation. As a tool that will be used by a diverse range of countries, REDD+ operationalization and implementation will need to be flexible in order to meet high ambition in this sector.

3. OPERATIONALIZATION AND IMPLEMENTATION

3.1 Early Lessons in REDD+

Having been introduced to the UNFCCC negotiations in 2007, and with the mechanism being complete in 2013, REDD+ is still a relatively new

---

[28] Boucher, D. et al. 2014. *Deforestation Success Stories: Tropical Nations where Forest Protection and Reforestation Policies have Worked.* Union of Concerned Scientists.

[29] Ibid.

[30] http://www.inpe.br/noticias/noticia.php?Cod_Noticia=3781.

[31] Boucher et al. (n 28). Assunção, J., Gandour, C.C.E. and Rocha, R. 2012. "Deforestation Slowdown in the Legal Amazon: Prices or Policies?" *Climate Policy Initiative.*

concept. Other international conservation and sustainability treaties have moved at a more rapid pace. CITES was written in 1973 and entered into force in 1975, while the Montreal Protocol was signed within 18 months of the discovery of the ozone hole. The CBD was adopted in 1992, after four years of ad hoc expert meetings on the issue. However, CITES, the Montreal Protocol and the CBD are not limited, like REDD+, by being embedded within a larger treaty. Even in these few years there are already many indications of success in REDD+. In Brazil, Guyana, Madagascar and Vietnam REDD+ programs have reduced or avoided emissions due to deforestation.[32] However, these emissions reductions have come at varying rates, and there does not appear to be any single approach or activity that can account for these successes across multiple examples.[33] Therefore, one of the major challenges to operationalization is how to incorporate adaptive management to keep moving towards scaled-up results.

3.2 Operational Challenges and Benefits of Adaptive Management

Adaptive management is a design system in which progress towards an explicit goal is iteratively assessed, and feedback loops are used to adjust approaches in order to consistently work at meeting the goal (Figure 14.2). It is an approach that has been applied to forestry and natural resource management since the late 1970s due to the uncertainty of cause and effect with actions taken across a long-term, multi-scale, multi-disciplinary approach.[34] More recently, adaptive management has been seen as a tool to link policy and implementation with natural resource management results.[35]

Operational challenges to adaptive management include:[36]

- Funding or implementation structures that do not allow for learning and adjusting.

---

32 Boucher et al. (n 28).
33 Ibid.
34 Stankey, G.H., Clark, R.N. and Bormann, B.T. 2005. "Adaptive Management of Natural Resources: Theory, Concepts, and Management Institutions." *Gen. Tech. Rep.* PNW-GTR-654. Portland (US Department of Agriculture, Forest Service, Pacific Northwest Research Station, 73 pp.).
35 Ibid.
36 Doremus, H., Andreen, W.L., Camacho, A., Farber, D.A., Glicksman, R.L., Zellmer, S.B., Jones, S. and Huang, Y. 2011. *Making Good Use of Adaptive Management*. Center for Progressive Reform White Paper #1104.

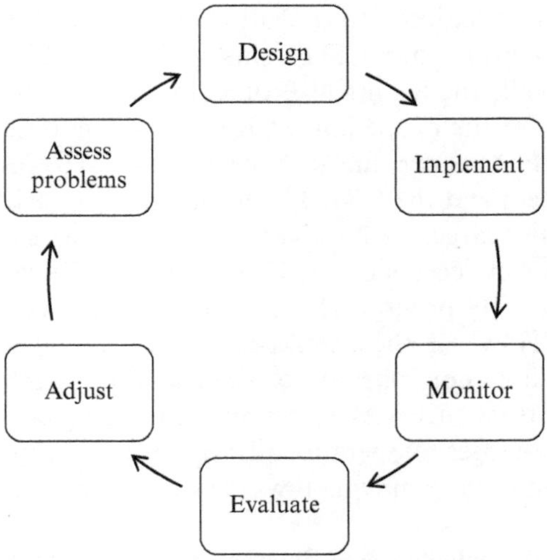

Figure 14.2 Adaptive management scheme

- Poorly framed adaptive management that can threaten management accountability.
- Adaptive management can be used as an excuse to avoid controversial or politically difficult actions.

Adaptive management is not appropriate for those aspects of REDD+ that can cause irreversible damage if not correctly operationalized from the start (i.e. social safeguards).[37] However, there are many benefits to using adaptive management. Based on early experiences in REDD+ one of the most important could be that adaptive management allows for the incorporation of a changing and improving scientific understanding over time. Adaptive management can be beneficial for addressing two of the main challenges to environmental regulation: incomplete understanding and changing systems.[38] By structuring policies to learn and evaluate progress towards achieving an agreed-upon goal, adaptive management can be an approach to reducing uncertainty in the system.[39] Doremus et al. concluded that there are three indicators of where adaptive management will be successful: (1) when there are information gaps, (2) for

[37] See Chapters 5, 6 and 7 (by Savaresi, Jodoin and Long, respectively) in this book.

[38] Doremus et al. (n 36).

[39] Ibid.

activities with good prospects of learning, and (3) when opportunities for adjustment exist.[40] The need for a flexible approach across a large range of implementing countries and the aim for continuous improvement indicate that REDD+ could be an ideal candidate for applying adaptive management.

3.3 Adaptive Management and Continuous Improvement

The principle and approach of continuous improvement, which is the fundamental basis for adaptive management, is integrated into UNFCCC REDD+ decisions. This indicates that adaptive management is an appropriate approach to operationalization. For example, the Cancún REDD+ decision "decides that [REDD+] activities undertaken by Parties . . . should be implemented in phases"[41] and

> Recognizes that the implementation of [REDD+] activities . . . including the choice of a starting phase . . . depends on the specific national circumstances, capacities and capabilities of each developing country Party and the level of support received.[42]

The Warsaw REDD+ Decision on monitoring calls for those systems to "be flexible and allow for improvement,"[43] and provides guidance for the technical assessment of reference levels to support:

> the capacity of developing country Parties for the construction and future improvements, as appropriate, to their forest reference emissions levels . . . subject to national capabilities and policy.[44]

The same decision, but in reference to MRV "encourages Parties to improve the data and methodologies used over time." Furthermore, the concept of continuous improvement also applies to operationalization of REDD+ finance. The Warsaw REDD+ decision "also recognizes the need to scale up and improve the effectiveness of finance for [REDD+] activities."[45]

---

40 Ibid.
41 FCCC/CP/2010/7/Add.1.
42 Ibid.
43 FCCC/CP/2013/10/Add.1.
44 Ibid.
45 Ibid.

3.4 Challenges to Applying Adaptive Management to REDD+

One of the main benefits of applying adaptive management is that it provides a method to address uncertainty in the face of enacting environmental policies, which is normally seen as a barrier or obstacle to operationalization of environmental regulations.[46] However, there are legal and regulatory challenges to operationalizing adaptive management. Even the more commonly used legal approach of Environmental Impact Assessments, which seek to avoid negative potential impacts of activities and use monitoring to ensure the outcomes, is not clearly grounded in international environmental law.[47] There are few domestic or international legal standards for applying adaptive management to international policies. In evaluating the legal foundation for adaptive management, Ruhl and Fischman conclude that "[the] gap between theory and practice leads to profound disparities between how agencies justify decisions and how adaptive management in practice arrives at the courthouse doorsteps."[48] However, they found three key themes by reviewing case law on adaptive management:[49]

> (1) Larger-scale plans are more likely to incorporate adaptive management plans that withstand judicial scrutiny than are smaller-scale ones; (2) the practice of tiering site-specific environmental impact analyses to an earlier, overarching, cumulative study is well suited to adaptive management, and adaptive management can reduce the need for supplemental analyses; and (3) adaptive management procedures, no matter how finely crafted, cannot substitute for showing that a plan will meet substantive management criteria required by law.

In addition to legal issues, there are other limitations and challenges to adaptive management. Doremus et al. state that:[50]

> Documented instances of successful adaptive management of public resources are rare. Funding structures and agency cultures often stand in the way of learning. Furthermore, unless carefully designed, adaptive management programs threaten management accountability and can be used to avoid politically controversial limits on economic activity.

Controversy and risks associated with adaptive management include perceptions that it does not provide sufficient regulatory certainty, that

---

46 Vinuales, J.E. 2010. "Scientific Uncertainty and Environmental Law." *Vanderbilt Journal of Transnational Law*, 43, 437.

47 Ibid.

48 Ruhl and Fischman (n 4).

49 Ibid.

50 Doremus et al. (n 36).

it places too much open-ended discretion in the hands of managers, that it falls short of the scientific ideal it is based upon, and that it can be used as an excuse to delay.[51] The last of these risks is especially critical for REDD+, where another challenge to adaptive management includes incentivizing countries to scale-up and move along the phases of REDD+ implementation to continue to work towards the collective goal.

Based on case studies from the United States, Doreumus et al. suggest the following best practices to adaptive management: (1) tailor the strategy to the problem; (2) ensure accountability and enforceability; (3) promote directed learning; and (4) ensure sufficient funding.[52]

3.5 The Role of a Global Goal in Successful Adaptive Management

One of the fundamental characteristics of adaptive management is consistent re-evaluation against the goal or purpose of actions, and having a clear goal appears to be a critical aspect of successful adaptive management.[53] The Cancún REDD+ decision provides a starting point for setting a global goal for REDD+, where Parties affirmed that they "should collectively aim to slow, halt and reverse forest cover and carbon loss, in accordance with national circumstances, consistent with the ultimate objective of the Convention, as stated in Article 2."[54] However, under the UNFCCC there is no mechanism to ensure that such a goal is being met through an evaluation of progress.

3.6 The FCPF: an Example of Adaptive Management in REDD+ Governance

Regardless of the legal gaps and scant international experiences in adaptive management, there is still interest in applying it to REDD+. The FCPF of the World Bank is a global partnership of governments, businesses, civil society and indigenous peoples that has created a REDD+ mechanism with two funding windows – one for capacity building and readiness, and another to pay for performance. The FCPF has attempted to operationalize adaptive management in its REDD+ approach. Its monitoring and evaluation framework includes adaptive management for both the facility level (the function of the fund) and at the country and

---

51 Ibid., p. 3, p. 5.
52 Ibid.
53 Ibid.
54 FCCC/CP/2010/7/Add.1.

pilot level.[55] However, this framework was only adopted in March 2013, so it remains to be seen how this approach requesting adaptive management is implemented.

3.7 Opportunities for Financing

Over the past few years, political will has moved away from using carbon markets as the primary source of funding for REDD+, and has instead focused on how policies can provide the capacity for the private sector to engage in reducing their impact on deforestation.[56] This may impact REDD+ in terms of making a closer link between those parties associated with the drivers of deforestation and their role in financing implementation. However, to date the private sector has only contributed to 0.1 percent of REDD+ financial commitments.[57]

There are numerous legal challenges to creating carbon-trading markets that include REDD+ offsets. For example, although lawmakers in California have created provisions within their cap and trade system to purchase REDD offsets, they have yet to implement these. A concern is that as a subnational entity it has limited international agreement capabilities and therefore limited capacity for enforcement in the REDD jurisdiction. The REDD Offsets Working Group of California concluded that:

> Any linkage arrangement that operates as a binding agreement or resembles any treaty as understood under public international law would run afoul of constitutional provisions in Brazil, Mexico, and the United States that prohibit states from entering into such agreements.[58]

An analysis of REDD+ financial flows to 14 different REDD+ countries found that US$7.3 billion had been pledged to REDD+ efforts by 2015, but substantially less has been tracked to providing implementation within REDD+ countries.[59] In addition to difficulties in tracking financing, addressing information gaps can reduce duplication of financing efforts,

---

[55] FCPF. 2013. *Carbon Fund Methodological Framework.*

[56] Boucher, D. and Elias, P. 2013. "From REDD to Deforestation-Free Supply Chains: The Persistent Problem of Leakage and Scale." *Carbon Management*, 4(5), 473–5.

[57] Canby et al. (n 5). The authors note that information on private sector REDD+ financing is difficult to obtain.

[58] Johnson, E. 2013. *California, Acre and Chiapas: Partnering to Reduce Emissions from Tropical Deforestation.* REDD Offsets Working Group.

[59] Ibid. As of 2012, 32 percent of committed funds for REDD+ have been disbursed.

lead to better understanding of the need for financial contributions, provide information on self-financing from REDD+ countries, and generate evidence of how REDD+ financing has been used and if there has been successful implementation in reducing deforestation.

3.8 Flattening the Forest Transition Curve through a Flexible Mechanism

The forest transition curve, the shift from declining forest cover towards forest recovery (Figure 14.1),[60] can be used to model the trend that many countries follow as they develop economically.[61] Therefore, one of the goals of REDD+ can be to change the shape of the curve, essentially making it flatter, while achieving economic development in tropical forest countries. This link between the goal of reducing forest loss and economic growth has legal implications for REDD+ implementation, including the need to evaluate performance at appropriate time scales and the legal frameworks that provide the opportunity to change economic growth paradigms.

Each country's forest transition is likely to be somewhat different, and experiences to date point to the need for domestic flexibility in order to implement REDD+ appropriately within the many contexts where it could work to shift the forest transition curve.[62] As REDD+ continues to gain momentum outside of the UNFCCC, there are multiple levels and locations at which fragmentation may occur. This could be due to multiple rules (i.e. UNFCCC, CBD, FCPF) or multiple implementing agencies (i.e. World Bank, various ministries, etc.). Ensuring that they are following a common set of guidelines, even though they have different governance structures, goals, and approaches, will be difficult, but important for avoiding fragmentation.[63]

3.9 Summary

Adaptive management, a system for iteratively assessing whether actions are achieving a specific goal, can be used to operationalize REDD+ in a way that still provides flexibility at the local level. There is a basis for such an approach in the many references to continuous improvement in the REDD+ UNFCCC decisions. However, there are many challenges to

---

60 Rudel et al. (n 16).
61 Uriarte et al. (n 17).
62 Boucher et al. (n 28).
63 See chapters 3 and 4 (by van Asselt and McDermott, and Young, respectively) in this book.

putting into place the legal and policy frameworks for adaptive management, and little evidence from operationalization that such an approach will be feasible for REDD+. Still, policymakers, such as those at the World Bank FCPF, are interested in applying this approach to REDD+.

As an international mechanism that needs to balance national flexibility with global environmental integrity, an operational approach of adaptive management can be used to structure REDD+ implementation and help countries flatten their forest transition curves as they develop economically.

4. CONCLUSIONS

Ambitiously reducing emissions from tropical deforestation and degradation is a global responsibility, and can contribute to addressing climate change and meeting the ultimate objective of the UNFCCC Convention. At the same time, REDD+ can help developing countries achieve economic development without following the traditional forest transition curve. Instead, paying for REDD+ performance can "flatten" the forest transition curve so that forests are conserved and the drivers of deforestation are decoupled from economic growth. Achieving such ambition will require the participation of multiple actors, including the private sector.

Although it is still a relatively new concept, and there have been challenges to producing and paying for results, recent successes in REDD+ provide the promise that ambition can be rekindled through flexible approaches and adequate financing.

A certain level of flexibility in REDD+ can provide the opportunity for the mechanism to be operationalized under a variety of different country circumstances, while still meeting some specific guidelines to ensure the validity of the results and that they have met required safeguards. An adaptive management loop approach could be used to guide such flexible operationalization and implementation. In the case of REDD+ the agreement among UNFCCC Parties to "collectively aim to slow, halt and reverse forest cover and carbon loss" from the Cancún Accords could be used as the goal to measure REDD+ against in the adaptive management loop. Furthermore, the idea of continuous improvement, fundamental to adaptive management, is already integrated into various UNFCCC REDD+ decisions. Such an approach, however, presents legal challenges. Although adaptive management recently has been seen as a tool to link policy and implementation with natural resource management results, there is little international legal foundation for such an approach.

Identifying and applying appropriate financing is also necessary for achieving ambitious emissions reductions from REDD+. In a flexible mechanism this could lead to using a large number of financial sources for implementation, which could lead to fragmentation. Therefore, efforts to reduce the variability among the guidelines of financial mechanisms – even if they have different governance structures – can be important for reducing fragmentation.

Existing UNFCCC decisions provide the foundation for REDD+ operationalization and implementation, although as a mechanism designed globally but applied locally it will not be without its challenges. Still, there is reason to expect that REDD+ can play an ambitious role in addressing the global climate challenge.

15. Adjudicating disputes across scales: global administrative law considerations for REDD+

*Kristen Hite**[1]

1. INTRODUCTION

Climate change requires global collaboration across any number of political, cultural and geographic boundaries. REDD+ is no exception: by integrating REDD+ into international efforts to address climate change, the global community now can incentivize efforts to capture more of the carbon stored in trees on faraway lands. National and local property laws, customary rights, international standards and obligations, and REDD-specific policies all influence who benefits from and has rights to forest carbon. In a perfectly governed world, these norms are all consistent and clear. But this is rarely the case, as each set of norms has its own system of rule-making and adjudicating disputes. Conflicts arise regarding who has rights to carbon and the forest on which it is dependent, exacerbated by implementation across scales and political boundaries. This chapter offers a global administrative law perspective to explore avenues to address various disputes that can arise out of competing claims to forests and the carbon they contain.

The two core functions of administrative law are rule-making and adjudication. Rule-making is the process of standard setting and application of norms at the institutional level. Adjudication is the process of applying and enforcing these institutional norms. At the international level, these two functions become slightly more complicated because they

* All websites cited in this chapter were accessed on 1 October 2015.

[1] The author is grateful to the Center for International Environmental Law, Rainforest Foundation Norway, and the Forest Carbon, Markets and Communities Program for USAID, for commissioning the following papers and authorizing their incorporation into this chapter: *A Complaint Mechanism for REDD+*, Rainforest Foundation Norway and Center for International Environmental Law (2011); and *Tenure Rights, Human Rights and REDD+: Knowledge, Skills and Tools for Effective Results, USAID-supported Forest Carbon Markets and Communities (FCMC) Program*, Washington, DC (2014).

operate both independently from and under the umbrella of treaty-based obligations. Many international institutions are created by treaty and thus have mandates limited to their authorized scope but also enjoy sovereign immunity, making the interplay between treaty-based obligations of nation States and the authorizing treaties of international institutions a challenging one to navigate.

Effective REDD+ implementation may require engaging various agencies, countries and actors across scales, which can create both explicit and implicit conflicts in choice of law as well as the venue for addressing disputes. In order to navigate this complexity, we consider both the standards and dispute resolution options available under various REDD+ regimes.

If properly implemented, REDD+ activities will not only benefit indigenous and other forest-dependent communities, but will also protect forest ecosystems and effectively reduce carbon emissions; however, if poorly implemented, REDD+ activities have the potential to disrupt forests and those who depend upon them, in addition to risks associated with carbon emissions. Moreover, recognizing that forests rarely lack inhabitants, REDD+ activities often occur on lands pertaining to indigenous and other forest-dependent communities. When these communities and the climate all benefit, REDD+ can be a success at the international level. But when there are trade-offs, it may require working across the international, national, local, community and potentially even household scales.

Because REDD+ interfaces the local and global scales by design, a cross-jurisdictional mechanism capable of addressing disputes related to carbon, rights, livelihoods and ecosystems can contribute to successful REDD+ outcomes. A complaint mechanism provides an opportunity to remedy situations and avoid undesired or unintended outcomes such as negative social and environmental impacts. The scope of complaints could include impacts on, inter alia, forest resources and associated lands, forest-dependent livelihoods, environment, just processes, legal and institutional frameworks, and misappropriation/abuse of funds.

To establish an objective basis for considering complaints, it is helpful to identify the obligations, rules and standards applicable to REDD+ activities. After that, we can consider options for resolving disputes based on the constellation of applicable obligations that apply to any given REDD+ activity.

2. REDD+ NORMS

This section considers obligations at these various scales to help scope the legal and political frameworks that underpin dispute settlement considerations for REDD+. The Parties to the UNFCCC have agreed on rules, methodologies and modalities for forest countries to take action to reduce deforestation and associated emissions. Funds and institutions beyond the UNFCCC are also used to support countries to develop and implement their own approaches to REDD+. As such, the policy framework for REDD+ is grounded in UNFCCC rules and supplemented by specific institutional policies and procedures as well as national and international law. A number of these rules and policies pertain to forest rights (see Table 15.1).

At the UNFCCC meetings in 2007, Parties to the UNFCCC affirmed that "the needs of local and indigenous communities should be addressed when action is taken to reduce emissions from deforestation and forest degradation in developing countries."[2] By 2010, countries better defined the scope of REDD+ measures, agreed they should "fully respect human rights" in all climate-related actions, and included a set of safeguards specific to REDD+. Parties also launched the development of safeguard policies and a complaint mechanism for all activities (not just REDD+) financed by the GCF. For REDD+ specifically, countries agreed that national REDD+ strategies or action plans should address land tenure issues, gender considerations, and promote and support safeguards including respecting indigenous and community rights and international obligations. By 2013, countries had adopted a more comprehensive series of decisions including a requirement to report on how these safeguards are being addressed and respected prior to accessing any results-based finance for REDD+.

Bilaterally and nationally, the policy framework for REDD+ varies, although all countries have agreed to the REDD+ framework adopted through the various UNFCCC decisions. With respect to rights, this requires promoting, supporting and providing information on safeguards, including that REDD+ actions "complement or are consistent with . . . relevant international conventions and agreements," and respect for rights and the full participation of indigenous peoples and local communities (including by taking into account international and national obligations). And while the particular instruments vary depending on the country, all countries are party to at least some international human rights treaties relevant to REDD+.

While the specific legal and policy framework that applies to a REDD+ activity will depend in part on the country, funding, activities and institutions involved, nearly all international organizations and national governments have policies and laws in place that support international obligations

[2] UNFCCC Decision 2/CP.13, chapeau.

Table 15.1 The various sources, types and actors supporting rights related to REDD+

	Tenure rights	Human rights
Sources: Statutory	National law • Constitution • Laws • Common law	Treaties • Conventions, covenants, protocols • Any other binding global, regional, or bilateral agreement where at least one State is a Party
Customary	Administrative decisions • Regulations • Licenses	International institutions and donor agencies • Operational policies • Finance agreements
	Traditional use	Customary international law
Types	"Bundle of rights": • Access • Withdrawal • Exclusion • Alienation • Management Authority to sanction	Procedural • Access to information, transparency • Decision-making, participation, consultation/consent • Access to justice and remedy Substantive • Equitable access and benefits • Cultural: non-discrimination, religion, traditional knowledge, territories, livelihoods • Natural resources: lands, territories, resources, access to food, water, ecosystems
Rights holders	Private • Collective/commons • Individuals • Companies Public • State-owned • State-managed	Individuals Groups and cultures • Indigenous, tribal, minorities • Women, youth, elders
Duty bearers	National Governments (primary duty bearers)	
	Subnational actors • Jurisdictional authorities • Local authorities • Community authorities	Transnational actors • International organizations • Donors • Private sector companies and project developers • NGOs

affirming the rights of indigenous peoples and local communities. As such, it helps to understand what conventions, agreements, and national and international obligations could apply in this context. These can be broken down into tenure rights and human rights (both procedural and substantive), described in more detail below.

2.1 Tenure Rights

Tenure rights derive from multiple sources. They may be granted as statutory rights through the power of the State as sovereign and ascribed in constitutions, laws and regulations or enforced through common law as decided by the courts. They may also derive from customary rights based on traditional or historic use – often by distinct cultures, communities or other specific groups. Customary rights may or may not be recognized by the State, but they may still exist and are often affirmed under international law – human rights law in particular. Owing to these different sources, tenure rights holders (including governments, individuals groups, collectives, etc.) may enjoy only partial, occasionally overlapping, or sometimes more complete rights to access, use and own forest resources.

Carbon rights and benefit-sharing rights are related to tenure rights. First, trees store and sequester carbon, so holders of rights to trees (either as land or as forest resources, depending on the specific legal framework for the area) may also have some rights to carbon or to the benefits associated with carbon sequestration. However, the precise relationship between tenure, carbon rights and benefit-sharing may depend on contractual agreements and underlying rights holders (such as whether/how carbon rights holders are recognized in relation to forest rights holders), as well as the source of the rights.

2.2 International Obligations

Regardless of the implementing agency, REDD+ activities must meet certain international obligations, including human rights treaties and other relevant international instruments that apply to the countries in which the REDD+ activities occur. Customary international law may also be relevant to a State that is not a Party to a particular human rights treaty, although virtually all rights relevant to REDD+ are reflected in one or several broadly applicable human rights treaties.

Human rights can be both procedural and substantive. Procedural rights generally relate to inputs into decision-making, and include access to information, access to and transparency of proceedings, the right to be consulted or consent to decisions that may affect certain rights holders, and access to justice. Substantive rights pertain more to outcomes and underlying interests and include, e.g., cultural, spiritual and natural resource rights (including forest ecosystems).

Sources of human rights include State-negotiated treaties, as well as customary international law, the latter of which has a similar legal status as treaties even if not explicitly codified. For example, many provisions of the Universal Declaration of Human Rights are widely respected by States and treated as legal obligations even though declarations approved by the UN General Assembly are not in themselves legally binding. Additionally, some instruments serve to explain how rights protections apply to specific groups. UNDRIP is one example.

International instruments enumerate and support various human rights relevant to REDD+ activities, including rights related to identity, due process, property, and protection of life and livelihoods. Many of these instruments have specific provisions guaranteeing protection of specific rights, while others contain broader language supporting these rights. While the specific obligations may vary depending on a particular instrument and/or country, international instruments generally support the following rights applicable to REDD+: self-determination; culture; religion; non-discrimination; access to effective remedies; access to justice; participation and prior and informed consent in decision-making; access to information; life, livelihood, an adequate standard of living, and health; property, land, territories and natural resources; work; and the right to a healthy environment/sustainable development.

All of these rights are recognized and protected by a variety of international agreements relevant to REDD+. For example, at least 13 instruments refer to the right to culture, including the ICESCR, ICCPR, ICERD, ILO Convention 169, UNDRIP and the CBD.[3] At least 11 instruments support the right to participation in decision-making, including ICCPR, ICERD, ILO Convention 160, UNDRIP and CBD.[4] No fewer than nine

---

[3] Seven other global instruments supporting the right to culture include the following: Universal Declaration of Human Rights; Convention Concerning the Protection of the World Cultural and Natural Heritage; Convention for the Safeguarding of the Intangible Cultural Heritage; Universal Declaration on Cultural Diversity; Convention on the Protection and Promotion of the Diversity of Cultural Expressions; Convention on the Rights of the Child; and Convention on the Elimination of All Forms of Discrimination against Women.

[4] Six other global instruments supporting the right to participation in decision-making include the following: Universal Declaration of Human Rights; Convention for the Safeguarding of the Intangible Cultural Heritage; Universal Declaration on Cultural Diversity; Convention on the Protection and Promotion of the Diversity of Cultural Expressions; Convention on the Rights of the Child;

agreements refer to the principle of non-discrimination,[5] and seven core global human rights instruments support each of the following rights: religion and sacred sites;[6] access to justice;[7] and access to information.[8]

Land-related rights implicated by REDD+ initiatives include: protection against illegal displacement; protection of the right to lands, territories and resources; recognition of legal personality of tribes, communities and other traditional collectives as indigenous peoples; and respect for FPIC. Many REDD-related policies generally call for protection of the rights of indigenous and other local communities; however, few provide specific measures to ensure that these rights are respected and protected.

Closely related to indigenous and other local communities' authority to decide how land is used are procedural rights implicated by REDD+. Such rights include the following: access to information regarding REDD+ activities; full and effective public participation in decision-making processes (including FPIC where appropriate); consideration and mitigation of adverse social and environmental impacts; and access to justice, which requires national legal and institutional frameworks that effectively protect rights, livelihoods and ecosystems.

To successfully implement REDD+ activities, considering the economic, social and cultural rights of indigenous peoples and forest-dependent communities includes measures supporting the equitable distribution of

---

and Convention on the Elimination of All Forms of Discrimination against Women.

[5] The following global human rights instruments reference the principle of non-discrimination: Universal Declaration of Human Rights; ICESCR; ICCPR; ICERD; ILO Convention 169; UNDRIP; Convention on the Protection and Promotion of the Diversity of Cultural Expressions; Convention on the Rights of the Child; and Convention on the Elimination of All Forms of Discrimination against Women.

[6] The following global human rights instruments reference the right to religion and sacred sites: Universal Declaration of Human Rights; ICESCR; ICCPR; ICERD; ILO Convention 169; UNDRIP; and Convention on the Rights of the Child.

[7] The right of access to justice is referenced by these global human rights instruments: Universal Declaration of Human Rights; ICCPR; ICERD; ILO Convention 169; UNDRIP; Convention on the Rights of the Child; and Convention on the Elimination of All Forms of Discrimination against Women.

[8] The following seven global instruments refer to the right of access to information: CBD; UNDRIP; Convention Concerning the Protection of the World Cultural and Natural Heritage; Convention for the Safeguarding of the Intangible Cultural Heritage; Universal Declaration on Cultural Diversity; Convention on the Protection and Promotion of the Diversity of Cultural Expressions; and Convention on the Rights of the Child.

benefits resulting from REDD+ projects, and protection of traditional forest-dependent lifestyles. The widespread international support of the rights to culture, religion and sacred sites also helps to guarantee protection of the property rights of communities to the lands and resources, as cultural and religious practices often coincide with territory that communities inhabit.[9]

2.3 National Obligations

Many countries have adopted a wide range of international human rights conventions and other international agreements that affirm basic human rights for all, with additional protections for specific groups such as indigenous peoples and women. In many signatory countries, national law and policies may also support these rights; however, domestic implementation of these rights may be uneven. Countries frequently maintain national policies and legislation on these and other rights, such as regulations supporting land and resource tenure rights. Government agencies, international organizations and private actors may apply administrative rules, policies and procedures related to some of the rights-related standards applicable to REDD+.

Respecting nationally and internationally recognized rights helps enable REDD-related decisions that are fair and equitable, and supported and implemented by those with direct access to forest resources. Because States have a primary obligation to protect human rights, as well as an obligation to provide recourse to vulnerable groups, it is important to consider the adequacy of both international- and national-level processes to respect and protect rights. In many cases, a need arises for some form of complaint mechanism capable of hearing claims of violations of rights so as to ensure that REDD+ activities do not jeopardize fundamental rights to life, lands, territories, resources, culture, livelihood and just processes.

---

[9] The link between the rights to culture, religion and sacred sites, and ownership and use of land and natural resources is exemplified in UNDRIP Article 25, which requires States Parties to respect the right of indigenous peoples to "their distinctive spiritual relationship with their traditionally owned or otherwise occupied and used lands, territories, waters and coastal seas and other resources." UNDRIP art. 25. All but seven REDD participants (Colombia, Kenya, Equatorial Guinea, Ethiopia, Papua New Guinea, Uganda and Vanuatu) voted in favour of UNDRIP, demonstrating the widespread support of the relationship between these three rights among REDD countries. For specific information on the instruments and related obligations, see Annex A.

2.4 Institutional Standards

As the foundational decisions for REDD+ were being negotiated and developed at the UNFCCC, multilateral, bilateral and national initiatives emerged to provide support to countries interested in developing REDD+ programmes, plans and activities. These programmes have their own legal and policy frameworks, which vary in the degree to which they explicitly include rights and tenure considerations. For example, the FCPF and Forest Investment Programme have separate charters and policies that reference the rights of indigenous peoples and forest communities, and apply broader institutional safeguards (the specifics of which depend in part on the implementing partner). The FCPF Charter clearly mandates compliance with the World Bank's Operational Policies and Procedures, "taking into account the need for effective participation of Forest-Dependent Indigenous Peoples and Forest Dwellers in decisions that may affect them, respecting their rights under national law and applicable international obligations."[10]

Meanwhile, the FAO, UNDP and UNEP combined efforts for the UN-REDD. UN-REDD's programme documents affirm the commitment to a rights-based approach that respects international obligations and the rights of indigenous peoples and forest-dependent communities, and include detailed guidance notes on topics such as FPIC. Additionally, UN-REDD and FCPF have published joint guidelines on stakeholder engagement. Combined, these multilateral initiatives cover over 60 countries implementing REDD+ programmes.

3. ADJUDICATION

Where disputes arise, rights holders may utilize available recourse mechanisms to advance rights, resolve disputes and remedy violations in order to facilitate meaningful, equitable and legal outcomes. Many of these are discussed below. There are often multiple venues available to address a complaint. Clear identification of the source of the rights helps in navigating remedy options in the event of overlapping claims or alleged rights violations. Many of the treaties and institutional policies and procedures described in subsequent sections specify at least one means for resolving disputes, and their identification should be a part of the process of identifying the legal and institutional framework described above.

---

[10] FCPF Charter Section 3.1(d).

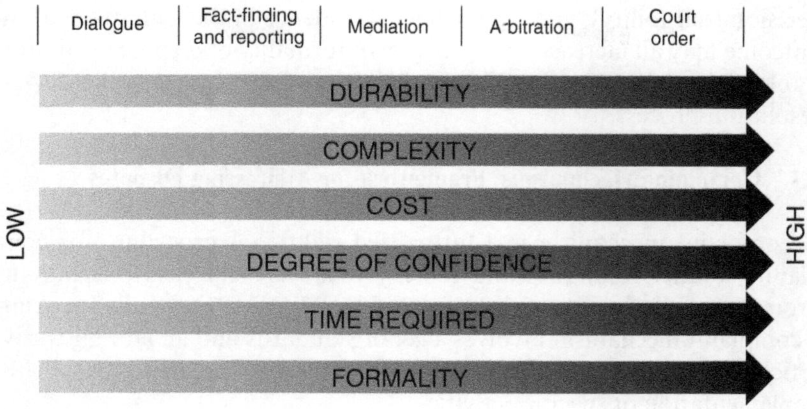

Figure 15.1 The spectrum of possibilities to address and resolve disputes, ranging from informal discussions to binding, enforceable decisions

Judicial and non-judicial mechanisms at scales ranging from the project to international can help resolve disputes related to tenure and human rights. While tenure rights tend to be addressed at the national or sub-national level and human rights may more frequently rise to the international level, it is important to consider the most appropriate forum on a case-by-case basis. The selection of the best venue for a particular case will depend on many factors, including the degree of conflict and complexity associated with resolving a dispute and the likelihood that Parties will be able to come to a facilitated agreement among themselves or whether they need to depend on a third party to adjudicate their dispute.

Given the different scales of activities affecting rights, mechanisms may be available at various levels to assert and help remedy rights.

The level of formality of these dispute resolution mechanisms varies, and disputes may transition between mechanisms – e.g. an ombudsman or grievance mechanism may be used initially before a dispute rises to more formal judicial complaints. Generally speaking, disputes may be easier to resolve in venues that are less formal (non-judicial) and more geographically specific (project/community level). However, in some cases disputes may be more complex, or there may be political barriers to effective resolution. In these cases, rights holders may prefer to present a claim to a more formal body or one with broader geographic jurisdiction. Where multiple venues are available to hear a dispute, considerations such as time, complexity, the reversibility or permanence of the decision (durability), and widely held confidence in the legitimacy of the outcome may all increase with the level of formality of dispute resolution. Table 15.2 presents some of the considerations for the format of a dispute resolution process.

3.1 Complaint Mechanisms: Framework for Addressing Disputes

A complaint mechanism is a formalized right to a procedure for complaint, conflict resolution and remedy that can help ensure rights and protect ecosystems potentially impacted by REDD+. Generally speaking, a complaint mechanism involves a set of standards and an administrative office, which determines whether those standards are being met in the implementation of specific activities.

International complaint mechanisms exist in many different forms, including fact-finding panels, tribunals, compensatory commissions and mediation offices. While national legal systems maintain any number of courts to address legal matters on a case-specific basis, the availability, costs, limited jurisdiction and procedural requirements for bringing a court case may not always provide an effective or timely solution to REDD-related complaints. A specialized international office to hear REDD+ complaints not effectively addressed or resolved at the national level can help the global REDD+ regime function in a more timely and efficient manner. The functions of a complaint mechanism can include fact-finding, advising, compliance assessment, dispute resolution, provision of remedy and award compensation.

3.2 Principles for an Effective Complaint Mechanism

A primary objective of a complaint mechanism for REDD+ is to avoid adverse impacts of REDD-related decisions and actions taken at the international, national and project/community level. This mechanism should be capable of effectively addressing international obligations that apply to the design, implementation and monitoring of REDD+ policies and programmes. An effective complaint mechanism should also have the authority to consider procedural violations at every level of decision-making – international, national, subnational and community – that could contribute to adverse impacts of REDD+ initiatives.

The 2008 Report of the Special Representative of the Secretary-General on the issue of human rights and transnational corporations and other business enterprises (hereinafter "Ruggie's Report") describes six principles for non-judicial grievance mechanisms: legitimacy,

Table 15.2 Examples of dispute resolution options at different scales of REDD+ implementation

	Project/ community	Jurisdiction	Country	Regional	International
Judicial	Community or municipality, and in some cases national courts (e.g., constitutional issues) may provide forum	Provincial or federal court	Specialized, constitutional or national court	Inter-American and African Courts of Human Rights; European Court of Justice	International Court of Justice
Non-judicial	Ombudsman Hearing at a provincial agency or office		National agency or office (e.g., National REDD+ Committee); national human rights contact point	African Commission on Human Rights; NAFTA; Commission for Environmental Cooperation – Submissions on Enforcement Matters; Aarhus Compliance Committee	World Bank Inspection Panel Committee on the Elimination of all forms of Racial Discrimination; UN Human Rights Council

accessibility, predictability, equitability, rights-compatibility and transparency.[11]

To evaluate options for a complaint mechanism, it is important to understand the six principles of an effective complaint mechanism, which Ruggie describes as follows:

- Legitimacy requires "clear, transparent and sufficiently independent governance structures to ensure that no party to a particular grievance process can interfere with the fair conduct of that process."[12] This means that a complaint mechanism should be governed by an independent body free of political influence, and should operate in a transparent manner based on clear procedures. As Ruggie warns, problems may arise if an actor is both defendant and judge.[13]
- Accessibility means that a "mechanism must be publicized to those who may wish to access it and provide adequate assistance for aggrieved parties who may face barriers to access, including lan-

[11] Report of the Special Representative of the Secretary-General on the issue of human rights and transnational corporations and other business enterprises, 7 April 2008, available at http://www.reports-and-materials.org/Ruggie-report-7-Apr-2008.pdf, at paras. 92–5. In the conclusion of the 2010 Report, the Special Representative undertook to provide a set of guiding principles for the operationalization of the framework, which could prove instructive to operationalization of the above-mentioned principles. See Report of the Special Representative of the Secretary-General on the issue of human rights and transnational corporations and other business enterprises, 9 April 2010, available at http://www reports-and-materials.org/Ruggie-report-2010.pdf, at para. 124. The 2009 and 2010 Reports summarized a seventh consideration – that a company or project-level mechanism should "operate[] through dialogue and engagement rather than the company itself acting as adjudicator." See Report of the Special Representative of the Secretary-General on the issue of human rights and transnational corporations and other business enterprises, 22 April 2009, para. 99 and Report of the Special Representative of the Secretary-General on the issue of human rights and transnational corporations and other business enterprises, 9 April 2010, available at http://www.reports-and-materials.org/Ruggie-report-2010.pdf, at para. 94; see also Report of the Special Representative of the Secretary-General on the issue of human rights and transnational corporations and other business enterprises, 7 April 2008, available at http://www reports-and-materials.org/Ruggie-report-7-Apr-2008.pdf, at paras. 92–5; http://www2.ohchr.org/english/bodies/hrcouncil/docs/11session/A.HRC.11.13.pdf (collectively, "Ruggie's Reports").

[12] Report of the Special Representative of the Secretary-General on the issue of human rights and transnational corporations and other business enterprises, 7 April 2008, para. 92, available at http://www.reports-and-materials.org/Ruggie-report-7-Apr-2008.pdf.

[13] Ibid. at para. 95.11.

guage, literacy, awareness, finance, distance, or fear of reprisal."[14] With respect to the potential actors involved in a REDD+ complaint, accessibility is crucial, particularly for complainants, including members of local communities and indigenous peoples. Unless information is widely disseminated in an understandable language and in a culturally sensitive manner as an early part of REDD+ readiness activities, it is very likely that potential complainants will not be able to access the complaint mechanism.

- Predictability requires "a clear and known procedure with a time frame for each stage and clarity on the types of process and outcome it can (and cannot) offer, as well as a means of monitoring the implementation of any outcome."[15] Predictability is particularly challenging for some of the issues that could form the subject of REDD+ complaints. Property disputes, for example, may take years – in some cases decades or longer – to resolve. In those cases where disputes are not easily resolved, it may be that the principle of predictability would encourage specific time limits to consider and address a complaint.
- Equitability means that a "mechanism must ensure that aggrieved parties have reasonable access to sources of information, advice and expertise necessary to engage in a grievance process on fair and equitable terms."[16] It is important to recognize that international actors may be more familiar with international processes than the local communities or indigenous peoples whose lands may be impacted by REDD-related activities. With respect to the emerging REDD+ regime, there may be significant disparities between the amount of information and expertise available to the different actors. An effective complaint mechanism should be aware of these disparities, identify those cases in which these asymmetries disadvantage local communities, and where appropriate, provide additional resources to help address the equitability concerns.
- Rights-compatibility requires that "a mechanism must ensure that its outcomes and remedies accord with internationally recognized human rights standards."[17] Considering the human rights obligations related to REDD+, it is clear that human rights standards are critical to the issues contemplated for consideration by a complaint mechanism.

---

14 Ibid. at para. 92.
15 Ibid.
16 Ibid.
17 Ibid.

- Transparency means that "a mechanism must provide sufficient transparency of process and outcome to meet the public interest concerns at stake and should presume transparency wherever possible; non-State mechanisms in particular should be transparent about the receipt of complaints and the key elements of their outcomes."[18]

A rights-based approach under an international system could be seen to include an obligation by donor governments or governments housing corporations or other private actors engaged in REDD-related activities to provide access to a remedy. Several key international human rights instruments and processes already support the right to an "effective remedy," which is a central element of a complaint mechanism. These treaties include ICCPR,[19] ICESCR,[20] ICERD,[21] ILO Convention 169[22] and the African Charter on Human and Peoples' Rights.[23] We can use these principles to evaluate the different options available for a complaint mechanism.

Application of these principles to REDD+ can help determine whether

---

[18] Ibid.

[19] ICCPR art. 2.3 (requiring States Parties to ensure the right to "an effective remedy," to be "determined by competent judicial, administrative or legislative authorities or by any other competent authority provided for by the legal system of the State," and to "have a decision in their favor enforced").

[20] ICESCR, opened for signature 19 December 1966, 993 UNTS 3, available at https://treaties.un.org/doc/Publication/UNTS/Volume%20993/v993.pdf at 3; see also *State Obligations to Provide Access to Remedy for Human Rights Abuses by Third Parties, Including Business: An Overview of International and Regional Provisions, Commentary and Decisions*, UN Doc. A/HRC/11/13/Add.1 (15 May 2009) at 92 (interpreting Article 2.1 of the ICESCR as implying the obligation to provide access to an effective remedy in the obligation of States "to take steps . . . [toward] achieving progressively the full realization of the rights recognized in the present Covenant by all appropriate means"); *Business and Human Rights: The Evolving International Agenda*, Corporate Social Responsibility Initiative Working Paper No. 38 (June 2007), at 23, available at http://www.hks harvard.edu/m-rcbg/CSRI/publications/workingpaper_38_ruggie.pdf.

[21] ICERD art. 6 (requiring Parties to provide "effective protection and remedies, through the competent national tribunals and other State institutions" for violations of the Convention).

[22] See ILO 169 art. 4 (requiring the adoption of special measures by States Parties to safeguard the rights of indigenous and tribal peoples, and noting further that arts. 15 and 16 contain several provisions relating to compensation for harm suffered through exploration, or use of resources, on indigenous and tribal peoples' lands).

[23] The African Commission has interpreted the African Charter on Human Rights to require remedies at the national level to be "available, effective and sufficient." *State Obligations to Provide Access to Remedy for Human Rights Abuses by Third Parties, Including Business: An Overview of International and*

BOX 15.1 WHAT IS A COMPLAINT MECHANISM? EXAMPLE: COMPLIANCE ADVISOR/ OMBUDSMAN

As the complaint mechanism for projects supported by the International Finance Corporation (IFC) and Multilateral Investment Guarantee Agency (MIGA), the Compliance Advisor/Ombudsman (CAO) of the World Bank Group addresses complaints by people affected by the social and environmental impacts of IFC and MIGA projects, whether or not there is an allegation of a violation of policies or procedures. The office first uses its ombudsman function to see whether a complaint can be resolved collaboratively, and if not, may use its compliance function to assess whether the IFC (or MIGA) violated its own policies, performance standards, guidelines, procedures and requirements.

The CAO process for addressing complaints is as follows:

1. The Ombudsman conducts an assessment of the issues and concerns raised in the complaint. The Ombudsman identifies key stakeholders to be consulted, and considers their views and incentives to reach resolution and what processes might be most useful to them. The assessment can include review of IFC/MIGA files, meetings with stakeholders, site visits and public meetings in the project area. The Ombudsman offers suggestions to the principal parties on how to proceed.
2. Based on the assessment, the Ombudsman works with the stakeholders to agree on a collaborative process for addressing the issues raised in the complaint. Collaborative processes can include various approaches, including facilitation and information sharing, joint fact-finding, dialogue and negotiation, and if agreed by all parties, conciliation and mediation.
3. If the collaborative phase does not result in progress, the Ombudsman can refer the complaint to the CAO's compliance function. An audit will then evaluate whether IFC or MIGA complied with its policies, performance standards, guidelines, and procedures.

Source: Center for International Environmental Law and Rainforest Foundation Norway, *A Complaint Mechanism for REDD+* (2011), at 4.

it is more effective to use existing institutional options or to create a new REDD-specific mechanism.

In 2008, the UN Human Rights Council approved a framework for addressing human rights in the context of private multilateral transactions, developed by the Special Representative of the Secretary-General on the issue of transnational corporations and other business enterprises

---

Regional Provisions, Commentary and Decisions, UN Doc. A/HRC/11/13/Add.1 (15 May 2009) at 92.

with regard to human rights.[24] The Human Rights Council is an intergovernmental body, created by the UN General Assembly in 2006 that periodically reviews the condition of human rights in specific countries and oversees various technical experts to assist in the reporting on the situation of human rights across the globe. The Council also manages a working group and forum on business and human rights, which was created following the work of the Special Representative that developed the framework. This framework has become known as the "Protect, Respect and Remedy" framework[25] and includes the following principles for duty bearers, which may be useful for REDD+:

- protect refers to the State's duty to protect rights holders from human rights abuses by third parties, through appropriate policies, regulations, and adjudications;
- respect refers to third parties' responsibilities with respect to human rights, including undertaking due diligence to avoid violations and addressing adverse impacts; and
- remedy means ensuring that rights holders have both judicial and non-judicial remedies available to address rights violations and concerns.

3.3 REDD+ Recourse

The wide range of concerns related to the protection of lands, livelihoods, resources and participatory processes illustrates the need for a mechanism that is capable of considering complaints arising from REDD+ initiatives. Stakeholder groups have not always been adequately involved in REDD+ planning, decision-making or implementation to date. Their greater involvement will be essential for successful and sustainable REDD+ interventions. Moreover, clarity around rights to forest resources (decision-making, ownership and use rights) can enhance the long-term sustainability of efforts and help ensure equitable future benefit-sharing.

Considering the scope of possible social, cultural and environmental impacts, there must be some means to ensure that REDD+ proposals are designed and implemented in a manner that protects human rights

---

[24] *Guiding Principles on Business and Human Rights*, available at http://www.ohchr.org/Documents/Publications/GuidingPrinciplesBusinessHR_EN.pdf.

[25] See *The UN "Protect, Respect and Remedy" Framework for Business and Human Rights*, available at http://www.reports-and-materials.org/Ruggie-protect-respect-remedy-framework.pdf.

and guarantees recourse for those adversely affected by REDD-related policies.

An effective complaint mechanism for REDD+ should be able to address the following impacts: harm to forest resources and associated lands; harm to forest-dependent livelihoods; environmental harm; harm to just processes, failure to consider and minimize adverse social and environmental impacts; lack of an adequate national legal and institutional framework to protect rights, livelihoods and ecosystems; and misappropriation/abuse of funds. In addition to these components, an effective mechanism should follow the basic principles outlined in Ruggie's reports: legitimacy, accessibility, predictability, equitability, rights-compatibility and transparency.[26] A threshold question in evaluating options for a REDD+ complaint mechanism is whether any existing mechanisms are adequate to address potential complaints, or whether a new mechanism should be created.

A number of options already exist to address REDD-related complaints. The UNFCCC has multiple mechanisms to resolve disputes but very little is available to non-State actors. The World Bank maintains an Inspection Panel, which is able to address many impact categories, including property rights, access to resources, some impacts to ecosystems and fiduciary standards, but there is limited authority to consider human rights as jurisdiction is limited to violations of the Bank's own policies. Moreover, the Inspection Panel may not be available to hear many REDD-related complaints due to certain restrictions regarding the trust funds that finance REDD-related activities. UN-REDD follows a rights-based approach to its activities and individual agencies are beginning to offer options to consider complaints, but these are generally in incipient stages, making it difficult to assess the adequacy and effectiveness of a complaint mechanism under UN-REDD. The international human rights system offers many options to hear impacts to livelihoods, rights and property, although it does not have the authority to hear the full scope of REDD-related complaints, and even the complaints that it does hear can take a long time to resolve. The Aarhus Convention and OECD NCPs offer opportunities to address procedural and substantive rights violations of European and other donor countries but those mechanisms are less available to potential complainants

[26] Special Representative of the Secretary-General on the Issue of Human Rights and Transnational Corporations and Other Business Enterprises, *Report of the Special Representative of the Secretary-General on the Issue of Human Rights and Transnational Corporations*, 92, UN Doc. A/HRC/8/5 (7 April 2008), available at http://www.reports-and-materials.org/Ruggie-report-7-Apr-2008.pdf.

in REDD-participant countries. These are all described in more detail below.

(a) UNFCCC

There is currently no specific mechanism within the UNFCCC to address REDD-related allegations of harm to livelihoods, ecosystems or processes. The GCF offers some form of grievance mechanism but is still in the process of becoming operational. Two additional options exist within the UNFCCC to resolve disputes and assess compliance, but neither of these options is available to non-State actors. Further, neither option has a mandate to address the specific concerns identified above related to REDD+. These two existing options include the dispute settlement mechanism of the UNFCCC and the Compliance Committee under the KP. Under the current UNFCCC framework for REDD+, it is unclear how either of these options has the authority to consider anything beyond the scope of emission reductions, such as the REDD+ safeguards adopted by the Parties in December 2010.

Article 14 of the UNFCCC and Article 19 of the KP envision a dispute settlement mechanism "in the event of a dispute between any two or more Parties concerning the interpretation or application of the Convention." The dispute settlement provisions have not been invoked to date and thus there is no experience to draw upon. But even if there were, the State-to-State character of the mechanism precludes non-State actors, such as communities or individuals impacted by REDD+, from being able to use Article 14 or Article 19.

With respect to the Compliance Committee, this body was designed to "facilitate, promote and enforce compliance with the commitments under the Protocol." The Compliance Committee has two branches, a facilitative branch and an enforcement branch (that theoretically can impose sanctions). At present, the compliance process can be triggered in two ways, either by a Party to the KP or by an expert review team tasked with reviewing national communications and emissions inventories. There is no process for an impacted person or community to formally raise concerns during the compliance process. Moreover, it is unclear whether the REDD+ safeguards adopted in December 2010 could be a part of the compliance process, particularly since REDD is not being negotiated under the KP. Even if the REDD+ safeguards were subject to the Compliance Committee, there is still no guarantee that the Committee could hear complaints from those whose rights, livelihoods or ecosystems may be impacted by REDD-related projects. At present, non-State actors have no direct means of having their complaints heard by the Compliance Committee. If information related to REDD+ safeguards is reported in national communications or emissions inventories *and* if non-State parties can supplement information contained in national communications, then it may be possible to find a way to address some of the identified REDD-related concerns articulated above, but at this point that appears to be an attenuated possibility at best.

(b) World Bank

The World Bank Inspection Panel considers allegations of violations of a robust set of policies and procedures that govern World Bank operations. As such, the FCPF and Forest Investment Programme are both subject to certain World Bank policies and procedures, and therefore subject to the jurisdiction of at least some Inspection Panel claims.

Established by the World Bank Board of Directors in 1993 in response to public pressure for increased accountability, the Inspection Panel was the first of its kind to allow non-State actors – citizens and their communities – to challenge decisions of international bodies through a clear and independently administered accountability and recourse process.[27] The creation of the Inspection Panel opened up new avenues for citizen involvement in a globalized world heavily influenced by international institutions.[28] The Inspection Panel supports a process initiated by local and affected people to ensure that the safeguards embodied in Bank policies are adhered to, and that in the case of non-compliance, corrective measures are initiated.[29] As an example of ways in which World Bank policies could apply to large-scale forest interventions, the Inspection Panel

---

[27] The World Bank Inspection Panel, BP 17.55, Annex A – Inspection Panel Resolution. IBRD Resolution 93-10 and IDA Resolution 93-6 adopted by the Bank's Board of Executive Directors on 22 September 1993.

[28] World Bank Inspection Panel, *Accountability at the World Bank: The Inspection Panel at 15 Years* (2009), at ix.

[29] See, e.g., World Bank Operational Policies, *OP 4.10 – Indigenous Peoples*, July 2005, available at http://go.worldbank.org/TE769PDWN0 (requiring a social assessment; the results of the free, prior, and informed consultation with the affected indigenous peoples' communities that was carried out during project preparation and its implementation; an action plan of measures to ensure distribution of benefits; and measures to avoid, minimize, mitigate or compensate adverse effects and accessible procedures appropriate to the project to address grievances by the affected indigenous peoples' communities arising from project implementation; further mandating consideration of culturally appropriate judicial recourse and customary dispute settlement mechanisms and benchmarks appropriate to the project for monitoring, evaluating, and reporting on the implementation of the policies); see also the World Bank Inspection Panel, *Accountability at the World Bank: The Inspection Panel at 15 Years* (2009), at x.

has previously issued findings related to communities and forests in the DR Congo.[30]

As described by the Inspection Panel, the process of considering complaints is as follows:[31]

Access to the Panel is intended to be an uncomplicated process: two or more people affected by a Bank-financed project may send a letter to the Panel asking for an investigation. Once the Panel has received and registered a Request, Bank Management has the opportunity to provide an initial response, which generally focuses on whether it has complied with the relevant Bank policies in that particular project. The Panel then examines the eligibility of the Request for a full investigation. If the Panel decides that the Request is eligible, it sends its recommendation for a full investigation to the Board of Executive Directors, which traditionally has agreed with the Panel's recommendations without interference in the Panel's work.

The Panel's methodology for an investigation includes field work, fact-finding, verification, public meetings, interviews with affected people and Bank operations staff, and review of relevant project documents and policies. Once the Panel completes its investigation, it sends its final report with findings to the Board and to Bank Management. Management, in consultation with the borrower and increasingly also with Requesters and affected populations, responds to the Panel's final report with recommendations and an action plan that lays out the process by which the project should be brought into compliance and the operational corrections that are to be initiated. The Board makes a decision regarding next steps based on both the Panel Report and Management's Response.

Notably, the Inspection Panel serves as a fact-finding body and not as a compliance body. In particular, the Panel may report on whether there have been violations of World Bank policies and procedures, but any remedial measures depend upon action by the World Bank Board and its management.

---

[30] See the World Bank, *Progress on Inspection Panel Action Plan*, 31 August 2009, available at http://go.worldbank.org/SZ8R5LRKK0 (discussing an "action plan for the forest sector, that monitors a moratorium on future logging concessions, supports the legal review on remaining logging contracts, integrates forest-dependent communities more widely into the Bank's activities and supports critical activities such as capacity building, participatory zoning, customary rights, law enforcement and independent monitoring in forthcoming forest-related operations").

[31] World Bank Inspection Panel, *Accountability at the World Bank: The Inspection Panel at 15 years* (2009).

If there were political will, it might be possible for the Inspection Panel to consider REDD+ complaints beyond its institutional walls, such as for complaints arising under the Multiple Delivery Partners function of the FCPF. One advantage is that the Panel is already established. In addition, it is more insulated from political pressures of REDD+ implementation than many of the other options described below. Although there may be significant administrative challenges in establishing this approach, it may be worth considering as an option. This would, of course, require agreement by the World Bank's Board of Directors. Even if the World Bank agreed, it is not practical to presume all complaints related to multilateral REDD+ projects could be handled by the Inspection Panel. This is due in part to the Panel's mandate to only consider violations of the World Bank's institutional policies and procedures.

In addition to the administrative challenges in expanding the Inspection Panel's mandate, the World Bank as an institution does not automatically apply international obligations beyond its own walls. For example, with respect to UNDRIP, the World Bank ought to comply with Article 42 (applying UNDRIP to Specialized Agencies of the UN), as it is one of 15 Specialized Agencies of the United Nations, organized under the purview of the ECOSOC according to the 1945 UN Charter.[32] The relationship between the UN and the World Bank was formalized in the 1947 Agreement between the UN and the International Bank for Reconstruction and Development.[33] While the agreement broadly outlines

---

[32] UN ECOSOC, UN Agencies, http://www.un.org/en/ecosoc/. Specialized Agencies are independent, international institutions that have entered into agreements with the UN pursuant to Articles 57 and 63 of the UN's 1945 Charter. See UN Charter arts. 57, 63, available at http://www un.org/en/documents/charter/intro.shtml. The UN defines these Specialized Agencies as "legally independent international organizations with their own rules, membership, organs and financial resources . . . brought into relationship with the United Nations through negotiated agreements." See UN Chief Executives Board for Coordination, United Nations System, available at http://www.unsceb.org/members/specializedagencies. In general, there are degrees of "independence" among Specialized Agencies, and the degree to which each agency deviates from mandates, conventions or requests of the UN varies depending on the specific agreement between the entities and the function of the organization, among other factors. See Mac Darrow, "Between Light and Shadow: The World Bank, the International Monetary Fund and International Human Rights Law," 1 *Studies in International Law*, at 124 (Hart Publishing 2005).

[33] Articles of Agreement of the International Bank for Reconstruction and Development, 27 December 1945, 60 Stat. 1440, 2 UNTS 134 (amended 17 December 1965); GA Res. 124(II), UN Doc. 124(II) (15 November 1947); see also Draft Agreements between the United Nations and International Bank for

the relationship between the two entities as a cooperative one, it explicitly notes that the World Bank "is, and is required to function as, an independent international organization."[34] It remains unclear how this agreement might be interpreted with respect to other entities or laws with respect to REDD+. Nothing in the "relationship agreement" between the two entities explicitly requires the Bank to comply with a decision of any organ of the United Nations, and the independence between the two entities is asserted throughout Bank and UN documents.[35] As such, it is unclear whether the Inspection Panel would have full jurisdiction to consider violations of UNDRIP as well as other human rights violations unless the World Bank maintains its own policies requiring compliance with rights obligations. Without explicit jurisdiction to fully consider complaints regarding basic human rights violations, this particular mechanism could not meet the principle of rights-compatibility.

(c) UN-REDD

UN-REDD follows a rights-based approach to its activities and has established an interim ombudsman process to receive complaints, including those alleging rights violations.[36] Formal procedures have not yet been detailed, so at present it is not possible to determine whether a complaint mechanism under UN-REDD could in fact consider the full scope of concerns needed for REDD+ or whether it would meet any of the principles for an effective grievance mechanism articulated by Ruggie. Nevertheless, considering that UN-REDD is a formal part of the UN system, follows a rights-based approach, has requirements to follow UNDRIP, and respects the standard of FPIC, a complaint mechanism under UN-REDD has significant potential to address some of the principal concerns regarding REDD+ activities.

4. INTERNATIONAL HUMAN RIGHTS SYSTEM

Individuals may bring claims of violations of many of the key human rights related to REDD+ before any of the bodies established by international

---

Reconstruction and Development and the International Monetary Fund, UN Doc. A/349 (2 September 1947), and note that the agreement came into force upon adoption by the General Assembly on 15 November 1947.

[34] Ibid. at art. 1, §2.

[35] Ibid.

[36] While UN-REDD policy is developing a more detailed ombudsman process to process complaints, at present claims are processed through the UN-REDD Secretariat and referred to the Policy Board.

human rights instruments. These rights include, inter alia, prohibition of discrimination; the right to culture; the right to religion and sacred sites; rights to lands, territories and resources; participatory rights; and the rights to life, livelihood and an adequate living standard (see Annex A). Four human rights treaties have formal bodies to consider complaints, including the ILO complaint mechanism, CESCR, Human Rights Committee on Civil and Political Rights (CCPR) and CERD. While the specific scope of their jurisdiction is defined by each of the underlying treaty obligations, individuals may bring claims of violations of the following rights before these human rights complaint mechanisms: self-determination; access to justice; participation in decision-making; property, land and resources; work; access to effective remedies; and FPIC.[37] Beyond these particular mechanisms, the Human Rights Council also supports special procedures, such as the Special Rapporteur on the Rights of Indigenous Peoples. Special Rapporteurs typically report on country- or issue-specific human rights concerns, sometimes at the request of concerned individuals and communities. While this is not a formal complaint resolution mechanism, it does provide some means of having a complaint considered.

While there are several means of recourse available to individuals claiming violations of international human rights instruments, some rights may be more easily enforced than others. As discussed below, the most developed and effective means of international recourse for REDD-related rights violations are the complaint mechanisms of the CESCR, CCPR, CERD, ILO and regional human rights bodies, such as the IACtHR. The rights of participation in decision-making and access to justice may be brought before all of these mechanisms except CESCR, which is the only mechanism that cannot consider complaints of violations of the rights to property. We briefly describe these bodies below.

4.1 Committee on Economic, Social, and Cultural Rights

To enforce these rights, the CESCR reviews reports on implementation regarding the ICESCR submitted by States Parties. CESCR can also hear claims brought against States Parties to the Optional Protocol to the International Covenant. Individuals or groups of individuals may inform the Committee of alleged Covenant violations by a State Party through written communications.

[37] Depending on the specific nature of the complaint, many claims of rights violations can be brought before CCPR, CESCR and/or the ILO complaint mechanisms described above.

Once a claim is brought before the CESCR, the Committee informs the State Party accused of the Covenant violation, and the State Party has six months to respond to the Committee with an explanation of the situation and a description of any remedy provided. After the CESCR considers the information brought before it, the Committee provides both Parties with its opinion and recommendations. States Parties involved in the dispute must submit another response to the Committee within six months of receiving the CESCR's opinion, describing actions taken in furtherance of the Committee's opinion. The Committee may continue to request information from the State Parties as it deems appropriate.

While the CESCR meets many of the complaint mechanism principles articulated by Ruggie, communications to the CESCR are subject to limitations on accessibility and predictability, as specified in OP-ICESCR Articles 3 and 4. Claimants first exhaust all domestic remedies (or demonstrate that such procedures are "unreasonably prolonged"), and cannot simultaneously pursue redress in other international forums. Claims of ICESCR violations related to REDD+ activities could be brought before the CESCR; however, the limitations previously described would likely reduce the effectiveness of a remedy issued by the Committee.

4.2 The Human Rights Committee

ICCPR Article 28 establishes the CCPR, which monitors treaty compliance with the ICCPR by reviewing reports[38] from States Parties and allowing States Parties and individuals to present claims of Covenant violations.[39] As with the CESCR, individuals may present claims in the form of written communications to the Committee.[40] Article 4 of the First Optional Protocol to the ICCPR ("First Optional Protocol") requires the CCPR to notify the State Party of claims brought against it, and allows the State Party up to six months to respond.[41] In cases of imminent harm, however, individuals can request protection before the Committee adopts

[38] Office of the UN High Commissioner for Human Rights, Human Rights Committee, available at http://www2.ohchr.org/english/bodies/hrc/index.htm [hereinafter "Human Rights Committee"]. States Parties must submit reports to the Committee within one year of the Covenant entering into force, and then when the CCPR so requests. ICCPR art. 40.1, opened for signature 19 December 1966, 999 UNTS 171.

[39] Ibid., art. 41.1; Optional Protocol to the ICCPR art. 1, opened for signature 19 December 1966, 999 UNTS 171 [hereinafter "FOP-ICCPR"].

[40] FOP-ICCPR art. 1.

[41] Ibid. art. 4.

its final views, and the Committee can make an urgent request to the States to provide necessary protection.

Similar to the accessibility and predictability challenges of the CESCR, the effectiveness of the CCPR mechanism is subject to limitations. Under Article 1 of the First Optional Protocol, only States Parties that have accepted the Protocol can be the subject of such communications to the Human Rights Committee.[42] Further, the First Optional Protocol imposes a number of limitations on the communications procedure. Article 5.2 excludes communications that have been examined under another international procedure, and those that have not exhausted all domestic remedies.[43] These limitations may interfere with the Committee's efficiency in providing adequate recourse to individuals and groups claiming ICCPR violations resulting from REDD+ activities.

Another option is to use the reporting functions of the special procedures to provide guidance and lessons learned regarding REDD+. For example, the Special Rapporteur on the situation of human rights and fundamental freedoms of indigenous peoples reports annually on his activities to the Human Rights Council. This mandate holder could also be requested to submit REDD-related reports to the UNFCCC or other international entities administrating REDD+ activities.

4.3 Committee on the Elimination of Racial Discrimination

The CERD oversees implementation of the International Convention on the Elimination of All Forms of Racial Discrimination (in this chapter, "Convention on Racial Discrimination") and addresses questions of noncompliance.[44] Like the CESCR and CCPR, CERD reviews reports from Parties and subsequently issues comments and recommendations to improve

---

42 FOP-ICCPR, art. 1. The FOP-ICCPR has 35 signatories and 113 parties. See UN Treaty Collection, *Chapter IV Human Rights: 5. Optional Protocol to the International Covenant on Civil and Political Rights* (2010), available at http://treaties.un.org/Pages/ViewDetails.aspx?src=TREATY&mtdsg_no=IV-5&chapter=4&lang=en. Twenty-four REDD participants have ratified this protocol: Argentina, Bolivia, Cameroon, Central African Republic, Chile, Colombia, Costa Rica, Democratic Republic of Congo, El Salvador, Equatorial Guinea, Ghana, Guatemala, Guyana, Honduras, Madagascar, Mexico, Nepal, Nicaragua, Panama, Paraguay, Peru, Republic of Congo, Suriname and Uganda. Ibid.

43 Ibid.

44 ICERD art. 9.1, adopted 21 December 1965, 660 UNTS 195. See also "Monitoring racial equality and non-discrimination," CERD, website of the Office of the UN High Commissioner for Human Rights, CERD, http://www2.ohchr.org/english/bodies/cerd/index.htm.

implementation.[45] Further, the CERD can receive complaints from States or individuals with respect to actions taken by Parties to the Convention.[46]

The CERD has very predictable procedures to help facilitate timely resolution of a complaint. First, a claimant must bring the complaint to a national body designated by the State Party; if no resolution is reached at the end of six months, the claimant may bring the issue before the CERD.[47] The Committee then notifies the State Party of the complaint, and the State Party must respond within three months, explaining the situation and any efforts to remedy the situation.[48] After considering the information provided, the CERD forwards its opinions and recommendations to both Parties to the dispute.[49]

In addition, the CERD has instituted two preventative measures of early warning and urgent procedures. Early warning measures may include suggesting that CERD members offer technical assistance to relevant States and submit a report to the UN Secretary-General.[50] These are intended to resolve imminent conflicts or prevent conflicts from escalating into more serious situations.[51]

Of particular relevance to REDD+, CERD General Recommendations have specifically addressed protecting indigenous peoples' rights under the Convention on Racial Discrimination. General recommendation No. 23 declares that States should promote sustainable development of indigenous peoples and secure property rights, informed consent, and effective participation in decisions related to these rights.[52] Recommendation No. 24

---

[45] Article 9.1 requires States Parties to submit reports every two years and upon request by CERD. Ibid.

[46] Ibid. arts. 11, 14.

[47] Ibid. arts. 14.2, 14.5.

[48] Ibid. art. 14.6.

[49] Ibid. art. 7(b).

[50] Ibid. arts. 13.1, 14.1, 15, 16, 19. Articles 15 and 16 interpret "lands" to "include the concept of territories, which covers the total environment of the areas which the peoples concerned occupy or otherwise use"; CERD, *Working Paper: Prevention of Racial Discrimination, Including Early Warning and Urgent Procedures*, Annex III, at 3–4, A/62/18, available at http://www2.ohchr.org/english/bodies/cerd/docs/A_48_18_Annex_III_English.pdf.

[51] CERD, "About the early-warning measures and urgent procedures," website of the Office of the UN High Commissioner for Human Rights, Early-Warning Measures and Urgent Procedures, available at http://www.ohchr.org/EN/HRBodies/CERD/Pages/EarlyWarningProcedure.aspx#about. Early-warning measures and urgent procedures became part of CERD's regular agenda in 1994. Ibid.

[52] CERD, *General Recommendation No. 23: Indigenous Peoples*, arts. 4–5, 18/08/97 Gen. Rec. No. 23. (18 August 1997).

promotes State recognition of all indigenous peoples in implementing the Convention, and securing the rights guaranteed therein.[53]

While the CERD broadly satisfies Ruggie's basic principles, it does not have jurisdiction to hear REDD-related complaints applicable to all international REDD actors and is therefore limited in its current use as a complaint mechanism tailored to REDD. Specifically, the CERD can only accept individuals' complaints against States that have recognized the Committee's competence to hear such claims.[54]

Further, CERD, like CESCR and CCPR, cannot hear claims of petitioners who have not exhausted all domestic remedies, unless such remedies are "unreasonably prolonged."[55] These features limit the CERD from providing effective redress for treaty violations arising under REDD+ activities.

4.4 ILO

As of May 2011, 22 countries had ratified ILO Convention 169, 15 of which are participants in REDD+ initiatives, plus four donor countries.[56] Should a State fail to uphold its obligations under ILO conventions, ILO Member States may file a complaint, and the Governing Body may call for formation of a Commission of Inquiry either upon receipt of such a complaint or on its own.[57] The Commission of Inquiry then issues a report containing recommendations for resolving the issue to the Director-General of the ILO.[58] After the Director-General publishes and transmits the report to the concerned Member States, each government must reply with its decision on whether to accept the recommendations and whether to refer the complaint to the International Court of Justice (ICJ).[59] If the concerned States fail to adhere to the Commission recommendations or to the ICJ decision, the "Governing Body may recommend to the Conference such action as it may deem wise and expedient to secure compliance therewith."[60]

---

[53] Ibid. arts. 1–2, 27/08/99 Gen. Rec. No. 24 (27 August 1999).

[54] ICERD art. 14.1, adopted 21 December 1965, 660 UNTS 195.

[55] Ibid. art. 7(a).

[56] Argentina, Bolivia, Brazil, Central African Republic, Chile, Colombia, Costa Rica, Denmark, Ecuador, Guatemala, Honduras, Mexico, Nepal, Netherlands, Nicaragua, Norway, Paraguay, Peru and Spain have all ratified. See status of ratification webpage for ILO, Convention No. C169 (2009), at http://www.ilo.org/dyn/normlex/en/f?p=NORMLEXPUB:1:0.

[57] Ibid. art. 26.

[58] Ibid. arts. 28–9.

[59] Ibid. art. 29.

[60] Ibid. art. 33. Note, however, that Article 33 has only been used once since the ILO's existence. See also ILO website regarding complaints, at http://www.ilo.

In addition, under Article 24 of ILO Convention 169, a form of complaint called a "representation" may be used to allege a government's violations of ILO conventions. A representation must be submitted to the ILO in writing by a workers' or employers' organization, and must identify the specific provisions of the Convention that are alleged to have been violated. If the ILO Governing Body determines that the representation is eligible to be considered, then it will appoint a Tripartite Committee (i.e. one government representative, one employer representative and one worker representative) to investigate the claim. The Tripartite Committee writes a report including its findings and recommendations (which is made available to the public), and submits it to the Governing Body for adoption. The Committee of Experts then addresses the recommendations within its regular supervision.

Regarding the adequacy of ILO-specific mechanisms to address REDD-related complaints, Convention 169 is able to address an important subset of impacts pertaining to the rights of indigenous peoples, including rights to lands and resources; displacement; FPIC; livelihoods; just processes; and national frameworks. However, ILO processes cannot easily address other impacts pertinent to REDD complaints, including many environmental harms, abuse of funds, or impacts associated with the resources or livelihoods of non-indigenous or non-tribal peoples. Additionally, the ILO's "representation" mechanism to receive complaints from affected peoples requires involvement in a workers' or employers' organization. This could render the mechanism inaccessible to many affected peoples. Nevertheless, the Committee's monitoring of implementation of ILO Convention 169 could be used as a means of ensuring that REDD+ activities do not infringe on at least some key REDD-related rights afforded to indigenous peoples under this Convention.

4.5 Regional Human Rights Bodies

In addition to international human rights bodies, regional institutions are instrumental in helping resolve rights-related complaints. The IACtHR, the IAComHR, the European Court of Human Rights and the African Commission on Human Rights all have the authority to consider case-specific allegations of rights violations. For example, to enforce compliance, the ACHR authorizes the IACtHR to interpret and apply the Convention, and to provide recourse for victims of relevant rights

---

org/global/standards/applying-and-promoting-international-labour-standards/complaints/lang--en/index.htm.

violations.[61] The IACtHR has issued landmark rulings for indigenous and tribal peoples in the Americas. Decisions by the Court can be internationally binding.[62] As such, eligible individuals claiming violation of their rights related to REDD+ activities may be able to seek recourse from the Court.

In terms of scope, the regional human rights courts have authority to hear claims regarding rights to lands, territories and resources, as well as just process. They have also increasingly considered environmental complaints related to livelihoods, but would not generally consider a complaint solely regarding carbon, ecosystems or financial flows. Due to their regional placement, they tend to be more accessible than a centralized international court. While the international community generally holds them to be legitimate, Member States have at times accepted their decisions and other times have ignored them. The courts by their very nature are rights-compatible, though they may vary in degree of transparency.

4.6 Summary of Human Rights Bodies

It is clear from the analysis that the current structures of international and regional human rights systems are not sufficiently strong and timely as to serve as a practical forum for direct attention to all complaints and demands from indigenous peoples or other forest-dependent communities allegedly aggrieved by acts or omissions directly related to REDD+ implementation activities. Interactions between REDD+ actors, including Annex I and Non-Annex I governments, indigenous peoples, carbon brokers and others are expected to increase dramatically in the immediate future. Based on the analysis above, it appears that the existing international and regional human rights systems are not well equipped to resolve many of the complaints that could arise alleging violations of the rights of indigenous peoples and local communities. In most cases, the human rights mechanisms are limited by the non-binding nature of their respective resolutions, their open procedural time frames, and their inability to have direct influence on REDD+ processes.

While utilizing the human rights system has the advantage of using existing human rights bodies to hear complaints rather than creating a new

---

[61] ACHR arts. 62.3, 63.1, opened for signature 22 November 1969, 1144 UNTS 123.

[62] Human Rights Education Associates, *The Inter-American Human Rights System*, available at http://www.hrea.org/learn/. The Court only has jurisdiction over States Parties to the American Convention on Human Rights that have recognized the Court's competence to hear claims against them. Ibid.

mechanism, it may be difficult to ensure impartial, credible, timely and full response to every complaint. Depending on the rights and policies to be applied, potential REDD-related complaints could reach beyond the collective jurisdiction of all the human rights bodies' mandates. Additionally, the human rights system might fail to fully satisfy the criteria of accessibility and predictability due to the relatively formal nature of addressing complaints under the human rights regime, added layers of bureaucracy, existing case backlogs and limited resources. All of these factors could result in delays to the resolution of a complaint.

In conclusion, existing human rights bodies provide several means of recourse for peoples and communities claiming violations of REDD-related rights based on international human rights treaties. However, none of the mechanisms within the human rights system can adequately address all of the functions for a recourse mechanism for REDD+. Particularly in light of the complex and technical nature of REDD-related activities and by virtue of the fact that inter-related activities may be implemented by many different actors at many different scales, existing human rights bodies may not be ideally suited to field the full spectrum of complaints related to REDD+. Therefore, it may be more helpful to consider the option of using existing human rights bodies as a non-exclusive one: while some complaints could be addressed by a particular court, committee or special procedure, many others would need an alternative forum for recourse.

Many entities within the human rights system have specialized expertise in addressing at least some potential REDD impacts. As such, it might be worthwhile to consider a means for a centralized REDD+ mechanism to utilize the expertise that does exist. To this effect, section 5 considers a new REDD-specific mechanism, including the option of referring complaints to existing entities, and this option may be particularly relevant here.

5. AARHUS CONVENTION

Individuals affected by REDD+ activities by a State Party to the Aarhus Convention may be able to present claims of related rights violations through the Aarhus Convention's non-compliance mechanism.[63] Article

[63] Convention on Access to Information, Public Participation in Decision-Making and Access to Justice in Environmental Matters ("Aarhus Convention"), art. 15, opened for signature 25 June 1998–21 December 1998, available at

15 of the Convention requires the Meeting of the Parties to arrange for optional review of States Parties' compliance when agreed to by consensus.[64] The public may participate in and present communications to the Meeting of the Parties.[65] Although it is a regional agreement, the Aarhus Convention allows non-UNECE States to become Parties through accession, provided they are members of the United Nations; thus, the non-compliance mechanism could potentially be used by all REDD+ participants that accede to the treaty.[66]

Another potential venue is the Aarhus Convention's Compliance Committee, which safeguards the participatory rights of indigenous peoples and forest-dependent communities, including the right to full and effective participation.[67] Any State Party, the Secretariat or members of the public may raise compliance issues before the Committee.[68] Additionally, NGOs that qualify as observers under the Aarhus Convention may nominate candidates to serve on the Committee.[69] The appointed experts' independence allows them to render their opinions without external diplomatic pressure, thereby elevating both the quality of their work and the overall functioning of the mechanism.[70]

Both the Aarhus Convention's non-compliance mechanism and Compliance Committee provide a means of recourse for those who are denied rights to just processes, including access to information, full and effective participation, and access to justice. The remaining impacts – to land, territories, resources, environment, fraud, etc. – would not generally be within the jurisdiction of the Aarhus mechanisms. Moreover, at present, the 44 Parties to the Aarhus Convention do not include any of the REDD+ implementing countries, though they do include many REDD+

---

http://www.unece.org/env/pp/documents/cep43e.pdf [hereinafter "Aarhus Convention"].

64 Ibid. art. 15.

65 Ibid.

66 Ibid. art. 19.3.

67 Ibid. art. 15 ("The Meeting of the Parties shall establish, on a consensus basis, optional arrangements of non-confrontational, non-judicial and consultative nature for reviewing compliance with the provisions of this Convention. These arrangements shall allow for appropriate public involvement and may include the option of considering communications from members of the public on matters related to this Convention.").

68 Meeting of the Parties of the Aarhus Convention, Decision I/7, *Review of Compliance*, parts IV–VI (2002).

69 Ibid. Annex 4 (2002).

70 Svitlana Kravchenko, "The Aarhus Convention and Innovations in Compliance with Multilateral Environmental Agreements," 18 *Colo. J. Int'l Envtl. L. & Pol'y* 1 (2007).

donor countries such as Norway, Denmark, Germany and the United Kingdom. Given that REDD+ participant countries have not acceded to the Convention (which originated as a regional treaty for Europe), these Aarhus-specific mechanisms may not be readily accessible to the indigenous peoples and forest-dependent communities affected by local and national REDD+ initiatives. Nevertheless, the Aarhus mechanisms do provide a legitimate and rights-compatible forum with solid expertise regarding procedural rights.

6. OECD NATIONAL CONTACT POINTS

The OECD country governments, including those that house corporations or other non-State actors engaged in REDD-related activities, maintain a system of national human rights institutions (NHRIs) and the National Contact Points (NCPs) of States adhering to OECD Guidelines. According to the research carried out under the Special Envoy of the Secretary-General (SESG), at least 40 of the 85 recognized NHRIs are able to handle grievances related to the human rights performance of private actors. Some NHRIs are limited to considering human rights abuses alleged against State-owned enterprises or private companies providing public services. Others can address grievances against a broader set of actors, but only with regard to specific kinds of human rights-related grievances, often discrimination. Another group of NHRIs – notably those in Africa – consider grievances against all companies with regard to any human rights concern.

Where NHRIs are able to address grievances, they can provide a means to hold both State and non-State actors accountable for their actions. NHRIs are well-positioned to use problem-solving approaches – whether adjudicative or mediation-based – that are culturally appropriate, accessible and expeditious. Even if they cannot themselves handle specific complaints, NHRIs can provide information and advice on other avenues of recourse to those seeking remedy. Through increased exchange of information, NHRIs can serve a facilitative role within the wider system of complaint mechanisms, linking local, national and international processes across countries and regions.

The 40 States that adhere to the OECD Guidelines for Multinational Enterprises must provide an NCP who is responsible for considering and addressing grievances. OECD provides procedural guidance, although individual NCPs have significant flexibility in applying the Guidelines. While they have been criticized at times for providing inadequate remedies, OECD procedures currently under revision may better satisfy Ruggie's principles for an effective complaint mechanism.[71] For this reason, the NCPs could be an important option to consider for REDD+.

NCPs stress the need for operational flexibility that reflects national circumstances, which helps respond to individual country needs. At the same time, to ensure the credibility of the system as a whole, there should be minimum performance criteria in line with those principles set out by Ruggie's reports. Certain NCPs, including those in the UK and the Netherlands, have developed innovative solutions to address this tension. Several States have engaged multiple government agencies, and created multi-stakeholder advisory groups. Perhaps most interesting is the decision of the Dutch Government to reorganize its NCP such that a four-person multi-stakeholder group handles grievances independent of, though supported administratively by, the government. Other alternatives include placing NCPs under the legislative branch or within an NHRI.[72]

---

[71] Past criticisms have noted challenges in the housing of some NCPs primarily or wholly within government departments tasked with promoting business, trade and investment, which raises questions about conflicts of interest; a lack of resources to undertake adequate investigation of complaints and the training to provide effective mediation; no clear time frames for the commencement or completion of the process; and inadequate reporting of outcomes. See generally Special Representative of the Secretary-General on the Issue of Human Rights and Transnational Corporations and Other Business Enterprises, *Business and Human Rights: Towards Operationalizing the "Protect, Respect and Remedy" Framework*, UN Doc. A/HRC/11/13 (22 April 2009) [hereinafter "*Business and Human Rights*"], available at http://www2.ohchr.org/english/bodies/hrcouncil/docs/11session/A.HRC.11.13.pdf; Special Representative of the Secretary-General on the Issue of Human Rights and Transnational Corporations and Other Business Enterprises, *State Obligations to Provide Access to Remedy for Human Rights Abuses by Third Parties, Including Business: An Overview of International and Regional Provisions, Commentary and Decisions*, UN Doc. A/HRC/11/13/Add.1 (15 May 2009) [hereinafter "*State Obligations*"], available at http://www2.ohchr.org/english/bodies/hrcouncil/docs/11session/A.HRC.11.13.Add.1.pdf.

[72] *Business and Human Rights: the Evolving International Agenda*, Corporate Social Responsibility Initiative Working Paper No. 38 (June 2007), at 20, available at http://www.hks harvard.edu/m-rcbg/CSRI/publications/workingpaper_38_ruggie.pdf; *State Obligations to Provide Access to Remedy for Human Rights Abuses by Third Parties, Including Business: An Overview of International and Regional Provisions, Commentary and Decisions*, UN Doc. A/HRC/11/13/Add.1 (15 May 2009).

7. CONCLUSION AND RECOMMENDATIONS

REDD+ by nature straddles administrative regimes across jurisdiction, with various intersections of international and national laws and norms governing forest and land-use activities across multiple scales. By examining the various recourse options available for associated REDD+ activities, we see that many existing bodies may be equipped to adjudicate at least some complaints likely to arise from REDD+ implementation. While none of the existing entities offers a comprehensive option to address the full scope of REDD-related complaints, many have specialized knowledge and capacity that could potentially address certain REDD-related impacts. However, it is clear that no single mechanism has the competency to effectively address and/or remedy all of the categories of REDD-related complaints in accordance with Ruggie's key principles.

The World Bank's Inspection Panel, UN-REDD Ombudsman, human rights bodies and OECD NCPs have specialized authority to consider at least some of the situations that could give rise to a complaint, and may be able to directly address the problems arising under those particular situations. However, none of these entities is able to consider all of the potential impacts created through internationally supported REDD+ activities. Moreover, as REDD+ financing is flowing independently of the existing recourse mechanisms, REDD+ funders may be increasing risks of harm by moving forward through financial mechanisms that do not provide sufficient recourse.

While it may be impractical to establish a new mechanism that could serve as a comprehensive forum competent to consider all aspects of REDD-related complaints, it might be possible to offer a centralized intake office with a more limited mandate to simply receive complaints and then refer claims to the existing mechanisms where appropriate. Recognizing that many existing mechanisms could provide valuable expertise to specific types of REDD-related claims, it might be possible for competent institutions/adjudicative bodies to enter into agreements for enhanced coordination, such as to screen, refer and/or investigate claims, which could help streamline the process.

Depending on the nature of the complaint and the adjudicative body or bodies involved, a centralized office could help refer complainants based on relief sought, such as:

- Declaration and public disclosure: issue and publicize findings of violation (compatible with fact-finding function).
- Injunction: halt violation (compatible with arbitration or other forms of dispute resolution such as fact-finding, if the terms of

reference for the relevant institution allow for recommendations and those recommendations are not rejected).
- Compensation: pay for harm caused by violation (compatible with mediation, arbitration, and fact-finding, where the terms of reference allow for recommendations and those recommendations are not rejected). For example, ILO Convention 169 provides in Article 4 that special measures "shall be adopted as appropriate" by State Parties to safeguard the rights of indigenous and tribal peoples. In terms of the substantive aspects of remedy, ILO Convention 169 contains several provisions relating to compensation for harm suffered through exploration, or use of resources, on indigenous and tribal peoples' lands.
- Sanction: punish violation (primarily compatible with adjudication but could be a component of fact-finding, depending on terms of reference).
- Restitution, i.e. restore to pre-harm state (compatible with adjudication and potentially awarded as component of mediation or fact-finding recommendations). Restitution is the remedy favoured by international law when it is practical.

In addition, a centralized office could compile annual reports from any national or international grievance mechanism or expert reviewing claims complaints received, decisions taken, lessons learned and recommendations for future action. It might also be possible for a centralized office to tap into the UNFCCC's systems for MRV. Monitoring, reporting and verifying compliance with obligations can help resolve disputes and in some cases may help satisfy due diligence obligations.

Regardless of whether we rely upon new or existing structures to implement REDD+, it is clear that international administrative adjudications can play important roles in addressing disputes that may arise, even as national courts and agencies work through their own systems to help resolve complaints. The hydra of legal and administrative regimes relevant to REDD+ presents challenges for administration, compounded exponentially by working across scales of intervention ranging from the hyper-local to global. Tapping the expertise of competent bodies to address complaints may prove challenging, especially where conflicts of law might emerge. A referral system can help but ultimately we are likely to end up with a system that mirrors REDD+ itself: decentralized efforts with competing norms and administrative challenges, which provide an opportunity to enhance both national and international cooperation while simultaneously carrying the risk of conflicting mandates and enforcement. Effective management and thoughtful system design are likely to reduce risk and enhance efficient administration of disputes, ultimately resulting in improved and lasting REDD+ outcomes.

ANNEX A: INTERNATIONAL STANDARDS APPLICABLE TO REDD+

The ILO Convention 169[73] is important to the discussion over indigenous peoples' rights. Presently, ILO Convention 169 has been ratified by 22 countries that collectively include over 899 million hectares of tropical forests, including a large portion of the Amazon basin and a large portion of the tropical forests in Central America. Sixteen of these countries are rainforest countries that have entered into REDD+ agreements. Large parts of these forest areas correspond to areas traditionally owned, occupied and/or utilized by indigenous peoples. Between 2000 and 2005, REDD+ countries with tropical forests party to ILO Convention 169 lost an aggregate total of 4.892 million hectares of forest area, representing 66.8 per cent, about two-thirds, of the total global deforestation.[74]

Several specific provisions of ILO Convention 169 are particularly relevant to REDD+. Article 7 grants all affected peoples[75] "the right to decide their own priorities for the process of development as it affects their lives, beliefs, institutions and spiritual well-being and the lands they occupy or otherwise use."[76]

The Convention references the rights of indigenous and tribal peoples to cultural identity, practices and customs;[77] "religious . . . values and practices";[78] health, livelihood and well-being;[79] ownership and possession of property, land and natural resources; and sustainable development.[80] Additionally, the treaty supports access to justice[81] and participation and

---

[73] Convention Concerning Indigenous and Tribal Peoples in Independent Countries, adopted 27 June 1989, 28 ILM 1382 [hereinafter "ILO Convention 169"].

[74] UN FAO, *State of the World's Forest 2009*, Annex table 2 (2009).

[75] ILO Convention 169 calls for the protection of the rights of both tribal and indigenous peoples, which is significant in that it can apply beyond groups traditionally considered "indigenous." See, e.g., *Saramaka People* v. *Suriname*, IACtHR No. 172 (28 November 2007). ILO 169 is quite flexible, as we have seen in granting the character of indigenous or tribal to any group that self-identifies as such. It is significant that the Convention allows for *self-identification* of groups, but not individuals, as indigenous or tribal peoples. See ILO Convention 169 art. 1.2 (calling for self-identification as indigenous or tribal to be a "fundamental criterion for determining the groups to which the provisions of this Convention apply").

[76] ILO Convention 169 art. 7.

[77] Ibid. 169 arts. 2, 5(a)–(b), 8.1–8.2.

[78] Ibid. 169 art. 5(a).

[79] Ibid. arts. 7.2, 23.1, 25.1.

[80] Ibid. arts. 7.2, 7.4, 30.1.

[81] Ibid. arts. 2, 12. Article 2 describes government responsibility in ensuring protection of indigenous and tribal peoples' rights; Article 12 states that "[t]he

Table 15.3 REDD+ Participant Countries Parties to ILO 169, respective total forest surface, net change in land use and annual rates of deforestation[82]

Country	Total forest surface, 2005 (in 1,000 ha.)	Net forest change, 2000–2005 (in 1,000 ha.)	Net % change, 2000–2005
Argentina	33,021	−150	−0.4%
Bolivia	58,740	−270	−0.5%
Brazil	477,698	-3103	−0.6%
Central African Republic	22,755	−30	−0.1%
Chile	16,121	57	0.4%
Costa Rica	2,391	3	0.1%
Colombia	60,728	−47	−0.1%
Ecuador	10,853	−198	−1.7%
Guatemala	3,938	−54	−1.3%
Honduras	4,648	−156	−3.1%
Mexico	64,238	−260	−0.4%
Nepal	3,636	−53	−1.4%
Nicaragua	5,189	−70	−1.3%
Paraguay	18,475	−179	−0.9%
Peru	68,742	−94	−0.1%
Venezuela	47,713	−288	−0.6%
Total	899,932	4,892	
Total net and % global deforestation in ILO 169 REDD+ Parties		7,317+	66.8%

informed consent in decision-making;[83] prohibits discrimination;[84] and addresses the right to work.[85] This is significant in the REDD+ context

peoples concerned shall be safeguarded against the abuse of their rights and shall be able to take legal proceedings, either individually or through their representative bodies, for the effective protection of these rights." Ibid.

82 UN FAO, *State of the World's Forest 2009* (2009) Annex table 2.

83 Id. arts. 2.1, 5, 6.1(a)–(b), 7, 12, 15, 16.2, 17.2, 23.1, 33.

84 Id. arts. 3.1, 20.2.

85 Ibid. arts. 5(c), 20, 23. Article 5(c) declares that "[p]olicies aimed at mitigating the difficulties experienced by these peoples in facing new conditions of life and work shall be adopted, with the participation and co-operation of the peoples affected"; Article 20 is concerned with ensuring equality and non-discrimination in employment and recruiting; and Article 23 encourages recognition of the economic, cultural and developmental significance of preserving "[h]andicrafts, rural and community-based industries, and subsistence economy and traditional activities of the peoples concerned, such as hunting, fishing, trapping and gathering." Ibid.

because carbon (or the ability to store carbon) is inherent in certain natural resources (namely forests) associated with the land.

REDD-related Provisions of ILO Convention 169

The ICESCR is relevant to REDD+ because it sets an important precedent for safeguarding several principal rights related to culture, identity and livelihood in the international community.[86] The ICESCR prohibits discrimination and supports the rights to self-determination; participation in cultural life; religion; health, livelihood and an adequate standard of living; and work.[87]

The UN ICCPR[88] specifically guarantees the rights to self-determination; minorities' rights to the enjoyment of culture; religion; and life.[89] The ICCPR also prohibits discrimination, supports the right to livelihood, and protects universal access to justice, effective remedies and participation in decision-making.[90]

Besides prohibiting discrimination based on race, the UN ICERD secures other rights pertaining to REDD+, including the rights to partake in cultural activities; religion; health care and social services; property ownership; and work.[91] The Convention also supports several procedural rights, including the rights of equality and equal treatment before the law, participation in public affairs and services, and access to effective remedies.[92]

The 1998 UNECE Aarhus Convention on Access to Information, Public Participation in Decision-making and Access to Justice ("Aarhus Convention") encapsulates Principle 10 of the Rio Declaration on Environment and Development, which combines three essential elements of "environmental democracy": the rights to access to information, public participation in environmental policy and decision-making processes, and access to justice.[93]

---

[86] ICESCR, opened for signature 19 December 1966, 993 UNTS 3.

[87] Ibid. arts. 2.2; 1.1 and 1.3; 15.1(a), 2.2 and 13.3; 1.2/11/12; and 6.1 and 7, respectively.

[88] ICCPR art. 40.1, opened for signature 19 December 1966, 999 UNTS 171.

[89] Ibid. arts. 1.1; 27; 18.1 and 27; and 6.1, respectively.

[90] Ibid. arts. 2.1, 26 and 27; 1.2; 16 ("Everyone shall have the right to recognition everywhere as a person before the law"); and 25 (calling for participation in public affairs, and protects universal suffrage and the rights to be elected and to receive public services), respectively.

[91] ICERD arts. 2.1 and 5.

[92] Ibid. arts. 5 and 6.

[93] Aarhus Convention, 25 June 1998, 2161 UNTS 447; UNCED, UN Doc. A/CONF.151/5/Rev.1 (14 June 1992), 31 ILM 874 (1992).

The ACHR guarantees several rights potentially impacted by REDD+. Specifically enumerated by the Convention are the rights to life, religion, "use and enjoyment" of property, participation in government and public affairs, and the right to "effective recourse."[94] Additionally, the Convention supports the right of access to justice.[95]

The UNDRIP affirms the rights of indigenous peoples in activities affecting their lands and resources.[96] Particular guarantees include the right of self-determination;[97] "the right to own, use, develop and control the lands, territories and resources that they possess by reason of traditional ownership or other traditional occupation or use";[98] the right to cultural identity, heritage, values and customs;[99] and provisions for FPIC.[100] This is especially relevant in the REDD+ context because REDD+ activities, in all likelihood, will affect lands and resources utilized by indigenous peoples. UNDRIP also requires States to secure available and effective methods of redress for the peoples concerned in the declaration;[101] and participation in decision-making and "in the political, economic, social and cultural life of the State."[102]

Although UNDRIP is a General Assembly Resolution, it is authoritative for UN bodies that may operationalize REDD+, expressing broadly accepted views of the particular application of international and customary law obligations regarding indigenous peoples.[103] Recognizing that much of the world's forests correspond to the lands, territories and resources of indigenous peoples, UNDRIP is an important instrument to protect the rights of those people.

---

[94] Organization of American States, ACHR, 22 November 1969, OASTS No. 36, 1144 UNTS 123, arts. 4, 12, 21.1, 23, and 25 (see also art. 8 guaranteeing the right to a fair trial), respectively.

[95] Ibid. art. 3.

[96] UNDRIP, UN Doc. A/RES/47/1 (2007).

[97] Ibid. arts. 3, 23, 33.1.

[98] Ibid. arts. 8.2(b), 10, 25, 26.1–26.2, 29.1.

[99] Ibid. arts. 8.2(a), 8.2(d)–(e), 10, 11.1, 15.1, 31.1, 34.

[100] Ibid. arts. 10, 19, 28, 29, 32.

[101] Ibid. arts. 8.2, 11.2, 20, 28.1, 32.2, 32.3.

[102] Ibid. 5, 18–19, 23, 27, 32.2, 38, 41.

[103] Although UNDRIP is not a legally binding instrument itself, commentators argue that the Declaration "has some kind of binding force both as a resolution of the General Assembly grounded in the authority of the United Nations Charter, and from the perspective of the substantive rights enshrined therein." UNPFII, *International Expert Seminar on the Role of UN Mechanisms with Specific Mandate Regarding the Rights of Indigenous Peoples*, 14, UN Doc. E/C.19/2009/CRP.17 (4–6 February 2009).

Index